I0803731

THE

PUBLICATIONS

OF THE

Lincoln Record Society

(FOR THE ANCIENT DIOCESE AND THE COUNTY OF LINCOLN)

FOUNDED IN THE YEAR

1910

VOLUME 19

FOR THE YEAR ENDING 30TH SEPTEMBER, 1921

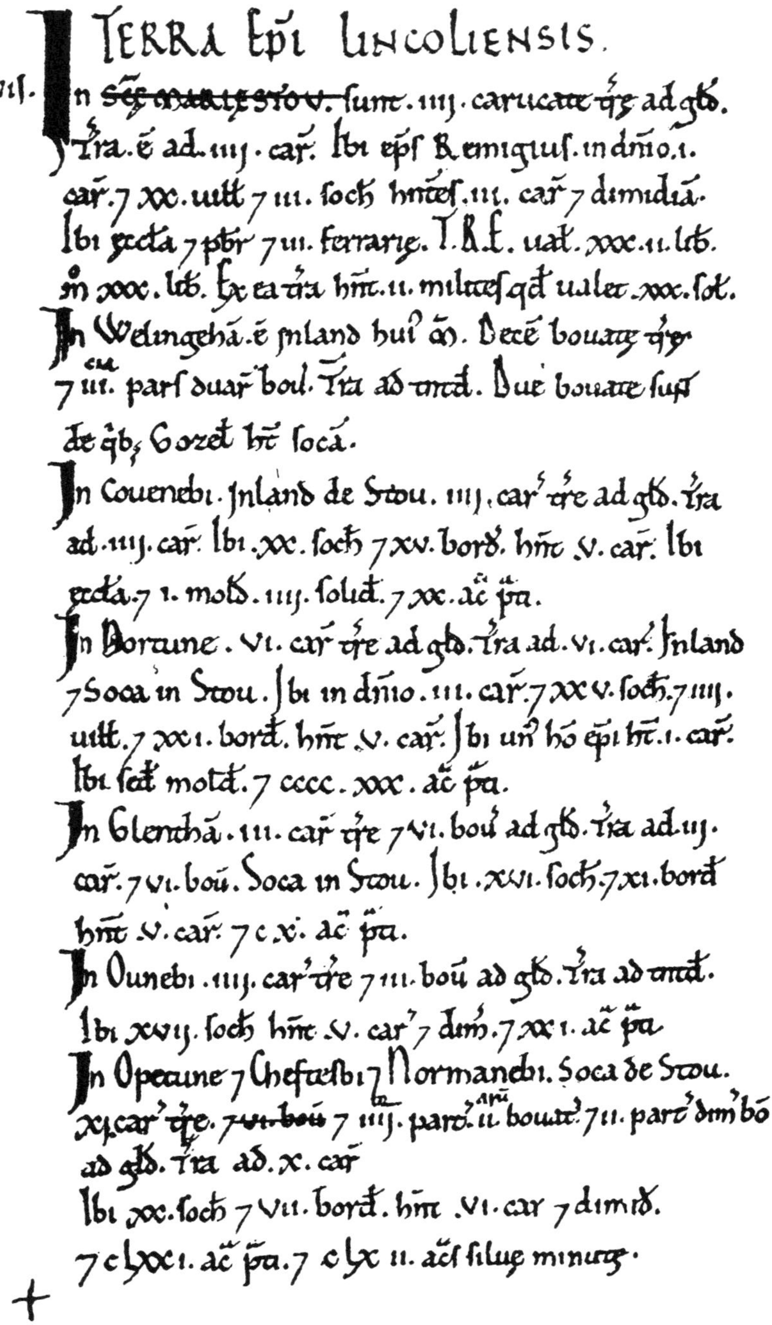

VII. TERRA EPI LINCOLIENSIS.

In ~~Sce Marie Stou~~ sunt. iiij. carucatæ træ ad gld. Tra. ē ad. iiij. car. Ibi eps Remigius. in dnio. i. car. 7 xx. uitt 7 iii. soch hntes. iii. car 7 dimidiā. Ibi æccta 7 pbr 7 iii. ferrariæ. T.R.E. uat. xxxii. lib. m̄ xxx. lib. Ex ea tra hnt. ii. milites qđ ualet. xxx. sol.

In Welingehā. ē inland hui⁹ m̄. Decē bouatæ træ 7 iii. pars duar boū. Tra ad. iii car. Duæ bouatæ sunt de qb; Gozet hīt socā.

In Couenebi. inland de Stou. iiij. car̄ træ ad gld. Tra ad. iiij. car. Ibi. xx. soch 7 xv. bord. hnt. v. car. Ibi æccta 7 i. molī. iiij. solid. 7 xx. ac̄ pti.

In Bortune. vi. car̄ træ ad gld. Tra ad. vi. car. Inland 7 Soca in Stou. Ibi in dnio. iii. car. 7 xxv. soch. 7 iiij. uitt. 7 xxi. bord. hnt. v. car. Ibi un̄ hō epi hīt. i. car. Ibi sedĕ molĭ. 7 cccc. xxx. ac̄ pti.

In Glenthā. iii. car̄ træ 7 vi. bou ad gld. Tra ad. iij. car. 7 vi. bou. Soca in Stou. Ibi. xvi. soch. 7 xi. bord hnt. v. car. 7 c. x. ac̄ pti.

In Ounebi. iiij. car̄ træ 7 iii. bou ad gld. Tra ad tntđ. Ibi xvij. soch hnt. v. car̄ 7 dim̄. 7 xxi. ac̄ pti.

In Opetune 7 Chefteslbi 7 Normanebi. Soca de Stou. xi. car̄ træ. ~~7 vi. bou~~ 7 iiij. part. ii bouatæ 7 ii. part dim̄ bō ad gld. Tra ad. x. car. Ibi. xx. soch 7 vii. bord. hnt. vi. car 7 dimid. 7 c lxxi. ac̄ pti. 7 c lx ii. ac̄ siluæ minutæ.

Domesday Book (folio 344, part of column 1), containing the first seven entries of the Bishop of Lincoln's Land (see below, pp. 47, 48).

THE

LINCOLNSHIRE DOMESDAY

AND THE

LINDSEY SURVEY

TRANSLATED AND EDITED BY

C. W. FOSTER, M.A., F.S.A.

CANON OF LINCOLN AND VICAR OF TIMBERLAND

AND

THOMAS LONGLEY, M.A.

CANON OF LINCOLN AND RECTOR OF CONISHOLME

WITH

AN INTRODUCTION

BY

F. M. STENTON, M.A.

PROFESSOR OF MODERN HISTORY, UNIVERSITY COLLEGE, READING

AND

APPENDIXES OF EXTINCT VILLAGES

BY

C. W. FOSTER, M.A., F.S.A.

PRINTED FOR

THE LINCOLN RECORD SOCIETY

1924

REPRINTED 1976

© Lincoln Record Society 1924

All Rights Reserved. Except as permitted under current legislation no part of this work may be photocopied, stored in a retrieval system, published, performed in public, adapted, broadcast, transmitted, recorded or reproduced in any form or by any means, without the prior permission of the copyright owner

First published 1924
Unaltered reprint 2005, 2013

ISBN 978-0-90150-375-6

Transferred to digital printing

A Lincoln Record Society Publication
Published by The Boydell Press
an imprint of Boydell & Brewer Ltd
PO Box 9, Woodbridge, Suffolk IP12 3DF, UK
and of Boydell & Brewer Inc.
668 Mt. Hope Avenue, Rochester NY 14620, USA
website: www.boydellandbrewer.com

A CIP record for this title is available
from the British Library

This publication is printed on acid-free paper

Printed in Great Britain by
4edge Ltd, Hockley, Essex

PREFACE

THE present work is intended to be the first of a series of three volumes. In the second volume, Canon Longley will bring together under one head the chief facts relating to each village which are to be found in *Domesday Book*, dispersed there under the heads of the several barons amongst whom the village was divided. Besides this reconstruction of the villages, the results of an exhaustive comparison of *Domesday Book* with the *Lindsey Survey* (A.D. 1115-18), will be set out; and also a systematic account will be given of the assessment of the villages, wapentakes, and county to the danegeld, an intricate subject to which Canon Longley has devoted many years of study. In a third volume it is proposed to trace the descent of the various fees within the county from 1066, the year when King Edward 'was alive and dead,' to about 1250. When using these two volumes, students will find it necessary constantly to refer to *Domesday Book*, for which, among other reasons, it has been decided to make a translation of that record the first volume of the series.

It is the third time that the Lincolnshire part of *Domesday Book* has been translated into English. In 1809, the Reverend William Bawdwen, vicar of Hooton Pagnell in Yorkshire, edited *A Translation of the Record called Domesday*, in so far as it relates to Yorkshire and parts of the counties of Lancaster, Westmoreland, and Cumberland, and to the counties of Derby, Nottingham, Rutland, and Lincoln. This was followed by another volume in 1812, relating to the counties of Middlesex, Hertford, Buckingham, Oxford, and Gloucester. In 1870, Mr. Charles Gowen Smith edited *A Translation of that part of Domesday Book which relates to Lincolnshire and Rutlandshire.*

A new translation is desirable on several grounds. Bawdwen says in his prospectus, 'On account of the high price of paper it is not intended to strike off more copies than are subscribed for.' In consequence of this, the book is now practically unobtainable. Copies of Smith's book, though not so scarce, are by no means plentiful. But, further, the work of later scholars, such as Professors Maitland, Vinogradoff, and Stenton, and Dr. J. H. Round, has done so much to increase the knowledge of *Domesday Book* that a new edition in English is fully justified. Also, the present edition embodies the first scientific attempt to give the modern names of the places mentioned in the record. This part of the work has involved an immense amount of research on the part of both the editors. Documents, both early and late, have been examined, many sites have been explored, and local information carefully sifted. Mistakes are unavoidable, but the identifications which are added to the text are put forward with a considerable degree of confidence. Bawdwen supplied identifications of the *Domesday* forms with some measure of success, and, being a wise man, he left many blanks. Mr. Smith corrected some of his predecessor's mistakes, and sometimes made alterations for the worse. He also filled in almost all Bawdwen's blanks, in many cases, seemingly, supplying identifications by guess-work, a peculiarly hazardous method, for Lincolnshire place-names afford many pitfalls for the unwary. In the first 238 pages of Smith's text, the actual misidentifications or failures to distinguish between places of the same name number about 220. One further advantage of the present edition may be mentioned, namely, that each entry in the text is numbered, thus making reference to any particular passage more precise as well as more expeditious.

The editors have added a translation of the text of the *Lindsey Survey* (British Museum, Cotton MS., Claudius, C. v), in order that it may be available for reference in the use of the other volumes of this series, and here also the places are identified. At page xliv below, Professor Stenton indicates the importance of this document, and gives particulars of the two previous editions in which the Survey has appeared.

To another feature of the present work attention may be directed, namely, the two appendixes of extinct villages and other forgotten places, of which a surprising number has been found. In many instances the cause of decay can only be surmised, but the cases of Dunsthorpe near Hameringham and West Wykeham (pp. liv-v, lxxii) suggest that the great pestilences of the fourteenth century were chiefly answerable for the depopulation of the villages. This conclusion is reinforced by the records of institutions to benefices which prove that, in a considerable number of cases, no incumbents were instituted after the end of the fourteenth century.

The present writer is responsible for the text of the volume, the identifications of places, the appendixes of extinct villages, the lists of wapentakes and villages, and the indexes, and also for seeing the volume through the press. Canon Longley read the translations of the Latin texts, and made many valuable suggestions ; and he has also read most of the proofs. Further, he has supplied indispensable help in the identification of places ; and the convenient plan of numbering each entry for the purpose of reference is due to his suggestion.

The Introduction by Professor F. M. Stenton is primarily intended to make the highly technical language of the Domesday Survey intelligible to those readers who have made no previous acquaintance with it. No attempt has been made to reconstruct the social condition of Lincolnshire in 1086, and the history of the persons whose names occur in the Survey is omitted from the introduction unless, as sometimes, though rarely, happens, it throws light on dark passages in the text. The writer also wishes to acknowledge his indebtedness to Professor Stenton for constant help and encouragement, and especially for his assistance when revising the translation of the two most difficult portions of *Domesday Book*, namely, the sections about Lincoln, Stamford, and Torksey at the beginning, and the *Clamores* at the end of the text ; and also for guidance in classifying the names of persons of native descent for the index.

Sir H. C. Maxwell Lyte, K.C.B., Deputy Keeper of the Public Records, kindly allowed the writer to use the proof sheets of Parts I and II of *The Book of Fees*, which have since been published ; and the

Director-General of the Ordnance Survey Department kindly supplied proof copies of the Ordnance Maps of Lincolnshire now in course of publication, which are, for the first time, ruled in squares for the purpose of reference. Thanks are also due to Captain W. A. Cragg, who lent a useful manuscript gazeteer of Lincolnshire, compiled by Mr. John Cragg, of Threckingham, about one hundred years ago—a work which supplied valuable evidence in connexion with some of the extinct villages.

The two maps which have been added to the volume have been drawn by Miss F. E. Thurlby, the writer's secretary. In these maps, the present coast-line has necessarily been followed, since the coast-line of 1086 cannot be traced with certainty. For during eight and a half centuries the sea has encroached upon the land here, and receded there. A single instance of each kind may be mentioned. On the one hand, in 1086, Guy of Craon's land in Wrangle which was assessed at two carucates, was waste *propter fluxum maris* (*D.B.*, 57/36) ; while on the other hand, the large tract of land which lies between North Somercotes and Grainthorpe Haven was reclaimed from the sea in the middle of the seventeenth century, a fact which made it difficult to determine the exact locality of the Swine haven (pp. lxiii, lxxxvii) which is mentioned in the *Clamores* of 1086.

C. W. Foster.

12 April, 1924.

CONTENTS

FRONTISPIECE

Part of *Domesday Book*, containing the first seven entries of the Bishop of Lincoln's land.

MAPS

OF LINCOLNSHIRE AND PART OF RUTLAND

(in the pocket at the end of the volume)

1. Divisions, Ridings, and Wapentakes, with the places mentioned in *Domesday Book* and *The Lindsey Survey*.
2. Outline Map of Divisions, Wapentakes, and Boroughs.

ABBREVIATIONS & EXPLANATIONS

D.B. *Domesday Book* (preserved in the Public Record Office). In the present translation the folios of the Record Commission edition of the text, volume i, are shewn, *a*, *b*, *c*, *d*, being added to specify the column. The pages of the photozincographed Facsimile are also given.

L.S. *The Lindsey Survey.* The modern numbers of the folios of the original text (British Museum, Cotton MS., Claudius, C. v) are given.

L Stands in the Indexes for *The Lindsey Survey.*

The method of referring to the numbered entries in this edition of *Domesday Book* and *The Lindsey Survey* is explained at page 261.

Identifications of place-names are enclosed in square brackets ; and the name of the wapentake in each case is added within round brackets.

⌈ ⌉ These signs indicate that the words or letters which they enclose are interlined.

⌊ ⌋ These signs indicate that the words or letters which they enclose have been added to elucidate the text.

* † ‡ These signs, as used in the Index of Persons and Places, are explained at page 261.

B.M. British Museum.

P.R.O. Public Record Office.

T.R.E. Tempore Regis Edwardi, *i.e.* A.D. 1066.

s. son (in the Index of Persons and Places).

Wap. Wapentake.

The following names of Wapentakes have been abbreviated in the Indexes :

Asward.	Aswardhurn
Ave.	Aveland
Axh.	Axholme
Belt.	Beltisloe
Bol.	Bolingbroke
Calce.	Calcewath

Cand.	Candleshoe
Corr.	Corringham
Flax.	Flaxwell
Hav.	Haverstoe
Horn.	Horncastle
Law.	Lawress
Louth.	Louthesk
Love.	Loveden
Lud.	Ludborough
Man.	Manlake
Skir.	Skirbeck
Walsh.	Walshcroft
Wrag.	Wraggoe
Yarb.	Yarborough

Latin christian names have been translated. Most of these names are well-known, but the following may be mentioned :

Alfred *for* Aluredus, Alvredus
Drew *for* Drogo
Geoffrey *for* Goisfridus, Gosfridus
Gocelin *for* Goislanus, Goscelinus, Goslinus, Gozlinus
Guy *for* Wido
Ilbert *for* Ilbertus
Payne *for* Paganus

MANUSCRIPTS

Bardney Cartulary	*Bardney Abbey Cartulary*, British Museum, Cotton MS., Vespasian, E. xx.
Croyland Cartulary	*Croyland Abbey Cartulary*, formerly at Wrest Park, Bedfordshire, now in the possession of Ashley K. Maples, Esq., of Spalding.
Feet of Fines	*Feet of Fines* in the Public Record Office.
Kirkstead Cartulary	*Kirkstead Abbey Cartulary*, British Museum, Cotton MS., Vespasian, E. xviii.
Reg.	*Episcopal Registers* in the Lincoln Diocesan Registry.
Sub.	*Lay Subsidy Rolls* in the Public Record Office.

PRINTED BOOKS

B.F.	*The Book of Fees* (Calendars of State Papers).
Cal. of Charter Rolls	*Calendar of the Charter Rolls* (Calendars of State Papers).

Cal. Inq.	*Calendar of Inquisitions post mortem* (Calendars of State Papers).
Danelaw Charters	*Documents illustrative of the Social and Economic History of the Danelaw*, ed. F. M. Stenton.
F.A.	*Feudal Aids* (Calendars of State Papers).
F.C., i	Lincolnshire Records—*Abstracts of Final Concords*, vol. i.
F.C., ii	*Final Concords of the County of Lincoln*, vol. ii, ed. C. W. Foster (Lincoln Record Society, vol. xvii).
L.R.S.	Publications of the Lincoln Record Society.
Monasticon	*Monasticon Anglicanum*, 1817-1830 edition.
O.S.	*Ordnance Survey*. The references are to the ruled squares in the one-inch-to-the-mile series, now in course of publication, unless either of the larger scale maps is specified.

INTRODUCTION

THE Lincolnshire portion of the Domesday Survey is an important and an interesting record, but neither its importance nor its interest lie upon the surface. Its seventy-two folios of almost unrelieved statistics contribute little to our knowledge of the actors in the Norman Conquest of England. Its value as the earliest record of the villages and hamlets of the modern map is not peculiar to itself. In most parts of England, Domesday Book is the topographer's starting point. It is as material for social history that the Lincolnshire Domesday fills a unique place. With each year that passes, the interest of the form of society that prevailed in Lincolnshire and the other regions of Danish settlement becomes more clearly apparent. Lincolnshire under William I was one of the richest counties in England. Its life had not been broken, as the life of Yorkshire was broken, by devastation following the Norman Conquest. Its prosperity meant that the masses of free peasants registered by Domesday under the name of sokemen could transmit their independence to their successors. Whatever direction may hereafter be given to the study of English social history, the Lincolnshire Domesday will never want its students.

The first step towards an edition of any part of the Domesday Survey is the precise identification of the place-names which it records. Every county presents its own problems of identification, but those presented by Lincolnshire are the most difficult of all. Most of them have been answered by reference to the recorded descent of the great feudal estates of the county. Others have yielded to an investigation of the ground, for the tofts and crofts of a deserted village sometimes leave their imprint on the ground for centuries. Some of them still remain unsolved. But it is now possible to attempt a reconstruction of the eleventh century wapentakes of Lincolnshire, to trace the distribution of the different peasant classes over the vast area contained within the county boundary, and to identify the scattered estates of the Conqueror's tenants in chief. The results of Canon Longley's work upon the assessment of the shire to the Danegeld and other public burdens are to form a second volume of this edition. In a third volume it is hoped to use the Domesday Survey as a foundation for the feudal history of Lincolnshire. All that will be attempted in this introduction is a discussion of the terminology of the Survey, regarded, as its compilers regarded it, as a record to serve the purposes of royal finance.

For the whole character of the Domesday Survey is governed by its fiscal purpose. It was compiled in order that the king might know how far assessment to public burdens corresponded to the facts of real life. The Danegeld, the heaviest of these burdens, belongs to the closing phase of Old English history, but in many shires Danegeld was paid in the eleventh century upon an assessment which had persisted from a far remoter age—from a time before the earliest Danish raids upon England.

Lincoln is not one of these shires ; but even in Lincolnshire it is certain that Kesteven and Holland bore a far heavier assessment than Lindsey, and there is no economic or geographical explanation of the severity with which Kesteven and Holland were treated. A description of all England according to a uniform plan was a necessary preliminary to the correction of such anomalies. The task of correction was to prove beyond the power of the king's financial officers. In the thirteenth century, it seems that the men of Kesteven and Holland were still taxed according to the ancient assessment of those parts, although by negociation with the Exchequer they secured a reduction of the rate at which taxes were actually levied upon them. The Domesday Survey was not used as a basis for financial reform, but it enabled the king to know the sources of his revenue with remarkable precision of detail.

A large, if indeterminate, part of that revenue was derived from the tax called Danegeld. The word appears for the first time in the description of Stamford in the Lincolnshire Domesday. Danegeld was a land tax, and in Lincolnshire it was a levy of so many shillings on each 'carucate to the geld' at which an estate was assessed. The rate at which Danegeld was taken was in the king's discretion, but in the twelfth century a levy of two shillings on the carucate became the rule. Regarded as a measure of land, the carucate of Domesday denoted the tract which could be cultivated by an eight ox plough team. The carucate was composed of eight bovates, and later evidence suggests very strongly that an average Lincolnshire bovate contained twenty acres of arable land, with the meadow and the rights of pasture which were annexed to such a tenement by local custom. There is reason to believe that this terminology represents a system of land division introduced by the Danish settlers of Lincolnshire. In the south and west of England, the regions which escaped Danish settlement, the unit of assessment was not the carucate or ploughland, but the ancient English 'hide,' or family land. It is probable that the Lincolnshire jurors spoke of 'plogslands' when the clerks of the Domesday commissioners wrote 'carucatæ.' The word 'plogsland,' which from its form must be of Scandinavian origin, is used for a ploughland in a Yorkshire document of the eleventh century and a Lincolnshire document of the twelfth. It had fallen out of use before documents were again generally written in English, but the word 'oxgang,' the English equivalent of 'bovata,' which is recorded a hundred years before the Conquest, is still one of the commonest terms in Lincolnshire records of the sixteenth and seventeenth centuries.

But Domesday Book is before all things the record of an assessment, and the carucates and bovates which pay to the geld—the *carucatæ* and *bovatæ ad geldum* of the survey—must always be clearly distinguished from the actual ploughlands and oxgangs of the village fields. When the survey records that Fulcheri had 11 carucates 7 bovates to the geld in Flixborough, it is telling nothing directly about the number of real ploughlands and oxgangs within Fulcheri's lordship, still less is it telling anything about its acreage. It is merely recording that Fulcheri's estate in Flixborough had answered for 11 carucates 7 bovates to the officers collecting the king's geld, that if, for example, Danegeld were taken at the rate of two shillings on the carucate a sum of twenty-three shillings and nine pence would be demanded from the property. In some parts of England—in some parts of Lincolnshire—assessment agrees very closely with agricultural facts. The village of Asgarby was assessed at three carucates to the geld, it was reputed to contain three ploughlands, and the twenty sokemen and two villeins who lived there had three teams among them. Coincidences like this are exceptional in Lincolnshire. It is true that a large village with many working teams will generally bear a high assessment. Even in the eleventh century taxation was not wantonly inequitable, and its framers tried to achieve a rough correspondence between the carucates to the geld and the teams and teamlands of real life. More than this they could not hope to do, and the study of the detailed assessment of any county will always bring out very clearly the conditions which limited their prospects of success.

From what has just been said it will be evident that the total assessment of a shire in carucates to the geld was not obtained by counting its actual, arable, ploughlands. It was a round sum, laid on the shire by the king and his council. It is more than probable that these high authorities in fixing this sum took into account what they knew of the agrarian condition of the shire which was thenceforward to answer for it. But the Old English state had not yet developed the administrative machinery which could make assessment correspond with reality. It was easier to handle round numbers, to cast an arbitrary number of carucates upon a shire, and to leave the shire to distribute them among its constituent wapentakes. The men of the wapentakes could then distribute among their villages the carucates for which the shire had ruled that they must answer. They had local knowledge enough to make the assessment of a village at least roughly proportionate to its size or to the fertility of its soil. The result is seen in the village assessments recorded in Domesday.

The process which has just been described may be illustrated by an example. Whatever the total assessment of all Lincolnshire may have been, there is good reason to believe that the parts of Kesteven were rated at exactly 1908 carucates to the geld. Of this sum, 132 carucates were laid upon the wapentake of Boothby. They were apportioned among the villages within the wapentake in the following way :—

	carucates		carucates
Boothby and Somerton -	12	Skinnand - -	3
Coleby - - - - -	24	Waddington -	24
Harmston - - -	24	Welbourn -	12
Navenby - - - -	12	Wellingore -	21

There is no mistaking the conventional character of this scheme. It was obviously framed by men who felt that a village ought to be assessed either at exactly twelve carucates or at some fraction or multiple of this sum. In Boothby wapentake they were able to carry out this idea with remarkable consistency. The neatness of the scheme is only broken by the twenty-one carucates assigned to Wellingore and the three carucates assigned to Skinnand. The exception is one of the sort which proves a rule. Skinnand, which has almost faded from the modern map, was a small place even in 1086. It was inhabited by only seven villeins who did not possess a complete ox team among them. It was evident that such a place could not bear a high assessment. Three carucates were assigned to it, Wellingore, which overlooks it from the edge, was let off rather lightly with twenty-one, and a neat combined assessment of twenty-four carucates was thus secured.

This habit of reckoning in twelves and sixes is characteristic of the northern portion of the great region called the Danelaw. It underlies the assessment of Yorkshire, Lincolnshire, Nottinghamshire, Derbyshire, Leicestershire, and northern Rutland, and it undoubtedly represents methods of computation which prevailed among the Anglo-Danish population of this region. The assessment of the centre and south of England was equally artificial, but in those parts assessment was distributed in fives and tens of hides. A normal Bedfordshire village, for example, will answer for five or ten hides. The duodecimal system of reckoning is confined to the parts of England settled by the Danes in 876 and 877, that is to the ancient kingdom of York and the territory of the Five Boroughs, Lincoln, Stamford, Nottingham, Leicester, and Derby. Its prevalence in this region is a remarkable illustration of the strength of early provincial custom and the vitality of ancient habits of thought.

Nevertheless it might easily escape the notice of anyone reading the Lincolnshire Domesday consecutively. Such a reader might, indeed, be struck by the curious recurrence of certain figures. He would probably notice that Freiston, Butterwick, Baumber, Harlaxton, Folkingham, Welbourn, Edenham, Aubourn, Grantham, Ruskington, Potter Hanworth, Digby, Dorrington, Rowston, Westborough, Branston, Gelston, Norton Disney, Carlton le Moorland, and Billinghay, are each assessed at twelve carucates precisely. He would hardly realise the significance of these figures unless he went on to reconstruct, village by village, the several wapentakes of the county. In 1086 most Lincolnshire villages were divided between two or more tenants in chief. The unit of assessment was not the lord's estate but the village as a whole. The assessments borne by the various estates within a village under divided lordship rarely suggest the influence of a governing system. The regularity with which the carucates of the geld were distributed in blocks of six and twelve over the villages of the county does not appear until the reader has before him the complete information given by Domesday about each individual village.

Even then in any given case it may happen that the complete assessment of a village works out at some irregular number of carucates and bovates to the geld. The assessment of a whole shire to public burdens was a difficult business. There were many interests to be consulted, wide differences of agrarian condition to be taken into account. And the actual work of apportioning among the villages of a wapentake the number of carucates which the court of the shire had decided that it should bear had to be done in an open and probably heated assembly by thegns and peasants little practised in reckoning. Moreover the clerks who wrote the Lincolnshire Domesday were not infallible and Roman figures were difficult to handle. A little slip, the confusion of *iiii*^{tam} *partem* with *iiii*^{or} *partes*, for example, and the round, duodecimal, total of a village assessment is hopelessly blurred. A chinese puzzle cannot be reconstructed if some of the pieces are broken.

A few examples may serve to illustrate the neatness with which the distribution of the carucates to the geld could be carried out, and, it should be added, the remarkable accuracy which distinguishes the Domesday clerks :

	Skirbeck	car.	bov.
12/67	Berewick of Drayton -	2	0
,,	Sokeland of Drayton -	9	6
29/33	Sokeland of Tattershall		2
		12	0

	Drayton in Swineshead	car.	bov.
11/6	Berewick of Dowdyke -	1	0
12/58	Manor, Greue - -		6
12/59	Manor, bishop Wulfwig	1	0
12/60	Manor, Ralf the Staller	8	2
57/56	Manor, Alestan - -		4
67/18	Manor, Wider - -		4
		12	0

	Marston	car.	bov.
12/45	Sokeland of Hough -	1	0
26/33	Manor, Alsi - -	1	0
	Sokeland of this manor	1	2
27/50	Manor, Ulsi - -	1	0
	Sokeland of this manor	1	0
54/1	Manor, Turvert ,, 'alius Turvert' }	6	0
57/35	Berewick of Haceby -		6
		12	0

	Barkston	car.	bov.
1/15	Sokeland of Grantham	8	0
14/89	Sokeland of Honington	1	2
54/2	Sokeland of Marston -	1	0
67/15	Berewick of Belton -		6
67/16	Sokeland of Belton -	1	0
		12	0

	Barholme and Stowe	car.	bov.
8/35	Berewick of Witham on the Hill - -	1	0
8/36	Sokeland of Peterborough - -	1	0
8/37	Sokeland of Witham on the Hill - -		4½
8/38	Sokeland of Peterborough - -		2
24/29	Sokeland of Edenham		4
24/35	Sokeland of Casewick		4
24/34	Sokeland of Edenham		6½
27/36	Sokeland of Uffington		1½
51/4	Manor, Aschil - -	1	0
51/5	Sokeland of Barholme		1½
		6	0

	Fishtoft	car.	bov.
57/37	Manor, Adestan - -	9	0
12/66	Sokeland of Drayton -	3	0
		12	0

	Little Bytham	car.	bov.
8/7	Berewick of 'Bergestorp'	4	0
30/31	Manor, Edward - -	7	0
51/8	Sokeland of Creeton -		4
59/10	Sokeland of Creeton -		4
		12	0

	Belton	car.	bov.
1/15	Sokeland of Grantham	5	0
31/1	Manor, Tori - -	4	0
57/25	Sokeland of Towthorpe		4
67/13	Manor, Rold - -	2	4
		12	0

	Long Bennington	car.	bov.
12/49	Manor, Ralf the Staller	14	0
	Sokeland of this manor	7	6
15/2	Inland of Carlton Scroop	1	2
	Sokeland of ,, ,,	1	0
		24	0

	Hougham	car.	bov.
7/54	Manor, Tori - -	14	0
7/55	(Robert the priest) -	1	0
26/34	Sokeland of Marston -	2	0
26/35	Manor, Azor - -	2	0
56/5	Manor, Estori - -	5	0
		24	0

	Somerby near Grantham	car.	bov.
1/15	Sokeland of Grantham	2	2
31/3	Manor, Tori - -	2	2
57/43	(Adelid) - - -		6
67/12	Manor, Ulsi - -		6
		6	0

	Hainton	car.	bov.
2/23	Sokeland of 'Torp' -	1	4
4/46	Manor, Rolf - -	1	7
16/12	Manor, Oudon - -	1	1
16/14	Manor, Clac - Manor, Sendi - }	1	0½
40/9	Manor, Code - -		3½
		6	0

CLAXBY AND NORMANBY LE WOLD

		car.	bov.
14/8	Manor, Godwin - -	1	2
14/9	Manor, Godric -		
	Manor, Siward -		
	Manor, Ulchel -	1	4
	Manor, Godwin -		
14/11	Manor, Alwin - -		3
28/23	Sokeland of Tealby -	1	1
30/36	Manor, Ulf - -		6
32/8	Manor, Chetel - -		2
	Manor, Godwin - -		1
44/15	Sokeland of Wyham -		5
		6	0

LUDFORD

		car.	bov.
14/61	Manor, Turold - -		5
22/21	Manor, Alsi - -	1	6
22/22	Manor, Wilac -		
	Manor, Siward -	3	0
22/23	Sokeland of Baumber -		2
25/18	Sokeland of Wykeham		2
40/16	Sokeland of Wykeham		1
		6	0

CROXBY

		car.	bov.
14/15	Manor, Siward - -		5
18/10	Sokeland of Binbrook -	1	0
32/9	Manor, Fulcheri - -		3
49/2	Manor, Asford - -	1	0
		3	0

These details of assessment are closely connected with one of the most interesting features presented by the Lincolnshire Domesday—the occasional appearance of an anomalous local division called the Hundred. We are told, for example, that the bishop of Durham's manor in Kelby lay in Aswardhurn wapentake and in Laythorpe hundred, that the 'men of the hundred' say that the soke of certain lands in Keisby ought to belong to Osgodby. The hundred was obviously an institution, quite distinct from the wapentake, which could speak for itself before the Domesday commissioners, but little that is definite is at present known about its origin or its functions.

One thing, however, which is certain is that each of these hundreds was assessed at exactly twelve carucates to the geld. In the description of Walter de Aincurt's fee, for example, Branston, which was rated at just twelve carucates, is described as a hundred by the insertion of the letters HUND' above the name of the village, and Blankney, which was rated at twenty-four carucates, is described as two hundreds. Belton, Little Bytham, Skirbeck, Fishtoft, Frampton, Horbling, Honington, Leake, Leverton, Drayton, Walcot near Timberland, Welby, Potter Hanworth, and Gelston, each of which has been observed to bear an exact assessment of twelve carucates, are each definitely called hundreds by Domesday. Long Bennington, assessed like Blankney at twenty-four carucates, was similarly described in Domesday as two hundreds. There can be no doubt that every Lincolnshire village assessed at twelve carucates was known as a hundred in the eleventh century.

But many villages, and in Lindsey nearly all villages, were assessed at a smaller sum than this, and many hundreds were therefore composed of two or more villages whose combined assessments amounted to the precise twelve carucates. Thealby, Derby, and Burton upon Stather, assessed together at twelve carucates, formed the hundred of Thealby. Hough on the Hill and Brandon together formed the hundred of Hough. The earl of Chester's estate which comprised the villages of Swaby, Belleau, South Thoresby, Claythorpe, and Tothill, and was assessed at twelve carucates, appears in the Lindsey Survey of the next generation as Swaby Hundred. We know on the best authority that the division of Lincolnshire into hundreds, each assessed at twelve carucates to the geld, was carried out consistently throughout the county. Of an odd two carucates in Pickworth we are definitely told that 'these are not in the 'tale (*in numero*) of any hundred, nor have they their like in Lincoln- 'shire (26/53).'

It is hard to say exactly what part these hundreds played in the life of the county, or what is the origin of their curious name. A passage which is inserted between the descriptions of Lincoln and Stamford proves at the least their importance. 'If the peace given by the king's 'hand and seal be broken it is emended by eighteen hundreds. Each 'hundred pays eight pounds. Twelve hundreds pay to the king, and six 'to the earl.' These hundreds were therefore combined in large groups to pay the fine incurred by an aggravated offence against the king's peace. This in turn suggests that they may have discharged police and judicial functions. Of this however nothing is at present known. But these hundreds are so closely connected with the assessment to the king's geld that we may fairly assume that the system of which they are a part was intended to secure the punctual payment of taxes. It was a highly artificial system. We can just see that the hundreds were not all continuous stretches of land. A carucate might be taken from one village assessed too highly to fit into a local group rated at twelve carucates and be added to another group to bring up its assessment to the neat, inevitable, total. No convincing explanation has yet been given of the application of the name hundred of these curious local divisions. They may have received this name because they were felt in some way to resemble the hundreds of southern England. If so, their function in matters of police and local government might safely be assumed. At present, their existence can only be noted as one of the many features which give a special character to the Domesday survey of the counties of the northern Danelaw.

In almost every entry, the essential statement of the property to the geld is followed by an estimate of the number of plough-teams that could be employed upon it. Few of the questions which arise in the study of Domesday terminology are more difficult than the interpretation to be put upon this estimate. In some counties, Bedfordshire is one, the words 'There is land for *x* teams' can be taken to mean precisely what they say. They record an estimate of the number of teams for which work would be found if the land were cultivated to its fullest capacity. In effect, they tell the king's financial officers whether the land will bear heavier taxation than is already laid upon it. This is what the king's officers really wanted to know. In Northamptonshire, which had recently enjoyed a reduction of its assessment to the geld, the information was given by a statement of the older, higher, assessment which the land had borne. It is highly probable that the same course was followed in Nottinghamshire. So long as the answer was relevant to the purpose of the inquiry it did not much matter at the time in what form it was cast.

It is obvious that in Lincolnshire there is often something artificial about this form. In many entries the number of estimated teamlands is exactly equal to the number of geldable carucates. In the soke of Ruskington, for example, Ruskington itself, Dorrington, Digby, and Rowston, are each assessed at 12 carucates, and are each estimated to contain land for exactly 12 teams. The 6 geldable carucates at Anwick and Dunsby near Cranwell are each balanced by 6 estimated teamlands. At Brauncewell and Rauceby there were parcels of sokeland assessed respectively at 9 carucates 2 bovates and at 6 carucates 2½ bovates, and in each case there was considered to be land for the same number of teams and oxen. On this great estate it is only at 'the other Rauceby' and at Evedon that the coincidence between assessment and estimate is broken.

This coincidence becomes more striking when it can be shown to occur in every entry relating to a village under divided lordship :

	Assessment		Teamlands		Demesne		Men's	
	car.	bov.	teams	oxen	teams	oxen	teams	oxen
				STOW ST. MARY				
7/1	4	0	4	0	1	0	3	4
7/12	1	1⅓	1	1⅓		no details		
12/41		4		4				4
20/3		4		4		no details		
28/6	1	0	1	0			1	0
	7	1⅓	7	1⅓	1	0	5	0
				BURGH LE MARSH				
12/78	1	4	1	4			1	4
24/50	8	0	8	0			6	0
29/18	1	2	1	2	1	0	1	0
29/25	1	0	1	0			1	0
29/26		1		1				2
	11	7	11	7	1	0	9	6
				ADDLETHORPE				
2/19		no details						
3/46		6		6			1	1
12/79		1		1				2
12/80	1	0	1	0				4
24/51	4	2	4	2			4	0
29/17		2		2				1
29/19	1	1	1	1				6
29/23	1	0	1	0				2
38/8	3	0	3	0	3	0	6	0
68/10		2		2				
	11	6	11	6	3	0	13	0
				POINTON				
12/54		4		4				4
24/98	2	2	2	2			6	0
26/38		4		4	1	0		
52/2		2		2				
57/13	1	0	1	0	1	0		
	4	4	4	4	2	0	6	4

These figures prove that the Lincolnshire teamland was not a measure of area. In these examples, the teamlands must be as artificial as the carucates of assessment, with which they coincide. The jurors seem, in effect, to be saying that the assessments of these villages correspond to their arable capacity. They are not putting forward any plea for a reduction of assessment, but they are making no admissions which might be held to justify an increase. The numerous cases in which the assessment of an estate is followed immediately by the statement that there is land for the same mumber of teams or oxen produce the same impression. 'In Creeton Fredgist and Brictmar had 12 bovates and 2 'thirds of 2 bovates assessed to the geld. There is land for as many 'oxen.' These words were not meant to be taken literally, but they told the commissioners all that they were really interested to know.

On the other hand, Domesday shows clearly that many Lincolnshire villages were under-assessed. Where the discrepancy between the carucates and bovates on which geld was paid and the teamlands and oxgangs of the open fields was sufficiently great the jurors will often estimate their teamlands at precisely double the carucates of assessment. 'In Rothwell Rolf had 13 bovates and a half and the third part of one 'bovate assessed to the geld. There is twice as much land for ploughing '(*Terra dupliciter ad arandum*).' More often in such cases the number of teamlands is expressed in figures :

BECKERING

	Assessment		Teamlands		Demesne		Men's	
	car.	bov.	teams	oxen	teams	oxen	teams	oxen
2/15		2		4			1	6
16/18		2		4				3
22/12		1½		3				2
28/30		½		1				1
32/12		2		4		2		2
	1	0	2	0		2	2	6

SWALLOW

	car.	bov.	teams	oxen	teams	oxen	teams	oxen
2/10	1	0	2	0				4
4/27	1	0	2	0			1	0
12/15		3		6				
12/17	1	4	3	0		4	1	4
16/2	1	0	2	0		4	1	0
27/6		3		6				1
	5	2	10	4	1	0	4	1

APPLEBY, RISBY, AND SAWCLIFF

	car.	bov.	teams	oxen	teams	oxen	teams	oxen
8/27		3		6	1	0		
17/2	9	5	19	2	4	0	6	0
							6	0
24/10	2	0	4	0	2	0	2	0
	12	0	24	0	7	0	14	0

GOXHILL

	Assessment		Teamlands		Demesne		Men's	
	car.	bov.	teams	oxen	teams	oxen	teams	oxen
7/23	1	0	2	0	2	0	1	0
27/1	1	2	2	4	1	0	2	0
30/2	2	0	4	0			3	0
34/6	1	2	2	4		4	2	4
68/40		4	1	0			1	0
	6	0	12	0	3	4	9	4

Here, again, it is evident that the jurors were making an estimate instead of recording facts. They were also saving themselves trouble. When a village was greatly under-assessed, it was much easier to say that it contained two bovates of arable for every bovate on which it paid geld than to make a careful estimate of the land that then was, or might thereafter come, under the plough. Moreover it was not always possible to say how many real teamlands or oxgangs belonged to the several estates within a village. A hundred years after the date of Domesday, the men of Willoughton could not distinguish the teamlands of Simon de Canci from those of Roger de Buslei (*Feodary of the Templars*, see *Monasticon Anglicanum*, vii, 827). The king's commissioners were satisfied with round figures. They learned that the village in question was assessed very materially below its arable capacity, and they would have learned nothing more useful from a series of detailed estimates. The jurors, on their part, dared not return an estimate which was flagrantly at variance with fact. Other juries might contradict them, and throughout the Middle Ages a jury suffered heavily when it was convicted of a false verdict.

Nevertheless the evidence for the conventional character of the Lincolnshire teamland should not be exaggerated. It is only conclusive when every entry relating to a village under divided lordship reveals the same ratio between the carucates of assessment and the teamlands. There are many cases in which no such ratio is observed :

ULCEBY

	Assessment		Teamlands		Demesne		Men's	
	car.	bov.	teams	oxen	teams	oxen	teams	oxen
7/22		6	2	0	1	0		
32/20		6	2	2	1	0		4
34/2	4	0	10	0	4	0	9	0
68/39		4	1	3	1	0		
	6	0	15	5	7	0	9	4

CANDLESBY

	car.	bov.	teams	oxen	teams	oxen	teams	oxen
12/81		2		3				4
24/49	1	0	1	0			2	0
29/22	4	2	5	3	5	4	2	4
68/8		4		5		4		
	6	0	7	3	6	0	5	0

Here, at least, there is no valid reason to doubt that the teamlands represent a genuine estimate of the existing arable. These figures clash sharply with the neat ratios shown by the tables relating to Burgh le Marsh or Goxhill. The discrepancy makes it impossible to give a comprehensive definition of the Lincolnshire teamland, but it is not in itself remarkable. To compel a large number of local juries to adopt an identical principle in framing a series of estimates was beyond the power of any eleventh century government. The Domesday commissioners did not attempt the impossible.

From the Lincolnshire Domesday it appears that the number of teams working within a village was often in excess of the number of teamlands which it was reputed to contain. On earl Hugh's sokeland in Swaby, Belleau, South Thoresby, Claythorpe, and Tothill, which was estimated at 18 teamlands, 46 sokemen, 22 villeins, and 38 bordars, had 31 teams. Cases like this are common. Whatever their explanation may be, they show that the Lincolnshire teamlands were estimates of the land actually under the plough, without reference to the possibility of creating new teamlands by breaking up waste. At Potter Hanworth, where there was considered to be land for 6 teams, Walter de Aincurt had 2 teams in demesne; 9 sokemen, 22 villeins, and 11 bordars had 9½ teams, a knight had 2 teams and 2 villeins with half a team. The jurors who said that there was land for 6 teams in this village were obviously making no allowance for the fresh teamlands that might be formed by bringing stretches of the Heath into cultivation. In part, at least, it is probable that the explanation of this excess of teams over teamlands lies in the social condition of the county. It may well have been that the free peasants of Lincolnshire were actually keeping up more teams than would have been required under a more efficient—a manorial—system of local economy. Moreover, the establishment of new demesne farms after the Conquest must often have disturbed the traditional balance of teamlands and teams. The village of Sibsey, a member of the soke of Bolingbroke, was assessed at 6 carucates and estimated to contain 6 teamlands. The men of the village had 6 teams among them, but Ivo Taillebois, the new lord, had also a demesne team of his own. The lord's team appears here very plainly as an innovation. In this and in similar cases it should not be assumed that the creation of new demesne was accompanied by the cultivation of new lands. In most cases, the new home farm must have arisen on ancient arable. Its establishment meant the employment of new teams without any corresponding increase in the number of the village teamlands.

In the description of a normal manor, the enumeration of the teams upon the lord's demesne is followed by an enumeration of the teams possessed by the men belonging to the estate—the sokemen, villeins, and bordars: 'Ivo has 2 teams there in demesne, and 2 villeins and 11 sokemen 'and 1 bordar with 2 teams' (14/22). Domesday makes no attempt to distinguish between the teams possessed by the members of these three classes of men, and concise entries like this obscure the important fact that the ordinary bordar owned no plough beasts. He was a cottager, with at most some five acres of arable, gaining his living as a hired labourer, or by the exercise of some craft. He might be a smith, carpenter, or wheelwright; he must often have been a herdsman, but he can rarely have contributed an ox to a co-operative plough team. It follows that the bordars should be left out of the reckoning when it is attempted to estimate the number of plough beasts possessed by the average member of a village community. This number was remarkably small. It is indeed possible to find a Lincolnshire sokeman with an entire plough team. At Ashby near Bottesford, a sokeman had a plough team and three acres of underwood (8/26); at Scopwick, a sokeman had a team and four acres of meadow (61/8). Such cases are rare. Upon an average, a Lincolnshire villein or sokeman of 1086 possessed two oxen, the quarter of a full team. At Dorrington, 28 sokemen, and 8 bordars who should be omitted from the calculation, had 7 teams (64/3). At Scothorne, St. Peter had 32 sokemen having 8 teams (8/2). At Little Ponton, 8 sokemen, 12 villeins, and 3 bordars—the last again to be ignored—had 5 teams (56/7). Many Lincolnshire peasants were still less well provided with oxen. At Whitton, for example, 10 villeins, 4 bordars, and 30 sokemen, had only 5 teams among them (21/1). At Snarford, 4 sokemen had half a team (35/17). Many other passages show the sokemen and villeins upon an estate possessing upon the average only one ox apiece. Sometimes it is even impossible to allow one ox to each enumerated peasant. At Thrunsco, 5 villeins had one ox amongst them (14/6). At Stickford in Bolingbroke soke, 28 sokemen and 2 villeins had only 3 teams (14/77); at Alvingham in Gayton soke, 14 sokemen, 7 villeins, and 5 bordars had only two (1/88). In these cases, and in many others, two or more villeins or sokemen must have combined to find an ox for a common team. Even where Domesday reveals a neat ratio between the number of villeins and sokemen and the number of their teams, it should not be assumed that each enumerated peasant possessed the same number of oxen. Round totals and neat quotients may conceal much real variety, and a Lincolnshire village of 1086 may have contained both large and small farmers as its successor contains them today. Some such conclusion follows indeed inevitably from the Domesday descriptions of the several estates in a village under divided lordship. There are, for example, three entries in Domesday relating to Harpswell. In the first, 6 sokemen have $2\frac{1}{2}$ teams, or twenty oxen (1/42); in the second, 5 sokemen and 1 villein have 6 oxen (2/27); in the third, 13 villeins have 3 teams or 24 oxen (28/11). Nevertheless, when all allowance has been made for variations masked by succinct statistics it may safely be said that the ordinary Lincolnshire sokeman and villein—for in this respect there was no material difference between these classes—was a man of two or three oxen.

This conclusion is more important than might at first appear. It proves that the remarkable independence which distinguished the sokemen among the Lincolnshire peasantry of the eleventh century was not the result of any superior economic position. There were many southern villages in which the average villein possessed more oxen than the average Lincolnshire sokemen. In Oxfordshire, for example, 16 villeins with 8 bordars at Mapledurham had 16 teams; 22 villeins with 5 bordars at Watlington had 11 teams; 19 villeins with 10 bordars at Kingham had 12 teams. Here, as in Lincolnshire, the bordars are not likely to have possessed plough oxen. The Lincolnshire sokemen as a class had inherited their independence from their predecessors, the Danish invaders of the ninth century, and the facts which have just been quoted are in their way evidence of the thoroughness of the Danish settlement. The existence of a large class of peasants who maintained their personal independence with a very modest agricultural equipment proves that this settlement was not merely the establishment of a few Danish chiefs over a subject English population. It was also a settlement of the men of the Danish army among the people whom they had conquered.

Among the miscellaneous sources of manorial revenue, mills were the most important. Domesday gives no direct information as to the way in which these mills came into being, but it suggests that in most cases some earlier lord of a village has built its mills. Of a village mill erected by the men of a village community there is no evidence in the Lincolnshire Domesday. On the other hand, the value of a mill to its owner is often measured in a way which suggests a somewhat remote origin for the owner's rights. In many cases, the value of a mill is set down at sixteen pence, or at some multiple of this sum. At Walesby and Otby there was a mill rendering 16 pence (14/13); at Kexby, there was another (26/22). At Billingborough, a mill rendered 5 shillings and 4 pence (26/36); at Normanby by Spital, two mills rendered the same amount (14/18). At Great Sturton, a mill rendered 10 shillings and 8 pence (29/1). At Donington on Bain, two mills rendered 17 shillings and 4 pence; and the two mills at Belchford were worth sixteen pence more than this (14/50, 14/45). At Kirkby Green and Scopwick, there were four mills rendering 21 shillings and 4 pence (31/14); and at Claxby and Normanby the quarter of a mill rendered 8 pence (30/36). These figures are interesting because sixteen pence was the value of the *ora*, or ounce of silver, a denomination introduced into England under Scandinavian influence. The recurrence of this unit suggests very strongly that the yearly render of a mill was often a traditional sum. Documents of the twelfth century will sometimes show a miller, on taking over a mill, pledging his faith to pay his lord the yearly sum required from him, and it may safely be assumed that a similar practice existed in the time before the Conquest. The same ancient unit of account was often used to measure the yearly render which a lord derived from his salt-pans. At Bicker, Guy de Craon had a salt-pan rendering 16 pence (57/44); at Stenning in Bicker, Robert de Veci had two salt-pans rendering 2 shillings and 8 pence (37/6); at Wainfleet, two salt-pans rendered 16 pence to Eudo son of Spirewic (29/20); and a single pan rendered 8 pence to a man of Gocelin son of Lambert (28/41). Here, again, it is probable that the figures recorded by Domesday represent payments which had already been established for many years.

Like a mill, a church was usually a source of profit to some owner. Domesday gives no complete list of churches, and rarely assigns a value to those which it mentions, but there is no mistaking the significance of the numerous entries which record that some fraction of a church belonged to this or that manor. At Scremby, the quarter of half a church was attached to a small parcel of sokeland belonging to a manor in West Keal (29/13). In the single village of Threckingham there were two separate churches, and each of them was much divided. The Bishop of Durham possessed a twelfth of a church of St. Peter, and a sixth of a church of St. Mary, with a sixth of four bovates which belonged to it (3/55). Odo the arblaster had the sixth of St. Peter's church, and the third of St. Mary's, with the third part of its four bovates (48/7).

Ulviet, a king's thegn, had a twelfth of St. Peter's church and a sixth of St. Mary's with a sixth of its four bovates (67/11). Of the remaining two thirds of St. Peter's church and the remaining third of St. Mary's, Domesday tells nothing. But it shows clearly enough that the remarkable arrangement which it records was the result of the partition of an estate in such a way that one person, whose share had passed to Odo the arblaster, had acquired as much land as two other persons who shared in the division. It shows, therefore, that the division of a property implied a corresponding division of the profits which might come to an owner from the church or churches built upon it. Many similar cases may be explained in this way. In others, the division of the church—or rather of its profits—must have existed from the very time of its foundation. When two or more lords contributed equally towards the building of a church and the endowment of a priest, all were held entitled to share equally in the ensuing profits. When a lord built a church at his own cost, it became his church, and it was long before the representatives of the founder were compelled, mainly by episcopal pressure, to assign a definite portion of the revenues of the church to the maintenance of the priest who served it. Even if the men of a village combined to build and endow a church, it would be hard for them to retain an interest in its profits. The legal ideas of the eleventh century did not include the conception of a rural community which could present a priest for institution to a benefice and make a collective bargain with him. Inevitably in such cases the church would pass into the power of the several lords of the village, if the village were under divided lordship. For centuries, the history of a Lincolnshire church might be influenced by the results of this primitive individualism. In the sixteenth century it is still possible to trace the six portions into which the church of Brocklesby had been divided in the time of Henry II, and the division of Brocklesby church amongst its several patrons answers precisely to the division of Brocklesby village between the various lords who had authority there in 1086.

The remaining sources of revenue raise few difficult questions. Something should however be said of the figures which express the total value of an estate in 1066 and in 1086. They are generally round figures—even numbers of shillings in the case of the smaller estates, even numbers of pounds in the case of the greater. Some of the exceptions to this rule are only apparent. In 1066, a small manor in Blyborough had been worth 26 shillings and 8 pence—in round figures, 20 *oræ* (14/16). Stow St. Mary and Barrow on Humber were each valued at £32 in 1066. £32 is the same as 48 *oræ* of 16 pence. To a Lincolnshire man of Edward the Confessor's time, practised in reckoning by twelves and sixteens, these were neat, round, figures. The roundness of these figures makes it impossible to suppose that the values which Domesday assigns to a manor represent the sum of the yearly payments made and the customary services done, to its lord. In many cases they are doubtless estimates of the sum which would be paid yearly by a lessee of the estate. In others, it is highly probable that the jurors are returning as the value of the property the sum that is actually being paid each year to its lord by the person who is holding it of him in farm. In the case of Westborough (64/15), for example, it is likely that Geoffrey Alselin was receiving each year from some lessee the £25 which Domesday returns as the value of the manor. Some such explanation is required to account for the frequent appearance in Domesday of a sum called a 'tailla' beside the sum which represents the 'value' of an estate in 1086. The great manor of Folkingham was 'worth' £40, but also produced a 'tailla' of £50 (24/82). This 'tailla' should not be identified with the taillage of later medieval custom—the sum exacted by a lord from his unfree tenants. In 1086, large payments were being exacted by way of 'tailla' from manors which contained only an insignificant proportion of villein peasants. The 'tailla' should rather be regarded as a sum of money paid directly to the lord, by both free and unfree tenants, and standing outside the sum for which the lessees of the manor answered to him. It is impossible to distinguish between the various kinds of render combined in this general payment, but in most cases they must have included the sums which a lord's free tenants were bound by custom to pay him yearly as an acknowledgement of his superiority. It is a rare exception when, as at Owston and Haxey (63/6, 7), 'tailla' was taken from a manor which included no peasants above the villein class.

It is impossible to discuss the statements of value which occur in Domesday without introducing the word 'manor' into the discussion. Nevertheless it is difficult to attach a definite meaning to the Domesday manor. One reason for this is that the word *manerium*—representing the French *manoir*—was imported into England by Norman clerks, and employed by them in Domesday with little regard for diversities of local usage. It was long before the word found its way into common employment in Lincolnshire. It is rarely used, for example, in Lincolnshire private charters of the twelfth century. Fundamentally, the word means no more than dwelling, or residence. Originally, it can have carried few if any seignorial associations, but already by the date of Domesday it seems to have become specialised to denote the dwelling of a man of higher standing than his neighbours—a man in a position to exact payments and services from the peasants around him. It had thus acquired very much the sense of the Old English *heafod botl*, a compound which passed into later law through the translation *capitale mesuagium*, 'chief messuage,' but before the Conquest had commonly denoted the dwelling of a thegn or other high important local person. Naturally, it is hard to define so indefinite a word. It covered earl Hugh's enormous estate of Greetham, with members in thirty-five villages, and also Outi's tenement in Hibaldstow, rated at 2 bovates, valued at 2 shillings, and cultivated by a lord—if the word is appropriate—who possessed one ox (68/33). It is unwise to read into Domesday Book the highly organised manor of the later middle ages, with its court, its free tenants, its economy resting on the labour of serfs, and its staff of officers. Already in 1086 estates of this type must have arisen even in Lincolnshire, but the conception of the Domesday manor was not derived from them.

The man whose house the local juries distinguished as a manor must in some way have differed from the men around him. The difference cannot always have consisted in his greater wealth. Many peasants must have held more land and owned more oxen than Outi of Hibaldstow. It is far more probable that the distinction was a matter of personal rank. There is reason to believe that most of the men who were possessed of 'manors' in 1066 were thegns, with a thegn's wergild of 1200 shillings, and the power which contemporary law gave to a thegn of swearing a weighty oath on behalf of his men involved in legal process. The Lincolnshire Domesday contains little evidence bearing directly upon this point. The Nottinghamshire Domesday is occasionally more explicit. "In Grove Alwi and Osmund had 4½ bovates assessed to the 'geld . . . . In Headon Godric and six other thegns had each his hall, 'and 8 bovates assessed to the geld amongst them . . . . In West Markham 'Godric had 4 bovates assessed to the geld'—these passages, which do not stand alone, create a strong impression that the normal possessor of a manor was a thegn. There is only one passage in the Lincolnshire Domesday which runs definitely counter to this impression. 'In Est 'depinge . . . . habuit sanctus Petrus de Burgo v soc' super v maneria de 'ii carucatis terre et vi bouatis ad geldum' (51/3). If the *soc'* of this entry is extended into *socmannos* it can only be translated 'In East Deeping 'St. Peter had five sokemen upon five manors assessed at 2 carucates and '6 bovates,' and it will afford a clear case of sokemen occupying manors before the Conquest. Even so, the entry will remain as exceptional in form as it is in matter. If the abbreviated *soc'* is extended into *socam*, and the first v is rejected as an anticipation of the second, the entry will read 'St. Peter had soke over five manors,' and its interpretation will present no difficulty. In any case, the difficulties raised by a single exceptional entry do not cancel the impression created by a long succession of normal entries that the essential part of a Lincolnshire manor of 1066 had been a thegn's house.

The problems presented by the Domesday berewick are different from those which attend consideration of the Domesday manor. For one thing, 'berewick' is an English word. The Old English *bere wic* meant originally a place where barley is stored, then, by natural development, a grange, or outlying portion of an estate. The common place name Berwick descends from the employment of the word in this sense. The berewick of the Lincolnshire Domesday is a detached portion of a manor. It might consist of an entire village—the whole village of Hundon formed a berewick of Caistor—or of a single bovate; its inhabitants might be many or few. In any case, the soil of the berewick was considered to belong to the lord of the manor of which it formed a part. A few valuable passages early in the Lincolnshire Domesday prove that another Old English word, 'inland' was interchangeable with the more usual berewick. The entry which records that of 7 carucates in Great Gonerby 3 were inland and 4 sokeland of Grantham is distinguished in the margin by the letters S, for Soca, and B, for Berewick (1/10). So is the following entry, which states that 9 carucates in Harlaxton were sokeland and 3 belonged to the hall of Grantham. These passages emphasise the lord's ownership of the soil of the berewick. They also mark the fundamental contrast between the berewick, a detached property belonging to the lord of a greater estate, and the sokeland annexed to a manor, of which the soil belonged to the men who were settled upon it.

For the lord's rights over his sokeland were far from amounting to ownership. In the twelfth century, and probably also in the eleventh, he held a court for the men who dwelt upon his sokeland, did justice between them, and took its profits. He undoubtedly received payments from them, in money or in kind. He may sometimes have required them to assist in the repair of the house which was the centre of the manor, and there is good evidence that before the Conquest they had helped him to perform the military service which was due from the estate. An important passage in an entry relating to Somerby near Grantham runs, 'This sokeland was such that it used to render nothing, 'but used to help in the king's host on land and at sea' (57/43). A lord cannot have exacted any onerous labour service from the tenants of his sokeland unless they happened to live in the immediate neighbourhood of the manor house, and sokeland often lay very remote from the manorial centre. Information which comes from the twelfth and later centuries shews conclusively that the tenant seated upon sokeland was then united to the chief manor by two principal ties—the customary rent which he was bound to pay, and the duty of attending the manorial court. This statement would undoubtedly be true if it were made in regard to the eleventh century, although Domesday tells nothing of manorial courts, and little as to the rents which were being exacted from the individual tenants of sokeland.

Much sokeland lay within the confines of the manor to which it belonged. 'In Tathwell earl Harold had 5 carucates of land assessed to 'the geld . . . . Two carucates are sokeland' (13/28). On such an estate, the tenants of sokeland may well have done a certain amount of labour service upon the lord's demesne—may, in particular, have done customary works there in hay-time and harvest. More important and more interesting is the type of estate which consisted of a manor with dependent parcels of sokeland scattered over a number of villages. The sokeland of Wragby lay in ten villages, that of Folkingham in twenty-five, that of Belchford in twelve. It is estates of this type to which the word 'soke' is properly applied. They are by no means confined to Lincolnshire. In Leicestershire, the soke of Melton Mowbray included nine members ; in Nottinghamshire, the bishop of Lincoln's soke of Newark included sixteen. Many of the sokes described by Domesday were destined to survive for centuries. The soke of Peterborough is not yet absorbed into Northamptonshire. It is easy to find medieval reference to the Lincolnshire sokes of Kirton in Lindsey, Caistor, Gayton, Horncastle, Bolingbroke, Waltham, Belchford, Greetham, and Grantham. Within these great estates, the tenants displayed remarkable tenacity in the conservation of the privileges and customs of the soke. It is more remarkable that many of the smaller sokes of Domesday, which are never mentioned in the great feudal records of the next centuries, are sometimes revealed as in being by some phrase in an obscure private charter. Walter de Aincurt's soke of Branston, for example, extended into only four villages (31/12-14). It was not the sort of estate which would be expected to offer much resistance to the forces which were to convert many sokes into groups of compact manors. Nevertheless, the grandson of the Domesday lord of Branston, when granting a toft in Scopwick to Thurgarton priory, thought it wise to record that the sitting tenants of this toft rendered two pence yearly *ad socam de Brauncetona* (Southwell Cathedral MSS., *Thurgarton Cartulary*, f. 133). It is easy to under-estimate the part which the soke played in the social and economic life of Lincolnshire and the adjacent counties in the twelfth and thirteenth centuries.

On a normal soke, the majority of the population recorded by Domesday consisted of men who are described as sokemen. The word is English, though it is not often found before the Conquest. By derivation, it denotes a man who is under an obligation to 'seek' some other person. By the date of Domesday there can be little doubt that it had come to denote a man bound to seek a lord, to do suit at his court, to render payments to him. It is necessary to use indefinite words like these for, to judge from later evidence, the sokeman's duty to his lord varied greatly between different estates. In the twelfth century, there was a wide difference between the sokemen of Gayton soke, with few burdens beyond rent and suit of court, and the abbot of Peterborough's sokemen of Scotter, bound to work for the abbot one day in the week throughout the year, and two days a week in August (*Black Book of Peterborough* (Camden Society), p. 164). In later medieval economy no clear line, of universal applicability, was ever established between the services of villeins and sokemen. Domesday tells nothing of the services due from men of either class, but it may safely be assumed that the distinction between them did not turn on the part which they respectively played in the economy of the manor.

Nevertheless the separate enumeration in Domesday of sokemen and villeins implies that some real distinction was felt to exist between them. The basis of that distinction is never stated, but it can be inferred from various suggestive facts. In the first place, it seems clear that while the sokemen paid the geld which was charged upon his tenement, the geld which lay upon the villein's tenement was paid by the villein's lord. The sokeman's responsibility for the geld must be the explanation of a formula which is very often employed in the surveys of Lincolnshire and Nottinghamshire. 'In Irnham Merlosuen had 7 carucates of land 'assessed to the geld. There is land for 7 teams. Ralf has 3½ teams 'there in demesne, and 7 sokemen on 2 carucates of this land and 29 'villeins and 9 bordars with 7 teams' (35/14). The point of the statement that the 7 sokemen held 2 carucates can only be that they paid the geld levied on their tenements—the carucates in question are carucates of assessment. This information was highly relevant to the main purpose of the Survey, the determination of the way in which responsibility for the geld was distributed. Later evidence entirely supports the conclusion that the sokeman answered for the geld that lay upon his holding. Early in the reign of Henry II, Ralf and William, sons of Spracli of Hawthorpe, granted seventeen acres of their land to Sempringham priory, and inserted into the charter of their gift the clause, 'We and our 'heirs after us will acquit this land . . . with our own substance towards 'the king and the king's servants and all our lords from all gelds and aids 'and customs' (*Danelaw Charters*, no. 438).

The grant which has just been quoted suggests another distinction which seems to have existed between the sokemen and the villeins of Domesday. The sokeman must have enjoyed a much wider freedom of alienating his tenement than can have belonged to the villein. Here again, it is necessary to invoke later evidence to explain the terminology of Domesday, but on this point the later evidence is conclusive. Whenever there is adequate later material for the history of a district where there were many sokemen in 1086, the successors of these sokemen can be seen alienating their land by written instrument,

Kirkstead abbey, for example, derived much of its property from the gifts of men who obviously represented eleventh century sokemen. The 167 sokemen within the soke of Gayton in 1086 were represented in the twelfth and thirteenth centuries by scores of free peasants, who made grants of land by charter to one another, and to such religious bodies as Lincoln cathedral, the priory of Alvingham, and the abbey of Louth Park. These men cannot have acquired during the twelfth century a power of alienation which did not belong to their predecessors in 1086. The eleventh century was a time of general depression for the peasantry, a period in which ancient liberties were often lost. As a class, the Lincolnshire sokemen were fortunate in retaining an exceptional measure of the liberty which they had inherited from the time before the Conquest. The power of alienation was perhaps the most notable sign of their inherited independence.

The tendencies of social history in the twelfth century should be remembered in any estimate of the condition of the Domesday villein. He should not be identified with his successor in name, the unfree tenant of later centuries. Even at the date of Domesday, serfdom of a rigorous sort may well have existed in many manors. The early surveys of the Lincolnshire possessions of Peterborough abbey show a highly developed manorial system in operation on such manors as Thurlby near Bourne, Scotter, and Fiskerton. On the other hand, it is certain that the *villani* of Domesday were a miscellaneous class. If there were serfs, and perhaps many serfs, among them there were also men whose personal freedom was unquestioned. A man might easily lose that power of dealing with his land as he would which distinguished those whom the Domesday clerks called sokemen. Inability to pay his taxes, inability to meet a private debt, even a couple of bad seasons, might compel a free man to become the dependent of a lord who would pay the taxes, settle with the creditor, or provide new stock. For those who for some such reasons fell on the wrong side of the line which separated, in Domesday, the sokeman from the villein, the descent into serfdom was easy. In the eleventh century, *villanus* was used as a convenient translation of the Old English *ceorl*, the indefinite native word which denoted the ordinary free householder. But the word *villanus* soon acquired servile associations, and in a generation or two the free man who had lost his tenurial independence lost also the right to be accounted wholly free. Nevertheless in the thirteenth and fourteenth centuries serfdom itself did not always imply in Lincolnshire the heavy burden of service which was usual in more southern counties. In particular, it by no means always involved that 'week work' which was generally the most onerous part of the villein's duty to his lord. Lincolnshire was a rich county, and many villeins must have been in a position to bargain with their lords for their release from the heavier portions of their service. But the descent from freedom into villeinage, which has been described, need not always have involved submission to all the burdens of full serfdom, and many Lincolnshire *villani* must have retained some trace of the higher status which had once belonged to their ancestors.

The law of the thirteenth century drew a clear distinction between land which a lord held 'in demesne' and that which he held 'in service'—land with which he could deal at his pleasure and land from which he only received rents and services. A lord was considered to hold *in dominico* the land of his villeins and bordars, he could remove them from their tenements at his will; their land was regarded as his land. Even though it is impossible to carry back to the eleventh century the strict conceptions of villein tenure which prevailed two hundred years later, this contrast between land *in dominico* and land *in servitio* is really anticipated in the Lincolnshire Domesday. Three successive entries under the fee of earl Alan are especially important in this connexion. 'In Brant Broughton, Ralf the Staller had 13 carucates of land assessed 'to the geld in demesne and 5 carucates . . . . of sokeland.' 'In Fulbeck 'and Leadenham, Ralf the Staller had 24 carucates of land in demesne 'and 15 carucates of sokeland assessed to the geld.' In Long Benning- 'ton, Ralf had 14 carucates of land assessed to the geld in demesne and '7 carucates and 6 bovates . . . of sokeland' (12/47–49). The demesne of these entries cannot bear the usual sense of land in the lord's immediate occupation. At Long Bennington, earl Alan had only 5 teams as against a demesne of 14 carucates; at Fulbeck and Leadenham he had only 6 teams against a demesne of 24 carucates. The demesne of these passages must cover not merely the lord's home farm but also the land of villeins and bordars. Already, that is, by 1086, it was possible to regard the villeins' land as the property of his lord. There are few passages in the whole of Domesday which require this construction—so few that the employment of demesne to cover villein land has often been regarded as an extension made by later generations. Nevertheless the force of the entries must be carefully weighed in any estimate of the position of the Domesday villein.

The importance of Lincolnshire in the eleventh century is illustrated by the existence of three boroughs within the county. Few shires north of Thames then included more than one borough—that from which the county derived its name. Moreover, the Lincolnshire boroughs, when measured by an eleventh century standard, were unusually populous. The size of Stamford cannot be precisely estimated, but it was certainly considerable. Lincoln, with 1150 inhabited messuages in 1066, had been one of the greatest of English boroughs, and its relative position was not seriously affected by the subsequent destruction of 166 messuages to clear a site for the castle, and by the decay of 74 messuages through misfortune, poverty, and fires. Even the 'suburb' of Torksey, with 213 messuages, was considerably larger than Nottingham in 1066, though the decay of more than half its messuages left only 102 burgesses resident 20 years later. Domesday tells nothing of the trade by which these boroughs lived, but the ports of Lincolnshire look towards the north and east. A new connexion with the Scandinavian lands had recently been established by Cnut's conquest of England, and Flemings were already visiting English trading centres. In a writ which must be earlier than 1069, William I forbids any man 'French or Flemish or English' to encroach upon the rights which archbishop Ealdred of York enjoyed in the shires where he held land (Farrer, *Early Yorkshire Charters*, i, 30). Primarily, the writ relates to Yorkshire, but the archbishop had land in Lincolnshire also, and it is probable that the Flemish element in Lincolnshire, which was to become highly important in the twelfth century, dates from the time before the Conquest.

The Scandinavian element in Lincoln undoubtedly created the most interesting feature of the organisation of the city—its twelve lawmen. A class of men especially learned in the law, and known as lawmen, existed in the Scandinavian countries. They gave judgment in cases brought before them. They collected and expounded customs. Domesday proves the existence of lawmen at Lincoln, Stamford, and Cambridge ; it refers to twelve *judices* at Chester who clearly held a similar position to the Lincoln lawmen. In the reign of Henry I, the title of lawmen was still known in York (*Visitations and Memorials of Southwell Minster* (Camden Society), 192). All these towns had formerly come under a strong Scandinavian influence, and it is probably a mere accident that there is no proof of a body of lawmen in Leicester, Nottingham, and Derby. In 1086, five of the twelve Lincoln lawmen were the sons of men who had held the same position in king Edward's day. Such a position inevitably tended to become hereditary. In Scandinavia itself, among the nineteen recorded lawmen of West Gothland, Algut, the sixteenth in the succession, was son of Sittrygg, the fifteenth, who was son of Algut, the twelfth, the son of Karli, the eleventh. In view of the Scandinavian origin of their office it is remarkable that only seven of the Lincoln lawmen of 1066 bore Scandinavian names. One of them, Suartin the son of Grimbold, had a father whose name is neither English nor Scandinavian, but Frankish. The names Brictric, Godric son of Eddeve, and Leuuine, are unambiguously English ; Aluuold may be either English or Scandinavian. These facts make it hard to believe that the lawmen of Lincoln represent a Scandinavian aristocracy imposed upon a subject English town, but they are quite in keeping with the blending of races which in later times was characteristic of the Danelaw at large.

There can be little doubt that in the tenth century the lawmen of Lincoln and Stamford had formed two benches of expert doomsmen. Whether they still effectively discharged this function in 1086 is less certain. According to the explicit definition given by Domesday, the lawmen were a group of privileged burgesses rather than the expert members of a borough moot. 'In this city there were twelve lawmen, that is, men having sake and soke'. The clerk who wrote the description of the city of Lincoln undoubtedly intended the phrase *habentes sacam et socam* to explain the unfamiliar word *lagaman*. The meaning of the former phrase is well established. To have sake and soke was to have the right to take the amercements of one's men ; it was coming to imply the right to hold a private court for the settlement of their disputes. Ulf son of Suertebrand, one of the Lincoln lawmen, possessed the rarer privileges of toll and team, the right of taking or of being exempt from toll, and the right of holding a court in which persons could be 'vouched to warranty'. At Stamford, the twelve lawmen of 1066 had sake and soke within their houses and over their men, though these privileges did not cover the forfeitures and amercements imposed in respect of the graver offences. As they are described in Domesday, the lawmen of Lincoln and Stamford may appropriately be compared with the persons who in the later middle ages possessed 'sokes' within the city of London. Within the lawman's property the profits of jurisdiction were the lawman's. The Domesday definition of the lawman as a man possessed of sake and soke would have been impossible if in 1086 the lawmen as a body had still held in fact the position of their predecessors in title. Individually, they were, no doubt, the leading men in their respective boroughs, and their opinion must have carried especial weight in the borough court, but their duty of declaring and expounding the law was becoming obsolete. In 1275, there were still 12 men in Stamford called lawmen, but their position could not be explained by a local jury except by reference to Domesday (*Rotuli Hundredorum*, i, 354).

The longest paragraph in the description of Lincoln relates to the property of Tochi son of Outi, the native lord of Ruskington and Westborough, and the predecessor of the Norman Geoffrey Alselin. He had possessed a hall in the city 'quit of all custom', two and a half churches, and thirty messuages. From each messuage he took a penny by way of land gavel—a payment which normally would have been made to the king—and he also exercised over his thirty messuages a right which Domesday represents by the word *locatio*. The meaning of this word is uncertain. There is good classical authority for the use of *locatio* in the sense of 'lease', and it need not be doubted that Tochi had been able to grant leases of such of his tenements as came into his hand. The difficulty is rather that while most, or all, important holders of tenements within the city must have possessed this right, the word *locatio* is introduced with an emphasis which suggests that it denoted something unusual. It may be observed that from a remote time the verb *locare* could be used to denote the hiring of an individual for some specific purpose. It is at least possible that the *locatio* of this passage means that Tochi had enjoyed the right of hiring persons resident within his messuages for work on his property. Such a power would, indeed, be exceptional, but it would be cognate with the familiar right which entitled a lord to call on his free tenants for occasional agricultural services. Apart from this difficult word, there are other abnormal features in the account of Tochi's Lincoln estate. He had held his hall *quietam ab omni consuetudine*, but the rights which he had enjoyed over those thirty messuages were evidently uncertain. Whereas the burgesses swore that the king had possessed the tolls and forfeitures arising from them, Ulviet the priest contradicted the burgesses, and offered to prove the truth of his contradiction by the ordeal. Tolls and forfeitures were probably included in the *consuetudo* from which Tochi was exempt in respect of his hall, but it did not follow that he had enjoyed a similar liberty in respect of his messuages. Moreover, the devolution of the messuages after Tochi's death or the confiscation of his lands was strikingly at variance with the cardinal principle which governed the Conqueror's distribution of the lands of Englishmen. Geoffrey Alselin was the successor in title of Tochi son of Outi, and he should therefore have received Tochi's property in the city, just as he received his rural estates. But bishop Remigius was holding the thirty messuages as part of the estate attached to the church of St. Mary, and Geoffrey Alselin had received nothing in exchange for them. It is not surprising that the property of Tochi son of Outi occupies an appreciable proportion of the space which the compilers of Domesday allotted to the city of Lincoln.

The compilers of Domesday did not attempt to give a complete list of the owners of property in Lincoln. A few persons are mentioned by name, but only because they enjoyed unusual liberties in respect of their tenements, or because there was some uncertainty as to their tenure. Ralf Paganel, for example, had a messuage 'quit of all custom' ; earl Hugh had a messuage with sake and soke, and two other messuages from which he took land-gavel ; Ivo Taillebois was claiming against the countess Judith the messuage which had been Stori's. Ivo's claim illustrates again the principle that the Norman who is an Englishman's successor in the country should also be his successor in the town. Stori had preceded Ivo as lord of Belchford and Bolingbroke, but he had also preceded the countess Judith in a manor at Hough on the Hill, and it was probably uncertain to which of these estates the messuage in Lincoln had been annexed. Similarly, earl Hugh's messuage had formerly belonged to earl Harold, and Ralf Paganel's messuage to Merlesuen—in each case the new, Norman, owner has succeeded in the borough a man whose estates in the shire have passed to him. With this principle in mind it becomes possible to identify Suen son of Suaue, Roger de Busli's predecessor in a Lincoln messuage, with the Suuen who in 1066 had held the manor in Greetwell which afterwards came to Roger (17/1). The Ulf whose messuage in Lincoln had passed to Gilbert de Gand was certainly identical with Ulf 'fenisc,' one of the greatest landowners in the pre-Conquest Danelaw, whose estates formed a considerable part of the Gant fee of later times. Siward, Gilbert's predecessor in another messuage, can safely be identified with the Siward whose lands in West Ashby and Driby (24/72-3) were Gilbert's in 1086. Nothing further is known of Siward, but if, as Domesday implies, he had held his Lincoln messuage 'quit of all custom,' he must have been a person of greater consequence than would be inferred from his brief appearance in the body of the Lincolnshire survey.

Like most, if not all, English boroughs of the eleventh century, Lincoln possessed a set of arable fields. They amounted to thirteen and a half teamlands. Many contemporary villages in Kesteven possessed more arable than this, and it is evident that the Lincoln of Domesday cannot have subsisted on the produce of its own fields. These fields were divided among a small number of important persons. One teamland belonged to a 'little manor' which bishop Remigius held outside the walls. In a passage which cannot be regarded as descriptive of conditions in 1086, eight teamlands are assigned to 'the king and the 'earl.' At the date of Domesday there was no earl of Lincoln, nor did Lincolnshire then form part of any larger district with an earl of its own. Here, and later in the survey, where it is said that Lincoln 'now' renders a hundred pounds 'between the king and the earl,' the clerks seem to be reserving the rights of the earldom, in view of some possible future appointment. This is the most probable explanation of the entry which states that beside their eight teamlands the king and the earl have 231 acres of arable as 'inland.' Before the Conquest, it would seem that the king and the earl had cultivated their respective portions of this land through reeves, and probably by means of hired servants. Nothing is said as to their treatment of their eight teamlands, but king William had given one of them to a certain Ulchel in return for a ship, and he doubtless held himself free to do as he would with the earl's share in the fields of Lincoln.

Of the remaining four and a half teamlands, two were possessed by persons who are known to have been lawmen of the city. In the fields, as among the lawmen, Sortebrand had followed his father Ulf, and the Norman Peter de Valognes had followed Godric son of Eddeve. The third teamland had been divided between Siward the priest, doubtless the lawman of that name, and a certain Outi of whom nothing else is known. One half of this teamland—presumably Outi's—had passed to a certain Alfnod. The other half was held in 1086 by Siward's son Norman, but at some time since the Conquest the king had imposed a fine of 40 shillings on Siward, and the land had therefore been taken into the king's hand. The statement in this entry that Unlof the priest had taken unlawful possession of the land and of Siward's wife while it was in the king's seisin remains enigmatical, but it may be conjectured that Unlof had paid the money due to the king, had taken possession of Siward's land without waiting for the king's writ, and had allowed Siward's widow to remain in occupation of her husband's house.

The remaining teamland and a half had been annexed to two Lincoln churches before the Conquest. The half teamland had belonged to the church of St. Mary, to which, before 1086, bishop Remigius had removed the seat of his bishopric. The teamland had belonged to the church of All Saints. Godric son of Garewine, who had possessed this church, had become a monk at Peterborough, and the abbot had therefore taken possession of the church and the land which belonged to it. His action gave occasion for the interesting statement that neither Garewine nor his son could grant their property to anyone outside the city, nor to anyone not of their kin, without the king's consent. This point was raised in favour of Ernuin the priest, a kinsman of Godric son of Garewine, and in king Edward's time the holder of a considerable property in Stamford which had passed by 1086 to Eudo, one of the king's stewards. In the county at large, Ernuin the priest held six bovates of the king's alms in South Witham (68/25), and he is probably identical with the Ernuin who held two bovates in Ingham 'of the king 'and the queen' (68/30). Before the Conquest, he had possessed half a carucate in Owersby which by the date of Domesday had passed to another priest, named Siward (68/42). He was one of many Englishmen who suffered heavily by the Norman Conquest, but received some small compensation from the new king, and might thus be dissuaded from rebellion.

The long list of persons who had withheld the geld due from their tenements in Lincoln includes a passage which deserves particular notice. The abbot of Peterborough possessed a house which Norman Crassus—a Lincoln lawman—claimed 'as of the king's fee,' *de feuo regis*, since Godred, Norman's predecessor, had received it in pledge for three and a half marks of silver (p. 7/20). The unusual phrase *de feuo regis* is probably intended to emphasise the fact that Norman claimed the house by virtue of the king's gift. It is also probable that Norman was asserting enfeoffment by the king in all the possessions of Godred (*cf.* Vinogradoff, *English Society in the Eleventh Century*, 233). If so, the word *feum* denotes the act of enfeoffment rather than the fee in which a man was enfeoffed. This explanation is supported by the fact that Godred, the name of Norman's predecessor in this house, is only a variety of the name Guret borne by Norman's predecessor in the office of lawman. In the twelfth century, for example, a man who appears as *Galfridus filius Gudredi* in one charter appears as *filius Gunrad* in a second, and as *filius Gurred* in a third. All these forms go back to a primitive Norse *GunnfrethuR*. In regard to property as in regard to office, Norman was claiming succession to Gured.

Already in the Conqueror's reign, the population of Lincoln was beginning to spread beyond the ancient limits of the city walls. Colsuain, the one great Lincolnshire tenant in chief of native descent, had received from the king a stretch of waste land outside the city. On this he had built and found inhabitants for thirty-six new houses. He also possessed, and may be presumed to have built, two churches, which in 1086 were not yet provided with any endowment in land. It may safely be assumed that Colsuain's houses and churches stood in the tract of low-lying land immediately to the south of the Witham, where the towers of the three late eleventh century churches of St. Benedict, St. Mary le Wigford, and St. Peter at Gowts, still survive. There is no direct evidence for the attribution of any of these churches to Colsuain, though in view of the present passage in Domesday it can hardly be doubted that two of them are of his foundation. As an inscription on the tower of the church of St. Mary le Wigford states that it was built by a man whose name, now almost illegible, should probably be read as Eirtig, it is at least possible that Colsuain's two churches were those of St. Benedict and St. Peter at Gowts.

The entry which follows the description of Colsuain's property raises a problem of another kind. It states that Alfred 'nepos' of Turold had three tofts in which he had all customs 'preter geldum regis 'de monedagio.' Fourteen years after the date of Domesday, Henry I, in his coronation charter, forbade the future exaction of a *monetagium commune* which had been taken from cities and shires, but had not been levied in king Edward's time. There is no doubt that the *monedagium* of Domesday and the *monetagium commune* of Henry I's charter are identical, but no early authority explains the meaning of the phrase. The tax was obviously connected with the coinage, but equally obviously it was not exacted from moneyers alone. The types of the early Norman currency were frequently changed, and it seems probable that the *monetagium commune* was a payment intended to induce the king to accept money of an earlier issue in discharge of the sums due to him from shires or boroughs. Lincoln, for example, rendered yearly a hundred pounds by tale 'between the king and the earl.' Strictly, no doubt, this sum should be paid in pennies of the current issue, and the king might hold himself entitled to demand some extra payment if money of an earlier type were tendered to him. It may be suggested that the earliest Norman kings—perhaps upon each change in the currency—had been exacting a general levy from each borough and shire, and in return had accepted payment of the sums due to them year by year in money of an earlier type. An exaction of this kind might easily be abused. The language of Henry I's charter suggests that it was an innovation since the Conquest, and it was discontinued before its nature could be illustrated by the abundant records of the late twelfth century Exchequer.

Like Thetford and Tamworth, Stamford is an ancient borough on the boundary between two shires. In 1086, five of its six wards were in Lincolnshire, the sixth, from which the abbot of Peterborough took rent and toll, was in Northamptonshire. The six wards were assessed at twelve and a half 'hundreds', that is, at 150 carucates, for army service, ship service, and danegeld. At Stamford, as at Lincoln, a body of lawmen still survived, though their numbers had fallen from twelve to nine during the Conqueror's reign. They were the leading members of a large community. In the five Lincolnshire wards, for which alone there is sufficient evidence, king Edward had taken, and it is implied that king William still took, all manner of customs from 136 messuages. Five messuages which had rendered customs to the king before the Conquest had been destroyed to make a site for the castle. The nine lawmen, from whose tenements it would appear that the king only derived geld, heriots, personal forfeitures above 40 ounces of silver, and penalties for larceny, held among them 51½ messuages. A class of men who are described as sokemen, and were so free that they could choose lords for themselves where they would, held 77 messuages. The king's rights over their tenements were limited in much the same way as his rights over the lawmen's property, except that he apparently received the forfeitures incurred for lesser offences than those emended by 40 ounces of silver. In addition to this, a special note was made in Domesday of six messuages which had rendered 'all customs' to the king before the Conquest, but no longer did so in 1086. In this way 270½ messuages are accounted for in the five northern wards. At this point Domesday proceeds to enumerate 136 more messuages, divided among eight persons, mostly of high rank. They included the king himself, who had succeeded to the 70 messuages which had belonged to queen Edith, the Confessor's widow, and had been annexed to the large estate in Rutland which her husband had given her. If these figures can be trusted, the Lincolnshire portion of Stamford contained 406 messuages, and the unsurveyed Northamptonshire ward must have included at least fifty messuages more. Stamford was undoubtedly one of the most populous of midland boroughs.

The most interesting feature of the description of Stamford is the appearance of a class of sokemen holding tenements within the borough. Domesday normally denotes the inhabitants of a borough by the word *burgenses*, and near the end of the survey of Stamford itself a paragraph reads *Lagemanni et burgenses habent cc et lxxii acras sine omni consuetudine*. Unless, which is highly improbable, no sokeman held any of this land, the word *burgenses* must have covered sokemen in this passage. In itself, this usage is not remarkable, for the old English word *burgware*, which Domesday represents by *burgensis* means nothing more definite than dweller in a borough. The passage relating to the Stamford sokemen is important because it gives for once a hint as to the status of the persons who composed a burghal community. Besides men bound to individual lords, men whose essential economic function was to supply the rural manors of their lord with such goods as could only be obtained in a borough market, there were in Stamford men who could choose lords at their will, who as Domesday states 'held their lands in 'demesne.' Men of this sort must have existed in other boroughs. If the burgesses of 1086 usually appear as an undifferentiated class, described by an indefinite word, this is largely because of the repetition in Domesday of a uniform terminology which conceals local variations of personal condition. Beneath this uniformity, as the Stamford sokemen prove, there may have existed as much variety between the different burgesses of a borough as existed between the different classes of free tenant upon a manor in the open country.

Apart from its reference to sokemen and the liberty which they enjoyed, the survey of Stamford raises few problems. The most difficult occurs in the entry relating to queen Edith's seventy messuages. She is said to have held them *cum omnibus consuetudinibus sine panificis*. The adjective which ends this phrase does not seem to occur elsewhere in Domesday. These *consuetudines panificæ* were evidently customs relating to the baking of bread, but their exact nature is uncertain. It is possible that the phrase denotes fines for baking bad bread, similar to the amercements for breaking the assize of bread of the later middle ages. This is a simple explanation, but it is not necessarily correct. In Lincoln in the twelfth century there existed a privilege called oven soke, which by analogy with fold soke and mill soke is best explained as the lord's right of compelling his tenants to bake their bread in his oven. Domesday might well describe such a right as *consuetudo panifica*. But the evidence is insufficient for a decision on this point, and it can only be left open.

Between Torksey, the smallest, and Lincoln, the greatest, of the three ancient boroughs of Lincolnshire, there existed a close connexion in the eleventh century. The burgesses of Torksey enjoyed the same customs as those of Lincoln, and in addition certain exemptions from toll, which probably outweighed the occasional duty of conducting the king's messengers by water to York. The fiscal connexion between Torksey and Lincoln was more remarkable. When the king took Danegeld, a round sum of money was cast upon the city of Lincoln. Torksey, with the adjacent village of Hardwick, was responsible for a fifth of this sum ; Torksey paying two thirds of the fifth and Hardwick the remaining third. It would be hard to find a parallel in Domesday to this arrangement. Scarcely less abnormal is the fact that before the Conquest queen Edith had held Torksey in demesne. Torksey, though a small, was an ancient borough. It had been a minting place in the reign of Æthelred II. In the twelfth century its court, like that of Lincoln city, was known as the 'Burewarmot' (British Museum *Cott. MSS.*, Vesp. E XVIII, f. 402), a word representing the Old English *burgwara gemot*, 'assembly of the burgesses.' It is only in ancient boroughs that an assembly with this name appears in the middle ages, and it is highly unusual for such boroughs in the eleventh century to be subject to any single lord other than the king. Domesday offers no explanation of the remarkable decline in the number of burgesses from 213 to 102 between 1066 and 1086. It may be conjectured that this decline was due to some obstruction of the Foss Dyke, which, when open to traffic, allowed ships to pass by inland waters from Boston to York. That the Foss Dyke was obstructed at or shortly after the date of Domesday is certain, for in 1121 it was re-opened for traffic (Simeon of Durham, *Historia Regum*, sub anno). In spite of the decay of the borough, its yearly 'farm' had been increased from £18 to £30 since the Conquest.

The Domesday descriptions of Yorkshire, Lincolnshire, and Huntingdonshire, are each distinguished by a very remarkable appendix. These appendices give for once some hint as to the number and variety of the disputes which must have arisen as a result of the replacement of English by Norman landowners. They also prove that the inquiry of which Domesday is the record must have had as one of its principal objects the settlement of suits between individuals as to the ownership of land. That the Domesday commissioners had fuller instructions under this head than the text of the survey suggests is probable. Most contemporary references to the Domesday inquiry ignore its judicial side, but from the work which was actually done in the settlement of disputed claims to land it may reasonably be argued that the commissioners held a position similar to that of the later justices in eyre. In any case, although it does not appear that the Domesday commissioners held any criminal pleas in the shires they visited, the Domesday inquest remains the great precedent for the later inquiries conducted by parties of justices itinerant. The work of the commissioners was not confined to the settlement of cases brought before them by interested parties—cases which must be settled before the entries concerning the land at issue could be made. In Lincolnshire, for example, they heard complaints as to new, and therefore presumably unlawful, tolls (69/39, 40 ; 70/1, 14). They must have been expected to take cognisance of encroachments upon the king's rights. In all matters of civil justice their powers were wide, and probably unprecedented. It was no new thing for persons of high rank to be sent down into a shire to hear some particular plea. The innovation of 1086 lay in the general and miscellaneous character of the business brought before the king's representatives in that year.

The method of the inquiry may be inferred, at least in outline, from various hints given in the course of the survey, and from comparison with the better known procedure followed in the eyres of the thirteenth century. The commissioners may be presumed to have sat in the county town. They presided over a meeting of the shire court, and the whole shire gave on occasion its collective testimony. There was also present a jury from each riding of Lindsey, and it would seem that separate juries appeared from Kesteven and Holland. Each wapentake was represented by a jury. In most counties each township was present through representatives, but in Lincolnshire it is probable that the township men were replaced by juries from the several hundreds of each wapentake. It was the men of the hundred who said that the soke of four bovates in Keisby belonged to Osgodby in Lavington (68/*22*). The function of the commissioners was to control the pleadings, to see that the questions of fact were properly laid before the appropriate jury, and that its verdict was duly recorded, and to refer questions which lay outside the competence of any jury to the king in person. There is little trace in Domesday of the pleadings in any suit before the commissioners. Even in the reign of John, an assize roll will often give little more than the names of the parties, the question at issue, and the judgment in a suit. Domesday is even more concise, and its terseness has tended to conceal the vast amount of strictly legal business which was incidental to the taking of the Domesday inquest.

One fundamental principle governed the settlement of the greater number of the pleas recorded in Domesday. A Frenchman who had received land from the king ought to occupy in relation to that land the exact legal position of the Englishman who had preceded him there. In the language of Domesday, the Englishman was the Frenchman's *antecessor*, and in most cases it was for a claimant to prove that in king Edward's time his *antecessor* had been possessed of the land or the rights at issue. Often, perhaps usually, it was impossible for either party to adduce conclusive written testimony in the plea. There can be no question that in the years which immediately followed 1066 king William often granted to a follower the lands of some Englishman in general terms, without any specification of quantity, service, or situation. For immediate purposes it was enough for the king to issue a writ commanding the sheriffs of the shires in which the Englishman had held land to put the Frenchman in seisin of all the lands which the Englishman had held in the several shires where they held office. It must, for example, have been in virtue of such a writ that Gilbert de Gant had entered into possession of the estates of Ulf Fenisc—Ulf of Fünen—in Lincolnshire, Nottinghamshire, Derbyshire, Huntingdonshire, and Cambridgeshire. This procedure left an opening for much subsequent dispute. Ulf's manor at Folkingham, for example, had extended into twenty seven villages : it is doubtful whether Gilbert could produce any title to this great property more definite than a writ directing the sheriff of Lincolnshire to give him possession of all the lands which had been Ulf's. In any dispute which might thereafter arise it was necessary to appeal to men who had local knowledge, and could speak with assurance as to Ulf's position on the day when king Edward died, or the day when king William gave Ulf's lands to Gilbert. 'They say that Oger holds nine oxgangs in Haconby unjustly, because 'Gilbert de Gant ought to have them through Ulf Fenisc, his *antecessor*, 'who had them in king Edward's time' (72/44). The verdict of the local jurors was conclusive, and the language of Domesday implies that judgment followed automatically upon it.

The situation with which the Domesday commissioners had to deal was seriously complicated by the fact that both before and after the Conquest one man might possess a piece of land and another might possess soke over it. Many Lincolnshire pleas in 1086 show that the right to a property did not imply any right to the profits of justice arising within it. 'Archbishop Thomas ought to have soke over Aschil's land 'in Willingham, which the bishop of Bayeux has, because the whole 'county bears witness that the archbishop's *antecessor* had sake and soke 'over this land, and the bishop's men have unjustly taken away the same 'soke from the archbishop' (69/28). This is an instructive passage, for it proves that there was no real difference in meaning between the word soke and the phrase sake and soke. By derivation, sake means a matter in dispute, and soke means the duty of *seeking* a lord—'seeking' his court, his fold, or his mill. 'Soke' is a vague word, and the rights which it might cover in the eleventh century were various. One important Lincolnshire entry goes far to prove that 'soke,' even when possessed by a man of moderate rank, might cover not merely the profits of justice but the right of holding a court. In the suit between Rainer de Brimou and Alfred of Lincoln touching the soke of three and a half bovates 'the men of the wapentake and riding say that Rainer ought to 'have nothing, but Roger of Poitou ought to have it in the house of Clac, 'his *antecessor*, in Hainton' (69/25). This explicit reference to Clac's house as the place where Roger ought to exercise his soke implies that Clac had held a court there before the Conquest. In the light of this passage it is permissible to argue that many other of king Edward's thegns held that their soke over their tenants entitled them to do justice in their own houses. Already before the Conquest the process was far advanced which was to make the manorial court an essential feature of every manor.

But the word 'soca' sometimes occurs in a less intelligible context. A man might have soke over a meadow or over a wood in another's possession. 'The men of the riding say that Ketelber ought to have 'twenty acres of wood in Hamby, and Ivo Taillebois the soke' (69/20). The exact sense of this passage is not obvious. Probably it means that Ivo received the amercements for scuffles and blows arising within those twenty acres. In any case it is certain that *soca*, in such a context, means something more than the mere receipt of money from the wood or meadow over which it was exercised. 'They say that in king 'Edward's time Leuric cilt witheld the 'warnode' from ten acres of meadow in Belton. Colegrim claims the soke of these ten 'acres' (72/61). Here, 'soke' is contrasted with 'warnode,' a difficult expression, but one that is explained clearly enough in later records as a rent which if not paid on the first day must be paid two-fold on the second, three-fold on the third, and so on, indefinitely. Contrasted, as in this passage, with a form of rent, 'soke' cannot well mean anything else than profits of justice. It seems to bear the same sense also in the passages which refer to the soke of a church. 'The men of Holland bear 'witness that the soke of Ketel's 'minster' in Long Sutton belongs to 'the king's manor of Tydd' (73/6). Speculation as to the way in which a man could have soke over a church is fortunately limited by a more explicit passage relating to a different part of the county. 'In Withcall 'hundred, Rainer claims the whole 'minster,' and the men of the riding 'say that it, and the third part of the soke belonged to his predecessor; 'and Ilbert de Laci has two thirds of the soke over the 'church' and 'the land which belongs to it' (69/11). The last words are important, for they show that soke over a church carried the profits of justice over the land with which it was endowed. Whether or not it also covered the amercements for breaches of the peace within and immediately around the church must be left an open question. At a later time, these offences were a matter for the ecclesiastical courts, but the strict distinction between secular and ecclesiastical justice cannot be carried back to the eleventh century. It may at least be said that to the men of that age there would have been nothing repugnant in the idea that the successors of the man who had founded the church should claim the penalties for offences committed in and around it.

The rights brought by the terminology of Domesday under the general head of soke were many and various. Among the Lincolnshire landowners of king Edward's day, none can have possessed more extensive privileges of this character than the church of St. Mary of Stow. 'The wapentake bears witness . . . that over the forfeiture of the 'wapentake St. Mary had two thirds of the soke, and the earl had one 'third. Now the king has it. Likewise in respect of heriot. Also if 'men should forfeit their land, St. Mary had two parts and the earl the 'third' (71/9). In the next entry, this information is brought up to date. 'Of all the thegns who have land in Well wapentake, St. Mary has two 'parts of the forfeiture and the earl has the third. Likewise touching 'heriot. Also if men should forfeit their land, two parts belong to St. 'Mary, and the third part is in the earl's hand. Now the king has it. 'Gilbert de Gant, Robert de Todeni, and Ralf de Mortemer are exempt 'from this custom, through their *antecessores*' (71/10). Before the end of the century, bishop Robert of Lincoln received from William II 'the 'third penny of Stow wapentake' for a yearly rent of ten pounds (Davis, *Regesta*, no. 374), and thus obtained possession of all the financial issues of the wapentake. They must have been considerable, for ten pounds was a large sum, and if William Rufus was the man to drive a hard bargain bishop Robert was not the man to offer a rent which left no margin of profit.

Domesday is probably referring to similar financial issues in a difficult passage which occurs near the beginning of the Lincolnshire portion of the survey, but of which nothing has yet been said. 'The customs of the 'king and the earl in South Lincoln—that is probably, Kesteven and 'Holland—amount to £28, those in the North Riding amount to £23, 'those in the West Riding to £12, those in the South Riding to £15' (pp. 7, 9). At first sight, these figures are not easy to reconcile with the sum which bishop Robert paid yearly for 'the third penny of Stow 'wapentake.' If the earl's third penny for a single wapentake in the West Riding amounted to £10, the sums received by the king and the earl from the whole riding must have amounted to more than £12. But there are two considerations to be set on the other side. It is very probable, in the first place, that in its general estimate of 'the customs 'of the king and the earl' Domesday is quoting a traditional figure. In any case, these figures must represent the sums which someone—the sheriff or the bailiff of each riding—was paying to the king for the right of collecting these issues, and the reign of William Rufus was a time in which payments of this nature were being greatly increased. It is no less probable that in other wapentakes the king's portion of the issues was often in the possession of local magnates. The long list of persons who had sake and soke, toll and team, in Lincolnshire, which includes the names of the greatest landowners of the county in king's Edward's time (p. 13), should probably be read in this connexion. A similar, though shorter, list is included in the miscellaneous matter which precedes the description of Yorkshire. It is headed with the statement 'These had sake and soke and toll and team *and all customs*' (*D.B.*, i, 298c). Domesday is still more explicit as to the right possessed by the pre-Conquest magnates of Nottinghamshire and Derbyshire. 'Here are set down those who had soke and sake and toll and team *and* '*the king's custom of the two pennies*' (*D.B.*, i, 280c). Each of these three lists was obviously made for the same purpose, to record the names of those persons who in king Edward's time had received the king's share of the forfeitures, heriots, and similar issues arising on their lands. The Lincolnshire list, highly compressed, and showing other signs of hurried writing, omits the reference to the king's customs, but it should certainly be interpreted in the light of the Yorkshire and Nottinghamshire evidence. A brief reference from the names which occur in the list to the description of the lands which they had held in the county will suffice to show the extent to which 'the king's customs' had passed into private hands before the death of Edward the Confessor.

Much that is now obscure in the Lincolnshire 'clamores' would be explained if more contemporary documents were available for comparison with Domesday. Of all the great mass of writs and charters which the Conqueror must have issued for his English dominions, barely three hundred have survived. Less than a score of these are original documents, and many of the remainder have been rewritten or interpolated by their later copyists. At the date of Domesday, few religious houses held land in Lincolnshire, and only one, Peterborough abbey, possessed a large estate there. On the other hand, an unusual amount of material exists for the early history of the Peterborough lands, and preserves some fragments of information about various individuals whose names occur in Domesday, but of whom there is no other memory.

Without any obvious reason, there is inserted into the Lincolnshire 'Clamores' an entry which runs: 'The shire bears witness that on 'and after the day when king Edward was alive and dead Aschil had 'these three manors, Scotton, Scotter, and Raventhorpe, of king 'Edward, at his own disposal (*in propria libertate*). In the same way, he 'had Muskham in Nottinghamshire, and one manor, Manton, he had of 'his brother, Brand the monk, on lease (*in presto*)' (71/15). This information is expanded, and also complicated, by a paragraph which occurs in a twelfth century list of benefactors to Peterborough[1] to the effect that Askil son of Toke gave to the abbey Walcot on Humber while he still lived, and that, after his death and that of Siric and Siworth his brothers, Brand the abbot, their brother, gave Muskham in Nottinghamshire, Scotter, and other Lincolnshire lands, which amounted to most, if not all, of the abbey's extensive property in the north of the county. In the text of Domesday, Aschil is represented as holding in 1066 the lands which afterwards came to the abbey in Scotton, Walcot, Appleby with Risby and Sawcliff, and Raventhorpe (8/15, 23, 27, 28). Manton, which Aschil was holding in lease of Brand, according to the 'Clamores,' was held, according to the text of Domesday, by a certain 'Rolft,'[2] who was also holding lands in Yawthorpe and Hibaldstow (8/14, 20, 22; 71/15), which, according to the list of benefactors, came to the abbey, like Manton, by the gift of Aschil and his brothers. Of the remaining property which they were believed to have given to the abbey, Scotter, according to the text of Domesday, was divided, in 1066, between Aschil and a certain Alnod, and to Alnod Domesday also assigns the manors in Riseholme, Cleatham, and Messingham which the abbey possessed at the date of Domesday (8/13, 17, 19, 31). It is evident that the history of these estates had really been much more complicated than would be gathered either from Domesday or from the list of benefactors to Peterborough. It is, no doubt possible to invent a plausible explanation of these conflicting statements—to conjecture, for example, that 'Rolft' and Elnod were the heirs of Siric and Siworth. It is better to take these discrepancies as an illustration of the complex facts of personal history which must often have lain behind the succinct entries in Domesday.

---

1 Hugh Candidus, *Historia Coenobii Burgensis*, ed. Sparke, p. 44.

2 It is hard to explain the final *t* in this name. Most probably it represents an abbreviation of some word intended to distinguish a man called Rolf from some other person of the same name. *Teinus*—'thegn'—is a possible extension of this enigmatical letter.

But the information about Aschil and his brothers is important for another reason. Of Aschil himself all that is known, apart from the passages which have been quoted, is the fact of his attestation as 'Askill 'Tokes sun,' to the charter by which Edward the Confessor confirmed Fiskerton to Peterborough abbey in 1060 (*Monasticon*, i, 385). But abbot Brand enters for a moment into English history at a very critical time, and any new facts which relate to him are welcome. Leofric his predecessor, the pluralist abbot of Peterborough, Coventry, Burton on Trent, Crowland, and Thorney, had joined the English army before the battle of Hastings, had fallen ill, and had died on 1st November, 1066. The monks chose as his successor Brand their 'provost,' and sent him for the confirmation of his election to Edgar the Atheling, whom they thought likely to become king. The Conqueror's anger at this was only appeased by the mediation of good men and the payment of 40 marks of gold (*Peterborough Chronicle*, sub anno 1066). It must have been at this time—probably at the Christmas of 1066—that abbot Brand obtained from the new king a charter confirming to his abbey 'the lands which 'his brothers or kinsmen held hereditarily and freely under king 'Edward' (Davis, *Regesta*, no. 3 ; *Monasticon* i, 383). The king's language implies that the abbot's brothers were dead or had withdrawn from the world. As Aschil was certainly alive for some time after the Confessor's death on 5th January, 1066, it is permissible to suggest that he had fallen in one of the two great fights of that year, at Stamford Bridge or at Hastings. Brand himself died on 27th November, 1069 ; but at the very end of the century, after the abbey had been ruled for twenty-eight years by the Norman abbot Thorold, the monks gave two hundred marks to William Rufus for liberty of election, and chose one of their own number, a brother of abbot Brand named Godric.

The list of benefactors which records the gifts of abbot Brand and his brothers supplies important information about other men of their kin. It states that a certain Elfgar of Dunsby gave Dunsby near Bourne to St. Peter, but that abbot Brand let it at rent to a kinsman of his own named Halden son of Tope, because king William had taken all his land from him and given it to Remi bishop of Lincoln, and that on this account the bishop unjustly took away Dunsby from St. Peter. Nothing is known as to the reasons for Halden's forfeiture, but the accuracy of this information is confirmed by the fact that in 1086 the bishop of Lincoln was holding manors in Grayingham, Bigby, Worlaby, Ulceby, Keelby, Dunsby, and Ringstone, which had belonged to 'Aldene' before the Conquest (7/16, 18, 20, 22, 27, 30, 32). The bishop's right to Dunsby is the subject of an entry in the 'Clamores' (72/45). The wapentake says that Aldene's land in Dunsby, which bishop Remi holds and the abbot of Peterborough claims, did not belong to St. Peter in king Edward's time. St. Peter never recovered possession of Dunsby, but there is no reason to doubt the story which is preserved in the list of benefactors to his house.

From the same list it also appears that a brother of Halden's named Ulf son of Tope, gave 'Manthorpe and Carlton' to St. Peter. The relationship between Ulf and Haldene, implying, as it does a relationship between Ulf and abbot Brand, is an important fact, for Ulf was a person of much consequence at the time of the Conquest. At the end of 1066, he attests king William's confirmation to Peterborough abbey of the lands of abbot Brand and his brothers. His fellow witnesses formed a distinguished company. They include Aldred archbishop of York, who had just crowned the king, Wulfwig bishop of Dorchester, Merleswein the sheriff of Lincolnshire, who had been king Harold's representative in the north at the time of the battle of Hastings, earl William fitz Osbern of Hereford, William Malet, who had been lord of Alkborough before the Conquest and became the first Norman sheriff of York, and Ingelric the priest, who had been one of the Confessor's chaplains. Ulf's signature in such company would prove his importance, even if nothing further were known about him.

A greater interest attaches to him from the fact that within three years from this time he and Madselin his wife planned, and probably carried out, a pilgrimage to Jerusalem. Before their departure they made a will—the first of the long series of Lincolnshire wills—of which a copy is preserved in a twelfth century cartulary of Peterborough abbey (Thorpe, *Diplomatarium*, p. 594). Its provisions were only imperfectly executed, but it throws light on various dark passages in Domesday, and it deserves analysis. Ulf and Madselin bequeath their land at Carlton Scroop to Peterborough, their land at Bytham to Crowland, and that at Sempringham to Ramsey. They state that archbishop Aldred is to receive their land at Lavington and 'æt Heordwican' 'for its full price,' and their land at Skillington, Hoby in Leicestershire, and at one of the many places called Morton, on which the archbishop had already advanced them eight marks of gold. These provisions explain an entry in the 'Clamores' which states that archbishop Aldred acquired Lavington and Skillington with the berewick of Hardwick from Ulf son of Tope for money which he gave him in the sight of the wapentake, and that afterwards the wapentake saw the king's seal by which the archbishop was reseised of those lands after Hilbold had disseised him (72/10). It would seem that Ulf and Madselin alienated these estates in order to raise the money necessary for their journey, and the fact that the archbishop could take possession, be disseised, obtain the king's writ, and be reseised before his death on 11th September, 1069, suggests that Ulf made his will very soon after his appearance at court at Christmas, 1066. The testators go on to provide that if they return, the archbishop shall have his money again ; if not, he shall expend for the benefit of their souls the sum by which the value of the land exceeds the money which he has gave for it, and that if the archbishop should die, abbot Brand should take over the land under the obligation which they had laid on it. Ulf then bequeaths his land at Manthorpe in Witham on the Hill to the abbot, and his land at an unknown place named Willabyg to Siferth his kinsman. Madselin leaves her land at Stoke to Leofgifu her kinswoman, and her land at Stroxton to a certain Ingemund, who gives her in return the west hall at Winterton. It is next provided that the testators' land at Cold Overton in Leicestershire should be sold, and the price expended for the benefit of their souls. Ulf then gives to his mother his lands at Kettleby near Wrawby and at Keelby Cotes, and she gives him her lands at Messingham and Kettleby. If Ulf does not return, Ingemund is to take his land at Kirmington. Ulf then gives his land at Claxby by Normanby to Healdene his brother—the Aldene of the *Clamores* (72/45)—his land at North Ormsby to the convent at Stow St. Mary, and provides that his servants (*cnihts*) shall have his land at Limber if he does not return. Finally, it is provided that Madselin's land shall be given to Thorney abbey.

The document is a remarkable combination of a last will and a settlement *inter vivos.* It is also remarkable among eleventh century wills for what it does not contain. The absence of any provision for the enfranchisement of the testator's unfree dependents is abnormal, but agrees very well with the fact that according to Domesday there were no slaves in Lincolnshire in the Conqueror's time. In regard to other, and more personal, matters, the evidence of the will with one important exception is in harmony with that of Domesday. It is evident, for example, from the will that Ulf's mother had possessed lands in Kettleby near Wrawby and Messingham. It cannot be coincidence that Domesday shows a woman holding a manor in each of those villages in that year. Her name was Eddeva, and she had also held in Melton Ross, Brocklesby, and Grayingham, lands which had passed to the Norman Ernis de Burun (34/1, 3, 8, 9, 27). There is an apparent, but perhaps only apparent, discrepancy between Domesday and the will in regard to Ulf's estate in North Ormsby. According to the will, Ulf states that he has given Ormsby to the the convent of Stow. According to the '*Clamores,*' 'the North Riding and all the Shire bear witness that Ulf's land of 'Ormsby, namely four and a half carucates was sold—or perhaps rather 'given in pledge—to St. Mary of Stow in king Edward's time, and 'belonged there on the day when king Edward was alive and dead, and 'bishop Remi was afterwards seised of it' (70/27). There is no necessary contradiction between these statements, for Ulf may have thought it wise to insert in his will a passage which would have the effect of confirming the convent in the possession of an estate which they had already bought from him.

The chief value of the will lies in its contribution to personal history. Ulf was the *antecessor* of the Domesday baron, Drew de Beurere, whom he had preceded in Lincolnshire at Kettleby near Wrawby, Kirmington, Limber, North Ormsby, Witham on the Hill, and Claxby by Normanby (30/6-8, 20, 32, 36). Here, the evidence of Domesday agrees well with that of Ulf's will. On the other hand, according to Domesday, Drew's predecessor at Stroxton, Stoke, Carlton le Moorland, and Castle Bytham, had been, not Ulf, but earl Morcar (30/22, 26, 27, 29), and the earl is also represented as holding, at the beginning of 1066, lands in Sempringham and Skillington which must be the estates of which Ulf was disposing by will at the end of the year. It would be presumptuous to offer any explanation of this discrepancy, for it puzzled the Domesday commissioners themselves. 'The claims which Drew de Beurere makes 'to Morcar's lands they refer to the king's judgment,' is an entry which stands alone in the Lincolnshire 'clamores' (72/50). Outside Lincolnshire, Ulf son of Tope may be identified with the Ulf who held with sake and soke manors at Cold Overton and Hoby in Leicestershire which had come to Drew de Beurere, and with Ulf, 'earl Waltheof's man,' who had possessed a manor at Chadstone in Northamptonshire which Drew was holding and earl Waltheof's widow, the countess Judith, was claiming, in 1086 (*D.B.*, i, 228a). In Yorkshire an Ulf who is probably identical with Ulf son of Tope had preceded Drew in the great manor of Aldborough, and in various smaller estates in the same region (*D.B.*, i, 324a-c). A man possessed of such large, if scattered, estates must have been one of the leading Danelaw thegns in 1066.

The importance of such a man was due as much to his influence with other land-holding families as to the extent of his own possessions. This makes the relationship which existed between Ulf and abbot Brand a fact of some significance. It is highly probable that king William was moved to grant his peace to abbot Brand in 1066 not merely by the proffer of 40 marks of gold and the mediation of good men, but by a sense that it would be indiscreet at that moment to indulge his anger against an abbot with powerful kinsmen in the unquiet Danelaw. At the time of the reconciliation, the attitude of the Danelaw magnates towards the new Norman king must have been highly uncertain. There was a real possibility that they would refuse to accept the battle of Hastings as a final decision, and would invite Swegn Estrithson of Denmark to assert his claim to the English kingdom. The Scandinavian ancestry of abbot Brand, and his kinsfolk is proved by the names which they bore: Toke, Tope, Askil, Siworth, Siferth, Brand, Haldene, Ingemund all belong to the stock of personal names imported into England as a result of the Danish settlement of the north and northern midlands. In 1066 the Scandinavian strain in the leading families of Lincolnshire was a fact which a wise, but alien, king would take into account in his dealings with that region. William the Conqueror was pre-eminently wise.

THE LINDSEY SURVEY

The Lindsey Survey (1115-1118), of which a translation is given at the end of this book, is the earliest of three similar records compiled during the reign of Henry I. The larger portion of a survey of Leicestershire, made between 1125 and 1130, was printed by Dr Round in *Feudal England*. A survey of Northamptonshire, of approximately the same date, was translated and compared with Domesday by Dr Round in Volume I of the Victoria History of that county. The Lindsey Survey, unlike the other two, is preserved in a contemporary text. It has long been known. It was first printed by Thomas Hearne in his edition of the Black Book of the Exchequer. In 1883, Mr. Chester Waters translated it, apparently from Hearne's text. He also compared it, entry by entry, with Domesday, but at that date the medieval topography of Lincolnshire was not sufficiently known to enable an exact comparison to be made. In 1884, Mr. Greenstreet published it in facsimile, with an index, but without any identification of places. Its date was first precisely determined by Dr Round, who also was the first to indicate its great value to the student of danegeld and its assessment. This value is largely due to the way in which the Survey is arranged. Domesday is arranged according to the fees of tenants in chief, and the wapentakes in which those fees lay are rarely indicated. The Lindsey Survey is drawn up riding by riding and wapentake by wapentake. Within each wapentake, the lands belonging to each fee are brought together, but the arrangement by wapentakes makes it easy to reconstruct the assessment of the several villages which each wapentake contained. Moreover, the survey of every wapentake is preceded by a statement of its assessment, giving the total number of twelve carucate hundreds which it contained. It was the Lindsey Survey which supplied the conclusive proof of Dr Round's epoch-making discovery that the assessment of the northern Danelaw was distributed on a duodecimal basis.

Canon Longley's detailed comparison of the Lindsey Survey with Domesday will form part of the second volume of this edition. But the value of the Lindsey Survey is not confined to its importance as a fiscal record. In feudal history, the reign of Henry I is a most obscure period. The Lindsey Survey shows the changes which had taken place among the tenants in chief of north Lincolnshire in the generation which followed 1086. Its information is no less important in quite a different direction. The clerk who compiled the existing text of the Survey was very conservative in his spelling of place names. He found much less difficulty than his Domesday predecessor in representing the uncouth combinations of sound which distinguished the local nomenclature of north Lincolnshire. The result is that his work supplies a sound basis for the interpretation of the place names of Lindsey. It also reveals many examples of Scandinavian influence upon the earliest English names of this region, which are not brought out by the clerk who wrote the Lincolnshire portion of Domesday Book. The Lindsey Survey will always be of primary value for the period to which it immediately relates, but like Domesday Book itself it can be used to illustrate the history of a far remoter time.

MODERN WORKS ON DOMESDAY BOOK

The modern study of Domesday Book begins with the publication of *Feudal England* by Dr J. H. Round in 1895. There had been many earlier studies of the Survey, but Dr Round was the first to demonstrate the artificial character of the figures which record assessment, and he thus relieved all future students from the hopeless task of attempting to establish a connexion between hides or carucates *ad geldum* and modern parish acreage. We also owe to Dr Round the discovery that the carucates of assessment in the northern Danelaw were normally grouped in multiples of six, a discovery which provided a new criterion of Scandinavian settlement in northern England.

In 1897, the late Professor Maitland published in *Domesday Book and Beyond* three long and brilliant essays which brought the Survey into relation with the pre-Conquest evidence on the one hand, and with later law and rural economy on the other. Not all the answers which Maitland gave to individual problems have withstood subsequent criticism. Nevertheless it would be hard to overestimate the stimulus which the book gave to Domesday studies. It remains a model of the way in which these questions should be approached. Many questions were for the first time propounded by Maitland, and all later inquirers have been influenced by the solutions which he advanced, though they may ultimately have come to different conclusions themselves.

In the first decade of this century, the study of Domesday Book as material for social history was notably advanced by two books by Professor (now Sir Paul) Vinogradoff. *The Growth of the Manor*, published in 1905, traced the development of English manorial institutions through the phases illustrated by Old English laws and land books to the feudal age, of which Domesday is the first great monument. *English Society in the Eleventh Century*, which appeared in 1908, is an indispensable introduction to the Domesday Survey as a whole. In such a work, the problems raised by the Lincolnshire Domesday are continually illustrated by material occurring in the descriptions of other counties, and a long appendix sets out in minute detail the different ratios between the carucates of assessment, the teamlands, and the teams, in the several entries of which the Lincolnshire Domesday is composed.

Little work has hitherto been done specifically upon the Lincolnshire Domesday. It has never formed the subject of monographs such as those written by Eyton upon the surveys of Dorset, Somerset, and Staffordshire, There is nothing for Lincolnshire comparable to Professor Tait's translation of, and introduction to, the Cheshire Domesday, or to Dr. Fowler's digest and discussion of the survey of Bedfordshire. In the Victoria Histories of the Counties of England the Yorkshire, Nottinghamshire, Leicestershire, and Northamptonshire Domesdays are translated, and explained in a series of introductions. The surveys of these neighbouring counties, especially those of Yorkshire and Nottinghamshire, inevitably throw much light on Lincolnshire problems, but in Domesday each county has its own individuality, and it is unsafe to argue automatically from one county to another. Work of a general character upon the northern Danelaw has from time to time necessitated reference to the Lincolnshire Domesday. In *Types of Manorial Structure in the Northern Danelaw* (1908) I used the Lincolnshire evidence in a discussion of the Domesday terminology of this region, and in the introduction to *Danelaw Charters* (1920) I have argued for the survival into the twelfth century of the forms of social organisation revealed by the Domesday description of Lincolnshire. If the Lincolnshire Domesday has received less than its due of attention from students, the explanation chiefly lies in the exceptional difficulties of medieval Lincolnshire topography. In Lincolnshire there are many examples of different villages bearing the same name, and many places recorded in Domesday cannot be found upon a modern map. The work of topographical identification, which is the foundation of detailed Domesday study, has hitherto been more difficult in Lincolnshire than in any other English county, with the possible exceptions of Devon and Cornwall. It may be hoped that this difficulty will be lessened by the publication of the present edition.

F. M. STENTON.

APPENDIX I

EXTINCT VILLAGES

AND OTHER FORGOTTEN PLACES

The schedule includes extinct villages and hamlets, and also other places which are of sufficient importance to be mentioned independently in medieval documents. After the name of each place there generally follow, within brackets, a reference to an early source, and to the appropriate square in the one inch *Ordnance Survey*. In some cases only the bare site, not the name, will be found since the place has not yet been entered in the map.

ACKTHORPE (Louthesk wap.—*F.C.*, i, 105—*O.S.*, 40, G 6), an extinct hamlet in the parish of South Elkington, which is now represented by Ackthorpe farm. *Circa* 1565, Hagthorp is returned as a hamlet containing one family (B.M., *Harleian MS.*, 618, f. 11).

ACREHOUSE, ACREHOLES, ACREHOLM (Walshcroft wap.—*Danelaw Charters*, 171, 174, 176, 192-3—*O.S.*, 39, E 9), an important grange of Newhouse abbey, with land in Claxby by Normanby and Normanby le Wold. The grange itself was situate in Claxby, just below the top edge of the cliff, in close no. 14 of the *O.S.*, 25 in. scale, 37/8. The buildings were demolished in the nineteenth century, and the present farmstead of Acrehouse [*O.S.*, 39, E 9] was built in their place, a little distance to the east, in the parish of Normanby.

ADEWELLE (Beltisloe wap.—*D.B.*), apparently an extinct hamlet near Bowthorpe (*O.S.*, 64, D 8) in the hamlet of Manthorpe and parish of Witham on the Hill. See below under BOWTHORPE.

ALDEFELD (Lawress wap.—*Monasticon*, vii, 952a—*O.S.*, 39, J 7), a grange of Bullington priory in the parish of Faldingworth, which is now represented by Faldingworth grange.

ALFLETBY (Well wap.—*F.C.*, ii, 40), probably a hamlet, which is now extinct, in the parish of Willingham by Stow (*O.S.*, 39, J 2).

ARMTREE (Horncastle wap.—P.R.O., *Feet of Fines*, 2 and 3 Elizabeth, Michaelmas, no. 31), an extinct place and manor in the parish of Coningsby (*O.S.*, 48, H 2). See Thompson, *The History and Antiquities of Boston*, 622.

Aswick (Elloe wap.—*O.S.*, 65, D 2), a hamlet and chapelry in the parish of Whaplode. The manor belonged to Croyland abbey, which had a grange there; and, in 1322, the monks founded a perpetual chantry in their chapel en le Brodedroue near Asewyk for the soul of their seneschal, Richard son of Peter de Hoddil of Cheyle [Cheal in Gosberton], who had expended 400 marks out of his own resources for their relief when their common substance was diminished by the inclemency of the weather, the common murrain among beasts, innumerable inundations, and various other causes (*Reg.*, iv, ff. 5, 5d.).

Autby (Haverstoe wap.—*D.B.*—*O.S.*, 40, E 5), an extinct village and parish, now represented by Autby or Audby house in the south-western part of the parish of North Thoresby. Traces of the ancient toftsteads are still visible in the north-west corner of Autby park (*O.S.* (6in. scale), 39 N.E.). See *F.C.*, ii, pp. liv, 343.

Avethorpe (Aveland wap.—*D.B.*), an extinct village, in the western part of the parish of Aslackby. No traces of its site survive. It is found in 1316 as a *uilla* (*F.A.*, iii, 188), and in 1327 and 1333 as *uillata de Haugthorp'* and *uillata de Hauthorp'* (*Sub.*, 135/10, mem. 3d.; 135/15, mem. 4); as *Auethorpe* (*Cal. Inq.*, i, no. 583), *Athorp* (*ibid.*, v, no. 522), *Awthorpe* (P.R.O., *Feet of Fines*, 7 Eliz., Easter, no. 1), Hauetorp (Peterborough Cathedral library, *Goxhill Leiger*, no. 127). Avethorpe has often been confused with Hawthorpe in the parish of Irnham, which probably adjoined it. It may be presumed that the site of the village is not far from a moated enclosure in the western part of the parish of Aslackby, called The Aveland, which was the traditional meeting-place of the wapentake. Mr. John Cragg of Threckingham in a manuscript gazetteer, which he compiled about 100 years ago, states that the vicar of Aslackby had the great and small tithes of Avethorpe but only the vicarial tithes of the rest of the parish. The tithe award, however, does not throw any light on this assertion (Lincoln Diocesan Registry, *Tithe Rentcharge Awards*, H. 455).

Bainthorpe (Horncastle wap.—*O.S.*, 48, C 2), probably an extinct hamlet in Little Sturton in the parish of Baumber, and presumably near the river Bain. A probable site is where the monks of Kirkstead had a mill on the west side of the river, at a place where a mill still exists. See Lancaster, *Chartulary of Bridlington Priory*, 354.

Banthorpe (Ness wap.—*D.B.*), an extinct hamlet in the parish of Braceborough. In 1316, Braussingburg cum Branthorp was a *uillata* (*F.A.*, iii, 187; cp. *Sub.*, 135/10, mem. 1d.). Banthorpe wood (*O.S.*, 6 in. scale, 146 s.w.), which lies to the north-west of Shillingthorpe hall, and Banthorpe lodge to the south-west of the hall (*O.S.*, 64, E 8), mark the approximate site.

Bassingham (Candleshoe wap.—*F.C.*, ii, 35—*O.S.*, 48, E 9), an extinct village or hamlet, in the parish of Scremby, which is now represented by Bassingham farm (*O.S.*, *ut supra*), and Bassingham plantation (*O.S.*, 6in. scale, 75, s.w.). The place must have become decayed at an early date, for the only documentary evidence of it that has been found is the mention of rent in Basingham in conjunction with the manor of Scremby, in 1246 (*F.C.*, ii, 35, where the place is misidentified as the modern parish of Bassingham).

BECKFIELD (Walshcroft wap.—*F.C.*, i, 320—*O.S.*, 40, F 2, 3), an extinct hamlet, in the parish of Binbrook. The site, which shews traces of foundations, is in the southern half of the grass close (*O.S.*, 6 in. scale, 46, N.E.), which is bounded on the south and east by the road from Binbrook to Kirmond le Mire, and on the west by a stream which divides the parishes of Binbrook and Kirmond le Mire. The hamlet was therefore close to the latter village. In 1316, Bynbrok cum Beckefeld and Irford was a *uillata* (*F.A.*, iii, 182).

BERGESTORP. See BREDESTORP.

BIRKWOOD (Gartree wap.—*F.C.*, i, 104—*O.S.*, 48, H 3), an extinct chapelry in the parish of Kirkby on Bain, and extending into the parish of Mareham le Fen, in which latter parish there is the moated site of Birkwood hall. In 1158, Henry II confirmed to Durham priory the church of Kirkby '*cum* capella de Birchewda' (*Charters of the Dean and Chapter of Durham*, 3, i, Regal. 1).

BOWTHORPE (Beltisloe wap.—*F.A.*—*O.S.*, 64, D 8), an extinct village which is now represented by Bowthorpe park farm in the south-western part of the hamlet of Manthorpe and in the parish of Witham on the Hill.

The house dates from the Tudor period, and contains a fine oak stair-case. It was evidently a place of some importance in former days. Near the house there is an oak-tree which is believed to be more than a thousand years old. Inside it a room has been formed in which a dozen people have dined with comfort. An engraving of the tree and house, from a drawing made by J. C. Nattes, in 1804, is given by Howlett in *A Selection of Views in the County of Lincoln*.

In 1316, Manthorp cum Beirethorp was a *uillata* (*F.A.* iii, 188); and the name of the *uillata* is given as Manthorp' cum Bourethorp' in 1327, and as Manthorp' cum Bourthorp in 1333 (*Sub.*, 135/10, mem. 4d; 135/15 mem 7). By the time of Henry VIII, Bowthorpe had dropped out of the subsidy rolls. In 1304, Gilbert de Gaunt had one knight's fee in Wytham, Manthorp, and Bourethorp (*Cal. Inq.*, iv, p. 154; cp. *D.B.*, 24/32). In 1226, the abbot of Croyland had the twenty-fifth part of a knight's fee in Burethorp (*F.C.*, i, 205). In 1253, the abbot and convent of Croyland had a grant of free warren in their demesne lands in Burthorpe (*Cal. Charter Rolls*, i, 419); in 1282, they were lords of the manor of Burthorpe, which is referred to as a village (*Chartulary of Bridlington Priory*, ed. Lancaster, 377); in 1535, they had rents in Manthorpe 7*l.* 9*s.* 9*d.*, and in Baurthorpe 11*l.* (*Valor Ecclesiasticus*, iv, 86a). In the *Croyland Cartulary* the name appears as Burthorpe (ff. 179-184). In 1545, the duke of Suffolk received a grant, *inter alia*, of the possessions of the collegiate church of Tattershall in Manthorp and Burthorp (*State Papers*, Henry VIII, xx, part i, 214a). In 1585, there was a final concord touching the manors of Burthorpe, Manthorpe, etc. (P.R.O., *Feet of Fines*, 27 Eliz., Trin., no. 19).

BRACHECOURT (Beltisloe wap.—*Monasticon*, v, 489—*O.S.*, 64, B 7), a place in the parish of Edenham, which was given to the monks of Castle Bytham as a new site for their monastery, to which they gave the name of Vaudey. See below VAUDEY.

BRAKENHOLM (Calcewath wap.—*F.C.*, i, 75), an island in the parish of Farlsthorpe (*O.S.*, 48, C 10).

Bredestorp *alias* Bergestorp (Beltisloe wap.—*D.B.*), which either is to be identified with the extinct village of Bowthorpe or is another extinct village in the parish of Careby. The weight of evidence seems to be on the side of the former alternative. The place is mentioned twice in *Domesday Book*, and it will be convenient to set out the relevant entries with the corresponding items in later surveys :

Domesday Book—Land of Saint Peter of Burg—
i. Manor—In Adewelle 5 carucates (8/5).
ii. In Witham and Mannetor and Toftlund, a berewic, half a carucate (8/6).
iii. In Bintham, a berewic of Bergestorp, 4 carucates (8/7).
iv. Manor—In Witham and Mannetorp and Toftland, 12 bovates (8/34).

Liber Niger Monasterii S. Petri de Burgo, c. 1100—
i. Breidestorp, 4½ carucates in demesne and half a carucate in socage.
ii. and iv. Witham (manor), 1 carucate in demesne and 1 carucate in socage.
iii. Bitham manor, 2 carucates in demesne and 2 carucates in socage.
(*Chronicon Petroburgense* (Camden Society), ed. Stapleton, 178-9).

Book of Fees, 1212—
The abbot of Burg' holds in Karlebi [*rectius* Careby] and Bihamel 2 knight's fees which Baldwin Wacke holds (p. 182).

Feudal Aids, 1303—Fees of the abbot of Burg—
Ranulph de Carleby [*sic*] holding 2 fees in Carleby [*rectius* Careby] (p. 146).

Feudal Aids, 1346—Fees of the abbot of Burgh Saint Peter—
John Bayous holds 2 fees in Careby, which Ralph de Careby formerly held (p. 202).

Domesday Book—Land of Drew de Beurere—
HUNDRED
Manor—In Bredestorp 7 carucates. It is sokeland belonging to Westbitham (*Soca in Westbitham*) (30/28).

Book of Fees, 1212—
The earl of Albemarle [Drew de Beurere's successor in title] holds Helewell in demesne of his barony (p. 182).

Each subsequent survey contains a similar entry (*B.F.*, 1050 ; *F.A.*, iii, 151, 204).

The identity of Bergestorp and Bredestorp cannot be justified by pure philology. Nevertheless it seems certain. The spelling Breidestorp, *circa* 1100 (*Chronicon Petroburgense*, 179) shows that the name is derived from the O.N. personal name Breithr, 'the broad,' which occurs again in Braceby, co. Lincoln, Bradeston, co. Norfolk, and Bracewell, co. York. Now the link between this form and Bergestorp is supplied by the spelling Brerchestorp given by Hugh Candidus in a list of the benefactors to Peterborough abbey, *temp.* Henry II, (ed. Spark 43). An independent copy of this list in *Lansowne MS.* 994, f. 147b, reads Breidestorp, thus preserving the original form. The early development of the forms, *berg*, *berch* seems to be due to the influence of neighbouring places with similar names, and in particular to Birthorpe in the wapentake of Aveland (derived from *berg*, a hill), and Barholme in the wapentake of Ness. It may be noted that when two r's occur in a word one of them is quite likely to change its place or to disappear.[1]

The philological evidence supplied by the ancient forms of Bowthorpe —Beirethorp, Baurthorpe, Bourethorpe, Burethrope, Burthorpe—is in favour of identifying Bredestorp *alias* Bergestorp with that place. But the tenurial evidence is not quite so strong. If, however, the name

[1] For the information in this paragraph the writer is indebted to Professor Stenton.

Bergestorp or Breidestorp does not occur amongst the possessions of Peterborough abbey after the date of the *Chronicon Petroburgense* this may be accounted for by the fact that later surveys suggest that the monks parted with their land in Witham on the hill, Manthorpe, Bowthorpe, Toft, and Lound at an early date.

It will be noticed that *D.B.* 8/7 states that the 4 carucates in Bintham are a berewic of [the manor of] Bergestorp, and yet the name of the manor under which the berewic is entered is Adewelle (D.B., 8/5). Adewelle has generally been identified with Holywell, the early form of which is Helewell; but there is little beyond their common termination to connect the two names, and there is no evidence that Peterborough abbey held any land in Holywell. Adewelle and Bergestorp or Bredestorp may be alternative names of a village; but it is more likely that Adewelle was a hamlet near Bergestorp, in which case a parallel may be found in the extinct hamlet of Holme (*D.B.*, 24/78) whose 24 carucates, in 1086, include the assessment of Beckingham and its hamlets. There are many springs and streams in the districts, and names compounded of *well* seem to have been common. In the parish of Witham on the Hill six of these names are recorded (*Chartulary of Bridlington Priory*, ed. Lancaster, 366, 374-7), besides the Caudell (cold well) springs close to Bowthorpe park farm; and three more are mentioned in a terrier of the glebe of Careby, dated 1577 (Lincoln Diocesan Registry, *Terriers*, i, ff. 69-72*d*).

The substitution in later documents of the name of Careby for that of Bergestorp or of Adewelle raises no difficulty; for when a tenement lay in two parishes, it was a common practice to call it indifferently by the name of either place. In the case of Drew de Beurere's land, *Domesday Book* itself (30/28) paves the way for the change of name from Bredestorp to Helewell by stating that the 7 carucates in Bredestorp, though the entry has a marginal *M*, were sokeland of West (or Castle) Bytham, of which parish Holywell was a hamlet.

Brethage, Brethawe (Wraggoe wap.—*Bardney Cartulary*, ff., 89, 90), a district and manor in the parish of Langton by Wragby (*O.S.*, 47, B 10), extending to the boundary of Hatton.

Buckland (Gartree wap.—*L.S.*—*O.S.*, probably 48, E 2), an extinct hamlet in the parish of Woodhall, and probably comprising the north-eastern part of that parish. Entries relating to the inhabitants of Buckland appear in the parish register of Woodhall as late as 1580-1600. The land of the hamlet of Torp, which is entered in *Domesday Book* (1/94; 4/51) in close association with Langton by Horncastle and Thimbleby, appears in 1115-18 and 1212 (*B.F.*, 169), under the name of Buckland.

Burgh, Burg (Aswardhurn wap.—*D.B.*), an extinct village, which, in 1086, was associated with Evedon and perhaps also with Kirkby by Laythorpe (*O.S.*, 55, C 9). The assessment of Burgh in *Domesday Book* is as follows:

	car.	bov.
Sokeland of Colegrim's manor of Ewerby with a church (*D.B.*, 67/3) - - - - - -		6
A manor held by Archil (*D.B.*, 67/5) - - - -		6½
A manor held by Archil (*D.B.*, 68/26) - - - -		5
	2	1½

It may be conjectured that the village of Burgh was grouped with Evedon (12 car. 4 bov.) and part of Quarrington (9 car. 2½ bov.) to make a double hundred of 24 carucates.

Colegrim's holding of 6 bovates in Burgh descended to the Clinton family together with his manor of 2 carucates in Ewerby (*D.B.*, 67/1) of which it was sokeland, and also with 2 bovates of sokeland in Evedon (67/4)—3 carucates in all ; and all this land belonged to Henry de Clinton's fee in 1212 (*B.F.*, 180). Towards the end of Henry II's reign, the mesne tenant of the 3 carucates was Nigel son of Alexander, who had been succeeded by Osbert son of Nigel in 1212 (*ibid.*). The immediate tenants were as follows : William son of Ranulf who, before 1185, gave one bovate in Evedon of this land to the Templars (*Monasticon*, vi, 826a). About that date, William's sons held his land, namely Nicholas (son of William) of Hoiland and Walter his brother, who paid rent to the Templars for 1 carucate and 6½ bovates (*ibid.* 826a, 826b). In 1212, the two brothers held the two carucates in Ewerby, which were returned as being free from service. In 1239, Robert de Rye, for 20 marks quit-claimed to William son of Nicholas 2 carcuates of land in Ewerby (*Iwardeby*) and 1 carucate in Evedon and Kirkby (*F.C.*, i, 303). These are the same 3 carcuates which Colegrim held in Ewerby, Burgh, and Evedon in 1086, and it is significant that, in 1239, Kirkby has taken the place of Burgh.

The evidence is sufficient to shew that if Burgh is not included in the present parishes of Kirkby and Evedon, it is at least in close proximity to them. The lane which runs from Kirkby to Ewerby is called Bar-gate, and Bargate hill lies to the south-east of it (*O.S.*, 6 inch scale, 106, N.E.). These names are old ones, and it might be thought that they had some connection with the extinct village of Burgh, were it not for the fact that there is no evidence for the form Burgate.

No trace of Archil's two manors in Burgh has been found after 1086. It is not improbable that they were given to the nuns of Haverholme, and are to be sought in the parish of Evedon.

BURRETH (Gartree wap.—*D.B.*—*O.S.*, 47, E 10), an extinct village and parish co-terminous with the present parish of Tupholme. See *F.C.*, ii, p. liii. Burreth was a *uillata* in 1316 (*F.A.*, iii, 180).

BUTYATE (Wraggoe wap.—*D.B.*—*O.S.* 47, D 10), an extinct hamlet in the parish of Bardney. It was no doubt one of the members of the *uillata* of Bardney mentioned in the subsidies (*F.A.*, iii, 179 ; *Sub.*, 135/10, mem. 9d.). Charters, especially those in the Bardney abbey cartulary (ff. 82d.—85), point to a site in the north-eastern part of the parish of Bardney, adjoining Gautby, and the foundation of the village, with clear indications of a moat, may still be traced in the grass close on the opposite side of the road to Bardney grange (*O.S.* (25 in. scale), 72/6, no. 228). A hundred years ago there was a mean farm-house on the moated site, known as Butchett farm. Robert Marmion gave the town, called Butheatha, to Bardney abbey in frank almoign (*Cal. Charter Rolls*, iv, 238). The place must early have declined in importance since its name hardly ever occurs after the early part of the thirteenth century. In 1592, however, it reappears as 'Budget' (L.R.S., xvii, 124).

CADEBY, SOUTH (Louthesk wap.—*D.B.*—*O.S.*, 40, H 4), an extinct village and parish, which is now included in Grimblethorpe and

Calcethorpe. See *F.C.*, ii, pp. lviii, lxix, 343. In 1316, Gayton, Cateby, and Grimpelthorp were a *uillata* (*F.A.*, iii, 177).

CARLTON, MIDDLE (Lawress wap.—*D.B.*—*O.S.*, 47, B 4), an extinct village and parish, which is now included in the parish of North Carlton. It was also called Little Carlton, Carlton Makerel, Barton, Barkeston, etc. See *F.C.*, ii, p. lvii. In 1333, Middle Carlton was associated with North Carlton, and in another subsidy with South Carlton, to form a *uillata* (*Sub.*, 135/11, mem. 26d ; 135/16, mem. 6d.).

CASTHORPE (Winnibriggs wap.—*D.B.*—*O.S.*, 55, F 1, 2), an extinct village consisting of East Casthorpe and West Casthorpe in the parish of Barrowby. The present Casthorpe lodge seems to mark the situation of the former, and Casthorpe house the approximate position of the latter. Casthorp cum Staynwath' was a *uillata* in 1327 and 1333 (*Sub.*, 135/10, mem. 6 ; 135/15, mem. 7d.).

CATLEY (Langoe wap.—*Monasticon*, v, 967-8—*O.S.*, 47, J 9), formerly a Gilbertine priory, in Walcot in the parish of Billinghay. The site shews many traces of buildings. See *Transcripts of Charters of Gilbertine Houses*, ed. Stenton (L.R.S., vol. xviii), 72-90.

CAWTHORPE (Ludborough wap.—*D.B.*—*O.S.*, 40, E 8), an extinct village in the eastern part of the parish of Covenham St. Bartholomew. See *F.C.*, ii, p. lxi.

CONESBY, NORTH, OR LITTLE CONESBY (Manley wap.—*D.B.*—*O.S.*, 33, J 2) an extinct hamlet and chapelry in the parish of Flixborough. Flikesburgh and Parva Conyngesby formed a *uillata* in 1316 (*F.A.*, iii, 185). The site of North Conesby was marked by a moated enclosure, which within the last twelve months has been buried beneath a huge mound of soil thrown up in the process of mining for iron-stone. The name occurs as Cunigesbi, Coningesby, etc. (*L.S.*, 1/14 ; *Cal. Inq.*, ix, p. 400).

CONESBY, SOUTH, or GREAT CONESBY (Manley wap.—*D.B.*—*O.S.*, 33, J 2), an extinct hamlet, which is now represented in the *O.S.* by Conesby farm close to the northern boundary of the parish of Crosby. The lordship of Conesby appears as a well-defined area in the estate maps of Sir Berkeley D.G. Sheffield, of Normanby Park. It extends to the river Trent on the west. The name appears as Cunesbi, Cunihingby, etc. (*D.B.*, 13/16 ; *Rotuli Hundredorum*, i, 373b.). Magna Conyngesby, Gunnesse, and Crosseby were a *uillata* in 1316 (*F.A.*, iii, 185) ; in 1333, the order of the names is Crosseby, Conyngesby, and Gunneys (*Sub.*, 135/16, mem. 2d. ; cp. 135/11, mem. 22).

CORRINGHAM, LITTLE (Corringham wap.—*F.A.*, iii, 185—*O.S.*, 39, G 1), an extinct village in the parish of Corringham. It appears as a *uillata* in 1316, 1327, and 1333 (*F.A.*, iii, 185 ; *Sub.*, 135/11, mem. 24 ; 135/16, mem. 27 ; *Cal. Pat. Rolls*, A.D. 1319, p. 269). Until comparatively recent times Corringham has been known by the name of Great Corringham in contradistinction from its hamlet. The tithe rentcharge award of the hamlet of Little Corringham, dated 23rd October, 1838, shews that the territory of the hamlet lay to the south of the village of Great Corringham, near Staple Gate house (Lincoln Diocesan Registry. *Tithe Rentcharge Awards*, D., 213).

COTELAND (Flaxwell wap.—*D.B.*—*O.S.*, 55, B 9), a depopulated place in the parish of Anwick, and possibly also in Ruskington. It occurs frequently in the Haverholme priory charters (*Lincolnshire Notes & Queries*, xvii, 9, 10, 13, 15, etc.).

COTES (Langoe wap.—*Kirkstead Cartulary*, ff. 32-39d., 63, 67d.—*O.S.*, 47, G 9), an extinct village, which was given, in the time of king Stephen, to Kirkstead abbey. The monks built a grange there which they named Linwood, and that name soon superseded Cotes as the name of the village and its territory. Portions of the grange are incorporated in the present house, the name of which has been changed to Linwood hall (*O.S.*). See *F.C.*, ii, p. lv.

COTES, NORTH, COTES, OR LITTLE COTES (Langoe wap.—*Cal. of Charter Rolls*, i, 383), a grange of Kirkstead abbey, probably in the parish of Dunston (*O.S.*, 47, G 8). See *F.C.*, ii, pp. liv, lv.

COTON (Yarborough wap.—*D.B.*—*O.S.*, 40, A 1), an extinct village now included in the parish of Brocklesby, but formerly in the parish of Keelby. It is known as Nun Coton on account of a priory of Cistercian nuns which was founded there in the time of king Stephen. See *F.C.*, ii, p. lxv.

CROSSHOLME (Aslacoe wap.—*F.C.*, i, 251—*O.S.*, 39, G 5), an extinct hamlet in the south part of the parish of Bishop Norton. The manor of Crossholme is still in existence. The hall stood in the close which lies to north-east of New Close plantation (*O.S.*, 25 in. scale, 44/3 and 4, no. 92), and the close immediately to the east is known locally as Crossholme field (*ibid*, no. 93).

DANMARK (Calcewath wap.—*F.C.*, ii, 287—*O.S.*, 48, D 12), probably a hamlet, which is now extinct, in Mumby Chapel in the parish of Mumby. See *F.C.*, ii, p. liii.

DRAYCOTE (Yarborough wap.—*F.A.*, iii, 182), an extinct hamlet, in the parish of Nettleton (*O.S.*, 39, D 9), the site of which has not yet been found. In 1316, Nettleton, Herwyk, Wikham, and Draycote were a *uillata* (*F.A.*, iii, 182).

DRAYTON (Kirton wap.—*D.B.*—*O.S.*, 55, E 13), a village which in very early times lost its separate existence, and became part of Swineshead, and is now represented by a cluster of houses south by south-east of that village. Drayton was a hundred of twelve carucates, and Count Alan's manor there had a considerable quantity of sokeland attached to it (*D.B.*, 12/58 ff ; *Cal. of Charter Rolls*, iii, 326-7).

DUNSTHORPE (Hill wap.—*F.A.*, iii, 245—*O.S.*, 48, F 4), an extinct village and parish, now included in the parish of Hameringham. The benefice was a rectory. In 1437, a petition was presented to the bishop of Lincoln by John Derman, rector of Hameringham, the prior and convent of Bullington, patrons of the church, and John Kighley, laic, patron of the church of Dunsthorpe, shewing that the church of Dunsthorpe, which was wont to be ruled by a secular rector, is so decreased on account of the lack of parishioners, the fewness of peasants, their low wages, the bareness of the lands, the lack of cultivation, pestilences, and epidemics with which the Lord afflicts his people for their sins, that it is hardly sufficient for the eighth part of the salary of a stipendiary chaplain, much less of a rector who has to bear necessary charges; and that there is no likelihood of its sufficing in the future since the world is going from bad to worse, and that the church of Dunsthorpe has no parishioners; and praying that the two churches may be united. Thereupon the bishop, on 7 February, 1437-8, decreed the union, and ordained that, to compensate John Kyghley for the loss of the patronage, the rector should be bound to observe, on 9 November every year, the anniversary of John himself and Alice his late wife, and also of Sir Robert Elkyngton and Joan his wife and John Greg, chaplain, both in the church of Hameringham and in that of Salmonby (*Reg.*, xx, ff. 77, 77d.). Terriers of the glebe of the rectory of Hameringham, dated 27 July, 1601, and 1634 (Lincoln Diocesan Registry, *Terriers*, iii, f. 97d., ix, f. 52), prove that Dunsthorpe comprised the southern portion of the present parish of Hameringham. The site of place is marked by 'The Grange' (see *O.S.*, 48, F 4), which is to be identified with Dunsthorpe grange. The terriers mention a little close or pingle, containing half a stong, called 'the Chappell yarde,' which is surrounded by the lands of Dunsthorpe grange on every side. This close has now been thrown into the adjoining grass field (*O.S*, 25 in. scale, 81/8, no. 119), but its boundaries can still be traced immediately to the east of the present grange. Many bones of men, women, and children have been found there. It is not improbable that Low Hameringham may have formed part of Dunsthorpe (See *F.C.*, ii, liv).

DUNSTHORPE (Louthesk wap.), a hamlet in the parish of South Elkington, which has lost its separate status. It is almost certainly to be identified with Thorpe or Elkington Thorpe (*O.S.*, 40, H 6) a group of houses which lies to the east of the village of South Elkington. It was a hamlet *circa* 1565 (B.M., *Harleian MS.*, 618, f. 11). See *Lincoln Cathedral Charters*, D ij, 69/2, no. 41. Dunesthorpe in *Feet of Fines* (P.R.O.), 3-4 Philip and Mary, Michaelmas, no. 33, and 4-5 Philip and Mary, Hilary, no. 18, seems to correspond with Lesthorpe in *Feet of Fines*, 3-4 Elizabeth, Michaelmas, no. 7.

DUNSTHORPE (Threo wap.—*D.B.*), an extinct village, now included in Old Somerby (*O.S.*, 55, G 4), Harrowby, and the borough of Grantham. See *F.C.*, ii, p, lxii. In 1316, Donston [*sic*] cum Herierby was a *uillata* (*F.A.*, iii, 191); while, in 1333, the names are given as Dunsthorp' cum Herierby and Westhorp (*Sub.*, 135/15, mem. 8d.).

FANTHORPE, FELMETHORP (Louthesk wap.—*B.F.*, 169—*O.S.*, 6 in. scale, 48, s.w.), in the parish of Louth, a grange of Tupholme abbey, now represented by Fanthorpe Lawn and certain cottages near the boundary of South Elkington. See *F.C.*, ii, p. lviii.

FEN (Skirbeck wap.—*B.F.*, 195), an extinct hamlet and chapelry in the parish of Fishtoft (*O.S.*, 56, D 4). See Thompson, *History and Antiquities of Boston*, 593-4.

FULSTHORPE, FUGHELESTHORP (Calcewath wap.—*F.A.*, iii, 178—*O.S.*, 48, A 10), a hamlet in the parish of Trusthorpe, which seems to have lost its separate status, though it is still marked by the name of Thorpe in the *O.S.* There is a moated site. Trusthorpe hall has seemingly been misnamed, since it is situate in Thorpe, and not in the village of Trusthorpe. Trussethorp and Foulesthorp formed a *uillata* in 1316 and 1327 (*F.A.*, iii, 178; *Sub.*, 135/11, mem. 19).

GANTHORPE (Winnibriggs wap.—*D.B.* (*Germuntorp*)—*O.S.*, 55, H 3), an extinct village in the south-eastern part of the parish of Great Ponton. The site is now a plantation, in the north-east corner of Stoke Rochford park, which bears the name of 'Ganthrops' (*O.S.*, 6in. scale, 122, S.E.). See *F.C.*, ii, p. lxiii.

GIPPLE (Threo wap.—*B.F.*, 1003 (Typpehall')—*O.S.*, 55, E 5), a grange of St. Katherine's priory, Lincoln, situate in the parish of Welby, close to Ermine street. The site is marked as Gappel on Armstrong's map (A D. 1778), but it cannot now be traced since the ground has long been under the plough. It was almost exactly opposite to Gipple cottages (*O.S.*) in the parish of Syston.

GREETHAM, LITTLE (Hill wap.—*F.A.*, iii, 180), an extinct hamlet in the parish of Ashby Puerorum. In 1316, Parva Askeby, Gretham, and Stanesby formed a *uillata* (*F.A.*, iii, 180; cp. *Sub.*, 135/11, mem. 13d.; 135/16, mem. 25d.).

GREINBY (Candleshoe wap.—*F.C.*, i, 82), an extinct hamlet probably in, but certainly near, the parish of Scremby. It is possibly to be identified with Scremby itself, or with Grebby, a hamlet of Scremby; but the evidence is slightly against such identification. The name in the final concord might be read as *Gremby*. The concord is registered in the *Bardney cartulary* (f. 45), where the place is given as *Geuerbby* and *Greinby*; but the text is untrustworthy. The bishop of Durham held land in Scremby and Grebby in 1086 (*D.B.* 3/43-6), and Pinceon was the tenant of the bishop's land *circa* 1115 (*L.S.*, 14/9). It seems that Greinby must be looked for in Scremby or Grebby, for the final concord was made in 1208 to settle a dispute as to whether 2 bovates of land and a toft in Greinby and half a bovate in Laisingtorp (*q.v.*) were the free alms of the masters of the hospital of Saint Mary Magdalene of Partney or the lay fee of Henry Bec, who was Pinceon's great grandson.

GUNNERBY (Haverstoe wap.—*D.B.*—*O.S.*, 40, D 3), formerly a hamlet in the parish of Hatcliffe. It is now represented by two or three houses, for which the name of Gunnerby is retained in the *O.S.* In 1327 and 1333, Haddeclyff and Gunnerby formed a *uillata* (*Sub.* 135/11, mem. 4; 135/16, mem. 12d.).

HAKERLEY, ACHE, HACCHÆ (Bolingbroke wap.—*Monasticon*, v, 454-5—*O.S.*, 56, A 2), a hermitage in the parish of Sibsey, the approximate site of which is probably represented in the *O.S.* by Akerley Bridge farm (56, A 2), where there is a bridge over what is now called Medlam drain. The hermitage was part of the grant of William I of Roumare, earl of Lincoln, for the foundation of Revesby abbey. Its existence suggests that there was in olden days a bridge or causeway which it was the hermit's duty to maintain.

HANBY (Calcewath wap.—*D.B.*—*O.S.*, 48, E 10), an extinct hamlet, in the parish of Welton le Marsh, which is now represented by Hanby hall (moated). See Oldfield, *Account of Wainfleet*, 276.

HANEHAITHE or ANEHEYTHE (Langoe wap.—*Kirkstead Cartulary*, ff. 71-77), the name given (*a*) to part of the great heath in the western parts of the parishes of Nocton, Dunston, Metheringham, Blankney, Harmston, Coleby, and Boothby Graffoe; and (*b*) to an important grange of Kirkstead abbey, which was sometimes called Kirkestedeheyth grange, some traces of the buildings of which remain in the farmstead called Metheringham lodge (*O.S.*, 47, H 7). See *F.C.* ii, pp. lvi, 343.

HARDWICK (Wraggoe wap.—*F.C.*, i, 230), an extinct hamlet in or near the parish of Panton (*O.S.*, 47, B 11), the site of which has not been found. Panton and Herdwyk were a *uillata* in 1316, 1327, and 1333 (*F.A.*, iii, 179; *Sub.*, 135/11, mem. 9d.; *ibid.*, 135/16, mem. 20).

HARDWICK (Yarborough wap.—*F.A.*, iii, 182—*O.S.*, 39, E 9), an extinct hamlet in the parish of Nettleton. The approximate site was marked by some cottages, known as Haddock houses, which were demolished many years ago, but within living memory. No traces of foundations remain. The site is about 740 yards east by north from Nettleton Top, in the south-easternmost corner of no. 233 of the *O.S.* (25 in. scale), sheet 38/1, where no. 233 adjoins no. 238. See *F.C.*, i, 28, 31-2, 72, 80, 297; ii, pp. lxv, 18, 72. In Dodsworth's transcript of the lost Hundred Roll of Yarborough wapentake in 1275 (Bod. Lib., *Dodsworth MS.* 89) this place, under the name of Heryewyke, is surveyed with Nettleton and Wykeham. Nettelton, Herwyk, Wikham, and Draycote formed a *uillata* in 1316 (*F.A.*, iii, 182).

HAVERCROFT (Corringham wap.—*F.A.*, iii, 187), a hamlet in the parish of Gainsborough, which has long been extinct. Its site is included in Thonock park (*O.S.*, 38, G 14). See *Cal. of Charter Rolls*, ii, p. 110 (4). In 1316, Gaynesburgh, Thunnek, and Havercroft formed a *uillata* (*F.A.*, iii, 187). In 1327 and 1333, Thunayke and Havercroft were a *uillata* (*Sub.*, 135/11, mem. 23d.; *ibid.*, 135/16, mem. 5).

HAVERHOLME (Calcewath wap.—*F.C.*, ii, 141), possibly a hamlet which is now extinct, near Mumby (*O.S.*, 48, C 11).

HAWTHORN (Horncastle wap.—P.R.O., *Feet of Fines*, 2 and 3 Edward VI, Hilary, [no. 1]—*O.S.*, 48, J 2), an extinct place in the ancient parish of Coningsby, now represented by Hawthorn hill.

HAYE, UPPER, and LOWER HAYE (Corringham wap.—*Danelaw Charters*, 60, 62, 63 (bis)), two islands in the parish of Redbourne. See *Monasticon* vii, 954, 982. The land in the neighbourhood has been drained, and the islands have disappeared; but their position is established approximately by the farm of Redbourne Hayes and by Hayes wood (*O.S.*, 39, D 5; and 6 in. scale, 27 S.E.).

HAYTHBY (Manley wap.—*D.B.*—*O.S.*, 33, G 2), an extinct hamlet in the parish of West Halton, lying to the south-west of Coleby. See *F.C.*, ii, p. lxi. In 1316, Colby, Teuelby, Haccheby, and Dorby were a *uillata* (*F.C.*, iii, 184; cp., *Sub.*, 135/16, mem. 2). See *F.C.*, ii, p. lxi.

HEYNINGS (Well wap.—*Monasticon*, v, 723a—*O.S.*, 38, J 14), a suppressed priory, in the parish of Knaith. Part of the priory church is used as the parish church of Knaith.

HOLE or HOOLE (Bradley wap.—*L.S.*—*O.S.*, 40, A 6), a hamlet in the parish of Clee, which has been swallowed up in the modern civil parish of Cleethorpes. The latter name means the thorpes of Clee, and is due to the grouping together of the thorpes of Hole and Itterby. Hole town street is now called Market street. See C. E. Watson, *A History of Clee and the Thorpes of Clee*, 98, 99. *Circa* 1565, there were thirteen families in Hole (B.M., *Harleian MS.* 618, f. 12d.)

Holme, or South Holme (Bradley wap.—*F.A.*, 361—*O.S.*, 40, A 5), a hamlet and manor in the parish of Clee, and now included in the borough of Great Grimsby. See *F.C.*, ii, p. lii.

Holme Spinney (Loveden wap.—*D.B.*—55, A 2), an extinct village adjoining Sutton in the parish of Beckingham. In *D.B.* 'Holm' included Beckingham and Sutton. Close no. 237, on sheet 95/6 of the *O.S.* (25 in. scale) is the site of the strongly fortified manor house of the Furnivals who were the lords of the manor in the thirteenth century. See *F.C.*, ii, pp. lx-i, for an account of the site, and of the chantry of the chapel of St. Leonard founded there.

Holtham (Wraggoe wap.—*D.B.*—*O.S.*, 40, H 1), an extinct village in the parish of Legsby, now represented by the farm of Holtham Garrs, or Holtham Garth, or Holtham Carrs. On the south-east side of the farmstead, adjoining the boundary of Sixle, the foundations of the village, and a moat, may be traced (*O.S.*, 25 in. scale, 54/2, no. 101). See *F.C.*, ii, p. lxiv.

Hornode (Yarborough wap.), a place in the parish of North Kelsey (*O.S.*, 39, D 7). On 16 August, 1420, the bishop of Lincoln granted to John Whyte of North Kelsey, hermit, that he might celebrate divine service in a certain chapel in Hornode St. Mary situated within the same parish, which he was to inhabit as long as the bishop pleased (*Reg.*, xvi, f. 210d.).

Houflet (Yarborough wap.—*D.B.*—*O.S.*, 34, J 8), an extinct place in the parish of Stallingborough, and one of the numerous medieval ports on the coast of Lincolnshire. Henry II granted to Grimsby abbey 'totam decimam piscium de portu meo de Houflet' (*Cal. of Charter Rolls*, iv, 311). Oldfleet drain (*O.S.*, 6in. scale, 14, s.w.), or Oldfleet Clough (*Bryant's Map*), which forms the boundary between the parishes of Stallingborough and Healing, and runs into the Humber, is probably a modernised form of Houflet. This evidence suggested the identification of the Wenflet of *D.B.* (4/29) which was sokeland of Stallingborough with the Houflet of Henry's charter. The name occurs elsewhere in Lincolnshire as Hoffleet Stow (*O.S.*, 55, F 13) in Wigtoft, and 'Holflete in pratis de Trentemersch,' probably in the neighbourhood of Gainsborough (Stenton, *Transcripts of Charters*, L.R.S., vol. xviii, p. 89).

Houghton (Winnibriggs wap.—*D.B.*—*O.S.*, 6 in. scale, 122, n.e.), an extinct village, now represented by Houghton farm in the ancient parish of Grantham See *F.C.*, ii, pp. lxiii-iv. The issues of the altar of the chapel of Horton' (which is probably to be identified with Houghton) formed part of the endowment of the southern mediety of the vicarage of Grantham in 1224-5 (L.R.S., ix, 136).

Huberdheythe (Langoe wap.—*Rotuli Hundredorum*, 390b—*O.S.*, 47, H 7), a grange of St. Katherine's priory, Lincoln, on Scopwick heath, in the western part of the parish of Scopwick. The farm called Scopwick lodge is probably close to the site of the grange.

Itterby (Bradley wap.—*D.B.*—*O.S.*, 40, A 6, B 6), a hamlet in the parish of Clee which is now, like Hole (q. v.), included in the modern civil parish of Cleethorpes. Itterby stood on rather higher ground than Hole, and a little to the south-east, near the present Cliff hotel. Sea

View street is the old town street of Itterby. *Circa* 1565, there were seventeen families in Itterby (B.M., *Harleian MS.* 618, f. 12d.).

LANGENE (Candleshoe wap.—*D.B.*), an extinct village, the name of which does not occur after *D.B.* The place is represented in later records by Irby in the Marsh (48, F 10). Land in Bretoft and Langene in 1086 (*D.B.*, 13/6) is entered as 11 carucates in Breitoft and Irebi in 1115-18 (*L.S.*, 14/7). Cp. *B.F.*, 164.

LANGWORTH or LANGWATH (Horncastle wap.—*Kirkstead Cartulary*, ff. 139-156d. *passim*—*O.S.*, 48, J 3), an important grange of Kirkstead abbey, in the parish of Coningsby.

LANGWORTH, EAST (Wraggoe wap.—*F.A.*, iii, 179—*O.S.*, *circa* 47, B 8), an extinct hamlet in the parish of Stainton by Langworth. Staynton, Reresby, Neubel and Langwath formed a *uillata* in 1316. In 1633, Langworth in the parish of Barlings and wapentake of Lawress was known as West Langworth (L.R.S., xvi, 347).

LAVINGTON, LITTLE (locally in Beltisloe wap., but assessed partly in Aveland wap.—*D.B.*—*O.S.*, 55, H 7), an extinct hamlet in the parish of Lavington *alias* Lenton, lying between Hanby on the north and Lavington on the south. In its history it is closely associated with Hanby.

In 1086, Offram had two carucates in Parva Lavintune (*D.B.*, 68/21), which correspond to the two carucates in Handebec, that is Hanby, which belonged to the Clinton fee in 1212, 1242, 1303, and 1346, constituting one-tenth of a knight's fee in 1212, and one twelfth of a knight's fee in 1242, 1303, and 1346 (*B.F.*, 183, 1049 ; *F.A.*, iii, 166, 210, where 'Hanbec' is wrongly indexed as Handbeck [*sic*] in Wilsford). At the last two dates Vaudey abbey was sub-tenant. These two carucates were not included in the hundred of Lavington, for Lavington, with its hamlets of Keisby and Osgodby (in part), is assessed at exactly 12 carucates (*D.B.*, 2/42 ; 8/8 ; 24/26 ; 57/41 ; 68/22).

In 1086, Gilbert de Gant held 4 carucates and $2\frac{2}{3}$ bovates in Lavintone, which were sokeland of the manor of Folkingham (*D.B.*, 24/86). Richard I confirmed to Vaudey abbey Reiner de Sally's gift of the grange which is called Parva Lanintona [*sic*], namely, 4 carucates of land, with all their appurtenances, and the quittance and liberties of the same land, which Alice de Gant, the countess, and Robert de Gant granted to them (Dugdale, *Monasticon*, v, 490b.). The jurors of the wapentake of Aveland, in 1275, state that

> the abbot of Vaudey holds 4 carucates in Parva Lavinton of Gerard le Saille in alms ; and they were geldable, but are not so now, but by what warrant they know not. Gerard holds them of Gilbert de Gaunt by mesne as one fee, and Gilbert holds them of the king in chief, by a service which is unknown. They are worth 20 pounds by the year (*Rotuli Hundredorum*, 254b, *cp.* pp. 256, 392).

The inclusion of these 4 carucates in the assessment of the wapentake of Aveland is no doubt due to the fact that they were sokeland of the manor of Folkingham.

In 1535, Vaudey abbey held demesne lands in Lavyngton cum Hambeke, worth 21 pounds and 4 pence a year (*Valor Ecclesiasticus*, iv, 90).

This evidence justifies the conclusion that Hanby grange, the site of which is marked in the *O.S.* (6 in. scale, 124, s.w.), is the grange spoken of above as Little Lavington. Vaudey abbey owned most of the land in both places, and their estate, including the grange, was probably known by either name. An award of the tithe rentcharge of Little Lavington, dated 17 May, 1848, shews that the territory of Little Lavington lay to the east of the road from Lavington to Sapperton and, with the exception of one close, on the south side of the road from Lavington to Folkingham ; and that it came to within a quarter of a mile of Lavington church on the south, and to within less than half a mile of Hanby grange on the north. In the award the place is described as 'the hamlet of Lavington otherwise called Lenton in the parish of Lavington otherwise called Lenton' (Lincoln Diocesan Registry, *Tithe Rentcharge Award*, H. 524). The following are the numbers in the *O.S.* of the closes in Little Lavington that are subject to tithe rentcharge—sheet 124/9, nos. 93-95, 98, and 101-103. The actual site of the village has not yet been found.

LAYSINGTHORPE, LAISINTORP (Candleshoe wap.—*F.C.*, i, 82), an extinct village or hamlet, probably situate in the parish of Scremby. Henry Bec, in 1208, granted to the hospital of St. Mary Magdalene of Partney two bovates of land and a toft in Greinby and half a bovate in Laisintorp in frank almoign (*F.C.*, i, 82) ; and the gift of Henry Bot [*sic*] to the hospital of these two bovates, which are described as two bovates in Laysingthorp in frank almoign was confirmed by the king to Bardney abbey in 1331 (*Cal. Charter Rolls*, iv, 253). See also Lincoln Cathedral muniments, D iv, 69/3, no. 4.

LAYTHORPE (Aswardhurn wap.—*D.B.*—*O S.*, 55, C 9), a village in the parish which is now called Kirkby Laythorpe. Laythorpe is now represented by a cluster of houses at the southern end of the parish of Kirkby Laythorpe, on the south side of the high road from Sleaford to Boston. The place has lost its separate status, and also its name which is now found only in the conflate form Kirkby Laythorpe. The modern form Kirkby la Thorpe is due to a misconception as to the origin of the name which is derived from the Scandinavian personal name *Leithulfr*. The site of an ancient chapel is marked in the *O.S.* (6in. scale) 106, N.E. Kirkeby Leylthorp was a *uillata* in 1316 and 1327 (*F.A.*, iii, 189 ; *Sub.* 135/10, mem. 7) ; while in 1333, the *uillata* is called Kyrkeby and Laylthorp' (*Sub.*, 135/15, mem. 10d.). Laythorpe is found as a separate place until early in the fourteenth century (P.R.O., *Feet of Fines*, 135/77, no 13). For the hundred of Laythorpe, see below, p. 34. See *F.C.*, ii, p. l.

LINDLEY (Corringham wap.—*Danelaw Charters*, 2), an extinct place in the parish of Lea (*O.S.*, 38, H 14), where the nuns of Bullington priory were first established. See *Calendar of Charter Rolls*, ii, 106.

LISSINGLEYS (Wraggoe wap.—*F.C.*, i, 98—*O.S.*, 39, J 8). A small extraparochial district of which the eastern part is called Lissingleys, is bounded on the north by Buslingthorpe, on the south by Wickenby, on the east by Lissington, and on the west by Friesthorpe (Lincoln Diocesan Registry, Award of the Tithe Rentcharge of Friesthorpe, F, 476).

LOBINGHAM (Yarborough wap.—*D.B.*), an extinct village of 6 carucates, of which the name has not been found in any document later than the *Lindsey Survey*. Its site is unknown, but it was no doubt in the present parishes of Killingholme and East Halton (*O.S.*, 34, G 5, H 5,

H 6) ; for territory that is described as Lobingham in 1086 is reckoned to be in Killingholme in 1115-18 and, later, in that place and East Halton. The present boundaries of these parishes were not established before the latter part of the twelfth century. In the charters of that period, South Killingholme included both North and South Killingholme ; and the church of St. Denis of South Killingholme was the church which is now known as the church of that dedication at North Killingholme ; while North Killingholme then meant East Halton. Nicholas de Areci, about 1155, gave to Newhouse abbey the portion which he had in the church of St. Peter of Nortkiluingholm 'que alio nomine uocatur Haltuna' (Stenton, *Danelaw Charters*, 213 ; cp. p. 169, also p. 459, columns a and b).

MARÆ (Axholme wap.—*D.B.*—*O.S.*, 33, H 1), an extinct hamlet the site of which is approximately represented by Mere Dyke Staith on the river Trent, in the parish of Luddington. Before the drainage of the district much of the land was, in the words of the ancient maps, 'fenny and marische soyle.' The Meredyke (*O.S.*), or Mare dyke as it is generally found in medieval documents, was an arm of the old river Don (Stonehouse, *History and Topography of the Isle of Axholme*, 52, 69 ; *Coucher Book of Selby*, ed. J. T. Fowler, ii, 286, 291, 392 ff.).

MARE. See SALTFLEETBY HAVEN, MARE, AND SWINE.

MAREHAM or COLD MAREHAM (Aswardhurn wap.—*D.B.*,—*O.S.*, 55, D 8), an extinct village in the present parish of Burton Pedwardine, of which the site is marked by a moated enclosure, containing about nine acres. It gave its name to the Roman road from Bourne to Sleaford, which is still called Mareham lane. Sempringham priory had a grange there, and one of the priory charters mentions 'illum montem qui uocatur 'þinghou iuxta Caldmarham' (*The Genealogist*, n.s., xvi, 77). As Thinghou means 'hill of assembly,' perhaps this *mons* was the meeting-place of the wapentake of Aswardhurn.

MEDLAM, MEDELHAM (Bolingbroke wap.—*Cal. of Charter Rolls* iv, 95—*O.S.*, 48, J 5), an extinct hamlet or place in the parish of Revesby, which was given to Revesby abbey by William III de Roumare.

MILLTHORPE (Aswardhurn wap.—*F.A.*, iii, 189), an extinct hamlet in the parish of Quarrington (*O.S.*, 55, C 7), the site of which has not yet been found. See *F.C.*, ii, p. l.

MINTING, LITTLE (Gartree wap.—*D.B.*), an extinct village, the site of which must be sought in the parish of Minting (*O.S.*, 48, C 1), or in Minting park.

NONGETUNE, NONGTONE (Winnibriggs wap.—*D.B.*—*O.S.*, 55, G 3), the name of a village which has not been found after 1086. The place may almost with certainty be identified with Spittlegate (see *F.C.*, ii, lxiv). The assessment of Nongetune is 4 carucates 1½ bovates, and this, when added to the 7 carucates 6½ bovates of Houghton near Grantham, makes a village of 12 carucates. In this community Walton also must no doubt be included. In 1316, 1327, and 1333, Houton, Walton, and Spitelgate constitute a *uillata* (*F.A.*, iii, 190 ; *Sub.*, 135/10, mem. 6 ; *ibid.*, 135/15, mem. 7d.) ; and the three places are often named together in other documents. They formed a lordship or manor at the time of the enclosure ; and Spittlegate Without (that is, so much of the place as has not been incorporated in the borough of Grantham), Houghton, and Walton now form a civil parish.

Norcotes (Horncastle wap.—*Cal. of Charter Rolls*, i, 111), an extinct village in the parish of West Ashby (*O.S.*, 48, D 3). See *Kirkstead Cartulary*, 169-173, 175d., 176d.

Ogarth (Threo wap.—*F.A.*, iii, 191), an extinct hamlet, probably in the parish of Ropsley (*O.S.*, 55, G 5), the site of which has not yet been discovered. It occurs as Ogarth in *F.A.* (iii, 191), and in *Sub.*, 135/10, mem. 6d., and as Osgarth in *Sub.*, 135/15, mem. 8d. The name appears again in the parish of Tathwell as Orgarth hill (*O.S.*, 48, A 5).

Osgodby (Wraggoe wap.—*D.B.*—*O.S.*, 47, D 10), an extinct village in the north-eastern part of the parish of Bardney. Charters, especially those in the Bardney abbey cartulary, shew that the village lay near Butyate (see above p. lii), to the east of Holme wood. The hamlet of Bardney Dairies represents the ancient village, and the form Osgarby Daries occurs in an administration bond in the Lincoln Consistory Court, dated 1646. Traces of the village may be seen in a grass close immediately to the south-east of Lodge farm (*O.S.*, 25 in. scale, 72/5, no. 161). It is probable that the stream which flows from Hatton through Langton and to the east of Lodge farm formed part of the boundary between Osgodby and Butyate, as it still divides two properties. Osgodby was no doubt one of the members of the *uillata* of Bardeney cum membris (*F.A.*, iii, 179; *Sub.*, 135/11, mem. 10; *ibid.*, 135/16, mem. 20d.).

Otby (Walshcroft wap.—*D.B.*—*O.S.*, 40, F 1), an extinct hamlet in the parish of Walesby, now represented by a farm. Walesby [and Otby] formed a *uillata* in 1327 (*Sub.* 135/11, mem. 1).

Ouseby (Aveland wap.—*D.B.*—*O.S.*, 55, G 9), an extinct hamlet in Birthorpe which was formerly in the parish of Stow by Threckingham, but is now in Sempringham. See *F.C.*, ii, p. li. Birthorp cum Useby was a *uillata* in 1316 (*F.A.*, iii, 189; cp. *Sub.*, 135/15, mem. 4), and Birthorp and Ouseby in 1327 (*Sub.*, 135/10, mem. 3d.).

Outhorpe (Loveden wap.—*O.S.*, 54, D 14, C 14), perhaps an extinct hamlet; now represented by a farm called Outhorpe in the parish of Long Bennington. A William Barn of Owthorp or Howthorp appears in 1331-2 in the charters of the family of Staunton of Staunton, co. Nottingham. As Outhorpe farm is only a mile from Staunton, William Barn is more likely to have come from there than from Owthorpe in Bingham wapentake, eleven miles away.

Poolham (Horncastle wap.—*B.F.*, 165—*O.S.*, 48, E 1), an extinct hamlet and chapelry in the parish of Edlington, which is now represented by Poolham hall. See Walter, *Parishes Round Horncastle*, 35-8, 43.

Riche (Kirton wap.—*D.B.*), an extinct village, now included mainly in the parish of Wigtoft, and perhaps partly in Algarkirk and Sutterton. The site is unknown. The hundred of Riche included 10 carucates in Riche and, no doubt, 2 carucates in Dowdyke. Swineshead abbey received, during the twelfth and thirteenth centuries, gifts of land in Richundred or Rikehundred (*Cal. of Charter Rolls*, iii, 324-5, 327; see also *Cal. of Inquisitions Miscellaneous*, ii, no. 1482). The use of the word 'hundred' in the case of these gifts suggests that the village was extinct when the gifts were made, or at least when the confirmatory charter, in which they are enumerated, was granted in 1316.

RINGSTHORPE (Threo wap.—*F.A.*, iii, 190—*O.S.*, 55, D 3), an extinct hamlet in the southern part of the parish of Barkston. Its site is in two grass closes, adjoining the village of Barkston, which shew faint traces of foundations. These closes lie on the west side of the river Witham, and on the north side of the road which leads from Barkston to Barkston railway station, and they are numbered 22 and 23 on sheet 114/1 of the *O.S.* (25 in. scale). Barkeston cum Ringstorp was a *uillata* in 1316 and 1333 (*F.A.*, iii, 190; *Sub.*, 135/15, mem. 8).

RINGSTONE (Aveland wap.—*D.B.*—*O.S*, 55, J 9), an extinct village in the parish of Rippingale. See *F.C.*, ii, p. li. In 1316, 1327, and 1333, Ringsdon was a *uillata* (*F.A.*, iii, 188; *Sub.*, 135/10, mem. 4; *ibid.*, 135/15, mem. 4d.).

RISBY, HIGH, or GREAT RISBY (Manley wap.—*D.B.*—*O.S.*, 33, H 3), formerly a *uillata* (*F.A.*, iii, 184), and a parish; now a hamlet in the parish of Roxby. Traces of the parish church of St. Bartholomew may still be seen, and a service is occasionally held on the site. Vicars were instituted until 1631. By 1662, the vicarage had been united to the vicarage of Roxby (Lincoln Diocesan Registry, *Liber Cleri*, 1662, f. 89d.).

RISBY, LOW, or LITTLE RISBY (Manley wap.—*F.A.*, iii, 184—*O.S.* (6 in. scale), 11 s.w), a *uillata* in 1316 (*F.A.*, iii, 184). In 1327 and 1333, Magna and Parva Rysby formed a *uillata* (*Sub.*, 135/11, mem. 21d.; *ibid.*, 135/16, mem. 2d.). It has now lost its separate status and, with High Risby, forms the hamlet of Risby in the parish of Roxby.

RISKENTON (Kirton wap.—*D.B.*), an extinct village, and hundred of twelve carucates, now included in the parish of Kirton (*O.S.*, 56, E 2). The site is unknown. Swineshead abbey in the twelfth or the thirteenth century, received gifts of land in Riskenton, Riskenton fenland, and 'Riskentonbrac in the territory of Kirketon,' and a mill in Ryskington hundred (*Cal. of Charter Rolls*, iii, 328). For the use of the word 'hundred' in these gifts, see RICHE above.

ST. ANNE'S (Threo wap.—B.M., *Harl. M.S.* 618, f. 5—*O.S.*, 55, F 3), a hamlet, formerly at the extreme western end of the parish of Somerby, but now included in New Somerby, in the borough of Grantham and the ecclesiastical parish of St. Anne's, Grantham. See *F.C.*, ii, p. lxii.

SALTFLEETBY HAVEN, MARE, and SWINE (Louthesk wap.—*D.B.*), three havens where there was a dispute in 1086 about a new toll that had been established. It will be convenient to deal with the names in reverse order

Swine Haven (*O.S.*, 40, D 9) was situated at the mouth of a stream which locally is still called Swine dike. It runs through the village of Grainthorpe, and anciently it formed the boundary between that parish and North Somercotes. Near the coast it joined the northern arm of the river Lud, and its mouth formed Swine haven. In later times there were some salt-works in North Somercotes on the south side of the haven, while on its northern side there was some rather higher land in Grainthorpe. Owing to the enclosure of Porter's marsh in North Somercotes, in 1635, and the disturbance of streams which it occasioned, the haven seems to have silted up, and a few years later a bank was made across the mouth of the stream, and a new channel was made on the west of the higher land, to carry the water to the old haven of Grainthorpe, which lay half a mile to the north of Swine haven. The present Grainthorpe haven, which was made in consequence of a nineteenth century enclosure, lies another half mile to the N.N.E. A small dike, which in an old parish map is called Swine creek, remains to represent the original course of Swine dike to the sea coast. *Temp.* Edward I, Alan de Conyngesholm made a fine with the king because, amongst other transgressions, he had allowed 40 sacks of wool going to parts beyond the sea to be brought to the haven (*portum*) of Swyne (*Placita de quo Waranto*, 399b.). Swine and Swinesbrigge occur in twelfth and thirteenth century charters of land in Grainthorpe (Lincoln Cathedral muniments, *Registrum Antiquissimum*, nos. 456, 463, 466).

Mare Haven (*O.S.*, 40, F 11) was evidently situated at the mouth of the Mar dike which runs through the villages of Saltfleetby St. Peter and Saltfleetby St. Clement. This stream, when it reaches the sand-hills on the sea-coast, now turns abruptly to the north and discharges itself into Saltfleet haven. Speed's map (A.D. 1610), however, shews that formerly it ran straight on into the sea. Mare and Maredich occur in charters of land in Saltfleetby in the twelfth and thirteenth centuries (Lincoln Cathedral muniments, *Registrum Antiquissimum*, nos. 479, 488, 492-4).

Saltfleetby Haven (*O.S.*, 40, G 11), was a haven at the mouth of the Great Ea or Eau or, as it is sometimes called, the Withern Ea, which formerly ran into the sea at the boundary of the parishes of Saltfleetby All Saints and Theddlethorpe St. Helen, as shewn in Speed's map (A.D. 1610). This stream, however, like Swine dike and Mar dike, has been diverted where it reaches the sand-hills at the coast, to the north, and now empties itself into Saltfleet haven.

It seemed obvious to identify the Salfluet of *D.B.* 69/39 with the present Saltfleetby Haven, which was an important harbour in the fourteenth century (*Cal. Patent Rolls*) ; but, *temp.* Edward I, a jury of the wapentake of Louthesk presented that Sir Alan de Conigholm' and his men gathered wreck of the sea from the haven of Saltfleteby as far as the haven of Marr,' and also from the haven of Marr' as far as the haven of Swyne, but by what warrant in each case they knew not (*Rotuli Hundredorum*, i, 336a). It may be assumed that the same three havens are referred to here and in *Domesday Book* ; and it is evident that here Mare haven lay between the other two. The present Saltfleet haven, however, is situated between Swine and Mare, and it may therefore be left out of account. A haven, however, at the south-eastern corner of Saltfleetby, where the Great Ea then flowed into the sea fits the evidence ; and also, it may be added, shews that the order in which the havens are named in *Domesday Book*—Salfluet, Mare, and Suine—is their geographical order from south to north. Further, if this theory be correct, it is evident that the present Saltfleet haven was formed by the confluence of the two diverted streams, the Mar dyke and the Great Ea, with two other streams converging to the same point, a channel being scoured by the increased volume of fresh water.

For information about these three havens the writer is much indebted to Canon Longley, without whose intimate knowledge of the locality they could scarcely have been identified.

Sapperton (Boothby wap.), said to be a hamlet in the parish of Welbourn (*O.S.*, 55, A 5), mentioned in the enclosure award. The little manor-house of Sapperton belonged to the Welby family, and is said to have stood by the side of the road from Lincoln to Grantham.

Saxedale (Louthesk wap.), a place or district in the parishes of Welton le Wold and Withcall (*O.S.*, 40, H 5, 6). See *Kirkstead Cartulary*, ff. 79-81 *passim*.

Scrane and Old Scrane (Skirbeck wap.—*B.F.*, 195), places in the parish of Frieston, in which Kirkstead abbey possessed a considerable quantity of land, and which are represented by Scrane End in the *O.S.* (56, D 4), about a mile south of Frieston church. See *Kirkstead Cartulary*, ff. 177d.—192d. See also, *B.F.*, 195 (Escrahinghe).

Scremthorpe (Candleshoe wap.—*B.F.*, 168—*O.S.*, 48, F 10), an extinct hamlet in the parish of Bratoft. *Circa* 1565, it contained nine families (B.M., *Harleian MS.*, 618, f. 9d.). See P.R.O., *Feet of Fines*, 9 Henry VIII, Trinity, no. 47 ; 6 Edward VI, Michaelmas, no. 30 : 3-4 Philip and Mary, Michaelmas, no. 7. A terrier of the glebe of Bratoft, dated 3 July, 1601, mentions land in Screventhorpe feeld which butted upon Browgh (Burgh le Marsh) on the north and had a highway from Somergates to Croft on the south (Lincoln Diocesan Registry, *Terriers*, iii, ff. 171-2). It would seem therefore that Scremthorpe lay in the westernmost part of Bratoft. *Temp.* Edward I, Philip of Kyme had land in Scripinthorp (*Placita de quo Waranto*, 397a). See *Calendar of State Papers*, Henry VIII, xx, part i, pp. 213b, 214a.

Seney Place (Wraggoe wap.—*Monasticon*, i, 641), a manor and grange of Bardney abbey in Southrey (*O.S.*, 47, F 10), in the parish of Bardney. Called Seny place *alias* Sotheray (P.R.O., *Feet of Fines*, 17 Eliz., Easter, no. 37). Cp. Sim Booth Grange below.

Silkby (Aswardhurn wap.—*F.A.*, iii, 128, 189—*O.S.*, 55, D 7), a hamlet and manor in the parish of Willoughby. The hamlet survives, being situate about a third of a mile to the west of the church, but it has lost its name and separate status, and is merged in the village of Willoughby, which is known by the conflate name of Silk Willoughby. Wylugby cum Silkeby was a *uillata* in 1316 (*F.A.*, iii, 189), and Wyllughby and Silkeby in 1327 and 1333 (*Sub.*, 135/10, mem. 7d. ; *ibid.*, 135/15, mem. 10). See *F.C.*, ii, p. l.

Silverys or Sellers (Gartree wap.—*O.S.*, *circa* 47, E 10), a hermitage in the parish of Burreth, of which the site has not been found. On 20 August, 1395, at Sleaford, the bishop of Lincoln granted a letter to Thomas de Gretham, hermit of the hermitage of Siluerys in the parish of Burreth, that he might celebrate divine service within the chapel of the hermitage for the space of two years, provided that he did nothing to the prejudice of the abbot and convent of Tupholme or to the vicar of the church of Burreth or his successors (*Reg.*, xi, f. 427). In 1526, the bishop's vicar general issued a notification that sir John Spynk, hermit of Sellers in the parish of Bureth, had been excommunicated for his contumacy in not appearing before him when cited (Lincoln Diocesan Registry, *Episcopal Court Books*, 1525-1562, f. 22d.). Possibly High Cell house (*O.S.*, 47, E 10) in the parish of Tupholme marks the approximate site of the hermitage.

Sim Booth Grange (Langoe wap.—*Valor Ecclesiasticus*, iv, 31—*O.S.*, 47, G 11), a grange of St. Katherine's priory, Lincoln, near the river Witham, in the Dales of the parish of Martin near Timberland. The place appears as 'Skynnybocke juxta aquam de Wyme' in *Rotuli Hundredorum*, i, 390b. The medieval form of the name is Senney Bothe. Cp. Seney Place above.

Southorpe (Beltisloe wap.—*D.B.*—64, A 6), an extinct village in the northern part of the parish of Edenham. It is placed in ancient county maps about one-and-a-half or two miles south-east of Irnham and a rather shorter distance south-west of Bulby. The Huntingfield family had a manor at Southorpe from 1183, with a chantry in their chapel for five weeks in the year; and Bridlington Priory held land there (*F.C.*, ii, 307-8; *Chartulary of Bridlington Priory*, ed. W. T. Lancaster, 361-4, 422). It seems to be a *uilla* in the aid of 1316 (*F.A.*, iii, 188), and it is certainly a *uillata* in the subsidies of 1327 and 1333 (*Sub.*, 135/10, mem. 5; *ibid.*, 135/15, mem. 5d.).

Southorpe (Louthesk wap.—*Danelaw Charters*, 112), an extinct hamlet in the parish of Gayton le Wold. It is perhaps represented on the map by Gayton grange (*O.S.*, 40, J 4), which formerly belonged to Kirkstead abbey.

Stainton by Wadingham (Manley wap.—*O.S.*, 39, E 5), a village which was contiguous to, and afterwards became incorporated with and indistinguishable from, the village of Wadingham. The united villages are now known by the name of Wadingham or Waddingham. It is not unlikely that Stainton comprised the western, and Wadingham the eastern part, of the place. The church of Wadingham was dedicated to St. Peter, and belonged to the patronage of Thornholme priory from the time of Henry III at the latest. Stainton church was dedicated to St. Mary, and belonged to the patronage of the Multon family. The church of Stainton in the thirteenth century is called Wadigham, Magna Wadingham, Wadingham St. Mary, Steynton in Wadingham. The two parishes were in different deaneries, Wadingham being in Aslackhoe and Stainton in Manlake. In a return of the value of benefices in 1603-4, it was certified by the parson of Owmby and the vicar of Bishop Norton that

> Waddingham Petri and Waddingham Marie twoe contiguous small rectories are not twoe seuerall competent livinges but mighte be helped by vnitinge them in one they are but one towne and both the churches stand in on churchyard (Diocesan Registry, *Liber Cleri*, 1603-4).

In August, 1602, it was certified about Wadingham St. Peter's that there were some defects in the repair of the church which would be speedily supplied, and that the chancel was in good repair and kept decently; and about Wadingham St. Mary's (*i.e.* Stainton) that the church and chancel were in 'reasonable good case bothe for repaire and decencie in the keapinge' (*ibid.*, 1602, ff. 25, 29). St. Peter's church was pulled down many years ago, and St. Mary's church remains with the dedication of St. Mary and St. Peter.

In 1316, Staynton and Wadingham were a *uilla* (*F.A.*, iii, 184), and in 1327 and 1333, Staynton cum Wadyngham formed a *uillata* (*Sub.*, 135/11, mem. 23; *ibid.*, 135/16, mem. 3d.).

STAPLEFORD, LITTLE (Loveden wap.—*F.A.*, iii, 191—*O.S.*—47, J 2), an extinct hamlet and chapelry in the parish of Brant Broughton, a mile or more distant, probably to the north-west, from the church of that place. Early in the thirteenth century part of the endowment of the church of Brant Broughton consisted in the tithes of 12 bovates of land in the fields of Parva Stapelford' 'que est capella de Bructon' (L.R.S., iii, 118). On 2 id. January [12 January], 1338-9, the bishop of Lincoln granted a commission to Ralf rector of Brendebroughton' to remove the wood and stones of a chapel in that parish in a place called Parva Stapelford, a mile or more distant from the church, and to use them for the fabric of the church or the bell-tower. On 20 February, 1231-2, a commission issued for taking an assize about a dike raised in Magna Stapelford to the hurt of people in Bructon and Parua Stapelford (*Cal. Pat. Rolls*, 1232, p. 512). In 1316, Broucton cum Parva Stapelford was a *uillata* (*F.A.*, iii, 191).

STENNING or ESTOVENING (Kirton wap.—*D.B.*—*O.S.*, 55, E 13), an extinct village of 3 carucates and 6 bovates, in the parish of Swineshead, represented by Estovening hall (*O.S.*, 55, E 13), which adjoins a piece of land called The Steyning, from which Steyning lane runs north-westwards (*O.S.*, 6 in. scale, 117 N.W.). Swineshead abbey received gifts of land in Stevenynges (*Cal. of Charter Rolls*, iii, 320-1, 325). Ralf son of Stephen held half a knight's fee in Stevaning in 1212 (*Book of Fees*, 194); and John de Hoyland held it in 1281 of Peter de Sabaudia (*Cal. Inq.*, ii, pp, 212, 217). In 1303, 1333, and 1335, final concords were made touching the manor of Steninge by Swynesheued or Steuenyng in Holand (P.R.O., *Feet of Fines*, 134/69, no. 14; 138/102, no. 14; 138/104, no. 48).

STOCKING (Loveden wap.—*F.A.*, iii, 192—*O.S.*), an extinct hamlet, which is associated with Dry Doddington (*O.S.*, 55, C 1). The site has not yet been found. Dodington cum Stockyng was a *uillata* in 1316, 1327, and 1333 (*F.A.*, iii, 192; *Sub.*, 135/10, mem. 10d.; *ibid.*, 135/15, mem. 14d.).

STRUBBY (Wraggoe wap.—*D.B.*—*O.S.*, 47, B 11), an extinct hamlet, in the parish of Langton by Wragby, now represented by Strubby hall. Langeton and Strubby formed a *uillata* in 1316 (*F.A.*, iii, 179).

STURTON, LITTLE (in Horncastle wap.—*D.B.*), an extinct village, now represented by Stourton hall in the parish of Baumber (*O.S.*, 48, C 2). There was a chapel there with a chantry in the twelfth and thirteenth centuries (*Chartulary of Bridlington Priory*, ed. W. T. Lancaster, 352, 356-7).

SUDTHORPE (Loveden wap.—*O.S.* (6 in. scale), 96 S.W.), a place in the parish of Fulbeck. The name has an ancient sound, but it has not been found in medieval documents.

SUDTONE (Gartree wap.—*D.B.*—*O.S.*, *circa* 48, C 1), an extinct village in the parish of Great Sturton. Eudo son of Spirewic's land there was assessed in *D.B.*, as a berewic of his manor of Little Sturton, at $3\frac{1}{4}$ bovates, and as sokeland of the same manor, at $1\frac{1}{2}$ bovates (29/2, 3, 15). The corresponding entry in *L.S.*, is 5 bovates in Strettuna in the wapentake of Gartree (13/9). All or most of this land was given to Kirkstead abbey (*Kirkstead Cartulary*, ff. 158d, 164d., 165d.). Gilbert de Gand also had 2 bovates in Sudtone, as sokeland of his manor of Baumber (24/1). It may be assumed that Sudtone lay to the south, and probably to the south-west, of the village of Great Sturton which in the twelfth century was generally known as North Sturton.

SUDWELLE (Beltisloe wap.—*D.B.*), an extinct village, which lay almost certainly in the parish of Swayfield (*O.S.*, 64, A 5). Walter de Aincurt's manor of 2 carucates in Sudwelle, with its berewic of half a carucate in Swinstead, in 1086 (*D.B.*, 31/7, 8), seem to be represented, in 1212, by Oliver de Aincurt's one third of a knight's fee in Swayfield and Swinstead (*B.F.*, 183) ; and, in 1242, by half a knight's fee in Swayfield which Oliver de Eyncurt held of ancient feoffment (*ibid.* 1078).

SUMMERLEDE is possibly a place, but probably a personal name which is given in error for Osgodby in Walshcroft wapentake (*D.B.*, 4/19, and note to that entry).

SWINE. See SALTFLEETBY HAVEN, MARE, AND SWINE.

SWINEFLEET (Kirton wap.—*F.C.*, ii, 98), probably a hamlet in the parish of Swineshead (*O.S.*, 55, E 13). See *Lincoln Wills*, ed. C. W. Foster, (L.R.S.), v, 56.

SYTHESBY, SCHICTHESBIA, SCITHESBI (Bolingbroke wap.—*Monasticon*, v, 454-6—*O.S.*, *circa* 48, G 5), an extinct village in the parish of Revesby. The name is given as Skydeby in an *inspeximus* of Henry III, confirming a charter of Richard I (*Cal. of Charter Rolls*, iv, 95). See THORESBY below.

TATEBI (Calswath wap.—*D.B.*—*O.S.*, probably 48, C 8), an extinct village in or near Ulceby by Alford. In 1086, the archbishop of York had 1 carucate in Tatebi, which, with land in Rigsby and Ailby, is described as sokeland of the manor of Rigsby, with the note, 'Hoc 'manerium fuit' (*D.B.*, 2/20).

In 1242, Thomas of Rigsby held one knight's fee in Rigsby, Ailby, Tothby, Alford, Well, and Sutton le Marsh, of the honour of the archbishop (*B.F.*, 1059), and Tothby is mentioned continually amongst the lands of the Rigsby family, whilst no mention is made of Tatebi. Hence, Tatebi has generally been identified with Tothby, and it is so identified in the text (2/20). But this conclusion must be revised in the light of new evidence. Tothby is found in Domesday Book, under the form 'Touedebi' (4/64), where it is assessed at half a carucate, amongst the lands of bishop Odo. This half carucate, together with 1 bovate in Well (*D.B.*, 4/62), had been acquired by the archbishop before 1118, and this is sufficient to account for the name of Tothby in later records amongst the archbishop's possessions. Professor F. M. Stenton has pointed out that there are very serious philological objections to the identification of Tatebi with Tothby. Further, a recent examination of the numerous early charters relating to the neighbourhood has produced evidence which suggests that there was a village of Tatebi in the northern, and probably the north-eastern, part of the parish of Ulceby by Alford, and therefore on the west side of Ailby, whereas Tothby lies to the east of that place. If the village disappeared before the thirteenth century, as the absence of its name from documents would suggest, the carucate of land which belonged to it in 1086 was probably attached to Well.

The evidence of the charters is as follows ; (1) By a composition, dated 1220, between W. de Welle, knight, and W. the chaplain, rector of the chapel of Well on the one part, and the prior and canons of St. Katherine's, Lincoln, on the other, to settle a dispute as to whether certain tithes belonged to the fee of Rigsby or to the fee of Gant, it was agreed, *inter alia*, that the tithes 'de magna cultura que vocatur Thateby' should remain to the church of Alford (B.M., *Harleian Charter* 57, F 51). (2) A grant in alms by Philip de Praeres to Kirkstead abbey of two selions in Vlesbi 'quantum se extendunt in longum a uia que 'uadit per medium uille de Vlesbi usque ad semitam de Tatebi' [etc.] (B.M., *Cotton MSS.*, Vesp. E. xviii, f. 20). (3) A similar grant by the same Philip to the abbey of all the land that he had in the fields of Vlesbi 'inter terram Ricardi filii Ricardi militis et curtem grangie 'monachorum in eadem uilla de Vlesbi ex nord parte grangie quantum se 'extendit in latum et in longum a magna uia que uadit uersus Hagh 'usque ad semitam de Tatebi' (*ibid.*). (4) An indenture between the monks of Kirkstead and Roger de Welle about land in Ulceby, recording that Roger has exchanged 'quicquid habuit de feodo Baldrici de 'Grendale quod iacet ex est parte Tatebigate et but[at] super croftum 'Arnaldi pro duabus acris et dimidia super Randolfwange ad caput del 'west de feodo quod Willelmus de Fuletebi dedit prefatis monachis in 'elemosinam' (*ibid.*, ff. 26, 26d.).

TETLEY (Manley wap.—*F.A.*, iii, 185—*O.S.*, 38, A 12), a hamlet in the parish of Crowle, which has lost its separate status, and is now reckoned as a part of Crowle. Crull, Est Toft, Aland, and Tettelay formed a *uillata* in 1316 (*F.A.*, iii, 185, where Tettelay is wrongly identified as Cottley).

THETFORD (Ness wap.—*Placita de quo Waranto*, 402b.—*O.S.*, 64, D 9), an extinct village and chapelry in the parish of Baston, now represented by the farmstead of Thetford. Croyland abbey owned much of the land (*Valor Ecclesiasticus*, iv, 86). There are institutions, in 1529 and 1539, to the vicarage of Tetforthe with the chapel of Baston annexed (*Reg.*, xxvii, ff. 45d., 46, 70); but this is putting the cart before the horse.

THORESBY (Bolingbroke wap.—*Monasticon*, v, 454-6—*O.S.*, *circa* 48, H 4), an extinct village in the parish of Revesby. William I de Roumare, earl of Lincoln, gave all his land in Revesbia and Thoresbi and Schicthesbia to the abbot of Rievaulx for the foundation of a Cistercian abbey at Revesby, recompensing his rustics in the three villages for their displacement, either by gifts of land elsewhere or by the liberty, for themselves and their families, of going and living where they would. Thoresby is supposed to have been situated near the present chapel of St. Lawrence; and Sythesby in the present park of Revesby, close to the Kangaroo pond (Stanhope, *Abstracts of the Deeds and Charters relating to Revesby Abbey*, 1, note).

THORLEY (Gartree wapentake), an extinct village. Later it appears as a manor which included a large part of the parishes of Minting and Gautby. The name of Thorley was afterwards superseded by that of Minting Park which appears in the *O.S.* (47, D 10). See *F.C.*, ii, p. liv.

THORPE (Loveden wap.—*F.A.*, iii, 191), an extinct hamlet in the parish of Westborough (*O.S.*, 55, C 1). It is called Parua Thorp in *B.F.*, p. 1041. See *Cal. Inq.*, iv, p. 168. The site has not yet been found.

West Burg with Thorp was a *uillata* in 1316 and 1333 (*F.A.*, iii, 191; *Sub.*, 135/15, mem. 14d.).

THORPE NEAR LANGTON. See BUCKLAND.

THORPE LE VALE, formerly FRUNTHORPE (Wraggoe wap.—*Sub.*, 242/113, mem. 5—*O.S.*, 40, G 3), a hamlet in the parish of Ludford Magna, which has lost its separate status. In the twelfth to the fourteenth centuries the place was known as Frunthorpe (*B.F.*, 171; *F.C.*, i, 308; P.R.O., *Feet of Fines*, 136/88, no. 7). In the first two of these references *Frunthorpe* should probably be read for *Frimthorpe*. *Temp.* Henry VIII, the place was called Frumthorpe *alias* Thorpe in le Myres (*Feet of Fines*, 22/175, no. 22); and *temp.* Elizabeth, Thorpe in le Myre (*ibid.*, 9 and 10 Eliz., Mich., part 2, no. 38; 17 Eliz., East., no. 37; 44 Eliz., East., no. 59); and Thorpe le Mire in Bryant's map, 1828. The adoption of the more euphonious form of Thorpe le Vale seems to be quite modern.

TILNEY (Langoe wapentake) an extinct hamlet in the village of Thorpe [Tilney] and in the parish of Timberland. Mention of the hamlet has been found in two charters registered in the cartulary of Thurgarton priory which is preserved in the library of Southwell cathedral (f. 106). On 4 July, 1545, John Broxholme and John Bellowe received a royal grant of three houses in Thorpe and Tylney, being possessions of the dissolved priory of Kyme (*Cal. State Papers*, Henry VIII, xx, part i, p. 659b). In the tithe rentcharge award of Thorpe Tilney a close about half way between the Car dike and the river Witham, and adjoining the boundary of Walcot on the south, is called 'Tilney end.' The close contains 7 acres, 3 roods, and 35 perches, and forms the southern half of close no. 79 in the *O.S.* (25 in. scale—86/6). The evidence is not sufficient to determine the site of the hamlet; but it is not unlikely that a slight hill on the east side of the Car dyke, where a farm-stead now stands (*O.S.*, 25 in. scale, 88/5, no. 42), may be the place. The village of Thorpe, or Timberland Thorpe as it was formerly called, is now known by the conflate name of Thorpe Tilney.

TOWTHORPE (Threo wap.—*D.B.*—*O.S.*, 55, E 3), an extinct hamlet, now included in the parish of Londonthorpe. A place in Belton park, partly surrounded by the river Witham, in the extreme south-eastern corner of the *O.S.* (6 in. scale) 113, N.E., known locally as Towthorpe Hollow, is the approximate site of the village. No traces of foundations remain, for the land has been levelled within the last fifty years. See *F.C.*, p. lxii. Lunderthorp cum Touthorp' was a *uillata* in 1327 and 1333 (*Sub.*, 135/10, mem. 69; *ibid.*, 135/15, mem. 8d.; cp., *F.A.*, iii, 190).

TRIC (Candleshoe wap.—*D.B.*—*O.S.*, *circa* 48, G 13), an extinct village, the name of which is not found after 1086. It seems to be represented by Skegness in subsequent records.

TUNSTALL (Corringham wap.—*Danelaw Charters*, 60, 62, 63 (bis)), an island in the south-eastern part of the parish of Redbourne (*O.S.*, 39, D 5). There was a house of Gilbertine nuns here which was afterwards united to the priory of Bullington. See *Monasticon*, vii, 954a.

TYTTON (Kirton wap.—*F.C.*, ii, 307-8—*O.S.*, 56, D 2), an extinct hamlet in the parish of Wyberton, now represented by Tytton hall.

VAUDEY (Beltisloe wap.—*F.A.*, iii, 127—*O.S.*, 64, B 7), an extinct place in Grimsthorpe park in the parish of Edenham, where there was an abbey of Cistercian monks. See above BRACHECOURT.

WALTON (Winnibriggs wap.—*F.A.*, iii, 190—*O S.*, 55, G 3), an extinct hamlet in the ancient parish of Grantham, and the modern civil parish of Spittlegate Without. It is not mentioned in *D.B.*, but was included in Houghton or in Nongetune (q. v.). See *F.C.*, ii, pp. lxiii, lxiv. Houton, Walton, and Spitelgate were a *uillata* in 1316 and 1327 (*F.A.*, iii, 190 ; *Sub.*, 135/10, mem. 5d.).

WATERTON (Axholme wap.—*D.B.*—*O.S.*, 33, H 1), an extinct village in the parish of Luddington, now represented by Waterton hall (*O.S.*) which is used as a farm-house (Stonehouse, *History and Topography of the Isle of Axholme*, 445 ff.). Ludington and Watterton were a *uillata* in 1316 and 1333 (*F.A.*, iii, 185 ; *Sub.*, 135/16, mem. 1d.).

WESTHORPE (Threo wap.—*D.B.*), an extinct hamlet, now included in the parish of Old Somerby (*O.S*, 55, G 4). See *F.C.*, ii, pp. lxii-iii. In 1333, Dunsthorp' cum Herierby and Westhorp' was a *uillata* (*Sub.*, 135/15, mem. 8d.).

WILLINGTHORPE (City of Lincoln—*Danelaw Charters*, 343 and note), formerly a suburb of Lincoln (*O.S.*, 47, D 5) which has not been identified.

WILLINGTON or KIRTON WILLINGTON (Kirton wap.—*Descriptive Catalogue of Ancient Deeds*, v, 286), probably an extinct hamlet in the parish of Kirton in Holland (*O.S.*, 56, E 2). The road which runs from Kirton to Kirton End is still called Willington road. See P.R O., *Feet of Fines*, 32 Eliz., Trinity, no. 26.

WOLMERSTY (Skirbeck wap.—*D.B.*), an extinct village in the parish of Wrangle. Ulmerestig is used in *D.B.* (p. 68) as the name of the wapentake instead of the more usual name of Skirbeck. Wolmersty survived as a manor till at least the reign of Henry IV (P.R.O., *Feet of Fines*, 144/152, no. 3). See Thompson, *History and Antiquities of Boston*, 593-4 ; *F.C.*, i, 179, 302, 359 ; *ibid.*, ii, p. lxii ; *Kirkstead Cartulary* ff. 177d.—192d. *passim*. It is not improbable that Wirmele (*F.C.*, i, 118, 340) should be identified with Wolmersty.

WOODHOUSE FARM (Corringham wap.), in the parish of Great Corringham (*O.S.*, 39, G 2). An award of tithes in the hamlet or division of Woodhouse Farm was made, 9 February, 1839 (Lincoln Diocesan Registry, *Tithe Rentcharge Award*, H 295).

WULFHOLM (Corringham wap.—*Danelaw Charters*, 63-4—*O.S.*, 39, E 6), a place in the parish of Redbourne. The name survives in the *O.S.* as Woofham hill. See *Monasticon*, vii, 954a.

WYKEHAM (Yarborough wap.—query *D.B.*—*O.S.* (6 in. scale), 38 N.W.), an extinct hamlet in the south-eastern part of the parish of Nettleton, extending on the south to the boundary of Normanby le Wold Lincoln Cathedral muniments, D ij, 85/2, nos. 29, 36). The approximate site is represented by Wykeham Well (*O.S.*). Nettleton, Herwyk, Wikham, and Draycote formed a *uillata* in 1316 (*F.A.*, iii, 182).

WYKEHAM, WEST (Louthesk wap.—*D.B.*—*O.S.*, 40, H 3), an extinct village and parish, which comprised and was co-terminous with the manor of Great Tows and Little Tows, and now forms part of the parish of Ludford Magna in the wapentake of Wraggoe. It was bounded on the north by Binbrook, on the south by Burgh on Bain, on the east by Ludford Magna, and on the west by Kelstern and East or Little Wykeham. In 1316, Est Wykham and West Wykham formed a *uillata* (*F.A.*, iii, 178). The church of West Wykeham was dedicated to St. Edward (Lincoln Cathedral muniments, Dij, 86/3/42), and was appropriated as to one mediety to Sixle priory and as to the other mediety to Markby priory. Vicars were instituted until 1382 on the alternate presentation of the two priories. On 7 March, 1396-7, the bishop of Lincoln, with the consents of the two priories, decreed the union and incorporation of the vicarage with the vicarage of Ludford Magna, since the parish of West Wykeham, having been attacked by divers pestilences, was so destitute of parishioners that the number of households or of the persons of parishioners did not reach ten, and since the parish had remained continuously desolate without the rule and solace of a pastor because no priest had hitherto been found who was so simple as to suffer himself to be joined to such a spouse, for which reason the church and the buildings of the vicarage had become altogether ruinous, and hospitality and the cure of souls had been utterly neglected, and the sacraments and sacramentals had not been ministered to the parishioners by their own priest, etc. (*Reg.*, xi, ff. 450d—451).

The sites of West Wykeham and South Cadeby (q.v.), in the heart of the Lincolnshire Wolds, are the two best examples in the county of extinct villages. The foundations of the church and homesteads of West Wykeham may be clearly traced as they lie on both sides of a little valley which slopes down to the river Bain, in the grass close numbered 166a and 166b in the *O.S.* (25 in. scale, 47/9 and 13); and the town street is seen to be part of the road which leads from South Cadeby, through East Wykeham, to Ludford Magna. The church, which stood in close no. 166a, about 220 feet from the north-east fence and 90 feet from the north-west fence, seems to have measured about 50 by 24 feet, while the churchyard was about 140 by 80 feet.

Great Tows was a grange of Markby priory, and when the village of West Wykeham disappeared, it supplied the name by which the place has ever since been known. The tithe award of the parish of Ludford Magna, dated 19 April, 1849 (Lincoln Diocesan Registry, *Tithe Rentcharge Award*, H. 648), states that all the tithes of the parish were commuted under the enclosure act of 31 George III, except the tithes of lands in the lordship of Ludford called Great Towes and Little Towes, containing 950 acres, well known by metes and bounds, which lands were protected from the render of tithes by a prescriptive payment of 1*l*. 10*s*. 0*d*. to the vicar of Ludford. Under the award this charge of 1*l*. 10*s*. 0*d*. was apportioned on an arable close called Snipewells, which lay between the Bain on the east and close no. 166a and 166b on the west.

As part of the parish of Ludford Magna, West Wykeham now lies in the wapentake of Wraggoe; but until the union of the two parishes it formed part of the wapentake of Louthesk, the river Bain being the boundary between the wapentakes as well as between the parishes.

APPENDIX II

BOROUGHS, WAPENTAKES, VILLAGES, AND OTHER PLACES

The schedules contain the places named in *Domesday Book*, *The Lindsey Survey*, *The Book of Fees*, and the Aid of 1316 (*Feudal Aids*, iii, 177-192), and some other villages, hamlets, and places, most of which are now extinct.

Italics denote that a place does not occur in *Domesday Book* or the *Lindsey Survey*.

BOROUGHS AND WAPENTAKES IN THE COUNTY OF LINCOLN

BOROUGHS

Lincoln	Stamford	Torksey with Hardwick

WAPENTAKES

PARTS OF HOLLAND

Elloe	Kirton	Skirbeck

PARTS OF KESTEVEN

Aswardhurn	Flaxwell	Ness
Aveland	Graffoe	Threo
Beltisloe	Langoe	Winnibriggs
Boothby	Loveden	

PARTS OF LINDSEY

NORTH RIDING

Bradley	Ludborough	Yarborough
Haverstoe	Walshcroft	

SOUTH RIDING

Bolingbroke	Gartree	Louthesk
Calcewath	Hill	Wraggoe
Candleshoe	Horncastle	

WEST RIDING

Aslacoe	Corringham	Manley
Axholme (or Epworth)	Lawress	Well

VILLAGES AND HAMLETS

AND OTHER PLACES

WAPENTAKE OF ASLACOE

IN THE WEST RIDING OF LINDSEY

Atterby (*F.A.*)
Blyborough
Caenby
Cammeringham
Cotes by Stow
Crossholme (*F.C.*, i)
Fillingham
Firsby, (East and West)
Glentham
Glentworth
Hackthorn
Hanworth, Cold
Harpswell
Hemswell
Ingham
Normanby by Spital
Norton, Bishop
Owmby
Saxby
Snitterby
Spital in the Street (*F.A.*)
Spridlington
Willoughton

WAPENTAKE OF ASWARDHURN

IN KESTEVEN

Asgarby (*Sub.*, 242/113)
Aswarby
Aunsby
Boughton (*B.F.*)
Burgh (by Evedon)
Burton Pedwardine
Crofton (*F.A.*)
Culverthorpe
Evedon (part)
Ewerby
Ewerby Thorpe
Hale, (Great and Little)
Heckington
Helpringham
Howell
Ingoldsby
Kelby
Kirkby by Laythorpe
Kyme, South
Laythorpe
Mareham
Millthorpe (*F.A.*)
Quarrington
Scredington
Silkby (*B.F.*)
Sleaford, Old
Swarby
Thorpe Latimer (*B.F.*)
Willoughby by Silkby

WAPENTAKE OF AVELAND

IN KESTEVEN

Aslackby
Avethorpe
Billingborough
Birthorpe
Bourne
Bridge End (*F.A.*)
Cawthorpe
Dembleby
Dowsby
Dunsby
Dyke
Folkingham
Graby, East
Graby, West
Haceby
Haconby
Hanthorpe
Horbling
Kirkby Underwood
Laughton, (East and West)
Millthorpe (*F.A.*)
Morton

WAPENTAKE OF AVELAND (CONT.)

Newton
Osbournby
Ouseby
Pickworth
Pointon
Ringstone
Rippingale
Sempringham
Spanby
Stainfield
Stow
Swaton
Threckingham
Walcot
Willoughby, Scott

WAPENTAKE OF AXHOLME (OR EPWORTH)

IN THE WEST RIDING OF LINDSEY

AFTERWARDS INCLUDED IN THE WAPENTAKE OF MANLEY[1]

Althorpe
Amcotts
Beltoft
Belton
Burnham, High
Burnham, Low
Butterwick, West
Crowle
Derrythorpe (*F.A.*)
Ealand (*F.A.*)
Eastlound
Eastoft (*F.A.*)
Epworth
Garthorpe
Graizelound
Gunthorpe (*F.A.*)
Haxey
Hirst (p. lxxxvi)
Keadby (*F.A.*)
Kelfield (*F.A.*)
Kinnard's Ferry, West, (*F.A.*)
Luddington
Maræ
Misson (*F.A.*)
Owston
Temple Belwood
Tetley (*F.A.*)
Upperthorpe
Waterton
Westwood
Wroot (*F.A.*)

WAPENTAKE OF BELTISLOE

IN KESTEVEN

Adewelle
Aunby (*F.A.*)
Bassingthorpe
Bitchfield
Bowthorpe
Brachecourt (p. xlix)
Bredestorp or Bergestorp
Bulby
Burton Coggles
Bytham, Castle
Bytham, Little
Careby
Colsterworth
Corby
Counthorpe
Creeton
Easton
Edenham
Elsthorpe
Grimsthorpe (*F.A.*)
Gunby St. Nicholas
Hanby (*B.F.*)
Hawthorpe
Holywell
Irnham
Keisby
Lavington
Lavington, Little

[1] Axholme is entered as a wapentake in *L.S.* (1115-1118). In *Sub.*, 242/113, mem. 1, (late twelfth century), its villages are entered as the last of the items under the title of the wapentake of Manley. It is called 'Epworth wapentake' in *D.B.*, 71/16.

WAPENTAKE OF BELTISLOE (CONT.)

Lobthorpe
Lound
Manthorpe
Osgodby
Scottlethorpe
Skillington
Southorpe
Stainby
Sudwelle
Swayfield
Swinstead
Toft
Twyford
Westby
Witham on the Hill
Witham, North
Witham, South
Woolsthorpe (in Colsterworth) (*F.A.*)

WAPENTAKE OF BOLINGBROKE

IN THE SOUTH RIDING OF LINDSEY

Asgarby
Bolingbroke
Enderby, Mavis
Eresby
Hagnaby
Halton Holgate
Hareby
Hundleby
Keal, East
Keal, West
Kirkby, East
Laythorpe (p. lxxxvii)
Lusby
Medlam (p. xli)
Miningsby
Raithby by Spilsby
Revesby
Sibsey
Spilsby
Steeping, Little
Stickford
Stickney
Sythesby (p. lxviii)
Thoresby (p. lxix)
Thorpe St. Peter
Toynton All Saints
Toynton St. Peter

WAPENTAKE OF BOOTHBY

IN KESTEVEN

Boothby
Coleby
Harmston
Navenby
Sapperton (p. lxv)
Skinnand
Somerton
Waddington
Welbourn
Wellingore

WAPENTAKE OF BRADLEY

IN THE NORTH RIDING OF LINDSEY

Aylesby
Bradley
Clee
Cotes, Great
Cotes, Little
Grimsby, Great
Healing
Hole
Holme, South, (p. lviii)
Holton le Clay
Humberstone
Irby upon Humber
Itterby
Laceby
Scartho
Swallow
Tetney
Thrunscoe
Weelsby

WAPENTAKE OF CALCEWATH

IN THE SOUTH RIDING OF LINDSEY

Aby
Ailby
Alford
Anderby (*B.F.*)
Asserby (*B.F.*)
Authorpe (in Mumby)
Beesby in the Marsh
Belleau
Bilsby
Bonthorpe
Calceby
Cawthorpe, Little, (*Sub.*, 242/113)
Claxby by Alford
Claythorpe
Cumberworth
Danmark (p. lxiv)
Farlesthorpe (*B.F.*)
Fulsthorpe (*B.F.*)
Gayton le Marsh (*B.F.*)
Hagnaby (*B.F.*)
Hanby
Hannah (*B.F.*)
Hasthorpe
Haugh
Hogsthorpe (*B.F.*)
Huttoft
Legbourne
Mablethorpe
Maltby le Marsh
Markby
Mawthorpe (*B.F.*)
Mumby
Reston, South, (*B.F.*)
Rigsby
Saleby
Sloothby
Stain
Strubby
Sutton in the Marsh
Swaby
Tatebi
Theddlethorpe (All Saints and St. Helen)
Thoresby, South
Thoresthorpe
Thurlby
Tothby
Tothill
Trusthorpe
Ulceby
Well
Willoughby in the Marsh
Withern
Woodthorpe

WAPENTAKE OF CANDLESHOE

IN THE SOUTH RIDING OF LINDSEY

Addlethorpe
Ashby by Partney
Bassingham (p. xlviii)
Boothby
Bratoft
Burgh in the Marsh
Candlesby
Croft
Dalby
Dexthorpe
Driby
Firsby (*B.F.*)
Fordington
Friskney
Grebby
Greinby (p. lvi)
Gunby St. Peter
Ingoldmells
Irby le Marsh
Langene
Laysingthorpe (p. lx)
Northolme (*F.A.*)
Orby
Partney
Scremby
Scremthorpe (*B.F.*)
Skegness (*B.F.*)
Skendleby
Steeping, Great
Sutterby
Tric
Wainfleet
Welton le Marsh
Winthorpe (*B.F.*)

WAPENTAKE OF CORRINGHAM

IN THE WEST RIDING OF LINDSEY

Aisby
Blyton
Cleatham
Corringham, [Great]
Corringham, Little, (F.A.)
Dunstall
Gainsborough
Gilby (F.A.)
Grayingham
Havercroft (F.A.)
Heapham
Kinnard's Ferry, East, (F.A.)
Kirton in Lindsey
Laughton
Lea
Morton
Northorpe
Pilham
Scotter
Scotterthorpe
Scotton
Somerby
Southorpe
Springthorpe
Stockwith, East, (F.A.)
Susworth
Thonock
Walkerith (F.A.)
Wharton
Wildsworth (F.A.)
Yawthorpe

WAPENTAKE OF ELLOE

IN HOLLAND

Aswick (p. xlviii)
Cowbit (*Sub.*, 138/491)
Croyland
Fleet
Gedney
Gedney Fen (*Sub.*, 138/491)
Holbeach
Lutton
Moulton
Pinchbeck
Spalding
Sutton, Long
Tydd St. Mary
Weston
Whaplode

WAPENTAKE OF FLAXWELL

IN KESTEVEN

Anwick
Ashby de la Laund
Bloxham
Brauncewell
Coteland
Cranwell
Digby
Dorrington
Dunsby St. Andrew
Evedon (part)
Hanbeck (B.F.)
Haverholme
Holdingham (F.A.)
Leasingham
Rauceby, North
Rauceby, South
Rowston
Roxham
Ruskington
Sleaford, New, (F.A.)
Temple Bruer (B.F.)

WAPENTAKE OF GARTREE

IN THE SOUTH RIDING OF LINDSEY

Asterby
Belchford
Bucknall
Burreth
Campney (p. lxxxvi)
Cawkwell

WAPENTAKE OF GARTREE (CONT.)

Donington on Bain
Gautby (*B.F.*)
Goulceby (*B.F.*)
Hemingby
Horsington
Kirkstead (*F.C.*,i)
Minting
Minting, Little
Ranby
Scamblesby
Silverys (p. lxv)
Stainton, Market
Stenigot
Stixwould
Sturton, Great
Sudtone
Thorley

WAPENTAKE OF GRAFFOE

IN KESTEVEN

Aubourn
Bassingham
Boultham
Carlton le Moorland
Doddington Pigot
Eagle
Haddington
Hykeham, North
Hykeham, South
Morton (*B.F.*)
Norton Disney
Scarle, North, (*B.F.*)
Skellingthorpe
Stapleford
Swinderby
Swinethorpe (*B.F.*)
Thorpe on the Hill
Thurlby
Whisby

WAPENTAKE OF HAVERSTOE

IN THE NORTH RIDING OF LINDSEY

Ashby by Fenby
Autby
Barnoldby le Beck
Beelsby
Beesby
Brigsley
Cabourn
Cadeby, North
Cotes, North
Cuxwold
Fenby
Fulstow
Grainsby
Gunnerby
Hatcliffe
Hawerby
Marshchapel
Newton le Wold
Ravendale, East
Ravendale, West
Rothwell
Swinhope
Thoresby, North
Waith
Waltham

WAPENTAKE OF HILL

IN THE SOUTH RIDING OF LINDSEY

Ashby Puerorum
Aswardby (*B.F.*)
Brinkhill
Claxby Pluckacre
Dunsthorpe (*F.A.*)
Enderby, Bag
Fulletby
Greetham
Greetham, Little, (*F.A.*)
Hagworthingham
Hameringham
Harrington (*B.F.*)
Ketsby
Langton by Spilsby
Ormsby, South
Oxcombe

WAPENTAKE OF HILL (CONT.)

Salmonby
Sausthorpe (*B.F.*)
Scrafield (*B.F.*)
Somersby
Stainsby (*F.A.*)
Tetford
Walmsgate
Winceby
Worlaby

WAPENTAKE OF HORNCASTLE

IN THE SOUTH RIDING OF LINDSEY

Armtree (p. xlvii)
Ashby, West
Bainthorpe[1] (see p. xlviii)
Baumber[1]
Birkwood[1] (p. xlix)
Buckland[1]
Coningsby[1]
Dalderby[1]
Edlington[1]
Enderby, Wood
Fulsby[1]
Haltham on Bain
Horncastle
Kirkby on Bain[1]
Langton by Horncastle[1]
Mareham le Fen
Mareham on the Hill
Martin by Horncastle[1]
Moorby
Norcotes (p. xlii)
Poolham (*B.F.*)
Roughton[1]
Scrivelsby[1]
Sturton, Little[1]
Tattershall[1]
Tattershall Thorpe[1]
Thimbleby[1]
Thornton by Horncastle[1]
Toynton, High
Toynton, Low
Tumby[1]
Waddingworth[1]
Wilksby[1]
Wispington[1]
Woodhall[1] (*B.F.*)

WAPENTAKE OF KIRTON

IN HOLLAND

Algarkirk
Bicker
Brothertoft
Burtoft
Cheal
Donington
Dowdyke
Drayton
Fosdyke (*Sub.*, 138/491)
Frampton
Gosberton
Kirton
Quadring
Riche
Riskenton
Stenning
Surfleet
Sutterton
Swineshead (*B.F.*)
Swinfleet
Wigtoft (*B.F.*)
Wyberton
Wykes (*B.F.*)

WAPENTAKE OF LANGOE

IN KESTEVEN

Billinghay
Blankney
Bracebridge
Branston
Canwick
Catley (p. liii)
Cotes (*in Blankney*) (p. liv)
Dogdyke (*F.C.*, i)
Dunston
Hanworth, Potter

[1] Afterwards transferred to the wapentake of Gartree.

WAPENTAKE OF LANGOE (CONT.)

Heighington (*F.A.*)
Kirkby Green
Kyme, North
Martin (*B.F.*)
Mere (*F.A.*)
Metheringham
Nocton
Scopwick
Sim Booth Grange (p. lxvi)
Thorpe [*Tilney*] (*B.F.*)
Tilney (p. lxx)
Timberland
Walcot
Washingborough

WAPENTAKE OF LAWRESS

IN THE WEST RIDING OF LINDSEY

Aisthorpe
Barlings
Brattleby
Broxholme
Burton by Lincoln
Buslingthorpe
Carlton, Middle
Carlton, North
Carlton, South
Dunham
Faldingworth
Fiskerton
Friesthorpe
Greetwell
Holme (in Sudbrooke)
Ingleby (High and Low *or* North and South)
Langworth, West, (*F.A.*)
Nettleham
Reepham
Riseholme
Ryland (*Sub.*, 242/113)
Saxilby
Scampton
Scothorn
Snarford
Sudbrooke
Thorpe in the Fallows
Torksey (a borough in *D.B.*)
Welton by Lincoln
Willingham, Cherry

WAPENTAKE OF LOUTHESK

IN THE SOUTH RIDING OF LINDSEY

Ackthorpe (p. xlvii)
Alvingham
Authorpe
Brackenborough
Burwell
Cadeby, South
Calcethorpe
Carlton, Castle
Carlton, Great
Carlton, Little
Cockerington, (North and South)
Conisholme (*B.F.*)
Dunsthorpe (p. lv)
Elkington, (North and South)
Esthorpe (p. lxxxvi)
Fanthorpe (*B.F.*)
Farforth
Gayton le Wold
Grainthorpe
Grimblethorpe
Grimoldby
Hallington
Haugham
Keddington
Kelstern
Lambcroft (*B.F.*)
Louth
Louth Park (*Sub.*, 242/113)
Ludney
Maidenwell
Maltby by Louth
Manby
Mare Haven
Muckton
Northorpe (p. lxxxvii)
Raithby by Louth
Reston, North
Ruckland
Saltfleet Haven
Saltfleetby
Saltfleetby Haven
Skidbrook
Somercotes, (North and South)
Southorpe (p.lxvi)

WAPENTAKE OF LOUTHESK (CONT.)

Stewton
Swine Haven
Tathwell
Welton le Wold
Withcall
Wykeham, East
Wykeham, West
Yarburgh

WAPENTAKE OF LOVEDEN

IN KESTEVEN

Ancaster (*part*) (*B.F.*)
Beckingham (*B.F.*)
Bennington, Long
Brandon
Broughton, Brant
Carlton Scroop
Caythorpe
Claypole
Doddington, Dry
Fenton (*B.F.*)
Foston
Frieston
Fulbeck
Gelston
Holme Spinney
Hough on the Hill
Hougham
Leadenham
Marston
Normanton
Outhorpe (p. lxii)
Stapleford, Little, (*F.A.*)
Stocking (*F.A.*)
Stragglethorpe (*B.F.*)
Stubton
Sudbrook (*B.F.*)
Sudthorpe (p. lxvii)
Sutton (*B.F.*)
Thorpe, Little, (*B.F.*)
Westborough
Willoughby, West

WAPENTAKE OF LUDBOROUGH

IN THE NORTH RIDING OF LINDSEY

Cawthorpe (in Covenham)
Covenham (St. Bartholomew and St. Mary)
Fotherby
Grimsby, Little
Ludborough
Ormsby, North
Utterby (*F.A.*)
Wyham

WAPENTAKE OF MANLEY

IN THE WEST RIDING OF LINDSEY

Alkborough
Appleby
Ashby
Bottesford
Broughton
Brumby
Burringham (*F.A.*)
Burton upon Stather
Butterwick, East, (*F.A.*)
Castlethorpe
Coleby
Conesby, North
Conesby, South
Crosby
Darby
Flixborough
Frodingham (*F.A.*)
Gainsthorpe
Gunhouse (*F.A.*)
Halton, West
Haythby
Hibaldstow
Holme
Manby
Manton
Messingham
Normanby
Raventhorpe

WAPENTAKE OF MANLEY (CONT.)

Redbourn
Risby, (Great and Little)
Roxby
Santon, (High and Low)
Sawcliffe
Scawby
Scunthorpe
Stainton by Wadingham
Sturton
Thealby
Twigmoor
Wadingham
Walcot
Whitton
Winteringham
Winterton
Yaddlethorpe

WAPENTAKE OF NESS

IN KESTEVEN

Banthorpe
Barholm
Baston
Braceborough
Carlby
Casewick
Deeping, East
Deeping, Market, (*Sub.*, 137/383)
Deeping, West
Greatford
Langtoft
Newstead (p. lxxxvii)
Obthorpe
Shillingthorpe (p. lxxxvii)
Stamford (a borough in *D.B.*)
Stowe
Tallington
Thetford (p. lxix)
Thurlby
Uffington
Wilsthorpe

WAPENTAKE OF SKIRBECK

IN HOLLAND

Benington (*B.F.*)
Boston (*B.F.*)
Butterwick
Fen (p. lv)
Fishtoft
Frieston
Leake
Leverton
Scrane (p. lxv)
Scrane, Old, (p. lxv)
Skirbeck
Wolmersty
Wrangle

WAPENTAKE OF THREO

IN KESTEVEN

Aisby
Ancaster (part) (*B.F.*)
Barkston
Belton
Boothby Pagnell
Braceby
Dunsthorpe
Gipple (*B.F.*)
Harrowby
Haydor
Honington
Humby
Londonthorpe
Manthorpe (*B.F.*)
Ogarth (*F.A.*)
Oseby
Ringsthorpe (*B.F.*)
Ropsley
St. Anne's (p. lxiii)
Sapperton
Somerby
Syston
Towthorpe
Welby
Westhorpe
Wilsford

WAPENTAKE OF WALSHCROFT

IN THE NORTH RIDING OF LINDSEY

Beckfield (*F.A.*)
Binbrook
Cauthorpe (p. lxxxvi)
Claxby by Normanby
Croxby
Holton le Moor
Irford
Kelsey, South
Kingerby
Kirkby (*F.A.*)
Linwood
Newton by Toft
Normanby le Wold
Osgodby
Otby
Owersby, (North and South)
Rasen, Market
Rasen, Middle
Rasen, West
Risby
Stainton le Vale
Tealby
Thoresway
Thorganby
Thornton le Moor
Toft by Newton
Usselby
Walesby
Willingham, North
Winghale

WAPENTAKE OF WELL

IN THE WEST RIDING OF LINDSEY

Alfletby (p. xlvii)
Brampton
Bransby
Burton, Gate
Fenton
Hardwick
Heynings (p. lvii)
Kettlethorpe (*Sub.*, 242/113)
Kexby
Knaith
Laughterton (*F.A*)
Marton
Newton upon Trent
Normanby by Stow
Stow St. Mary
Sturton by Stow
Upton
Willingham by Stow

WAPENTAKE OF WINNIBRIGGS

IN KESTEVEN

Allington, (East and West)
Barrowby
Belvoir (*part*) (*F.A.*)
Casthorpe, (East and West)
Denton
Ganthorpe
Gonerby, Great
Gonerby, Little
Grantham
Harlaxton
Houghton
Hungerton
Newbo (p. lxxxvii)
Nongetune
Ponton, Great
Ponton, Little
Sedgebrook
Spittlegate (*F.A.*)
Stenwith
Stoke, North
Stoke, South
Stroxton
Walton (*B.F.*)
Woolsthorpe (near Grantham)
Wyville

WAPENTAKE OF WRAGGOE

IN THE SOUTH RIDING OF LINDSEY

Apley
Bardney
Barkwith, (East and West)
Beckering
Benniworth
Biscathorpe

WAPENTAKE OF WRAGGOE (CONT.)

Bleasby
Bullington
Burgh upon Bain
Butyate
Calcote (or Collow)
Fulnetby
Girsby
Hainton
Hardwick (*B.F.*)
Hatton
Helethorpe (*B.F.*)
Holtham (in Legsby)
Holton by Beckering
Kingthorpe
Kirmond le Mire
Langton, Low
Langton by Wragby
Langworth, East, (*F.A.*)
Legsby
Lissington
Ludford (Magna et Parva)
Newball
Osgodby
Panton
Rand
Reasby
Sixle
Snelland
Sotby
Southrey
Stainfield
Stainton by Langworth
Strubby
Swinthorpe
Thorpe le Vale or Frunthorpe or Frinthorpe (*B.F.*)
Torrington, East
Torrington, West
Westlaby
Wickenby
Willingham, South
Wragby

WAPENTAKE OF YARBOROUGH

IN THE NORTH RIDING OF LINDSEY

Audleby
Barnetby le Wold
Barrow on Humber
Barton on Humber
Bigby
Bodebi (p. lxxxvi)
Bonby
Brocklesby
Burnham
Cadney
Caistor
Clixby
Coton, Nun
Croxton
Draycote (*F.A.*)
Elsham
Ferriby, South
Fonaby
Glanford Brigg (*F.A.*)
Goxhill
Grasby
Habrough
Halton, East
Hardwick (*B.F.*)
Horkstow
Houflet
Howsham
Hundon
Immingham
Keelby
Kelsey, North
Kettleby
Kettleby Thorpe
Killingholme, (North and South)
Kirmington
Limber, Great
Limber, Little
Lobingham
Melton Ross
Nettleton
Newsham *or* Newhouse
Owmby
Riby
Roxton (*B.F.*)
Saxby All Saints
Searby
Somerby by Brigg
Stallingborough
Thornton Curtis
Ulceby
Wootton
Worlaby
Wrawby
Wykeham

APPENDIX III

ADDITIONAL EXTINCT VILLAGES

AND OTHER FORGOTTEN PLACES

BODEBI (Yarborough wap.—*D.B.*), probably an extinct hamlet in or near the parish of Thornton Curtis (*O.S.*, 34, H 4). The identification of Bodebi (*D.B.*, 36/2) with Bonby is suggested at p. 155 ; but further consideration shews that this is improbable. The *D.B.* form of Bonby is Bundebi (25/1 ; 36/3), whereas Bodebi is elsewhere the equivalent of Boothby.

CAMPNEY (Gartree wap.—*O.S.*, 47, E 11) seems to have been a hamlet in the parish of Bucknall, which is now represented by Campney grange. The road which runs south-westwards from the grange is known as Campney lane. Campney occurs in the *Feet of Fines* (6 Eliz., East., [8] ; 8-9 Eliz., Mich., [61] ; 40 Eliz., East., part 2, [6] ; 43 Eliz., Trin., [16]).

CAUTHORPE (Walshcroft wap.), was returned, *circa* 1565, as a hamlet of Thornton le Moor (*O.S.*, 39, E 7), containing six families (B.M., *Harleian MS.* 618, f. 14). Its approximate site is probably indicated by a close called Cauthorp Close which lies to the south-east of Thornton le Moor church on the southern boundary of the parish. (*O.S.*, 39, F 7 ; *O.S.* (25in. scale), 37/10/109).

ESTHORPE (Louthesk wap.), was returned, *circa* 1565, as a hamlet of North Elkington (*O.S.*, 40, G 6), containing one family (B.M., *Harleian MS.* 618, f. 11d.) ; but it does not exist now.

FULSBY (Horncastle [*afterwards* Gartree] wap.—*D.B.*—*O.S.*, 48, G 3), an extinct hamlet in Tumby in the parish of Kirkby on Bain.

HELETHORPE (Wraggoe wap.—*B.F.*, 172), an extinct hamlet in the parish of Rand (*O.S.*, 47, B 9), the site of which has not been found. The name appears in various forms—Helghetorp, Belethorp [*sic*], Ellethorp (*B.F.*, 172, 1061, 1093). *Circa* 1565, Halithorp was returned as a hamlet of Rand, containing one family (B.M., *Harleian MS.* 618, f. 14d.).

HIRST (Axholme wap.—*O.S.*, 38, A 12), in the parish of Belton, the site of an Augustinian priory, now represented in the *O.S.* by the mansion called Hirst priory.

HOLME (Lawress wap.—*D.B.*—*O.S.*, 47, C 7), an extinct hamlet in the parish of Sudbrooke, which is represented in the *O.S.* by the modern mansion of Sudbrooke Holme. In 1316, Sudbrok, Holm, and Langwath formed a *uillata* (*F.A.*, iii, 186) ; and in 1327 and 1333, Sudbrok' and Holm' were a *uillata* (*Sub.*, 135/11, mem. 25d. ; *Sub.*, 135/16, mem. 6d.).

KETTLEBY (Yarborough wap.—*D.B.*—*O.S.*, 39, B 7), an extinct village in the parish of Bigby, now represented in the *O.S.* by Kettleby house (moated). In 1316, Bekeby, Ketelsby, and Thorp in Mora formed a *uillata* (*F.A.*, iii, 181). *Circa* 1565, Kettleby was returned as a hamlet of Bigby, containing one family (B.M., *Harleian MS.* 618, f. 13).

KETTLEBY THORPE (Yarborough wap.—*D.B.*—*O.S.*, 39, B 7), an extinct hamlet of the extinct village of Kettleby (*q.v.*), in the parish of Bigby, now represented in the *O.S.* by the farm of Kettleby Thorpe. In 1316, it appears as Thorp in Mora (*F.A.*, iii, 181). *Circa* 1565, it was returned by the name of Thorp as a hamlet of Bigby, containing five families (B.M., *Harleian MS.* 618, f. 13).

LAYTHORPE (Bolingbroke wap.—*O.S.*, 48, G 6), was returned, *circa* 1565, as a hamlet of West Keal, containing six families (B.M., *Harleian MS.* 618, f. 9).

NEWBO (Winnibriggs wap.), in the parish of Barrowby (*O.S.*, 55, F 2), the site of a Premonstratensian abbey.

NEWSTEAD [BY STAMFORD] (Ness wap.—*O.S.*, 64, F 7), in the parish of Uffington, the site of an Augustinian priory.

NORTHORPE (Louthesk wap.—*O.S.*, 40, E 9), was returned, *circa* 1565, as a hamlet of North Somercotes, containing 26 families (B.M., *Harleian MS.* 618, f. 11). It is to be identified with the hamlet, lying to the north-west of the village of North Somercotes, which appears in the *O.S.* as The Bank, and was formerly called The Bank Village. It takes its name from its position near the old sea bank from which the sea was pushed northwards and eastwards by the enclosure of Porter's marsh (*O.S.*, 40, E 9) by Endymion Porter in 1635. It is interesting to note that the main village of North Somercotes seems to lie along an older sea bank which is probably the original Roman bank (*Ex informatione* Canon Longley).

SANTON (Manley wap.—*D.B.*—*O.S.*, 39, A 4 and 33, J 4), an extinct village in the parish of Appleby, which is represented in the *O.S.* by High Santon and Low Santon, places which are now scarcely more than farmsteads. In 1316, 1327, and 1333, Saunton was a *uillata* (*F.A.*, iii, 184 ; *Sub.*, 135/11, mem. 21 ; *Sub.*, 135/16, mem. 3).

SHILLINGTHORPE (Ness wap.—*F.C.*, i, 115, 361—*O.S.*, 64, G 8), an extinct hamlet in the parish of Braceborough, which is represented in the *O.S.* by Shillingthorpe hall. It appears as Skeldintorp and Scheldingthorp (*op. cit.*) ; as Scleldingthorp, Sceldingthorp and Scheldingthorp (*Rotuli Hundredorum*, 344, 345, 395) ; and as Shillyngthorp (*P.R.O.*, *Fcet of Fines*, 145/162, no. 48). Shillingthorpe was returned, *circa* 1565, as a hamlet of Braceborough, containing one family (B.M., *Harleian MS.* 618, f. 8). The place has sometimes been confused with Skellingthorpe.

SWINE HAVEN (see pp. lxiii f.)—A charter of 1250 to Nun Ormsby priory refers to a fishery in Grainthorpe extending *a portu que vocatur Shuyn usque in profundum maris* (Lincoln Record Society Publications, xviii, 49). That *Shuyn* is a possible, though abnormal, form of *Swine* is proved by the thirteenth century representation of the personal name Swein by Swayn or Schuyn indifferently. In *Ancient Deeds*, L2945 (P.R.O.), a man who grants as David filius Schuynn' of Skidbrooke appears on his seal as David filius Suain.

TOTHBY (Calcewath wap.—*D.B.*—*O.S.*, 48, B 9), an extinct hamlet in the parish of Alford. The moated manor house survives as a farm-house, and appears in the *O.S.* as Tothby manor. In 1316, Alford, Welle, Toutheby, and Malthorp formed a *uillata* (*F.A.*, iii, 178). In 1327, Salby, Thoresthorp, and Touwythby were a *uillata* (*Sub.*, 135/11, mem. 20). *Circa* 1565, Tothby was still a hamlet of Alford (B.M., *Harleian MS.* 618, f. 10).

ADDITIONS AND CORRECTIONS

p. xiv, l. 9 from foot; and 1/64, l. 1—*for* Derby *read* Darby.

p. xlii, l. 21 and l. 12 from foot—Hardwick and Willabyg may now be identified with Hardwick and Wilby, two adjoining villages near Wellingborough, in Northamptonshire. In 1086, Alan held of the countess Judith in Hardwick (*Herdewiche*, *Hardewiche*) (*a*) a manor of one hide which Ulf held with sake and soke in 1066, and (*b*) a tenement of 1 hide which is entered in the form generally used in the case of a berewic or sokeland (*D.B.* (Record Com.), i, f. 229a, col. 1). The land in the latter entry may have been a berewic of Ulf's manor of Hardwick, or even of his manor of Chadstone (*Cedestone*), a few miles to the south, which Drew de Beurere held in 1086 (*ibid.*, 228a, col. 1); and the description of it as the berewic of Harduic' in the *Clamores* (*D.B.* 72/10) may well be intended to distinguish it from Ulf's manor in the same village.

In 1066, Ulf had land at Witham on the Hill (*D.B.*, 30/32), which was held by Drew de Beurere in 1086, and afterwards seemingly passed to Croyland abbey. He bequeathed his land in Manthorpe in the parish of Witham on the Hill to his brother Brand, abbot of Peterborough (see above, p. xlii); and this land also seems to have come into the possession of Croyland abbey. He also disposed of his land at Willabyg and his berewic of Heordwican by will (*ibid.*) In view of these facts, it is not without significance that, in the twelfth and thirteenth centuries, Croyland abbey held land in Witham on the Hill and Manthorpe and also in Wilby and Hardwick near Wellingborough (*Croyland Abbey Cartulary* (in the possession of Ashley K. Maples), ff. 179-184, 236-238). True it is that Ulf does not appear in *Domesday Book* as the tenant of land in Wilby in 1066; but neither does he appear as holding Skillington of which he disposes by will soon after that year (*D.B.*, 2/37); and it is not unlikely that there were appurtenances in Wilby of his manor of Hardwick, or even of his manor of Chadstone. It may be added that the principles of philology forbid the identification of Willabyg with Willoughby or any other known place in Lincolnshire, and that they are entirely in favour of Wilby as its equivalent.

p. l, l. 11—*for* Toftland *read* Toftlund.
p. lvii, l. 3—*Circa* 1565, Harwicke was returned as a hamlet in the parish of Panton, containing two families (B.M., *Harleian MS.* 618, f. 14d.).
p. lviii—*s.v.* HOLTHAM—Howdome was returned, *circa* 1565, as a hamlet of Legsby, containing four families (*ibid.*).
p. lxiv, l. 32—*for* Saltfleetby *read* Saltfleet.
p. lxxx, under Kirton Wap.—*for* Swinfleet *read Swinefleet* (p. lxviii).
p. lxxxi, under Langoe Wap.—*for* Sim Booth Grange *read Sim Booth Grange.*
under Lawress Wap.—note that Saxilby, although it does not appear in the Lincolnshire *Domesday*, is found under Nottinghamshire as Saxebi (*D.B.*, i, 291 b., col. 1).
p. 11/13, l. 2—*for* Hambledon *read* Hambleton.
1/9, l. 6—*for* teams in demesne *read* carucates in demesne.
1/39, p. 20, l. 25, and 1/58, l. 1—*for* Bromby *read* Brumby.
1/66, l. 2—*for* Housham *read* Howsham.
1/94, ll. 1, 2, and 4/51, ll. 1, 2—Langton Thorpe seems to be the equivalent of Buckland (see p. li).
2/20, l. 2—*for* Tothby *read* Tatebi (see page lxviii).
2/21, l. 1; 2/22, l. 1; 2/28, l. 1—*for* Hille *read* Hill.
2/25, l. 4—*for* slaughter-house *read* shearing-house.
2/31, l. 1—*for* Graby *read* East Graby.
2/36, l. 6; 2/37, l. 8—*for* gelt *read* geld.
3/10, l. 3; 3/11, ll. 3, 4; 29/1, l. 1; 29/6, l. 3; 29/7, l. 4; 29/15, l. 4—*for* [Great Sturton (Gartree)] *read* [Little Sturton (Horncastle)].
p. 32, note 6—*for* 0/29 *read* 70/29.
3/36, l. 1—*for* (Aswardhurn) *read* (Flaxwell).
4/17, l, 1—*for* Tofti *read* Tosti.
p. 43, note 2—*after* 29/34 *add* and 3/15.
4/58, l. 3—*for* Cockrington *read* Cockerington.
7/3, l. 1—*for* Cainby *read* Caenby.
8/5, l. 1—*for* Bowthorpe in Manthorpe *read* (see above, p. xlvii.).
8/7, l. 2—*for* Bowthorpe in Manthorpe *read* (see above, pp. l, li.).
8/36, l. 1; and 12/84, l. 1—*for* place *read* places.
8/39, l. 3—insert a bracket after *Goisfridus.*
12/89, l. 1; and 37/6, l. 1—*for* Bicker *read* Swineshead.
13/6, l. 2; 68/9, l, 1; and L 14/7, l. 6—*for* Braytoft *read* Bratoft.
13/45, l. 1—*for* Newbold *read* Newball.
16/18, l. 1—*for* Holton by Beckering *read* Beckering in Holton.
22/23, l. 3—*for* (Gartree) *read* (Horncastle).
24/21, l. 1—*for* [Little Sturton in Baumber (Horncastle)] *read* [an extinct place in Great Sturton (Gartree)].
24/79, l. 1—*for* Silk Willoughby (Aswardhurn) *read* Scott Willoughby (Aveland).
24/98, l. 1—*for* Poynton *read* Pointon.
29/2, l. 1; and 29/15, l. 1—*for* Little Sturton *read* an extinct place in Great Sturton.
30/11, l. 3—*for* (Bradley) *read* (Yarborough).
30/25, l. 2—*for* (Threo) *read* (Winnibriggs).

30/28, l. 1— *omit=probably* Careby *or* Holywell. *See* above *pp. l, li.*
36/2, ll. 1, 2—Bodebi is probably an extinct hamlet of Thornton Curtis (see p. lxxxvi).
51/8, l. 1—*for* Castle Bytham *read* Bytham.
51/9, l. 1—*for* Little Bytham *read* Castle Bytham.
56/4, l. 5—*for* Martinsley *read* Witchley.
57/51, l. 1—*query* may be omitted.
69/3, l. 3—*for* Lambert *read* Lanbert.
69/14, l. 4—*for* Comberworth *read* Cumberworth.
69/33, l. 1—*for* Hornecastle *read* Horncastle.
69/39, l. 1 ; and 69/40, l. 1—*for* Saltfleet *read* Saltfleetby.
72/10, l. 2—*for* [co. Rutland] *read* [co. Northampton].
L 1/14, l. 4—*for* Croxby *read* Crosby.
L 2/3, l. 1—*for* Wadingeheim *read* Wadingheheim.
L 3/19, l. 6—*the last four letters of* B[ar]linga *must* be considered doubtful.
L 4/8, l. 5—*for* Monte *read* Mont[begon].
L 6/6, l. 1—*for* [Burton by Lincoln] *read* [Gate Burton].
L 11/7, l. 2—*for* Wragby *read* Wrawby.
L 16/15, l. 1—*for* Wllingeheim *read* Wllingheheim.
l. 2—*for* Willlam *read* William.
L 19/10, l. 3—*for* Sturton *read* Little Sturton.

E

[CIVITAS LINCOLIA]

D. B., f. 336a. *Facsimile, p. 1a.*

1. In CIVITATE LINCOLIA . erant tempore regis Eduuardi nouies centum et lxx . mansiones hospitatę . Hic numerus anglice computatur . i . centum pro . c^tum^ xx^ti^ . In ipsa ciuitate erant . xii . lageman . idest habentes sacam et socam . Hardecnut . Suartin . filius . Grimboldi . Vlf filius Suertebrand . qui habuit thol et theim . Walrauen . Aluuold . Britric . Guret . Vlbert . Godric . filius . Eddeue . Siuuard [presbyter] . Leuuine [presbyter] . Aldene [presbyter].

2. Modo sunt ibi totidem . habentes similiter sacam et socam . [.i.] Suardinc loco Hardecnut patris sui . [.ii.] Suartinc . [.iii.] Sortebrand loco Vlf patris sui . [.iiii.] Agemund loco Walrauen patris sui . [.v.] Aluuold . [.vi.] Goduinus filius Brictric . [vii.] Normannus Crassus loco Guret . [.viii.] Vlbert frater Vlf adhuc uiuit . [.ix.] Petrus de Ualonges loco Godric filii Eddeue . [.x.] Vlnodus presbyter loco Siuuard . presbyteri . [xi.] Buruolt loco patris sui Leuuine qui modo . est monachus . [.xii.] Leduuinus filius Rauene loco Aldene presbyteri.

3. Tochi filius Outi habuit in ciuitate .xxx. mansiones pręter suam hallam . et ii. ęcclesias et dimidiam . et suam hallam habuit quietam ab omni consuetudine . et super alias xxx. mansiones habuit locationem . et pręter hoc de una quaque unum denarium idest landgable . Super has .xxx. mansiones habebat rex theloneum et forisfacturam . ut burgenses iurauerunt . Sed his iurantibus contradicit Vluiet presbyter . et offert se portaturum iudicium quod non ita est sicuti dicunt . Hanc aulam tenet Goisfridus Alselin . et suus nepos Radulfus . Remigius episcopus tenet supradictas .xxx. mansiones in ęcclesia Sancte Marię . ita quod Goisfridus Alselin nichil inde habet . neque scangium neque aliam redditionem . Isdem Goisfridus habet .i. mansionem extra murum . unde habet landgable . sicut habuit Tochi.

4. Radulfus Pagenel habet .i. mansionem quę fuit Merlesuen . quietam ab omni consuetudine.

5. Ernuin presbyter habet .i. mansionem Morcari [comitis] cum saca et soca . et sic de rege tenet sicut Morcar habuit . ut ipse dicit.

6. Gislebertus de Gand habet .i. mansionem . Vlf . cum saca et soca . et aliam mansionem unde habebat .i. denarium . et iterum .i. mansionem . Siuuard quietam ab omni consuetudine.

7. Comes Hugo habet .i. mansionem comitis Heroldi . cum saca et soca . et ii. mansiones unde habet landgable.

8. Rogerus de Busli habet .i. mansionem Suen . filii . Suaue . cum saca et soca.

[THE CITY OF LINCOLN]

D. B., f. 336a. *Facsimile, p. ia.*

1. IN THE CITY OF LINCOLN there were T. R. E. 970 inhabited messuages. This number is reckoned according to the English method, 100 counting for 120. In the same city there were 12 lawmen, that is [men] having sake and soke :—Hardecnut ; Suartin son of Grimbold ; Ulf son of Suertebrand, who had toll and team ; Walraven ; Alwold ; Britric ; Guret ; Ulbert ; Godric son of Eddeve ; Siward [the priest] ; Lewine [the priest] : and Aldene [the priest].

2. Now there are as many there having sake and soke in like manner :—[1] Suardinc in the place of his father Hardecnut ; [2] Suartinc ; [3] Sortebrand in the place of his father Ulf ; [4] Agemund in the place of his father Walraven ; [5] Alwold ; [6] Godwin son of Brictric ; [7] Norman Crassus in the place of Guret ; [8] Ulbert, brother of Ulf, who is still living ; [9] Peter of Valognes in the place of Godric son of Eddeve ; [10] Ulnod the priest in the place of Siward the priest ; [11] Buruolt in the place of his father Lewine who is now a monk ; [12] Ledwin son of Ravene in the place of Aldene the priest.

3. Tochi son of Outi had in the city 30 messuages besides his hall and 2½ churches. And he had his hall quit of all custom. And with respect to other 30 messuages he had by way of letting ; and in addition to this [he had] from each [messuage] one penny, that is '*l*andgable.'[1] Upon these 30 messuages the king used to have toll and forfeiture, as the burgesses made oath. But Ulviet the priest gainsays what they say thus upon their oath, and proffers himself to prove by the ordeal of fire that it is not as they say. Geoffrey Alselin holds this hall, and his *nepos* Ralf. Bishop Remigius holds the aforesaid 30 messuages in respect of the church of Saint Mary, so that Geoffrey Alselin has nothing therein either by way of exchange or other render. The same Geoffrey has 1 messuage outside the wall, wherefrom he has 'landgable,' as Tochi had.

4. Ralf Pagenel has 1 messuage, which was Merlesuen's, quit of all custom.

5. Ernuin the priest has 1 messuage [which was] [Earl] Morcar's, with sake and soke ; and he holds it of the king in the same way as Morcar had [it], as he himself says.

6. Gilbert of Gant has 1 messuage, [which was] Ulf's, with sake and soke ; and another messuage wherefrom he used to have 1 penny ; and yet again, 1 messuage, [which was] Siward's, quit of all custom.

7. Earl Hugh has 1 messuage, [which was] Earl Harold's, with sake and soke ; and 2 messuages wherefrom he has 'landgable.''

8. Roger de Busli has 1 messuage, [which was] Suen the son of Suaue's, with sake and soke.

---

[1] This payment reappears in the penny known as 'landtoll' which was due to the king from many tenements within the city of Lincoln in the twelfth and thirteenth centuries (*Dean and Chapter muniments*, Dij, 74/1, no. 2 ; 74/3, no. 4 ; 75/1, no. 32 ; 76/2, no, 52 ; 79/1, no. 133 ; etc.).

9. Judita comitissa . habet .i. mansionem Stori sine saca et soca . et hanc calumniatur Iuo Taillebosc per burgenses.

10. Remigius episcopus habet .i. maneriolum cum .i. carucata contiguum[1] ciuitati[2] Lincolię[3] . cum saca et soca et cum thol et theim . et super iii. mansiones similiter . et super .ii. ęcclesias . et super .lxx viii. mansiones similiter . prȩter geldum regis quod dant cum burgensibus . Ex his sunt .xx. mansiones wastę . De tribus superioribus mansionibus est .i. quieta ab omnibus rebus . duę uero sunt in geldo cum burgensibus.

*D. B., f. 336*b. *Facsimile, p. i*b.

11. In campis Lincolię extra ciuitatem sunt xii. carucatę terrę et dimidia . prȩter carucatam episcopi ciuitatis . De hac terra habent rex et comes .viii. carucatas in dominio . Ex his dedit unam rex Willelmus cuidam Vlchel pro una naui quam ab eo emit . Ille uero qui uauim uendidit mortuus . est . et hanc carucatam terre nullus habet nisi rege concedente . Prȩter has .viii. carucatas . habet rex et comes cc et xxx.i. acras terrę arabilis inland . et c. acras prati.

12. De reliqua terra idest .iiii. carucate et dimidia : T. R. E. habuit Vlf .i. carucatam . nunc habet filius eius Sortebrand.

13. Aliam carucatam . T. R. E. habuerunt Siuuard presbyter et Outi . et vi . acras terrę quas tenet Vluiet presbyter . Nunc habet Alfnod medietatem huius carucatę . et Norman filius Siuuard presbyteri alteram medietatem . Hanc uero predictam medietatem istius terre . et uxorem Siuuardi presbyteri inuasit Vnlof presbyter dum erat in saisitione regis propter .xl. solidos quos ipsemet rex imposuerat super Siuuardum presbyterum.

14. Terciam carucatam habet Petrus de Valongies . quam habet Godricus T. R. E.

15. Quarta carucata adiacuit in ęcclesia omnium sanctorum . T. R. E. et xii. toftes . et iiii. croftes . Hanc ęcclesiam et terram ęcclesię et quicquid ad eam pertinet . habuit Godricus filius Gareuinę . Sed eo facto monacho . abbas de Burg[4] obtinet . Burgenses uero omnes Lincolię dicunt quod injuste habet . quia nec Gareuin nec Godricus filius eius nec ullus alius dare potuerit extra ciuitatem nec extra parentes eorum . nisi concessu regis . Hanc ęcclesiam et que ibi pertinent clamat Ernuin presbyter[4] hereditate Godrici consanguinei sui.

16. Residuam dimidiam carucatam terrę habuit et habet sancta Maria de Lincolia . in qua nunc est episcopatus.

17. Inter ęcclesias Lincolię et burgenses . habuerunt .xxx. vi. croftes in Lincolia . exceptis .xii. et dimidia carucatis terrę quę [supra] enumeratę sunt.

18. Ex predictis mansionibus quę T. R. E. fuerunt hospitatę . sunt modo waste .cc. anglico numero .*id.* cc.xl. et eodem numero septies centum et lx. sunt modo hospitatę.

---

[1] *contiguum* has been interlined by way of correction above *in*.

[2] *ti* has been interlined by way of correction above the final *te* of *ciuitate*.

[3] ę has been interlined by way of correction above the final *a* of *Lincolia*.

[4] There is a blank space here of about a quarter of an inch.

9. Countess Judith has 1 messuage, [which was] Stori's, without sake and soke; and Ivo Taillebosc claims this through the burgesses.

10. Bishop Remigius has 1 little manor with 1 carucate [of land] near[1] the city of Lincoln with sake and soke and with toll and team [over it]; and likewise over 3 messuages, and over 2 churches, and likewise over 78 messuages, except for the king's geld which they give with the burgesses. Of these messuages 20 are waste. Of the 3 messuages aforesaid one is quit of all things, but two geld with the burgesses.

*D. B., f. 336*b. *Facsimile, p. ib.*

11. In the fields of Lincoln outside the city there are 12½ carucates of land, besides the carucate of the bishop of the city. Of this land the king and the earl have 8 carucates in demesne. Of these King William gave one [carucate] to a certain Ulchel for a ship which he bought from him. But he who sold the ship is dead, and no one has this carucate of land unless the king grant [it]. In addition to these 8 carucates the king and the earl have 231 acres of arable land [which is] inland, and 100 acres of meadow.

12. Of the rest of the land, that is 4½ carucates, Ulf had T. R. E. 1 carucate: now his son Sortebrand has it.

13. Siward the priest and Outi had another carucate T. R. E., and 6 acres of land which Ulviet the priest holds. Now Alfnod has a moiety of this carucate, and Norman son of Siward the priest has the other moiety. But Unlof the priest invaded this aforesaid moiety of this land and Siward the priest's wife, while it was in the seisin of the king on account of [a fine of] 40 shillings which the king himself had laid upon Siward the priest.

14. Peter de Valognes has the third carucate, which T. R. E. Godric had.

15. The fourth carucate belonged to the church of All Saints T. R. E., and 12 tofts and 4 crofts. Godric son of Gareuine had this church, and the church's land, and whatever belonged to it; but, on his becoming a monk, the abbot of Peterborough obtains it. But all the burgesses of Lincoln say that he has it unjustly, because neither Gareuine nor his son Godric nor any one else could give it outside the city or outside their kindred, except by grant of the king. This church and what belongs thereto Ernuin the priest claims by inheritance from his kinsman Godric.

16. Saint Mary of Lincoln, in which the bishopric now is, had and has the remaining half carucate of land.

17. The churches of Lincoln and the burgesses had among them 36 crofts in Lincoln, excepting the 12½ carucates of land which are enumerated [above].

18. Of the aforesaid messuages which were inhabited T. R. E., there are now waste 200 by English reckoning, that is 240; and by the same reckoning 760 are now inhabited.

---

[1] See notes 1–3.

19. Hi subscripti non dederunt geldum regis sicut debuissent . Terra sancte Marie in qua Tedbertus manet in magno uico . non dedit geldum . neque terra episcopi ad sanctum Laurentium posita . non dedit geldum de .i. domo.

Abbas de Burg de .i. domo et de .iii. toftis non dedit geldum . Hugo [comes] de omni terra sua non dedit geldum . neque Turaldus de Greteuilla . neque Losuardus . neque Chetelbertus . Hugo . filius . Baldrici non dedit geldum de .ii. toftis . Neque Goisfridus Alselin . similiter de .ii. toftis.

Neque Gislebertus de .iii. domibus dedit geldum . Neque Petrus de Ualonges de sua domo . Neque Judita [comitissa] de sua domo . Neque Radulfus Pagenel de .i. domo . Neque Radulfus de Badpalmas de sua domo . Neque Ertaldus de sua domo.

20. Domum de qua abbas de Burg ut dictum est non dedit . geldum ;

D. B., f. 336c. *Facsimile, p. iia.*

ipsam clamat Normannus [Crassus] de feuo regis . Ipsam enim habuit Godredus antecessor suus in uadimonio pro tribus markis argenti et dimidia.

21. Colsuen habet in Lincolia ciuitate .iiii. toftes de terra Cole nepotis sui . et extra ciuitatem habet xxx. vi. domos et ii. ęcclesias in quibus nichil adiacet . quas hospitauit in wasta terra quam rex sibi dedit . et quę nunquam ante hospitata fuit . Modo habet rex omnes consuetudines ex eis.

22. Aluredus nepos Turoldi habet .iii. toftes de terra Sybi . quam rex sibi dedit . in quibus habet omnes consuetudines . pręter geldum regis de monedagio.

23. Abbas de Elyg habet dimidiam mansionem de terra Edstan.

24. Hugo . filius . Baldrici . habet .ii. toftes quas rex sibi dedit.

25. De predictis wastis mansionibus . propter castellum destructę fuerunt c.lx.vi. Relique .lxx.iiii. wastatę sunt extra metam castelli . non propter oppressionem uicomitum et ministrorum ! sed propter infortunium et paupertatem . et ignium exustionem.

26. T. R. E. reddebat ciuitas Lincolia regi .xx. libras . et comiti .x. libras . Modo reddit .c. libras ad numerum . inter regem et comitem . Moneta uero reddit .lxx.v. libras.

[COMITATUS LINCOLNIE]

27. Consuetudines regis et comitis in SUDLINCOLIA ! reddunt .xxviii. libras.

28. In NORTTREDING consuetudines regis et comitis ! reddunt .xx.iiii. libras.

19. Those written below have not paid the king's geld as they ought:

The land of Saint Mary[1] on which Tedbert dwells in the high street has not paid geld; nor has the bishop's land situate at Saint Laurence's paid geld in respet of 1 house.

The abbot of Peterborough has not paid geld in respect of 1 house and 3 tofts.

[Earl] Hugh has not paid geld in respect of any of his land; nor [has] Thorold of Greetwell (Lawress), nor Losuard, nor Chetelbert.

Hugh son of Baldric has not paid geld in respect of 2 tofts; nor Geoffrey Alselin likewise in respect of 2 tofts.

Nor has Gilbert paid geld in respect of 3 houses. Nor has Peter de Valognes in respect of his house. Nor [has] the [Countess] Judith in respect of her house. Nor [has] Ralf Pagenel in respect of 1 house. Nor [has] Ralf of Bapaume in respect of his house. Nor [has] Ertald in respect of his house.

20. The house in respect of which the abbot of Peterborough has not, as they say, paid geld* Norman [Crassus] claims [as] of the king's

**D. B., f. 336c.* *Facsimile, p. iia.*

fee, for Godred his predecessor had it in gage for 3½ marks of silver.

21. Colsuen has in the city of Lincoln 4 tofts of his *nepos* Cole's land; and outside the city he has 36 houses and 2 churches to which nothing belongs, which he built on the waste land that the king gave him, and that was never before built upon. Now the king has all the customs from them.

22. Alfred, Thorold's *nepos*, has 3 tofts from Sybi's land, which the king gave him, in which he has all customs except the king's geld in respect of minting.

23. The abbot of Ely has half a messuage from Edstan's land.

24. Hugh son of Baldric has 2 tofts which the king gave him.

25. Of the aforesaid waste messuages, 166 were destroyed on account of the castle. The remaining 74 are waste outside the castle boundary, not because of the oppression of the sheriffs and officers but by reason of misfortune and poverty and the ravage of fires.

26. T. R. E. the city of Lincoln used to render to the king 20 pounds and to the earl 10 pounds. Now it renders 100 pounds by tale between the king and the earl. The mint, however, renders 75 pounds.

[THE COUNTY OF LINCOLN]

27. The customs of the king and the earl in SOUTH LINCOLN render 28 pounds.

28. In the NORTH RIDING the customs of the king and the earl render 24 pounds.

---

[1] This may be the land which appears in twelfth century charters as belonging to the cathedral church in 'uenella de sancte Marie' or 'Sayntemaristyg' near the 'uicus magnus' or high street, *Dean and Chapter muniments* (Dij, 80/3, nos. 13, 14, 52, 55).

29. In WESTREDING consuetudines regis et comitis: reddunt .xii. libras.

30. In SUDTREDING consuetudines regis et comitis: reddunt .xv. libras.

[PAX REGIS]

31. Pax manu regis uel sigillo eius data . si fuerit infracta; emendatur per xviii. hundrez.

32. Vnum quodque hundredum soluit .viii. libras . Duodecim hundreda emendant regi . et vi. comiti.

33. Siquis pro aliquo reatu exulatus fuerit a rege et a comite et ab hominibus uicecomitatus: nullus nisi rex sibi dare pacem poterit.

*D. B., f. 336*d. *Facsimile, p. ii*b.

[STANFORD BURGUM REGIS]

1. STANFORD BVRGVM REGIS . dedit geldum T. R. E. pro .xii. hundrez et dimidio . in exercitu . et naüigio . et in danegeld . Ibi fuerunt et sunt .vi. custodie . Quinque in Lincolescyre . et sexta in Hantunescyre . quę est ultra pontem . et tamen ipsa reddebat omnem consuetudinem cum aliis . pręter gablum et theloneum . quod abbas de Burg habebat et habet.

2. In his .v. custodiis T. R. E. fuerunt .cxl et i. mansiones . et dimidium molendinum . quę reddebant omnes consuetudines . Sed etiam modo totidem sunt . pręter .v. quę propter opus castri sunt wastę.

3. In his custodiis sunt .vi. mansiones quę T. R. E. dabant omnes consuetudines . modo autem non dant . Brand habet .iiii^{or}. et Vlchetel filius Mereuuine .ii^{as}.

4. In his custodiis sunt lxx vii. mansiones sochemanorum . qui habent terras suas in dominio . et qui petunt dominos ubi uolunt . super quos rex nichil . aliud habet nisi emendationem forisfacturę eorum . et heriete . et theloneum . et i. molindinum de .xxx. solidis quod abstulit [Eustacius] de Huntedune . Illud erat unius sochemani.

5. In Stanford . T. R. E. erant .xii. lagemanni . qui habebant infra domos suas sacam et socam . et super homines suos . pręter geld et heriete . et forisfacturam corporum suorum de xl. oris argenti . et pręter latronem . Hoc idem modo habent . Sed non sunt nisi nouem . Vnus eorum habet xvii. mansiones sub se . et dimidium molindinum .xv. solidorum . Alter .xiiii^{cim}. mansiones . una ex his . est wasta . Tercius .ii^{as}. mansiones . Quartus .ii^{as}. et dimidiam . Quintus . quinque . Sextus .iiii^{or}. Septimus .iii^{es}. Octauus . unam . Nonus .iii^{es}. sed Hugo Musard[us] duas ei abstulit.

29. In the WEST RIDING the customs of the king and the earl render 12 pounds.

30. In the SOUTH RIDING the customs of the king and the earl render 15 pounds.

[THE KING'S PEACE]

31. If the peace given by the king's hand or by his seal be broken, let a fine be paid by 18 hundreds.

32. Each hundred pays 8 pounds. Twelve hundreds pay the fine to the king, and six to the earl.

33. If any one for any crime shall have been outlawed by the king and by the earl and by the men of the shrievalty, no one but the king can give him peace.

*D. B., f. 336*d. *Facsimile, ii*b.

[THE ROYAL BOROUGH OF STAMFORD]

1. The royal borough of Stamford gave geld T. R. E. for 12½ hundreds for army service and boat service and for danegeld. There were and are 6 wards there, five in Lincolnshire, and the sixth in Northamptonshire which is beyond the bridge; and yet this [sixth ward] used to render every custom together with the others except [land]gable and toll, which the abbot of Peterborough used to have and has.

2. In these 5 wards there were T. R. E. 141 messuages and half a mill, which used to render all customs. And also there are as many [messuages] now except 5 which are waste on account of the work of the castle.

3. In these wards there are 6 messuages which T. R. E. used to give all customs, but now they do not give them. Brand has four [of them], and Ulchetel son of Merewine two.

4. In these wards there are 77 messuages of sokemen, who have their lands in demesne, and seek lords where they will; over whom the king has nothing except the fines of their forfeiture, and heriot, and toll. And there is 1 mill rendering 30 shillings, which [Eustace] of Huntingdon took away. It belonged to one of the sokemen.

5. In Stamford there were T. R. E. 12 lawmen who used to have sake and soke within their own houses and over their own men, excepting geld, and heriot, and forfeiture of their bodies up to 40 ores of silver, and excepting larceny. The same have this now, but there are only nine [of them]. One of them has 17 messuages under him, and half a mill rendering 15 shillings. The second [has] 14 messuages, one of them is waste. The third [has] two messuages. The fourth [has] 2½. The fifth [has] 5. The sixth [has] 4. The seventh [has] 3. The eighth [has] one. The ninth [has] 3, but Hugh Musard has taken 2 away from him.

6. In his custodiis adhuc sunt .xxii. mansiones . et ii. ęcclesię cum .xii. acris terrę de xiiii. solidis . quas habębat Ernuin presbyter . T. R. E. et Ezi habebat .i. mansionem . has .xx. iii. mansiones habet modo Eudo dapifer . Super eas habebat rex omnem consuetudinem . modo non habet.

7. In eadem uilla habuit Azor .vii. mansiones et dimidium molindinum . T. R. E. modo habet Gunfridus de Cioches . Ad has pertinent .lxx. acrę extra uillam.

8. Eduuard cild habuit .xiiii. mansiones et lxx. acras . extra uillam . modo habet Judita comitissa.

9. Edded regina habuit .lxx. mansiones quę iacuerunt in Roteland cum omnibus consuetudinibus . sine panificis . Ad has adiacent ii. carucatę terrę et dimidia . et i. caruca arans . et xl v. acre prati extra uillam . Modo habet Rex . W . et ualet vi. libras . T. R. E. ualuit .iiii. libras.

10. Abbas de Burg habuit et habet in Stanford x. mansiones pertinentes ad Lincolesyre . et i. molindinum .xl. solidorum . et v. solidos de domibus et de viii. acris.

11. Leuuinus habebat .ix. mansiones . modo Aluredus habet . Item Leuuinus .i. mansionem ad omnem consuetudinem . sine geldo . quam modo habet Wido de Re*n*budcurt.

12. Fastolf habuit unam ęcclesiam de rege quietam cum .viii. acris.

13. Albertus unam ęcclesiam sancti Petri cum .ii[abus]. mansionibus et dimidia carucata terre quę iacet in Rotelande in Hemeldune . Valet .x. solidos

14. Terram arabilem extra uillam in Lincolescire habet rex .dc. acras.

15. Lagemanni et burgenses habent .cc. et lxx ii°. acras . sine omni consuetudine.

16. T. R. E. dabat Stanford .xv. libras. modo dat ad firmam .l. libras . De omni consuetudine regis . modo dat .xxviii. libras.

D. B., f. 337a. *Facsimile, p. iiia.*

[TORCHESEY]

1. In Torchesey . T. R. E. fuerunt . cc. et xiii. burgenses . Easdem consuetudines habebant omnes quas et Lincolienses . et tantum plus quod quicunque eorum mansionem in eadem uilla habebat . neque intrans neque exiens theloneum dabat nec consuetudinem . Hoc autem eorum erat . ut si legati regis illuc uenirent : homines eiusdem uici cum nauibus suis et aliis instrumentis nauigationis usque Eboracum eos conducerent . et uicecomes uictum legatorum et nautarum ex firma sua inueniret . Quod si aliquis burgensium alibi uellet abire . et domum quę esset in eadem uilla uendere : sine scientia [et licentia] prepositi si uellet posset facere.

6. In these wards there are still 22 messuages and 2 churches with 12 acres of land rendering 14 shillings, which Ernuin the priest used to have T. R. E.; and Ezi used to have 1 messuage. Eudo the sewer has these 23 messuages now. The king used to have every custom over them; now he has [it] not.

7. In the same vill Azor had 7 messuages and half a mill T. R. E. Now Gunfrid de Cioches has [them]. To these [messuages] belong 70 acres outside the vill.

8. Edward 'cild' had 14 messuages and 70 acres outside the vill. Now Countess Judith has [them].

9. Queen Edith had 70 messuages which belonged to Rutland, with all customs except those touching bread. To these [messuages] there belong 2½ carucates of land, and 1 ploughing team, and 45 acres of meadow outside the vill. Now King William has [it]; and it is worth 6 pounds. T. R. E. they were worth 4 pounds.

10. In Stamford the abbot of Peterborough had and has 10 messuages belonging to Lincolnshire, and 1 mill rendering 40 shillings, and 5 shillings in respect of houses and of 8 acres.

11. Lewin used to have 9 messuages; now Alfred has [them]. Lewin also [used to have] 1 messuage with every custom except geld, which [messuage] Guy de Re*n*budcurt has now.

12. Fastolf had 1 church of the king, quit, with 8 acres.

13. Albert [had] one church, [that] of Saint Peter, with 2 messuages, and half a carucate of land which belongs to Hambledon in Rutland. It is worth 10 shillings.

14. The king has 600 acres of arable land outside the vill in Lincolnshire.

15. The lawmen and burgesses have 272 acres without any custom.

16. T. R. E. Stamford used to give 15 pounds; now it gives by way of farm 50 pounds. In respect of all the king's custom it now gives 28 pounds.

*D. B., f. 337*a. *Facsimile, p. iii*a.

[TORKSEY]

1. In Torksey there were T. R. E. 213 burgesses. All these used to have the same customs as the people of Lincoln, and this in addition, that whoever of them had a messuage in the same vill used to give neither toll nor custom either coming in or going out. This, however, was their duty, that if the king's messengers should come thither, the men of the same town should conduct them to York with their ships and their means of navigation, and the sheriff should find the messengers' and sailors' food out of his farm. But if any of the burgesses should wish to go elsewhere, and to sell [his] house which was in the same vill, he could do it, if he wished, without the knowledge [and licence] of the reeve.

2. Hoc suburbium Torchesyg et Harduic manerium ei contiguum habuit Eddid regina in dominio . et habebat foris urbem .ii. carucatas terrę sine geldo . Modo habet rex in dominio . et sunt ibi . cii. burgenses manentes . wastę sunt uero . c. xi. mansiones . Ad hanc uillam pertinent xx. acre prati . et lx. acre siluę minutę . et xi. piscarię . Vna ex his. est Bereng*eri* de Todeni . T. R. E. inter regem et comitem . ualet . xviii. libras . modo .xxx. libras.

3. T. R. E. reddebant Torchesiy et Harduic in Lincolia quintum denarium de geldo ciuitatis . Ad hanc quintam partem dabat Torchesyg .ii. denarios . et Harduic tercium . De hac Torchesig habebat Morcar. tercium denarium de omnibus consuetudinibus.

4. In Harduic habuerunt Suen et Godric .i. carucatam terrę . et ibi manebant .xii. homines . Modo habet Rogerus de Busli medietatem . et episcopus Lincoliensis aliam medietatem . ad sanctam Mariam de Stou . Ibi cadit tercia pars geldi regis . quod rex non habet de illa quę pertinet ad Dorchesyg.

2. Queen Edith had this suburb of Torksey and the manor of Hardwick adjoining it in demesne, and she used to have 2 carucates of land exempt from geld outside the city. Now the king has [them] in demesne; and there are 102 burgesses dwelling there, but 111 messuages are waste. To this vill belong 20 acres of meadow and 60 acres of underwood and 11 fisheries. One of these [fisheries] is Berenger de Todeni's. T. R. E. it [*i.e.* Torksey and Hardwick] was worth 18 pounds between the king and the earl; now 30 pounds.

3. T. R. E. Torksey and Hardwick used to render in Lincoln the fifth penny of the city's geld. To this fifth part Torksey used to give 2 pennies and Hardwick the third. From this Torksey [Earl] Morcar used to have the third penny of all customs.

4. In Hardwick Suen and Godric had 1 carucate of land, and 12 men used to dwell there. Now Roger de Busli has a moiety, and the Bishop of Lincoln the other moiety in respect of Saint Mary of Stow. On this there falls the third part of the king's geld which the king now has from that which belongs to Torksey.

D. B., f. 337a. *Facsimile, p. iiia.*

HERE ARE WRITTEN THOSE WHO HAD SAKE AND SOKE AND TOLL AND TEAM IN LINCOLNSHIRE.

Bishop of Lincoln
Queen Edith
Abbot of Peterborough (*Burg*)
Abbot of Ramsey
Abbot of Croyland
[Earl] Harold
[Earl] Morcar
[Earl] Waltref
[Earl] Ralf
Vlf Fenisc
Merlesuen
Turgot
Tochi [son of Outi]
Stori
Ralf [the Staller (*Stalre*)]
Siward Barn
Harold [the Staller (*Stalre*)]
Fyach
Rolf son of Sceldeware
Godric [son of Toruert]
Achi son of Siward and Wilac his brother in respect of their father's land
Lewine [son of Alwine]
Azer [son of Sualeua]
Ailric [son of Marfete]
Outi [son of Azer]
Adestan [son of Godran]
Tori [son of Rold]
Toli [son of Alsi]
Azer [son of Burg]
Wlward [Wite]
Vlf
Haminc
Bardi
Suan [son of Suaue]

[THE LANDHOLDERS OF LINCOLNSHIRE IN 1086]

1. The land of the King
2. Of the Archbishop of York
3. Of the Bishop of Durham
4. Of the Bishop of Bayeux
5. Of the Bishop Osmund of Salisbury
6. Of the Bishop of Coutances
7. Of the Bishop of Lincoln
8. Of the Abbot of Peterborough (*Burg*)
9. Of the Abbot of Westminster
10. Of the Abbot of Ramsey (*Ramesyge*)
11. Of the Abbot of Croyland
12. Of Count Alan
13. Of Earl Hugh
14. Of Ivo Taillebosc
15. Of William of Warren
16. Of Roger of Poitou
17. Of Roger de Busli
18. Of Robert de Todeni
19. Of Berenger de Todeni
20. Of Ilbert de Laci
21. Of Henry de Ferrers
22. Of William de Percy
23. Of Gilbert Tison
24. Of Gilbert of Gant
25. Of Hugh son of Baldric
26. Of Colsuan
27. Of Alfred of Lincoln
28. Of Gocelin son of Lanbert
29. Of Eudo son of Spirewic
30. Of Drew de Brurere
31. Of Walter de Aincurt
32. Of Norman de Arci (*Adreci*)
33. Of Norman Crassus
34. Of Ernis de Burun
35. Of Ralf Pagenel
36. Of Ralf de Mortemer
37. Of Robert de Veci
38. Of Robert the Steward (*dispensatoris*)
39. Of Guy de Re*n*budcurt
40. Of Rayner de Brimou
41. Of Osbern de Arcis
42. Of Oger the Breton
43. Of Ranulf de Sancto Walarico
44. Of Durand Malet
45. Of Martin
46. Of Waldin the Breton
47. Of Waldin the Engineer (*ingeniosi*)
48. Of Odo the Arblaster (*balistarii*)
49. Of William Blund
50. Of Restold
51. Of Godfrey of Ca*m*brai
52. Of Gunfrid de Ciochis
53. Of Osbern the priest and
54. Of Ralf the Sewer (*dapiferi*)
55. Of Ansgot
56. Of Countess Judith
57. Of Guy of Craon (*Credun*)
58. Of Robert Malet
59. Of Robert of Stafford
60. Of Peter of Valognes (*Valonges*)
61. Of Heppo the Arblaster (*balistarii*)
62. Of Ralf son of Hubert
63. Of Geoffrey de Wirce
64. Of Geoffrey Alselin
65. Of Baldwin the Fleming (*flandrensis*)
66. Of William Taillebosc
67. Of Colegrim
68. Of Sortebrand
69. Of Chetelbern and others
70. Of the King's Thanes

D. B., f. 337c. *Facsimile, p. iva.*

I. THE KING'S LAND

ASWARDETIERNE WAPENTAKE [ASWARDHURN]

1. M. In Cherchebi[1] [Kirkby by Laythorpe (Aswardhurn)] Earl Morcar had 5 carucates of land [assessed] to the geld. There is land for 4 teams. Now the king has there 1 team [in demesne], and 14 sokemen with 2 teams, and 5 villeins and 5 bordars with 1 team. There is half a church there. T. R. E. it was worth 4 pounds; now 8 pounds by weight and assay (*cum pondere et arsione*).

2. B. Evedune [Evedon (Aswardhurn)] belongs to (*iacet in*) the above-mentioned manor, 10 bovates of land [assessed] to the geld. There is land for 1 team. 2 sokemen [and] 2 villeins have 1 team there. There is a mill there rendering 5 shillings and 4 pence, and the site of 1 mill, and 6 acres of meadow.

3. To the same manor belongs this Soke[land]—
   Oustorp [Ewerby Thorpe (Aswardhurn)] [1 carucate]
   Welle [Howell (Aswardhurn)] [2½ bovates]
   Hechintone [Heckington (Aswardhurn)] [1 bovate]
   Cornintone [Quarrington (Aswardhurn)] [1 bovate]

Altogether 1½ carucates and half a bovate [assessed] to the geld. There is land for 1½ teams. In these [members] the king has 7 sokemen having 1 team. There is one mill there rendering 12 shillings, and 13 acres of meadow, and 11 acres of underwood, and 20 acres of marsh (*maresch*).

4. M. In Chime [South Kyme (Aswardhurn)] [Earl] Morcar had 4 carucates and 2 bovates of land [assessed] to the geld. There is land for 2 teams. Now the king has half a team there [in demesne], and 12 villeins and 3 bordars with 2 teams. There are two churches there, and one priest, and 2 acres of meadow, and 6 fish ponds (*piscine*) rendering 4 shillings. There is wood[land] for pannage throughout the territory (*per loca*) 210 acres, and 700 acres of marsh (*maresc*). T. R. E. it was worth 40 shillings; now 60 shillings by weight and assay (*cum pondere et arsione*).

5. M. In Bodebi [Boothby Graffoe (*Boothby*)] [Earl] Morcar had 8 carucates of land [assessed] to the geld. There is land for 9 teams. The king has 2 teams there [in demesne], and 20 villeins and 2 bordars having 4 teams, and 11 sokemen on (*de*) 3 carucates having 3 teams. There is a church there, and a priest. One carucate [of land] belongs to (*iacet in*) the church. There is one mill there rendering 3 shillings, and 120 acres of meadow. T. R. E. it was worth 20 pounds; now likewise 20 pounds by weight (*cum pensione*).

6. M. In Wellingoure [Wellingore (Boothby)] [Earl] Morcar had 18 carucates of land [assessed] to the geld. There is land for as many teams. Now the king has 2 teams there [in demesne], and 7 villeins and

---

[1] See 72/34.

7 bordars with 1 team, and 28 sokemen with 7 teams. There is a church there, and a priest, having 2 carucates and 2 bovates of the same land. And the said church belongs to the church of Saint Peter in Lincoln. There are 129 acres of meadow there, and [other] 14 acres belonging to the church. T. R. E. it was worth 30 pounds; now 15 pounds by weight (*cum pensione*).

7. M. In Colebi [Coleby (Boothby)] Siward had 7 carucates of land [assessed] to the geld. There is land for as many teams. Now the king has 1 team there [in demesne], and 5 villeins and 6 bordars with 1 team, and 10 sokemen with 2 teams, and 30 acres of meadow. T. R. E. it was worth 4 pounds. King W[illiam], however, placed (*apposuit*) this land in Washingeburg [Washingborough (Langoe)], and there it is valued (*appreciatur*). There is a priest, and a church, having 1 bovate of this land.

D. B., f. 337d. *Facsimile, p. iv*b.

8. S. and B. In the same Colebi there are 12 carucates of land [assessed] to the geld. There is land for as many teams. Of these [carucates] 1 carucate is inland in Washingeburg; but 11 are soke[land] (*in soca*). Ralf the staller (*stalre*) had this land. Now the king has 14 sokeman and 7 villeins there with [8[1]] teams, and 60 acres of meadow. The value (*precium*) of this is in Washingeburg.

9. In Grantham [Grantham (Winnibriggs)] Queen Edith had 12 carucates [assessed] to the geld. There is no arable land there outside the vill. No one had sake or soke there except Elsuid the nun, who gave [it] to Saint Peter of Burg [Peterborough Abbey]; and now Colegrim has this with sake and soke. Queen Edith had a hall (*aulam*), and 2 teams in demesne, and land for 3 teams exempt from geld. There were 111 burgesses, [and] 77 tofts of the sokemen of the thanes.[2] Now the king has the like number (*similiter*). Ivo[3] found 1 team,[4] and it is still [there] (*adhuc est*), and 72 bordars. There is 1 church with 8 tofts, and 4 mills rendering 12 shillings, and 8 acres of meadow exempt from geld. Of the above-mentioned tofts the Bishop of Durham claims 7 tofts which Ernuin the priest has, and the hundred bears testimony in the bishop's favour. T. R. E. all Granham was soke[land] [farmed] at 52 pounds (*fuit soca ad lii libras*); now it renders 100 pounds by weight (*ad pondus*). The church was then [farmed] at 8 pounds; now it is [farmed] at 10 pounds; but it is only worth 100 shillings.

10. S. and B. In Gunfordebi [Great Gonerby (Winnibriggs)] there are 7 carucates of land [assessed] to the geld. There is land for 9 teams. Three carucates are inland, and 4 [are] soke[land] belonging to (*in*) Grandham. Now the king has 1 team there [in demesne], and 21 sokemen and 1 villein and 1 bordar having 6 teams, and 105 acres of meadow.

11. S. and B. In Herlavestune [Harlaxton (Winnibriggs)] there are 12 carucates of land [assessed] to the geld. There is land for 16 teams. Nine [carucates] are soke[land] (*in soca*), and 3 belong to

[1] Interlined above 9, which however is not marked for deletion.

[2] This phrase is unique in Domesday, and its meaning is uncertain.

[3] *I.e.*, Ivo Taillebois, who was probably sheriff.

[4] The correct extension of the *car'* of the original is uncertain, but this rendering seems the most probable.

(*sunt in*) the hall of Granham. Now the king has 10 villeins and 2 bordars there with 2 teams, and 58 sokemen having 14 teams. There are 2 mills there rendering 2 shillings, and 60 acres of meadow, and 60 acres of thicket (*spineti*).

12. S. In Sudstoches [South Stoke (Winnibriggs)] [6], and Nortstoches [North Stoke (Winnibriggs)] [3], there are 9 carucates of land [assessed] to the geld. There is land for 12 teams. Now the king has 1 team there [in demesne], and 16 villeins with 3 teams, and 10 sokemen with 2 teams, and 2 mills rendering 21 shillings and 4 pence. Of meadow there is 9 furlongs in length and 3 in breadth, and 20 acres.

13. S. In Nongtone [*probably* = Spittlegate[1] (Winnibriggs)] there are 3 carucates and 5 bovates [and a half] of land [assessed] to the geld. There is land for as many teams. It is soke[land] belonging to (*in*) Gra*n*ham. The king has 13 sokemen and 6 villeins there with 4 teams, and 1 mill rendering 13 shillings and 4 pence, and 3 acres of meadow.

14. M. and S. In Great Panptune [Great Ponton (Winnibriggs)] Queen Edith had 12 carucates of land [assessed] to the geld. There is land for 10 teams. Now this land is soke[land] belonging to (*in*) Granham. There are now 10 villeins and 3 bordars and 12 sokemen there, and half a team. [Ivo[2] found the same there.] There is underwood 8 furlongs in length and 3 in breadth.

15. To Granham [Grantham] belongs this Soke[land]—
Sumerdebi [Somerby (Threo)] [2 carucates and 2 bovates].
Sapretone [Sapperton (Threo)] [5 carucates] and
Breizbi [Braceby (Threo)] [5 carucates].
Wellebi [Welby (Threo)] [8 carucates].
Beltone [Belton (Threo)] [5 carucates].
Herigerbi [Harrowby (Threo)] [4 carucates].
Dunetorp[3] [Dunsthorpe (Threo)] [2 carucates].
Lundetorp [Londonthorpe (Threo)] [5 carucates and 6 bovates].
Barchestone [Barkston (Threo)] [8 carucates].
Dentone [Denton (Winnibriggs)] [10 carucates].

Altogether 55 carucates [assessed] to the geld. There is land for 60 teams. This land is all in Asuuardetierne[4] wapentake.

D. B., f. 338a. *Facsimile, p. v*a.

16. In Summerdebi [Somerby (Threo)] the king has [2½ carucates and [2 bovates] and[5]] 8 sokemen with 2½ teams.

17. In Sapretone and Brezbi [Sapperton and Braceby (Threo)] there are 24 sokemen and 5 villeins and 2 bordars with 9 teams, and 140 acres of meadow, and 46 acres of wood[land] for pannage, and 64 acres of underwood, and 1 church.

---

[1] *See* Appendix I.
[2] *I.e.*, Ivo Taillebois, who was probably sheriff. *Cp.* 71/4.
[3] A depopulated vill, near Harrowby.
[4] This statement is quite possibly a mere mistake. On the other hand it is possible that the soke of Grantham was temporarily annexed for fiscal purposes to Aswardhurn wapentake. In that case the arrangement would be comparable to the division of Alstoe wapentake in Rutland between the two Nottinghamshire wapentakes of Broxtow and Thurgarton.
[5] Cancelled.

18. In Wellebi [Welby (Threo)] there are 37 sokemen and 7 villeins and 4 bordars with 10 teams, and 160 acres of meadow, and 150 acres of underwood, and a church with a priest.

19. In Beltone [Belton (Threo)] there are 18 sokemen and 14 bordars with 4 teams, and 68 acres of meadow.

20. In Herigerbi [Harrowby (Threo)] there are 16 sokemen with 4 teams, and 34 acres of meadow.

21. In Dunetorp[1] [Dunsthorpe (Threo)] there are 5 villeins and 1 bordar and 8 sokemen with 2 teams, and 20 acres of meadow.

22. In Lundertorp [Londonthorpe (Threo)] there are 21 sokemen and 6 villeins with 5 teams, and 44 acres of meadow, and 1 mill rendering 10 shillings.

23. In Barchestone [Barkston (Threo)] there are 35 sokemen and 10 bordars with 6 teams, and 70 acres of meadow, and 2 mills which Turued [son of Vlued] had. Their soke belongs to (*in*) Granham.[2]

24. In Dentone [Denton (Winnibriggs)] there are [8]0 acres of meadow.

25. In Schillintune [Skillington (Beltisloe)] there is soke[land] of Granham, 3 carucates of land [assessed] to the geld. There is land for 3 teams. 14 villeins and 2 bordars and 1 sokeman have 3 teams there, and 10 acres of meadow, and 140 acres of underwood. Its value (*precium*) [is] in Granham.

26. M. In Basingeham [Bassingham (Graffoe)] [Earl] Morcar had 24 carucates of land [assessed] to the geld. There is land for 16 teams. The king has 2 teams there [in demesne], and 35 villeins and 8 bordars and 1 sokeman having 6 teams, and 2 mills rendering 32 shillings. There is a church there, and a priest, and 420 acres of meadow. The whole [is] 16½ furlongs in length and 15 furlongs in breadth. T. R. E. it was worth 35 pounds; now 16 pounds.

27. In Torp [Thorpe on the Hill (Graffoe)] there is soke[land] of this manor, 6 bovates of land [assessed] to the geld. There is land for 5 oxen. There is 1 sokeman there with half a team, and 5 acres of meadow.

28. M. In Tite [Tydd St. Mary (Elloe)] [Earl] Algar had 5 carucates and 1 bovate of land [assessed] to the geld. There is land for 3 teams. The king has 1 team there [in demesne], and 16 villeins and 5 bordars and 1 sokeman having 8 teams, and 80 acres of meadow. T. R. E. it was worth 8 pounds, and 1 fishery with a wood used to render 70 shillings less 4 pence; now the whole is worth 15 pounds.

29. M. In Luctone [Lutton (Elloe)] [Earl] Algar had 4 carucates of land [assessed] to the geld. There is land for 2 teams. The king has 6 oxen there [in demesne], and 16 villeins with 4 teams, and 1 fishery rendering 12 pence, and 60 acres of meadow. T. R. E. it was worth 8 pounds; now the like amount.

30. In Tite [Tydd (Elloe)] there is a berewic of this manor, 2 carucates and 1 bovate of land [assessed] to the geld. Now there are 8 villeins and 1 sokeman there having 1 team and 2 oxen, and 30 acres of meadow.

---

[1] A depopulated vill, near Harrowby.

[2] This sentence refers to Turued's two mills.

31. In Gadenai [Gedney (Elloe)] [Earl] Algar had 8 carucates of land [assessed] to the geld. There is land for 4 teams. The king has 6 oxen there [in demesne], and 18 villeins with 3 teams, and 30 acres of meadow, and a fishery rendering 12 pence. [The land is] 20 furlongs in length and 12 in breadth. T. R. E. it was worth 8 pounds ; now 6 pounds.

*D. B., f. 338*b. *Facsimile, p. v*b.

32.[1] In Holebech [Holbeach (Elloe)] there is soke[land] of this manor, 8 carucates and 6 bovates of land [assessed] to the geld. The king has there 26 sokemen and 5 borders with 11 teams, and 80 acres of meadow. This soke[land] is valued (*appreciata*) at 17 pounds exclusive of (*extra*) the aforesaid amount (*numerum*).[2]

33. In the same Holebech and Copelade [Whaplode (Elloe)] there are 5 carucates of land [assessed] to the geld, which Count Alan used to hold ; now they are in the king's hand.

34. In Fleot [Fleet (Elloe)] [Earl] Algar had 6 carucates of land [assessed] to the geld. There is land for 4 teams. The king has there 6 oxen [in demesne], and 8 villeins with 2½ teams, and 1 fishery rendering 16 pence, and 2 salt-pans rendering 2 shillings, and 500 acres of meadow. [The land is] 1 league in length and 1 in breadth. T. R. E. it was worth 4 pounds ; now 50 shillings.[3]

35. M. In Netelham [Nettleham (Lawress)] [Queen] Edith had 12 carucates of land [assessed] to the geld. There is land for 16 teams. The king has there 3 teams [in demesne], and 28 villeins and 12 bordars and 1 sokeman having 11 teams. The whole [is] 20 furlongs in length and 20 in breadth. T. R. E. it was worth 24 pounds ; now 30 pounds.

36. In Duneham [Dunham (Lawress)] there is soke[land] of this manor, 8 carucates of land [assessed] to the geld. There is land for as many teams. There are 18 sokemen there with 6 teams, and 50 acres of meadow. Of this land Odo the Arblaster has 2½ carucates.

37. In Sonetorp [6 bovates] and Wichingebi [1 carucate] [Swinthorpe and Wickenby (Wraggoe)] there is soke[land] belonging to (*in*) Netelham. In Reresbi [Reasby (Wraggoe)] there are [2 bovates] of soke[land] belonging to Nettleham (*soca ibidem*).[4]

38. M. In Chirchetone [Kirton in Lindsey (Corringham)] [Earl] Edwin had 8 carucates of land [assessed] to the geld. There is land for 16 teams. Now the king has 4 teams there in demesne, and 80 villeins and 37 bordars with 18 teams, and 1 mill rendering 12 pence, and 200 acres of meadow. [It is] 2 leagues in length and 20 furlongs in breadth. T. R. E. it was worth 24 pounds ; now 80 pounds.

39. To this Manor belongs this Soke[land]—

Glenteuurde [Glentworth (Aslacoe)] [6 carucates and 2½ bovates].

---

[1] This entry is a duplicate of 12/84.

[2] That is the 6 pounds at which Gedney is valued.

[3] The vacant space of 3 inches in the original between entries 34 and 35 marks the passage from Holland to Lindsey.

[4] This entry is contained in a single line which is a contemporary insertion into the text.

Helmeswelle [Hemswell (Aslacoe)] [4 carucates and 2 bovates].
Herpeswelle [Harpswell (Aslacoe)] [2 carucates and 6½ bovates].
Esnetrebi [Snitterby (Aslacoe)] [4 bovates].
Sassebi [Saxby near Market Rasen (Aslacoe)] [1 carucate].
Grangeham [Grayingham (Corringham)] [4 carucates].
Coringeham [Corringham (Corringham)] [1 carucate].
Asebi [Aisby in Corringham (Corringham)] [1 carucate].
Iopeham [Heapham (Corringham)] [2½ carucates].
Springetorp [Springthorpe (Corringham)] and
Coringeham [Corringham (Corringham)] [6 carucates].
[Mortum [Morton in Gainsborough (Corringham)] [9 bovates][1]].
Sumerdebi [Somerby in Corringham (Corringham)] [2 carucates].
Blitone [Blyton (Corringham)] [3 carucates].
Pileham [Pilham (Corringham)] [1 carucate].
Torp [Northorpe *and query* Southorpe (Corringham)] [2 carucates].
Aschebi [Ashby in Bottesford (Manley)] [1 carucate].
Hiboldestone [Hibaldstow (Manley)] [2½ carucates].
Staintone [Stainton near Waddingham (Manley)] [6 bovates].
Reburne [Redbourne (Manley)] [9 bovates].
Brunebi [Bromby (Manley)] [5 carucates].
Aschebi [Ashby in Bottesford (Manley)] [13 bovates].
Budlesforde [Bottesford (Manley)] [2 carucates].
Iadulfestorp [Yaddlethorpe (Manley)] [1 carucate].
Witrintone [Winterton (Manley)] [4 carucates].
Escumetorp [Scunthorpe (Manley)] [3 carucates and 6 bovates and 2 parts of 1 bovate].

Altogether there are 59 carucates of land [assessed] to the geld. There is land for 68 teams.

D. B., f. 338c. *Facsimile, p. via.*

[SOKELAND OF KIRTON IN LINDSEY—*cont.*].

40. In Glenteuurde [Glentworth (Aslacoe)] there are 24 sokemen and 6 bordars with 5 teams, and 212 acres of meadow.

41. In Helmeswelle [Hemswell (Aslacoe)] there are 17 sokemen and 1 villein and 7 bordars with 3 teams, and 173 acres of meadow.

42. In Herpeswelle [Harpswell (Aslacoe)] there are 6 sokemen with 2½ teams, and 150 acres of meadow.

43. In Esnetrebi [Snitterby (Aslacoe)] there are 9 sokemen with 2 teams.

44. In Sassebi [Saxby (Aslacoe)] there are 4 sokemen with 1 team, and 6 acres of meadow.

45. In Grangeham [Grayingham (Corringham)] there are 7 sokemen and 14 villeins with 4 teams.

---

[1] Written in the margin.

46. In Coringham [Corringham (Corringham)] there are 4 sokemen and 1 bordar with 2 teams.

47. In Aseby [Aisby (Corringham)] there are 7 sokemen and 1 bordar with 2 teams.

48. In Iopeham [Heapham (Corringham)] there are 16 sokemen with 4 teams, and 120 acres of meadow.

49. In Springetorp [and Coringeham] [Springthorpe and Corringham (Corringham)] there are 41 sokemen with 10 teams, a church, and a priest.

50. In Summerdebi [Somerby (Corringham)] there are 6 sokemen with 1½ teams, and 45 acres of meadow.

51. In Blittone [Blyton (Corringham)] there is nothing.

52. In Pileham [Pilham (Corringham)] there are 8 sokemen with 2 teams, and 16 acres of meadow.

53. In Torp [Northorpe *and query* Southorpe (Corringham)] there are 6 sokemen with 2½ teams, and 60 acres of meadow.

54. In Aschebi [Ashby (Manley)] there are 9 sokemen with 1½ teams.

55. In Hiboldeston [Hibaldstow (Manley)] there is 1 team in demesne, and 16 villeins and 2 bordars with 2 teams, and 222 acres of meadow, and 120 acres of underwood.

56. In Staintone [and Wadingham] [Stainton and Waddingham (Manley)] there are 3 sokemen having 5 oxen and 16 acres of meadow.

57. In Reburne [Redbourne (Manley)] there are 4 sokemen with 1 team, and 30 acres of meadow.

58. In Brunebi [Bromby (Manley)] there are 14 sokemen with 3 teams, and 80 acres of meadow.

59. In Aschebi [Ashby (Manley)] there are 7 sokemen with 1½ teams.

60. In Budlesforde [Bottesford (Manley)] there are 2 sokemen with 2 oxen, and 30 acres of meadow.

61. In Iadulftorp [Yaddlethorpe (Manley)] there is nothing except 15 acres of meadow and 12 acres of underwood.

62. In Wintretune [Winterton (Manley)] there are 9 sokemen and 1 bordar with 5 oxen.

63. In Escumetorp [Scunthorpe (Manley)] there are 20 sokemen with 2 teams and 2 oxen, and 80 acres of meadow.

Altogether there are 223 sokemen, 16 bordars, [and] 15 villeins, with 50 teams.

64. In Tedulbi[1] and Derbi and Burtone [Thealby, Derby, and Burton upon Stather (Manley)] the king has 6 tofts, and half a market belonging to Chirchetone [Kirton in Lindsey (Corringham)]. Hibaldston is a berewic, not soke[land]; and in Grangeham [Grayingham (Corringham)] there are 2 carucates of inland; and in Springetorp [Springthorpe (Corringham)] half a carucate is inland. All the rest is soke[land].

65.[2] M. and B. In Castre and Humendone [Caistor and Hundon (Yarborough)] [Earl] Morcar had 3 carucates of land [assessed] to the

[1] See 71/18.

[2] See 70/6.

geld. There is land for 6 teams. The king has 1 team there in demesne, and 40 villeins and 12 sokemen with 3 teams. There is a church there, and a priest, which the bishop of Lincoln claims. There are 4 mills there rendering 13 shillings and 4 pence, and 60 acres of meadow. T. R. E. it was worth 30 pounds ; now 50 pounds.

66. To the hall of this manor belong Catenai and Usun [Cadney and Housham (Yarborough)], 4 carucates of land [assessed] to the geld. There is land for 8 teams. There are 2 teams there in demesne, and 20 villeins and 15 sokemen and 10 bordars having 9 teams. There are 360 acres of meadow there.

*D. B., f. 338*d. *Facsimile, p. vi*b.

TO THE SAME MANOR BELONGS (*iacet*) THIS SOKE[LAND]

67. In Linberge[1] [Great Limber (Yarborough)] $4\frac{1}{2}$ carucates and half a bovate of land. There is 1 team there in demesne, and 33 sokemen and 5 villeins with 3 teams, and 30 acres of meadow.

68. In Norchelsei [North Kelsey (Yarborough)] 5 carucates of land. There are 50 sokemen and 2 villeins there with 6 teams, and 700 acres of meadow.

69. In Fuldenebi [Fonaby in Caistor (Yarborough)] $1\frac{1}{2}$ carucates. There are 18 sokemen there with 3 teams, and 3 acres of meadow.

70. In Clisbi [Clixby (Yarborough)] $1\frac{1}{2}$ carucates of land [which is] inland and soke[land]. There is 1 team there in demesne, and 14 villeins and 2 sokemen with 3 teams, and 30 acres of meadow.

71. In Chernitone [Kirmington (Yarborough)] 4 carucates and 6 bovates of land. There are 20 sokemen and 1 villein and 14 bordars there with $3\frac{1}{2}$ teams.

72. In Crochestune [Croxton (Yarborough)] 2 bovates of land. There are 3 sokemen there with half a team.

73. In Linberge [Little Limber (Yarborough)] 3 bovates of land. There are 3 sokemen there.

74. In Grosebi [Grasby (Yarborough)] half a carucate of land belonging to the church of Castre, with 1 villein having 1 ox. This is valued (*appreciatur*) at 6 shillings and 8 pence.

75. In Odenebi [Owmby in Searby (Yarborough)] 5 bovates of land [which is] inland. There is nothing there except 10 acres of meadow.

76. In Sourebi [Searby (Yarborough)] 1 bovate of land [which is] inland. There is 1 villein there with 2 oxen.

77. In Haburne and Neuhuse [Habrough and Newsham (Yarborough)] 2 carucates and 2 bovates and 2 parts of 1 bovate of land. There are 8 sokemen and 2 bordars there with $1\frac{1}{2}$ teams, and 1 salt-pan rendering 12 pence, and 200 acres of meadow.

78. In Chelebi [Keelby (Yarborough)] 15 bovates of land [assessed] to the geld. There 13 sokemen and 3 bordars have 2 teams.

79. In Colesi [South Kelsey (Walshcroft)] 3 carucates of land. There 35 sokemen and 12 bordars have $5\frac{1}{2}$ teams, [and] meadow 1 league in length and two and a half furlongs in breadth.

---

[1] See 14/31 ; 70/3.

80. In Hoctune [Holton le Moor (Walshcroft)] $2\frac{1}{2}$ carucates of land. There 26 sokemen have $3\frac{1}{2}$ teams, and 60 acres of meadow. Of this soke[land] Ivo [Talgebosc] has 1 carucate.

Altogether [in numbers 67–80] there are 28 carucates and 1 bovate of land [assessed] to the geld. There is land for 58 teams. In all there are 211 sokemen and 24 villeins and 28 bordars with 30 teams.

81. M. In Gettune [Gayton le Wold (Louthesk)] [Queen] Edith had 3 carucates of land [assessed] to the geld. There is land for 4 teams. There the king has $1\frac{1}{2}$ teams in demesne, and 18 sokemen and 4 bordars with 5 teams. There is a church there, and 50 acres of meadow. [It is] $7\frac{1}{2}$ furlongs in length and 7 in breadth. T. R. E. it was worth 15 pounds; now 45 pounds.

SOKE[LAND] OF THIS MANOR

82. In Salflatebi [Saltfleetby (Louthesk)] 2 carucates of land. There are 40 sokemen and 9 bordars there having 4 teams, and 120 acres of meadow.

83. In Mannebi [Manby (Louthesk)] 3 carucates of land. There are 20 sokemen there with 4 teams.

84. In Grimalbi [Grimoldby (Louthesk)] 4 carucates of land. There 6 sokemen and 5 bordars have 3 teams, and 100 acres of meadow.

85. In Germundstorp [Grainthorpe (Louthesk)] 2 carucates of land. There 13 sokemen and 6 villeins have 2 teams, and 6 salt-pans rendering 6 shillings.

86. In Summercotes [Somercotes (Louthesk)] 3 carucates of land. There 30 sokemen and 7 villeins and 8 bordars have 6 teams, and 80 acres of meadow.

87. In Gereburg [Yarborough (Louthesk)] $2\frac{1}{2}$ carucates and 1 bovate and the third part of 1 bovate of land.

D. B., f. 339a. *Facsimile, p. viia.*

88. In Alvingham [Alvingham (Louthesk)] 1 carucate of land. There are 14 sokemen and 7 villeins and 5 bordars there with 2 teams, and 40 acres of meadow.

89. In Schitebroc [Skidbrook (Louthesk)] 3 carucates of land. There 24 sokemen and 3 villeins have $8\frac{1}{2}$ teams, and 60 acres of meadow.

90. In Welletone [Welton le Wold (Louthesk)] 4 carucates of land. There 20 sokemen and 14 villeins have $5\frac{1}{2}$ teams, and 40 acres of meadow.

Altogether [in numbers 82–90] there are $25\frac{1}{2}$ carucates and 1 bovate and the third part of a bovate [assessed] to the geld. There is land for 38 teams. In these [members] there are 167 sokemen and 37 villeins and 27 bordars having 34 teams.

91. M. In Hornecastre [Horncastle (Horncastle)] [Queen] Edith had 3 carucates of land exempt from the geld. There is land for 4 teams. [The king has] 2 teams there in demesne, and 29 villeins and 12 bordars having 3 teams. There are 2 mills there rendering 26 shillings, and 100 acres of meadow. T. R. E. it was worth 20 pounds; now 44 pounds.

SOKE[LAND] OF THIS MANOR

92. In Stimblebi [Thimbleby (Horncastle)] 4 carucates of land. There 22 sokemen and 18 villeins have 4½ teams, and 240 acres of meadow.

93. In Todintune [uel Tintune] [High *or* Low Toynton (Horncastle)] 3 carucates of land. There 23 sokemen and 2 villeins and 7 bordars have 4 teams, and 300 acres of meadow.

94. In Langetone and Torp [Langton by Horncastle and Langton Thorpe (Horncastle)] 3 carucates of land. There 13 sokemen and 24 villeins have 4 teams, and 1 mill rendering 9 shillings, and 120 acres of meadow, and 250 acres of wood[land] for pannage.

95. In Folesbi [Fulsby in Tumby (Horncastle)] half a carucate of land. There 3 sokemen have half a team, and 8 acres of meadow, and 120 acres of wood[land] for pannage throughout the territory.

96. In Cuningesbi [Coningsby (Horncastle)] 1½ carucates of land [which are] inland. There are 8 villeins and 3 bordars there with 1½ teams, and 5 fisheries rendering 5 shillings, and 12 acres of meadow, and 60 acres of underwood.

97. In Holtham [Haltham on Bain (Horncastle)] 2 carucates and 6 bovates of land. There 7 sokemen have 1½ teams, and 32 acres of meadow, and 20 acres of wood[land] for pannage.

98. In Folesbi [Fulsby (Horncastle)] 1 carucate of land. There 1 sokeman has 1 team.

99. In Rocstune [Roughton (Horncastle)] 12 bovates of land. There 8 sokemen have 1½ teams, and 15 acres of meadow, and 40 acres of wood[land] for pannage.

100. In Scriuelesbi [Scrivelsby (Horncastle)] 3 carucates and 7 bovates of land. There 20 sokemen and 12 bordars have 6 teams, and 200 acres of meadow, and 6 acres of underwood.

101. In Morebi [Moorby (Horncastle)] 3 carucates of land. There 8 sokemen and 10 bordars have 4 teams. There is a church there, and 240 acres of meadow, and 6 acres of underwood.

102. In Marun [Mareham le Fen (Horncastle)] 3 carucates of land. There 21 sokemen and 11 bordars have 4 teams. There is a church there, and a priest, and 60 acres of meadow, and 300 acres of underwood.

103. In Endrebi [Wood Enderby (Horncastle)] 3 carucates of land. There 16 sokemen and 6 bordars have 4 teams, and 60 acres of meadow, and 450 acres of wood[land] for pannage.

104. In Wilchesbi [Wilksby (Horncastle)] 1½ carucates of land. There 4 sokemen and 5 bordars have 1 team, and 20 acres of underwood.

105. In Aschebi [West Ashby (Horncastle)] 6 carucates of land. There 45 sokemen and 5 villeins and 13 bordars* have 8 teams, and 500 acres of meadow and pasture.

**D. B., f. 339*b. *Facsimile, p. vii*b.

106. In Tedlintune [High *or* Low Toynton (Horncastle)] 4 carcuates of land. There 21 sokemen and 8 villeins and 3 bordars have 8 teams, and 400 acres of meadow.

In all these members [numbers 92–106] there are 42 carucates of land [assessed] to the geld.[1] There is land for 58 teams. In these [members] there are 212 sokemen and 66 villeins and 70 bordars having 55 teams.

D. B., f. 339c. *Facsimile, p. viiia.*

2. LAND OF THE ARCHBISHOP OF YORK

1. Two M. In Vlingeham[2] [South Willingham (Wraggoe)] Elmer had 3 carucates of land [assessed] to the geld. There is land for 4 teams. Archbishop Thomas has it now, and William has it of him. There are 2½ teams in demesne, and 11 villeins and 2 bordars having 2 teams, and 77 acres of meadow. T. R. E. it was worth 4 pounds and 10 shillings; now the like amount.

2. In Barcuurde [Barkwith (Wraggoe)] there is soke[land] of this manor, 6 bovates of land [assessed] to the geld. There is land for 1½ teams. There 7 sokemen and 1 bordar have 1 team. There are 13 acres of meadow there.

3. M. In Pantone [Panton (Wraggoe)] Aluric had 2 carucates of land [assessed] to the geld. There is land for 3 teams. Now Gilbert, the archbishop's man, has in demesne 1½ teams, and 1 villein and 12 sokemen with 1½ teams, and 17 acres of meadow. T. R. E. it was worth 30 shillings; now 40 shillings.

4. In Barcuurde [Barkwith (Wraggoe)] there is soke[land] of this manor, 6 bovates of land [assessed] to the geld. There is land for 1 team. It is waste. There are 15 acres of meadow there.

5. M. In Grisebi [Girsby (Wraggoe)] Ælmar had 2 carucates and 2 bovates of land [assessed] to the geld. There is land for 4½ teams. Now William, the archbishop's man, has 2 teams in demesne, and 8 villeins and 7 bordars and 18 sokemen having 4½ teams, and 20 acres of meadow. T. R. E. it was worth 3 pounds; now the like amount; and tallage 20 shillings.

6. Two M. In Stalingeburg[3] [Stallingborough (Yarborough)] Elaf had 1 carucate and 2 bovates of land [assessed] to the geld. There is land for 2½ teams. Herbert, the archbishop's man, has there 1 team in demesne, and 5 villeins and 3 sokemen and 1 bordar with 1 team. There is half a mill there rendering 32 pence, and 2 salt-pans, and 80 acres of meadow. T. R. E. it was worth 30 shillings; now 50 shillings.

---

[1] Here in the original there is a *T*. This is probably due to the scribe beginning to write the word *Terra* which he eventually decided to put at the beginning of the next line.

[2] See 4/53; 69/28.

[3] See 70/9.

SOKE⌊LAND⌋ OF THIS MANOR

7. Heghelinge ⌈1 bovate⌉ Cleia ⌈3 bovates⌉ Ternescou ⌈2 bovates⌉ [Healing, Clee, and Thrunscoe (Bradley)], that is 6 bovates of land ⌊assessed⌋ to the geld. There is land for 1 team and 2 oxen. There 5 sokemen and 3 villeins have 1 team, and 25 acres of meadow.

8. M. In Chelebi[1] [Keelby (Yarborough)] Elaf had $4\frac{1}{2}$ bovates of land ⌊assessed⌋ to the geld. There is land for 1 team and 1 ox. William, the archbishop's man, has half a team there ⌊in demesne⌋, and 2 sokemen and 2 bordars, and half a mill rendering 3 shillings and 4 pence. T. R. E. it was worth 10 shillings ; now the like amount.

9. M. In Cucualt[2] [Cuxwold (Haverstoe)] Fulchri had 7 bovates and 3 parts of 1 bovate of land ⌊assessed⌋ to the geld. There is land for 1 team and 6 oxen. William, the archbishop's man, has 1 team there ⌊in demesne⌋, and 1 villein and 1 bordar and 1 sokeman. They have 1 team. T. R. E. it was worth 20 shillings ; now the like amount.

10. In Svalun [Swallow (Bradley)] there is soke⌊land⌋ ⌈and inland⌉ of this manor, 1 carucate of land ⌊assessed⌋ to the geld. There is land for 2 teams. There are 3 sokemen and 1 bordar there with half a team.

11. M. In Lessintone [Lissington (Wraggoe)] Lanbecarle had 4 carucates of land ⌊assessed⌋ to the geld. There is land for 10 teams. Herbert, the archbishop's man, has 2 teams there in demesne and 16 villeins and 8 bordars and 4 sokemen having 5 teams. There are 80 acres of meadow there, and 80 acres of underwood. T. R. E. it was worth 4 pounds ; now 7 pounds and 10 shillings ; tallage 40 shillings.

D. B., f. 339d. *Facsimile, p. viii*b.

INLAND AND SOKE⌊LAND⌋ OF THIS MANOR

12. In Sonetorp [Swinthorpe (Wraggoe)] $1\frac{1}{2}$ carucates of land ⌊assessed⌋ to the geld. There is land for 2 teams. There is 1 team ⌊in demesne⌋, and 2 villeins, and $12\frac{1}{2}$ acres of meadow.

13. In Esnelent [Snelland (Wraggoe)] 2 bovates of land ⌊assessed⌋ to the geld. There is land for half a team. It is waste. There are 3 acres of meadow there.

14. In Houtune [Holton Beckering (Wraggoe)] 1 carucate of land ⌊assessed⌋ to the geld. There is land for 2 teams. There 5 sokemen and 5 villeins have 3 teams, and 13 acres of meadow.

15. S. In Bechelinge [Beckering (Wraggoe)] 2 bovates of land ⌊assessed⌋ to the geld. There is land for half a team. There 4 sokemen have 1 team and 6 ploughing oxen.

16. M. In Beningurde[3] [Benniworth (Wraggoe)] Godwin has $2\frac{1}{2}$ carucates of land ⌊assessed⌋ to the geld. There is land for $3\frac{1}{2}$ teams. Now Osbern the priest has ⌊it⌋ of the archbishop. There are 2 teams in demesne, and 7 villeins and 2 bordars and 6 sokemen having $1\frac{1}{2}$ teams. There is a church there, and the site of 1 mill, and 60 acres of meadow. T. R. E. it was worth 30 shillings ; now 70 shillings.

---

[1] See 70/11. [2] See 70/23. [3] See 69/27.

17. Two M. In Agetorne [Hackthorn (Aslacoe)] Alwin had 1 carucate and 5 bovates of land ⌊assessed⌋ to the geld, and Auti 3 bovates of land ⌊assessed⌋ to the geld. There is land for 3½ teams. William, the archbishop's man, has 1 team there ⌊in demesne⌋, and 6 villeins and 7 bordars and 2 sokemen have 3 teams and 5 oxen. There is half a church there, and 2 mills rendering 4 shillings, and 60 acres of meadow. T. R. E. it was worth 60 shillings ; now 40 shillings. In the soke of this manor [of Auti's] Archbishop T⌊homas⌋ has 3 bovates ⌊assessed⌋ to the geld.

18. M. In Rigesbi [Rigsby (Calswath)] Aldene had 6 bovates of land ⌊assessed⌋ to the geld. There is land[1] for 1 team and 2 oxen. Herbert, the archbishop's man, has 1 team there ⌊in demesne⌋, and 3 villeins and 4 bordars with 2 oxen. There is a church there, and a priest, and 90 acres of woodland for pannage, and 60 acres of underwood. T. R. E. it was worth 60 shillings ; now the like amount.

19. In Sudtune and Dreuistorp [Sutton in the Marsh and Trusthorpe (Calswath)] and Herdetorp [Addlethorpe (Candleshoe)] there is inland of this manor, half a carucate of land ⌊assessed⌋ to the geld. There is land for 1 team. There 6 villeins have half a team, and 40 acres of meadow.

SOKE⌊LAND⌋ OF THE SAME MANOR.

20. Righesbi ⌊4 bovates⌋, Halebi 3 [bovates], Tatebi [Rigsby, Ailby, Tothby (Calswath)] [1 carucate ; this was a manor], that is 15 bovates of land ⌊assessed⌋ to the geld. There is land for 3½ teams. In those ⌊members⌋ 7 sokemen and 2 villeins and 1 bordar have 1½ teams, and 20[2] acres of meadow, and 12 acres of wood⌊land⌋, and 20 acres of under⌊wood⌋. This soke T. R. E. was worth 4 pounds ; now 40 shillings.

21. Two M. In Tesforde [Tetford (Hille)] Elmer and Arnui had 3 carucates of land ⌊assessed⌋ to the geld. There is land for 4 teams. There Gilbert, the archbishop's man, has 2 teams and 1 ox ⌊in demesne⌋, and 8 villeins and 7 sokemen with 2 teams. There is a church there, and 1 mill rendering 4 shillings, and 120 acres of meadow, and 6 acres of underwood. T. R. E. it was worth 30 shillings ; now 4 pounds.

22. In Ormesbi [South Ormsby (Hille)] there is soke⌊land⌋ of this manor, half a carucate of land ⌊assessed⌋ to the geld. There is land for 6 oxen. There is there 1 sokeman, and 1 villein with half a team, and 20 acres of meadow.

D. B., f. 340a. *Facsimile, p. ixa.*

23. In Haintone [Hainton (Wraggoe)] there is soke⌊land⌋ of Torp [*unidentified*], 1½ carucates of land ⌊assessed⌋ to the geld. There is land for 3 teams. There 3 sokemen and 3 bordars have 5 ploughing oxen, and 80 acres of meadow. Elmer had ⌊it⌋. William has ⌊it⌋ of the archbishop.

24. In the soke of Linberge [Limber (Yarborough)] the archbishop has 3 bovates of land ⌊assessed⌋ to the geld. There is land for 1 team.

---

1 *Terra* is repeated in the text.

2 This number is uncertain. It has been altered either from *xl* to *xx* or from *xx* to *xl*.

25. In Stalinburg [Stallingborough (Yarborough)] there is inland of Linberge, half a bovate of land [assessed] to the geld. There is land for 1 ox. The archbishop has there 1 villein ploughing with 1 ox, and the site of a mill, and half a slaughter-house (*laninam*).

26. In Neutone [Newton on Trent (Welle)] the archbishop has 100 acres of meadow. It belongs to Lanun (Laneham, co. Nottingham[1]).

27. M. In Herpeswelle [Harpswell (Aslacoe)] Alwin had $5\frac{1}{2}$ bovates of land [assessed] to the geld. There is land for 1 team. William, the archbishop's man, has there 1 villein and 5 sokemen ploughing with 6 oxen, and 39 acres of meadow. T. R. E. it was worth 16 shillings ; now 10 shillings.

28. M. In Wlvricesbi [Worlaby (Hille)] Aluric had 2 carucates of land and 2 bovates [assessed] to the geld. There is land for 3 teams. Now the archbishop has there 1 team [in demesne], and 1 villein and 10 sokemen with 1 team, and 20 acres of meadow. T. R. E. it was worth 3 pounds ; now 40 shillings.

29. M. In Dusebi [Dowsby (Aveland)] Aldene had 3 carucates of land [assessed] to the geld. There is land for 3 teams. Now Hugh, the archbishop's man, has there 1 team [in demesne], and 9 villeins and 3 bordars and 1 sokeman having 2 teams, and 1 mill rendering 3 shillings, and 32 acres of meadow, and 20 acres of underwood. T. R. E. it was worth 3 pounds ; now 4 pounds ; tallage 20 shillings.

30. In Bichere [Bicker (Kirton in Holland)] there is inland of this manor, $1\frac{1}{2}$ bovates of land [assessed to the geld]. There is land for as many teams. It is waste. There is 1 salt-pan there which is waste.

31. In Greibi [Graby (Aveland)] there is soke[land] of the same manor, 1 carucate of land. There is land for 1 team. There 6 sokemen have 1 team and 1 ox.

32. M. In Billingeburg [Billingborough (Aveland)] Turchil had 5 bovates of land [assessed] to the geld. There is land for 5 oxen. Now Walter [de Aincurt] has it of the archbishop. There is half a team there in [demesne], and 1 villein and 1 bordar, and 7 acres of meadow, and 1 site of a mill. It is worth 10 shillings.

33. M. In Horbelinge [Horbling (Aveland)] Turchil had 4 carucates of land [assessed] to the geld. There is land for as many teams. Now Walter has it of the archbishop. There is 1 team in demesne, and 9 villeins and 1 bordar and 8 sokemen having 3 teams. There is a church there, and 20 acres of meadow. The arable land is 1 league in length and 1 in breadth. T. R. E. it was worth 6 pounds ; now 40 shillings ; tallage 20 shillings.

34. M. In Wime [North Witham (Beltisloe)] Bacon (*Baco*) had 1 carucate of land [assessed] to the geld. There is land for 1 team, and M.[2] Ulwine had 1 carucate [assessed] to the geld. There is land for 1 team. Now Walchelin, the archbishop's man, has there 2 teams [in demesne], and 4 villeins and 2 bordars with 1 team. There is a church there of which Edward [cilt] has the third part, and 1 site of a mill, and 27 acres of meadow. T. R. E. it was worth 40 shillings ; now 50 shillings ; tallage 11 shillings.

---

[1] Laneham was a manor of the archbishop's in 1086 (*V.C.H.*, *Nottinghamshire*, p. 225).
[2] *I.e.* Manor.

35. In Tuiforde [Twyford (Beltisloe)] there is soke⌊land⌋ of Nortwine [North Witham (Beltisloe)], half a carucate of land ⌊assessed⌋ to the geld. There is land for half a team. There are 2 bordars there ploughing with 2 oxen.* There are 3 acres of meadow there, and 27 acres of underwood.

*D. B., f. 340b. *Facsimile, p.* ixb.

36. M. In Wime [North Witham (Beltisloe)] Alwin had 2 carucates of land ⌊assessed⌋ to the geld. There is land for 2 teams. Walchelin, the archbishop's man, has 2 teams there ⌊in demesne⌋, and 6 villeins and 2 sokemen and 1 *censor*.[1] There are 89 acres of meadow there, and 120 acres of woodland which belong to Drew for the purpose of defence against the gelt (*in Warnode Drogonis*), and 40 acres of underwood. T. R. E. it was worth 20 shillings ; now 25 shillings ; tallage 5 shillings.

37. In Schillintone [Skillington (Beltisloe)] ⌊Earl⌋ Morcar had 3 carucates of land ⌊assessed⌋ to the geld, and Friguist and Bridmer[2] 1 carucate of land ⌊assessed⌋ to the geld. There is land for 5½ teams. The *frigesoca* belongs to (*in*) Schillintune. Walchelin, the archbishop's man, has 2 teams there ⌊in demesne⌋, and 13 villeins and 5 sokemen having 4 teams. There are 121½ acres of meadow there, and 60 acres of woodland for pannage which belong to Bishop Remigius for the purpose of defence against the gelt (*in Warnode episcopi Remigii*). T. R. E. it was worth 4 pounds ; now the like amount ; tallage 20 shillings.

38. M. There [in Skillington] ⌊and⌋ in Estone [Easton (Beltisloe)] Siward had 3 carucates of land ⌊assessed⌋ to the geld. There is land for 3 teams and 6 oxen. Osbern, the archbishop's man, has 1 team there ⌊in demesne⌋, and 12 villeins and 6 bordars. There is half a church there, and one mill rendering 8 shillings, and 10 acres of meadow, and 200 acres of wood for pannage, and 240 acres of underwood. T. R. E. it was worth 40 shillings ; now 40 shillings.

39. S. In Colstewrde [Colsterworth (Beltisloe)] [Earl] Morcar had 3 carucates of land ⌊assessed⌋ to the geld. There is land for 3 teams. The soke belongs to (*in*) Schellintune [Skillington (Beltisloe)]. Four sokemen and 4 villeins have 2 teams there, and 120 acres of wood⌊land⌋ for pannage throughout the territory.

40. M. In Belingei [Billinghay (Langoe)] Swen had 12 carucates of land ⌊assessed⌋ to the geld. There is land for 4 teams. Walchelin, the archbishop's man, and the two sons of Swen have 2 teams there ⌊in demesne⌋, and 3 villeins and 15 sokemen having 4 teams. There are 16 acres of meadow there, and 3 sites of fisheries (*sed' piscar'*). T. R. E. it was worth 4 pounds ; now the like amount and 5 shillings more.

41. In Walecote [Walcot in Billinghay] (Langoe) there is inland of this manor, 8 carucates of land ⌊assessed⌋ to the geld. There is land for 6 teams. Fifteen sokemen and 1 villein have 6 teams there, and 4 acres of meadow, and 46 acres of underwood.

---

[1] *I.e.*, a tenant who paid a rent.

[2] *Rectius* Brictmer.

42. M. In Lavintone[1] [Lavington (Beltisloe)] Ulf[2] had 4 carucates of land [assessed] to the geld. There is land for 5 teams. Rannulf, the archbishop's clerk, has 2 teams there in demesne, and 12 villeins and 1 sokeman and 4 bordars having 6 teams. There are 36 acres of meadow there, and 110 acres of underwood. It belongs to Guy of Craon for defence against the geld (*in Warnode Widonis de Credun*). The arable land and the feedings (*pascuę*) are 2 leagues in length and 6 furlongs in breadth. T. R. E. it was worth 4 pounds ; now 60 shillings.

D. B., f. 340c. *Facsimile, p. xa.*

3. LAND OF THE BISHOP OF DURHAM

1. M. In Brotulbi [Brattleby (Lawress)] Stepiot had 5 bovates of land [assessed] to the geld. [The soke belongs to the same place (*soca ibidem*)]. There is land for 6 oxen. Now the Bishop of Durham [has] this land, and Colswen has it of him, and cultivates it. T. R. E. [it was worth] 3 shillings ; now 4 shillings.

2. M. In Snardesforde [Snarford (Lawress) Siward had 2 carucates and 2 bovates of land [assessed] to the geld. There is land for 2 teams and 6 oxen. Now the Bishop of Durham, and under him (*de eo*) Colsuan, has 1 team [in demesne], and 14 sokemen with 2 teams, and 60 acres of meadow. T. R. E. [it was worth] 20 shillings ; now 30 shillings, and tallage 10 shillings.

3. M. In Berlinge [Barlings (Lawress)] Dane had 9 bovates of land [assessed] to the geld. There is land for 1½ teams. Now Colsuan [has it] of the bishop. There is 1 team in demesne, and 2 villeins and 1 bordar with 1 team, and 20 acres of meadow, and 20 acres of underwood. T. R. E. it was worth 16 shillings ; now 20 shillings.

4. M. In Bliburg [Blyborough (Aslacoe)] Redulf had 7 bovates of land [assessed] to the geld. There is land for 2 teams. Now the monks of Durham have 2 teams there [in demesne], and 3 villeins and 1 bordar and 1 sokeman with 1 team, and 20 acres of meadow, and half a church between the bishop and Gocelin [son of Lanbert]. T. R. E. it was worth 20 shillings ; now 30 shillings.

NORTTREDING [NORTH RIDING]

5. M. In Brachelesbi [Brocklesby (Yarborough)] Godwin had 1 carucate of land [assessed] to the geld. There is land for 2 teams. Nigel, the bishop's man, has 3 villeins there with 1 ox, and 30 acres of meadow. T. R. E. it was worth 40 shillings ; now 10 shillings.

---

[1] See 72/10. [2] *I.e.*, Ulf son of Tope (72/10).

6. Two M. In Fugelestou[1] [Fulstow (Haverstoe)] Aldene and Elmar had 1 carucate and 2 bovates of land ⌊assessed⌋ to the geld. There is land for 2½ teams. Walbert, the bishop's man, has 16 villeins and 10 bordars there with half a team, and 1 team in demesne, and 11 salt-pans rendering 2 shillings, and 60 acres of meadow. T. R. E. it was worth 60 shillings ; now 4 pounds.

7. Two M. In Neutone[2] [Wold Newton (Haverstoe)] Grinchel had 11 bovates of land ⌊assessed⌋ to the geld. There is land for 2 teams. Walbert, the bishop's man, has 1 team there ⌊in demesne⌋, and 2 villeins and 2 bordars with half a team. There is a church there, and 40 acres of meadow. And in Turgrimbi [Thorganby (Walshcroft)] there is 1 mill [and 10 acres of meadow] which Norman de Areci holds unjustly.[2] T. R. E. it was worth 100 shillings ; now 30 shillings. There is a hall (*halla*) there ⌊with a toft and soke and sake⌋.

SUD TREDING [SOUTH RIDING]

8. M. In Bolintone [Bullington (Wraggoe)] Aluric had 3½ bovates of land ⌊assessed⌋ to the geld. There is land for 1 team. Nigel, the bishop's man, has half a plough there ⌊in demesne⌋, and 6 villeins with 1 team, and 10 acres of meadow, and 160 acres of underwood. T. R. E. it was worth 20 shillings ; now 10 shillings.

9. M. In Hardwic [Hardwick in Panton (Wraggoe)] Aluric had 2 bovates and the third part of 1 bovate of land ⌊assessed⌋ to the geld. There is land for 5 oxen. Nigel has it of the bishop, and it is waste. There are 27 acres of meadow there. T. R. E. it was worth 10 shillings ; now 3 shillings.

10. In Langetona[3] [Langton by Wragby (Wraggoe)] there are 3 bovates of land ⌊assessed⌋ to the geld. There is land for 6 oxen. The soke belongs to (*est in*) Stratone [Great Sturton (Gartree)], and there are 65 acres of underwood there.

11. S. and B. In Wispinctune [Wispington (Horncastle)] there are 2 carucates of land ⌊assessed⌋ to the geld. There is land for 4[4] teams. It is inland and soke⌊land⌋ belonging to (*in*) Stratone [Great Sturton (Gartree)] and Cherchebi [Kirkby on Bain (Horncastle)]. There are 9 sokemen and 6 bordars there with 3 teams.

D. B., f. 340d. *Facsimile, p.* xb.

12. S. In Waldingurde [Waddingworth (Horncastle)] there are 6 carucates of land ⌊assessed⌋ to the geld. There is land for 6 teams. The soke belongs to (*in*) Stratone and to Cherchebi. There are 20 sokemen there with 4 teams, and 20 acres of meadow, and 25 acres of underwood.

13. M. In Chirchebi [Kirkby on Bain (Horncastle)] Harold had 10 bovates of land ⌊assessed⌋ to the geld. There is land for 13 oxen. The Bishop of Durham has 3 villeins and 2 bordars there with half

---

[1] See 70/21. [2] See 70/25. [3] See 69/22.

[4] Perhaps this number should be *3*, since the first of the four minims which represent *4* may be intended to be cancelled.

a team, and 12 acres of meadow and 170 acres of wood[land] for pannage throughout the territory. T. R. E. it was worth 100 shillings ; now the like amount.

14. In Martone [Martin (Horncastle)] there is soke[land] of this manor, 12 bovates of land [assessed] to the geld. There is land for 2 teams. There 3 sokemen and 2 bordars have 1 team, and 34 acres of meadow, and 33 acres of wood[land] for pannage, and 60 acres of underwood.

15. In Torp [Tattershall Thorpe (Horncastle)] there is inland and soke[land] of the same manor, 2 carucates of land [assessed] to the geld. There is land for 2 teams. 16 villeins and 1 sokeman and 4 bordars have 1 team there, and the third part of 2 mills rendering 8 shillings, and 3 fisheries rendering 7 shillings and 6 pence, and 15 acres of meadow, and 120 acres of wood[land] for pannage. Eudo[1] claims it[2].

16. M. In Covenham [Covenham (Ludborough)] Esbern had $2\frac{1}{2}$ carucates of land [assessed] to the geld. There is land for 3 teams, and 6 oxen. Now Saint Karilef[3] has it [from the bishop]. There are $2\frac{1}{2}$ teams [in demesne], and 12 villeins and 6 sokemen with $1\frac{1}{2}$ teams. There is a church there, and 60 acres of meadow, and 2 salt-pans rendering 3 shillings. T. R. E. it was worth 60 shillings ; now 4 pounds ; tallage 20 shillings.

17[4] In Scitebroc [Skidbrook (Louthesk)] there is inland of Couenham, 7 bovates of land [assessed] to the geld. There is land for 9 oxen. Saint Karilef has 6 men there with 2 teams, and 9 acres of meadow.

[LUDES [LOUTHESK] WAPENTAKE[5]]

18.[4] In Germundtorp [Grainthorpe (Louthesk)], there is soke[land] of Couenham, $4\frac{1}{2}$ bovates of land [assessed] to the geld. 6 villeins have 1 team and 2 oxen there, and 50 acres of meadow.

19. In Grimesbi [Little Grimsby (Ludborough)] there is soke[land] of this manor, 2 bovates of land [assessed] to the geld. There is land for 3 oxen. It was waste ; now it is cultivated.

20. Two M. In Fdrebi[6] [Fotherby (Ludborough)] Su*m*merled and Archil had 7 bovates [assessed] to the geld. There is land for 2 teams and 5 oxen. Turstin, the bishop's man, has 1 sokeman [and] 6 villeins there having 1 team, and 42 acres of meadow. T. R. E. it was worth 4 pounds ; now 20 shillings.

21. M. In Endrebi and Radebi [Mavis Enderby and Raithby by Spilsby (Bolingbroke)] Elnod had $4\frac{1}{2}$ bovates [assessed] to the geld. There is land for 5 oxen. Now there is half a team there [in demesne], and 1 villein, and half the site of a mill, and 10 acres of meadow. T. R. E. it was worth 10 shillings ; now the like amount.

---

1 *I.e.*, Eudo son of Spirewic.

2 *K* in the margin calls attention to the claim. *Cp.*, 4/55, 29/34.

3 The monastery of St. Carilef, now St. Calais ; department of Sarthe, France.

4 These entries are written at the foot of the column, and a sign indicates that they should come where they are printed.

5 Crowded into the margin.

6 See 18/97 ; 0/29.

22. M. In Spilesbi and Iresbi and Torp [Spilsby and Eresby and Thorpe St. Peter (Bolingbroke)] Aschil had 6 carucates of land ⌊assessed⌋ to the geld. There is land for 6 teams. The bishop has 1 team there ⌊in demesne⌋, and 5 villeins and 5 sokemen and 1 bordar having 1 team, and 2 mills rendering 9 shillings, and 12 acres of meadow. T. R. E. it was worth 20 shillings; now the like amount. [Eudo[1] claims it[2]].

23. In the same places (*ibidem*) there is soke⌊land⌋ of Gredbi [Grebby (Candelshoe)] and Estrecale [East Keal (Bolingbroke)], 2 carucates of land ⌊assessed⌋ to the geld. There is land for three teams. 12 sokemen have 2 teams there.

24.[3] In Hundelbi [Hundleby (Bolingbroke)] there are 4 acres of land.

25. M. In Estrecale [East Keal (Bolingbroke)] Elnod had 6 bovates of land ⌊assessed⌋ to the geld. There is land for 6 oxen. 2 villeins plough there with 2 oxen. There are 5 acres of meadow there. T. R. E. it was worth 10 shillings; now the like amount. Eudo[1] claims the soke.

26. In Totintune [Toynton All Saints and Toynton St. Peter (Bolingbroke)] there is soke⌊land⌋ of Spilesbi [Spilsby (Bolingbroke)] 2 bovates of land ⌊assessed⌋ to the geld. There is land for 2 oxen. There is 1 sokeman there, and 6 acres of meadow.

*D. B., f. 341*a. *Facsimile, p. xi*a.

SUDTREDING [SOUTH RIDING]

27. Two M. In Caditon [Keddington (Louthesk)] Harold and Artor had $9\frac{1}{2}$ bovates of land ⌊assessed⌋ to the geld. There is land for $1\frac{1}{2}$ teams. Turstin, the bishop's man, has 1 team there ⌊in demesne⌋, and 15 sokemen and 12 villeins with 4 teams, and $3\frac{1}{2}$ mills rendering 20 shillings, and 12 acres of meadow. T. R. E. it was worth 40 shillings; now 60 shillings.

28. In Salflatebi [Saltfleetby (Louthesk)] there is soke⌊land⌋ of this manor, 1 bovate of land ⌊assessed⌋ to the geld. There is land for 2 oxen. There are 3 sokemen and 1 villein there with 4 oxen.

29. In Salflatebi there is 1 bovate ⌊assessed⌋ to the geld.[4]

30. In Crochinton [Cockerington (Louthesk)] there is other soke⌊land⌋, half a bovate of land ⌊assessed⌋ to the geld. There is land for 1 ox. There is 1 villein there ploughing with 1 ox.

WINEGEBRIGE [WINNIBRIGGS] WAPENTAKE

31. M. In Gunfordebi [Great Gonerby (Winnibriggs)] Morcar had $1\frac{1}{2}$ carucates of land ⌊assessed⌋ to the geld. There is land for 2 teams. Lanbert, the bishop's man, has 1 team there ⌊in demesne⌋, and 5 villeins and 2 bordars with 1 team, and 2 mills rendering 16 shillings, and $22\frac{1}{2}$ acres of meadow. T. R. E. it was worth 40 shillings; now the like amount.

---

[1] *I.e.*, Eudo son of Spirewic.

[2] *Eudo clamat* is written in the right hand margin, and the letter *K*, in the opposite margin of the column, is apparently intended to direct attention to the claim.

[3] This entry is written in the margin of the column opposite no. 22.

[4] This entry is given as a note at the foot of f. 341b, and a sign indicates that its proper place is where it is printed.

AVELUNT [AVELAND] WAPENTAKE

32. In Neutone[1] [Newton near Folkingham (Aveland)] Uluric Wilde had 7 bovates of land [assessed] to the geld. There is land for 2 teams. The Bishop of Durham has a moiety, and Uluiet and his wife have the other [moiety] of the king. The whole of this land was his wife's mother's. The bishop has half a team there [in demesne], and 3 villeins with half a team, and 6 acres of meadow, and 35 acres of underwood. Uluiet has half a team [in demesne], and 3 villeins with half a team, and 6 acres of meadow, and 35 acres of underwood. The whole T. R. E. was worth 40 shillings; now the bishop's part [is worth] 25 shillings; and Uluiet's part [the bishop claims it] 25 shillings.

HAZEBI [HACEBY] HUNDRED

33. Two M. In Picheurde [Pickworth (Aveland)] Swen and Agemund had 1 carucate and 5 bovates of land [assessed] to the geld. There is land for 2 teams and 2 oxen. Now Gocelin (*Goislan*), the bishop's man, has 1 team there [in demesne], and 5 villeins and 3 bordars ploughing with 5 oxen. There is half a church there, and 16 acres of meadow, and 33 acres of wood[land] for pannage throughout the territory. T. R. E. it was worth 40 shillings; now the like amount.

TREHOS [THREO] WAPENTAKE

34. In Brezbi [Braceby (Threo)] [hundred] there is soke[land] of this manor, 1 carucate of land [assessed] to the geld. There is land for 1 team. 1 sokeman has half a team there, and 30 acres of meadow, and 21 acres of wood[land] for pannage throughout the territory.

ASWARDETIERNE [ASWARDHURN] WAPENTAKE

LEDULFTORP [LAYTHORPE] HUNDRED

35. Three M. In Chelebi [Kelby in Haydor (Aswardhurn)] Aslac, Brictric, and Archil had 6 carucates and 3 bovates of land [assessed] to the geld. There is land for 8 teams. Now Almod, the bishop's man, has 2 teams there [in demesne], and 7 villeins and 3 sokemen and 3 bordars with 2 teams. T. R E. it was worth 70 shillings; now 6 pounds. There are 70 acres of meadow there, and 90 acres of underwood, which bishop R.[2] and Colegrim and their fellows hold. The bishop has the soke.

FLAXEWELLE [FLAXWELL] WAPENTAKE

HASCHEBI [ASHBY DE LA LAUND] HUNDRED

36. M. In Evedune [Evedon (Aswardhurn)] Turuert had $2\frac{1}{2}$ carucates [assessed] to the geld. There is land for 3 teams. Colsuan, the bishop's man, has 1 team there [in demesne], and 4 villeins and 2 bordars with 1 team and 2 oxen, and 20 acres of meadow. T. R. E. it was worth 4 pounds; now 20 shillings.

*D. B. f. 341*b. *Facsimile, p. xi*b.

37. In Rosbi [hundred] and the other Rosbi [hundred] [North and South Rauceby (Flaxwell)] there is soke[land] belonging to (*in*) Wilgebi

---

[1] See 67/10, 72/52.

[2] *I.e.* Remigius bishop of Lincoln.

and Chirchebie [Silk Willoughby and Kirkby by Laythorpe (Aswardhurn)], 3 carucates and 1 bovate of land [assessed] to the geld. There is land for 4 teams. Almod, the bishop's man, has 15 sokemen there and 6 bordars having 5 teams, and half a church. These are valued (*appreciantur*) in the above-mentioned manor.

38. In Evedune [Evedon (Aswardhurn)] there is soke[land] of Cherchebi [Kirkby by Laythorpe (Aswardhurn)], 1 bovate of land [assessed] to the geld. There are 1 villein and 2 bordars there, and 2 acres of meadow.

NORT TREDING [NORTH RIDING] BRADELAI [BRADLEY] WAPENTAKE

ALESBI [AYLESBY] HUNDRED

39. M. In Alesbi [Aylesby (Bradley)] Aben had $6\frac{1}{3}$ bovates of land [assessed] to the geld. There is land for 1 team. Nigel, the bishop's man, has half a team there [in demesne], and 3 sokemen and 1 villein and 1 bordar with half a team, and the site of 1 mill. T. R. E. it was worth 40 shillings; now 20 shillings.

HAWARDESHOU [HAVERSTOE] WAPENTAKE

FENBI [FENBY] HUNDRED

40. M. In Ravenedal [Ravendale (Haverstoe)] Grinchel had 2 bovates of land [assessed] to the geld. There is land for half a team. Walbert, the bishop's man, ploughs it with 3 oxen. T. R. E. it was worth 20 shillings; now 5 shillings.

SVD TREDING [SOUTH RIDING]

WARAGEHOU [WRAGGOE] WAPENTAKE

41. Three M. In Biscopetorp [Biscathorpe (Wraggoe)] Godric and his two brothers had 3 carucates of land [assessed] to the geld. [There is land for 6 teams[1]]. Two served the third. Now two men of the bishop's have 2 teams there [in demesne], and 3 villeins and 7 bordars and 9 sokemen with $2\frac{1}{2}$ teams, and 2 mills rendering 5 shillings, and 24 acres of meadow. T. R. E. it was worth 60 shillings; now the like amount.

42. M. In Torp [Tattershall Thorpe (Horncastle)] Godwine and Gunnewate had $5\frac{1}{3}$ bovates of land [assessed] to the geld. There is land for 6 oxen. The bishop has 1 team there [in demesne], and 5 villeins and 1 bordar with 1 team, and a fourth part of 1 mill rendering 12 pence, and $1\frac{1}{2}$ fisheries rendering 3 shillings, and the third part of a church, and 8 acres of meadow, and 46 acres of wood[land] for pannage. T. R. E. it was worth 3 pounds; now 33 shillings and 4 pence.

CALNODESHOU [CANDLESHOE] WAPENTAKE

43. M. In Screnbi [Scremby (Candleshoe)] Fenchel had 1 carucate of land [assessed] to the geld. There is land for 1 team. Now the same man has it of the bishop. There is 1 team there [in demesne], and 4 villeins ploughing with 5 oxen. T. R. E. it was worth 40 shillings; now 20 shillings.

---

[1] In margin.

44. In Aschebi [Ashby by Partney (Candleshoe)] there is soke[land] of this manor, 1 carucate of land [assessed] to the geld. There is land for 1 team. [There are] 2 villeins there, and 5 acres of meadow.

45. In Screnbi there is soke[land] of Estrecale [East Keal (Bolingbroke)], 2 bovates of land [assessed] to the geld.

46. In Heretorp [Addlethorpe (Candleshoe)] there is inland of Estrecale and Heresbi and Greibi [East Keal and Orby and Grebby (Candleshoe)], 6 bovates of land [assessed] to the geld. There is land for 6 oxen. 6 villeins and 1 sokeman have 1 team and 1 ploughing ox there, and 120 acres of meadow.

47. B. In Wenflet [Wainfleet (Candleshoe)] three brothers had 7 bovates [and a half] of land [assessed] to the geld. There is land for 1 team. This is inland belonging to (*in*) the above-mentioned manor. Now Bundo and Ralf have 10 villeins and 1 bordar there with 1 team, and 2 oxen [[1]], and 2 salt-pans rendering 8 pence, and 83 acres of meadow.

Ludes [Louthesk] Wapentake

48. Two M. In Catebi [South Cadeby (Louthesk)] Summerde and Osgot had $4\frac{1}{2}$ bovates of land [assessed] to the geld.* There is land for 1 team and 2 oxen. Turstin, the bishop's man, has 1 team there[2] [in demesne], and 3 villeins and 1 bordar ploughing with 2 oxen, and 10 acres of meadow. T. R. E. it was worth 20 shillings ; now 18 shillings.

**D. B., f. 341c.* *Facsimile, p. xiia.*

49. In Welletone [Welton le Wold (Louthesk)] there is soke[land] of this manor, 1 carucate of land [assessed] to the geld. There is land for 1 team. 2 sokemen have half a team there, and the third part of the site of 1 mill, and 10 acres of meadow.

Calsvad [Calcewath] Wapentake

50. M. In Hage and Calesbi [Haugh and Calceby (Calcewath)] Aldene had 2 bovates of land [assessed] to the geld. There is land for 3 oxen. Now William, the bishop's man, has half a team there [in demesne], and 1 bordar. T. R. E. it was worth 10 shillings ; now 10 shillings.

51. M. In Brunetorp [Bonthorpe in Willoughby (Calcewath)] Tori had 1 carucate of land [assessed] to the geld. There is land for 2 teams. Nigel, the bishop's man, has 1 team there [in demesne], and 6 villeins and 4 bordars with 1 team, and 9 acres of meadow. T. R. E. it was worth 60 shillings ; now 60 shillings.

52. B. In Slodebi [Sloothby in Willoughby (Calcewath)] there is inland [of Bonthorpe], half a carucate of land [assessed] to the geld. There is land for 7 oxen. There are 6 villeins and 2 bordars there with half a team, and 20 acres of meadow.

53. Two M. In Fullobi [Fulletby (Hill)] Siward and Edric had 3 carucates and 6 bovates of land [assessed] to the geld. There is land for 5 teams. William, the bishop's man, has 2 teams there [in demesne],

---

[1] A blank space in the original.

[2] *Ibi* is repeated in the original.

and 5 villeins and 19 sokemen having 2 teams and 2 oxen. There are 50 acres of meadow there. T. R. E. it was worth 4 pounds; now 100 shillings.

54. In Oxetune [and Wluricebi] [Oxcombe and Worlaby (Hill)] there is soke[land] of this manor, 1½ carucates of land [assessed] to the geld. There is land for 2 teams. 11 sokemen have 2 teams there, and 60 acres of meadow.

55. B. In Trichingheham [Threckingham (Aveland)] there is inland of Neutone [Newton near Folkingham (Aveland)], 5 bovates and a sixth part of 2 bovates of land [assessed] to the geld. There are 1 sokeman and 3 villeins there having half a team. The Bishop of Durham has a twelfth part of one church of Saint Peter there, and a sixth part of one church of Saint Mary, and a sixth part of 4 bovates of land which belong to (*iacent in*) the church of Saint Mary. In the same hundred and in this same vill a certain Uluiet has of the king's alms as many parts of the land and of the churches and of the teams and of the men as it is said above the bishop has, for they divide Neutone and what belongs thereto in halves.

[Brunetorp[1]]

D. B., f. 342a. *Facsimile, p. xiiia.*

4. LAND OF THE BISHOP OF BAYEUX (*Baiocensis*)

1. M. In Carlentone [South Carlton (Lawress)] Aldreman had 1 carucate of land [assessed] to the geld. There is land for 1 team. The Bishop of Bayeux has 4 sokemen there with 1½ teams, and 1 church. T. R. E. it was worth 10 shillings and 8 pence; now the like amount; tallage 13 shillings and 4 pence. Ralf the sewer (*dapifer*) and Gilbert of Gand have this land by (*per*) the seal of the Bishop of Bayeux. Ernuin the priest says that it ought to be the king's [land].

2. Two M. In Englebi [Ingleby (Lawress)] Chetel and Ulchil had 3 carucates and 6 bovates of land [assessed] to the geld. There is land for 4 teams. Colsuan and Wadard, the Bishop of Bayeux' men, have 2 teams there [in demesne], and 12 villeins and 2 sokemen and 4 bordars having 1½ teams, and 90 acres of meadow, and 110 acres of underwood. T. R. E. it was worth 30 shillings; now 50 shillings; tallage 20[2] shillings.

3. M. In Stratone[3] [Sturton by Stow (Well)] Ulchil, Asfort, Restelf, and Ulmer had 8 carucates of land [assessed] to the geld. There is land for 8 teams. Ilbert, the bishop's man, has 4 teams there [in

[1] Written in the margin just below the level of the last line of no. 55. The rest of the page is blank.

[2] There is a space of ¾ inch between *xx* and *solid'*.

[3] See 71/9.

demesne], and 16 villeins with 2 teams, and 30 acres of meadow, and 80 acres of underwood. T. R. E. it was worth 7 pounds; now 4 pounds; tallage 40 shillings.

4. M. In Welingeham [Willingham by Stow (Well)] Archil had $1\frac{1}{2}$ carucates [assessed] to the geld. There is land for 12 oxen. Now Ilbert, the bishop's man, has 1 team there [in demesne], and 2 villeins and 3 sokemen with 1 team. T. R. E. it was worth 20 shillings; now the like amount.

5. M. In Ingeham [Ingham (Aslacoe)] Gamel had 1 carucate of land [assessed] to the geld. There is land for 12 oxen. Now Ilbert has 2 teams there [in demesne], and 2 villeins and 3 bordars and 3 sokemen having 1 team, and 10 acres of meadow. T. R. E. it was worth 5 shillings; now 20 shillings; tallage 10 shillings.

6.[1] B. In Cotes [Cotes by Stow (Aslacoe)], [there is] inland of Ingeham, half a carucate of land [assessed] to the geld. There is land for half a team. Ilbert has there 3 villeins and 2 bordars [who] have 1 team.

7. M. In Glentewrde [Glentworth (Aslacoe)] Estan had 7 bovates of land [assessed] to the geld. There are 4 bovates of land there [assessed] to the geld. It is soke[land] belonging to (*in*) Glandham [Glentham (Aslacoe)]. There is land for 10 teams. Now Wadard, the bishop's man, has half a team [in demesne], and 6 sokemen and 1 villein with half a team, and 50 acres of meadow. T. R. E. it was worth 15 shillings and 4 pence; now 40 shillings and 8 pence.

8. M. In Helmeswelle [Hemswell (Aslacoe)] Elnod had 4 bovates of land [assessed] to the geld. There is land for 1 team. Now Losoard, the bishop's man, has 1 villein and 2 bordars there with 1 team, and $27\frac{1}{2}$ acres of meadow. T. R. E. it was worth 20 shillings; now 10 shillings.

9. Two M. In Glandham [Glentham (Aslacoe)] Adestan and Ulmær had 10 bovates of land [assessed] to the geld. There is land for 10 oxen. Wadard [has] 2 villeins and 1 sokeman[2] there with 1 team. He himself [has] 1 team [in demesne], and 40 acres of meadow. T. R. E. it was worth 15 shillings and 4 pence; now 60 shillings.

10. M. In Normanestou [Normanby by Spital (Aslacoe)] Tor had 1 carucate of land [assessed] to the geld. There is land for 2 teams. Now Ilbert, the bishop's man, has 2 sokemen with 1 team, and 10 acres of meadow. T. R. E. it was worth 10 shillings; now 12 shillings.

11. Two M. In Frisebi [East and West Firsby (Aslacoe)] Alwi and Aschil had 3 carucates and 5 bovates of land [assessed] to the geld. Now Ilbert, the bishop's man, has 2 teams there [in demesne], and 8 villeins and 8 bordars* and 6 sokemen with 2 teams. There is a church there, and 30 acres of meadow. T. R. E. it was worth 60 shillings; now the like amount; tallage 10 shillings.

**D. B., f.* 342b. *Facsimile, p. xiii*b.

[1] This entry comes between nos. 21 and 22, but a sign indicates that it is to be inserted here.

[2] Or possibly *2 sokemen*. It seems that *ii soch'* was first written, the first *i* being then changed into the sign for *and* in forgetfulness that that sign was already in the text.

12.[1] In Neutone [Newton by Toft (Walshcroft)] there is soke⌊land⌋ of Frisebi, 6 bovates of land ⌊assessed⌋ to the geld. There is land for 2 teams. Ilbert has 5 sokemen there with 1½ teams, and 20 acres of meadow.

13. M. In Torp [Northorpe (Corringham)] Aschil had 10 bovates ⌊assessed⌋ to the geld. There is land for 2 teams. Now Ilbert, the bishop's man, has 1 team there ⌊in demesne⌋, and 5 villeins and 3 bordars with 1 team, and 10 acres of meadow. T. R. E. it was worth 20 shillings; now 20 shillings.

14. M. In Cletham [Cleatham (Corringham)] Aschil had 6 bovates of land ⌊assessed⌋ to the geld. There is land for 12 oxen. Ilbert, the bishop's man, has 1 team ⌊in demesne⌋, and 3 villeins and 2 bordars with 1 team, and 6 acres of meadow. T. R. E. it was worth 30 shillings; now 40 shillings.

15. M. In Stantone and Widingeham [Stainton and Waddingham (Manley)] Ardegrip had 6 bovates of land ⌊assessed⌋ to the geld. There is land for 1 team. Ilbert, the bishop's man, has [himself 1 team] ⌊in demesne⌋ there, ⌊and⌋ 6 villeins and 2 bordars with 1 team, [and 16 acres of meadow]. T. R. E. it was worth 20 shillings; now 15[2] shillings.

16. M. In Elesham [Elsham (Yarborough)] Chetelbern had 7 bovates of land ⌊assessed⌋ to the geld. There is land for 2 teams. Ilbert, the bishop's man, has 6 villeins and 1 bordar there with 1 team, and 47 acres of meadow. T. R. E. it was worth 20 shillings; now 15 shillings.

17. Three M. In Aldulvebi [Audleby (Yarborough)] Tofti, Turuet, and Ernui had 10 bovates of land ⌊assessed⌋ to the geld. There is land for 3 teams. Now there are 3 teams in demesne, and 15 villeins and 3 sokemen and 6 bordars with 2 teams, and 60 acres of meadow. T. R. E. it was worth 100 shillings; now 8 pounds. The whole ⌊is⌋ 15 furlongs in length and 6 in breadth.

SOKE⌊LAND⌋ OF THIS MANOR

18. In Neutone [Newton by Toft (Walshcroft)] there are 10 bovates of land ⌊assessed⌋ to the geld. There is land for 3 teams. 10 sokemen have 3 teams there.

19. In Summerlede[3] [Osgodby (Walshcroft)] there are 5 bovates of land ⌊assessed⌋ to the geld. There is land for 1½ teams. 8 sokemen have 1 team and 2 ploughing oxen there.

20. In Risebi [Risby in Walesby (Walshcroft)] there is 1 carucate of land ⌊assessed⌋ to the geld. There is land for 2 teams. 14 sokemen and 4 villeins have 3 teams there, and 31 acres of meadow, and 12 acres of underwood. ⌊It is⌋ 3 leagues in length, and 3 furlongs in breadth.

---

[1] This entry is written at the foot of column *b*, but a sign indicates that it is connected with no. 11.

[2] *15* is a rather uncertain reading. The numeral seems to have been altered from *xi* to *xv*.

[3] This entry seems to be a duplicate of no. 22 below, which is probably the more correct version. It is impossible to account for the name *Summerlede* unless perhaps it is the result of confusion with a personal name. In Old English *Sumerlida* represents the Old Norse personal name Sumarlithi. *Cp.* 3/20.

21. In Chenebi [Kingerby (Walshcroft)] there are 5 bovates of land [assessed] to the geld. There is land for 2 teams. 8 sokemen have 1 team and 2 ploughing oxen there.[1]

22. In Osgotebi [Osgodby (Walshcroft)] there are 5 bovates of land [assessed] to the geld. There is land for 10 oxen. 9 sokemen have 1 team and 2 ploughing oxen there. It is soke[land] belonging to (*in*) Aldulvebi [Audleby (Yarborough)].

23. Two M. In Neteltone [Nettleton (Yarborough)] Chetelber and Gamel had 1 carucate and 6 bovates of land [assessed] to the geld. There is land for 3½ teams. Now Ernegis and Wadard, the bishop's men, have 2 teams there [in demesne], and 13 villeins and 5 bordars with 1 team and 2 oxen, and 2 mills [rendering] 3 shillings, and 60 acres of meadow. T. R. E. it was worth 60 shillings; now 4 pounds.'

24. In Toresbi and Alwoldebi [Autby[2] and North Thoresby (Haverstoe)] there is soke[land] of this manor, 2 bovates of land [assessed] to the geld. There are 4 villeins there, and 3 salt-pans, and 20 acres of meadow.

25. In Rodowelle [Rothwell (Haverstoe)] there is 1 bovate of land [assessed] to the geld. 1 sokeman has 1 ox there.

D. B., f. 342c. *Facsimile, p. xiv*a.

26. In Grosbi [Grasby (Yarborough)] Ulchil had 2 carucates of land [assessed] to the geld. There is land for 4 teams. Now there are 2 teams there in demesne, and 6 villeins and 6 bordars and 11 sokemen having 2 teams. There is a church there, and priest, and 1 mill [rendering] 3 shillings, and 40 acres of meadow. T. R. E. it was worth 60 shillings; now 100 shillings.

27. In Sualun [Swallow (Bradley)] there is soke[land] of this manor, 1 carucate of land [assessed] to the geld. There is land for 2 teams. There are 8 sokemen there with 1 team.

28. M. In Chelebi [Keelby (Yarborough)] Sigar had 4½ bovates of land [assessed] to the geld. There is land for 9 oxen. Wadard, the bishop's man, has 1 team there [in demesne], and 2 villeins and 3 sokemen ploughing with 2 oxen. T. R. E. it was worth 30 shillings: now the like amount.

29. In Wenflet [*perhaps* Houflet[3] in Stallingborough (Yarborough)] there are 2 bovates [assessed] to the geld. There is land for 2 oxen.

30. In Stalinburg [Stallingborough (Yarborough)] there is [inland[4]] of this manor, 5½ bovates of land [assessed] to the geld. There is land for 11 oxen. 8 villeins and 2 sokemen have 1 team there, and 180 acres of meadow, and half a mill rendering 3 shillings.

31. M. In Hegelinge [Healing (Bradley)] Sigar had 7 bovates of land [assessed] to the geld. There is land for 1 team and 6 oxen. Wadard, the bishop's man, has 1 team there [in demesne], and 3 villeins and 5

---

[1] Cotes, no. 6, was inserted here, and a sign indicates that no. 22 is to follow no. 21, as it does follow when Cotes is removed to its proper place.

[2] A depopulated vill in North Thoresby, now represented by a farm called 'Autby' in that parish.

[3] In a grant of Henry II to Grimsby abbey, the king speaks of his port of Houflet (*Cal. Charter Rolls*, iv, 311).

[4] Corrected from *soke[land]*.

bordars and 2 sokemen with 1 team, and 5 acres of meadow. T. R. E. it was worth 30 shillings; now 40 shillings; tallage 20 shillings.

32. In Cleia [Clee (Bradley)] there is soke[land] of this manor, 3 bovates of land [assessed] to the geld. There is land for half a team. 4 sokemen and 2 villeins and 1 bordar have 5 ploughing oxen there, and 25 acres of meadow.

33. In Ternesco [Thrunsco in Clee (Bradley)] there are 2 bovates of land [assessed] to the geld. There is land for half a plough. 1 villein and 3 sokemen have half a plough there.

34. M. In Sudcotes [Little Cotes (Bradley)] Azor had 15 bovates of land [assessed] to the geld. There is land for 4 teams. Now there are 16 sokemen there having 3 teams, and 40 acres of meadow. T. R. E. it was worth 20 shillings; now 40 shillings.

35. In Cotes [Great Cotes (Bradley)] there are 6 [or 3] bovates of land [assessed] to the geld. There is land for 6 oxen. It is soke[land] belonging to (*in*) Sudcotes [Little Cotes]. 2 sokemen have 2 ploughing oxen there, and 100 acres of meadow.

36. M. In Cleia [Clee (Bradley)] Algar had half a carucate of land [assessed] to the geld. There is land for 1 team. Now Ilbert has it of the bishop, and it is waste. There are 40 acres of meadow there. T. R. E. it was worth 10 shillings; now 20 shillings.

37. In Itrebi [Itterby[1] in Clee (Bradley)] there is inland [and soke[land]] of this manor, 1 carucate of land [assessed] to the geld. There is land for 1½ teams. Ilbert has 5 sokemen and 2 villeins having 1½ teams there.

38. M. In Rase [West Rasen (Walshcroft)] Rolf had 5⅓ bovates of land [assessed] to the geld. There is land for 1½ teams. Wimund, the bishop's man, has 1 team there [in demesne], and 7 villeins and 3 bordars with 1 team, and 2 mills rendering 6 shillings, and 61 acres of meadow. T. R. E. it was worth 20 shillings; now 30 shillings.

39. M. In Rasa [Middle Rasen (Walshcroft)] Ulgrin, Broclos, Ulf, Goduin, Alwin, and Levric had 2 carucates and 1 bovate of land [assessed] to the geld. There is land for 5 teams. Wadard, the bishop's man, has 18 villeins and 11 bordars having 5 teams there. There is a church there, and a priest, with 2 bordars. One bovate of this land belongs to the church. There are 120 acres of meadow there. T. R. E. it was worth 70 shillings; now 4 pounds.

D. B., f. 342d. *Facsimile, p. xiv*b.

40. M. In Tofte [Toft by Newton (Walshcroft)] Azor had 14⅓ bovates of land [assessed] to the geld. There is land for 4 teams. Wadard, the bishop's man, has 1 team there [in demesne], and 3 villeins and 11 sokemen having 5 teams, and 60 acres of meadow. T. R. E. it was worth 10 shillings; now 60 shillings; tallage 20 shillings.

41. M. In Tavelesbi [Tealby (Walshcroft)] Rolf had half a carucate of land [assessed] to the geld. There is land for 1 team. Losoard, the bishop's man, has 1 team there [in demesne], and 3 villeins ploughing

---

[1] A hamlet which is now included in Cleethorpes.

with 3 oxen, and 1 mill rendering 2 shillings, and another mill which belongs to Grosbi [Grasby (Yarborough)]. T. R. E. it was worth 20 shillings ; now the like amount.

42. M. In Toresbi and Alwoldebi [North Thoresby and Autby (Haverstoe)] Toruet had 4 carucates and $3\frac{1}{6}$ bovates of land [assessed] to the geld. There is land for 6 teams. Ilbert, the bishop's man, has 2 teams there [in demesne], and 23 villeins and 5 bordars with 2 teams and 5 oxen, and 27 sokemen having 5 teams less 2 oxen. There are 80 acres of meadow there, and turbary (*toruelande*), rendering 10 shillings, and 16 salt-pans rendering 16 shillings. T. R. E. it was worth 8 pounds ; now the like amount ; tallage 40 shillings. Edward [1] exchanged (*cambiauit*) this land with the Bishop of Bayeux.

43. M. In Stratone [Great Sturton (Gartree)] Grinchel had 3 carucates and 2 bovates and two parts of 1 bovate of land [assessed] to the geld. [There is land for 4 teams]. Now Ilbert, the bishop's man, has 1 team there [in demesne], and 3 villeins and 3 bordars and 23 sokemen having 4 teams. There is a church there, and 1 mill rendering 8 shillings, and 120 acres of meadow. T. R. E. it was worth 40 shillings ; now 50 shillings ; tallage 10 shillings.

44. In Randebi [Ranby (Gartree)] there is inland and soke[land] of this manor, 9 bovates of land [assessed] to the geld. There is land for 2 teams. Now there is 1 team there in demesne, and 3 villeins and 1 bordar and 4 sokemen having 1 team, and 200 acres of meadow. There is a church there, to which belong 40 acres of land and 5 acres of meadow. There is a priest there having half a team.

45. In Burgrede [Burreth (Gartree)] there is soke[land], 3 bovates of land [assessed] to the geld. There is land for half a team. There is 1 villein and 1 bordar there having 1 ploughing ox, and 15 acres of meadow, and 120 acres of wood[land] for pannage, and 100 acres of underwood.

46. M. In Haintone [Hainton (Wraggoe)] Rolf had 15 bovates of land [assessed] to the geld. There is land for 3 teams and 6 oxen. Ilbert, the bishop's man, has half a team there [in demesne], and 9 villeins and 2 bordars and 1 sokeman having 2 teams, and 100 acres of meadow. T. R. E. it was worth 40 shillings ; now the like amount.

47. In Sutreie[2] [Southrey (Wraggoe)] there is inland belonging to (*in*) Haintone, 2 bovates of land [assessed] to the geld. There is land for half a team. 2 villeins have half a team there, and 4 acres of meadow, and 20 acres of wood[land].

48. In Strubi [Strubby near Hainton (Wraggoe)] there are 2 bovates of land assessed to the geld. There is land for half a team. [It is soke[land]]. 3 sokemen have half a team there.

49. In Bacwrde [Barkwith (Wraggoe)] there are 3 bovates of land [assessed] to the geld. There is land for 6 oxen. 3 sokemen have half a team there.

50. M. In Sotebi [Sotby (Wraggoe)] Ulnod had 4 carucates of land [assessed] to the geld. There is land for 6 teams. Ralf, the

[1] This blank seems to be intended for a name which has not been filled in.

[2] This entry has been inserted at the foot of the column, and a sign shews that its proper place is where it is printed in the text.

bishop's man, has 16 sokemen and 3 villeins there with 4 teams. There is no demesne there. There is a church there, and 150 acres of meadow. T. R. E. it was worth 3 pounds; now 4 pounds.

51. In Langetone and in Torp [Langton by Horncastle and Langton Thorpe (Horncastle)] Lepsi had 1 carucate of land [assessed] to the geld. There is land for 1½ teams. One of the bishop's men has* 1 team there [in demesne], and 26 villeins and 3 sokemen having 5 ploughing oxen, and 60 acres of meadow, and 80 acres of wood[land] for pannage throughout the territory. T. R. E. it was worth 40 shillings; now the like amount.

**D. B., f. 343a.* *Facsimile, p. xva.*

52. In Stinblebi [Thimbleby (Horncastle)] there is inland and soke[land] of this manor, 10 bovates of land [assessed] to the geld. There is land for 14 oxen. 5 villeins and 3 sokemen have 2 teams there, and 12 acres of meadow, and 30 acres of underwood.

53. M. In Vlingeham[1] [South Willingham (Wraggoe)] Aschil had 6½ bovates of land [assessed] to the geld. There is land for 13 oxen. Wadard has 1 team there [in demesne], and 4 villeins and 1 bordar with 1 team, and 36 acres of meadow. T. R. E. it was worth 20 shillings; now 40 shillings.

54. M. In Chirchebi [Kirkby on Bain (Horncastle)] Wlmar had 10 bovates of land [assessed] to the geld. There is land for 1½ teams. Ilbert, the bishop's man, has 1 team there [in demesne], and 10 villeins and 4 bordars with 1 team, and the site of a mill, and 12 acres of meadow, and 160 acres of wood[land] for pannage throughout the territory. T. R. E. it was worth 40 shillings; now 20 shillings.

55.[2] In Torp [Tattershall Thorpe (Horncastle)] Ulmar had 2 carucates of land [assessed] to the geld for a manor. There is land for 2 teams. There are 18 villeins and 4 bordars there with 1 team, and 16 acres of meadow, and 120 acres of wood[land] for pannage, and a third part of 2 mills worth (*de*) 7 shillings, and 3 fisheries worth (*de*) 30 pence. It was worth and is worth 20 shillings. Eudo holds it of the king.

56. M. In Sisse [Sixle (Wraggoe)] Gudmunt had 6 bovates [and a half] of land [assessed] to the geld. There is land for 9 oxen. Ilbert, the bishop's man, has 1 team there [in demesne], and 3 villeins and 1 bordar and 2 sokemen having half a team.' There is a church there, and 25[3] acres of meadow. T. R. E. it was worth 20 shillings; now 20 shillings.

57. M. In Cocrintone [Cockerington (Louthesk)] Aschil and Ulgrin had 3 carucates [and 1 bovate] of land [assessed] to the geld. There is land for 6 teams. Ilbert, the bishop's man, has 2 teams there [in demesne], and 7 villeins and 4 bordars and 27 sokemen having 3 teams. There are 80 acres of meadow there, and 60 acres of underwood, and 2 parts of 1 mill rendering 2 shillings. T. R. E. it was worth 60 shillings; now the like amount; tallage 20 shillings.

---

[1] See 2/1, 69/28.

[2] This entry has been inserted at the foot of the column, and a sign shews that its proper place is where it is printed in the text. It is a duplicate of 29/34.

[3] *xx* is written in the line, and *v* above the line.

58. In Alvingeham [Alvingham (Louthesk)] there are 4 bovates and 2 parts of one bovate of land ⌊assessed⌋ to the geld. There is land for 1 team. ⌊It is⌋ soke⌊land⌋ of Cocrint' [Cockrington]. 4 sokemen have 1 team there, and 7 acres of meadow.

59. M. In Abi [Aby (Calcewath)] Ulstan and Aschil had 14 bovates of land ⌊assessed⌋ to the geld. There is land for 2 teams and 6 oxen. Wadard, the bishop's man, has 1 team there ⌊in demesne⌋, and and [*sic*] 12 villeins and 4 sokemen and 2 bordars having 2½ teams, and 80 acres of meadow, and 27 acres of wood⌊land⌋ for pannage, and 300 acres of underwood. T. R. E. it was worth 3 pounds; now 4 pounds.

60. In Strobi [Strubby (Calcewath)] there are 1 carucate and 2 bovates of land ⌊assessed⌋ to the geld. There is land for 2½ teams. 5 sokemen and 4 villeins have 2 teams there. ⌊It is⌋ soke⌊land⌋ belonging to (*in*) Abi.

61. M. In Rigesbi [Rigsby (Calcewath)] Turulf and Outbert had 10 bovates of land ⌊assessed⌋ to the geld. There is land for 2 teams. Losoard, the bishop's man, has 1 team there ⌊in demesne⌋, and 5 villeins and 3 bordars with half a team, and 120 acres of wood⌊land⌋ for pannage, and 60 acres of underwood. T. R. E. it was worth 60 shillings; now the like amount.

62. In Welle[1] [Well (Calcewath)] there is 1 bovate of land ⌊assessed⌋ to the geld. There is land for 3 oxen. ⌊It is⌋ soke⌊land⌋ in Rigesbi. There are 1 sokeman and 2 villeins there.

63. In Alebi [Ailby (Calcewath)] there are 5 bovates of land ⌊assessed⌋ to the geld. There is land for 10 oxen. ⌊It is⌋ soke⌊land⌋ belonging to (*in*) Rigesbi.* 3 sokemen and 2 bordars have 1 team there, and 12 acres of meadow, and 12 acres of wood⌊land⌋ for pannage, and 40 acres of underwood.

**D. B., f.* 343b. *Facsimile, p. xv*b.

64. In Touedebi [Tothby in Alford (Calcewath)] there is half a carucate of land ⌊assessed⌋ to the geld. There is land for 10 oxen. ⌊It is⌋ soke⌊land⌋ ⌊in⌋ Rigesbi. There are 3 sokemen ploughing with 3 oxen, and 20 acres of meadow, and 12 acres of wood⌊land⌋.

65. M. In Aschebi [Ashby Puerorum (Hill)] Odincarle [and Chiluert] had 4 carucates of land ⌊assessed⌋ to the geld. There is land for 5 teams. Now the bishop has 1 team there in demesne, and 9 villeins and 2 bordars and 14 sokemen having 3 teams, and 2 mills rendering 3 shillings and 6 pence, and 31 acres of meadow. T. R. E. it was worth 3 pounds; now 7 pounds.

66. In Andrebi [Bag Enderby (Hill)] [3 bovates] and Marchebi [Markby (Calcewath)] [4 bovates], there are 7 bovates of land ⌊assessed⌋ to the geld. There is land for 1 team. It is soke⌊land⌋ ⌊in⌋ Aschebi [Ashby Puerorum (Hill)]. 15[2] sokemen and 10 villeins and 1 bordar have 2 teams there, and 12 acres of meadow.

67. M. In Aschebi [Ashby near Fenby (Haverstoe)] Algar had 9 bovates of land ⌊assessed⌋ to the geld. There is land for 2 teams and 2 oxen. Ilbert, the bishop's man, has half a team there ⌊in demesne⌋,

---

[1] See 24/68; 69/13.

[2] The numeral is doubtful; *xiii* seems to have been altered into *xv*.

and 2 villeins and 2 bordars and 8 sokemen with 1 team, and 1 mill rendering 3 shillings, and 30 acres of meadow, and 6 acres of underwood. T. R. E. it was worth 30 shillings; now 40 shillings; tallage (*tailla*) 20 shillings.

68. In Brigeslai and Wade and Rauenedal [Brigsley and Waith and Ravendale (Haverstoe)] there are 2 carucates and 5½ bovates of land ⌊assessed⌋ to the geld. There is land for 4 teams and 6 oxen. It is sokeland belonging to (*in*) Aschebi [Ashby near Fenby]. 13 sokemen and 10 villeins have 4 teams there, and 25 acres of meadow.

69. Three M. In Levesbi and Bredelou and Scarhou [Laceby and Bradley and Scartho (Bradley)] Swen, Arich, and Tosti had 9 carucates of land ⌊assessed⌋ to the geld. There is land for 16 teams. The Bishop of Bayeux has 3 teams there in demesne, and 4 villeins and 5 bordars and 85 sokemen having 13½ teams. There are 3 churches there with priests, and 2 mills rendering 8 shillings, and 360 acres of meadow, and 100 acres of underwood.

70. In Grimesbi[1] [Grimsby (Bradley)] the customs and the ferry (*passagium*) render 40 shillings. T. R. E. it was worth 12 pounds; now 30 pounds.

71. In Grimesbi[1] [11 bovates] and Cleia [3⅓ bovates] and Itrebi [4 bovates] and Ternescou [7 bovates] [Grimsby, Clee, Itterby, and Thrunsco (Bradley)] there is soke⌊land⌋ of this manor, 3 carucates and 1 bovate of land[2] [assessed] to the geld.[3] There is land for 5 teams and 7 oxen. 55 sokemen and 1 villein have 6 teams there, and 54 acres of meadow.

72. Two M. In Wichale [Withcall (Louthesk)] Aschil and Outgrim had 3½ carucates less a third of 1 bovate of land ⌊assessed⌋ to the geld. There is land for 6 teams. Ilbert, the bishop's man, has 1 team there ⌊in demesne⌋, and 4 villeins and 42 sokemen having 6 teams, and 2 parts of a mill rendering 26 pence, and 56 acres of meadow. T. R. E. it was worth 4 pounds; now the like amount; tallage 20 shillings.

73. M. In Stivetone[4] [Stewton (Louthesk)] Aschil had 3 bovates of land ⌊assessed⌋ to the geld. There is land for 6 oxen. Ilbert has 1 team there ⌊in demesne⌋, and 1 bordar, and 3 acres of meadow, and 60 acres of wood⌊land⌋ for pannage. T. R. E. it was worth 20 shillings; now 15 shillings.

74. M. In Aresbi[5] [Owersby (Walshcroft)] Gamel had 2[6] carucates of land ⌊assessed⌋ to the geld. There is land for 4 teams. Wadard, the bishop's man, has 1 team there ⌊in demesne⌋, and 5 villeins and 4 bordars and 26 sokemen having 5 teams, and 130 acres of meadow. T. R. E. it was worth 40 shillings; now 60 shillings; tallage 20 shillings.

75. M. In Torgrebi [Thorganby (Walshcroft)] Aluric had 15 bovates of land ⌊assessed⌋ to the geld.* There is land for 3 teams and

**D. B., f. 343c.* *Facsimile, p. xvia.*

[1] See 70/13.
[2] One-third of a bovate is omitted in this total.
[3] *Ad geld* is repeated.
[4] See 27/26; 69/10.
[5] See 70/16.
[6] The numeral must be regarded as rather doubtful since it has perhaps been altered.

6 oxen. The bishop has 1 team there [in demesne], and 8 acres of meadow. T. R. E. it was worth 40 shillings ; now 20 shillings.

76. M. In Dodintune [Dry Doddington (Loveden)] Gladuine had 6 bovates of land [assessed] to the geld. There is land for 6 oxen. Baldric, the bishop's man, [has] 2 villeins and 2 bordars there with 1 team, and half a mill rendering 3 shillings, and 10 acres of meadow. It is worth 10 shillings.

77. M. In Claipol [Claypole (Loveden)] Turuert had 3 carucates and 1 bovate of land [assessed] to the geld. There is land for 3 teams. The bishop has 1 team there [in demesne], and 6 villeins and 3 bordars with 1½ teams, and 15 acres of meadow. T. R. E. it was worth 40 shillings ; now 30 shillings.

78. M. In Kaschingetorp [Casthorpe (Winnibriggs)] Turuert had 1½ carucates of land [assessed] to the geld. There is land for 14 oxen. Swen, the bishop's man, has 5 villeins and 1 bordar there with 1 team, and 10 acres of meadow. T. R. E. it was worth 40 shillings ; now 30 [shillings].

79. M. In Stapleforde [Stapleford (Graffoe)] Turuert had 2 carucates of land [assessed] to the geld. There is land for 1 team. Tor, the bishop's man, has 1 team there [in demesne], and 3 villeins and 1 bordar ploughing with 6 oxen. There are 1½ furlongs of meadow. T. R. E. it was worth 20 shillings ; now the like amount.

80. In Canuic [Canwick (Langoe)] Escule had 1½ carucates [assessed] to the geld. There is land for 12 oxen. Ilbert has 2 teams there, and 2 [*blank*] and 1 bordar, and 27 acres of meadow.

81. Two M. In Ounebi [Owmby (Aslacoe)] Rolf and Siward had 5 bovates of land [assessed] to the geld. There is land for 5 oxen. Ilbert and Wadard have 5 oxen in a plough, and 9 acres of meadow. T. R. E. it was worth 15 shillings ; now 20 shillings and 8 pence.

*D. B., f. 343*d. *Facsimile, p. xvi*b.

5. THE LAND OF BISHOP OSMUND [OF SALISBURY]

1. In Lundetorp [Londonthorpe (Threo)] there are 15 bovates of land [assessed] to the geld. There is the land of 2 teams. This land belongs to the church of Grantha*m*, and it is quit from all services. Bishop Osmund has 7 villeins there with 1 team, and 13 acres of meadow.

2. In Nongetune [*query* Spittlegate[1] (Winnibriggs)] Saint Wlfrann of Grantham has half a carucate of land [assessed] to the geld. There is land for 4 oxen. 1 villein ploughs there with 2 oxen.

[1] See 1/13.

3. In Gunfordebi [Gonerby (Winnibriggs)] Saint Wlfrann of Grantham has 1 carucate of land ⌊assessed⌋ to the geld with sake and soke. There is land for 12 oxen.

The value (*precium*) of this land [*i.e.*, numbers 1–3] is reckoned together with ⌊that of⌋ the church of Grantham.

6. [LAND] OF BISHOP GEOFFREY [OF COUTANCE]

1.[1] Two M. In Canuic and Brachebrige [Canwick and Bracebridge (Langoe)] Ulf had 6 carucates of land ⌊assessed⌋ to the geld. There is land for as many teams. Bishop Geoffrey has 1½ teams there ⌊in demesne⌋, and 2 sokemen on (*de*) 11 bovatès of this land, and 12 villeins and 11 bordars having 2½ teams, and 3 fisheries rendering 3 shillings, and 80 acres of meadow. T. R. E. it was, and now is, worth 60 shillings; tallage 10 shillings.

*D. B., f. 344*a. *Facsimile, p. xvii*a.

7. LAND OF THE BISHOP OF LINCOLN

1. In Saint Mary's, Stou [Stow (Well)], there are 4 carucates of land ⌊assessed⌋ to the geld. There is land for 4 teams. Bishop Remigius ⌊has⌋ 1 team there in demesne, and 20 villeins and 3 sokemen having 3½ teams. There is a church there, and a priest, and 3 iron-works (*ferrarię*). T. R. E. it was worth 32 pounds; now 30 pounds. Of this land 2 knights (*milites*) hold as much as is worth 30 shillings.

2. In Welingeham [Willingham by Stow (Well)] there is inland of this manor, 10 bovates and the third part of 2 bovates of land. There is land for as many ⌊oxen⌋. There are 2 bovates of which Gocelin has the soke.

3. In Couenebi [Cainby (Aslacoe)] there is inland of Stou, 4 carucates of land ⌊assessed⌋ to the geld. There is land for 4 teams. 20 sokemen and 15 bordars have 5 teams there. There is a church there, and 1 mill rendering 4 shillings, and 20 acres of meadow.

---

[1] See 72/18.

4. In Nortune [Bishop Norton (Aslacoe)] there are 6 carucates of land [assessed] to the geld. There is land for 6 teams. It is inland and soke[land] belonging to (*in*) Stou. There are 3 teams there in demesne, and 25 sokemen and 4 villeins and 21 bordars have 5 teams. One of the bishop's men has 1 team there [in demesne]. There is the site of a mill there, and 430 acres of meadow.

5. In Glentham [Glentham (Aslacoe)] there are 3 carucates and 6 bovates of land [assessed] to the geld. There is land for 3 teams and 6 oxen. It is soke[land] belonging to (*in*) Stou. 16 sokemen and 11 bordars have 5 teams there, and 110 acres of meadow.

6. In Ounebi[1] [Owmby by Normanby (Aslacoe)] there are 4 carucates and 3 bovates of land [assessed] to the geld. There is land for as many [teams and oxen]. 17 sokemen have 5½ teams there, and 21 acres of meadow.

7. In Opetune and Chestesbi and Normanebi [Upton and Kexby and Normanby by Stow (Welle)], there is soke[land] of Stou, 11 carucates [*and 6 bovates*[2]] and 4 parts of 2 bovates and 2 parts of half a bovate of land [assessed] to the geld. There is land for 10 teams. 20 sokemen and 7 bordars have 6½ teams there, and 171 acres of meadow, and 162 acres of underwood.[3]

8. M. In Welletone [Welton by Lincoln (Lawress)] Swen had 12 carucates of land [assessed] to the geld. There is land for 16 teams. Now 6 canons of Lincoln have 5 teams [there] in demesne, and 48 sokemen and 4 bordars having 11 teams, and 5 mills rendering 40 shillings, and 150 acres of meadow, and 40 acres of underwood. T. R. E. it was worth 16 pounds; now 11 pounds; tallage 40 shillings. It is 3 leagues in length and 1 in breadth.

9. In Burton [Burton by Lincoln (Lawress)] there is soke[land] of this manor, 1 carucate of land [assessed] to the geld. There is land for 1 team. 6 sokemen have 1 team there.

10. M. In Brantune [Brampton (Well)] Saint Mary of Stou had 4 carucates of land [assessed] to the geld. There is land for 4 teams. Now there are 4 teams there in demesne, and 4 villeins and 1 sokeman with 2 teams, and 40 acres of meadow, and underwood 10 furlongs in length and 4 in breadth. The whole manor is 16 furlongs in length and 9 in breadth. T. R. E. it was worth 12 pounds; now the like amount.

11. In Cheneide [Knaith (Well)] there are 12 bovates [and 2 parts of 1 bovate] [assessed] to the geld. There is land for 13 oxen. Saint Mary has 3 sokemen there with 2 teams, and 25 acres of meadow, and 26 acres of wood[land].

12. In Stou [Stow (Well)] there is soke[land] of Brantune, 1 carucate and 2 parts of 2 bovates [assessed to the geld]. There is land for as many [teams and oxen].

13. In the same place (*ibidem*) Alsi [had] 1 toft belonging to (*in*) the soke of Bishop Remigius; W. de Perci holds it.

---

[1] See 14/20; 28/4; 71/12.

[2] Cancelled.

[3] There is a cross in the margin immediately below this entry, and a space of half an inch.

*D. B., f. 344*b. *Facsimile, xvii*b.

14. [fð[1]] M. In Ingeham [Ingham (Aslacoe)] Acum had 6 bovates of land ⌊assessed⌋ to the geld. There is land for 1 team. Erchenold, the bishop's man, has 5 ploughing oxen there ⌊in demesne⌋, and 1 villein and 1 sokeman ploughing with 6 oxen, and 12 acres of meadow. T. R. E. it was worth 20 shillings; now 25 shillings; tallage 5 shillings.

15. [fð[1]] M. In Cotes [Cotes by Stow (Aslacoe)] Acum had half a carucate of land ⌊assessed⌋ to the geld. There is land for as many ⌊oxen⌋. Erchenold has 1 team there ⌊in demesne⌋. T. R. E. it was worth 20 shillings; now 30 shillings.

16. M. In Graingeham [Grayingham (Corringham)] Aldene had 1 carucate of land ⌊assessed⌋ to the geld. There is land for 1½ teams. Malger, the bishop's man, has 1 team there ⌊in demesne⌋, and 8 villeins with 1 team, and 20 acres of meadow. T. R. E. it was worth 40 shillings; now 30 shillings.

17. [fð[1]] M. In Messingeham [Messingham (Manley)] Rolf had 2 carucates and 2 bovates of land ⌊assessed⌋ to the geld. There is land for as many ⌊teams⌋. Malger has 1 team there ⌊in demesne⌋, and 1 villein, and 1 mill rendering 5 shillings, and 10 acres of meadow. T. R. E. it was worth 40 shillings; now 15 shillings; tallage 5 shillings.

18. M. In Bechebi [Bigby (Yarborough)] Aldene [Tope] had 1 carucate of land ⌊assessed⌋ to the geld. There is land for 2 teams. Ranulf, the bishop's man, has 1½ teams there ⌊in demesne⌋, and 11 villeins and 1 sokeman with 1½ teams. There is a priest there, and a church. T. R. E. it was worth 50 shillings; now 40 shillings; tallage 10 shillings.

19. M. In Eleham [Elsham (Yarborough)] Ulmar had 2 carucates and 2 bovates of land ⌊assessed⌋ to the geld. There is land for 9 teams. Gocelin (*Goislan*), the bishop's man, has 3 teams there ⌊in demesne⌋, and 10 villeins and 5 bordars and 2 sokemen having 2 teams, and 100 acres of meadow, and the site of a mill. T. R. E. it was worth 6 pounds; now 70 shillings; tallage 10 shillings.

20. [fð[1]] Two M. In Vluricebi [Worlaby (Yarborough)] Ulmar and Alden had 2½ carucates of land ⌊assessed⌋ to the geld. There is land for 5 teams. Gocelin (*Goislanus*) has 4 teams there ⌊in demesne⌋, and 10 villeins and 5 bordars with 2 teams. T. R. E. it was worth 100 shillings; ⌊now⌋ 3 pounds and 10 shillings; tallage 10 shillings.

21. M. In Vdetone [Wootton (Yarborough)] Ulmar had 2 carucates of land ⌊assessed⌋ to the geld. There is land for 4 teams. Roger, the bishop's man, has 2 teams there ⌊in demesne⌋, and 4 villeins and 6 sokemen with 1½ teams. T. R. E. it was worth 40 shillings; now the like amount; tallage 10 shillings.

22. [fð[1]] M. In Ulvesbi [Ulceby near Brigg (Yarborough)] Alden had 6 bovates of land ⌊assessed⌋ to the geld. There is land for 2 teams. Ranulf, the bishop's man, has 1 team there ⌊in demesne⌋. T. R. E. it was worth 10 shillings; now the like amount.

23. [fð[1]] M. In Golse [Goxhill (Yarborough)] Auti had 1 carucate

[1] In margin. The meaning of this word is uncertain, *Cp.* 'f' in 8/14, 18, 19, 20, etc.

of land ⌊assessed⌋ to the geld. There is land for 2 teams. Roger, the bishop's man, has 2 teams there ⌊in demesne⌋, and 8 villeins and 8 sokemen with 1 team, and 80 acres of meadow. T. R. E. it was worth 32 shillings; now 40 shillings; tallage 10 shillings.

24. [fð[1]] M. In Widun [Wyham (Ludborough)] Rolf had 2 carucates of land ⌊assessed⌋ to the geld. There is land for 3 teams. Malger has 1 team there ⌊in demesne⌋, and 1 villein and 1 bordar and 11 sokemen having 2 teams, and 4 acres of meadow, and 10 acres of underwood. T. R. E. it was worth 30 shillings; now 40 shillings; tallage 20 shillings.

25. S. In Ormesbi[2] [North Ormsby (Ludborough)] there is soke⌊land⌋ of this manor, 13 bovates of land ⌊assessed⌋ to the geld. There is land for 3 teams. 5 sokemen have 1 team there, and 8 acres of meadow, and 4 acres of underwood.

26. M. In Crochestone [Croxton (Yarborough)] Auti had 2 bovates of land ⌊assessed⌋ to the geld. It belongs to (*de*) [Grinchil's] soke. There is land for half a team. Gocelin (*Goislan*) has 1 team there ⌊in demesne⌋, and 2 villeins. T. R. E. it was worth 20 shillings; now 5 shillings.

*D. B., f. 344*c. *Facsimile, p. xviii*a.

27. M. In Chelebi [Keelby (Yarborough)] Aldene had 5 bovates and the third part of 1 bovate of land ⌊assessed⌋ to the geld. There is land for 11 oxen. Ranulf, the bishop's man, has 1 team there ⌊in demesne⌋, and 4 villeins and 1 bordar with 2 oxen, and 1 mill rendering 6 shillings and 8 pence, and 6 acres of meadow. T. R. E. it was worth 30 shillings; now the like amount; tallage 10 shillings.

28. M. In Aresbi [Owersby (Walshcroft)] Outi had 2 carucates of land ⌊assessed⌋ to the geld. There is land for 4 teams. Gocelin (*Goislanus*), the bishop's man, has 2 teams there ⌊in demesne⌋, and 3 villeins and 6 bordars and 20 sokemen with 3 teams, and 1 mill rendering 3 shillings, and 110 acres of meadow. T. R. E. it was worth 3 pounds; now 40 shillings; tallage 20 shillings.

29. [fð[1]] B. In Sudtrie [Southrey (Wraggoe)] there is inland of Vlingeham [Cherry Willingham (Lawress)], 2 bovates of land ⌊assessed⌋ to the geld. There is land for half a team. Osbern, [the bishop's clerk], has 2 villeins there with half a team.

30. M. In Dunesbi[3] [Dunsby near Bourne (Aveland)] Aldene had 5 carucates of land ⌊assessed⌋ to the geld. There is land for as many teams. Ralf, the bishop's man, has 2 teams there ⌊in demesne⌋, and 6 villeins and 6 bordars and 13 sokemen having 7 teams. There is a priest there, and a church, and 100 acres of meadow, and 100 acres of wood⌊land⌋ for pannage throughout the territory. T. R. E. it was worth 60 shillings; now 4 pounds; tallage 20 shillings.

31. S. In Hacunesbi [Haconby (Aveland)] there is soke⌊land⌋ of this manor, 4½ bovates ⌊assessed⌋ to the geld. There is land for as many ⌊oxen⌋. 5 sokemen have 1 team there, and 10 acres of meadow, and 10 acres of underwood.

---

[1] See above p. 49, note 1. [2] See 70/27. [3] See 72/45.

32. M. In Ringesdune [Ringstone (Aveland)] Aldene had 2 carucates and 2 bovates of land ⌊assessed⌋ to the geld. There is land for as many ⌊teams and oxen⌋. Adam, the bishop's man, has 1 team there ⌊in demesne⌋, and 10 villeins and 6 bordars with 2 teams. There is a priest there, and the third part of a church, and 20 acres of meadow, and 60 acres of underwood. T. R. E. ⌊it was worth⌋ 3 pounds; now 40 shillings; tallage 20 shillings.

33. B. In Dunesbi[1] [Dunsby near Bourne (Aveland)] there is inland of this manor, 1 carucate of land ⌊assessed⌋ to the geld. There is land for 1 team. 2 villeins have half a team there, and 20 acres of meadow, and 43[2] acres of wood⌊land⌋.

34. M. In Ceila [Cheal in Gosberton (Kirton)] Azor and his brothers had 2 carucates and 2 bovates of land ⌊assessed⌋ to the geld. There is land for as many ⌊teams and oxen⌋. Malger, the bishop's man, has 1 team there ⌊in demesne⌋, and 6 villeins with 2½ teams, and 8 acres of meadow, and 1 salt-pan rendering 8 pence. Its assessment (*precium*) is in Gozeberdecherca [Gosberton (Kirton in Holland)].

35. In Quadheueringe [Quadring (Kirton)] there is inland of this manor, 1 carucate of land ⌊assessed⌋ to the geld. There is land for 1 team. Malger has 8 villeins there with 1 team.

36. M. In Gozeberdecherca [Gosberton (Kirton)] Asli had 1 carucate and 6 bovates of land ⌊assessed⌋ to the geld. There is land for 1 team and 6 oxen. Malger has 1 team there [in demesne], and 12 villeins and 9 bordars with 3 teams, and 1 salt-pan rendering 4 pence, and 12 acres of meadow, and 1 sokeman on (*de*) his own enclosure (*orto*). T. R. E. it was worth 6 pounds; now 4 pounds; tallage 20 shillings.

37. In Quadheueringe [Quadring (Kirton)] there is [inland], 1½ carucates ⌊assessed⌋ to the geld.

38. M. In Carlebi [Carlby (Ness)] Bardi had 1 carucate and half a bovate of land ⌊assessed⌋ to the geld. There is land for as many ⌊teams and oxen⌋. Erchenold, [the bishop's man], has 1 team there ⌊in demesne⌋, and 10 villeins and 11 bordars with 2 teams, and 10 acres of meadow, and 40 acres of wood⌊land⌋ for pannage throughout the territory. T. R. E. it was worth 30 shillings; now 50 shillings; tallage 10 shillings.

39. M. In Corbi [Corby (Beltisloe)] Bardi had 8 carucates of land ⌊assessed⌋ to the geld. There is land for 8 teams. Walter, the bishop's man, has 2 teams there ⌊in demesne⌋, and 17 villeins[3]* and 12 bordars and 22 sokemen having 5 teams, and 1100 acres of wood⌊land⌋ for pannage. T. R. E. it was worth 7 pounds; now 7 pounds; tallage 40 shillings.

**D. B.*, *f.* 344d. *Facsimile*, *p. xviii*b.

40. In Billesfelt [Bitchfield (Beltisloe)] there is soke⌊land⌋ of this manor, 2 carucates and 2 bovates of land ⌊assessed⌋ to the geld. There is land for 3 teams. Walter, the bishop's man, has 2 teams there ⌊in demesne⌋, and 3 villeins and 8 bordars and 6 sokemen having 3 teams. There is a church there, and a priest, and 1 mill rendering 12 pence, and

---

1 See 72/45.
2 *iii* is interlined above *xl*.
3 *and 17 villeins* is repeated at the beginning of the next column.

13 acres of meadow, and 700 acres of wood⌊land⌋ for pannage throughout the territory. T. R. E. it was worth 20 shillings; now 60 shillings; now 20 shillings.[1]

41. In Suafeld [Swayfield (Beltisloe)] there is soke⌊land⌋ belonging to (*in*) Corbi [Corby (Beltisloe)], 2 carucates ⌊assessed⌋ to the geld. There is land for 2 teams. 10 sokemen have 3 teams there, and 8 acres of wood⌊land⌋.

42. In Suinham [Swinstead (Beltisloe)] there are 2 carucates ⌊assessed⌋ to the geld. There is land for 2 teams.

43. M. In Eslaforde [Old Sleaford (Aswardhurn)] Bardi had 11 carucates of land ⌊assessed⌋ to the geld. There is land for 11 teams. The bishop has 3 teams there in demesne, and 29 villeins and 6 sokemen and 11 bordars having 14 teams. There is a priest there, and a church, and 8 mills rendering 10 pounds, and 320 acres of meadow, and 1 acre of underwood, and 330 acres of marsh (*maresc*). T. R. E. it was worth 20 pounds; now 25 pounds.

44. ⌈M.⌉ In Lopintorp [Lobthorpe (Beltisloe)] there are 2 carucates ⌊assessed⌋ to the geld. There is land for 2 teams. It was worth 20 shillings.[2]

45. In Geresbi [Ewerby (Aswardhurn)] there are 13 bovates of land ⌊assessed⌋ to the geld. There is land for 10 oxen. It is soke⌊land⌋ belonging to (*in*) Eslaforde [Old Sleaford]. There are 2 sokemen there ploughing with 2 oxen, and 16 acres of meadow, and 13 acres of underwood.

46. In Welle [Howell (Aswardhurn)] there are 5 carucates and 3 bovates of land ⌊assessed⌋ to the geld. There is land for 4 teams. It is soke⌊land⌋ in like manner.[3] There are 10 sokemen and 7 bordars there having 4½ teams. There is a priest there, and a church, and 32 acres of meadow.

47. In Echintune [Heckington (Aswardhurn)] there is ⌈soke⌊land⌋⌉ ⌊of this manor⌋, 2 bovates of land ⌊assessed⌋ to the geld. There is 1 villein there having 2 oxen, and 3 acres of meadow.

48. [fð[4]]. In Corninctune[5] [Quarrington (Aswardhurn)] Bardi had 9 carucates and 2½ bovates of land ⌊assessed⌋ to the geld. There is land for 9 teams and as many oxen.[6] There are 32 sokemen and 15 bordars there with 7½ teams, and 2 mills rendering 16 shillings, and 60 acres of meadow. In this soke⌊land⌋ Osmund has 2 teams in demesne, and it is worth 60 shillings. Also in this soke⌊land⌋ Hugh Rufus has 1 carucate of land and 1 team in demesne, and it is worth 25 shillings.

49. In Leduluetorp [Laythorpe, now included in Kirkby Laythorpe (Aswardhurn)] there is ⌈soke⌊land⌋⌉ ⌊of this manor⌋, 2 carucates of land ⌊assessed⌋ to the geld, and there is land ⌈for⌉ 11 oxen. There are 5 sokemen and 2 bordars there with 2 teams.

50. In Evedune [Evedon (Aswardhurn)] there are 4 carucates and

[1] See note to no. 44.

[2] This entry has been inserted as a continuation of the last line of no. 43. No figure is given for the present value; but it may be conjectured that the unaccountable words 'now 20 shillings' at the end of no. 40 may properly belong to this entry.

[3] *I.e.*, belonging to Eslaforde.

[4] See above p. 49, note 1.

[5] See 72/33.

[6] *I.e.*, 2½ oxen.

3 bovates of land [assessed] to the geld. There is land for 4 teams. The bishop has 13 sokemen there with 5 teams, and 20 acres of meadow, and 100 acres of marsh (*maresc*), and 16 acres of underwood. Of this soke[land] Osmund has 11 bovates of land, and 1½ teams in demesne. It is worth 30 shillings.

51. In Canvic [Canwick (Langoe)] Welraven had [soke[land]], 2 carucates and 1½ bovates of land [assessed] to the geld. There is land for 2 teams and 1½ oxen. William, the bishop's man, has 1 team there [in demesne], and 3 villeins and 3 bordars with 1 team, and 55 acres of meadow. T. R. E. it was worth 60 shillings; now 20 shillings.

52. M. In Lessingham [Leasingham (Flaxwell)] Barne had 6 carucates of land [assessed] to the geld. There is land for 6 teams. Adam, the bishop's man, has 2 teams there [in demesne], and 16 villeins* and 1 sokeman and 4 bordars having 4 teams, and 30 acres of meadow. T. R. E. it was worth 6 pounds; now 100 shillings.

**D. B., f. 345a. Facsimile, p. xixa.*

53. M. In Wilgebi [Silk Willoughby (Aswardhurn)] Archel had 1 carucate of land [assessed] to the geld. There is land for 2 teams. Ralf, the bishop's man, has 2 teams there [in demesne], and 5 villeins and 2 sokemen having 2 teams, and 30 acres of meadow. T. R. E. it was worth 30 shillings; now 50 shillings.

54. [fδ[1]] M. In Hacam [Hougham (Loveden)] Tori had 14 carucates of land [assessed] to the geld. There is land for 9½ teams. Hugh, the bishop's man, has 2 teams there [in demesne], and 21 villeins and 4 sokemen and 1 bordar have 9 teams. There is a church there, and a priest, and 2 mills rendering 13 shillings and 4 pence, and 40[2] acres of meadow. T. R. E. it was worth 4 pounds; now 7 pounds.

55. In this vill Robert the priest had 1 carucate of land of the king in alms, and now with the same land he has been made [a monk] in Stou St. Mary's [Stow (Well)]; but it is not lawful[3] for anyone to have the land except by grant of the king. T. R. E. it was worth 10 shillings; now the like amount.

56. M. In Ludes [Louth (Louthesk)] the Bishop of Lincoln had 12 carucates of land [assessed] to the geld. There is land for 12 teams. Now the bishop has 3 teams there in demesne, and 80 burgesses, and 1 market rendering 29 shillings, and 40 sokemen and 2 villeins. Amongst them all they have 13 teams, and 13 mills rendering 60 shillings. 2 knights (*milites*) have 2 teams there, and 21 acres of meadow, and 400 acres of wood[land] for pannage throughout the territory. [It is] 1 league and 8 furlongs in length and 10 furlongs in breadth. T. R. E. it was worth 12 pounds; now 22 pounds; tallage 3 pounds.

57. M. In Reburne [Redbourne (Manley)] Archil had 1 carucate of land [assessed] to the geld. There is land for 2 teams. Now Bishop Remigius and the canons of Saint Mary have 2 villeins ploughing with 3 oxen, and 24 acres of meadow. T. R. E. it was worth 20 shillings; now 10 shillings.

58. In Chenebi [Kingerby (Walshcroft)] Gocelin (*Goislan*) holds of

---

[1] See above p. 49, note 1.
[2] *et xl* has been corrected from *T.R.*, which the scribe had written in error.
[3] *licet* has been written on an erasure.

the bishop 2 carucates of land [assessed] to the geld. There is land for 6 teams. Outi held it T. R. E. There are 2 teams there [in demesne], a priest, and a church, and 20 villeins and 5 bordars with 5 teams, and a mill rendering 4 shillings, and 400 acres of meadow. It was worth and is worth 4 pounds.

59. In Gullingham [Cherry Willingham (Lawress)] there are 10 bovates of land [assessed] to the geld There is land for 10 oxen. There are 8 villeins and 1 sokeman there with 1½ teams, and 20 acres of meadow. Formerly it was worth 20 shillings ; now 30 shillings.

D. B., f. 345c. *Facsimile, p. xx*a.

8. LAND OF SAINT PETER OF BURG [PETERBOROUGH]

1. M. In Fiscartune [Fiskerton (Lawress)] there are 3 carucates of land [assessed] to the geld. There is land for 3 teams. This manor was and is Saint Peter of Burg's. There are 3 teams there in demesne, and 18 villeins and 3 bordars having 4 teams. There is a church there, and a priest, and 3½ fisheries rendering 21 pence, and 120 acres of meadow. There is wood[land] for pannage 10 furlongs in length and 9 in breadth. The whole is 20 furlongs in length and 9 in breadth. T. R. E. it was worth 14 pounds ; now 17 pounds ; tallage 3 pounds.

2. In Scoltorne and Holme and Sutbroc [Scothorne and Holme and Sudbrooke (Lawress)] there is soke[land] of this manor, 5½ carucates of land [assessed] to the geld. There is land for 6 teams. Saint Peter has 32 sokemen there having 8 teams.

3. In Refaim[1] [Reepham (Lawress)] there is inland of this manor, 4 carucates [and 6 bovates] of land [assessed] to the geld. There is land for 4 teams [and 6 oxen]. 12 villeins and 2 bordars have 4 teams there, and 60 acres of meadow. There is underwood 8 furlongs in length and 4 in breadth.

4. M. In Turolvebi [Thurlby (Ness)] Saint Peter of Burg had and has 3 carucates and 5 bovates of land[2] [assessed] to the geld. There is land for as many teams and oxen. There is 1 team there in demesne, and 10 villeins and 2 sokemen have 1½ teams. Of this land 2 of the abbot's men have 2 carucates, and there are 1½ teams there [in demesne], and 7 villeins and 2 sokemen with 1 team. There are 20 acres of meadow there, and 80 acres of woodland for pannage throughout the territory. T. R. E. it was worth 60 shillings ; now the like amount ; tallage 10 shillings.

---

[1] See 43/5 ; 71/8.
[2] The first letter of *terre* has been corrected from the sign for *et*, which the scribe had written in error.

5. M. In Adewelle [Bowthorpe[1] in Manthorpe (Beltisloe)] Saint Peter of Burg had and has 5 carucates of land ⌊assessed⌋ to the geld. There is land for 5 teams. Now there are 2 teams there in demesne, and 10 villeins and 2 bordars and 2 sokemen having 3½ teams, and 18 acres of meadow. There are 180 acres of wood⌊land⌋ for pannage, and 60 acres of underwood. T. R. E. it was worth 60 shillings ; now the like amount ; tallage 12 shillings.

6. In Witham and Mannetor and Toftlund[2] [Witham on the Hill and Manthorpe and Toft with Lound (Beltisloe)] there is a berewic ⌊of this manor⌋, half a carucate of land ⌊assessed⌋ to the geld. There is land for 4 oxen. 2 villeins have half a team there, and 8 acres of meadow, and 40 acres of underwood. T. R. E. it was worth 5 shillings and 4 pence ; now the like amount. Ansfrid holds it.

7. In Bintham[3] [Bytham (Beltisloe)] there is a berewic of Bergestorp [Bowthorpe in Manthorpe (Beltisloe)] 4 carucates of land ⌊assessed⌋ to the geld. There is land for 4 teams. This land is demesne ⌊land⌋ of Saint Peter of Burg. Now 6 villeins have 2 teams and 2 oxen there. There, Saswalo, the abbot's man, has of this land 2 carucates of land and half a team in demesne, and 3 villeins with 1 team, and 25 acres of meadow, and 100 acres of underwood. T. R. E. this soke⌊land⌋ was worth 30 shillings ; now 20 shillings.

8. M. In Osgotebi [Osgodby in Lavington (Beltisloe)] Saint Peter of Burg had and has 5 carucates of land ⌊assessed⌋ to the geld. There is land for 5 teams. Now Anschitill, the abbot's man, has 2 teams there ⌊in demesne⌋, and 13 villeins with 4 teams, and 14 acres of meadow. Of wood⌊land⌋ for pannage there is 13 furlongs in length and 4 in breadth. T. R. E. it was worth* 60 shillings ; now 100 shillings ; tallage 20 shillings. The arable land is 14 furlongs in length and 6 in breadth. Two carucates of this manor belong to (*iacent in*) Lavintone [Lavington] hundred.

**D. B., f.* 345d. *Facsimile, p. xx*b.

9. M. In Walecote [Walcot near Folkingham (Aveland)] Saint Peter of Burg had and has 5 carucates of land ⌊assessed⌋ to the geld. There is land for 6 teams. Now Gilbert, the abbot's man, has 1 team there ⌊in demesne⌋, and 6 villeins and 5 bordars with 2 teams, and a church, and 14 sokemen on (*de*) 2 carucates, having 4 teams. One moiety of the soke belongs to Saint Peter, and the other belongs to Gilbert de Gant in Folchingeham [Folkingham]. There are 30 acres of meadow there. T. R. E. it was worth 8 pounds ; now 4 pounds.

10.[4] In Hedebi[5] [Haythby in West Halton (Manley)] there is soke⌊land⌋ of Walecote [Walcot on Trent (Manley)], 2 bovates of land ⌊assessed⌋ to the geld. There is land for 1½ oxen. 1 sokeman ploughs there with 2 oxen. Ivo holds it.

11. M. In Duninctune [Donington (Kirton)] Saint Peter of Burg had and has 3 carucates of land ⌊assessed⌋ to the geld. There is land

---

1 See Stapleton, *Chronicon Petroburgense*, 178*n*, 179.

2 See 24/32 ; 30/32 ; 72/6.

3 See 72/7.

4 No. 10 follows no. 11 in the text, but a sign indicates that it is to precede it. Its proper place, however, is no. 30, where it is repeated. The scribe was evidently misled by the occurrence of the two Walcots in nos. 9 and 28.

5 Altered from *Hodebi*. *See* no. 30 below.

for 3 teams. Now there is 1 team there in demesne, and[1] 12 villeins and 20 bordars with 2 teams, and 16 salt-pans rendering 20 shillings, and 12 acres of meadow. T. R. E. it was worth 60 shillings; now the like amount.

12. In Hoctune [Houghton in Grantham (Winnibriggs)] Saint Peter of Burg has half a carucate of land [assessed] to the geld, with sake and soke. 3 villeins have 1 team there. Colegrim holds it.

13. M. In Risun[2] [Riseholme (Lawress)] Elnod had 4 bovates of land [assessed] to the geld. There is land for half a team. Now Colsuan has it of Abbot T[horald], and he [Colsuan], [has] 2 bordars there. T. R. E. it was worth half a mark of silver; and now the like amount.

14. [f'[3]] M. In Iolestorp [Yawthorpe (Corringham)] Rolft had half a carucate of land [assessed] to the geld. There is land for 4 oxen. Abbot T[horald] has 1 team there [in demesne], and 3 acres of meadow. T. R. E. it was worth 12 shillings; now 5 shillings.

15. M. In Scotone[4] [Scotton (Corringham)] Aschil had 6 carucates of land [assessed] to the geld. There is land for 6 teams. Richard,[5] the abbot's man, has there under the abbot 3 teams [in demesne], and 22 villeins and 5 bordars and 17 sokemen having 2 teams. In Lincoln (*Lincolia*) there are 3 burgesses rendering 5 shillings, and 50 acres of meadow, and 36 acres of underwood. T. R. E. it was worth 100 shillings; now 4 pounds; tallage 40 shillings.

16. In Torp[6] [Northorpe (Corringham)] there is soke[land] of this manor, 1 carucate of land [assessed] to the geld. There is land for 1½ teams. 4 sokemen have 2 villeins and 1 bordar there with 1 team.

17. Two M. In Scotere[4] [Scotter (Corringham)] Alnod and Aschil had 8 carucates of land [assessed] to the geld. There is land for 12 teams. Now Abbot Thorald has 4 teams there [in demesne], and 32 villeins and 13 bordars with 4 teams, and 15 sokemen with 3 teams, and 1 mill, and a moiety of 2 [mills], rendering 8 shillings, and 2 fisheries rendering 15 shillings, and 120 acres of meadow, and 28 acres of wood[land] for pannage. T. R. E. it was worth 11 pounds; now 10 pounds. It is 3 leagues in length and 1 in breadth.

18. [f'[3]]. In Scaltorp [Scotterthorp (Corringham)] there is soke[land] of this manor, 3 carucates of land [assessed] to the geld. There is land for 2 teams. 8 sokemen and 4 villeins have 4 teams there,* and 30 acres of meadow.

*D. B., f. 346a. *Facsimile, p. xxia.*

19. [f'[3]] M. In Cletham [Cleatham (Corringham)] Ælnod had 7 bovates of land [assessed] to the geld. There is land for 1½ teams. Roger, the abbot's man, has 1 team there [in demesne], and 4 villeins ploughing with 5 oxen, and 7 acres of meadow. T. R. E. it was worth 40 shillings; now 30 shillings.

---

[1] The scribe first wrote *x*, and then altered it into the sign for *and*.

[2] See 26/2; 71/2.

[3] The meaning of this letter, which is written in the margin, is uncertain. *See* Index of Subjects, *s.v.* F'. Cp. 7/14 and note.

[4] See 71/15.

[5] Rectius *Ralf* (cp. 71/13).

[6] See 71/13.

20. [f'[1]] M. In Mameltune[2] [Manton (Manley)] Rolft had 2 carucates of land ⌊assessed⌋ to the geld. There is land for 4 teams. Ralf, the abbot's man, has 1 team there ⌊in demesne⌋, and 5 villeins and 4 bordars with 1 team, and 20 acres of meadow. T. R. E. it was worth 12 pounds; now 60 shillings; tallage 20 shillings. It is 2 leagues in length and 1 in breadth.

21. In Cletham [Cleatham (Corringham)] there is soke⌊land⌋ of this manor, 1 bovate of land ⌊assessed⌋ to the geld. There is 1 sokeman there ploughing with 1 ox.

22. M. In Hiboldestou [Hibaldstow (Manley)] Rolft had 10 bovates of land ⌊assessed⌋ to the geld. There is land for 3 teams. Gilbert, the abbot's man, has 2 teams there ⌊in demesne⌋, and 11 villeins and 1 sokeman and 3 bordars having 2½ teams, and 1 mill rendering 4 shillings, and 111 acres of meadow, and 60 acres of underwood. T. R. E. it was worth 6 pounds; now 70 shillings; tallage 20 shillings.

23. [f'[1]] M. In Rageneltorp[2] [Raventhorpe (Manley)] Aschil had 2 carucates of land ⌊assessed⌋ to the geld. There is land for 4 teams. Ralf, the abbot's man, has 1 team there ⌊in demesne⌋, and 5 villeins and 4 bordars with 1 team, and 12 acres of meadow. T. R. E. it was worth 6 pounds; now 30 shillings; tallage 10 shillings.

24.[3] In Cletham [Cleatham (Corringham)] there are 2 bovates ⌊assessed⌋ to the geld.

25. [f'[1]]. In Holm [Holme in Bottesford (Manley)] there is soke⌊land⌋ of this manor, 3 carucates of land ⌊assessed⌋ to the geld. There is land for 3 teams. 6 sokemen have 2 teams there, and 1 mill rendering 4 shillings, and 12 acres of underwood.

26. In Aschebi [Ashby in Bottesford (Manley)] there is other soke⌊land⌋ ⌊of this manor⌋, 3 bovates of land ⌊assessed⌋ to the geld. There is land for 3 oxen. 1 sokeman has 1 team there, and 3 acres of underwood.

27. [f'[1]] M. In Aplebi and Risebi and Saleclif [Appleby and Risby and Sawcliff (Manley)] Aschil had 3 bovates of land ⌊assessed⌋ to the geld. There is land for 6 oxen. Ralf, the abbot's man, has 1 team there ⌊in demesne⌋, and 12 acres of meadow. T. R. E. it was worth 20 shillings; now 16 shillings.

28. [f'[1]] M. In Walecote [Walcot in Alkborough (Manley)] Aschil had 6 carucates and 5 bovates of land ⌊assessed⌋ to the geld. There is land for as many teams and oxen. Now Ivo has it of the abbot. There is 1 team there ⌊in demesne⌋, and 7 villeins and 2 bordars and 10 sokemen with 2 teams, and 380 acres of meadow, and 60 acres of underwood. T. R. E. it was worth 6 pounds; now 40 shillings; tallage 10 shillings.

29. [f'[1]]. In Alchebarge [Alkborough (Manley)] there is a berewic of this manor, 1 carucate of land ⌊assessed⌋ to the geld. There is land for 1½ teams. 3 villeins plough there with 3 oxen.

30. In Hedebi[4] [Haythby in West Halton (Manley)] there is soke⌊land⌋ ⌊of this manor⌋, 2 bovates of land ⌊assessed⌋ to the geld. There is land for 1½ oxen. 1 sokeman ploughs there with 2 oxen.

---

[1] See above p. 56, note 3.

[2] See 71/15.

[3] This entry is inserted at the end of no. 23.

[4] See no. 10 above, and note.

31. M. In Messingeham [Messingham (Manley)] Elnod had 5 carucates of land [assessed] to the geld. There is land for 5 teams and 2 oxen. William, the abbot's man, has 2 teams there [in demesne], and 5 villeins and 4 bordars and 18 sokemen having 3 teams, and 20 acres of meadow. T. R. E. it was worth 4 pounds ; now the like amount ; tallage 20 shillings.

32. In Escumetorp [Scunthorpe (Manley)] there is a berewic of this manor, 1 bovate and a third part of 1 bovate of land [assessed] to the geld. There is land for 1 ox. 1 villein has 2 oxen there in a team.

*D. B., f. 346*b. *Facsimile, p. xxi*b.

33. In Offintone[1] [Uffington (Ness)] Saint Peter of Burg has 48 acres of meadow exempt from geld. Geoffrey and [also] the abbot's villeins hold these [acres] (*Hos tenet Goisfrid' . et uill' abbatis*). T. R. E. it was worth 90 shillings ; now the like amount.

34. M. In Witham and Mannetorp and Toftlund [Witham on the Hill and Manthorpe and Toft with Lound (Beltisloe)] Hereward had 12 bovates of land [assessed] to the geld. There is land for 1½ teams. Asfort (*Asuert*), Abbot Thorald's man, has 6 villeins and 4 bordars and 2 sokemen there with 2 teams, and 20 acres of meadow, and 40 acres of wood[land]. T. R. E. it was worth 40 shillings ; now the like amount.

35. In Bercaham[2] and Estou [Barholme and Stowe (Ness)] there is a berewic of this manor, 1 carucate of land [assessed] to the geld. There is land for 1 team. Asford has 2 villeins and 2 bordars there with 1 team.

36. In the same place there is 1 carucate of land [assessed] to the geld. There is land for 1 team. It is soke[land] belonging to (*in*) Burg [Peterborough]. Now Godfrey, the abbot's man, has 9 sokemen and 1 villein and 2 bordars with 2 teams. Robert holds half. T. R. E. it was worth 20 shillings ; now likewise 20 [shillings].

37. In Estou [Stowe (Ness)] there is soke[land] belonging to (*in*) Witham, 4½ bovates of land [assessed] to the geld. There is land for as many [oxen]. Asfort has of the abbot 1 villein and 2 sokemen there with half a team.

38. In the same place there are 2 bovates of land [assessed] to the geld. There is land for 2 oxen. It is soke[land] belonging to Saint Peter's fabric (*Soca in werche Sancti Petri de Burg*). Godfrey has there under (*de*) the abbot 1 villein and 2 sokemen with half a team. T. R. E. it was worth 3 shillings ; now the like amount.

39. In Turolvebi[3] [Thurlby (Ness)] Elnod had 1½ carucates [assessed] to the geld. There is land for 1½ teams. It is *frigsoca* under Aslac. Geoffrey (*Goisfridus* has there under the abbot 1 team and 1 villein and 4 bordars, and 30 acres of underwood. T. R. E. it was worth 20 shillings ; now likewise 20 shillings.

---

[1] See 56/4 ; 72/2. [2] See 72/4. [3] Altered from *Turoldebi*.

9. LAND OF SAINT PETER OF WESTMINSTER

1. M. In Dodinctone[1] [Doddington Pigot (Graffoe)] Ailric had 6 carucates of land ⌊assessed⌋ to the geld. There is land for 4 teams. Saint Peter of Westminster has 1 team there ⌊in demesne⌋, and 14 villeins and 6 bordars with 4 teams. There is a priest there, and a church. There is meadow half a league in length and half in breadth. There is wood⌊land⌋ for pannage 1½ leagues in length and half a league in breadth. T. R. E., with all things to this manor belonging, it was worth 20 pounds; now what Saint Peter has is worth 4 pounds.

2. B. In Torp [Thorpe on the Hill (Graffoe)] there are 6 carucates and 2 bovates of land ⌊assessed⌋ to the geld. There is land for 6 teams. It is soke⌊land⌋ of the same manor. 30 sokemen have 7½ teams there. The meadow is 2 furlongs in length and 2 in breadth.

D. B., f. 346c. *Facsimile, p. xxiia.*

10. LAND OF SAINT BENEDICT OF RAMSEY (*Ramesig*)

1. M. In Cornincturne[2] [Quarrington (Aswardhurn)] Saint Benedict of Ramesy had and has 1 carucate and 6 bovates of land ⌊assessed⌋ to the geld. There is land for as many teams and oxen. Now there is 1 team there ⌊in demesne⌋, and 3 villeins and 1 bordar and 1 sokeman with 1 team. There are 2 churches there, and 1 mill rendering 21 shillings and 4 pence, and 14 acres of meadow. T. R. E. it was worth 40 shillings; now 4 pounds.

2. In Eslaforde [Old Sleaford (Aswardhurn)] there is soke⌊land⌋ of this manor, 1 carucate of land ⌊assessed⌋ [to the geld]. There is land for 1 team. 1 sokeman and 2 villeins have 1 team there, and 27 acres of meadow.

3. In Dunnesbi [Dunsby St. Andrew in Brauncewell (Flaxwell)] there is other soke⌊land⌋ ⌊of this manor⌋, 6 carucates of land ⌊assessed⌋ to the geld. There is land for as many teams. Now 11 sokemen and 3 bordars have 3 teams there, and 6 acres of meadow.

4. M. In Trichingham [Threckingham (Aveland)] Saint Benedict of Ramesy had and has half a carucate of land ⌊assessed⌋ to the geld. There is land for 4 oxen. 1 villein has half a team there. T. R. E. it was worth 5 shillings; now the like amount.

5. In Coteland [Coteland in Anwick (Flaxwell)] Saint Benedict has half a carucate of meadow ⌊assessed⌋ to the geld in Cranewelle [Cranwell (Flaxwell)].

---

[1] See 65/5; 72/27.

[2] See 72/32.

*D. B., f. 346*d. *Facsimile, p. xxii*b.

11. LAND OF SAINT GUTHLAC OF CROYLAND (*Cruiland*)

1. M. In Holeben and Copelade [Holbeach and Whaplode (Elloe)] Saint Guthlac had and has 1 carucate of land [assessed] to the geld. There is land for 6 oxen. Now there is 1 team there in demesne, and 3 villeins with half a team, and 12 acres of meadow. T. R. E. it was worth 20 shillings; now the like amount.

2. In Spallinge [Spalding (Elloe)] there is a berewic of Croiland, 2 carucates of land [assessed] to the geld. There is land for 1½ teams. 7 villeins and 4 bordars have 3 teams there. T. R. E. it was worth 20 shillings; now the like amount.

3. M. In Langetof [Langtoft (Ness)] Saint Guthlac had and has 6 carucates of land [assessed] to the geld. There is land for 6 teams. Now there is 1 team there in demesne, and 8 villeins and 4 bordars and 20 sokemen having 5 teams, and 100 acres of meadow. There is wood-[land] rendering 2 shillings. There is marsh (*maresc*) 2 leagues in length and 2 in breadth. There is arable land 15 furlongs in length and 9 in breadth. T. R. E. it was worth 4 pounds; now 60 shillings; tallage 10 shillings.

4. M. In Bastune [Baston (Ness)] Saint Guthlac had and has 4 carucates of land [assessed] to the geld. There is land for 4 teams. Now there is 1 team there in demesne, and 5 villeins and 2 bordars and 7 sokemen with 2 teams. There is a church there, and half a mill, and 45 acres of meadow. There is marsh (*maresc*) 16 furlongs in length and 8 in breadth. There is arable land 8 furlongs in length and 8 in breadth. T. R. E. it was worth 40 shillings; now the like amount.

5. M. In Duuedic [Dowdyke in Sutterton (Kirton)] Saint Guthlac had and has 2 carucates of land [assessed] to the geld. There is land for 2 teams with sake and soke. Now there is 1 team there in demesne, and 13 villeins with 1 team, and 20 acres of meadow. T. R. E. it was worth 40 shillings; now the like amount. Colegrim holds it.

6. In Draitone [Drayton in Swineshead (Kirton)] there is a berewic of this manor, 1 carucate of land [assessed] to the geld. There is land for 1 team. 5 villeins there do not plough. There are 4 salt-pans rendering 5 shillings and 4 pence, and 6 acres of meadow.

7. In Alfgare [Algarkirk (Kirton)] there is another berewic [of this manor] 12 bovates of land [assessed] to the geld. There is land for 10 oxen. Now it is waste. Colegrim holds it of the abbot.

8. In Burtoft [Burtoft in Wigtoft (Kirton)] Saint Guthlac had and has 1 bovate of land which belongs to (*iacet in*) Duuedic. The king has the soke thereof.

9. M. In Buchehale [Bucknall (Gartree)] Gamel had 10 bovates of land [assessed] to the geld. There is land for 10 oxen. In the

same place (*ibidem*) there is soke⌊land⌋ belonging to (*de*) Badesford [Belchford (Gartree)], 10 bovates of land ⌊assessed⌋ to the geld. There is land for 10 oxen. Now Saint Guthlac has 1 team there in demesne, and 5 villeins and 2 bordars and 8 sokemen having 1 team. There are 120 acres of meadow there, and 50 acres of wood⌊land⌋ for pannage, and 70 acres of underwood. T. R. E. it was worth 30 shillings; now the like amount. Thorald [the sheriff] gave this land to Saint Guthlac for his soul.

D. B., f. 347a. *Facsimile, p. xxiii*a.

12. LAND OF COUNT ALAN

1. Two M. In Bortone[1] [Gate Burton (Well)] Gonnewate and Godric had 4 carucates and 6 bovates of land ⌊assessed⌋ to the geld. There is land for 5 teams. Now Count Alan has 1 team there ⌊in demesne⌋, and 10 sokemen having 3 teams, and 40 acres of meadow, and 70 acres of brushwood (*broce*). T. R. E. it was worth 3 pounds; now 30 shillings; tallage 10 shillings.

2. In Martone [Marton (Well)] there is soke⌊land⌋ of this manor, 6 bovates of land ⌊assessed⌋ to the geld. There is land for 1 team. It is waste.

3. M. In Welingeham [Willingham by Stow (Well)] Staigrim had 12 bovates of land ⌊assessed⌋ to the geld. There is land for 12 oxen.
M. In the same place (*ibidem*) Gunnewate had 6 bovates and the third part of 2 bovates of land ⌊assessed⌋ to the geld. There is land for as many oxen. Count Alan has 1 team there in demesne, and 5 villeins and 2 sokemen with 1 team. T. R. E. it was worth 40 shillings; now 20 shillings.

4. Four M. In Lea [Lea (Corringham)] Fulcheri and his two brothers had $3\frac{1}{2}$ carucates of land ⌊assessed⌋ to the geld. In the same place (*ibidem*) Ulchil had half a carucate of land ⌊assessed⌋ to the geld. There is land for 5 teams. Now Robert, the count's man, has 1 team there ⌊in demesne⌋, and 16 villeins and 2 sokemen with 3 teams, and half a fishery rendering 10 pence, and 1 ferry (*passagium*) rendering 12 pence, and 100 [and 15] acres of meadow, and 100 acres of underwood. T. R. E. it was worth 100 shillings; now 30 shillings; tallage 20 shillings.

5. In Iopeham [Heapham (Corringham)] there is a berewic of this manor and soke⌊land⌋, 4 bovates of land ⌊assessed⌋ to the geld. There is land for half a team. Now 4 sokemen plough there with 2 oxen. There are there 20 acres of meadow.

6. In Sumerdebi [Somerby (Corringham)] there is other soke⌊land⌋ ⌊of this manor⌋, half a carucate of land ⌊assessed⌋ to the geld. There is land for 4 oxen. 2 sokemen plough there with 3 oxen. There are 10 acres of meadow there, and 10 acres of underwood.

[1] See 71/10.

7. Six M. In Cheluingeholm [Killingholme (Yarborough)] Radolf, Welgrim, Aschil, Archel, Sagrim, and Ernuin [the priest] had 2½ carucates of land [assessed] to the geld. There is land for 6 teams. Now Landric, the count's man, has 2 teams there [in demesne], and 11 villeins with 1 team, and 100 acres of meadow. T. R. E. it was worth 4 pounds; now 30 shillings; tallage 10 shillings.

8. M. In Chernitone [Kirmington (Yarborough)] Aschilbar had 4 bovates of land [assessed] to the geld. There is land for 1½ teams. Now there is 1 team there in demesne, and 1 villein and 4 sokemen with 1 team. T. R. E. it was worth 40 shillings; now 20 shillings.

9. M. In Nortchelesei [North Kelsey (Yarborough)] Grimbold Crac had 1 carucate of land [assessed] to the geld. There is land for 2 teams. Now there is 1 villein there with 6 oxen, and 1 mill rendering 7 shillings. T. R. E. it was worth 20 shillings; now the like amount.

10. In Seurebi[1] [Searby (Yarborough)] there is a berewic of this manor, 3 bovates of land [assessed] to the geld. There is land for 6 oxen. 1 villein ploughs there with 3 oxen.

11. In Catenase and Usun [Cadney and Housham (Yarborough)] there is another berewic, 5 bovates and a third part of 1 bovate of land [assessed] to the geld,* and as much [land] for ploughing. 5 villeins have 2 teams there, and 100 acres of meadow. It is worth (*val'*) 40 shillings.

**D. B., f.* 347b. *Facsimile, p. xxiii*b.

12. In Odenebi [Owmby in Searby (Yarborough)] there is another berewic, 3 bovates of land [assessed] to the geld. 1 villein ploughs there with 3 oxen. There are 8 acres of meadow there.

13. M. In Catenase and Usun [Cadney and Housham (Yarborough)] Grimbold Crac had 5 bovates and a third part of a bovate of land [assessed] to the geld. There is land for as many oxen. 6 [men] together with the lord have 3½ teams. T. R. E. it was worth 60 shillings; now 40 shillings.

14. M. In Alesbi [Aylesby (Bradley)] Orm had 2 carucates of land and 6 bovates and 2 parts of 1 bovate [assessed] to the geld. There is land for 5 teams. Now Picot, the count's man, has 2 teams there [in demesne], and 6 villeins and 3 bordars and 20 sokemen having 2 teams and 2 oxen. There is a church there, and a priest, and 1½ mills rendering 9 shillings. T. R. E. it was worth 5 pounds; now 4 pounds; tallage 20 shillings.

15. In Sualun [Swallow (Bradley)] there is soke[land] of this manor, 3 bovates of land [assessed] to the geld. There is land for 6 oxen. Now there is 1 bordar there.

16. In Cotes [Great Cotes (Bradley)] there is other soke[land] [of this manor], 1 bovate of land [assessed] to the geld. It is waste.

17. M. In Sualun [Swallow (Bradley)] Sbern had 1½ carucates [assessed] to the geld. There is land for 3 teams. Picot has half a team there [in demesne], and 5 villeins and 1 bordar and 9 sokemen with 1½ teams. T. R. E. it was worth 20 shillings; now 60 shillings; tallage 20 shillings.

---

[1] See 70/7.

18. M. In Holtun [Holton le Clay (Bradley)] Turgot had 2 bovates and 5 acres [and 2 virgates] of land ⌊assessed⌋ to the geld. Wimund, the count's man, has 2 villeins there ploughing with 5 oxen, and 5 acres of meadow. T. R. E. it was worth 3 shillings; now 8 shillings.

19. Two M. In Fugelestou[1] [Fulstow (Haverstoe)] Rolf and Sbern had 2 carucates and 2 bovates of land ⌊assessed⌋ to the geld. There is land for 3½ teams. Picot has of (*de*) the count 2 teams there ⌊in demesne⌋, and 14 villeins and 7 bordars and 2 sokemen with 2 teams, and 8 salt-pans rendering 8 shillings, and 260 acres of meadow. T. R. E. it was worth 40 shillings; now 4 pounds; tallage 20 shillings.

20. Three M. In Grenesbi [Grainsby (Haverstoe)] Spille, Adestan, and Lepsi had 3 carucates of land ⌊assessed⌋ to the geld. There is land for 5 teams. Wimund, the count's man, has 1½ teams there ⌊in demesne⌋, and 12 villeins and 4 bordars and 13 sokemen having 3½ teams, and 51 acres of meadow and turf-land (*toruelande*) rendering 5 shillings and 4d. T. R. E. it was worth 70 shillings; now 4 pounds; tallage 20 shillings.

21. M. In Waltham [Waltham (Haverstoe)] Ralf the Staller (*Stalre*) had 6 carucates of land ⌊assessed⌋ to the geld. There is land for 12 teams. Now Count Alan has 4 teams there ⌊in demesne⌋, and 12 villeins and 1 bordar and 18 sokemen having 9½ teams. There is a church there, and a priest, and 68 acres of meadow. T. R. E. it was worth 20 pounds; now 45 pounds; tallage 15 pounds. The whole ⌊manor⌋ is 15 furlongs in length and 9 in breadth.

22. In Wade [Waith (Haverstoe)] there is soke⌊land⌋ of this manor, 11 bovates of land ⌊assessed⌋ to the geld. There is land for 11 oxen. 12 sokemen have 1½ teams there, and 20 acres of meadow.

23. In Aschebi [Ashby by Fenby (Haverstoe)] there is other soke⌊land⌋ ⌊of this manor⌋, 6 bovates of land ⌊assessed⌋ to the geld. There is land for 12 teams. 5 sokemen have 1 team there, and 25 acres of meadow, and 5 acres of underwood.

24. In Bernulfbi [Barnoldby le Beck (Haverstoe)] there is soke⌊land⌋ ⌊of this manor⌋, 6 carucates of land ⌊assessed⌋ to the geld. There is land for 12 teams.* There are 26 sokemen and 9 bordars there having 9½ teams, and 200 acres of meadow.

**D. B., f. 347c.* *Facsimile, p. xxiva.*

25. S. In Fendebi [Fenby (Haverstoe)] there is soke⌊land⌋ ⌊of this manor⌋, 3 carucates of land ⌊assessed⌋ to the geld. There is land for 6 teams. There are 15 sokemen and 2 bordars there having 3½ teams, and 20 acres of meadow.

26. S. In Ravenedal and the other Ravenedale [East and West Ravendale (Haverstoe)] there is soke⌊land⌋ ⌊of this manor⌋, 3 carucates of land ⌊assessed⌋ to the geld. There is land for 6 teams. 14 sokemen have 2 teams there.

27. S. In Cadebi [North Cadeby (Haverstoe[2])] there is soke⌊land⌋ ⌊of this manor⌋, 3 carucates of land ⌊assessed⌋ to the geld. There is land for 4 teams. 14 sokemen have 3 teams there.

---

[1] See 3/6; 38/14; 70/21-22.

[2] North Cadeby is now in Ludborough wapentake.

28. S. In Besebi [Beesby near Hawerby (Haverstoe)] there is soke[land] [of this manor], 3 carucates of land [assessed] to the geld. There is land for 4 teams. Count Alan has 1 team there [in demesne], and 1 sokeman, and 16 acres of meadow, and 6 acres of underwood.

29. M. In [the same] Basebi [Beesby] Ingemund and Oune, Edric, and Eculf had 3 carucates and 3 bovates and 3 parts of 1 bovate and also a third part of 1 bovate of land [assessed to the geld]. There is land for 4 teams. Now the count has 1 sokeman and 8 villeins there with 1½ teams, and 16 acres of meadow, and 6 acres of underwood. T. R. E. [it was worth] 20 shillings; now 30 shillings. William Blund had Eculf's land [5½ bovates] on that day on which Ernuin the priest was taken (*captus*), and before.

30. S. In Neutone[1] [Newton le Wold (Haverstoe)] there is soke[land] [of this manor], 3 carucates and half a bovate of land [assessed] to the geld. There is land for 5 teams. 20 sokemen and 2 bordars have 4 teams there.

31. Four M. In the same Neutone[2] Ingemund and his three brothers had 3 bovates of land [assessed] to the geld. There is land for 1 team. Wimund, the count's man, has 1 team there [in demesne].

SOKE[LAND] BELONGING TO (*in*) WALTHAM

32. S. In Hawardebi [Hawerby (Haverstoe)] there is soke[land] [of this manor], 2 carucates and 3 bovates of land [assessed] to the geld. There is land for 4 teams. There are 14 sokemen and 1 villein and 1 bordar there with 3 teams.

33. S. In Suinhope [Swinhope (Haverstoe)] there is soke[land] [of this manor], 15 bovates and a fourth part of 1 bovate of land [assessed] to the geld. There is land for 4 teams. 16 sokemen have 2 teams there.

34. S. In Gunresbi [Gunnerby in Hatcliffe (Haverstoe)] there is soke[land] [of this manor], 2 carucates of land [assessed] to the geld. There is land for 4 teams. 6 sokemen and 5 bordars have 4 teams there, and 1 mill rendering 6 shillings, and 10 acres of meadow.

35. S. In Hadeclive [Hatcliffe (Haverstoe)] there is soke[land] [of this manor], 4 carucates of land [assessed] to the geld. There is land for 7 teams. 9 sokemen and 9 bordars have 4 teams there, and 2 mills rendering 8 shillings, and 20 acres of meadow.

36. S. In Belesbi [Beelsby (Haverstoe)] there is soke[land] [of this manor], 4 carucates of land [assessed] to the geld. There is land for 8 teams. 24 sokemen and 7 bordars have 7 teams there, and 2½ mills rendering 12 shillings, and 30 acres of meadow.

37. M. In Welletune [Welton le Wold (Louthesk)] Siward had 1 carucate of land [assessed] to the geld. There is land for 2 teams. Landric, the count's man, has 2 teams there [in demesne], and 11 villeins and 2 sokemen with 1½ teams, and 1 mill rendering 10 shillings, and 20 acres of meadow, and the fourth part of a church. T. R. E. it was worth 4 pounds; now 3 pounds.

HAWARDESHOU WAPENTAKE [HAVERSTOE]

38. S. In Toresbi [North Thoresby (Haverstoe)] there is soke[land]

[1] See 70/25. [2] See 70/26.

of Waltham, 9½ bovates of land ⌊assessed⌋ to the geld. There is land for 14 oxen. 14 sokemen and 2 bordars have 2 teams there,* and 2 salt-pans rendering 2 shillings, and 16 acres of meadow.

**D. B., f.* 347d. *Facsimile, p. xxiv*b.

39. S. In Brigeslai [Brigsley (Haverstoe)] there is soke⌊land⌋ of Waltham, 1½ carucates of land ⌊assessed⌋ to the geld. There is land for 3 teams. 17 sokemen and 1 bordar have 3 teams there, and 10 acres of meadow.

Bolinbroc [Bolingbroke] Wapentake

40. M. In Haltun [hundred] and Stepi [Halton Holegate and Little Steeping (Bolingbroke)] Ælric had 3 bovates[1] of land ⌊assessed⌋ to the geld. There is land for 3 teams. Eudo, the count's man, has 1 team there ⌊in demesne⌋, and 80 acres of meadow. T. R. E. it was worth 10 shillings ; now the like amount.

Welle [Well] Wapentake

41. S. In Stou [Stow (Well)] Count Alan has half a carucate of land ⌊assessed⌋ to the geld. It is soke⌊land⌋. There is land for half a team. 2 sokemen have half a team there.

Aslacheshou [Aslacoe] Wapentake[2]

42. M. In Spredelintone [Spridlington (Aslacoe)] Cnut had 2 carucates and 1½ bovates of land ⌊assessed⌋ to the geld. There is land for 3 teams and 2 oxen. The count has 1 team there in demesne, and 6 villeins and 6 bordars and 6 sokemen having 3 teams and 2 oxen, and 8 acres of meadow. T. R. E. it was worth 30 shillings ; now the like amount ; tallage 10 shillings.

Lovedune [Loveden] Wapentake[2]

Hag [Hough on the Hill] Hundred

43. M. In Hache [Hough on the Hill (Loveden)] Ralf [the Staller (*Stalre*)] had 7 carucates and 6 bovates ⌊assessed⌋ to the geld. There is land for 12 teams. Count Alan has 4 teams there ⌊in demesne⌋, and 17 villeins and 14 sokemen and 7 bordars having 12 teams. There is a priest there, and a church, and 4 mills rendering 30 shillings, and 100 acres of meadow. T. R. E. it was worth 12 pounds ; now 16 pounds ; tallage 4 pounds ; for horse-provender 50 shillings (*ad uictum equorum*).

Hundred

44. In Cheuelestune [Gelston (Loveden)] there is a berewic of this manor, 12 carucates of land ⌊assessed⌋ to the geld. There is land for 16 teams. Now 18 villeins and 6 bordars and 2 sokemen have 6 teams there, and 146 acres of meadow, and 200 acres of underwood, and a warren for hares (*leporum*).

45.[3] In Merestune [Marston (Loveden)] there is 1 carucate of land ⌊assessed⌋ to the geld. It is soke⌊land⌋ of Hach [Hough on the Hill]. There is land for 12 oxen.

---

[1] Rectius *carucates*.

[2] The title is written in the margin.

[3] This entry is written at the foot of the column, and a mark indicates its position in the text.

46. In Carletune[1] [Carlton Scroop (Loveden)] there is 1 carucate of land [assessed] to the geld. It is soke[land] of Hach [Hough on the Hill].

HUNDRED

47. M. In Burtune [Brant Broughton (Loveden)] Ralf [the Staller (*Stalre*)] had 13 carucates of land [assessed] to the geld in demesne, and 5 carucates of land [assessed] to the geld of (*de*) soke[land]. There is land for 18 teams. Count Alan has 3 teams there in demesne, and 36 villeins and 9 bordars and 15 sokemen and 11 other bordars having altogether 15 teams. There is a priest there, and a church, and 1 mill rendering 12 shillings, and 200 acres of meadow. Of the above-mentioned soke[land] Cadiou holds 6 bovates of land and has there 6 ploughing oxen. T. R. E. it was worth 15 pounds; now 18 pounds; tallage 100 shillings; for horse-provender 50 shillings.

FOUR HUNDREDS

48. In Fulebec and Ledeneham [Fulbeck and Leadenham (Loveden)] Ralf the Staller (*Stalre*) had 24[2] carucates of land [*in demesne, and 15 carucates of* (de) *soke[land] assessed to the geld*[3]], [assessed] to the geld. There is land for 24 teams. Count Alan has 6 teams there in demesne, and 69 villeins and 4[4] bordars and 44[2] sokemen having together 28 teams. There are 2 churches there, and 2 priests, and half a mill rendering 10 shillings. Of this land Colegrim and Derinc have 5 carucates and 6 bovates, and they have 2½ teams there. T. R. E. it was worth 30 pounds; now 32 pounds; tallage 8 pounds; for horse-provender 100 shillings.

D. B., f. 348a. *Facsimile, p. xxv*a.

49. M. In Beningtun[5] [Long Bennington (Loveden)] [2 hundreds] Ralf [the Staller (*Stalre*)] had 14 carucates of land [assessed] to the geld in demesne, and 7 carucates and 6 bovates of land [assessed] to the geld of (*de*) soke[land]. Count Alan has 5 teams there in demesne, and 19 villeins and 5 bordars and 20 sokemen having together 12 teams. There is a priest there, and a church, and 300 acres of meadow. Of this land Hervey holds 1 carucate and 3 bovates, and he has 1 team there. T. R. E. it was worth 26 pounds; now 32 pounds; tallage 8 pounds; for horse-provender 100 shillings. There are 4 mills there rendering 4 pounds.

50. In Foztune [Foston (Loveden)] [hundred] there is a berewic of this manor, 12 carucates of land [assessed] to the geld [*in demesne, and 7 carucates of land [assessed] to the geld of* (de) *soke[land]*[3]]. Now the count has 2 teams there [in demesne], and 10 villeins and 5 bordars and 46 sokemen having together 11 teams, and 100 acres of meadow. There is arable land for 14[6] teams.

51. M. In the same Foztun Turvert had 1 carucate of land [assessed] to the geld. There is land for 2 teams. Hervey, the count's man, has 1 team there [in demesne], and 2 villeins and 1 bordar with half a team. T. R. E. it was worth 16 shillings; now 10 shillings.

---

[1] See 15/1; 72/38.
[2] The numbers have been corrected in the original.
[3] Cancelled.
[4] *ii* is written in the line and *ii* above the line. The two amounts are intended to be added together.
[5] See 15/2; 72/38.
[6] *xii* is written in the line and *ii* above the line. The two amounts are intended to be added together.

BELTESLAWE [BELTISLOE] WAPENTAKE
BERTUN [BURTON COGGLES] HUNDRED

52. M. In Westbi [Westby in Bassingthorpe (Beltisloe)] Carle had 6 bovates of land [assessed] to the geld. There is land for 6 oxen. Colegrim, the count's man, has 1 villein and 1 bordar there with 1 team, and 7½ acres of meadow, and 29 acres of underwood. T. R. E. it was worth 10 shillings; now 12 shillings.

AVELUNT [AVELAND] WAPENTAKE[1]

53. M. In Cherchebi [Kirkby Underwood (Aveland)] Wider had 5 bovates of land [assessed] to the geld. There is land for 5 oxen. Godric, the count's man, has 2 villeins and 1 bordar ploughing with 2 oxen, and 4 acres of meadow, and 60 acres of underwood. T. R. E. it was worth 20 shillings; now 10 shillings.

HUNDRED

54. In Pochinton [Pointon (Aveland)] there is soke[land] of this manor, half a carucate of land [assessed] to the geld. There is land for 4 oxen. 1 sokeman and 2 bordars have half a team there.

55. M. In Bilingeburg[2] [Billingborough (Aveland)] [hundred] Carle had 1 carucate of land [assessed] to the geld. There is land for 1 team. Colegrim, the count's man, has 1 team there in demesne, and 2[3] villeins and 2 bordars with half a team, and 15 acres of meadow. T. R. E. it was worth 20 shillings: now the like amount.

HUNDRED

56. M. In Horbelinge [Horbling (Aveland)] Greve had 4 carucates of land [assessed] to the geld. There is land for 4 teams. Stefan, the count's man, has 2 team's there [in demesne], and 9 villeins and 1 bordar and 3 sokemen having 3 teams, and 20 acres of meadow. T. R. E. it was worth 40 shillings; now the like amount.

TREHOS [THREO] WAPENTAKE

57. M. In Herigerbi [Harrowby (Threo)] [and] [Orbelinge[4]] [Horbling (Aveland)] Wider had 1 carucate of land [assessed] to the geld. There is land for 1 team and 2 oxen. Godric, the count's man, has half a team there in demesne, and 4 villeins having 5 ploughing oxen, and 2 mills rendering 10 shillings, and 10 acres of meadow. T. R. E. it was worth 12 shillings; now 16 shillings.

HUNDRED

58. M. In Draitone [Drayton in Swineshead (Kirton)] Greve had 6 bovates of land [assessed] to the geld. There is land for 6 oxen. Toli, the count's man, has 1 team there in demesne, and 4 villeins and 4 bordars with 1 team, and 10 acres of meadow, and half a salt-pan rendering 8 pence. T. R. E. it was worth 16[5] shillings; now the like amount.

---

1 This title is written in the margin.
2 See 72/51.
3 This number is nearly illegible, and the reading is somewhat doubtful.
4 This name is superscript above *Herigerbi* which, however, is not cancelled.
5 This number has been corrected, and the reading is somewhat doubtful.

D. B., f. 348b. *Facsimile, p.* xxvb.

59. In the same Draitone[1] bishop Wlwi[2] had 1 carucate of land [assessed] to the geld. There is land for 1 team. This belonged to Saint Benedict of Ramesy [Ramsey, co. Hunt.] according to the witness of the men of the wapentake, who say that they do not know through whom the bishop held it. Count Alan has 2 bordars there, and 8 acres of meadow, and 1 salt-pan rendering 16 pence. T. R. E. it was worth 3 shillings; now 2 shillings.

DRAITONE [DRAYTON] HUNDRED

60. M. In Draitone itself (*ipsa*) Ralf [the Staller (*Stalr'*)] had 8 carucates and 2 bovates of land [assessed] to the geld. There is land for 8 teams. This land is soke[land] in the vill itself. Now Count Alan has 6 villeins and 6 sokemen and 1 bordar there having 5 teams. There are 4½ salt-pans there rendering 6 shillings, and 40 acres of meadow. T. R. E. Draitone with all things belonging to it was worth 30 pounds; now 70 pounds; tallage 20 pounds.

CHIRCHET' [KIRTON] WAPENTAKE

61.[3] M. In Donnintune [Donington in Holland (Kirton)] Ralf had 6 bovates of land [assessed] to the geld for a manor. There is land for 6 oxen. There are 4 villeins and 3 bordars there with half a team, and 2 acres of meadow, and 2 salt-pans rendering 32 pence. It was worth, and is worth, 20 shillings.

62. In Donninctune there is a berewic of this manor, 5 carucates and 6 bovates of land [assessed] to the geld. There is land for as many teams and oxen. Count Alan has 3 teams there in demesne, and 26 villeins with 5 teams, and 9 salt-pans rendering 12 shillings, and 60 acres of meadow.

ULMERESTIG[4] [WOLMERSTY] WAPENTAKE

63. In Weranghe [Wrangle (Skirbeck)] there is soke[land] belonging to (*in*) Draitone, 10 carucates of land [assessed] to the geld. There is land for 5 teams. 7 sokemen have 1 team there.

LECHE [LEAKE] HUNDRED

64. In Leche [Leake (Skirbeck)] there is soke[land] of Drait' [Drayton], 12 carucates of land [assessed] to the geld. There is land for 10 teams. 32 sokemen and 30 villeins and 15 bordars have 11 teams there, and 26 salt-pans, and 34 acres of meadow. Of this soke[land] 2 of the count's men have 2 carucates, and [they have] 2 teams there, and 1 bordar, and 15 salt-pans, and 10 villeins with 1 team.

LEVRETUNE [LEVERTON] HUNDRED

65. In Levretune [Leverton (Skirbeck)] there is soke[land] of Drait' [Drayton], 12 carucates of land [assessed] to the geld. There is land for as many teams. 25 sokemen and 15 villeins and 24 bordars have 12

---

[1] See 73/1.

[2] *I.e.*, Wulfwig, bishop of Dorchester, A.D. 1053-1067. In the time of Remigius, his successor, the seat of the bishopric was removed to Lincoln.

[3] This entry, with the exception of the *M.* at the beginning, is written in the margin.

[4] Wolmersty was in Wrangle (Thompson, *History and Antiquities of Boston*, 593*n*, 594*n*). The later name of the wapentake is Skirbeck.

teams there. There is a priest there, and a church, and 60 acres of meadow. Of this soke⌊land⌋ 2 of the count's men have 2 carucates and 3 bovates of land, and they have 3 teams ploughing there.

TOFT [FISHTOFT] HUNDRED

66. In Toft [Fishtoft (Skirbeck)] there is soke⌊land⌋ of Drait' [Drayton], 3 carucates of land ⌊assessed⌋ to the geld. There is land for 3 teams. 17 sokemen have 5½ teams there, and 20 acres of meadow.

67. In Schirebec [Skirbeck] ⌈hundred⌉ there is a berewic of Drait' [Drayton], 2 carucates of land ⌊assessed⌋ to the geld, and in the same ⌊place⌋ there is soke⌊land⌋ belonging to (*in*) Drait' [Drayton] 9 carucates and 6 bovates of land ⌊assessed⌋ to the geld. There is land for 8 teams. 19 sokemen and 13 villeins have 8 teams there. The count himself ⌊has⌋ 1 team in demesne. There are 2 churches there, and 2 priests, and 2 fisheries rendering 10 shillings, and 40 acres of meadow.

68. In Wibertune [Wyberton (Kirton)] ⌈hundred⌉ there is soke⌊land⌋ of Drait' [Drayton], 9 carucates and 3 bovates of land ⌊assessed⌋ to the geld. There is land for 12½ teams. 34 sokemen have 11 teams there. There is a church there, and 12 acres of meadow.

69.[1] In Wibertune [Wyberton (Kirton)] he [Count Alan] has 10 bovates of land ⌊assessed⌋ to the geld. There is land for 13 teams. Edelric held it. It was worth, and is worth, 20 shillings.

FRANETON [FRAMPTON] HUNDRED

70. In Franetone [Frampton (Kirton)] there is a berewic of Drait' [Drayton], 7 carucates and 6 bovates of land ⌊assessed⌋ to the geld. There is land for 10 teams. Count Alan has 2 teams there in demesne, and 12 sokemen and 16 villeins and 2 bordars having 8 teams. There are 15 salt-pans there rendering 20 shillings, and 100 acres of meadow.

71. In Cherchetune [Kirton (Kirton)] hundred there is soke⌊land⌋ of Drait' [Drayton], 10 carucates and 1 bovate* and a third part of 1 bovate of land ⌊assessed⌋ to the geld. There is land for 12 teams. Count Alan has 30 sokemen and 16 bordars there having 10 teams, and there are 2 salt-pans rendering 16 pence. There is a church there, and 60 acres of meadow.

**D. B., f. 348c.* *Facsimile, p. xxvia.*

72. S. In Reschintone [Riskenton[2] (Kirton)] ⌈hundred⌉ there is soke⌊land⌋ ⌊of Drayton⌋, 12 carucates of land ⌊assessed⌋ to the geld. There is land for as many teams. 29[3] sokemen and 12 bordars have 6 teams there, and 30 acres of meadow.

73. S. In Alfgare[4] [Algarkirk (Kirton)] ⌈hundred⌉ there is soke⌊land⌋ of Drait' [Drayton], 10 carucates and 5 bovates of land ⌊assessed⌋ to the geld. There is land for 9 teams. 42 sokemen have 6 teams there, and 5 acres of meadow.

---

[1] This entry is written in the margin.

[2] Riskenton seems to have been in Kirton in Holland (see *Calendar of Charter Rolls*, iii, 328).

[3] *xx* is written in the line, and *ix* above it; and it is intended that the two numbers should be added together.

[4] Probably a part of Algarkirk. See *Calendar of Miscellaneous Inquisitions*, ii, no. 1482—'Twenty acres of land in Algerkyrk, lying in a place called 'Alger hundred' and in Est Langholm, and forty acres of land in Algerkyrk, lying in a place called 'Estcroft' in Riche hundred.'

Riche Hundred

74. S. In Riche [Riche[1] (Kirton)] there is soke⌊land⌋ of Drait' [Drayton], 10 carucates of land ⌊assessed⌋ to the geld. There is land for 10 teams. 35 sokemen and 28 bordars have 7 teams there, and 12 acres of meadow.

Bichere [Bicker] Hundred

75. S. In Bichere [Bicker (Kirton)] there is soke⌊land⌋ of Drait' [Drayton], 5 carucates and 7 bovates of land ⌊assessed⌋ to the geld. There is land for as many teams and oxen. There are 19 sokemen and 18 villeins and 1 bordar there having 5 teams. There is a church there, [and a priest], and 20 salt-pans rendering 30 shillings, and 20 acres of meadow.

76. S. In Gosebertechirche[2] [Gosberton (Kirton)] there is soke⌊land⌋ of Drait' [Drayton], 3 carucates and 2 bovates of land ⌊assessed⌋ to the geld. There is land for 3 teams and 2 oxen. Of this land Ulbert has 6 bovates. There is 1 team there ⌊in demesne⌋, and 2 villeins and 10 bordars with 1 team, and 6 acres of meadow, and 2 salt-pans rendering 12 pence. The other 2 carucates and 4 bovates belong to (*in*) the soke of Drait' [Drayton]. Aðestan held (*ten'*) 6 bovates, and [Earl] Ralf had the soke, and T. R. E. these 6 were worth 4 shillings ; now 40 shillings.

Sud Treding[3] [South Riding]

77. S. In Tric [= Skegness[4] (Candleshoe)] there is soke⌊land⌋ of Drait' [Drayton], half a carucate of land ⌊assessed⌋ to the geld. There is land for 4 oxen. There is 1 bordar there, and 60 acres of meadow.

78. S. In Burch [Burgh in the Marsh (Candleshoe)] there is soke⌊land⌋ of Drait' [Drayton], 1½ carucates ⌊assessed⌋ to the geld. There is land for 12 oxen. 3 sokemen and 2 villeins and 3 bordars have 1½ teams there.

79. S. In Herdetorp [Addlethorpe (Candleshoe)] there is soke⌊land⌋ of Drait' [Drayton], 1 bovate of land ⌊assessed⌋ to the geld. There is land for 1 ox. There are 2 villeins ploughing there with 2 oxen, and 20 acres of meadow.

80. M. In the same Hardetorp [Addlethorpe (Candleshoe)] Elnod had 1 carucate of land ⌊assessed⌋ to the geld. There is land for 1 team. Eudo, the count's man, has 3 sokemen there with half a team, and 100 acres of meadow. T. R. E. it was worth 20 shillings ; now 2 shillings and 8 pence.

Hundred[3]

81. S. In Calnodesbi [Candlesby (Candleshoe)] there is soke⌊land⌋ of this manor, 2 bovates of land ⌊assessed⌋ to the geld. There is land for 3 oxen. 2 villeins have half a team there, and 100 acres of marsh (*maresc*).

82. S. In Hacberdingham [Hagworthingham (Hill)] there is other soke⌊land⌋ ⌊of this manor⌋, 6 bovates of land ⌊assessed⌋ to the geld. There is land for 9 oxen. Eudo, the count's man, ⌊has⌋ 4 sokemen and 2 villeins there having 1 team, and 30 acres of meadow.

---

[1] See p. 69, note 4.
[2] See 73/5.
[3] This title is written in the margin.
[4] This tenement appears as Skegness in later documents.

ELLEHO [ELLOE] WAPENTAKE

83. B. In Holobech[1] and Copolade [Holbeach and Whaplode (Elloe)] [Earl] Algar had 1 carucate of land [assessed] to the geld. There is land for 6 oxen. It is a berewic belonging to (*in*) Flet [Fleet (Elloe)]. [Count] Alan has it, but the king's officers (*ministri*) claim it to the use of the king. There are 3 villeins there with 3 oxen in a team.

84. S. In the same place (*ibidem*) [Earl] Algar had 13 carucates and 6 bovates[2] of land [assessed] to the geld. There is land for 9 teams and 2 oxen. It is soke[land] belonging to (*in*) Gadenay [Gedney (Elloe)]. Of this land [Count] Alan has 5 carucates. Landric holds [it] of him. He has 2 teams there [in demesne], and 29 villeins with 5 teams, and 80 acres of meadow. It is worth 8 pounds. This is deraigned (*deratiocinata*) to the use of the king.[3]

*D. B., f. 348*d. *Facsimile, p. xxvi*b.

HYLLE [HILL] WAPENTAKE

85. M. In Hacberdingham [Hagworthingham (Hill)] Holchetel had half a carucate[4] of land [assessed] to the geld. There is land for 1 team. Eudo, the count's man, has 16 acres of meadow there. Of this land 30 acres are soke[land] belonging to (*in*) Bizebi [Beesby in the Marsh (Calcewath)]. Its value (*precium*) belongs to (*in*) other manors.

CALSUAD [CALCEWATH] WAPENTAKE

86. M. In Maltebi [Maltby le Marsh (Calcewath)] Brocles had 6 bovates of land [assessed] to the geld. There is land for 6 oxen. Eudo, [holding] under the count, has 3 sokemen and 4 villeins with 1 team, and 20 acres of meadow. T. R. E. it was worth 10 shillings; now the like amount.

87. In Strobi [Strubby (Calcewath)] there is soke[land] belonging to (*in*) Lecheburne [Legbourne (Calcewath)], 2½ bovates of land [assessed] to the geld. There is land for 5 oxen. 2 sokemen have half a team there, and 10 acres of meadow.

CHIRCHETONE [KIRTON] WAPENTAKE

88. M. In Chirchetune [Kirton (Kirton)] Edric had 10 bovates of land [assessed] to the geld. There is land for 1 team and 5 oxen. Toli, the count's man, has 1 team there [in demesne], and 4 villeins have 1 team, and 8 acres of meadow. T. R. E. it was worth 40 shillings; now 20 shillings.

BICHERE [BICKER] HUNDRED[5]

89. M. In Steveninge[6] [Stenning in Bicker (Kirton)] Aldene had 3 carucates of land [assessed] to the geld. There is land for 3 teams. Geoffrey (*Goisfridus*) [Tornai], the count's man, has 2 teams there [in demesne], and 8 villeins having half a team, and 6 salt-pans rendering 8 shillings, and 50 acres of meadow. T. R. E. it was worth 20 shillings; now the like amount.

---

[1] See 73/7.
[2] 8 carucates and 6 bovates of this land are duplicated in 1/32.
[3] See 1/33.
[4] See note to no. 96.
[5] This title is written in the margin.
[6] See 73/3.

DUNNINT' [DONINGTON] HUNDRED[1]

90. M. In Quedhaveringe[2] [Quadring (Kirton)] Turchil had 1 carucate of land [assessed] to the geld. There is land for 1 team with sake and soke except 2 bovates over which the count has the soke. Guert, the count's man, holds this land, but the men of the wapentake know not through whom. There are 3 villeins there, and 6 acres of meadow, and 2 salt-pans rendering 12 pence. T. R. E. it was worth 10 shillings; now the like amount.

WINEB' [WINNIBRIGGS] WAPENTAKE[1]

91. M. In Stoche[3] [Stoke Rochford (Winnibriggs)] Ralf [the Staller (*Stalr*)] had 3 carucates of land [assessed] to the geld. There is land for 3 teams. Colegrim, the count's man, has 2 teams there belonging to his hall (*ad aulam*), and 7 villeins and 1 bordar with 2 teams, and 2 mills rendering 7 shillings and 4 pence, and 30 acres of meadow, and 140 acres and 6 perches of wood[land] for pannage. T. R. E. it was worth 30 shillings; now 60 shillings.

HUNDRED

92. M. In Northniche[4] [North Hykeham (Graffoe)] Siward had 4 carucates of land [assessed] to the geld. There is land for 2 teams. Colegrim, the count's man, has 1 team there [in demesne], and 2 villeins ploughing with 2 oxen, and 1 mill rendering 5 shillings, and 26 acres of meadow. T. R. E. it was worth 20 shillings; now the like amount. Sortebrant claims it.[5]

MUNDEBI [MUMBY] HUNDRED

93. M. In Mundebi[6] [Mumby (Calcewath)] Arnui had 3 carucates of land [assessed] to the geld. There is land for 4 teams. Eudo, the count's man, has 3 teams there [in demesne], and 16 villeins and 8 bordars have 1½ teams, and 200 acres of meadow.

94. In Clachesbi [Claxby (Calcewath)], a berewic of this manor, Count Alan has 15 acres of land.

CALSUAD [CALCEWATH] WAPENTAKE[1]

95. In Telagestorp [Theddlethorpe (Calcewath)] there is soke[land] [belonging to (*in*) Mundebi] [Mumby (Calcewath)], 3 bovates of land [assessed] to the geld. There is land for 3 oxen. 5 sokemen and 1 bordar have half a team there, and 30 acres of meadow.

96. Six M. In Hacberdingham[7] [Hagworthingham (Hill)] [and] Mundebi [Mumby (Calcewath)] Ormchetel, Siuert, Elric, Suen, Suaue, [and] Holmchethel had 8 carucates of land [assessed] to the geld. There is land for 11 teams and 5 oxen. Eudo, the count's man, has 3

---

[1] This title is written in the margin.
[2] See 73/4.
[3] See 72/23.
[4] See 72/29.
[5] *Sortebrant calumniatur* is written in the right hand margin, and a *K* in the left hand margin calls attention to the claim. See 72/29.
[6] See 24/55; 69/18.
[7] This name is underlined, and is probably intended to be cancelled. The assessment of the land in Mumby was probably 7 carucates and 4 bovates, and perhaps the remaining 4 bovates may be a duplicate of no. 85.

teams there in demesne, and 40 villeins and 4 sokemen and 12 bordars having 5 teams and 6 ploughing oxen, and 310 acres of meadow. T. R. E. these 7[1] manors were worth 10 pounds; now 16 pounds.

HOTOT [HUTTOFT] HUNDRED

97. S. In Sudtone [Sutton in the Marsh (Calcewath)] there is 1 bovate of land ⌊assessed⌋ to the geld. 2 villeins have 20 acres of meadow there. It is soke⌊land⌋ belonging to (*in*) Combreuorde [Cumberworth (Calcewath)].

D. B., f. 349a. *Facsimile, p. xxvii*a.

13. LAND OF EARL HUGH

1. M. In Grandham [Greetham (Hill)] [Earl] Harold had 2 carucates of land exempt from the geld (*sine geldo*). There is land for 6 teams. Two bovates of this land are soke⌊land⌋ (*in soca*). Earl Hugh has 4 teams there in demesne, and 46 villeins and 8 bordars and 1 sokeman having 8 teams. There is a priest there, and a church, and 1 mill rendering 8 shillings, and 300 acres of meadow. It is 1 league and 1 furlong in length and 1 league in breadth. T. R. E. it was worth 40 pounds and half a mark of gold; now 60 pounds; tallage 70 pounds.

[SOKE⌊LAND⌋ OF GREETHAM]

2. In Lecheburne [Legbourne (Calcewath)] there is soke⌊land⌋ ⌊of this manor⌋, 10 carucates of land ⌊assessed⌋ to the geld. There is land for 12 teams. There are 31 sokemen and 18 villeins and 19[2] bordars there having 16 teams, and 40 acres of meadow, and 80 acres of wood⌊land⌋ for pannage throughout the territory.

3. In Suabi and Elgelo and Toresbi and Clactorp[3] and Totele [Swaby and Belleau and South Thoresby and Claythorpe and Tothill (Calcewath)] there is soke⌊land⌋ ⌊of this manor⌋, 12 carucates of land ⌊assessed⌋ to the geld. There is land for 18 teams. There are 46 sokemen and 22 villeins and 38 bordars there having 31 teams, and 6 mills rendering 4 pounds and 16 pence, and 20 acres of meadow, and 600 acres of wood⌊land⌋ for pannage.

4. In Widerne and Abi and Hage and Calesbi [Withern and Aby and Haugh and Calceby (Calcewath)] there is soke⌊land⌋ ⌊of this manor⌋, 7[4] carucates of land [*and a half*[4]] ⌊assessed⌋ to the geld. There is land for 6½ teams. 17 sokemen and 10 villeins have 6½ teams there, and 16 acres of meadow, and 92 acres of wood⌊land⌋ for pannage and underwood.

---

[1] That is, the manors in entries 93 and 96.

[2] *xi* is written in the line, and *viii* above the line. The two numbers are probably intended to be added together.

[3] See 69/12.

[4] *vi* has been altered into *vij*, and the words *et dim'* cancelled. The scribe probably first copied the number of teams in error.

5. In Sutrebi and Dalbi and Dristorp [Sutterby and Dalby and Dexthorpe (Candleshoe)] there is soke[land] [of this manor], 15 carucates of land [assessed] to the geld. There is land for 16 teams. There are 47 sokemen and 8[1] villeins and 11 bordars there having 11 teams. In Dalbi [Dalby] the earl has 1 team in demesne, and 2 churches, and 80 acres of meadow.

6. In Fortintone and Aschebi[2] and Bretoft and Langene [Fordington and Ashby by Partney and Braytoft and Langene[3] (Candleshoe)] there is soke[land] [of this manor], 18½ carucates of land [assessed] to the geld. There is land for 18 teams. Now 49 sokemen and 26 villeins and 22 bordars have 18 teams there. There are 3 churches there, and 620 acres of meadow.

7. In Wenflet [Wainfleet (Candleshoe)] and Haghe and Calesbi and Tedlagestorp[4] and Malbertorp [Haugh and Calceby and Theddlethorpe and Mablethorpe (Calcewath)] there is soke[land] [of this manor], 20 carucates and 2 bovates of land [assessed] to the geld. There is land for as many teams. 83 sokemen and 33 villeins and 35 bordars have 18½ teams there, and 1,000 acres of meadow, and 20 salt-pans rendering 10 shillings, and 80 acres of underwood.

8. In Hotot and Toruluesbi and Sutune and Druistorp and Billesbi and Marchesbi [Huttoft and Thurlby in Bilsby and Sutton in the Marsh and Trusthorpe and Bilsby and Markby (Calcewath)] there is soke[land] [of this manor], 18 carucates of land [assessed] to the geld. There is land for 20 teams. 69 sokemen and 19 villeins and 23 bordars have 16 teams there, and 780 acres of meadow.

HYLLE [HILL] WAPENTAKE

9. In Langetune and Hacberdincham and Salmundebi and Tedforde and Brincle and Winzebi and Clachesbi [Langton by Spilsby and Hagworthingham and Salmonby and Tetford and Brinkhill and Winceby and Claxby Pluckacre (Hill)] there is soke[land] [of this manor], 29 carucates of land [assessed] to the geld. There is land for 33 teams. There are 150 sokemen and 20 bordars and 12 villeins there having 39 teams, and 9 mills rendering 20 shillings, and 350 acres of meadow.

All this land or soke[land] belongs to (*pertinet ad*) Grandham [Greetham].* Altogether there are 131[5] carucates [assessed] to the geld. There is land for 144 teams. There are 376 sokemen, 148 villeins, and 168 bordars, having 156 teams.

**D. B., f. 349*b. *Facsimile, p. xxvii*b.

10. In Haltone [West Halton (Manley)] [Earl] Harold had 8 carucates of land [assessed] to the geld. There is land for 6 teams. Of this land 4 carucates are soke[land] (*in soca*). Now Earl Hugh has it, and William son of Neal [holds it] of him. There are 4 teams in demesne, and 3 villeins and 9 bordars and 14 sokemen having 2 teams, and 30 acres of meadow. T. R. E. it was worth 19 pounds ; now 10 pounds ; tallage 5 pounds.

---

[1] The numeral has been corrected in the original.
[2] See 69/35.
[3] Langene was probably in Irby in the Marsh.
[4] See 69/15.
[5] The details add up to 131 carucates 6 bovates, including the manor of Greetham (no. 1).

[SOKE⌊LAND⌋ OF THE MANOR OF WEST HALTON]

11. In Walecote [Walcot in Alkborough (Manley)] there is a berewic of this manor, 3 bovates of land ⌊assessed⌋ to the geld. There is land for 3 oxen.

12. In Wintrintune [Winterton (Manley)] there is soke⌊land⌋ ⌊of this manor⌋, 4 carucates of land ⌊assessed⌋ to the geld. There is land for 4 teams. 16 sokemen and 7 bordars have 2½ teams there.

13. In Colebi [Coleby in West Halton (Manley)] there is soke⌊land⌋ ⌊of this manor⌋, 15 bovates of land ⌊assessed⌋ to the geld. There is land for 2 teams. 3 sokemen plough there with 1 ox, and there are 9 acres of meadow.

14. In Hedebi [Haythby in West Halton (Manley)] there is soke⌊land⌋ ⌊of this manor⌋, 3 carucates of land ⌊assessed⌋ to the geld. There is land for 2 teams. Now 9 sokemen and 1 bordar have 2 teams there, and 80 acres of meadow, and 20 acres of underwood.

15. In Tedulfbi [Thealby in Burton on Stather (Manley)] there is soke⌊land⌋ ⌊of this manor⌋, 10½ carucates of land ⌊assessed⌋ to the geld. There is land for 9 teams. Now 16 sokemen and 15 bordars have 4½ teams there, and 50 acres of meadow, and 70 acres of underwood.

16. In Cropesbi and Cunesbi [Crosby and South Coneysby in Crosby (Manley)] there is soke⌊land⌋ ⌊of this manor⌋, 6 carucates and 6 bovates of land ⌊assessed⌋ to the geld. There is land for 6 teams and 6 oxen. Now 25 sokemen and 10 bordars have 6 teams there, and 80 acres of meadow.

NORT TREDING [NORTH RIDING]

17. M. In Bernodebi [Barnetby le Wold (Yarborough)] [Earl] Harold had 6[1] carucates of land ⌊assessed⌋ to the geld. There is land for 12 teams. Three carucates are soke⌊land⌋ (*in soca*). William, Earl H's man, has 3 teams there in demesne, and 4 villeins and 60 sokemen and 10 bordars having 7½ teams. T. R. E. it was worth 14 pounds; now 20 pounds; tallage 10 pounds.

18. In Bertone [2 bovates] and Bechebi [1 carucate] and Wirichebi [2 carucates] and Sumertebi [half a carucate] and Haburne [1 bovate] [Barton upon Humber and Bigby and Worlaby and Somerby and Habrough (Yarborough)] and 2 parts of 1 bovate ⌊assessed⌋ to the geld. There is land for 7 teams. There are 36 sokemen and 1 villein there having 4½ teams, and 40 acres of meadow. This soke⌊land⌋ belongs to (*pertinet ad*) Bernodebi [Barnetby le Wold].

19. Also in Lobingeham [*probably* in East Halton (Yarborough)] [4 carucates and 1 bovate] and Irebi [Irby on Humber (Bradley)] [1½ carucates] and Ribi [Riby (Yarborough)] [4½ carucates], altogether 10 carucates and 1 bovate of land ⌊assessed⌋ to the geld. There is land for 20 teams and 2 oxen. It is soke⌊land⌋ belonging to (*in*) Bernodebi [Barnetby le Wold]. There are 52 sokemen and 11 villeins and 7 bordars there having 11 teams, and 315 acres of meadow.

20. In Ribi [Riby (Yarborough)] Erneis, the earl's man, has 2 teams in demesne. He himself holds that soke⌊land⌋ of the earl. William, Ralf, and Azelin, the earl's men, hold the others (*alias tenent*).[2]

---

[1] *iii* has been altered into *vi*.

[2] The sokelands in nos. 18 and 19 seem to be referred to.

21. In Fugelestou [Fulstow (Haverstoe)] Godric had 6 bovates of land [assessed] to the geld. There is land for 11 oxen. Rozelin, the earl's man, has 1 team there [in demesne], and 7 villeins and 1 bordar with 1 team, and 100 acres of meadow. T. R. E. it was worth 20 shillings; now 40 shillings.

D. B., f. 349c. *Facsimile, p. xxviiia.*

22. M. In Hamingebi [Hemingby (Gartree)] Lambecarl had 6 bovates of land [assessed] to the geld. There is land for 6 oxen. Baldric, the earl's man, has 1 team there [in demesne], and 2 villeins and 2 bordars and 7 sokemen having 2 teams, and half a mill rendering 7 shillings, and 30 acres of meadow. T. R. E. it was worth 30 shillings; now 25 shillings.

23. In Buchehale and Horsitone [Bucknall and Horsington (Gartree)] there is soke[land] of this manor, 9 bovates of land [assessed] to the geld. There is land for 1 team and 2 oxen. 10 sokemen and 3 bordars have 2 teams there, and 62 acres of meadow, and 20 acres of wood[land] for pannage throughout the territory.

SUD TREDING [SOUTH RIDING]

24. M. In Staintune [Stainton by Langworth (Wraggoe)] Godric had 3 carucates of land [assessed] to the geld. There is land for 4 teams; half a carucate is the sokemen's. Osbern, the earl's man, has 2 teams there [in demesne], and 5 villeins and 4 bordars and 4 sokemen with 2 teams, and 1 mill rendering 12 pence, and 80 acres of meadow, and 140 acres of underwood. T. R. E. it was worth 3 pounds; now the like amount.

25. In Reresbi [Reasby (Wraggoe)] there is a berewic of this manor, 6 bovates of land [assessed] to the geld. There is land for 6 oxen.

26. M. In Bolintone [Bullington (Wraggoe)] Lambecarl had 3½ bovates of land [assessed] to the geld. There is land for 1 team. Colsuan, the earl's man, has 1 team there [in demesne], and 2 villeins and 3 bordars having half a team, and 10 acres of meadow, and 160 acres of underwood. T. R. E. it was worth 20 shillings; now the like amount.

27. In Cuningesbi [Coningsby (Horncastle)] there is inland belonging to (*in*) Tedintone [Toynton (Horncastle)], 1 bovate of land [assessed] to the geld. 1 villein ploughs there with 2 oxen, and there is 1 fishery rendering 30 pence, and 2 acres of meadow, and 20 acres of wood[land].

28. M. In Tadewelle[1] [Tathwell (Louthesk)] [Earl] Harold had 5 carucates of land [assessed] to the geld. There is land for 20 teams. Two carucates are soke[land] (*in soca*). [Earl] Hugh has 6 teams there in demesne, and 12 villeins and 4 bordars and 24 sokemen having 3 teams. There is a church there, and 1 mill rendering 16 pence, and 8 acres of meadow, and 80 acres of wood[land] for pannage. T. R. E. it was worth 15 pounds; now 20 pounds; tallage 100 shillings.

29. In Halintun [and Chelesturne] and Radresbi and Maltebi [Hallington and Kelstern and Raithby by Louth and Maltby by Raithby (Louthesk)] there is soke[land] of this manor, 9 carucates [and 2 bovates] of land [assessed] to the geld. There is land for 9 teams [and a half]. 41[2] sokemen and 20 villeins have 6 teams there, and 10 acres of meadow.

---

[1] See 69/2. [2] *xl* appears to have been altered into *xli*.

30. M. In Rocheland [Ruckland (Louthesk)] Godric had 1 carucate of land ⌊assessed⌋ to the geld. There is land for 3 teams. Brisard, the earl's man, has 1 team there ⌊in demesne⌋, and 6 villeins and 3 bordars with 1 team. There is a church there, and 1 mill rendering 2 shillings, and 30 acres of meadow. T. R. E. it was worth 4 pounds ; now 40 shillings.

31. M. In Farforde [Farforth (Louthesk)] Lambecarl had 1½ carucates of land ⌊assessed⌋ to the geld. There is land for 2 teams. One bovate is soke⌊land⌋ (*in soca*). Baldric, the earl's man, has 1 team there ⌊in demesne⌋, and 10 villeins and 2 sokemen and 6 bordars with 2 teams. There is a church there, and 1 mill rendering 3 shillings, and 8 acres of meadow. T. R. E. it was worth 3 pounds ; now the like amount.

32.[1] In Oxecumbe [Oxcombe (Hill)] there is soke⌊land⌋ belonging to (*in*) Farforde, 1½ carucates of land ⌊assessed⌋ to the geld. There is land for 2 teams. 12 sokemen and 1 villein have 2 teams there, and 60 acres of meadow. T. R. E. and now ⌊worth⌋ 40 shillings.

33. Three M. In Welle[2] [Maidenwell (Louthesk)] Allef, Edric, and Godric had 2 carucates [less 1 bovate] of land ⌊assessed⌋ to the geld. There is land for 3 teams. Half a bovate is soke⌊land⌋ (*in soca*). Osbern, the earl's man, has 3 teams there ⌊in demesne⌋, and 8 villeins and 2 sokemen with 1 team, and 1 salt-pan, and 34[3] acres of meadow, and 5 acres of underwood. T. R. E. it was worth 100 shillings ; now 4 pounds ; tallage 5 shillings.

*D. B., f. 349*d. *Facsimile, p. xxviii*b.

34. M. In Wadintune [Waddington (Boby)] [Earl] Harold had 24 carucates of land ⌊assessed⌋ to the geld. There is land for as many teams. 9 carucates and 2 bovates are soke⌊land⌋ (*in soca*). Earl Hugh has 4 teams there in demesne, and 15 villeins and 9 bordars and 24 sokemen having 11 teams. There is a church there, and a priest, and 2 mills rendering 11 shillings, and 270 acres of meadow. T. R. E. it was worth 100 pounds less 4 pounds ; now 20 pounds ; tallage 10 pounds.

35. In Medricesham [Metheringham (Langoe)] there is a berewic of this manor, 8½ carucates of land ⌊assessed⌋ to the geld. There is land for 4 teams and 2 oxen. The earl has 2 teams there ⌊in demesne⌋, and 10 villeins and 6 bordars with 2 teams, and 1 mill rendering 8 shillings, and 190 [90][4] acres of meadow, and 120 acres of underwood.

36. In Timbrelund [Timberland (Langoe)] there is a berewic ⌊of this manor⌋, 6 bovates of land ⌊assessed⌋ to the geld. There is land for 4 oxen. 2 bordars have half a team there, and 50 acres of underwood.

37. In Hermodestune [Harmston (Boby)] there is soke⌊land⌋ of Wadintone, 20½ carucates of land ⌊assessed⌋ to the geld. There is land for as many teams. 38 sokemen and 11 bordars have 10 teams there. There is a church there, and a priest, and 1 fishery rendering 50 score and 5 eels.

---

[1] This entry is written at the foot of the column, and a sign indicates that its proper place is where it is printed in the text.

[2] See 69/6.

[3] *xxx* is written in the line and *iiii* above the line.

[4] *cxc* is written in the line and *nonag'* above the line over the last two figures. The number intended to be recorded is probably 190.

38. M. In Exewelle [Ashwell, co. Rutland] [Earl] Harold had 2 carucates of land [assessed] to the geld. There is land for 6 teams. Gocelin, Earl H's man, has 2 teams [in demesne], and 13 villeins and 2 bordars having 5 teams, and 16 acres of meadow. T. R. E. it was worth 100 shillings ; now 6 pounds.[1]

39. M. In Fullobi[2] [Fulletby (Hill)] [Earl] Harold had 2 carucates of land [assessed] to the geld. There is land for 3 teams. Baldric, the earl's man, has 1 team there [in demesne], and 9 sokemen and 5 villeins and 4 bordars having 1½ teams, and 60 acres of meadow. T. R. E. it was worth 40 shillings ; now the like amount.

40. The priest of the same vill has [of the king] 2 bovates of land [assessed] to the geld, and 12 acres of meadow.

41. M. In Ormesbi [South Ormsby (Hill)] Godric had 3 carucates of land [assessed] to the geld. There is land for 4 teams. Hugh, the earl's man, has 2 teams there [in demesne], and 7 villeins and 1 bordar and 11 sokemen having 2 teams, and 1 mill rendering 32 pence, and 80 acres of meadow. T. R. E. it was worth 70 shillings ; now 4 pounds.

42. M. In Chetelesbi [Ketsby (Hill)] Godric had 3 carucates of land [assessed] to the geld. There is land for 4 teams. Hugh, the earl's man, has 3 teams there [in demesne], and 6 villeins and 1 bordar and 11 sokemen having 2½ teams, and 1 mill rendering 32 pence, and 60 acres of meadow. T. R. E. it was worth 4 pounds ; now 100 shillings.

43. In Walmesgar [Walmsgate (Hill)] there is soke[land] of this manor, 1 carucate of land [assessed] to the geld. There is land for 14 oxen.

44. Three M. In Hecham[3] [Haugham (Louthesk)] Elueua, Godric, and Edric had 2 carucates of land [assessed] to the geld. There is land for 6 teams. The monks of Saint Sever have 3 teams there [in demesne], and 29 villeins and 3 bordars with 6 teams, and 46 acres of meadow, and wood[land] for pannage throughout the territory 1 league in length and 3 furlongs in breadth. T. R. E. it was worth 6 pounds ; now 8 pounds.

45. M. In Neuberie [Newbold (Wraggoe)] Godric had 3 carucates of land [assessed] to the geld. There is land for 3 teams. Osbern, the earl's man, has 2 teams there [in demesne], and 13 villeins and 2 bordars with 2 teams, and 120 acres of meadow, and 500 acres of wood[land] for pannage. T. R. E. it was worth 60 shillings ; now 100 shillings.

---

[1] This entry appears again in the Rutland section of *Domesday Book*, f. 293*d*.
[2] Corrected from *Fulnodebi* by an interlineation
[3] See 69/6.

*D. B., f. 350*a. *Facsimile, p. xxix*a.

14. LAND OF IVO TAILLEBOIS (*Taillgebosc*)

1. Two M. In Tatenai [Tetney (Bradley)] Turgisle and Suen had 4 carucates of land ⌊assessed⌋ to the geld. There is land for 8 teams. 1 carucate and 2 bovates and the third part of 2 bovates of this land are soke⌊land⌋ (*in soca*). Now Ivo Taillebosc has 6 teams there in demesne, and 25 villeins and 7 bordars and 12 sokemen having 6 teams. There is 1 mill there rendering 16 shillings, and 13 salt-pans rendering 12 shillings, and 140 acres of meadow. T. R. E. it was worth 10 pounds; now 20 pounds; tallage 20 pounds.

2. In Holtone [Holton le Clay (Bradley)] there is soke⌊land⌋ of this manor, 2 carucates of land ⌊assessed⌋ to the geld. There is land for 4 teams. 14 sokemen have 3 teams there. It is worth 40 shillings.

3. M. In the same place (*ibidem*) Esbern had 1 carucate of land ⌊assessed⌋ to the geld. There is land for 2 teams. Hermer, Ivo's man, has 5 villeins and 2 bordars ploughing there with 5 oxen. There is the site of a mill there, and 14 acres of meadow. T. R. E. ⌊it was⌋, and now is, worth 40 shillings.[1]

4. In Humbrestone [Humberstone (Bradley)] there is soke⌊land⌋ of Tatenai [Tetney (Bradley)], 6 carucates of land ⌊assessed⌋ to the geld. There is land for 12 teams. 67 sokemen have 18 teams there, and 200 acres of meadow.

5. M. In Cleia [Clee (Bradley)] Grimbold had 2 bovates and 2 parts of 1 bovate of land ⌊assessed⌋ to the geld. There is land for half a team. Wimund, Ivo's man, has half a team there ⌊in demesne⌋, and 16 acres of meadow. T. R. E. it was worth 20 shillings; now 10 shillings.

6. M. In Ternescrou [Thrunsco (Bradley)] Grinchel had 5 bovates of land ⌊assessed⌋ to the geld. There is land for 10 oxen. Wimund has 1 team there ⌊in demesne⌋, and 5 villeins with 1 ox, and 12 acres of meadow. T. R. E. it was, and now ⌊is⌋, worth 20 shillings.

WALESCROS [WALSHCROFT] WAPENTAKE

7.[2] In Wifilingham [North Willingham (Walshcroft)] Ivo has half a carucate of land belonging to the soke of Eriz (*de soca Eriz*).

8. M. In Clachesbi and Normanesbi [Claxby by Normanby and Normanby le Wold (Walshcroft)] Godwin had 10 bovates of land ⌊assessed⌋ to the geld. There is land for 2½ teams.

9. Three M. In the same places (*ibidem*) Godric, Siward, Ulchel, and Godwin had 12 bovates of land ⌊assessed⌋ to the geld, and 1 toft with sake and soke. There is land for 3 teams. Hugh, Ivo's man, has 2 teams there ⌊in demesne⌋, and 48 sokemen and 4 bordars with 6 teams. There are 2 churches there, and 100 acres of meadow, and 40 acres of underwood. T. R. E. it was worth 40 shillings; now 4 pounds; tallage 4 pounds.

---

[1] See below, no. 35 and note.

[2] See 28/21.

10. In Osgotebi and Tauelebi [Osgodby and Tealby (Walshcroft)] there is inland [2 bovates] and soke[land] [1 bovate] of this manor, 3 bovates of land [assessed] to the geld. There is land for 6 oxen. 4 sokemen and 1 villein plough there with 6 oxen, and there is 1 mill there rendering 3 shillings, and 3 acres of meadow.

11. M. In Clachesbi[1] [Claxby by Normanby (Walshcroft)] Alwin had 3 bovates of land [assessed] to the geld. There is land for 6 oxen. Geoffrey, Ivo's man, has 1 team there [in demesne], and 2 villeins who do not plough (*non arant'*), and 1 mill rendering 2 shillings, and 13 acres of meadow, and 6 acres of underwood. T. R. E. it was worth 15 shillings; now 13 shillings.

12. M. In Torgrebi [Thorganby (Walshcroft)] Grimbald had 2 bovates of land [assessed] to the geld. There is land for 5 oxen. Odo, Ivo's man, has 1 team there [in demesne], and 2 villeins, and 3 parts of 1 mill rendering 5 shillings, and 9 acres of meadow. T. R. E. it was worth 20 shillings; now 30 shillings.

13. M. In Walesbi and Otesbi [Walesby and Otby (Walshcroft)] Grimbold had 1 carucate of land [assessed] to the geld. There is land for 2 teams. Geoffrey, Ivo's man, has 1 team there [in demesne], and 20 villeins with 2 teams, and 1 mill rendering 16 pence, and 20 acres of meadow,* and 5 acres of underwood. T. R. E. it was worth 40 shillings; now the like amount; tallage 10 shillings.

**D. B., f. 350*b. *Facsimile, p. xxix*b.

14. M. In Toreswe [Thoresway (Walshcroft)] Grimbold had 2 bovates of land [assessed] to the geld. There is land for 6 oxen. Odo, Ivo's man, has 1 villein ploughing there with 1 ox, and 15½ acres of meadow. T. R. E. it was worth 20 shillings; now 9 shillings and 4 pence.

15. M. In Crosbi[2] [Croxby (Walshcroft)] Siward had 5 bovates of land [assessed] to the geld. There is land for 2 teams. 5 acres of the land are soke[land] (*in soca*). Odo, Ivo's man, has 1½ teams there [in demesne], and 6 villeins and 1 bordar with 1 team, and 3 mills rendering 8 shillings, and 18 acres of meadow. T. R. E. it was worth 30 shillings; now 40 shillings.

16. M. In Bliburg [Blyborough (Aslacoe)] Gamel had 5½ bovates [assessed] to the geld. There is land for 11 oxen. Neal, Ivo's man, has 2 teams there [in demesne], and 7 villeins and 5 bordars with 1 team, and 1 mill rendering 12 pence, and 20 acres of meadow. T. R. E. it was worth 26 shillings and 8 pence; now 50 shillings; tallage 20 shillings.

17. M. In Glantham [Glentham (Aslacoe)] Turgisle had 3 carucates of land [assessed] to the geld. There is land for 4 teams. 2 carucates and 2 bovates of land of this land are soke[land] (*in soca*). Rainfrid, Ivo's man, has 2 teams there [in demesne], and 2 villeins and 13 bordars and 19 sokemen with 2½ teams, and 90 acres of meadow. T. R. E. it was worth 30 shillings; now 60 shillings; tallage 20 shillings.

---

[1] See 28/23; 70/19.

[2] See 70/20.

18. M. In Normanebi [Normanby by Spital (Aslacoe)] Code had 5 carucates of land ⌊assessed⌋ to the geld. There is land for 8 teams. 1½ carucates are soke⌊land⌋ (*in soca*). Now Ivo has 4 teams there ⌊in demesne⌋, and 15 villeins and 14 sokemen having 5 teams. There is a church there, and a priest, and 2 mills rendering 5 shillings and 4 pence, and 67½ acres of meadow. T. R. E. it was worth 50 shillings; now 100 shillings; tallage 20 shillings.

19. In Esnetrebi [Snitterby (Aslacoe)] there is soke⌊land⌋ of this manor, 1 bovate of land. There are 3 sokemen there ploughing with 6 oxen, and 40 acres of meadow.

20. M. In Ounebi[1] [Owmby (Aslacoe)] Code had 4 bovates of land ⌊assessed⌋ to the geld. There is land for half a team. Peter, Ivo's man, has 1 team there ⌊in demesne⌋, and 2 villeins, and 10 acres of meadow. T. R. E. it was worth 10 shillings; now 20 shillings. In the same place (*ibidem*) Ivo has 1 bovate of land belonging to (*de*) the soke of Bishop R⌊emigius⌋.

21. M. In Summertebi [Somerby (Corringham)] there are 7 bovates of land ⌊assessed⌋ to the geld. There is land for 7 oxen. Ivo has 1 bordar there, and 20 acres of wood⌊land⌋ for pannage. T. R. E. it was worth 20 shillings; now 5 shillings.

22. M. In Tonestale [Dunstall (Corringham)] Gamel had 2 carucates of land ⌊assessed⌋ to the geld. There is land for 2½ teams. 10 bovates of this land are soke⌊land⌋ (*in soca*). Ivo has 2 teams there in demesne, and 2 villeins and 11 sokemen and 1 bordar with 2 teams. There is a church there, and a priest, and 1 mill rendering 2 shillings, and 7 acres of meadow. T. R. E. it was worth 40 shillings; now 4 pounds.

23. M. In Mortune [Morton in Gainsborough (Corringham)] Gamel had 3 bovates of land ⌊assessed⌋ to the geld. There is land for 6 oxen. Ivo has 4 villeins there ploughing with 2 oxen, and 10 acres of meadow. There are moors (*morę*) and underwood half a league in length and half in breadth. T. R. E. it was worth 4 shillings; now 10 shillings.

24. M. In Scotone [Scotton (Corringham)] Gamel had 2½ carucates of land ⌊assessed⌋ to the geld. There is land for 2½ teams. Half a carucate of this land is soke⌊land⌋ (*in soca*). Gocelin, Ivo's man, has 2 teams there ⌊in demesne⌋, and 15 villeins and 3 bordars and 6 sokemen with 2 teams, and 31 acres of meadow, and 18 acres of underwood, and the site of a mill. T. R. E. it was worth 30 shillings; now 50 shillings; tallage 10 shillings.

D. B., f. 350c. *Facsimile, p. xxx*a.

MANELINDE [MANLEY] WAPENTAKE

25. Two M. In Hiboldestou [Hibaldstow (Manley)] Gamel had 1½ carucates of land ⌊assessed⌋ to the geld. There is land for 3 teams. Ivo has 4 teams there ⌊in demesne⌋, and 18 villeins and 2 bordars with 2 teams, and 1 mill rendering 5 shillings, and 111 acres of meadow, and 60 acres of underwood. T. R. E. it was worth 100 shillings; now 100 shillings; tallage 20 shillings.

---

[1] See 7/6; 28/4; 71/12.

26. M. In Gamelstorp [Hilboldestou[1]] [Hibaldstow and Gainsthorpe (Manley)] Ulgar had 2 bovates of land.[2] He has this in exchange for 1 bovate and 2 fisheries belonging to (*de*) Crul [Crowle (Manley)]. There is 1 team there ⌊in demesne⌋. T. R. E. and now ⌊worth⌋ 10 shillings.

27. B. In Straitone and Scallebi [Sturton and Scawby (Manley)] there is inland ⌊of this manor⌋, 3 bovates of land ⌊assessed⌋ to the geld. One of Ivo's men ⌊has⌋ 1 team there ⌊in demesne⌋, and 1 villein. T. R. E. it was worth 5 shillings and 4 pence ; now 20 shillings.

28. M. In Alchebarge [Alkborough (Manley)] William Malet had 5 carucates of land ⌊assessed⌋ to the geld. There is land for 6 teams. 3 carucates of this land are soke⌊land⌋ (*in soca*). Ivo has 3 teams there ⌊in demesne⌋, and 8 villeins and 20 sokemen with 5 teams. T. R. E. it was worth 100 shillings ; now 4 pounds ; tallage 40 shillings.

29. Two M. In Saxebi [Saxby (Yarborough)] Siward [and Turgisle] had 4 carucates of land ⌊assessed⌋ to the geld. There is land for 7[3] teams [and a half]. Roger, Ivo's man, has 2 teams there ⌊in demesne⌋, and 8 villeins and 2 sokemen with 3 teams, and 3 fisheries rendering 3 shillings. T. R. E. it was worth 4 pounds ; now 50 shillings ; tallage 10 shillings.

30. Three M. In Chelvingehou [Killingholme (Yarborough)] Briford, Siward, and Turgis ⌊had⌋ 2 carucates and 7 bovates of land ⌊assessed⌋ to the geld. There is land for 3 teams. 1 carucate and 1 bovate and 2 tofts are soke⌊land⌋ (*in soca*). Odo, Ivo's man, has 3 teams there ⌊in demesne⌋, and 4 villeins and 19 sokemen with 3 teams, and half a mill rendering 3 shillings, and 212 acres of meadow. T. R. E. it was worth 5 pounds ; now 3 pounds ; tallage 20 shillings.

31.[4] M. In Linberge [Limber (Yarborough)] Alwin had 9 bovates of land ⌊assessed⌋ to the geld. There is land for 4 teams. 1 bovate of this land is soke⌊land⌋ (*in soca*). Neal, Ivo's man, has 3 teams there ⌊in demesne⌋, and 1 villein. T. R. E. it was worth 40 shillings ; now 60 shillings.

32. M. In Neuhuse [Newsham (Yarborough)] Alwin had 5 bovates of land ⌊assessed⌋ to the geld. There is land for 10 oxen. Roger, Ivo's man, has 1 team there ⌊in demesne⌋, and 6 villeins with 1 team, and 1 mill rendering 2 shillings, and 30 acres of meadow. T. R. E. it was worth 22 shillings ; now 40 shillings.

33. M. In Iribi [Irby on Humber (Bradley)] Seward had 1 carucate of land ⌊assessed⌋ to the geld. There is land for 2 teams. Odo, Ivo's man, has 1 team there ⌊in demesne⌋, and 5 villeins and 10 bordars ploughing with 3 oxen. T. R. E. it was worth 10 shillings and 8 pence ; now 20 shillings.

34. In Hoctune [Holton le Moor (Walshcroft)] Ivo has 1 carucate of land ⌊assessed⌋ to the geld, ⌊which he has⌋ in exchange. There is land for 2 teams. There is 1 team there. Odo has it, and it is worth 15 shillings.

---

1 *Hilboldestou*, which is interlined above *Gamelstorp*, must be treated as an addition, not as a correction (cp. *L.S.*, 1/18).

2 The usual formula *ad geldum* does not occur here.

3 *iiij* has been corrected to *vij*.

4 See 1/67 ; 70/3.

35.[1] S. In Wade [Waith (Haverstoe)] there are 2 bovates ⌊assessed⌋ to the geld. There is land for 2 oxen. 4 villeins and 1 sokeman have half a team there, and 5 acres of meadow.

36. In Haburne [Habrough (Yarborough)] Turgis had 3 bovates and the third part of a bovate ⌊of land⌋ ⌊assessed⌋ to the geld. It is soke⌊land⌋ belonging to (*in*) Haltune [East Halton (Yarborough)]. It is waste.

37. M. In Brochelesbi [Brocklesby (Yarborough)] Alwin had 3 bovates of land ⌊assessed⌋ to the geld. There is land for 1 team. 1 bovate is soke⌊land⌋ (*in soca*). Neal, Ivo's man, has 2 sokemen there ploughing with 2 oxen. T. R. E. it was worth 16 shillings; now 3 shillings.

D. B., f. 350d. *Facsimile, p. xxx*b.

38. M. In Caburne [Cabourn (Haverstoe)] Unlof had 1 carucate and 3 bovates of land ⌊assessed⌋ to the geld. There is land for 3 teams. Roger, Ivo's man, has 2 teams there ⌊in demesne⌋, and 3 villeins and 5 bordars and 11 sokemen with 2½ teams, and 100 acres of meadow. T. R. E. it was worth 30 shillings; now 60 shillings; tallage 20 shillings.

39. M. In Cucvalt [Cuxwold (Haverstoe)] Alwin had 1½ bovates of land ⌊assessed⌋ to the geld. There is land for half a team. Gocelin, Ivo's man, has 1 team there ⌊in demesne⌋. T. R. E. it was worth 20 shillings; now 16 shillings.

40. M. In Reburne [Redbourne (Manley)] Gamel had 1 carucate and half a bovate of land ⌊assessed⌋ to the geld. There is land for 1 team and half an ox. Peter, Ivo's man, has 1 team there ⌊in demesne⌋, and 5 villeins and 1 sokeman and 1 bordar with 1 team, and 24 acres of meadow. T. R. E. it was worth 21 shillings; now 30 shillings; tallage 10 shillings.

41. M. In the same place (*ibidem*) Aldene had 3 bovates of land ⌊assessed⌋ to the geld. Ivo has 1 villein there with 1 ox, and 8 acres of meadow. It is worth 5 shillings.

42. M. In Westledebi [Westlaby (Wraggoe)] Harold had 7 bovates of land ⌊assessed⌋ to the geld. There is land for 14 oxen. Odo, Ivo's man, has half a team there ⌊in demesne⌋, and 2 villeins and 2 bordars with half a team, and 20 acres of meadow. T. R. E. it was worth 20 shillings; now 16 shillings.

43. M. In Lobingeham [Lobingham[2] (Yarborough)] Alwin had 6 bovates of land ⌊assessed⌋ to the geld. There is land for 12 oxen. Odo, Ivo's man, has 1 bordar there ploughing with 1 ox, and 30 acres of meadow. T. R. E. it was worth 20 shillings; now 12 shillings.

44. M. In Chelebi [Keelby (Yarborough)] Alwin had 2 bovates of land ⌊assessed⌋ to the geld. There is land for 4 oxen. Neal, Ivo's man, has half a team there ⌊in demesne⌋, and 2 villeins and 1 bordar ploughing with 1 ox. There is the site of a mill there, and 27 acres of meadow. T. R. E. it was worth 10 shillings; now 20 shillings.

---

[1] This entry is written at the foot of the column, and a mark indicates that it is to be placed after no. 34. It is probable that there is a confusion between Holton le Moor and Holton le Clay, and that its proper place is after no. 3 above.

[2] In East Halton or Killingholme.

HAWARDESHOU [HAVERSTOE] WAPENTAKE[1]

45. M. In Beltesford [Belchford (Gartree)] Stori had 6 carucates of land ⌊assessed⌋ to the geld. There is land for 8 teams. 2 carucates of this land are soke⌊land⌋ (*in soca*). Ivo has 5 teams there in demesne, and 9 villeins and 15 bordars and 45 sokemen having 9 teams. There are 2 mills there rendering 18 shillings and 8 pence, and 360 acres of meadow, and 3 acres of underwood. It is 1 league in length and 1 in breadth. T. R. E. it was worth 15 pounds ; now 33 pounds ; tallage 27 pounds.

SOKE⌊LAND⌋ OF THIS MANOR [nos. 46–56]

46. In Colchesbi [Goulceby (Gartree)] there are 3 carucates of land ⌊assessed⌋ to the geld. There is land for 3 teams. 16 sokemen and 2 villeins have 6 teams there, and 1 mill rendering 4 shillings, and there is a priest, and a church, and 120 acres of meadow.

47. In Hamingebi [Hemingby (Gartree)] there are 3 carucates ⌊assessed⌋ to the geld. There is land for 3 teams. 22 sokemen and 7 villeins and 6 bordars have 7 teams there, and 120 acres of meadow.

48. In Scamelesbi [Scamblesby (Gartree)] there are 6 carucates of land ⌊assessed⌋ to the geld. There is land for 7 teams. Ivo has 1 team there ⌊in demesne⌋, and 27 sokemen and 11 villeins and 3 bordars have 5 teams, and 240 acres of meadow.

49. In Calchewelle [Cawkwell (Gartree)] there are 1½ carucates of land ⌊assessed⌋ to the geld. There is land for as many ⌊teams and oxen⌋. 12 sokemen and 1 villein have 2 teams there, and 60 acres of meadow.

50. In Duninctune [Donington on Bain (Gartree)] there are 6 carucates of land ⌊assessed⌋ to the geld. There is land for 8 teams. Ivo has 3 teams there ⌊in demesne⌋, and 28 sokemen and 6 bordars have 6 teams, and there are 2 mills rendering 17 shillings and 4 pence, and 240 acres of meadow.

51. In Stangehou [Stenigot (Gartree)] there are 3 carucates of land ⌊assessed⌋ to the geld. There is land for 3 teams. Ivo has 2 teams there ⌊in demesne⌋, and 23 sokemen and 5 villeins have 4 teams,* and 120 acres of meadow, and 20 acres of underwood.

**D. B., f. 351*a. *Facsimile, p. xxxi*a.

52. In Estrebi [Asterby (Gartree)] there are 3 carucates of land ⌊assessed⌋ to the geld. There is land for 3 teams. There are 9 sokemen and 2 villeins and 7 bordars there having 3 teams, and 120 acres of meadow.

53. In the two Mentinghes [Minting and Little Minting (Gartree)] there are 7 carucates of land ⌊assessed⌋ to the geld, and 5 bovates and the fifth part of a bovate ⌊assessed⌋ to the geld. There is arable land for twice as many ⌊teams and oxen⌋ (*terra arabilis duplex*). Ivo has 2 teams there in demesne, and 27 sokemen and 10 villeins and 20 bordars having 9 teams, and 260 acres of meadow, and 100 acres of wood⌊land⌋ for pannage, and 1010 acres of underwood.

54. In Stigeswald [Stixwould (Gartree)] there are 2 carucates and 2 bovates of land ⌊assessed⌋ to the geld. There is land for 2 teams and 2 oxen. 10 sokemen and 3 villeins and 4 bordars have 3 teams there, and 40 acres of meadow, and 80 acres of wood⌊land⌋ for pannage.

[1] *Rectius* Gartree Wapentake.

55. In Horsintone [Horsington (Gartree)] there is 1 carucate of land ⌊assessed⌋ to the geld. There is land for 1 team. 4 villeins and 4 sokemen have 1 team there, and 50 acres of meadow, and 25 acres of underwood.

56. In Burgrede and Turlai [Burreth and Thorley (Gartree)] there are 1 carucate and 3[1] bovates and the third part of a bovate of land ⌊assessed⌋ to the geld. There is arable land for as many ⌊teams and oxen⌋. 9 sokemen have 3 teams there, and 175 acres of meadow, and 180 acres of wood⌊land⌋ for pannage, and 500 acres of underwood.[2]

57. M. In Bolintone [Bullington (Wraggoe)] Lambe had 5 bovates of land ⌊assessed⌋ to the geld. There is land for 2 teams. Odo, Ivo's man, has 1 team there ⌊in demesne⌋, and 13 villeins[3] and 1 villein and 2 bordars with 1 team, and 5 acres of meadow, and 80 acres of underwood. T. R. E. it was worth 16 shillings ; now 20 shillings ; tallage 10 shillings.

58. Two M. In Beningurde[4] [Benniworth (Wraggoe)] Siward [and Turgot] had 3 carucates [and a half] of land ⌊assessed⌋ to the geld. There is land for 6[5] teams. Of this land half a carucate is soke⌊land⌋ (*in soca*). Odo, Ivo's man, has 3 teams there ⌊in demesne⌋, and 11 villeins and 10 bordars and 18 sokemen having 6 teams, and 140 acres of meadow. T. R. E. it was worth 4 pounds ; now 5 pounds ; tallage 20 shillings.

59. M. In Chinetorp [Kingthorpe (Wraggoe)] Bertor had $2\frac{1}{2}$ bovates and the third part of half a bovate ⌊of land⌋ ⌊assessed⌋ to the geld. There is arable land for twice as many ⌊teams and oxen⌋ (*terra arabilis duplex*). Odo has 2 villeins ploughing there with 2 oxen, and 5 acres of meadow, and 80 acres of wood⌊land⌋ for pannage throughout the territory. T. R. E. it was worth 10 shillings ; now the like amount.

60. In Strubi [Strubby (Wraggoe)] there are 2 bovates ⌊assessed⌋ to the geld.[6]

61. M. In Ludesforde [Ludford (Wraggoe)] Thorald had 5 bovates of land ⌊assessed⌋ to the geld. There is land for 10 oxen. Odo has 1 team there ⌊in demesne⌋, and 8 villeins with 1 team, and 1 mill rendering 12 pence, and 10 acres of meadow. T. R. E. it was worth 40 shillings ; now 30 shillings.

62. M. In Ellingetone [Edlington (Horncastle)] Gamel had 2 carucates of land ⌊assessed⌋ to the geld. There is land for 2 teams. Walter, Ivo's man, has 2 teams there ⌊in demesne⌋, and 4 villeins and 6 sokemen and 3 bordars with 1 team, and 1 mill rendering 8 shillings, and 30 acres of meadow, and 30 acres of underwood, and a church. T. R. E. it was worth 40 shillings ; now 60 shillings.

63. Two M. In Widun [Wyham (Ludborough)] Alwin had 2 carucates of land ⌊assessed⌋ to the geld. There is land for 3 teams. Wimund, Ivo's man, has 2 teams there ⌊in demesne⌋, and 4 villeins and 4 sokemen with 1 team, and 8 acres of meadow. T. R. E. it was worth 40 shillings ; now the like amount ; tallage 20 shillings.

---

[1] *ii* has been written in the line, and *i* above the line with the last two letters of *tres* above it.
[2] The letter *r* is placed in the margin opposite this entry.
[3] *Villeins* is probably a mistake for *sokemen*.
[4] See 2/16 ; 69/27.
[5] *v* seems to have been corrected to *vi*.
[6] This entry has been squeezed in as a continuation of the last line of no. 59.

D. B., f. 351b. *Facsimile, p. xxxib.*

64. M. In Ormesbi[1] [North Ormsby (Ludborough)] Alwin had 2 carucates and 2 bovates of land [assessed] to the geld. There is land for 3½ teams. Wimund, Ivo's man, has 2 teams there [in demesne], and 13 sokemen and 2 villeins with 2 teams, and 16 acres of meadow, and 8 acres of underwood. T. R. E. it was worth 50 shillings ; now 40 shillings ; tallage 20 shillings.

65. M. In Bolinbroc [Bolingbroke (Bolingbroke)] Stori had 2 carucates of land [assessed] to the geld. There is land for 2 teams. 1 carucate of this land is sokeland (*in soca*). Now Ivo has 2 teams there [in demesne], and 12 villeins and 8 bordars and 12 sokemen with 3 teams. There is a church there, and a new market, and 3 mills rendering 10 shillings, and 70 acres of meadow. T. R. E. it was worth 30 pounds ; now 40 pounds ; tallage 80 pounds with all things appertaining.

SOKE[LAND] OF THIS MANOR [nos. 66–82]

66. In Harebi [Hareby (Bolingbroke)] there are 4 carucates of land [assessed] to the geld. There is land for 4 teams. 33 sokemen and 5 villeins and 5 bordars have 4 teams there, and 100 acres of meadow.

67. In Melingesbi [Miningsby (Bolingbroke)] there are 6 carucates of land [assessed] to the geld. There is land for 6 teams. 36 sokemen and 8 villeins and 4 bordars have 6 teams there, and 40 acres of meadow.

68. In Asgerebi [Asgarby near Spilsby (Bolingbroke)] there are 3 carucates of land [assessed] to the geld. There is land for 3 teams. 20 sokemen and 2 villeins have 3 teams there, and 80 acres of meadow.

69. In Endrebi [Mavis Enderby (Bolingbroke)] there are 5 carucates of land [assessed] to the geld. There is land for 5 teams. 24 sokemen and 5 bordars have 5 teams there, and 100 acres of meadow.

70. In Radebi [Raithby by Spilsby (Bolingbroke)] there are 3 carucates and 7 bovates of land [assessed] to the geld. There is land for as many teams and oxen. 18 villeins[2] and 3 villeins and 5 bordars have 4 teams there. There is a church there, and a mill rendering 12 shillings, and 40 acres of meadow.

71. In Hundelbi [Hundleby (Bolingbroke)] there are 4 carucates of land [assessed] to the geld. There is land for 4 teams. 25 sokemen and 12 villeins have 4 teams there. There is a church there, and a mill rendering 5 shillings, and 80 acres of meadow. In this land Tor had 4 acres of land which belong to the Bishop of Durham's manor of Spilesbi [Spilsby (Bolingbroke)].

72. In Haltun and Stepi [Halton Holegate and Little Steeping (Bolingbroke)] there are 9 carucates of land [assessed] to the geld. There is land for 9 teams. Ivo has 1 team there [in demesne], and 58 sokemen and 4 villeins with 9 teams. There is a church there, and 4 mills rendering 24 shillings, and 120 acres of meadow.

73. In Torp [Thorpe St. Peter (Bolingbroke)] there are 2 carucates and 5 bovates of land [assessed] to the geld. There is land for as many teams and oxen. 18 sokemen and 8 villeins have 3 teams there. There is a church there, and 280 acres of meadow.

---

[1] See 30/20 ; 70/28.

[2] *villani* is seemingly a clerical error for *sockmanni*.

74. In Totintun [Toynton All Saints (Bolingbroke)] there are 3 carucates of land ⌊assessed⌋ to the geld. There is land for 3 teams. 14 villeins and 13 sokemen have 3 teams there. There is a church there, and 30 acres of meadow, and 5½ acres of underwood.

75. In Stichenai [Stickney (Bolingbroke)] there are 3 carucates of land ⌊assessed⌋ to the geld. There is land for 3 teams. 33 sokemen and 5 villeins have 3 teams there. There is a church there, and 40 acres of meadow.

76. In Sibolci [Sibsey (Bolingbroke)] there are 6 carucates of land ⌊assessed⌋ to the geld. There is land for 6 teams. 51 sokemen and 16 villeins and 10 bordars have 6 teams there. Ivo himself has 1 team there ⌊in demesne⌋, and there is a church, and 120 acres of meadow.

77. In Stichesforde [Stickford (Bolingbroke)] there are 2½ carucates of land ⌊assessed⌋ to the geld. There is land for as many teams. 28 sokemen and 2 villeins have 3 teams there. There is a church there, and 30 acres of meadow.

78. In Estrecale [East Keal (Bolingbroke)] there are 4½ carucates of land ⌊assessed⌋ to the geld. There is land for as many teams. Ivo has 1 team there ⌊in demesne⌋, and 7 sokemen and 12 villeins and 4 bordars with 4½ teams. There is half a church there, and 20 acres of meadow.* Summerled had a manor there, and T. R. E. it was worth 20 shillings ; now the like amount.

**D. B., f. 351c.* *Facsimile, p. xxxii*a.

79. In Westrecale [West Keal (Bolingbroke)] there are 4 carucates of land ⌊assessed⌋ to the geld. There is land for 5 teams. 35 sokemen and 8 villeins and 6 bordars have 6 teams there, and 100 acres of meadow.

80. In Totintun [Toynton St. Peter (Bolingbroke)] there are 5 carucates and 2 bovates of land ⌊assessed⌋ to the geld. There is land for 6 teams. 40 sokemen and 7 villeins and 3 bordars have 6 teams there. There is a church there, and 70 acres of meadow, and 10 acres of underwood.

81. In Hagenebi [Hagnaby (Bolingbroke)] there are 2 carucates and 5 bovates of land ⌊assessed⌋ to the geld. There is land for as many teams and oxen. 14 sokemen and 4 villeins and 2 bordars have 3 teams there, and 73 acres of meadow.

82. In Cherchebi and Resvesbi [East Kirkby and Revesby (Bolingbroke)] there are 12 carucates of land ⌊assessed⌋ to the geld. There is land for 12 teams. 54 sokemen and 14 villeins have 12 teams there. Ivo has 1 team there ⌊in demesne⌋, and 2 churches, and 180 acres of meadow.

The whole manor with all things appertaining to it is 6 leagues in length and 6 in breadth.

83. M. In Archintone [Elkington (Louthesk)] Esbern had 4 carucates of land ⌊assessed⌋ to the geld. There is land for 8 teams. Of this land 2½ carucates are sokeland (*in soca*). Geoffrey (*Goisfridus*), Ivo's man, has 2 teams there ⌊in demesne⌋, and 19 sokemen and 5 villeins with 3 teams. There is half a church there, and half the site of a mill, and 60 acres of meadow. T. R. E. it was worth 60 shillings ; now 6 pounds ; tallage 40 shillings.

84. In Grimesbi [Little Grimsby (Ludborough)] there is soke⌊land⌋ ⌊of this manor⌋, 1½ carucates of land ⌊assessed⌋ to the geld. There is land for 2 teams. Geoffrey (*Goisfridus*) has 1 team there ⌊in demesne⌋, and 5 villeins and 6 sokemen with 1 team, and 10 acres of meadow.

85. B. and S. In Lodeby [Sloothby (Calcewath)] there are 7 bovates of land ⌊assessed⌋ to the geld. There is land for 1½ teams. It is inland, ⌈6 bovates⌉, belonging to (*in*) Hundebi[1] [Hanby in Welton le Marsh (Calcewath)], and soke⌊land⌋, ⌈1 bovate⌉, belonging to (*in*) Clachesbi [Claxby by Alford (Calcewath)]. 8 villeins and 3 bordars have 1 team there, and 15 acres of meadow.

86. M. In Brune [Bourne (Aveland)] Sewen had 3 bovates of land ⌊assessed⌋ to the geld. There is land for 3 oxen. Odo, Ivo's man, has 3 villeins and 1 bordar there with half a team, and the sixth part of a mill rendering 20 pence, and 3 fisheries rendering 8 pence, and 3½ acres of meadow, and 15 acres of underwood. T. R. E. it was worth 6 shillings; now 10 shillings.

87. In Brezbi and Sapretone [Braceby and Sapperton (Threo)] there is 1 carucate of land ⌊assessed⌋ to the geld. There is land for 1 team. It is soke⌊land⌋ belonging to (*in*) Bergebi [Barrowby (Threo)]. 2 villeins and 1 bordar have 1 team there, and 16 acres of meadow, and 30 acres of wood⌊land⌋ for pannage, and 5 acres of underwood.

88. In Hundintone[2] [Honington (Threo)] there are 9 carucates of land ⌊assessed⌋ to the geld. There is land for 9 teams. It is soke⌊land⌋ belonging to (*in*) Bergebi [Barrowby (Threo)]. Ivo has 2 teams there ⌊in demesne⌋, and 16 villeins and 4 bordars and 10 sokemen having 3½ teams. There is a church there, and a priest, and the site of a mill, and 105 acres of meadow. T. R. E. it was worth 6 pounds; now 5 pounds; tallage 20 shillings.

89. In Barchestone [Barkston (Threo)] there are 10 bovates of land ⌊assessed⌋ to the geld. There is land for 10 oxen. It is soke⌊land⌋ belonging to (*in*) Hundintune[3] [Honington]. There is 1 team there in demesne, and 1 sokeman and 1 villein and 3 bordars with 1 team, and 13 acres of meadow.

90. In Sidestan [Syston (Threo)] there are 2 bovates of land ⌊assessed⌋ to the geld. It is soke⌊land⌋ belonging to (*in*) Hundintone. It is waste.

91. M. In Chinetorp [Kingthorpe (Wraggoe)] Bertor and Thorald (*Torul*) had 7½ bovates and the third part of half a bovate ⌊assessed⌋ to the geld. There is arable land for twice as many ⌊teams and oxen⌋ (*ad duplum*). Odo, Ivo's man, has 1 team there in ⌊demesne⌋, and 10 villeins with 1 team, and 15 acres of meadow, and 80 acres of wood⌊land⌋ for pannage throughout the territory. T. R. E. it was worth 50 shillings; now 40 shillings.

D. B., f. 351d. *Facsimile, p. xxxii*b.

92. M. In Wiuelestorp [Wilsthorpe (Ness)] Bernac ⌈and Bole⌉ had 4[4] carucates of land ⌊assessed⌋ to the geld. There is land for 4 teams.

[1] See 14/100; 69/20. [2] See 24/84; 72/63. [3] Corrected from *Huntindune*.
[4] *ii* is written in the line, and *ii* above the line. These numbers are intended to be added together.

Of this land 2 carucates are soke⌊land⌋ (*in soca*). Odo, Ivo's man, ⌊has⌋ 1 team there ⌊in demesne⌋, and 10 sokemen and 10 villeins having 2½ teams, and [2] mills rendering 20 shillings, and 40 acres of meadow, and 12 acres of underwood. T. R. E. it was worth 40 shillings; now 80 shillings; now[1] 30 shillings.

SOKE⌊LAND⌋ ⌊OF THIS MANOR⌋

93. In Opestorp [Obthorpe (Ness)] there are 2 bovates of land ⌊assessed⌋ to the geld. There is land for 2 oxen. There are 2 sokemen there with half a team, and 4 acres of meadow.

94. M. In Bertune and Torp [Burton Coggles and Bassingthorpe (Beltisloe)] he[2] had 14 bovates of land ⌊assessed⌋ to the geld. There is land for 14 oxen. Azor, Ivo's man, has 3 villeins and 2 bordars there with 2 teams, and 300 acres of underwood, and 13 acres of meadow. T. R. E. it was worth 30 shillings; now 20 shillings. This belongs to (*iacet in*) Bergebi [Barrowby (Winnibriggs)].

95. In Helpericham [Helpringham (Aswardhurn)] there are 6 bovates of land ⌊assessed⌋ to the geld. There is land for 6 oxen. It is soke⌊land⌋ belonging to (*in*) Wiuelestorp [Wilsthorpe (Ness)]. There are 3 sokemen and 1 bordar there with 1 team, and 1 acre of meadow.

96. M. In Spallinge [Spalding (Elloe)] [Earl] Algar had 9 carucates of land ⌊assessed⌋ to the geld. There is land for as many teams. Ivo has 4 teams there in demesne, and 40 villeins and 33 bordars having 13 teams. There is a market there [rendering 40 shillings], and 6 fisheries rendering 30 shillings, and 20 shillings from salt-pans, and a wood of alders rendering 8 shillings. T. R. E. it was worth 23 pounds and 2 shillings and 8 pence; now 30 pounds; tallage 30 pounds.

97. In Tite [Tydd St. Mary (Elloe)] there are 3 carucates and 2 bovates of land ⌊assessed⌋ to the geld. There is land for 2 teams. It is a berewic belonging to (*in*) Spallinge [Spalding]. 9 villeins and 1 bordar have 3 teams there. Ivo has 2 teams there in demesne, and a church.

98. In Picebech [Pinchbeck (Elloe)] there is soke⌊land⌋, 10 carucates of land ⌊assessed⌋ to the geld. There is land for 10 teams. 22 sokemen and 16 villeins and 12 bordars have 9 teams there, and [4] fisheries rendering 1500 eels.

99. In Westune and Multune [Weston and Moulton (Elloe)] there is soke⌊land⌋, 10 carucates and 1 bovate of land ⌊assessed⌋ to the geld. There is land for as many teams and oxen. 26 sokemen and 31 villeins and 20 bordars have 20 teams there.

100. In Waletone and Bodebi [Welton le Marsh and Boothby in Welton (Candleshoe)] there are 2 carucates and 2 bovates of land ⌊assessed⌋ to the geld. There is land for 3 teams. It is soke⌊land⌋ belonging to (*in*) Hunbia[3] [Hanby in Welton le Marsh]. 7 sokemen and 2 villeins and 5 bordars have 4 teams and 1 mill rendering 2 shillings. W nd [*sic*] has it.

---

[1] Perhap *modo* is a mistake for *tailla*.
[2] The former tenant's name has probably been accidentally omitted.
[3] See 14/85; 69/20.

15. LAND OF WILLIAM OF WARENNE (*Warene*)

1. M. In Carletune [Carlton Scroop (Loveden)] [Earl] Harold had 5 carucates of land [assessed] to the geld. There is land for 7 teams. Aldelin, William of Warenne's man, has 3 teams there in demesne, and 21 sokemen on (*de*) 2 carucates of this land and 11 villeins and 6 bordars with 5 teams. There is a priest there, and a church,[1] and 50 acres of meadow. T. R. E. it was worth 6 pounds ; now 10 pounds.

2. B. and S. In Beningtone[2] [Long Bennington (Loveden)] there are 2 carucates and 2 bovates of land [assessed] to the geld. There is land for 3 teams. It is inland [10 bovates] and soke[land] [1 carucate] of the same manor. There is 1 team there in demesne, and 3 sokemen and 1 bordar have 1 team, and 20 acres of meadow.

D. B., f. 352a. *Facsimile, p. xxxiii*a.

16. LAND OF ROGER OF POITOU (*Pictavensis*)

1. M. In Ribi [Riby (Yarborough)] Stanchil had 12 bovates of land [assessed] to the geld. There is land for 3 teams. Ernuin, Roger of Poitou's man, has 1 team there [in demesne], and 5 villeins and 5 sokemen with 1 team, and 12 acres of meadow. T. R. E. it was worth 30 shillings ; now the like amount ; tallage 10 shillings.

2. M. In Sualun [Swallow (Bradley)] Stanchil [and Ernuin] had 1 carucate of land [assessed] to the geld. There is land for 2 teams. Wimund, Roger's man, has half a team there [in demesne], and 3 villeins and 3 sokemen with 1 team. T. R. E. it was worth 40 shillings ; now 20 shillings.

3.[3] M. In Rase [Middle Rasen (Walshcroft)] there are 3 bovates of land [assessed] to the geld. There is land for 7 oxen. Mainard, Roger's man, has 4 villeins there with half a team. T. R. E. it was worth 10 shillings ; now 22 shillings.

4. M. In Colesi [South Kelsey (Walshcroft)] Ernui had 3 carucates of land [assessed] to the geld. There is land for 6 teams. Roger, Roger of Poitou's man, has 1½ teams there [in demesne], and 4 villeins and 6 bordars and 20 sokemen having 3 teams. T. R. E. it was worth 100 shillings ; now 6c shillings.

5. In Torentun [Thornton le Moor (Walshcroft)] Grimbold had 2 bovates of land [assessed] to the geld. There is land for 6 oxen Roger of Poitou has 1 team there [in demesne], and 1 villein. T. R. E. it was worth 10 shillings ; now 5 shillings.

---

[1] See 72/37. [2] See 12/49 ; 72/38.
[3] The letter *K*, probably representing *Kalumpnia*, is written in the margin against this entry.

6.[1] In the same place (*ibidem*) Roger has 11 bovates[2] of land ⌊assessed⌋ to the geld. There is land ⌊for⌋ 14 oxen, and 364 acres of meadow.

7. M. In Hoctun [Holton le Moor (Walshcroft)] Ernui had half a carucate of land ⌊assessed⌋ to the geld. There is land for 1 team. Roger, Roger of Poitou's man, has 1 team there ⌊in demesne⌋, and 4 sokemen with half a team, and 5 acres of meadow. T. R. E. and now worth 10 shillings.

8.[1] M. In Oresbi [Owersby (Walshcroft)] Ernui had 1½ carucates of land ⌊assessed⌋ to the geld. There is land for 3 teams. This land belongs to (*iacet in*) the church of Wingeham [Winghale priory]. 2 bordars plough there with 2 oxen. Roger of Poitou has 76 acres of meadow there ⌊in demesne⌋. T. R. E. it was worth 30 shillings; now 10 shillings.

9. M. In Osgotebi [Osgodby (Walshcroft)] Ingemund had 2½ bovates of land ⌊assessed⌋ to the geld. There is land for 5 oxen. Geoffrey (*Goisfridus*), Roger's man, has 4 villeins and 1 bordar and 1 sokeman there with half a team, and 1 mill rendering 3 shillings of which bishop Remigius has the soke, and 20 acres of meadow. T. R. E. it was worth 20 shillings; now 5 shillings.

10. Two M. In Tavelesbi [Tealby (Walshcroft)] Swen and Brinot had 1½ carucates of land ⌊assessed⌋ to the geld. There is land for 2½ teams. Roger, Roger of Poitou's man, has 1 team there ⌊in demesne⌋, and 4 villeins and 5 bordars and 3 sokemen ploughing with 5 oxen. There are 4 mills there rendering 16 shillings and 4 pence, and 78 acres of meadow.

SOKE⌊LAND⌋ OF THIS MANOR

11. In Rase [8½ bovates], in Osgotebi [1 bovate], in Walesbi [1 carucate], in Otebi [1 carucate], [Market Rasen, Osgodby, Walesby, and Otby (Walshcroft)] there are 3 carucates and 1½ bovates of land ⌊assessed⌋ to the geld. There is land for 7 teams. There are 41 sokemen there having 4 teams, and 60 acres of meadow, and 1 mill rendering 3 shillings.

12. M. In Haintone [Hainton (Wraggoe)] Oudon had 9 bovates of land ⌊assessed⌋ to the geld. There is land for 2 teams and 2 oxen. Hacon (*Acun*), Roger's man, has 1 team there ⌊in demesne⌋ and 8 villeins and 2 bordars with 1½ teams, and 60 acres of meadow. T. R. E. it was worth 30 shillings; now 40 shillings.

13. In Strubi [Strubby in Langton by Wragby (Wraggoe)] there is soke⌊land⌋ of this manor, 2 bovates of land ⌊assessed⌋ to the geld. There is land for 4 oxen. 1 sokeman and 2 bordars plough there with 2 oxen.

14. Two M. In Haintone[3] [Hainton (Wraggoe)] Clac and Sendi had 1 carucate and half a bovate ⌊assessed⌋ to the geld. There is land for 2 teams. Albert, Roger's man, has 1 team there ⌊in demesne⌋, and 3 villeins ploughing with 3 oxen, and 54 acres of meadow. T. R. E. it was worth 50 shillings; now 60 shillings.

---

[1] The letter *K*, probably representing *Kalumpnia*, is written in the margin against these entries.

[2] See 22/5.

[3] See 69/25.

15.[1] In Blasebi [Bleasby (Wraggoe)] there are 2 bovates of wood⌊land⌋ which belongs to (*iacet in*) Haintun.

16.[1] In Sisse [Sixle (Wraggoe)] there is soke⌊land⌋ belonging to (*in*) Haintune, 2½ carucates and half a bovate of land ⌊assessed⌋ to the geld. There is land for 3 teams. 30 sokemen have 3 teams there and 320 acres of meadow.

17. In Barcuurde and Sutrei [West Barkwith and Southrey (Wraggoe) there is inland [2 bovates] and soke⌊land⌋ [3 bovates] of this manor ⌊assessed⌋ to the geld. 6 sokemen and 2 villeins have 2 teams there. There is 1 fishery there, and 16 acres of meadow, and 20 acres of wood⌊land⌋ for pannage.

D. B., f. 352b. *Facsimile, p. xxxiii*b.

18. M. In Bechelinge [Holton by Beckering (Wraggoe)] Alric had 2 bovates of land ⌊assessed⌋ to the geld. There is land for 4 oxen. 3 villeins and 4 bordars plough there with 3 oxen. There are 3 acres of meadow there. T. R. E. it was worth 10 shillings ; now 20 shillings.

19. In Terintone [West Torrington (Wraggoe) there is soke⌊land⌋ ⌊of this manor⌋, 5 bovates of land ⌊assessed⌋ to the geld. There is land for 10 oxen. 3 sokemen and 3 villeins and 1 bordar have 1 team and 1 ploughing ox there, and 8 acres of meadow.

WESTREDING [WEST RIDING]

20. M. In Suardesforde [Snarford (Lawress)] Ulchil had 3 bovates of land ⌊assessed⌋ to the geld. There is land for 4 oxen. Now Mainard and Thorald have it of Roger, and it is waste. There are 16 acres of meadow there. T. R. E. it was worth 10 shillings.

21.[2] In Hagetone [Hackthorn (Aslacoe)] there is soke⌊land⌋ belonging to (*in*) Snereforde [Snarford], 3 bovates ⌊assessed⌋ to the geld.

22. Three M. In Torp [Northorpe (Corringham)] Sperri had 6 bovates of land ⌊assessed⌋ to the geld. There is land for 1 team. And Frane and Alnod ⌊had⌋ 6 carucates[3] of land ⌊assessed⌋ to the geld. There is land for 2 teams. Roger of Poitou has there 4 villeins and 8 sokemen having 3 teams. He himself ⌊has⌋ 5 ploughing oxen there ⌊in demesne⌋, and 24 acres of meadow. T. R. E. it was worth 4 pounds; now 60 shillings ; tallage 10 shillings.

23. In Tunec [In Warton[4]] [Thonock, Wharton (Corringham)] there are 1½ carucates ⌊assessed⌋ to the geld. There is land for 2 teams. It is inland and soke⌊land⌋ ⌊of this manor⌋. 6 sokemen and 4 villeins and 1 bordar have 1½ teams there, and 20 acres of meadow. There is wood⌊land⌋ for pannage 1 league in length and half ⌊a league⌋ in breadth.

24. In Tonestele [Dunstall (Corringham)] there are 1 carucate and 2 bovates of land ⌊assessed⌋ to the geld. There is land for 12 oxen. It is inland [4 bovates], and soke⌊land⌋ [6 bovates]. There are 1 villein and 1 sokeman there with half a team. Ivo has 2 bovates and renders soke.

---

[1] These entries follow no. 34 in the text, and a sign indicates that they should be inserted where they appear in the text.

[2] This entry is written in the margin.

[3] This is probably a mistake for *6 bovates*.

[4] *In Warton* is interlined, but *In Tunec* is not cancelled. *Tunec* seems to have been written upon an erasure. In the later records the tenement is described as *Thonock.*

25.[1] In the other Torp [Southorpe (Corringham)] there are 2 bovates of land ⌊assessed⌋ to the geld. It is inland belonging to (*in*) the above-mentioned manor of Torp [Northorpe]. Roger of Poitou has nothing there.

26.[1] In Ioletorp [Yawthorpe (Corringham)] there is half a carucate ⌊assessed⌋ to the geld. It is soke⌊land⌋ ⌊of this manor⌋.

27. M. In Torp [Northorpe (Corringham)] Godric had 1½ carucates of land ⌊assessed⌋ to the geld. There is land for 2 teams. Roger, Roger of Poitou's man, has 2 teams there ⌊in demesne⌋, and 1 villein and 6 bordars ploughing with 2 oxen. T. R. E. it was worth 40 shillings; now 20 shillings.

28.[2] M. In Lastone[3] [Laughton (Corringham)] Swen had 1½ carucates of land ⌊assessed⌋ to the geld. There is land for 2 teams. Blancard, Roger of Poitou's man, has 1 team there ⌊in demesne⌋, and 3 villeins ploughing with 3 oxen, and half a mill rendering 12 pence, and half a fishery rendering 2 shillings, and 15 acres of meadow. T. R. E. it was worth 30 shillings; now 20 shillings.

29. In Scotone [Scotton (Corringham)] there are 2 bovates of land ⌊assessed⌋ to the geld. It is soke⌊land⌋ belonging to (*de*) Lastone[4] [Laughton].

30. M. In the same Lastone [Laughton] Leduin had 10 bovates of land ⌊assessed⌋ to the geld. There is land for 12 oxen. 5 sokemen have 6 ploughing oxen there, and 8 acres of meadow. T. R. E. it was worth 30 shillings; now 10 shillings.

31.[5] In Blitone [Blyton (Corringham)] there are 2 bovates of land ⌊assessed⌋ to the geld. It is soke⌊land⌋ of this manor.

32. M. In Stantone [Stainton by Waddingham (Manley)] Gamel had 6 bovates of land ⌊assessed⌋ to the geld. There is land for 6 oxen. Roger, Roger's man, has half a team there ⌊in demesne⌋, and 6 villeins with 1 team, and 16 acres of meadow. T. R. E. it was worth 20 shillings; now 10 shillings.

33. M. In Elesham [Elsham (Yarborough)] William had 9 bovates of land ⌊assessed⌋ to the geld. There is land ⌊for⌋ 2½ teams. Ernui, Roger's man, has 1 team there ⌊in demesne⌋, and 5 villeins and 1 bordar ploughing with 2 oxen, and 60 acres of meadow. T. R. E. it was worth 60 shillings; now 20 shillings; tallage 10 shillings.

34. In Catenai [Cadney (Yarborough)] there is inland of this manor, 5 bovates and 3 parts of 1 bovate of land ⌊assessed⌋ to the geld. 5 villeins have 1 team there.

35. M. In Alduluebi [Audleby (Yarborough)] Grimchil had 5 bovates of land ⌊assessed⌋ to the geld. There is land for 1 team. Blancard, Roger of Poitou's man, has half a team there ⌊in demesne⌋, and 5 villeins and 4 bordars.

D. B., f. 352c. *Facsimile, p. xxxiv*a.

36. Two M. In Catebi [South Cadeby (Louthesk)] Godric and

[1] These two entries have been inserted as a continuation of no. 24.
[2] The letter *K*, probably representing *Kalumpnia*, is written in the margin against this entry.
[3] See 71/14.
[4] Corrected from *Lestone*.
[5] This entry has been inserted at the end of the last line of no. 30.

Siward had 4 bovates [and a half] of land ⌊assessed⌋ to the geld. There is land for 1 team. Now Roger has half a team there ⌊in demesne⌋, and 2 villeins and 1 sokeman with 1 team, and 10 acres of meadow. T. R. E. it was worth 30 shillings ; now the like amount.

37.[1] In Wicham [East Wykeham (Louthesk)] there is half a bovate of land ⌊assessed to the geld⌋. It is inland of Catebi [South Cadeby].

38. In Welletune [Welton le Wold (Louthesk)] there is half a carucate of land ⌊assessed⌋ to the geld. There is land for 12 oxen. It is soke⌊land⌋ of this manor. 4 sokemen and 3 villeins have 1½ teams there, and 2 parts of 1 site of a mill.

39. M. In Lecheburne [Legbourne (Calcewath)] Hambe had 1 carucate of land ⌊assessed⌋ to the geld. There is land for 1½ teams. Girard, Roger's man, has 8 sokemen and 11 bordars there with 1 team, and 20 acres of meadow, and 142 acres of underwood. T. R. E. it was worth 30 shillings ; now 20 shillings.

40. In Summercotes [Somercotes (Louthesk)] there are 3 parts of 1 carucate ⌊assessed⌋ to the geld. There is land for half a team. 3 sokemen plough there with 2 oxen.

41. M. In Ingeham [Ingham (Aslacoe)] Aluui had 4 bovates of land ⌊assessed⌋ to the geld. There is land for 6 oxen. Roger has 3 sokemen and 2 bordars and 1 villein there with 1 team, and 10 acres of meadow. T. R. E. it was worth 10 shillings ; now the like amount. Mainard holds it.

42. In Cotes [Cotes by Stow (Aslacoe)] there is 1 bovate of land ⌊assessed⌋ to the geld. It is inland belonging to (*in*) Ingeham [Ingham].

43. M. In Filingeham [Fillingham (Aslacoe)] Turgot had 2 carucates and 1 bovate of land ⌊assessed⌋ to the geld. There is land for 3½ teams. Anschitil, Roger's man, has 2 teams there ⌊in demesne⌋, and 9 sokemen and 2 villeins with 2½ teams, and 80 acres of meadow. T. R. E. it was worth 30 shillings ; now 40 shillings ; tallage 10 shillings.

44. M. In Neteltone [Nettleton (Yarborough)] Grimchil had 5 bovates of land ⌊assessed⌋ to the geld. There is land for 2 teams. Blancard, Roger's man, has 5 villeins and 4 bordars and 1 sokeman there with 1 team, and 2 mills rendering 10 shillings, and 40 acres of meadow. T. R. E. it was worth 40 shillings ; now 30 shillings.

45. M. In Crocestone [Croxton (Yarborough)] Aschil had 6 bovates of land ⌊assessed⌋ to the geld, There is land for 12 oxen. Anschitil, Roger's man, has 1 team there ⌊in demesne⌋, and 5 villeins and 7 sokemen with 1 team. T. R. E. it was worth 40 shillings ; now the like amount.

46. M. In Blochesham [Bloxham (Flaxwell)] Turuer had 9 carucates and 5 bovates of land ⌊assessed⌋ to the geld. There is land for as many teams and oxen. Roger of Poitou has 1 team [and a half] there in demesne, and 18 sokemen and 2 villeins having 5 teams, and 13 acres of meadow. T. R. E. it was worth 4 pounds ; now 3 pounds.

47. M. In Canewic and Bragebruge [Canwick and Bracebridge (Langoe)] Strui had 2 carucates of land ⌊assessed⌋ to the geld. There is land for 2 teams. Ernuin, Roger's man, has 1 team there ⌊in demesne⌋, and 4 sokemen and 5 villeins and 1 bordar ploughing with 6 oxen. There

[1] This entry is written as a continuation of no. 36.

is a church there, and a priest, and 40 acres of meadow, and 2 fisheries rendering 2 shillings. T. R. E. it was worth 30 shillings ; now 40 shillings.

48. In the same places (*ibidem*) there is 1 carucate of land ⌊assessed⌋ to the geld. There is land for 1 team. It belongs to (*iacet in*) Branzuic [*unidentified*].

49. M. In Aclei [Eagle (Graffoe)] Archilbar had 13 bovates of land ⌊assessed⌋ to the geld. There is land for 10 oxen. There are 5 villeins and 16 acres of meadow there. T. R. E. and now worth 20 shillings.

50. In Haneurde [Cold Hanworth (Aslacoe)] there are 3 bovates of land ⌊assessed⌋ to the geld. There is land for 1 team. It is soke⌊land⌋ belonging to (*in*) Snerteforde [Snarford (Lawress)]. Thorald [the priest] has 1 sokeman and 2 bordars ploughing there with 2 oxen.

D. B., f. 352d. *Facsimile, p. xxxiv*b.

17. LAND OF ROGER DE BUSLI

1. M. In Grentewelle [Greetwell (Lawress)] Swen had 3 carucates of land ⌊assessed⌋ to the geld. There is land for 5 teams. Thorald, Roger de Busli's man, has 3 teams there ⌊in demesne⌋, and 15 villeins and 6 bordars with 4 teams. There is a church there, and a priest, and 2 fisheries rendering 15 pence, and 1 mill rendering 5 shillings, and 16 acres of meadow. T. R. E. it was worth 8 pounds ; now the like amount.

2. M. In Aplebi and Risebi and Saleclif [Appleby and Risby and Sawcliff (Manley)] Gamel had 9 carucates and 5 bovates of land ⌊assessed⌋ to the geld. There is land for 19 teams and 2 oxen. Roger de Busli has 4 teams there in demesne, and 31 villeins and 2 bordars with 6 teams, and 31 sokemen with 6 teams. There is a church there, and a priest. There is wood⌊land⌋ for pannage half a league in length and 1 furlong in breadth, and 20 acres of meadow. T. R. E. it was worth 8 pounds ; now 10 pounds ; tallage 3 pounds.

3. In Sanctone [Santon (Manley)] there is soke⌊land⌋ ⌊of this manor⌋, 1 carucate of land ⌊assessed⌋ to the geld. There is land for 1 team. 12 sokemen have 2 teams there, and 6 acres of meadow.

18. LAND OF ROBERT DE TODENI

1. M. In Englebi[1] [Ingleby (Lawress)] Turgot [the lawman (*lag'*)] had 4 carucates of land ⌊assessed⌋ to the geld. There is land for 4 teams. Berenger, ⌊who holds⌋ of Robert de Todeni, has 2 teams there ⌊in demesne⌋, [and 5 sokemen] and 8 villeins with 2 teams, and 180 acres of

[1] See 22/30.

meadow. There is wood⌊land⌋ for pannage 6 furlongs in length and 3 in breadth. T. R. E. it was worth 8 pounds; now 11[1] pounds; tallage 40 shillings. Of this land 1½ carucates ⌊are⌋ soke⌊land⌋ (*in soca*).

2. In Broxholme [Broxholme (Lawress)] there are 10 carucates of land ⌊assessed⌋ to the geld. There is land for 10 teams, soke⌊land⌋ [9 carucates] and inland [1 carucate]. There is 1 team there in demesne, and 24 sokemen and 2 villeins with 8½ teams. There is a church there, and 200 acres of meadow.

3. M. In Esetorp [Buslingthorpe (Lawress)] Turgot had 2 carucates of land ⌊assessed⌋ to the geld. There is land for 3 teams. Berenger, ⌊who holds⌋ of Robert, has 1½ teams there ⌊in demesne⌋, and 12 villeins and 2 sokemen with 3 teams, and 60 acres of meadow, and 33 acres of wood⌊land⌋ for pannage. Half a carucate ⌊is⌋ soke⌊land⌋. T. R. E. it was worth 40 shillings; now the like amount; tallage 10 shillings.

4. M. In Branzbi [Bransby (Well)] Turgot had 2 carucates of land ⌊assessed⌋ to the geld. There is land for 2 teams. Beren*ger*, ⌊who holds⌋ of Robert, has 1 ⌊team⌋ there ⌊in demesne⌋, and 6 villeins and 3 sokemen with 1½ teams, and 14 acres of meadow, and 50 acres of underwood. T. R. E. it was worth 60 shillings; now 50 shillings.

5.[2] In Burtone [Burton by Lincoln (Lawress)] there is 1 carucate of land ⌊assessed⌋ to the geld. There is land for 1 team. It is inland ⌊belonging to⌋ Branzbi [Bransby]. 2 bordars have 1 team there.

6. M. In Coringeham [Corringham (Corringham)] Turgot had 2 carucates of land ⌊assessed⌋ to the geld. There is land for 2 teams. Beren*ger*, ⌊who holds⌋ of Robert, has 1 team there ⌊in demesne⌋, and 5 villeins and 3 bordars with 1½ teams. There is wood⌊land⌋ for pannage 5 furlongs in length and 5 in breadth. T. R. E. it was worth 50 shillings; now 30 shillings.

D. B., f. 353a. *Facsimile, p. xxxv*a.

7. M. In Binnibroc [Binbrook (Walshcroft)] Turgot [the lawman (*Lag'*)] had 8 carucates and 4½ bovates of land ⌊assessed⌋ to the geld. There is land for 24 teams. Now Robert de Todeni, and Ber*enger* ⌊who holds⌋ of him, has 4 teams in demesne, and 6 villeins and 4 bordars and 44 sokemen with 8 teams. There is a church there, and a priest, and 2 mills rendering 20 shillings, and 100 acres of meadow. T. R. E. it was worth 7 pounds; now 15 pounds; tallage 10 pounds. Of this land 4 carucates and 4½ bovates are soke⌊land⌋.

8. S. In Ludeburg [Ludborough (Ludborough)] there are 8 carucates of land ⌊assessed⌋ to the geld. There is land for 12 teams. It is soke⌊land⌋ of the above-mentioned manor. Beren*ger* has 3 teams there ⌊in demesne⌋, and 38 sokemen with 5 teams, and 200 acres of meadow.

9. S. In Fodrebi[3] [Fotherby (Ludborough)] [4 carucates and 5 bovates], and Turgrebi [Thorganby (Walshcroft)] [1 carucate], there are 5 carucates and 5 bovates of land ⌊assessed⌋ to the geld. There is land for 9 teams. Ber*enger* has 1 team there ⌊in demesne⌋, and 33 sokemen and 2 bordars with 6 teams, and 120 acres of meadow, and 4 salt-pans rendering 2 shillings.

---

[1] The second figure of *xi* is very uncertain, and the number may possibly be *x*.

[2] This entry is written at the foot of the column, and a sign indicates that its proper place is where it is printed in the text.

[3] See 3/20; 70/29.

10. S. In Crosbi [Croxby (Walshcroft)] there is 1 carucate of land ⌊assessed⌋ to the geld. There is land for 3 teams. 14 sokemen and 4 bordars have 3 teams there, and 3 acres of meadow.

11. M. In Offintune [Uffington (Ness)] Erneber had 2 carucates of land ⌊assessed⌋ to the geld. There is land for 2 teams. Robert de Todeni has 2 teams there ⌊in demesne⌋, and 8 villeins and 2 bordars with 2 teams, and 10 acres of meadow. T. R. E. and now worth 40 shillings; tallage 10 shillings.

12. Two M. In Talintune [Tallington (Ness)] Alwin and Erneber had $5\frac{1}{2}$ carucates of land ⌊assessed⌋ to the geld. There is land for as many teams. William and Roger, Robert's men, have $1\frac{1}{2}$ teams there ⌊in demesne⌋, and 5 villeins with 1 team, and 17 acres of meadow. T. R. E. it was worth 40 shillings; now 30 shillings.

13. M. In Griteforde [Greatford (Ness)] Turgot [the lawman (*lag'*)] had $5\frac{1}{2}$ carucates of land ⌊assessed⌋ to the geld. There is land for as many teams. Bere*nger*, ⌊who holds⌋ of Robert, has 2 teams there ⌊in demesne⌋, and 10 villeins and 10 sokemen and 2 bordars with $3\frac{1}{2}$ teams, and 2 mills rendering 10 shillings, and 60 acres of meadow, and 20 acres of wood⌊land⌋ for pannage throughout the territory. T. R. E. it was worth 8 pounds; now 9 pounds; tallage 3 pounds.

14. S. In Breseburc and Barnetone [Braceborough and Banthorpe (Ness)] there are $5\frac{1}{2}$ carucates of land ⌊assessed⌋ to the geld. There is land for as many teams. 17 sokemen and 6 villeins have $5\frac{1}{2}$ teams there, and 40 acres of meadow.

15. M. In Ringesdune [Ringstone (Aveland)] Aslac and Dane had 4 carucates and 7 bovates and 2 parts of 1 bovate of land ⌊assessed⌋ to the geld. There is land for as many teams and oxen. Ivo, Robert's man, has 2 teams there ⌊in demesne⌋, and 9 villeins and 6 sokemen and 1 bordar with $1\frac{1}{2}$ teams, and 46 acres of meadow, and 120 acres of underwood, and the third part of a church. T. R. E. it was worth 50 shillings; now 60 shillings.

16. In Cherchebi [Kirkby Underwood (Aveland)] there are 2 bovates of land ⌊assessed⌋ to the geld. There is land for 2 oxen. 2 villeins plough there with 3 oxen, and there are 2 acres of meadow, and 40 acres of underwood. It is inland.

17. M. In Greibi [West Graby in Aslackby (Aveland)] Erneb*er* had 2 carucates and 2 bovates of land ⌊assessed⌋ to the geld. There is land for as many teams and oxen. Gunfrid, Robert's man, has [2 teams] there ⌊in demesne⌋, and 3 sokemen and 1 bordar ploughing with 2 oxen. There are 11 acres of meadow there, and 209 acres of wood⌊land⌋ for pannage. T. R. E. it was worth 4 pounds; now 40 shillings.

18. M. In Scachetorp [Scottlethorpe (Beltisloe)] Erneber had 10 bovates of land ⌊assessed⌋ to the geld. There is land for as many oxen. Now it is waste. T. R. E. it was worth 100 shillings; now at the most (*utcunque*) 10 shillings.

*D. B., f. 353*b. *Facsimile, p. xxxv*b.

19. M. In Aslachebi[1] [Aslackby (Aveland)] Erneber had 6 caru-

[1] See 72/9.

cates and half a bovate of land ⌊assessed⌋ to the geld. There is land for as many teams. Now Robert has 7 villeins and 1 bordar there having 2 teams, and 40 acres of meadow, and 24 acres of underwood. Gilbert de Gand has the soke of 2 carucates ⌊of this land⌋ as belonging to his manor of Fulchingeham [Folkingham (Aveland)] (*de duabus carucatis habet . . . socam in Fulchingeham*).

20. M. In Avetorp [Avethorpe in Aslackby (Aveland)] Erneber had 2½ carucates of land ⌊assessed⌋ to the geld. There is land for 3 teams. Gunfrid, Robert's man, has half a team there ⌊in demesne⌋, and 4 sokemen and 1 bordar with 1 team. There are 12 acres of meadow there, and 130 acres of meadow.[1] T. R. E. it was worth 6 pounds ; now 40 shillings ; tallage 20 shillings.

21. S. In Loctone [Laughton (Aveland)] there are 5 bovates and the third part of 1 bovate of land ⌊assessed⌋ to the geld. There is land for as many oxen. 11 sokemen have 1 team there, and half a church, and 8 acres of underwood.

22. S. In Aslachebi [Aslackby (Aveland)] there are 6½ bovates of land ⌊assessed⌋ to the geld. There is land for 1 team. 6 sokemen have 2 teams there, and 6 acres of meadow, and 12 acres of underwood.

23. S. In Sepingeham [Sempringham (Aveland)] there is 1 carucate of land ⌊assessed⌋ to the geld. There is land for 1 team. 4 sokemen have 1 team there, and 10 acres of meadow, and 6 acres of underwood.

24. M. In Ripeslai [Ropsley (Threo)] Tori had 8 carucates of land ⌊assessed⌋ to the geld. There is land for 9 teams. Ivo, Robert's man, has 2 teams there ⌊in demesne⌋, and 2 villeins and 29 sokemen with 8½ teams. There is a church there, and 120 acres of wood⌊land⌋ for pannage, and 450 acres of underwood. T. R. E. it was worth 6 pounds ; now 100 shillings ; tallage 40 shillings. There is soke⌊land⌋ amounting to 6 bovates (*Soca .vi. bouatarum*).

25. M. In Dentune or Huuelle [Denton or Wyville (Winnibriggs)] Eddiva had 6 carucates of land ⌊assessed⌋ to the geld. There is land for as many teams. Robert has 3 teams there in demesne, and 13 villeins with 4 teams. T. R. E. it was worth 4 pounds and 5 shillings and 4[2] pence ; now 100 shillings ; tallage 20 shillings.

26. In Hungretune [Hungerton (Winnibriggs)] there are 6 carucates of land ⌊assessed⌋ to the geld. There is land for 6 teams. It is inland. 13 villeins have 6 teams there, and 50 acres of meadow, and 87 acres of underwood. This wood⌊land⌋ belongs to (*est in*) the soke of Grantham.

27. M. In Vlestanetorp [Woolsthorpe (Winnibriggs)] Levric had 4 carucates of land ⌊assessed⌋ to the geld. There is land for as many teams. Robert has 1 team there in demesne, and 6 villeins and 3 bordars and 8 sokemen having 3 teams, and 3 mills rendering 15 shillings. T. R. E. and now worth 40 shillings.

28. Two M. In the same place (*ibidem*) Godwin and Archel had 4 carucates of land ⌊assessed⌋ to the geld. There is land for as many teams. Robert has 1½ mills there rendering 8 shillings and 6 pence, and 11 villeins with 1 team. There is a church there, and a priest having half a carucate of this land. There are 30 acres of meadow and 3 virgates there. T. R. E. and now worth 40 shillings.

---

[1] Perhaps the second *prati* is a mistake for *silue pastilis* or for *silue minute*.

[2] *ii* is written in the line and *ii* above the line.

29. M. In Aburne [Aubourn (Graffoe)] Turgot [the lawman (*lag'*)] had 12 carucates of land [assessed] to the geld. There is land for as many teams. Berenger, [who holds] of Robert, has 2 teams there in demesne, and 14 villeins and 4 bordars and 1 sokeman with 4 teams. There is a church there, and a priest, and 1 mill rendering 20 shillings, and 1 fishery rendering 1000 eels, and 100 acres (*acras*) of meadow. T. R. E. it was worth 5 pounds ; now 6 pounds.

D. B., f. 353c. *Facsimile, p. xxxvi*a.

30. In Hadinctone [Haddington (Graffoe)] there are 3½ carucates of land [assessed] to the geld. There is land for 2 teams. It is a berewic belonging to (*in*) Aburne [Aubourn]. 2 villeins have half a team there, and 6 acres of meadow, and 3 acres of underwood.

31. M. In Adelinctune [Allington (Winnibriggs)] Godwin had 3 carucates of land [assessed] to the geld. There is land for 6 teams. Robert has 2 teams there in demesne, and 14 sokemen and 5 villeins and 5 bordars with 4 teams. There is a church there, and 140 acres (*acras*) of meadow. Warin, his [Robert's] man, has 1 carucate there, and 1 bordar having 2 bovates of land. T. R. E. it was worth 3 pounds ; now 6 pounds.

32. M. In Nortchime [North Kyme (Langoe)] Mere had 6 carucates of land [assessed] to the geld. There is land for 8 teams. Ivo, Robert's man, has 3 teams there [in demesne], and 12 villeins and 2 bordars with 4 teams, and 56 acres of meadow, and 30 acres of wood[land] for pannage. T. R. E. it was worth 3 pounds and 13 shillings [and 8 pence] ; now 7 pounds.

19. LAND OF BERENGER DE TODENI

1. Two M. In Adelingetone [Allington (Winnibriggs)] Ulfchetel and Godwin had 6 carucates of land [assessed] to the geld. There is land for 5 teams. Berenger [de Todeni] has 1 team there [in demesne], and 14 sokemen and 5 villeins and 5 bordars having 4 teams. There is a church there, having half a carucate of this land, and 140 acres of meadow. T. R. E. it was worth 3 pounds ; now 6 pounds.

20. LAND OF ILBERT DE LACI

1. M. In Duneham [Dunham (Lawress)] Alrich had 2 carucates of land [assessed] to the geld. There is land for 2 teams. Now Ilbert de Laci has it. A 'knight' (*miles*) of his [has] of him 1 team in demesne, and 2 sokemen and 2 villeins with 1 team, and 17 acres of meadow. T. R. E. it was worth 20 shillings ; now 16 shillings ; tallage 4 shillings.

2. B. In Scotorne [Scothorn (Lawress)] there are 7 bovates of land ⌊assessed⌋ to the geld. There is land for 9 oxen.

3. S. In Stou [Stow (Well)] there is half a carucate of land ⌊assessed⌋ to the geld. There is land for half a team. It is inland and soke⌊land⌋.

4. M. In Welingeham [Willingham by Stow (Well)] Deincora had 12 bovates of land ⌊assessed⌋ to the geld. There is land for 12 oxen. On this land dwells one 'knight' (*miles*) of Ilbert's. T. R. E. and now worth 20 shillings.

21. LAND OF HENRY DE FERRERES

1. M. In Witenai [Whitton (Manley)] Seubar had 12 carucates of land ⌊assessed⌋ to the geld. There is land for 8 teams. Saswalo, Henry's man, has 2 teams there ⌊in demesne⌋, and 10 villeins and 4 bordars and 30 sokemen having 5 teams, and 300 acres of meadow. T. R. E. it was worth 10 pounds ; now 7 pounds ; tallage 3 pounds.

2. B. In Wintrintone [Winterton (Manley)] there are 2 bovates of land ⌊assessed⌋ to the geld. There is land for 2 oxen. It is inland, and it is waste.

D.B., f. 353d. *Facsimile, p. xxxvi*b.

22. LAND OF WILLIAM DE PERCI

1. M. In Imungeham [Immingham (Yarborough)] Alwin had 4 carucates and 1½ bovates of land ⌊assessed⌋ to the geld. There is land for 8 teams. William de Perci has 4 teams there in demesne, and 12 villeins and 14 bordars and 13 sokemen having 4 teams, and 80 acres of meadow. T. R. E. it was worth 8 pounds ; now the like amount ; tallage 40 shillings.

2.[1] In Lenesbi[2] [Laceby (Bradley)] there is half a bovate of land ⌊assessed⌋ to the geld. It is soke⌊land⌋.

3. M. In Aburne [Habrough (Yarborough)] Alcude had 6 bovates of land ⌊assessed⌋ to the geld. There is land for 12 oxen. Norman, William's man, has half a team there ⌊in demesne⌋, and 2 villeins and 4 bordars and 5 sokemen ploughing with 1 team and 2 oxen, and 60 acres of meadow. T. R. E. it was worth 14 shillings ; now 20 shillings ; tallage 4 shillings.

[1] This entry is inserted as a continuation of the last line of no. 1.

[2] The clerk in transcribing has perhaps written *n* for *u* in this name.

4. S. In Lobingeham [Lobingham[1] (Yarborough)] there are 1½ bovates of land ⌊assessed⌋ to the geld. There is land for 3 oxen. There is 1 sokeman ploughing there with 2 oxen, and 20 acres of meadow.

5. In Torentone[2] [Thornton le Moor (Walshcroft)] Alwin had 2 carucates and 6 bovates of land ⌊assessed⌋ to the geld. There is land for 4 teams. There are 12 sokemen and 3 bordars and 2 villeins there with 1½ teams. And upon 11 bovates of this land (*super has .xi. bouatas terre*) Roger of Poitou has 11 oxen in the same manner as William ⌊de Perci⌋, and the same William ought to have them by the witness of the men of the wapentake. There are 364 acres of meadow there. It is soke⌊land⌋ belonging to (*in*) Oresbi [Owersby (Walshcroft)].

6.[3] In Bernetebi [Barnetby le Wold (Yarborough)] there are 2 bovates of land ⌊assessed⌋ to the geld. There is land for 4 oxen. It is waste. It is inland belonging to (*in*) Torentune [Thornton le Moor].

7. M. In Oresbi [Owersby (Walshcroft)] Alwin had 7 bovates and 2 parts of 1 bovate of land ⌊assessed⌋ to the geld. There is land for 2 teams. William has 2 teams there in demesne, and 3 villeins and 10 sokemen with 1 team. There is a church there, and a priest, and 1 mill rendering 3 shillings, and 80 acres of meadow. T. R. E. it was worth 40 shillings ; now 50 shillings ; tallage 10 shillings.

8. M. In Caburne [Cabourn (Haverstoe)] Grinchil had 1 carucate of land ⌊assessed⌋ to the geld. There is land for 2 teams. Norman, William's man, has 1 team there ⌊in demesne⌋, and 1 villein and 1 bordar, and 12 acres of meadow belonging to (*in*) Chelsi [North Kelsey (Yarborough)] T. R. E. it was worth 30 shillings ; now 26 shillings.

9. In Cucualt[4] [Cuxwold (Haverstoe)] there is 1 bovate of land ⌊assessed⌋ to the geld. It is inland belonging to (*in*) Caburne.

10. M. In Wichingebi [Wickenby (Wraggoe)] Turgot had 2 carucates of land ⌊assessed⌋ to the geld. There is land for 3 teams. Osbern, William's man, has 2 teams there ⌊in demesne⌋, and 8 villeins and 2 sokemen with 2 teams, and 15 acres of meadow. There is underwood 1 league in length and 5 furlongs in breadth. T. R. E. and now worth 3 pounds.

SOKE⌊LAND⌋ OF THIS MANOR

11. S. In Westledebi [Westlaby (Wraggoe)] there are 9 bovates of land ⌊assessed⌋ to the geld. There is land for 18 oxen. Ralf, William's man, has 6 sokemen there with 2 teams, and 30 acres of meadow.

12. S. In Bechelinge [Beckering (Wraggoe)] there are 1½ bovates of land ⌊assessed⌋ to the geld. There is land for 3 oxen. Robert, William's man, has 1 sokeman and 1 bordar there ploughing with 2 oxen, and 1 acre of meadow.

13. S. In Reresbi [Reasby (Wraggoe)] there is half a carucate of land ⌊assessed⌋ to the geld. There is land for 4 oxen. Norman, William's man, has 1 sokeman there with half a team, and 10 acres of meadow.

---

[1] In East Halton or Killingholme.

[2] See 16/6.

[3] This entry is inserted at the foot of the column, and a sign indicates that it should be placed where it appears in the text.

[4] See 25/10 ; 70/24.

14. S. In Sneleslunt [Snelland (Wraggoe)] there are 4 bovates of land ⌊assessed⌋ to the geld. There is land for 1 team. Waldin, William's man, has 3 sokemen there with 1 team, and 6 acres of meadow, and 6 acres of underwood.

15. S. In Reresbi[1] [Reasby] there are 4 bovates of land ⌊assessed⌋ to the geld. There is land for 4 oxen. It belongs to (*iacet in*) Sneleslunt [Snelland].

16. M. In Stainfelde[2] [Stainfield (Wraggoe)] Siward had 1½ carucates of land ⌊assessed⌋ to the geld. There is land for 1 team. William has 1 team there ⌊in demesne⌋, and 8 villeins and 6 bordars and 4 sokemen with 4 teams, and 40 acres of meadow, and 264 acres of wood⌊land⌋ for pannage.* T. R. E. it was worth 30 shillings ; now 60 shillings.

**D.B., f.* 354a. *Facsimile, p. xxxvii*a.

17. S. In the same place (*ibidem*) Tona had 1½ carucates of land ⌊assessed⌋ to the geld. It is soke⌊land⌋ belonging to (*in*) Berlinge [Barlings (Lawress)]. William has 4 sokemen and 1 bordar there with 2 teams, and 20 acres of meadow, and 117 acres of wood⌊land⌋ for pannage.

18. S. In Apeleia [Apley (Wraggoe)] there are 7 bovates of land ⌊assessed⌋ to the geld. There is land for 12 oxen. 10 sokemen have 3 teams there, and 15 acres of meadow, and 110 acres of underwood.[3]

19.[4] S. In the same place (*ibidem*) Tona had 7 bovates of land ⌊assessed⌋ to the geld. There is land for 12 oxen. It is soke⌊land⌋ belonging to (*in*) Berlinge [Barlings]. William has 10 sokemen there with 3 teams, and 10 acres of meadow and 110 acres of underwood.[3]

20.[4] S. In the same place (*ibidem*) Alfric (*Aluric*) had 2 bovates of land ⌊assessed⌋ to the geld. It is soke⌊land⌋ belonging to (*in*) Bolintone [Bullington (Wraggoe)]. William has 2 sokemen there ploughing with 1 ox.

21. M. In Ludeforde [Ludford (Wraggoe)] Alsi had 1 carucate and 6 bovates of land ⌊assessed⌋ to the geld. There is land for 3½ teams. And [22.] Two M. In the same place (*ibidem*) Wilac and Siward had 3 carucates of land ⌊assessed⌋ to the geld. There is land for 6 teams. William de Perci has 3½ teams there in demesne, and 28 villeins and 8 sokemen with 4 teams, ⌊and⌋ 60 acres of meadow. T. R. E. and now worth 4 pounds ; tallage 20 shillings.

23. In the same place (*ibidem*) Tona had 2 bovates of land ⌊assessed⌋ to the geld. There is land for 4 oxen. It is soke⌊land⌋ belonging to (*in*) Badeburg [Baumber (Gartree)]. It is waste. There are 4 acres of meadow there.

24. M. In Cheuremont [Kirmond le Mire (Wraggoe)] Elsi had 3 carucates of land ⌊assessed⌋ to the geld. There is land for 6 teams. William has 4 teams there in demesne, and 18 villeins and 4 bordars and 2 sokemen having 4 teams. There is a church there, and 1 mill rendering 2 shillings, and 20 acres of meadow. T. R. E. it was worth 3 pounds ; now 4 pounds.

---

[1] See 28/26. [2] See 69/30.

[3] It will be observed that the details in nos. 18 and 19 are almost exactly the same, but there is no ground for thinking that they relate to the same land.

[4] The letter *K*, the initial of *Kalumpnia*, which is written in the margin against entries 19 and 20, is seemingly intended to call attention to the *clamores* in 69/31 and 69/32 which relate to nos. 19 and 20 respectively.

25. M. In Grimesbi [Little Grimsby (Ludborough)] Alric had 1 carucate and 2 bovates of land ⌊assessed⌋ to the geld. There is land for 3 teams. Fulk, William's man, has 1 team there ⌊in demesne⌋, and 3 villeins and 5 sokemen with 1 team. There is a church there, and 11 acres of meadow, and 1 salt-pan rendering 6 pence. T. R. E. it was worth 30 shillings ; now 25 shillings ; tallage 5 shillings.

26. Three M. In Covenham [Covenham (Ludborough)] Alsi and Chetel and Turuer had 3½ carucates of land ⌊assessed⌋ to the geld. There is land for 4 teams. William has 3 teams there in demesne, and 18 villeins and 17 sokemen with 5½ teams, and 5 salt-pans rendering 2 shillings, and 150 acres of meadow. T. R. E. it was worth 110 shillings ; now 4 pounds ; tallage 30 shillings. Chetel and Turuer were brothers, and after their father's death they divided the land, in such wise however that when Chetel was doing the king's service he should have his brother Turuer's aid. William [Perci] has Chetel's [and Ailsi's] land from (*de*) the king ; but he the same William bought Turuer's land from Anschitil, the late (*quondam*) cook, in the time of King William.

27.[1] S. In Germundtorp [Grainthorpe (Louthesk)] there are 3½ bovates of land ⌊assessed⌋ to the geld. There is land for as many oxen. It is soke⌊land⌋ belonging to (*in*) Covenham. 3 sokemen have 1 team there, and 50 acres of meadow.

28. M. In Alchinton [Elkington (Louthesk)] Ælsi had 8 carucates of land ⌊assessed⌋ to the geld. There is land for 16 teams. Fulk, William's man, has 2 teams there ⌊in demense⌋, and 38 sokemen with 7½ teams. There is a church there, and a mill rendering 3 shillings, and the site of another mill, and 20 acres of meadow. T. R. E. it was worth 3 pounds ; now 4 pounds ; tallage 40 shillings. 6½ carucates of this land are soke⌊land⌋.

D. B., *f.* 354b. *Facsimile*, *p.* *xxxvii*b.

29. M. In Ristone and Carletone[2] [North Reston and Little Carlton (Louthesk)] Alsi had 3 carucates of land ⌊assessed⌋ to the geld. There is land for 4 teams. Osbern, William's man, has 2 teams there ⌊in demesne⌋, and 4 villeins and 4 bordars and 18 sokemen with 4 teams. There is a church there, and 2 mills rendering 5 shillings, and 30 acres of meadow, and 100 acres of wood⌊land⌋ for pannage. T. R. E. [it was worth], and now is worth 40 shillings ; tallage 20 shillings. A moiety of this land is soke⌊land⌋.

30. M. In Englebi[3] [Ingleby (Lawress)] Gunnewate had 2 carucates and 2 bovates of land ⌊assessed⌋ to the geld. There is land for as many teams and oxen. William has 1 team there ⌊in demesne⌋, and 5 villeins and 1 sokeman with half a team. There is a priest there, and 50 acres of meadow, and 50 acres of underwood. T. R. E. it was worth 20 shillings ; now 25 shillings ; tallage 5 shillings.

31. M. In Odenebi [Owmby by Searby (Yarborough)] Grinchel had 2 carucates and 3 bovates of land ⌊assessed⌋ to the geld. There is land for 4 teams and 6 oxen. William, William's man, has 3 teams there

[1] This entry follows no. 28 in *D.B.*, and a sign indicates that it is to be inserted here.
[2] See 69/7.
[3] See 18/1.

⌊in demesne⌋, and 7 villeins and 11 sokemen with 3 teams, and 1 mill rendering 2 shillings, and 40 acres of meadow. T. R. E. it was worth 40 shillings ; now 60 shillings ; tallage 20 shillings. Of this land 9 bovates are soke⌊land⌋ (*in soca*).

32. M. In Stainton [Stainton le Vale (Walshcroft)] Grinchel had 4 bovates of land ⌊assessed⌋ to the geld. There is land for 12 oxen. Alulf, William's man, has 2 teams there ⌊in demesne⌋, and 6 villeins with 1 team, and 1 mill rendering 12 pence, and 26 acres of meadow. T. R. E. it was worth 30 shillings ; now 50 shillings.

33. M. In Fodrebi [Fotherby (Ludborough)] Sberne had half a carucate of land ⌊assessed⌋ to the geld. There is land for 12 oxen. Fulk, William's man, has it and tills it. There are 4 acres of meadow there. T. R. E. it was worth 10 shillings ; now 3 shillings.

34. M. In Wighingesbi [Wickenby (Wraggoe)] Godric had 5 bovates of land ⌊assessed⌋ to the geld. There is land for 7 oxen. Robert, William's man, has 1 team there ⌊in demesne⌋, and 1 villein with 1 ox, and 10 acres of meadow. T. R. E. and now worth 20 shillings.

35. M. In Lagesbi [Legsby (Wraggoe)] Alsi had 1 carucate of land ⌊assessed⌋ to the geld. There is land for 2 teams. Evrard, William's man, has 2 teams there ⌊in demesne⌋, and 6 villeins and 1 bordar with 1 team, and 1 mill rendering 6 pence, and 12 acres of meadow, and 12 acres of wood⌊land⌋ for pannage throughout the territory. T. R. E. worth 30 shillings ; now 40 shillings.

36.[1] S. In Houten [Holtham in Legsby (Wraggoe)] there is soke⌊land⌋ belonging to (*in*) Lagesbi [Legsby], 10 bovates of land ⌊assessed⌋ to the geld. There is land for 2 teams. Evrard, William's man, has 6 sokemen and 4 villeins and 2 bordars there with 2 teams, and 30 acres of meadow.

37. S. In the same place (*ibidem*)[2] there are 4 bovates of land ⌊assessed⌋ to the geld. It is soke⌊land⌋ belonging to (*in*) Waragebi [Wragby (Wraggoe)]. It is waste.

38. S. In Summertebi [Somerby near Brigg (Yarborough)] Salecoc had 2½ carucates of land ⌊assessed⌋ to the geld. There is land for 5 teams. It is soke⌊land⌋ belonging to (*in*) Brune [Burnham (Yarborough)]. 14 sokemen have 5 teams there, and 80 acres of meadow, and 20 acres of underwood.

23. LAND OF GILBERT TISON

1. M. In Ferebi [South Ferriby (Yarborough)] Godwin had 2 carucates and 7 bovates and the eighth part of a bovate of land ⌊assessed⌋ to the geld. There is land for 4 teams. Anschitill, Gilbert Tison's man,

---

[1] This entry precedes no. 29 in *D.B.*, and a sign indicates that it is to be inserted here.

[2] The reference is to Legsby. No. 37 follows no. 35 in the original (see note 1 above). See 34/14 ; 69/26.

has 1 team there [in demesne], and 6 sokemen on (*de*) 9 bovates of this land and 17 villeins having 4½ teams. There is a church there, and 1 mill rendering 10 shillings, and 1 ferry (*passagium*) rendering 60 shillings, and 210 acres (*acras*) of meadow. T. R. E. it was worth 8 pounds ; now the like amount.

D. B., f. 354c. *Facsimile, p. xxxviiia.*

24. LAND OF GILBERT DE GAND

1. M. In Scantone [Scampton (Lawress)] Ulf Fenisc had 6½ carucates of land [assessed] to the geld. There is land for 10 teams. Gilbert de Gand has 4 teams there in demesne, and 16 villeins and 12 sokemen and 6 bordars with 7 teams. There is a church there, and a priest, and 1 mill rendering 2 shillings, and 166 acres of meadow. T. R. E. it was worth 6 pounds ; now 8 pounds ; tallage 4 pounds.

2. B. In Risun [Riseholme (Lawress)] there are 1½ carucates [assessed] to the geld. There is land for 1½ teams. It is a berewic belonging to (*in*) Scant' [Scampton]. Colsuan, [Gilbert's man], has 1 team there, and 1 mill rendering 12 pence, and 36 acres of meadow.

3. S. In Burtone [Burton by Lincoln (Lawress)] there are 3 carucates of land [assessed] to the geld. There is land for 2 teams. There are 11 sokemen and 9 bordars there with 3 teams.

4. S. In Carletone [Middle Carlton (Lawress)] there are 6 bovates of land [assessed] to the geld. There is land for as many oxen. 2 sokemen plough there with 5 oxen, and there are 4 acres of meadow.

5. M. In Wilingeham [Cherry Willingham (Lawress)] Ulf had 14 bovates of land [assessed] to the geld. There is land for as many oxen. Gilbert has 2 teams there [in demesne], and 12 villeins and 1 sokeman with 2 teams. There is a church there, and a priest, and 2 fisheries rendering 32 pence, and 40 acres (*acras*) of meadow. T. R. E. it was worth 100 shillings ; now 4 pounds.

SOKE[LAND] OF SCANTON [SCAMPTON]

6. S. In Brotulbi and Torp [Brattleby and Thorpe in the Fallows (Lawress)] there are 3 carucates of land [assessed] to the geld. There is land for 3 teams. 5 sokemen and 2 bordars have 3 teams there, and 2 oxen, and 8 acres of meadow. Also[1]

7. S. In Torp and Æstorp [Thorpe in the Fallows and Aisthorpe (Lawress)] there are 5 carucates and 2 bovates of land [assessed] to the geld. There is land for 6 teams. There are 10 sokemen and 1 bordar there with 3½ teams. One of Gilbert's men has 6 sokemen and 5 bordars with 1 team, and 101 acres of meadow.

8. B. In Netelham [Nettleham (Lawress)] there are 2 bovates of land [assessed] to the geld. It is inland belonging to (*in*) Wilingeham [Cherry Willingham (Lawress)].

---

[1] This word connects nos. 6 and 7 which both relate to Thorpe in the Fallows.

9. In Stou [Stow (Well)] Ulf [had] 4 tofts, with sake and soke belonging to (*in*) Scantone [Scampton].

10. M. In Aplebi and Risebi and Saleclif [Appleby and Risby and Sawcliff (Manley)] Ulf had 2 carucates of land [assessed] to the geld. There is land for 4 teams. Robert, Gilbert's man, has 2 teams there [in demesne], and 10 villeins and 2 bordars with 2 teams. There is a priest there, and a church, and 12 acres of meadow. T. R. E. it was worth 50 shillings ; now 40 shillings ; tallage 10 shillings.

11. B. In Roxebi [Roxby (Manley)] there are 2 bovates of land [assessed] to the geld. There is land for 3 oxen. 1 villein has 2 oxen there.

12. M. In Wintringeham[1] [Winteringham (Manley)] Ulf had 12 carucates of land [assessed] to the geld. There is land for as many teams. Robert, Gilbert's man, has 4 teams there in demesne, and 40 villeins and 5 sokemen and 10 bordars with 7 teams. There is a priest there, and a church, and 3 mills rendering 37 shillings and 4 pence, and 1 ferry (*passagium*) rendering 13 shillings, and the site of a fishery. T. R. E. and now worth 10 pounds ; tallage 40 shillings.

13. M. In Bertone [Barton on Humber (Yarborough)] Ulf had 13 carucates of land [assessed] to the geld. There is land for 27 teams. Gilbert has 7 teams there in demesne, and 63 villeins and 16 bordars with 9 teams, and 42 sokemen and 67 bordars with 10 teams. There is a church there, and a priest, and 2 mills rendering 40 shillings, and 1 market (*mercatum*), and a ferry (*passagium*) rendering 4 pounds.

14. S. In Ferebi [South Ferriby (Yarborough)] there are 3 carucates of land less 1 bovate, and the eighth part of 1 bovate, [assessed] to the geld.[2] It is soke[land] belonging to (*de*) Bertone [Barton on Humber]. There is land for 5½ teams. There are now 34 sokemen and 13 bordars there with 8 teams, and 1 ferry (*passagium*) rendering 3 pounds, and 210 acres of meadow, and 260 acres of marsh (*maresc*). T. R. E. it was worth 38 pounds and 16 shillings ; now 30 pounds ; tallage 10 pounds.

D. B., f. 354d. *Facsimile, p. xxxviii*b.

15. S. In Horchetou [Horkstow (Yarborough)] there are 4 carucates of land [assessed] to the geld. There is land for 7 teams. It is soke[land] and inland belonging to (*in*) Bertone [Barton on Humber]. Gilbert has 1½ teams there, and 7 villeins and 20 sokemen with 8½ teams.

16. In Langetone[3] [Langton by Wragby (Wraggoe)] Gilbert has 140 acres of wood[land] for pannage.

17. M. In Bardenai [Bardney (Wraggoe)] Ulf had 2 carucates of land [assessed] to the geld. There is land for 3 teams. Gilbert has 1 team there [in demesne], and 16 villeins and 5 bordars and 6 sokemen with 2 teams, and 1 mill rendering 8 shillings, and 5 fisheries rendering 5 shillings and 4 pence, and 20 acres of meadow, and 500 acres of wood[land] for pannage. T. R. E. and now worth 20 pounds ; tallage 30 pounds.

18. S. In Osgotebi [Osgodby in Bardney (Wraggoe)] there is soke[land] of this manor, 2 carucates of land [assessed] to the geld.

---

[1] See 71/17. [2] *ad geld'* is repeated. [3] See 38/11 ; 69/23.

There is land for 3 teams. 16 sokemen have 3 teams there, and 60 acres of meadow, and 240 acres of wood[land] for pannage throughout the territory.

19. B. In Sutreie [Southrey (Wraggoe)] there is inland belonging to (*in*) Wilingeham [Cherry Willingham (Lawress)], 2 bovates of land [assessed] to the geld. There are 3 villeins there ploughing with 6 oxen, and 1 fishery, and 4 acres of meadow, and 20 acres of wood[land] for pannage.

20. M. In Badeburg[1] [Baumber (Horncastle)] Ulf had 12 carucates of land [assessed] to the geld. There is land for 10 teams. Gilbert has 5 teams there [in demesne], and 21 villeins, and 6 bordars, and 20 sokemen and their 16 bordars. Amongst them all [they have] 7 teams, and 1 mill rendering 8 shillings, and 140 acres of wood[land] for pannage. T. R. E. it was worth 10 pounds; now 12 pounds; tallage 3 pounds. Of this land 6 carucates are soke[land] (*in soca*).

21.[2] In Sudtone [Little Sturton in Baumber (Horncastle)] there are 2 bovates of land [assessed] to the geld. There is land for 3 oxen. Gilbert has a flock of sheep there.

22. M. In Ellingetone[3] [Edlington (Horncastle)] Ulf had 10 carucates of land [assessed] to the geld. There is land for 10 teams. Egbert, Gilbert's man, has 4 teams there [in demesne], and 25 sokemen and 7 villeins and 14 bordars with 6 teams, and 1 mill rendering 16 shillings, and 90 acres of meadow, and 210 acres of underwood. T. R. E. it was worth 10 pounds; now 11 pounds; tallage 3 pounds.

23. B. In Sanctone [Santon (Manley)] there is inland belonging to (*in*) Risebi [Risby (Manley)], 1 bovate of land [assessed] to the geld. It is waste.

24. M. In Luzebi [Lusby (Bolingbroke)] Tonne had 3 carucates of land [assessed] to the geld. There is land for 4 teams. William, Gilbert's man, has 5 teams there [in demesne], and 17 sokemen and 8 villeins having 9 teams. There is a church there, and a priest, and 1 mill rendering 3 shillings, and 180 acres of meadow. T. R. E. it was worth 14 pounds; now 10 pounds; tallage 100 shillings.

25. M. In Edeham [Edenham (Beltisloe)] Ulf had 12 carucates of land [assessed] to the geld. There is land for 12 teams. Gilbert has 5 teams there [in demesne], and 32 villeins and 24 sokemen and 4 bordars with 9 teams, and 29 acres of meadow, and 400 acres of wood[land] for pannage throughout the territory. T. R. E. it was worth 10 pounds; now 18 pounds; tallage 6 pounds.

26. B. In Offran[4] [*query* Keisby (Beltisloe)] there is a berewic [of this manor], $3\frac{1}{2}$ carucates of land [assessed] to the geld. There is land for 5 teams. There are 2 teams there in demesne, and 5 villeins with 3 teams, and 80 acres of meadow, and 120 acres of underwood.

---

[1] See 69/33.

[2] This entry has been inserted at the foot of the preceding column, and a sign indicates that it should be placed where it is printed in the text.

[3] See 69/34.

[4] It seems probable that this holding should be sought in Keisby. *Offran* cannot be identified with any modern place-name, and it is possible that it is a personal name which has been inserted here by mistake. Cp. p. 39, note 3.

27. B. In Bacstune [Baston (Ness)] there is a berewic [of this manor], 2 carucates of land [assessed] to the geld. There is land for 2 teams. Ivo, Gilbert's man, has half a team there [in demesne], and 8 sokemen on (*de*) 1 carucate of this land and 4 villeins and 3 bordars with 2 teams, and 40 acres of meadow. It is worth 50 shillings.

28. S. In Griteford [Greatford (Ness)] there are 2 bovates of land [assessed] to the geld. It is soke[land] [of this manor]. There are 4 sokemen there with 1 team.

29. S. In Bercham [Barholme (Ness)] there is half a carucate of land [assessed] to the geld. There is land for 4 oxen. It is soke[land] [belonging to (*in*)] Edeham [Edenham]. There are 4 sokemen there ploughing with 2 oxen. And it is worth 8 shillings.

D. B., f. 355a. *Facsimile, p. xxxix*a.

30. S. In Braseborg and Barnetorpi [Braceborough and Banthorpe (Ness)] there is half a carucate [assessed] to the geld. There is land for 4 oxen.

31. S. In Opetorp [Obthorpe (Ness)] there are 13 bovates of land [assessed] to the geld. There is land for as many oxen. 17 sokemen have 3 teams there, and 20 acres of meadow, and 20 acres of wood[land] for pannage.

32. S. In Witham[1] and Mannetorp and Totf [and] Lund [Witham on the Hill and Manthorpe and Toft and Lound (Beltisloe)] there are 8 carucates and the third part of 1 carucate of land [assessed to the geld]. There is land for as many teams. 45 sokemen and 10 bordars have 10 teams there. There is a church there, and 40 acres of meadow, and 40 acres of wood[land] for pannage, and 1 mill rendering 20 shillings. Of this land Berewold holds 1 carucate of land, and has 1 team there, and 1 mill rendering 12 shillings, and 2 villeins and 4 bordars with half a team. T. R. E. it was worth 20 shillings; now 40 shillings.

33. S. In Carlebi [Carlby (Ness)] there are 15 bovates of land [assessed] to the geld. 8 sokemen and 1 bordar have 2 teams there. T. R. E. it was worth 20 shillings; now the like amount; tallage 7 shillings. Ivo has this land, and Berewold [has it] under him, and he himself [*query* Berewold] [has] half a team there.

34. S. In Estou [Stowe (Ness)] there are 6½ bovates of land [assessed] to the geld. 5 sokemen have half a team there.

35. S. In Bercham[2] [Barholm (Ness)] there is half a carucate of land [assessed] to the geld. There is land for 4 oxen. It is soke[land] belonging to (*in*) Casuic[3] [Casewick (Ness)].

36. M. In Cranewelle [Cranwell (Flaxwell)] Ulf had 12 carucates of land [assessed] to the geld. There is land for as many teams. Geoffrey (*Goisfridus*), Gilbert's man, has 1 team there in demesne, and 21 sokemen on (*de*) 9 carucates of this land and 2 villeins and 5 bordars with 8 teams, and 29 acres of meadow. The arable land is 22 furlongs in length and 7½ in breadth. The pasture (*pascua*) is 10 furlongs in length and 7½ in breadth. T. R. E. it was worth 100 shillings; now 7 pounds.

37. M. In Torp [Culverthorpe (Aswardhurn)] Tunne had 3 carucates and 3 bovates of land [assessed] to the geld. There is land for 4

[1] See 8/6; 30/32; 72/6. [2] See 72/3. [3] See 52/1.

teams. Gilbert has 5 teams there [in demesne], and 8 villeins with 2 teams. There is a priest there, and a church, and 120 acres of meadow. T. R. E. it was worth 18 pounds; now 25 pounds.

SOKE[LAND] OF THIS MANOR

38. S. In Oustorp and Ieresbi [Ewerby Thorpe and Ewerby (Aswardhurn)] there are 3 carucates of land [assessed] to the geld. There is land for 2 teams. 9 sokemen and 9 bordars have 4 teams there. There is a church there, and a priest, and 24 acres of meadow, and 20 acres of underwood.

39. S. In Huuelle [Howell (Aswardhurn)] there is 1 carucate and half a bovate. There is land for 1 team. 3 sokemen have 1 team and 2 ploughing oxen there, and 8 acres of meadow.

40. B. and S. In Hechintune [Heckington (Aswardhurn)] there are inland [3 carucates] and soke[land] [5 carucates] [of this manor], 8 carucates of land [assessed] to the geld. There is land for as many teams. Gilbert has 2 teams there in demesne, and 22 sokemen[1] and 7 villeins and 15 bordars with 8 teams. There is a priest there, and a church, and 100 acres of meadow, and 3 fisheries rendering 5 shillings and 4 pence.

41. S. In Hale [Great Hale (Aswardhurn)] there are 8½ carucates [assessed] to the geld. There is land for 10 teams. 38 sokemen have 12 teams there. Ralf, Gilbert's man, has 3 teams there in demesne. It is soke[land].

42. S. In Haberdingham [Hagworthingham (Hill)] there are 6 bovates of land [assessed] to the geld. There is land for 10 oxen. Gretham [Greetham (Hill)] [has] the soke. And there are 10 acres of meadow.

43. B. In the same place (*ibidem*) there is 1 carucate of land [assessed] to the geld. There is land for 12 oxen. It is a berewic belonging to (*in*) Luzebi [Lusby (Bolingbroke)]. There is 1 team there in demesne, and 1 villein and 1 bordar ploughing with 1 ox, and 20 acres of meadow, and 1 mill rendering 12 pence.

44. S. In the same place (*ibidem*) there is 1 carucate of land [assessed] to the geld. There is land for 2 teams. It is soke[land] belonging to (*in*) Luzebi [Lusby]. There are 2 bordars there with 1 ox, and 30 acres of meadow.

D. B., f. 355b. *Facsimile, p. xxxix*b.

SOKE[LAND] BELONGING TO (*in*) BARDENAI [BARDNEY]

45. S. In Partene [Partney (Candleshoe)] there is soke[land], 5 carucates of land [assessed] to the geld. There is land for as many teams. Gilbert has 17 sokemen and 27 bordars there with 5 teams. There is a market there rendering 10 shillings, and 100 acres of meadow.

46. S. In Scheueldebi [Skendleby (Candleshoe)] there are 6 carucates of land [assessed] to the geld. There is land for 6 teams. Gilbert has 3 teams there in demesne, and a church, and 2 mills rendering 13 shillings, and 40 acres of meadow. He found 28 sokemen and 9 bordars there with 9 teams.[2]

---

[1] There is a blank space here of about half an inch.

[2] This is an unusual statement. Probably for once the clerks have left what the original returns must have had, a statement of the number of men and their teams on the land when it was given to Gilbert. One cannot, however, argue from this to the position in 1086.

47. S. In Screnbi[1] [Scremby (Candleshoe)] there are 4½ carucates of land ⌊assessed⌋ to the geld. There is land for 4 teams. There are 15 sokemen and 8 bordars there with 5 teams, and 100 acres of meadow, and 1 church.

48. S. In Stepinge [Great Steeping (Candleshoe)] there are 11½ carucates of land ⌊assessed⌋ to the geld. There is land for as many teams. 61 sokemen and 11 bordars have 10 teams there, and 2 churches, and 80 acres of meadow.

49. S. In Calnodesbi [Candlesby (Candleshoe)] there is 1 carucate of land ⌊assessed⌋ to the geld. There is land for 1 team. 13 sokemen and 6 bordars have 2 teams there.

50. S. In Burg [Burgh in the Marsh (Candleshoe)] there are 8 carucates of land ⌊assessed⌋ to the geld. There is land for 8 teams. 21 sokemen and 11 villeins and 3 bordars have 6 teams there, and ⌊there is⌋ 1 church, and 500 acres of meadow.

51. S. In Herdetorp [Addlethorpe (Candleshoe)] there are 4 carucates and 2 bovates of land ⌊assessed⌋ to the geld. There is land for as many teams. 18 sokemen and 17 villeins have 4 teams there, and [400] and 40 acres of meadow.

52. B. In Wemflet [Wainfleet (Candleshoe)] there is 1 bovate of land ⌊assessed⌋ to the geld. It is waste. It is inland.

53. S. In Haberdingham [Hagworthingham (Hill)] Gocelin son of Lanbert has 1 church, and half a carucate of land ⌊assessed⌋ to the geld, whereof Gilbert [de Gand] has the soke.

54. M. In Wilgebi[2] [Willoughby in the Marsh (Calcewath)] Tunne had 2 carucates of land ⌊assessed⌋ to the geld. There is land for 4 teams. Roger, Gilbert's man, has 2 teams there ⌊in demesne⌋. 4 sokemen on (*de*) half a carucate of land there have 2 teams, and 40 acres of meadow, and 40 acres of marsh (*maresc*), and 120 acres of wood⌊land⌋ for pannage, and 60 acres of underwood. T. R. E. it was worth 4 pounds ; now 8 pounds.

55. B. In Mundebi[3] [Mumby (Calcewath)] there is a berewic ⌊of this manor⌋, 2 bovates of land ⌊assessed⌋ to the geld. There is land for 3 oxen. Gilbert has 1 villein there ploughing with 1 ox.

56. B. In the same place (*ibidem*) there is a berewic ⌊of this manor⌋, 4 bovates of land ⌊assessed⌋ to the geld. There is land for 6 oxen. There are 6 villeins and 8 bordars there with 1 team, and 30 acres of meadow. The lord ⌊has⌋ 80 acres of meadow.

57. B. In Haroldestorp [Hasthorpe (Calcewath)] there is 1 carucate of land ⌊assessed⌋ to the geld. There is land for 2 teams. 4 sokemen on (*de*) half a carucate of land and 2 villeins and 2 bordars plough there with 6 oxen. Roger has 1 team there, and 30 acres of marsh (*maresch*).

58. B. In Slodebi [Sloothby (Calcewath)] there are 3 bovates of land ⌊assessed⌋ to the geld. There is land for 6 oxen. Roger has 2 villeins there ploughing with 3 oxen, and 10 acres of marsh (*maresch*).

59. B. In Wilgebi [Willoughby in the Marsh (Calcewath)] there are 3 bovates of land with sake and soke ⌊assessed⌋ to the geld. There is land for 5 oxen. There is 1 church there having half a carucate. T. R. E. it was worth 20 shillings ; now 10 shillings.

---

[1] See 69/36. [2] See 69/19. [3] See 12/93 ; 69/18.

60.[1] In Waletune and Bodebi [Welton in the Marsh and Boothby in Welton (Candleshoe)] there is 1 carucate of land ⌊assessed⌋ to the geld. There is land for 1 team. It is soke⌊land⌋ belonging to (*in*) Wilgebi [Willoughby].

61. M. In Clachesbi [Claxby St. Andrew (Calcewath)] Tonne had 6 bovates of land ⌊assessed⌋ to the geld. There is land for 12 oxen. Rademer, Gilbert's man, has 2 teams there ⌊in demesne⌋, and 6 villeins with 1 team. There are 660 acres of underwood there. T. R. E. and now worth 8 pounds. In the same vill Gilbert has 80 acres of underwood and other 120 acres of underwood. Of three parts of these acres Guy de Credun has the soke.

62. B. In Slodebi [Sloothby (Calcewath)] there is inland belonging to (*de*) Clachesbi [Claxby St. Andrew], half a carucate of land ⌊assessed⌋ to the geld.* There is land for 1 team. There are 6 villeins and 1 bordar there with 1 team, and 60 acres of meadow.

**D. B., f. 355c.* *Facsimile, p. xla.*

63. S. In Besebi [Beesby in the Marsh (Calcewath)] there is soke⌊land⌋ ⌊of this manor⌋, 3 carucates of land ⌊assessed⌋ to the geld. There is land for as many teams. 20 sokemen and 8 bordars have 5½ teams there, and 90 acres of meadow, and 180 acres of underwood.

64. S. In Maltesbi [Maltby le Marsh (Calcewath)] there are 2 carucates and 6 bovates of land ⌊assessed⌋ to the geld. There is land for 3 teams. 14 sokemen have 2 teams there, and 60 acres of meadow, and 5 acres of underwood.

65. B. In Salebi [Saleby (Calcewath)] there is half a carucate of land ⌊assessed⌋ to the geld. There is land for 4 oxen. There are 2 villeins there ploughing with 1 ox, and 10 acres of meadow, and 30 acres of underwood.

66. S. In Widerne [Withern (Calcewath)] there are 3½ carucates of land ⌊assessed⌋ to the geld. There is land for 4 teams. Rauemer, Gilbert's man, has 2 teams there ⌊in demesne⌋, and 20 sokemen and 13 villeins with 3 teams, and 1 mill rendering 15 shillings, and 180 acres of meadow. There is a priest there, and a church. [The soke belongs to H⌊ugh⌋ son of Baldric].

67. S. In Strobi [Strubby (Calcewath)] there are 2½ bovates ⌊assessed⌋ to the geld. There is land for 5 oxen. 2 villeins have half a team there, and 10 acres of meadow.

68. M. In Welle[2] [Well (Calcewath)] Tonne had 1 carucate of land ⌊assessed⌋ to the geld. There is land for 3 teams. Rauemer, Gilbert's man, has 2 teams there ⌊in demesne⌋, and 4 sokemen on (*de*) 2 bovates of this land and 12 villeins with 1 team, and 1 mill rendering 15 shillings, and 1½ acres of meadow, and 22 acres of wood⌊land⌋. T. R. E. it was worth 8 pounds; now 7 pounds.

69. S. In Ulesbi [Ulceby by Alford (Calcewath)] there are 2 bovates of land ⌊assessed⌋ to the geld. There is land for 4 oxen. There is 1 sokeman there with 1 team.

---

[1] This entry has been inserted at the foot of the column, and a sign indicates that it should be placed where it is printed in the text.

[2] See 4/62; 69/13.

70. S. In Alforde [Alford (Calcewath)] there are 6½ bovates of land [assessed] to the geld. There is land for 12 oxen. There are 2 sokemen and 3 villeins and 1 bordar there with 1 team, and 10 acres of meadow.

71. B. In Maltetorp [Mablethorpe (Calcewath)] there is half a carucate of land [assessed] to the geld. There is land for 1 team. 4 villeins have 1 team there, and 20 acres of meadow.

72. M. In Aschebi [West Ashby (Horncastle)] Siward had 1½ carucates of land [assessed] to the geld. There is land for 2 teams. Roger, Gilbert's man, has 2 teams there [in demesne], and 5 villeins and 5 bordars with half a team, and 100 acres of meadow, and 6 acres of underwood. T. R. E. it was worth 30 shillings; now 40 shillings; tallage 3 shillings.

73. M. In Dribi [Driby (Candleshoe)] Siward had 5½ carucates of land [assessed] to the geld. There is land for 5 teams. Ivo, Gilbert's man, has 4 teams there, in demesne, and 7 sokemen on (*de*) 2 carucates of land and 3 villeins and 5 bordars with 3 teams, and 1 mill rendering 12 pence, and 60 acres of meadow. T. R. E. it was worth 6 pounds; now 100 shillings; tallage 20 shillings.

74. M. In Croft [Croft (Candleshoe)] Odincarl had 2 carucates and 2 bovates of land [assessed] to the geld. There is land for 2 teams and 2 oxen. Ralf, Gilbert's man, has 2 teams there [in demesne], and 9 sokemen and 3 villeins and 3 bordars with 3 teams, and 1 salt-pan rendering 6 pence, and 120 acres of meadow. T. R. E. it was worth 20 shillings; now 4 pounds.

75. B. In Wemflet [Wainfleet (Candleshoe)] there is a berewic [of this manor], 2 bovates of land [assessed] to the geld. There are 6 villeins there with 2 oxen, and 6 salt-pans rendering 3 shillings.

76. M. In Chime [South Kyme (Aswardhurn)] Tunne had 14 bovates of land [assessed] to the geld. There is land for 1½ teams. Egbriht, Gilbert's man, has half a team there [in demesne], and 6 villeins with half a team, and 1 acre of meadow, and 82 acres of underwood, and 3 fisheries rendering 2 shillings. T. R. E. it was worth 20 shillings; now 40 [shillings].

77. In Mortun[1] and Hermodestorp [Morton and Hanthorpe (Aveland)] there are 2½ carucates and the fourth part of 1 carucate and the fourth part of 1 bovate of land [assessed] to the geld. There is land for as many teams and oxen. It is soke[land] belonging to (*in*) Edeham [Edenham (Beltisloe)].* There were 14 sokemen and 5 bordars there with 3 teams. There are 45 acres of meadow there, and 40 acres of wood[land] for pannage.

**D. B., f.* 355d. *Facsimile, p. xl*b.

78.[2] M. In Holm [Holme near Sutton in Beckingham (Loveden)] Ulf had 12 carucates of land in demesne and 12 carucates of land [which was] soke[land] [assessed] to the geld. There is land for as many teams. Gilbert has 4 teams there in demesne, and 28 sokemen and 28 villeins

[1] See 42/15.
[2] The letter *r* is written in the margin opposite this entry.

and 3 bordars having 14 teams. There are 2 priests there, and 2 churches, and 1 mill rendering 13 shillings and 4 pence. T. R. E. it was worth 10 pounds; now the like amount; tallage 3 pounds.

79. In Wilgebi [Silk Willoughby (Aswardhurn)] Gilbert has the fourth part of a church. It is soke⌊land⌋ belonging to (*in*) Wardebi [Aswarby].

80.[1] M. In Burgelai [Burley on the Hill (Alstoe, co. Rutland)] Ulf had 2 carucates of land ⌊assessed⌋ to the geld. There is land for 7 teams. Geoffrey (*Goisfridus*), Gilbert's man, has 2 teams ⌊in demesne⌋, and 30 villeins and 7 bordars with 4 teams, and 30 acres of meadow. There are wood⌊lands⌋ 1 league in length and 3 furlongs in breadth. T. R. E. it was worth 4 pounds; now 100 shillings.

81. M. In Bodebi [Boothby Pagnell (Threo)] Siwate had 5 carucates of land ⌊assessed⌋ to the geld. There is land for 5 teams. Roger, Gilbert's man, has 1 team there in demesne, and 4 villeins and 2 bordars and 12 sokemen on (*de*) 3 carucates of this land having 3 teams. There is a church there, and 6 acres of meadow, and 40 acres of wood⌊land⌋ for pannage, and 60 acres of underwood. T. R. E. it was worth 60 shillings; now the like amount. Guy de Credun renders soke in respect of 3½ bovates of this land.

82. M. In Folchingeham [Folkingham (Aveland)] Ulf had 12 carucates of land ⌊assessed⌋ to the geld. There is land for as many teams. Gilbert has 5 teams there in demesne, and 24 villeins and 5 sokemen and 9 bordars with 7 teams. There is a church there, and 1 mill rendering 10 shillings and 8 pence, and 100 acres of meadow, and 80 acres of underwood. T. R. E. it was worth 50 pounds; now 40 pounds; tallage 50 pounds.

83. B. In Cranewelle [Cranwell (Flaxwell) there is inland of this manor, 1½ carucates of land ⌊assessed⌋ to the geld. Azor had the soke of this land. Geoffrey (*Goisfridus*), Gilbert's man, has 6 villeins and 1 bordar there with 1 team, and 17½ acres of meadow. T. R. E. ⌊it was worth⌋ 20 shillings; now 10 ⌊shillings⌋.

SOKE⌊LAND⌋ OF THIS MANOR ⌊OF FOLKINGHAM⌋ [nos. 84–105]

84. S. In Hondintone[2] [Honington (Threo)] there are 3 carucates of land ⌊assessed⌋ to the geld. There is land for 3 teams. Fulbert, Gilbert's man, has 12 sokemen and 1 bordar there with 3 teams, and 35 acres of meadow. ⌊It is worth⌋ 60 shillings.

85. S. In Asedebi [Oseby in Haydour (Threo)] there are 5 carucates of land ⌊assessed⌋ to the geld. There is land for 7 teams. 18 sokemen and 3 bordars have 6 teams there, and 40 acres of meadow, and 30 acres of underwood.

86. S. In Lavintone [Lavington (Beltisloe)] there are 4 carucates and the third part of 1[3] carucate of land ⌊assessed⌋ to the geld. There is land for 5 teams.[4] Azelin, Gilbert's man, has 2 teams there in demesne, and 10 villeins and 3 bordars with 3 teams, and 30 acres of meadow. It is worth 100 shillings.

---

[1] This entry is duplicated in the *Domesday* Survey of Rutland (folio 293, col. 4) where the number of the bordars is given as 8, and of the villeins' teams as 3.

[2] See 14/88; 72/63.

[3] A space of a quarter of an inch is left blank here.

[4] *ad geld'* is duplicated, and *Terra v carucatis* is added in the margin.

87. S. In Picheworde [Pickworth (Aveland)] there are 2 carucates and half a bovate of land [assessed] to the geld. There is land for 2½ teams. Gilbert, has 21 sokemen there with 4 teams, and 16 acres of meadow, and 50 acres of underwood, and 20 acres of wood[land] for pannage.

88. S. In Hazebi [Haceby (Aveland)] there is 1 carucate of land [assessed] to the geld. There is land for 12 oxen. 13 sokemen and 5 bordars have 3 teams there, and 5 acres of meadow.

89. S. In Denbelbi [Dembleby (Aveland)] there is 1 carucate of land [assessed] to the geld. There is land for 12 oxen. 20 sokemen and 3 bordars have 3 teams there, and 18 acres of meadow, and 12 acres of underwood.

90. S. In Esbernebi [Osbournby (Aveland)] there are 4 carucates of land [assessed] to the geld. There is land for 5½ teams.* 16 sokemen and 8 bordars have 8 teams there ; and there is 1 church there.

**D. B., f. 356*a. *Facsimile, p. xli*a.[1]

91. S. In Trichingeham [Threckingham (Aveland)] there is 1 carucate of land [assessed] to the geld. There is land for 1 team. There is a market (*forum*) there rendering 40 shillings, and 11 sokemen and 8 bordars.

92. S. In Stou [Stow near Threckingham (Aveland)] there are 5½ carucates of land [assessed] to the geld. There is land for as many teams. Robert, Gilbert's man, has 21 sokemen and 14 bordars there having 5 teams. There is 1 team there in demesne, and 1 church, and 16 acres of meadow. The value (*precium*) [is] 100 shillings.

93. S. In Walecote [Walcot near Folkingham (Aveland)] there are 4 carucates of land [assessed] to the geld. There is land for 5 teams. There are 22 sokemen and 4 bordars there, and half a church, and 26 acres of meadow.

94. S. In Bellingeburg [Billingborough (Aveland)] Gilbert has the soke over (*super*) half a carucate of land.

95. S. In Berchetorp [Birthorpe (Aveland)] there are 15 bovates of land [assessed] to the geld, There is land for 2 teams. 8 sokemen and 8 bordars have 3 teams there, and 27 acres of meadow.

96. S. In Loctone [Laughton near Folkingham (Aveland)] there are 4 carucates of land [assessed] to the geld. There is land for 4 teams. 14 sokemen and 4 bordars have 3½ teams there, and 9 acres of meadow, and 13 acres of underwood.

97. S. In Aslachebi [half a carucate] and Spingeham [2 carucates and 6 bovates] [Aslackby and Sempringham (Aveland)] there are 3 carucates and 2 bovates of land [assessed] to the geld. There is land for 3½ teams. There are 13 sokemen and 1 bordar there having 3 teams, and [there are] half a church, and the sixth part of another church, and 24 acres of meadow, and 40 acres of underwood.

98. S. In Pochinton [Poynton (Aveland)] there are 2 carucates and 2 bovates of land [assessed] to the geld. There is land for as many teams and oxen. 16 sokemen have 6 teams there, and 32 acres of meadow, and 40 acres of [under]wood.

99. S. In Goldesbi[2] [Ingoldsby (Aswardhurn)] there are 3 caru-

---

[1] *Huuelle* is written upside-down at the head of this column.

[2] See 58/3 ; 72/35.

cates and 1 bovate of land [assessed] to the geld. There is land for 3 teams. 17 sokemen and 2 bordars have 5 teams there, and 25 acres of meadow, and 100 acres of underwood.

100. S. In Hag and Brandune [Hough on the Hill and Brandon (Loveden)] there are 3 carucates and 3 bovates of land [assessed] to the geld. There is land for 5 teams. 13 sokemen have 6 teams there, and 6 acres of meadow. All this Derinc holds of Gilbert, and he has half a team there in demesne. It is worth 40 shillings.

101. S. In Chirchebi [Kirkby by Laythorpe (Aswardhurn)] there are 7 carucates of land [assessed] to the geld. There is land for 5 teams. 31 sokemen and 6 bordars have 6 teams there.

102. S. In Wilgebi [Silk Willoughby (Aswardhurn)] there are 5 carucates of land [assessed] to the geld. There is land for 10 teams. 29 sokemen and 1 bordar have 6 teams there. There is a priest there, and a church, and 140 acres of meadow, and 24 acres of meadow [*sic*].

103. S. In Aswardebi [Aswarby (Aswardhurn)] there are 4½ carucates and 1 bovate of land [assessed] to the geld. There is land for 9 teams. 41 sokemen and 3 bordars have 18 teams there. There is a priest there, and a church, and 2 parts of 1 church, and 180 acres of meadow. Ralf the priest has 3½ carucates of this land, and he has 4 teams there in demesne.

104. S. In Scredintune [Scredington (Aswardhurn)] there are 10½ carucates of land [assessed] to the geld. There is land for 9 teams. 40 sokemen and 1 villein have 14 teams there. There is a priest there, and a church, and 21 acres of meadow.

105. In Helperincham [3 carucates and 2 bovates] and Burton [2 carucates] [Helpringham and Burton Pedwardine (Aswardhurn)] there are 5 carucates and 2 bovates of land [assessed] to the geld. There is land for 8 teams. 35 sokemen and 7 bordars have 10 teams there, and 26 acres of meadow.

*D. B., f. 356*b. *Facsimile, p. xli*b.

25.[1] LAND OF HUGH SON OF BALDRIC

1. Six M. In Bundebi [Bonby (Yarborough)] Grinchel and Merdo and Aldene and three other thanes had 3 carucates of land [assessed] to the geld. There is land for 6 teams. Hugh son of Baldric has 3 teams there in demesne, and 14 villeins and 7 bordars with 4 teams. T. R. E. it was worth 4 pounds ; now 6 pounds ; tallage 20 shillings. 3 bovates of this land [are] soke[land].

2. M. In Uluricebi [Worlaby near Brigg (Yarborough)] Grinchel had half a carucate of land [assessed] to the geld. There is land for 1 team. Ralf, Hugh's man, has 1 team there [in demesne], and 2 villeins having 2 oxen in a team. T. R. E. and now worth 20 shillings.

[1] The text has *.xxxv.* by a clerical error.

3. Two M. In Linberge [Great Limber (Yarborough)] Siward and Ulf had $2\frac{1}{2}$ carucates of land [assessed] to the geld. There is land for $5\frac{1}{2}$ teams. Hugh son of B. has 2 teams [in demesne], and 10 villeins and 4 bordars and 20 sokemen on (*de*) 5 bovates of this land. Amongst them all there are 4 teams and 2 oxen in a team. T. R. E. it was worth 100 shillings: now the like amount; tallage 20 shillings.

4. In Caburne [Cabourn (Haverstoe)] there is half a bovate of land. It is soke[land] belonging to (*in*) Linberge [Great Limber].

5. M. In Chernitone [Kirmington (Yarborough)] Tope had 2 bovates of land [assessed] to the geld. There is land for 2 teams. Hamelin, Hugh's man, has 1 team there [in demesne], and 5 villeins and 8 bordars and 10 sokemen with 1 team, having 18 tofts. T. R. E. it was worth 40 shillings; now 30 shillings; tallage 10 shillings.

6. M. In Crocestone [Croxton (Yarborough)] Siward had 10 bovates of land [assessed] to the geld. There is land for $2\frac{1}{2}$ teams. Hamelin, Hugh's man, [has] 1 team there [in demesne], and 6 villeins and 3 bordars and 2 sokemen with $1\frac{1}{2}$ teams. 1 bovate [is] soke[land]. There are 8 acres of meadow there. T. R. E. and now worth 40 shillings.

7. M. In Stalinburg [Stallingborough (Yarborough)] Siward and Gamel and Ulchil had 1 carucate of land [assessed] to the geld. There is land for 2 teams. Hugh has 1 team there [in demesne], and 2 sokemen on (*de*) 5 tofts, and 2 villeins and 1 bordar, and $2\frac{1}{2}$ mills rendering 10 shillings, and $2\frac{1}{2}$ salt-pans rendering 2 shillings, and 200 acres of meadow. T. R. E. and now worth 30 shillings.

8. M. In Staintone [Stainton le Vale (Walshcroft)] Bertor had 1 carucate of land [assessed] to the geld. There is land for 3 teams. Hugh has 1 team there [in demesne], and 4 sokemen on (*de*) 1 bovate of land, and 11 villeins and 3 bordars with 1 team and 2 oxen in a team, and 55 acres of meadow. T. R. E. it was worth 3 pounds; now 40 shillings; tallage 10 shillings.

9. M. In Caburne [Cabourn (Haverstoe)] Grinchel had 2 carucates and $3\frac{1}{2}$ bovates of land [assessed] to the geld. There is land for 5 teams. Hugh has 2 teams there [in demesne], and 12 sokemen on (*de*) 1 carucate of land, and 1 villein and 3 bordars with 3 teams, and 20 acres of meadow. T. R. E. it was worth 30 shillings; now 60 shillings; tallage 20 shillings.

10.[1] B. In Cucualt [Cuxwold (Haverstoe)] there is a berewic [of this manor], 3 bovates of land [assessed] to the geld. There is land for 6 oxen. There are 4 villeins and 3 sokemen there with 1 team.

11. M. In Crocestone [Croxton (Yarborough)] Grinchel had half a carucate of land [assessed] to the geld. There is land for 1 team. Hamelin, Hugh's man, has 1 team there [in demesne], and 9 sokemen on (*de*) 2 bovates of land and 6 villeins and 1 bordar having $1\frac{1}{2}$ teams, and 8 acres of meadow. T. R. E. and now worth 40 shillings.

12. S. In Toresbi and Alwoldesbi [North Thoresby and Autby in North Thoresby (Haverstoe)] there is 1 bovate and 5 parts of 1 bovate [assessed] to the geld. There is land for 2 oxen. [It is] soke[land] belonging to (*in*) Caburne [Cabourn (Haverstoe)]. There are 2 villeins there, and 2 salt-pans rendering 2 shillings, and 15 acres of meadow.

---

[1] *K* in the margin for *Kalumpnia* directs attention to a disputed claim (see 22/9; 70/24).

D. B., f. 356c. *Facsimile, p. xliia.*

13. 2 M. In Torp [Kettleby Thorpe (Yarborough)] Claç and Lewin had 10 bovates of land [assessed] to the geld. There is land for 2½ teams. Gilbert, Hugh's man, has 1½ teams [in demesne], and 2 sokemen on (*de*) 5½ bovates of land and 12 villeins and 5 bordars with 1½ teams, and 60 acres of meadow. T. R. E. it was worth 60 shillings ; now 50 shillings ; tallage 10 shillings.

14. B. In Bechebi [Bigby (Yarborough)] there is a berewic [of this manor], 5½ bovates of land [assessed] to the geld. There is land for 1 team. 1 villein and 1 bordar have 1 ox in a team there.

15. M. In Hamingebi [Hemingby (Gartree)] Edric had 6 bovates of land [assessed] to the geld. There is land for 6 oxen. Hugh has 2 teams there [in demesne], and 13 sokemen on (*de*) 2 bovates of land and 3 villeins with 2 teams, and 60 acres of meadow. T. R. E. it was worth 60 shillings ; now 100 shillings ; tallage 20 shillings.

SOKE[LAND]

16. S. In Buchehale [Bucknall (Gartree)] there are 6½ bovates of land [assessed] to the geld. There is land for as many oxen. 5 sokemen and 2 villeins have 1 team there, and 65 acres of meadow, and 9 acres of wood[land] for pannage, and 5 acres of underwood.

17. S. In Horsintone [Horsington (Gartree)] there are 2 carucates and 6½ bovates of land [assessed] to the geld. There is land for 3 teams. 16 sokemen and 2 bordars have 3 teams there, and 153 acres of meadow, and 15 acres of underwood.

18. S. Ludeforde [Ludford (Wraggoe)] there is soke[land] belonging to (*in*) Wicham [West Wykeham (Louthesk)], 2 bovates of land [assessed] to the geld. There is land for 4 oxen. 2 sokemen have half a team there, and 4 acres of meadow.

19. M. In Clachesbi [Claxby St. Andrew (Calcewath)] Dane had 1 carucate of land [assessed] to the geld. There is land for 14 oxen. Guy,[1] Hugh's son-in-law, has 2 teams there [in demesne], and 1 sokeman on (*de*) 3 bovates of land and 5 villeins with 1½ teams. There is a church there, and a priest, and 1 mill rendering 2 shillings, and 120 acres of underwood, whereof (*inde*) Gilbert de Gand has 2 parts and Guy the other 3 parts. T. R. E. it was worth 8 pounds ; now 9 pounds.

SOKE[LAND] OF THIS MANOR.

20. S. In Widerne [Withern (Calcewath)] there are 6 bovates of land [assessed] to the geld. There is land for 1 team. 8 sokemen and 2 villeins have 2 teams there, and 12 acres of meadow, and 60 acres of underwood.

21. S. In Endretorp [Woodthorpe (Calcewath)] there are 2½ carucates of land [assessed] to the geld. There is land for 5 teams. 19 sokemen and 9 bordars have 4 teams there. There is underwood half a league in length and as much in breadth.

22. S. In Strobi [5 bovates] and Malteby [2[bovates]] [Strubby and Maltby in the Marsh (Calcewath)] there are 7 bovates of land [assessed] to the geld. There is land for 12 oxen. 5 sokemen have 5 oxen in a team there, and 30 acres of meadow.

---

[1] *I.e.* Guy of Craon (*Credun*).

23. S. In Saleby [Saleby (Calcewath)] there are 2 carucates of land [assessed] to the geld. There is land for 2 teams. 2 sokemen and 2 villeins have 2 teams there.

24. S. In Thuorstorp [Thoresthorpe (Calcewath)] there are 2 carucates of land [assessed] to the geld. There is land for 2 teams. 5 sokemen and 2 bordars have 2½ teams there, and 40 acres of meadow, and 40 acres of underwood.

25. M. In Slodebi [Sloothby (Calcewath)] Dane had 3 bovates of land [assessed] to the geld. There is land for 1 team. Guy,[1] Hugh's son-in-law, has 4 villeins and 3 bordars there with half a team, and 4 acres of meadow. T. R. E. it was worth 20 shillings ; now 6 shillings.

[d . . . .[2]]

D. B., f. 356d. *Facsimile, p. xlii*b.

26.[3] LAND OF COLSUAIN

1. M. In Brotulbi [Brattleby (Lawress)] Chetel had 3 carucates of land [assessed] to the geld. There is land for 3½ teams. Colsuan has 2 teams there in demesne, and 9 sokemen on (*de*) 7 bovates of this land, and 6 villeins and 1 bordar with 4 teams. T. R. E. it was worth 40 shillings ; now 60 shillings ; tallage 20 shillings.

2. M. In Risun[4] [Riseholme (Lawress)] Lepsi had 1 carucate of land [assessed] to the geld. There is land for 1 team. Colsuan has 2 teams there [in demesne], and 3 villeins and 1 bordar with 1 team, and 1 mill rendering 2 shillings. T. R. E. it was worth 20 shillings ; now 60 shillings.

3. M. In Falingeurde [Faldingworth (Lawress)] Sberne had half a carucate of land [assessed] to the geld. There is land for 4 oxen. 3 villeins of Colsuan's have half a team there, and 8 acres of meadow. T. R. E. [worth] 10 shillings ; now 5 shillings and 4 pence.

4. M. Scotstorne and Holme and Sudborc [Scothorne and Holme and Sudbrooke (Lawress)] Turulf had 3 carucates and 5 bovates of land [assessed] to the geld. There is land for 4 teams. Colsuan has 1 team there [in demesne] and 11 sokemen on (*de*) 2½ carucates of land, and 1 villein and 1 bordar with 3 teams, and 64 acres of meadow. T. R. E. it was worth 40 shillings ; now 60 shillings ; tallage 20 shillings.

5. In the same places (*ibidem*) Godric had 4 bovates [and a half] of land [assessed] to the geld. There is land for 1 team. 1 villein and 1 bordar have 2 oxen in a team there. T. R. E. and now worth 5 shillings.

6. In the same places (*ibidem*) Colsuan has 1 carucate of land of the King, as he says ; and therefor he renders custom in Fiscartone [Fiskerton (Lawress)] to Saint Peter of Burg [Peterborough]. He has 1 mill there, and 3 villeins with 1 team. T. R. E. [it rendered], and now renders, 10 shillings.

---

[1] *I.e.* Guy of Craon (*Credun*).
[2] *Sic* ; in the bottom margin.
[3] The text has *.xxxvi.* by a clerical error.
[4] See 8/13 ; 71/2.

7.[1] M. In Berlinge [Barlings (Lawress)] Col had 6 bovates of land ⌊assessed⌋ to the geld. There is land for 1 team. Colsuan has 1 team there ⌊in demesne⌋, and 3 villeins with half a team, and 1 church. T. R. E. it was worth 10 shillings; now 4 pounds.

8. B. In Refan [Reepham (Lawress)] there are 6 bovates of land ⌊assessed⌋ to the geld. There is land for 1 team. It is a berewic ⌊of this manor⌋. Colsuan ⌊has⌋ 1 team there ⌊in demesne⌋, and 4 villeins with half a team, and 18 acres of meadow.

9. M. In Cameslingeham [Cammeringham (Aslacoe)] Chenut and Elnod and Ulchel and Sbern had 4½ carucates of land ⌊assessed⌋ to the geld. There is land for 5 teams. Colsuan has 4 teams there in demesne, and 8 sokemen on (*de*) half a carucate of this land, and 11 villeins and 2 bordars with 3 teams, and 70 acres of meadow. T. R. E. it was worth 3 pounds; now 4 pounds; tallage 20 shillings.

10. M. In Ingeham [Ingham (Aslacoe)] Frane and Summerled had 1 carucate of land ⌊assessed⌋ to the geld. There is land for 1½ teams. Roger and Anschitil, Colsuan's men, have 1½ teams there ⌊in demesne⌋, and 4 villeins and 1 bordar with 3 oxen in a team, and 16 acres of meadow. T. R. E. it was worth 50 shillings; now 30 shillings; tallage 10 shillings.[2]

11. S. In Frisetorp [Friesthorpe (Lawress)] there are 3 carucates of land ⌊assessed⌋ to the geld. There is land for 3 teams. It is soke⌊land⌋ belonging to (*in*) Ingeham [7 bovates] and Felingeham [17 bovates] [Ingham and Fillingham (Aslacoe)]. 10 sokemen and 3 bordars have 3 teams there, and 50 acres of meadow, and 20 acres of underwood.

12.[3] S. In Faldingeurde [Faldingworth (Lawress)] there are 2 carucates of land ⌊assessed⌋ to the geld. There is land for 2½ teams. It is soke⌊land⌋ belonging to (*in*) Figelingeham [6 bovates], and Sperlintone [1 carucate], and Lageham[4] [2 bovates] [Fillingham and Spridlington and Ingham (Aslacoe)]. 9 sokemen have 1 team there, and 26 acres of meadow, and 1 acre of wood⌊land⌋.

13. M. In Haneurde [Cold Hanworth (Aslacoe)] Frane had 6 bovates of land ⌊assessed⌋ to the geld. There is land for 12 oxen. Thorald the priest has 1 team there ⌊in demesne⌋, and 6 villeins and 1 bordar having 1 team, and 10 acres of meadow. T. R. E. it was worth 20 shillings; now 30 shillings.

14. B. In Hagetorne [Hackthorn (Aslacoe)] there is a berewic ⌊of this manor⌋, 3 bovates and the fourth part of 1 bovate ⌊assessed⌋ to the geld. There is land for 4 oxen.

D. B., f. 357a. *Facsimile, p. xliii*a.

15. M. In the same Hagetorne [Hackthorn] Chenut had 3 bovates of land ⌊assessed⌋ to the geld. There is land for 4 oxen. Colsuan has 2 oxen there in a team ⌊in demesne⌋, and 8 acres of meadow. T. R. E. it was worth 5 shillings and 4 pence; now the like amount.

---

[1] A sign against this entry answers to a similar sign against no. 21, the intention being seemingly to direct attention to the fact that the two entries relate to the same vill.

[2] A sign, answering to a similar sign against no. 23, shews that that entry should follow no. 10.

[3] A sign against this entry answers to a similar sign against no. 24. The intention being seemingly to connect the two notices of Fillingham.

[4] *La* in this name seems to be a misreading for *In*.

16. M. In Scalebi and Stratone [Scawby and Sturton (Manley)] Turulf had 11 bovates of land ⌊assessed⌋ to the geld. There is land for 2 teams. Alfred, Colsuan's man, has 1 team there ⌊in demesne⌋, and 5 sokemen on (*de*) 1 carucate of this land, and 3 villeins with 1½ teams. T. R. E. it was worth 10 shillings ; now 20 shillings ; tallage 5 shillings.

17. B. In Reburne [Redbourne (Manley)] there are 2 bovates of land and 4 parts of 1 bovate[1] ⌊assessed⌋ to the geld. There is land for 5½ oxen. Colsuan has it, and it is waste.

18. S. In Hiboldestou [Hibaldstow (Manley)] there is the third part of 2 bovates ⌊assessed⌋ to the geld. It is soke⌊land⌋ belonging to (*in*) Scal' [Scawby].

19. M. In Risun and Carlentun [Riseholme and South Carlton (Lawress)] Alsi had half a carucate of land ⌊assessed⌋ to the geld. There is land for 6 oxen. Matthew, Colsuan's man, has 1 team there ⌊in demesne⌋, and 4 villeins with half a team, and 20 acres of meadow, and 160 acres of wood⌊land⌋ for pannage. T. R. E. it was worth 15 shillings ; now 30 shillings.

20. M. In Cocrinton [Cockerington (Louthesk)] Elnod had 1 bovate of land ⌊assessed⌋ to the geld. There is land for 2 oxen. Matthew has half a team there ⌊in demesne⌋. T. R. E. and now worth 3 shillings.

21.[2] M. In Berlinge [Barlings (Lawress)] Osgot had 6 bovates of land ⌊assessed⌋ to the geld. There is land for 1 team. Colsuan has 1 team there ⌊in demesne⌋, and 2 villeins and 3 bordars with half a team, and 20 acres of meadow, and 20 acres of underwood. T. R. E. it was worth 30 shillings ; now 40 shillings.

22. M. In Cheftesbi [Kexby (Well)] Aschil had 3 carucates and 3 bovates [and a half] of land ⌊assessed⌋ to the geld. There is land for as many teams and oxen. Adelelm, Colsuan's man, has 2 teams there ⌊in demesne⌋, and 9 villeins and 3 bordars with 1½ teams, and 1 mill rendering 16 pence and 58 acres of meadow, and 40 acres of underwood. T. R. E. and now worth 40 shillings ; tallage 10 shillings.

23. S. In Cotes [Cotes by Stow (Aslacoe)] there are 2 bovates of land ⌊assessed⌋ to the geld. There is land for 2 oxen. It is soke⌊land⌋ belonging to (*in*) Ingeham [Ingham (Aslacoe)].[3]

24.[4] Five M. In Filingeham [Fillingham (Aslacoe)] Frane and Elnod and Aschil and Elnod and Godric had 7 carucates and 1 bovate of land ⌊assessed⌋ to the geld. There is land for 11 teams. Colsuan has 4 teams there ⌊in demesne⌋, and 32 sokemen on (*de*) 4½ teams of this land and 12 villeins with 3½ teams. There is a church there, and 240 acres of meadow. T. R. E. it was worth 4 pounds ; now 5 pounds ; tallage 40 shillings.

25. M. In Sperlinctone [Spridlington (Aslacoe)] Ebrard and his two brothers had 2 carucates and 5½ bovates of land ⌊assessed⌋ to the geld.

---

[1] It is possible that *iiii part'* may be a mistake for *iiii pars*. If the fraction is ¼, the holdings in Redbourne make a vill of 12 carucates (1/39 ; 7/57 ; 14/40, 41 ; 26/17 ; 28/15 ; 41/2 ; 48/3 ; 61/10). The clerks were not always accurate in their syntax : cp. 27/22 where they wrote *vi pars* after *habuit*.

[2] See note to no. 7 above.

[3] A sign shews that this entry should follow no. 10 above (see note to no. 10).

[4] See note to no. 12 above.

There is land for 3 teams. Colsuan has 2 teams there ⌊in demesne⌋, and 4 sokemen on (*de*) 1 bovate of this land and 16 villeins and 4 bordars with 2 teams, and 8 acres of meadow. T. R. E. it was worth 21 shillings; now 40 shillings; tallage 10 shillings.

26. M. In Oustorp [Ewerby Thorpe (Aswardhurn)] Eddive had $3\frac{1}{2}$ carucates and 1 bovate of land ⌊assessed⌋ to the geld. There is land for 3 teams. Colsuan has 2 teams there ⌊in demesne⌋, and 8 villeins with 1 team, and 44 acres of meadow, and 23 acres of underwood. T. R. E. it was worth 30 shillings; now 60 shillings.

27. Two M. In Hechintune[1] [Heckington (Aswardhurn)] Turchil and Algar had 1 carucate and 6 bovates of land ⌊assessed⌋ to the geld. There is land for 1 team and 5 oxen. Conded, Colsuan's man, has 1 villein there, and 18 acres of meadow. T. R. E. it was worth 36 shillings; now 30 shillings.

28. B. In Helpericham [Helpringham (Aswardhurn)] there are 2 bovates of land ⌊assessed⌋ to the geld. There is land for 2 oxen. There is 1 villein there, and 2 acres of meadow. This land is almost (*pene*) waste.

D. B., f. 357b. *Facsimile, p. xliii*b.

29.[2] In Huuelle [Howell (Aswardhurn)] hundred there are $2\frac{1}{2}$ bovates ⌊assessed⌋ to the geld. There is land for 2 oxen. It is soke⌊land⌋ belonging to (*in*) Cherchebi [Kirkby by Laythorpe (Aswardhurn)].

30. Two M. In Ledulvetorp [Laythorpe by Kirkby)] Tor and Aschil had $5\frac{1}{2}$ carucates of land ⌊assessed⌋ to the geld. Conded and Anchitil, Colsuan's men, have 4 teams there ⌊in demesne⌋, and 7 villeins and 10 bordars and 1 sokeman with $1\frac{1}{2}$ teams, and half a church, and[3] with half a priest. T. R. E. it was worth 4 pounds; now the like amount; tallage 20 shillings.

31. M. In Dodintone [Dry Doddington (Loveden)] Outi had 6 bovates of land ⌊assessed⌋ to the geld. There is land for as many oxen. Colsuan has 2 villeins and 2 bordars there with half a team, and ⌊he has⌋ half a mill rendering 3 shillings, and 10 acres of meadow. T. R. E. and now worth 10 shillings.

32. S. In the same place (*ibidem*) there are 6 bovates of land ⌊assessed⌋ to the geld. There is land for 6 oxen. It is soke⌊land⌋ belonging to (*in*) Merestone [Marston (Loveden)]. 2 sokemen and 2 bordars have 2 oxen there. The lord ⌊has⌋ half a team, and 10 acres of meadow.

33. M. In Merestone [Marston (Loveden)] Alsi had 1 carucate of land ⌊assessed⌋ to the geld in demesne and 10 bovates of soke⌊land⌋ (*x bouatas terre in soca*). There is land for 3 teams. Walter, Colsuan's man, has 1 team there ⌊in demesne⌋, and 4 sokemen and 5 bordars with 1 team and 1 ox, and the site of 1 mill, and 32 acres of meadow. T. R. E. it was worth 30 shillings; now 50 shillings.

34. S. In Hacham [Hougham (Loveden)] there are 2 carucates of land ⌊assessed⌋ to the geld. There is land for 12 oxen. It is soke⌊land⌋

[1] See 72/31.
[2] This entry has been inserted in the top margin.
[3] *and* seems to be superfluous.

belonging to (*in*) Merest⌊one⌋ [Marston]. 4 sokemen and 1 bordar have half a team there, and 4 acres of meadow.

35. M. In Hacham [Hougham (Loveden)] Azor had 2 carucates of land ⌊assessed⌋ to the geld. There is land for 3 teams. William, Colsuan's man, has 1 team there ⌊in demesne⌋, and 5 villeins and 5 bordars with 1 team, and 2 oxen, and 2½ acres of meadow. T. R. E. and now worth 30 shillings.

36. M. In Bolinburg [Billingborough (Aveland)] Suen had 2 carucates and 7 bovates of land ⌊assessed⌋ to the geld. Brunel, Colsuan's man, has 1½ teams there ⌊in demesne⌋, and 8 villeins and 2 bordars with 1½ teams. There is half a church there, and 1 mill rendering 5 shillings and 4 pence, and 27 acres of meadow, and 26 acres of underwood. T. R. E. it was worth 40 shillings ; now 60 shillings.

37. M. In Uluesbi [Ouseby in Birthorpe (Aveland)] Alsi had 2 carucates and 1½ bovates of land ⌊assessed⌋ to the geld. There is land for 18 oxen. Brunel, Colsuan's man, has 1½ teams there ⌊in demesne⌋, and 8 villeins with 2 teams. There is half a church there, and 1 mill rendering 5 shillings and 4 pence. T. R. E. and now worth 60 shillings.

38. S. In Podintone [Pointon (Aveland)] there is half a carucate of land ⌊assessed⌋ to the geld. There is land for 4 oxen. Conded, Colsuan's man, has 1 team there, and 3 bordars, and 4 acres of meadow.

39. S. In Spanebi [Spanby (Aveland)] there are 2 carucates of land ⌊assessed⌋ to the geld. There is land for 3 teams. 12 sokemen have 2 teams there, and 20 acres of meadow.

40. Two M. In Neutone [Newton by Folkingham (Aveland)] Turchil [and Godwin] had 10 bovates of land ⌊assessed⌋ to the geld. There is land for 2 teams. Ralf, Colsuan's man, has 1 team there ⌊in demesne⌋, and 4 villeins and 4 bordars with half a team, and 18[1] acres of meadow, and 72 acres of underwood. T. R. E. and now ⌊worth⌋ 70 shillings ; tallage 20 shillings.

41. B. In Uluesbi [Ouseby in Birthorpe (Aveland)] there are 6 bovates and the third part of 1 bovate of land ⌊assessed⌋ to the geld. There is land for 1 team. It is inland belonging to (*in*) Neutone [Newton]. There is now 1 bordar there, and the site of 1 mill, and 9 acres of meadow.

42. B. In Trinchigeham [Threckingham (Aveland)] there are 14 bovates and the third part of 1 bovate ⌊assessed⌋ to the geld. There is land for 2½ teams. It is inland. There are 1 sokeman and 5 villeins and 3 bordars there with 1½ teams.

43. M. In Delbebi [Dembleby (Aveland)] Gonchel had 1 carucate of land ⌊assessed⌋ to the geld. There is land for 10 oxen. Rainald, Colsuan's man, has 1 team there ⌊in demesne⌋, and 4 sokemen and 1 bordar with 1 team; and 16 acres of meadow, and 20 acres of underwood. T. R. E. and now ⌊worth⌋ 20 shillings.

D. B., f. 357c. *Facsimile, p. xliva.*

44. M. In Suavetone [Swaton (Aveland)] Auti had 7 carucates of land ⌊assessed⌋ to the geld. There is land for 9 teams. Colsuan has 3 teams there ⌊in demesne⌋, and 40 sokemen on (*de*) 5 carucates of this

---

[1] *xiii* has been corrected to *xvi*, and *ii* has been interlined above it.

land, and 7 villeins and 2 bordars with 10 teams, and 80 acres of meadow. T. R. E. it was worth 8 pounds ; now 4 pounds ; tallage 40 shillings.

45. M. In the same vill Alsi and Adestan had 1 carucate of land ⌊assessed⌋ to the geld. There is land for 10 oxen. Alfric (*Aluricus*) their brother had the soke over them in Hazebi [Haceby (Aveland)] only in the king's service (*solummodo in seruitio regis*). Colsuan has half a team there ⌊in demesne⌋, and 3 villeins with half a team, and 13 acres of meadow. T. R. E. and now ⌊worth⌋ 10 shillings.

46. M. In Horbelinge [Horbling (Aveland)] Suen had 3 carucates and 2 bovates of land ⌊assessed⌋ to the geld. There is land for as many teams and oxen. Matthew, Colsuan's man, has 1 team there ⌊in demesne⌋, and 11 sokemen on (*de*) 1 carucate of this land and 3 villeins with 3 teams, and 15 acres of meadow. T. R. E. and now worth 40 shillings ; tallage 20 shillings.

47. M. In Asebi [Aisby in Haydour (Threo)] Aslac had 3 carucates of land ⌊assessed⌋ to the geld. There is land for 4 teams. William, Colsuan's man, has 9 sokemen and 2 bordars there having 4 teams, and 100 acres of meadow. T. R. E. it was worth 60 shillings ; now the like amount ; tallage 20 shillings.

48. M. In Bertone and Billesfelt [Burton Coggles and Bitchfield (Beltisloe)] Letfled had 6 bovates of land ⌊assessed⌋ to the geld. There is land for 1 team. William, Colsuan's man, has half a team there ⌊in demesne⌋, and 3 villeins and 2 bordars with half a team, and 4 acres of meadow, and 150 acres of wood⌊land⌋ for pannage throughout the territory. T. R. E. it was worth 16 shillings ; now 20 shillings.

49. Two M. In Aschebi [Ashby de la Launde (Flaxwell)] Outi and Aschil had 3½ carucates of land ⌊assessed⌋ to the geld. There is land for 4 teams. Colsuan has 1½ teams there ⌊in demesne⌋, and 12 villeins and 2 sokemen on (*de*) 1 bovate of this land and 1 bordar with 2 teams, and 15 acres of meadow. T. R. E. worth 50 shillings ; now 70 shillings.

50. M. In Nortchime [North Kyme (Langoe)] Outi had 5 carucates and 2 bovates of land ⌊assessed⌋ to the geld. There is land for 2 teams. Colsuan has 1 team there ⌊in demesne⌋, and 1 fishery rendering 8 pence, and 20 acres of meadow, and 5 acres of underwood. T. R. E. it was worth 40 shillings ; now 4 pounds.

51. S. In Westbi [Westby (Beltisloe)] there are 10 bovates of land ⌊assessed⌋ to the geld. There is land for 10 oxen. It is free soke⌊land⌋ (*frisoca*) belonging to (*in*) Heidure [Haydour (Threo)]. 1 sokeman and 6 villeins have 2 teams there, and 12 acres of meadow, and 50 acres of wood⌊land⌋ for pannage throughout the territory.

52. B. In Evedune [Evedon (Aswardhurn)] there are 2 carucates of land ⌊assessed⌋ to the geld. There is land for 2 teams. It is inland belonging to (*in*) Cherchebi [Kirkby by Laythorpe (Aswardhurn)]. There are 6 acres of meadow there, and 8 acres of underwood, and 40 acres of marsh (*maresch*).

53. M. In Picheuorde[1] [Pickworth (Aveland)] Outi had 2 carucates

[1] See 72/54.

of land [assessed] to the geld. There is land for 3 teams. These 2 carucates are not enumerated in any hundred (*non sunt in numero alicuius hund'*) nor have they their like (*pares*) in Lincolnshire (*Lincolescyra*). William, Colsuan's man, has 1 team there [in demesne], and 6 villeins and 2 bordars with 1 team. There is a priest there, and half a church. In this land a certain free man (*francus homo*) has 1 carucate. And[1]

54. In the same vill there are 2½ bovates of land [assessed] to the geld. There is land for 3½ oxen. It is soke[land] belonging to (*in*) Picheuorde [Pickworth]. 2 villeins have 2 oxen there. T. R. E. and now worth 40 shillings.

D. B., f. 357d. *Facsimile, p. xliv*b.

27. LAND OF ALFRED (*Alvredi*) OF LINCOLN

1. M. In Golse[2] [Goxhill (Yarborough)] Siward had 1 carucate [and 2 bovates] of land [assessed] to the geld. There is land for 2½ teams. Ralf, Alfred's man, has 1 team there [in demesne], and 16 sokemen on (*de*) 2 bovates of this land and 6 villeins with 2 teams, and 60 acres of meadow. T. R. E. it was worth 30 shillings; now 40 shillings; tallage 10 shillings.

2. M. In Haburne [Habrough (Yarborough)] Alwin had 5 bovates of land [assessed] to the geld. There is land for 10 oxen. Ralf, Alfred's man, has 1 team there [in demesne], and 1 villein and 2 bordars with 2 oxen, and 1 mill rendering 2 shillings, and 20 acres of meadow. T. R. E. and now [worth] 30 shillings.

3. M. In Cotes[3] [Great Cotes (Bradley)] Morcar had 5 bovates of land [assessed] to the geld. There is land for 10 oxen. Bernard, Alfred's man, has there 2 villeins and 2 bordars and 8 sokemen on (*de*) 1 bovate of this land with 2 teams, and 100 acres of meadow. T. R. E. it was worth 30 shillings; now 24 shillings.

4. B. In Alesbi [Aylesby (Bradley)] there is half a bovate of land [assessed] to the geld. There is land for 2 oxen. 1 villein has 1 ox there. It is soke[land] belonging to (*in*) Cotes [Great Cotes].

5. M. In Hechelinge [Healing (Bradley)] Morcar had 2 carucates [of land] [assessed] to the geld. There is land for 4 teams. Bernard, Alfred's man, has 2 teams there [in demesne], and 13 sokemen on (*de*) half a carucate of this land and 2 villeins and 2 bordars with 2½ teams, and half a mill rendering 3 shillings, and 26 acres of meadow. T. R. E. it was worth 40 shillings; now 50 shillings; tallage 10 shillings.

6. B. In Sualun [Swallow (Bradley)] there are 3 bovates of land [assessed] to the geld. There is land for 6 oxen. It is inland of this manor. 1 villein has 1 ox in a team there.

---

[1] The conjunction connects nos. 53 and 54.
[2] See 30/2; 70/5.
[3] See 44/8; 70/12.

7. Two M. In Lindude [Linwood (Walshcroft)] William and Grinchel and Asford had 1½ carucates of land [assessed] to the geld. There is land for 4 teams. Alfred has 2 teams there in demesne, and 20 villeins and 5 bordars with 4 teams, and 2 parts of a mill rendering 2 shillings, and 280 acres of meadow. T. R. E. it was worth 65 shillings; now 50 shillings; tallage 10 shillings.

8. B. In Rase [Middle Rasen (Walshcroft)] there are 4 bovates of land [assessed] to the geld. There is land for 12 oxen. It is inland of this manor. 3 villeins have 2 oxen in a team there.

9. S. In the other Rase [Market Rasen (Walshcroft)] there are 4½ bovates of land [assessed] to the geld. There is land for 1 team. It is sokeland. 10 sokemen have 1 team there, and 1 mill rendering 12 pence, and 10 acres of meadow.

10. Two M. In Toreswe [Thoresway (Walshcroft)] Rolf and Code had 5 carucates and 7 bovates of land [assessed] to the geld. There is land for 13 teams. Alfred has 2 teams there [in demesne], and 56 sokemen and 5 villeins with 5 teams, and 2 mills rendering 3 shillings, and 40 acres of meadow in the soke of William de Perci's manor of Castre [Caistor (Yarborough)]. T. R. E. it was worth 4 pounds; now 100 shillings; tallage 40 shillings.

11. In Tauelesbi [Tealby (Walshcroft)] Alfred has 1 mill in the soke of the Bishop of Bayeux.

12. M. In Cucualt [Cuxwold (Haverstoe)] Leduin had 3 bovates of land [assessed] to the geld. There is land for 6 oxen. Gleu, Alfred's man, has 1 team there [in demesne], and 2 villeins and 1 bordar. T. R. E. and now worth 20 shillings.

13. S. In Caburne [Cabourn (Haverstoe)] there is 1 bovate of land [assessed] to the geld. It is soke[land] belonging to (*in*) Cucualt [Cuxwold]. 1 villein and 1 bordar have 1 ox in a team there.

14. Two M. In Rodewelle [Rothwell (Haverstoe)] Grinchil and William had 4 carucates and 1 bovate [*and 2 parts of 1 bovate*[1]] of land [assessed] to the geld. There is land for 8 teams. Gleu, Alfred's man, has 1½ teams there [in demesne], and 12 sokemen on (*de*) 7 bovates of this land and 7 villeins and 1 bordar with 2½ teams, and 2 mills rendering 3 shillings, and 46 acres of meadow, and 1 church. T. R. E. it was worth 4 pounds; now 3 pounds; tallage 10 shillings.

15.[2] M. In Rodewelle [Rothwell (Haverstoe)] Torchetel had half a carucate of land [assessed] to the geld. There is land for 1 team. Alfred has 1 sokeman and 2 bordars there with half a team. T. R. E. and now worth 6 shillings.

16.[2] In Toresbi and Aldulvebi [North Thoresby and Autby[3] (Haverstoe)] Alfred has 1 saltpan belonging to (*in*) Rodewelle [Rothwell].

*D. B., f. 358*a. *Facsimile, p. xlv*a.

17. S. In Cucualt [Cuxwold (Haverstoe)] there is 1 bovate of land [assessed] to the geld. 3 sokemen have 1 team there.

18. S. In Caburne [Cabourn (Haverstoe)] there are 2½ bovates of land [assessed] to the geld. It is waste.

---

[1] Cancelled by being struck through.

[2] Nos. 15 and 16 are written in the bottom margin of the column.

[3] *Aldulvebi* is the *D. B.* form of *Audleby* rather than of *Autby* (cp. 4/17; 16/35); but Autby seems to be the place referred to here. Perhaps the clerks confounded the two places.

19. M. In Stigeswalt [Stixwould (Gartree)] Siward had 6 bovates of land [assessed] to the geld. There is land for 12 oxen. The same has of Alfred 4 villeins with 1 team there, and 20 acres of meadow, and 40 acres of wood[land] for pannage. T. R. E. and now worth 10 shillings.

20. S. In Terintone [Torrington (Wraggoe)] Rolf had 3½ bovates of land [assessed] to the geld. There is land for 1 team. It is soke[land] belonging to (*in*) the vill itself. Gocelin, Alfred's man, has 2½ sokemen having 2½ oxen in a team there, and 11 acres of meadow.

21. S. In the same place (*ibidem*) Clac had 3½ bovates of land [assessed] to the geld. There is land for 1 team. It is soke[land] belonging to (*in*) Haintone [Hainton]. 2½ sokemen have 2½ oxen in a team there. Gocelin holds it of Alfred.

22. M. In Alvingeham [Alvingham (Louthesk)] Edric had 5½ bovates and the sixth part (*pars* rectius *partem*) of 1 bovate of land [assessed] to the geld. There is land for 1½ teams. Gocelin, Alfred's man, has 1 team there [in demesne], and 5 villeins with half a team. Two bovates of this land are soke[land] (*in soca*), and there are 20 acres of meadow. T. R. E. it was worth 20 shillings ; now 30 shillings.

23. S. In Brachenberg [Brackenborough (Louthesk)] there is 1 bovate of land [assessed] to the geld. There is land for 2 oxen. Ranulf, Alfred's man, has 1 team there [in demesne], and 4 villeins with half a team. It is soke[land] belonging to (*in*) Alvingham [Alvingham], and there are 10 acres of meadow.

24. Two M. In the vill itself [Brackenborough] Edric and Hoch had 6 bovates of land [assessed] to the geld. There is land for 14 oxen. Ranulf, Alfred's man, has 1 villein and 10 sokemen there with 2 teams, and 4 parts of 1 mill rendering 2 shillings, and 18 acres of meadow. T. R. E. it was worth 16 shillings ; now 40 shillings.

25.[1] Three M. In Cocrintone [Cockerington (Louthesk)] Edric and Macus had 7 bovates of land [assessed] to the geld. There is land for 14 oxen. Alfred and Gocelin his man have half a team there [in demesne], and 1 sokeman on (*de*) 1 toft and 2 villeins with half a team, and half a mill rendering 3 shillings, and 70 acres of meadow, and 58 acres of underwood. T. R. E. it was worth 21 shillings ; now 30 shillings.

26. M. In Stivetone[2] [Stewton (Louthesk)] Elmer had 13 bovates of land [assessed] to the geld. There is land for 3 teams and 2 oxen. Alfred has 2 teams there [in demesne], and 10 sokemen on (*de*) half a carucate of land, and 8 villeins with 1 team, and 200 acres of wood[land] for pannage. T. R. E. it was worth 20 shillings ; now 60 shillings.

27. M. In Catebi [South Cadeby (Louthesk)] Macus had 7 bovates of land [assessed] to the geld. There is land for 14 oxen. Alfred has 1 team there [in demesne], and 1 sokeman on (*de*) 4 bovates of this land and 4 villeins with 1 team, and 13 acres of meadow. T. R. E. it was worth 30 shillings ; now 20 shillings.

28. S. In Grimoldbi [Grimoldby (Louthesk)] there is 1 bovate of land [assessed] to the geld. It is soke[land] belonging to (*in*) Catebi

[1] The letter *K*, probably for *Kalumpnia*, is placed in the left hand margin against this entry.

[2] See 4/73 ; 69/10.

[South Cadeby]. Alfred has two parts and William[1] the third. It is waste.

29. S. In Salflatebi [Saltfleetby (Louthesk)] there is 1 bovate of land ⌊assessed⌋ to the geld. There is land for 1½ oxen. It is soke⌊land⌋ belonging to (*in*) Catebi [South Cadeby]. Alfred has two parts and William[1] the third.

30. M. In Torp ⌈Catebi⌉[2] [*query* Calcethorpe (Louthesk)] Rolf had 5 bovates of land ⌊assessed⌋ to the geld. There is land for 10 oxen. Alfred has 1 team there ⌊in demesne⌋, and 1 sokeman on (*de*) 2½ bovates of this land and 3 villeins having 2 oxen in a team, and 6 acres of meadow. T. R. E. it was worth 30 shillings; now 60 shillings.

31. S. In Wicham [East Wykeham (Louthesk)] there is half a bovate of land ⌊assessed⌋ to the geld. There is land for 1 ox. It is soke⌊land⌋ belonging to (*in*) Torp [*query* Calcethorpe]. It is waste.

32. S. In the same Wicham [East Wykeham] there are 5 bovates of land ⌊assessed⌋ to the geld. There is land for 10 oxen. It is soke⌊land⌋ belonging to (*in*) Catebi [South Cadeby]. 5 sokemen have half a team there, and 10 acres of meadow.

D. B., f. 358b. *Facsimile, p. xlv*b.

33. Two M. In Chelestorne [Kelstern (Louthesk)] Rolf and Machus had 2 carucates and 6 bovates of land ⌊assessed⌋ to the geld. There is land for 5½ teams. Alfred has 1 team there ⌊in demesne⌋, and 9 sokemen on (*de*) 15 bovates of this land and 4 villeins with 2 teams. T. R. E. it was worth 30 shillings; now 40 shillings.

34.[3] M. In Offintone[4] [Uffington (Ness)] Erneber had 7 carucates of land ⌊assessed⌋ to the geld. There is land for as many teams. Alfred has 2 teams there in demesne, and 16 sokemen on (*de*) 4 carucates of this land and 31 villeins with 7 teams, and 3½ mills rendering 40 shillings. There is a church there, and a priest, and 100 acres of meadow. T. R. E. it was worth 7 pounds; now 11 pounds; tallage 3 pounds.

35. M. In the same vill Leduin had 1 carucate of land ⌊assessed⌋ to the geld. There is land for 1 team. Alfred has 4 sokemen there on (*de*) 4 bovates of this land and 3 villeins with 1 team, and 9 burgesses of Stanford [Stamford] render (*redd'*) 4 shillings, and there are 20 acres of meadow. T. R. E. and now worth 30 shillings.

36. S. In Estou [Stowe (Ness)] there are 1½ bovates ⌊assessed⌋ to the geld. There is land for 1½ oxen. Alfred has 1 church there which belongs to (*iacet in*) Offintone [Uffington].

37. M. In Casuic[4] [Casewick (Ness)] ⌈Ulviet⌉ had 6 bovates of land ⌊assessed⌋ to the geld. There is land for 6 oxen. Boso, Alfred's man, has 1 team there ⌊in demesne⌋, and 2 villeins and 1 bordar with 2 oxen in a team. T. R. E. it was worth 10 shillings; now 20 shillings.

38. M. In Talintone[4] [Tallington (Ness)] Olviet had 6½ carucates [of land] ⌊assessed⌋ to the geld. There is land for as many teams. He [Alfred] has 2 teams there ⌊in demesne⌋, and 14 sokemen on (*de*) 4 caru-

---

1 *Query* William Blund (cp. 49/5, 6).
2 *Catebi* is interlined above *Torp* which, however, is not cancelled.
3 A star is placed in the left hand margin against this entry for no apparent reason.
4 See 72/1.

cates of land and 9 villeins with 4 teams, and 1 mill rendering 12 shillings, and 80 acres of meadow. T. R. E. it was worth 3 pounds; now 4 pounds; tallage 20 shillings.

39. In Estdepinge[1] [East Deeping (Ness)] there are 4 bovates of land [assessed] to the geld. There is land for half a team. It is soke[land] of this manor. 6 villeins and 2 bordars have 1½ teams there, and 20 acres of meadow, and 1 fishery [rendering 5 pence].

40. M. In Cretone [Creeton (Beltisloe)] Turchil had 6 bovates and 3 parts of 2 bovates of land [assessed] to the geld. There is land for as many oxen. Ralf, Alfred's man, has half a team there [in demesne], and 2 villeins, and 2 acres of meadow, and 30 acres of underwood. T. R. E. and now [worth] 20 shillings.

41. M. In Greneham and Awartorp and Bolebi [Irnham and Hawthorpe and Bulby (Beltisloe)] Aldene had 2 carucates and 7 bovates of land [assessed] to the geld. There is land for as many teams and oxen. Alfred has 2 teams there [in demesne], and 4 sokemen on (*de*) 10 bovates of this land and 2 villeins with 2 teams, and 8 acres of meadow, and 320 acres of wood[land] for pannage throughout the territory. T. R. E. it was worth 30 shillings; now 40 shillings; tallage 20 shillings.

42. M. In Aiglestorp [Elsthorpe (Beltisloe)] Siward had 2 carucates of land [assessed] to the geld. There is land for 2 teams. Alfred has 1 team there [in demesne], and 5 sokemen on (*de*) 6 bovates of this land and 5 villeins with 2 teams, and 18 acres of meadow, and 240 acres of wood[land]. T. R. E. it was worth 30 shillings; now 40 shillings; tallage 20 shillings.

43. M. In Stigandebi [Stainby (Beltisloe)] Siward had 6 carucates of land [assessed] to the geld. There is land for 8 teams. Alfred has 2 teams there [in demesne], and 2 mills rendering 2 shillings, and 8½ acres of meadow, and 40 acres of underwood. 4 carucates of the same land there are soke[land]. T. R. E. it was worth 20 shillings; now 40 shillings; tallage 20 shillings.

44. M. In Rochesham [Roxham (Flaxwell)] Alden had 2 carucates and 6 bovates of land [assessed] to the geld. There is land for as many teams and oxen. Ralf, Alfred's man, has 1½ teams there [in demesne], and 8 villeins, with 2 teams, and 40 acres of meadow. T. R. E. it was worth 40 shillings; now 50 shillings.

D. B., f. 358c. *Facsimile, p. xlvia.*

45. M. In Branzewelle [Brauncewell (Flaxwell)] Aldene had 2 carucates and 6 bovates of land [assessed] to the geld. There is land for as many teams and oxen. Alfred has 3 villeins and 2 bordars there with 3 oxen in a team. T. R. E. [worth] 20 shillings; now 10 shillings.

SOKE[LAND] OF THIS MANOR

46. S. In Blochesham [Bloxham (Flaxwell)] there are 2 carucates and 3 bovates of land [assessed] to the geld. There is land for as many teams and oxen. There are 2 sokemen there with half a team.

47. M. In Wime [South Witham (Beltisloe)] Siward had 4 carucates of land [assessed] to the geld. There is land for 4 teams. Gleu, Alfred's man, has 1 team there [in demesne], and 11 villeins and 3 bordars

[1] See 72/1.

with 3 teams, and 100 acres of meadow less 6, and 80 acres of wood⌊land⌋ for pannage. T. R. E. it was worth 40 shillings ; now 50 shillings ; tallage 10 shillings. This soke⌊land⌋ belongs to (*est in*) Tisteltune [Thistleton (Alstoe, co. Rutland)].

48[1] M. In Tisteltune [Thistleton (Alstoe, co. Rutland)] Siward had half a carucate of land ⌊assessed⌋ to the geld. There is land for 1 team. Gleu, Alfred's man, has 1 team there ⌊in demesne⌋, and 3 villeins and 2 bordars with half a team. Its value (*precium*) belongs to (*in*) Wime [South Witham (Beltisloe)].

SOKE⌊LAND⌋

49. S. In another (*alia*) Tisteltune [Thistleton (Alstoe, co. Rutland)] there is 1 carucate of land ⌊assessed⌋ to the geld. There is land for 1 team. 2 sokemen have 3 oxen there in a team.

50. M. In Merestone [Marston (Loveden)] Ulsi had 1 carucate of land in demesne, and 1 carucate of land ⌊which is⌋ soke⌊land⌋ (*in soca*). There is land for 3 teams. Walefrid, Alfred's man, has 1 team there ⌊in demesne⌋, and 8 villeins and 2 bordars and 1 sokeman with 3 teams, and 2 mills rendering 8 shillings, and 32 acres of meadow. T. R. E. it was worth 20 shillings ; now 40 shillings.

51. M. In Brune [Bourne (Aveland)] Turchil had 6 bovates of land ⌊assessed⌋ to the geld. There is land for 6 oxen. Dodin, Alfred's man, has 1 team there ⌊in demesne⌋, and 2 villeins and 4 bordars with 1 team, and the third part of 1 mill rendering 3 shillings and 4 pence, and 6 fisheries rendering 16 pence, and 6 acres of meadow, and 30 acres of wood⌊land⌋ for pannage. T. R. E. and now worth 20 shillings.

52. B. In Torulfbi [Thurlby (Ness)] there is half a carucate of land ⌊assessed⌋ to the geld. There is land for 4 oxen. 4 villeins have half a team there. It is inland belonging to (*in*) Brune [Bourne].

53. M. In Repinghale [Rippingale (Aveland)] Turchil had 15 bovates and 2 parts of 1 bovate of land ⌊assessed⌋ to the geld. There is land for as many oxen. Dodin, Alfred's man, has half a team there ⌊in demesne⌋, and 7 villeins and 3 bordars with 1½ teams. There is a priest there, and the third part of a church, and 20 acres of meadow, and 60 acres of underwood. T. R. E. and now worth 30 shillings.

54. M. In Cherchebi [Kirkby Underwood (Aveland)] Turuert had 1½ carucates of land ⌊assessed⌋ to the geld. There is land for 12 oxen. Alfred has half a team there ⌊in demesne⌋, and 4 sokemen on (*de*) 4 bovates of this land and 4 villeins and 2 bordars with 1 team, and 16 acres of meadow, and 60 acres of underwood. T. R. E. and now ⌊worth⌋ 30 shillings.

55. M. In the same place[2] (*ibidem*) Offran had 5 bovates of land ⌊assessed⌋ to the geld. There is land for as many oxen. The same Offran has there, ⌊holding⌋ of Alfred, 2 oxen in a team ⌊in demesne⌋, and 2 villeins, and 5 acres of meadow, and 60 acres of underwood. T. R. E. it was worth 20 shillings ; now 10 shillings.

---

[1] This entry is duplicated in the Domesday Survey of Rutland (folio 293, col. 3), where the mention of the sub-tenant is omitted, and in place of the reference to 'Wime' we find 'T. R. E. it was worth 20 shillings ; now 60 shillings.' See *V.C.H.* for Rutland, pp. 130-1.

[2] See 72/47.

56. M. In Avetorp [Avethorpe (Aveland)] Offran had half a caru cate of land [assessed] to the geld. There is land for 6 oxen. Suen, Alfred's man, has 1 team there [in demesne], and 2 villeins and 1 bordar, and 4 acres of meadow. T. R. E. it was worth 5 shillings ; now the like amount.

57. M. In Stepingeham [Sempringham (Aveland)] Morcar had 4 carucates and 2 bovates of land [assessed] to the geld. There is land for as many teams and oxen. Gocelin, Alfred's man, has 1 team there [in demesne], and 14 sokemen on (*de*) $2\frac{1}{2}$ carucates of this land, and 8 villeins and 2 bordars, and the fourth part of 1 church, and 11 acres of meadow, and 7 acres of underwood. T. R. E. and now worth 40 shillings ; tallage 20 shillings.

*D. B., f. 358*d. *Facsimile, p. xlvi*b.

58. M. In Bellingeburg [Billingborough (Aveland)] Toli had 1 carucate of land [assessed] to the geld. There is land for 1 team. Gocelin, Alfred's man, has 1 team there [in demesne], and 2 villeins and 1 bordar with 2 oxen in a team, and 14 acres of meadow. T. R. E. and now [worth] 10 shillings.

59. M. In Bodebi and Summertune [Boothby Graffoe and Somerton (Boby)] Aldene [and Offerd] had 4 carucates of land [assessed] to the geld. There is land for 4 teams and 6 oxen. Gocelin, Alfred's man, has $2\frac{1}{2}$ teams there [in demesne], and 6 sokemen on (*de*) 1 carucate of this land and 4 villeins and 6 bordars with 2 teams, and 55 acres of meadow. T. R. E. it was worth 30 shillings ; now 40 shillings.

60. M. In Hotot[1] [Huttoft (Calcewath)] Stepi had 1 bovate of land [assessed] to the geld. There is land for $1\frac{1}{2}$ oxen. Dodo, Alfred's man, has half a team there [in demesne], and 1 villein, and 40 acres of meadow. T. R. E. and now worth 10 shillings.

61. M. In the same place[1] (*ibidem*) Siward had 1 bovate of land [assessed] to the geld. There is land for $1\frac{1}{2}$ oxen. Bernard, Alfred's man, has there 2 oxen in a team [in demesne], and 40 acres of meadow. T. R. E. and now worth 5 shillings and 4 pence.

62. S. In Tedlagestorp [Theddlethorpe (Calcewath)] there is half a carucate of land [assessed] to the geld. There is land for 4 oxen. 4 sokemen and 1 villein have 2 oxen there in a team, and 40 acres of meadow.

63. S. In Haburne [Habrough (Yarborough)] there is 1 bovate of land [assessed] to the geld. There is land for 2 oxen. It is soke[land] belonging to (*in*) Neuhuse [Newsham]. Alfred has it, and it is waste.

64.[2] S. In Brochelesbi [Brocklesby (Yarborough)] there are $1\frac{1}{2}$ bovates of land [assessed] to the geld. There is land for 3 oxen. It is soke[land] belonging to (*in*) Neuhuse [Newsham]. Alfred has 1 sokeman there with 2 oxen in a team, and 11 acres of meadow.

---

[1] See 69/16.

[2] The letter *K*, probably for *Kalumpnia*, is placed in the left hand margin against this entry.

D. B., f. 359a. *Facsimile, p. xlviia.*

28. LAND OF GOCELIN SON OF LANBERT

1. M. In Bliburg[1] [Blyborough (Aslacoe)] Toui had 6 bovates of land ⌊assessed⌋ to the geld. There is land for 2 teams. Gocelin son of Lanbert has 2 teams there in demesne, and 1 sokeman on (*de*) 1 bovate of this land and 8 villeins with 1 team, and 20 acres of meadow. T. R. E. it was worth 20 shillings ; now 33 shillings ; tallage 7 shillings.

2. M. In Glentewrde [Glentworth (Aslacoe)] Godric had 7 bovates of land ⌊assessed⌋ to the geld. There is land for 12 oxen. Gocelin has 4 sokemen there on (*de*) 4 bovates of this land with half a team. Anschitil his man has 1 team there ⌊in demesne⌋, and 30 acres of meadow. T. R. E. it was worth 10 shillings and 8 pence ; now 20 shillings.

3. M. In Normanebi and Ounesbi [Normanby by Spital and Owmby (Aslacoe)] Agemund had half a carucate of land ⌊assessed⌋ to the geld. There is land for 4 oxen. Colsuan, Gocelin's man, has half a team there ⌊in demesne⌋, and 1 villein, and 4 acres of meadow. T. R. E. it was worth 8 shillings ; now 10 shillings.

4. In the same places[2] (*ibidem*) Gocelin has 9 bovates of land ⌊assessed⌋ to the geld whereof Bishop Remigius has the soke. There is land for 9 oxen.

5. Two M. In Wilingeham [Willingham by Stow (Well)] Aslac and Ernui had 5 carucates and the third part of 1 carucate of land ⌊assessed⌋ to the geld. There is land for as many teams. Walo, Gocelin's man, has 1 team there ⌊in demesne⌋, and 5 sokemen on (*de*) 3 carucates and 3 bovates of this land and 1 bordar with 1 team. T. R. E. it was worth 60 shillings ; now 40 shillings.

6. S. In Stou [Stow (Well)] there is 1 carucate of land ⌊assessed⌋ to the geld. There is land for 1 team. It is soke⌊land⌋ belonging to (*in*) Wilingeham [Willingham by Stow]. 4 sokemen have 1 team there.

7. Two M. In Ingeham [Ingham (Aslacoe)] Alnod and Aslac had 1 carucate of land ⌊assessed⌋ to the geld. There is land for 12 oxen. Anschitil, Gocelin's man, has 1 team there ⌊in demesne⌋, and 1 sokeman on (*de*) 2 bovates of this land and 1 bordar with 1 ox in a team, and 6 acres of meadow. T. R. E. it was worth 20 shillings ; now 10 shillings.

8. M. In Cotes [Cotes by Stow (Aslacoe)] Aslac had half a carucate of land ⌊assessed⌋ to the geld. There is land for 4 oxen. 1 villein has there 1 ox in a team. T. R. E. it was worth 20 shillings ; now 5 shillings.

9. S. In the same place (*ibidem*) there is 1 bovate of land ⌊assessed⌋ to the geld. It is soke⌊land⌋ belonging to (*in*) Ingeham [Ingham]. It is waste.

10. S. In Esnetrebi [Snitterby (Aslacoe)] there is 1 bovate of land ⌊assessed⌋ to the geld. It is soke⌊land⌋ belonging to (*in*) Wadingham [Wadingham (Manlake)]. It is waste.

---

[1] See 3/4.

[2] See 7/6 ; 14/20 ; 71/12.

11. Four M. In Herpeswelle [Harpswell (Aslacoe)] Agemund [and Sichet] and two other brothers had 2 carucates [and a half] of land [assessed] to the geld. There is land for 3 teams. Gocelin has 2 teams there [in demesne], and 13 villeins with 3 teams, and half a church, and 109 acres of meadow. T. R. E. it was worth 9 shillings ; now 50 shillings ; tallage 10 shillings.

12. Two M. In Hagetorne and Haneworde [Hackthorn and Cold Hanworth (Aslacoe)] Sighet and Briteua had 2 carucates and 1 bovate of land [assessed] to the geld. There is land for 4 teams.

13. S. B. In the same places (*ibidem*) there are 4 bovates of land [assessed] to the geld. It is [sokeland] belonging to (*in*) Herpeswelle [Harpswell]. And other 2 bovates of land [assessed] to the geld. It is inland belonging to (*in*) Dunebi[1] [Owmby (Aslacoe)]. There is land for 1 team. Gocelin has 2 teams there in demesne, and 11 sokemen on (*de*) 13 bovates of this land and 3 villeins and 11 bordars with 3 teams, and 1 mill rendering 16 pence, and 40 acres of meadow. T. R. E. and now worth 60 shillings ; tallage 20 shillings.

14. M. In Wadingeham [and Staintone] [Wadingham and Stainton (Manley)] Stangrim and Agemund had 6 bovates of land [assessed] to the geld. There is land for 6 oxen. Gocelin has 1 team there [in demesne], and 20 villeins with 1 team and 2 oxen in a team, and 20 acres of meadow. T. R. E. it was worth 40 shillings ; now 30 shillings ; tallage 10 shillings.

15. Three M. In Reburne [Redbourne (Manley)] Agemund and Bruhise and Scale had 7 carucates and 1 bovate of land [assessed] to the geld.* There is land for 14 teams and 2 oxen. Gocelin and a certain man of his have 3 teams there in demesne, and 6 sokemen on (*de*) 10 bovates of this land and 21 villeins and 4 bordars with $3\frac{1}{2}$ teams, and 1 mill rendering 3 shillings, and 140 acres of meadow. T. R. E. it was worth 13 pounds ; now 100 shillings ; tallage 20 shillings.

**D. B., f.* 359b. *Facsimile, p. xlvii*b.

16. M. In Scallebi and Stratone [Scawby and Sturton (Manley)] Agemund had 13 bovates of land [assessed] to the geld. There is land for $2\frac{1}{2}$ teams. Baldric, Gocelin's man, has 1 team there [in demesne], and 6 sokemen on (*de*) 3 bovates of this land and 1 villein and 3 bordars with 1 team. T. R. E. it was worth 20 shillings ; now 30 shillings ; tallage 10 shillings.

17. M. In Bulesforde [Bottesford (Manley)] Agemund had 1 carucate of land [assessed] to the geld. There is land for 1 team. Gocelin and a certain 'knight' (*miles*) of his have 2 teams there [in demesne], and 1 sokeman and 6 villeins and 4 bordars with 1 team, and the site of 1 mill, and a church, and 15 acres of meadow, and 30 acres of underwood. T. R. E. it was worth 4 pounds ; now 30 shillings ; tallage 10 shillings.

18. B. In Cletham [Cleatham (Corringham)] there are 2 bovates of land [assessed] to the geld. It is inland of this manor. 1 villein has 1 ox there.

19. M. In Rase [Middle Rasen (Walshcroft)] Tor had 3 bovates of land [assessed] to the geld. There is land for 5 teams. Walo, Gocelin's

[1] *Dunebi* is seemingly a mistake of the copyist for *Ounebi*.

man, has there 2 oxen in a team, and 1 sokeman on (*de*) half a bovate of this land and 4 villeins with half a team. T. R. E. it was worth 10 shillings; now 24 shillings.

20. M. In Tavelesbi[1] [Tealby (Walshcroft)] Edric had 1 carucate of land ⌊assessed⌋ to the geld. There is land for 12 oxen. Godard, Gocelin's man, has 1 team there ⌊in demesne⌋, and 4 sokemen on (*de*) 1 bovate of this land, and 10 villeins with 1½ teams, and 3 mills rendering 16 shillings, and 61 acres of meadow. T. R. E. it was worth 60 shillings; now 100 shillings; tallage 60 shillings.

21. S. In Wiuilingeham [North Willingham (Walshcroft)] there is soke⌊land⌋ of this manor, 15 bovates of land ⌊assessed⌋ to the geld. There is land for 3½ teams. 28 sokemen and 10 bordars have 2½ teams there, and 200 acres of meadow. Ivo has half a carucate there.[2]

22.[3] S. In Summerlede [Osgodby (Walshcroft)] there is 1 bovate of land ⌊assessed⌋ to the geld. There is 1 bordar there.

23. S. In Clachesbi[4] and Normanesbi [Claxby by Normanby and Normanby le Wold (Walshcroft)] there are 9 bovates of land ⌊assessed⌋ to the geld. There is land for 2 teams and 2 oxen. 14 sokemen have there 11 oxen in a team, and 40 acres of meadow, and 40 acres of underwood.

24.[5] S. In Osgotesbi [Osgodby (Walshcroft)] there is 1 bovate of land ⌊assessed⌋ to the geld. There is land for 2 oxen. There is 1 bordar there.

25. M. In Sneleslunt [Snelland (Wraggoe)] Agemund had 1 carucate of land ⌊assessed⌋ to the geld. There is land for 2 teams. Rayner, Gocelin's man, has 1 team there ⌊in demesne⌋, and 3 sokemen on (*de*) 2 bovates of this land and 1 villein with half a team, and 10 acres of meadow, and 14 acres of underwood. T. R. E. and now worth 30 shillings.

26. S. In Reresbi[6] [Reasby (Wraggoe)] there are 1½ carucates of land ⌊assessed⌋ to the geld. It is soke⌊land⌋ of this manor. There is land for 12 oxen. 4 sokemen have 1 team there, and 5 acres of meadow, and 10 acres of underwood. Of this soke⌊land⌋ W. de Perci holds 4 bovates.

27. S. In Sonetorp [Swinthorpe (Wraggoe)] there are 6 bovates of land ⌊assessed⌋ to the geld. There is land for 1 team. There is 1 sokeman there, and 6 acres of meadow.

28. S. In Wichingebi [Wickenby (Wraggoe)] there are 3 bovates of land ⌊assessed⌋ to the geld. There is land for 5 oxen. There are 4 sokemen there, and 6 acres of meadow.

29. M. In Blesebi [Bleasby (Wraggoe)] Agemund had 14½ bovates of land ⌊assessed⌋ to the geld. There is land for 3 teams. Herman, Gocelin's man, has 1½ teams there ⌊in demesne⌋, and 2 sokemen on (*de*) 2½ bovates of this land, and 2 villeins and 2 bordars with 1 team and 2 oxen, and 120 acres of meadow, and 120 acres of underwood. T. R. E. ⌊it was worth⌋ 22 shillings; now 40 shillings.

---

1 See 40/14; 70/18.
2 See 14/7.
3 This entry seems to be duplicated in no. 24 below, in the same way as 4/19 is duplicated in 4/22. For Summerlede, see the footnote to 4/19.
4 See 14/11; 70/19.
5 See note to 28/22 above.
6 See 22/15.

30. S. In Bechelinge [Beckering (Wraggoe)] there is half a bovate of land [assessed] to the geld. There is land for 1 ox. 1 sokeman ploughs there with 1 ox, and [has] half an acre of meadow.

D. B., f. 359c. *Facsimile, p. xlviii*a.

31. S. In Houtone [Holton by Beckering (Wraggoe)] there is 1 carucate of land [assessed] to the geld. There is land for 2 teams. There are 4 sokemen there with 9 oxen in a team, and 10 acres of meadow. Herman has it under Gocelin.

32. M. In Besebi and Maltebi [Beesby in the Marsh and Maltby in the Marsh (Calcewath)] Agemund had 6 bovates of land [assessed] to the geld. There is land for 6 oxen. Eurold, Gocelin's man, has half a team there [in demesne], and 1 sokeman on (*de*) 4 tofts of this land and 1 villein with 2 oxen in a team, and there is a church. T. R. E. and now worth 10 shillings.

33. M. In Adredebi [Bag Enderby (Hill)] Lesinc had 1 carucate of land [assessed] to the geld. There is land for 12 oxen. Baldric, Gocelin's man, has 1 team there [in demesne], and 3 sokemen and 5 villeins with $5\frac{1}{2}$ teams, and 1 mill rendering 2 shillings. T. R. E. worth 40 shillings ; now 30 shillings.

34. In Hacberdingeham [Hagworthingham (Hill)] Gocelin has 1 mill rendering 2 shillings.

35. M. In Tedforde [Tetford (Hill)] Britnod had 2 carucates and 2 bovates of land [assessed] to the geld. There is land for 3 teams. Walter, Gocelin's man, has 1 team there [in demesne], and 5 sokemen on (*de*) 6 bovates of this land, and 3 villeins with $1\frac{1}{2}$ teams. T. R. E. it was worth 20 shillings ; now 30 shillings.

SOKE[LAND] BELONGING TO (*in*) HAMERINGAM [HAMERINGHAM (HILL)]

36. M. In Summerdebi [Somersby (Hill)] Agemund had 1 carucate of land [assessed] to the geld. There is land for 12 oxen. 5 sokemen have $1\frac{1}{2}$ teams there, and half a mill rendering 10 pence.

37. M. In the same place (*ibidem*) Snarri had 1 carucate of land [assessed] to the geld. There is land for 12 oxen. Rayner, Gocelin's man, has 6 sokemen there with 1 team, and half a mill rendering 10 pence. T. R. E. it was worth 10 shillings ; now 16 shillings.

38. M. In Andrebi [Bag Enderby (Hill)] Lefsi had 6 bovates of land [assessed] to the geld. There is land for 1 team. Lanbert, Gocelin's man, has there 3 oxen in a team [in demesne], and 6 sokemen and 1 villein and 1 bordar with 1 ox in a team. T. R. E. it was worth 8 shillings ; now 10 shillings.

39. S. In the same place (*ibidem*) there is 1 bovate of land [assessed] to the geld. There is land for 2 oxen. It is soke[land] belonging to (*in*) Aschebi [Ashby Puerorum (Hill)]. 1 sokeman and 1 villein have there 1 ox in a team.

ALSO SOKE[LAND]

40. S. In Marchebi [Markby (Calcewath)] there is 1 bovate of land [assessed] to the geld. 1 sokeman has there 1 ox in a team.

41. S. In Wenflet [Wainfleet (Candleshoe)] there are 2 bovates of land [assessed] to the geld. There is land for 2 oxen. 2 villeins have there 2 oxen in a team, and 20 acres of meadow, and 1 salt-pan rendering 8 pence.

42. M. In Wizebi and Clachesbi [Winceby and Claxby Pluckacre (Hill)] Agemund had 1 carucate of land ⌊assessed⌋ to the geld. There is land for 1 team. Walter, Gocelin's man, has 1 team there ⌊in demesne⌋, and 1 villein, and 1 mill rendering 4 shillings. T. R. E. and now worth 20 shillings.

43. S. In Waletone and Bodebi [Welton in the Marsh and Boothby (Candleshoe)] there are 2 carucates and 2 bovates of land ⌊assessed⌋ to the geld. There is land for 3 teams. It is soke⌊land⌋ belonging to (*in*) Clasbi [Claxby Pluckacre]. Rayner, Gocelin's man, has half a team there ⌊in demesne⌋, and 14 sokemen have 3 teams.

*D.B., f. 359*d. *Facsimile, p. xlviii*b.

29. LAND OF EUDO SON OF SPIREWIC

SUD TREDING [SOUTH RIDING]

1. M. In Stratone [Great Sturton (Gartree)] Godwin and Gonewate had 2 carucates of land ⌊assessed⌋ to the geld. There is land for 5 teams. Eudo son of Spirewic has 5 teams there in demesne, and 16 villeins with 2 teams, and 1 mill rendering 10 shillings and 8 pence, and 200 acres of meadow less 10. T. R. E. it was worth 100 shillings ; now 8 pounds ; tallage 40 shillings.

2.[1] B. In Sudtone [Little Sturton (Gartree)] there is a berewic, 3 bovates and the fourth part of 1 bovate of land ⌊assessed⌋ to the geld. There is land for 4 oxen. There are 2 villeins there.

3.[1] S. In the same place (*ibidem*) Godwin ⌊had⌋ 1½ bovates of land ⌊assessed⌋ to the geld. There is land for 2 oxen. Eudo has 3 sokemen and 3½ villeins there with 1 team, and 25 acres of meadow. T. R. E. and now worth 10 shillings.

4. M. In Chirchebi [Kirkby on Bain (Horncastle)] Godwin and Gonewate had half a carucate of land ⌊assessed⌋ to the geld. There is land for 5 oxen. Eudo has 1 team there ⌊in demesne⌋, and 8 acres of meadow, and 80 acres of wood⌊land⌋ for pannage throughout the territory. T. R. E. and now worth 10 shillings.

5. S. In Martone [Martin (Horncastle)] there is 1 carucate [and a half] of land ⌊assessed⌋ to the geld. There is land for 2 teams. 2 sokemen and 3 bordars have 1 team there, and 34 acres of meadow, and 34 acres of wood⌊land⌋ for pannage, and 200 acres of underwood less 10. It is soke⌊land⌋ of the above-mentioned manor.

6. In Wadingurde [Waddingworth (Horncastle)] there are 6 carucates of land ⌊assessed⌋ to the geld. There is land for 6 teams. It is soke⌊land⌋ belonging to (*in*) Stratone [Great Sturton (Gartree)] and to (*in*) Cherchebi[2] [Kirkby on Bain]. A moiety is the Bishop of Durham's, and a moiety is Eudo's. 40 sokemen have 8 teams there, and 80 acres of meadow, and 100 acres of underwood.

---

[1] Nos. 2 and 3 are duplicated in no. 15 below.

[2] *K* in the margin for *Kalumpnia* directs attention to a claim.

7. In Wispinctune [Wispington (Horncastle)] there are 4 carucates of land [assessed] to the geld. There is land for 8 teams. It is soke[land], likewise divided into 2 parts between the bishop and Eudo, belonging to (*in*) Stratone [Great Sturton (Gartree)] and to (*in*) Chirchebi[1] [Kirkby on Bain]. 18 sokemen and 16 bordars have 6 teams there, and 140 acres of meadow. Eudo claims parts of the land of both places against the bishop (*clam' super episcopum utriusque partes terrę*).

8.[2] M. In Torp [Tattershall Thorpe (Horncastle)] Godwin and Gonewate had 2 carucates of land [assessed] to the geld. There is land for 2 teams. Now there are 2 teams there in demesne, and 16 villeins and 4 bordars have 2 teams. There is a church there, and $4\frac{1}{2}$ fisheries rendering 10 shillings, and the third part of 2 mills rendering 7 shillings, and 24 acres of meadow, and 140 acres of wood[land] for pannage. T. R. E. and now worth 100 shillings. Of this vill the Bishop of Durham has a third part, Eudo two-thirds.

9. M. In Tunbi [Tumby (Horncastle)] Godwin and Gonewate had $2\frac{1}{2}$ carucates of land [assessed] to the geld. There is land for 3 teams. Eudo has 1 team there [in demesne], and 10 villeins and 5 bordars and 2 sokemen on (*de*) 2 bovates of this land with 2 teams. There are 20 acres of meadow there, and $1\frac{1}{2}$ fisheries rendering 2 shillings, and 2 mills rendering 20 shillings, and 370 acres of wood[land] for pannage throughout the district. T. R. E. it was worth 40 shillings; now 60 shillings.

10. M. In Estrecale [East Keal (Bolingbroke)] Siwat had 6 bovates of land [assessed] to the geld. There is land for 6 oxen. Eudo has half a team there [in demesne], and 2 villeins, and 5 acres of meadow. T. R. E. and now [worth] 10 shillings.

11. M. In Westrecale [West Keal (Bolingbroke)] Godwin had 6 bovates of land [assessed] to the geld. There is land for 1 team. Eudo has 1 team there [in demesne], and 3 bordars. There is a church there, and 1 mill rendering 3 shillings, and 24 acres of meadow. T. R. E. it was worth 60 shillings; now 10 shillings.

12. B. In Hagenebi [Hagnaby (Bolingbroke)] there are 3 bovates of land [assessed] to the geld. There is land for as many oxen. It is a berewic. 3 villeins have 3 oxen there in a team, and 7 acres of meadow.

13. S. In Screnbi [Scremby (Candleshoe)] there are 2 bovates of land [assessed] to the geld. There is land for 2 oxen. 1 villein has 1 ox there, and there are the four parts (*iiii . part'*) of half a church.

14.[3] S. In Sudtone [Sutton in the Marsh (Calcewath)] there are 5 bovates and the fourth part of 1 bovate of land [assessed] to the geld. There is land for 7 oxen. It is soke[land] belonging to (*in*) Burg [Burgh in the Marsh (Candleshoe)]. 4 sokemen and 2 villeins and 2 bordars have there 6 oxen in a team, and 80 acres of meadow.

15.[3] B. In the same place[4] (*ibidem*) [*rectius* Sudtone = Little Sturton (Gartree)] there are 3 bovates and the fourth part of 1 bovate of land

[1] *K* in the margin for *Kalumpnia* directs attention to a claim.
[2] This entry is a duplicate of the $5\frac{1}{3}$ bovates of 3/42 + the $10\frac{2}{3}$ bovates of 29/28.
[3] Nos. 14 and 15 are written in the bottom margin.
[4] No. 15 relates to Little Sturtŏn in Gartree wapentake. It is a duplicate of nos. 2 and 3 above. The twice repeated *ibidem* in no. 15 is a mistake resulting from confusion between two places of the name of Sudtone. No. 15 relates, not to the same place as no. 14, but to a place of the same name.

⌊assessed⌋ to the geld. There is land for 4 oxen. It is a berewic belonging to (*in*) Stratone [Great Sturton (Gartree)]. In the same place[1] (*ibidem*) there are 1½ bovates of land ⌊assessed⌋ to the geld. There is land for 2 oxen. 3 sokemen and 3½ villeins have 1 team there, and 25 acres of meadow. T. R. E. and now worth 10 shillings.

D. B., f. 360a. *Facsimile, p. xlixa.*

16. B. In Wenflet [Wainfleet (Candleshoe)] there are 2½ bovates of land ⌊assessed⌋ to the geld. There is land for as many oxen. It is a berewic belonging to (*in*) Cale [West Keal]. 2 villeins and 1 bordar have half a team there.

17. B. In Herdetorp [Addlethorpe (Candleshoe)] there are 2 bovates of land ⌊assessed⌋ to the geld. There is land for 2 oxen. It is a berewic belonging to (*in*) Cale [West Keal]. 1 villein has 1 ox in a team there.

CALNODESHOU [CANDLESHOE] WAPENTAKE

18. M. In Burg [Burgh in the Marsh (Candleshoe)] Godwin and Tochi and Godric had 10 bovates of land ⌊assessed⌋ to the geld. There is land for as many oxen. Eudo and 2 men of his have 1 team there ⌊in demesne⌋, and 5 villeins and 4 bordars and 3 sokemen with 1 team, and 85 acres of meadow. T. R. E. it was worth 40 shillings; now 23 shillings.

19. B. In Herdetorp [Addlethorpe (Candleshoe)] there are 1 carucate and 1 bovate of land ⌊assessed⌋ to the geld. There is land for 9 oxen. Of these, 4 bovates are waste. It is inland belonging to (*in*) Burg [Burgh in the Marsh]. 1 sokeman has 6 oxen in a team there. There are 160 acres of meadow there.

20. B. In Wenflet [Wainfleet (Candleshoe)] there is 1 bovate of land ⌊assessed⌋ to the geld. There is land for 1 ox. It is inland belonging to (*in*) Burg [Burgh in the Marsh]. 3 villeins have 2 oxen in a team there, and 4 acres of meadow, and 2 salt-pans rendering [16 pence].

21. In Tric [= Skegness (Candleshoe)] there are 2 bovates of land ⌊assessed⌋ to the geld. There is land for 2 oxen. It is soke⌊land⌋ belonging to (*in*) Burg [Burgh in the Marsh]. 1 man has 1 ox in a team there, and 30 acres of meadow.

22. M. In Calnodesbi [Candlesby (Candleshoe)] Grinchel and Clac had 4 carucates and 2 bovates of land ⌊assessed⌋ to the geld. There is land for 5 teams and 3 oxen. Eudo has 5½ teams there ⌊in demesne⌋, and 10 sokemen on (*de*) 1 carucate of this land, and 4 villeins and 11 bordars with 2½ teams, and 2 churches. T. R. E. it was worth 108 shillings; now 8 pounds and 12 pence.

23. B. In Herdetorp [Addlethorpe (Candleshoe)] there is 1 carucate of land ⌊assessed⌋ to the geld. There is land for 1 team. 3 villeins have 2 oxen in a team there, and 100 acres of meadow.

24. S. In Tric [= Skegness (Candleshoe)] there is soke⌊land⌋ ⌊of this manor⌋, 2 bovates of land ⌊assessed⌋ to the geld. There is land for 2 oxen. 2 villeins have 2 oxen in a team there, and 30 acres of meadow.

25. S. In Burg [Burgh in the Marsh (Candleshoe)] there is soke⌊land⌋ ⌊of this manor⌋, 1 carucate of land ⌊assessed⌋ to the geld. There is land for 1 team. 1 sokeman has 1 team there.

---

[1] See note 4 on preceding page.

26. S. In the same place (*ibidem*) Sortebrand [had] 1 bovate of land [assessed] to the geld. There is land for 1 ox. It is soke[land] belonging to (*in*) Gunnebi [Gunby (Candleshoe)]. 1 sokeman has 2 oxen in a team there. Eudo has it.

27. M. In Dreistorp [Dexthorpe (Candleshoe)] two brothers had 1 carucate and 5 bovates of land [assessed] to the geld. There is land for 13 oxen. Ivo, Eudo's man, has 1 sokeman there with 2 oxen, and 3 acres of underwood. T. R. E. it was worth 10 shillings ; now 8 shillings.

WARAG'[1] [WRAGGOE] WAPENTAKE

28. M. In Torp [Tattershall Thorpe (Horncastle)] Godwin and Gonewate had 10 bovates and 2 parts of 1 bovate of land [assessed] to the geld. There is land for as many oxen. Eudo has 1 team there [in demesne], and 10 villeins and 2 bordars with 1 team. He has 2 parts of a church there, and the fourth part of 2 mills rendering 6 shillings, and 3 fisheries rendering 6 shillings and 8 pence, and 16 acres of meadow, and 100 acres less 8 of wood[land] for pannage. T. R. E. it was worth 6 pounds ; now 66 shillings and 8 pence.

ASLACHESHOU [ASLACOE] WAPENTAKE

29. M. In Sassebi [Saxby (Aslacoe)] Aschil had $2\frac{1}{2}$ carucates of land [assessed] to the geld. There is land for 3 teams. Eudo has 2 teams there [in demesne], and 1 sokeman on (*de*) 2 bovates of this land, and 12 villeins with 2 teams, and 2 mills rendering 3 shillings, and 6 acres of meadow. T. R. E. and now worth 40 shillings.

NORT TRED' [NORTH RIDING]

BOLINBROC [BOLINGBROKE] WAPENTAKE

30. M. In Endrebi [Mavis Enderby (Bolingbroke)] Godwin had half a carucate of land [assessed] to the geld. There is land for 4 oxen. Eudo has 1 team there [in demesne], and 1 bordar, and 10 acres of meadow. T. R. E. and now worth 10 shillings.

31. B. In Radebi [Raithby (Bolingbroke)] there is a berewic, half a bovate of land [assessed] to the geld, and half the site of a mill.

32. B. In Mundebi [Mumby (Calcewath)] there are 6 bovates of land [assessed] to the geld. There is land for 1 team. 1 villein and 1 bordar have there 2 oxen in a team, and 10 acres of meadow.

33. S. In Scirebec [Skirbeck (Skirbeck)] there are 2 bovates of land [assessed] to the geld. There is land for 1 ox. 8 villeins have 1 team there. It is soke[land] belonging to (*in*) Tateshale.

34.[2] In Torp [Tattershall Thorpe (Horncastle)] Ulmar had 2 carucates of land [assessed] to the geld. There is land for 2 teams which are there with 18 villeins and 4 bordars. It is worth (*val'*) 20 shillings.

---

[1] *Rectius* Horncastle Wapentake. This title is written in the margin.
[2] This entry is written in the bottom margin. It is duplicated in 3/15 and also in 4/55.

*D. B., f. 360*b. *Facsimile, p. xlix*b.

30. LAND OF DREW DE BEURERE

WESTREDING [WEST RIDING[1]]

1. M. In Barewe [Barrow on Humber (Yarborough)] [Earl] Morcar had 9 carucates and 2 bovates of land ⌊assessed⌋ to the geld. There is land for 18½ teams. Drew de Beurere has 4 teams there ⌊in demesne⌋, and 50 sokemen on (*de*) 2 carucates of this land and 7 villeins with 8 teams, and 1 mill rendering 13 shillings and 4 pence. T. R. E. it was worth 32 pounds; now 15 pounds; tallage 100 shillings.

SOKE⌊LAND⌋ OF THIS MANOR

2. In Golse[2] [Goxhill (Yarborough)] there are 2 carucates of land ⌊assessed⌋ to the geld. There is land for 4 teams. 20 sokemen have 3 teams there, and 300 acres of meadow.

3. M. In Normanebi[3] [Normanby in Burton on Stather (Manley)] 3 brothers had 5 carucates of land ⌊assessed⌋ to the geld. There is land for 5 teams. Gocelin, Drew's man, has 1 team there ⌊in demesne⌋, and 16 sokemen and 4 villeins and 3 bordars with 4 teams and 2 oxen, and the site of 1 mill, and 100 acres of meadow, and 72 acres of underwood. T. R. E.[4]

4. S. In Tedulfbi [Thealby (Manley)] there is 1 carucate of land ⌊assessed⌋ to the geld. There is land for 1 team. It is soke[land] belonging to (*in*) Normanebi [Normanby]. There are 3 sokemen there with 1 team, and 8[5] acres of meadow.

5. Two M. In Barewe [Barrow on Humber (Yarborough)] Ernuin and Siward had 2 carucates of land ⌊assessed⌋ to the geld. There is land for 4 teams. Tetbald, Drew's man, with 4 villeins has 1 team. T. R. E. it was worth 40 shillings; now it is valued in the above-mentioned manor [of Barrow, no. 1].

6. M. In Chetelbi [Kettleby (Yarborough)] Ulf had 3 bovates and the third part of 1 bovate of land ⌊assessed⌋ to the geld. There is land for 1 team. Rayner, Drew's man, has 1 team there ⌊in demesne⌋, and 5 villeins having 5 oxen in a team, and 13 acres of meadow. T. R. E. it was worth 40 shillings; now 30 shillings.

7. M. In Chernitone [Kirmington (Yarborough)] Ulf had 4 bovates of land ⌊assessed⌋ to the geld. There is land for 12 oxen. Robert, Drew's man, has 1 team there ⌊in demesne⌋, and 1 villein. T. R. E. it was worth 40 shillings; now 20 shillings.

8. M. In Linbergham [Limber (Yarborough)] Ulf had 1 carucate of land ⌊assessed⌋ to the geld. There is land for 4 teams. It is waste. T. R. E. it was worth 40 shillings.

---

[1] *Rectius* North Riding. [2] See 27/1; 70/5. [3] See 71/19.

[4] The *T. R. E.* seems to be superfluous since the land is evidently valued in no. 1.

[5] There is a space of half an inch between *viii* and *ac'*.

9. M. In Chelebi [or Cotes] [Keelby or Coton[1] in Keelby (Yarborough)] Rolf had 1 carucate of land [assessed] to the geld. There is land for 3 teams. Robert, Drew's man, has 1 team there [in demesne], and 10 villeins and 1 bordar with 2 teams, and 1 salt-pan rendering 12 pence, and 40 acres of meadow. T. R. E. it was worth 40 shillings; now 30 shillings; tallage 10 shillings.

10.[2] B. In Cheluingholme [Killingholme (Yarborough)] there is half a carucate of land [assessed] to the geld. There is land for 10 oxen. It is a berewic belonging to (*in*) Cotes [Coton]. It is waste. There are 30 acres of meadow there.

11. S. In Lobingeham [Lobingham (Yarborough)] there are 3 bovates of land [assessed] to the geld. There is land for 6 oxen. It is soke[land] belonging to (*in*) Cotes [Coton (Bradley)]. 1 sokeman has 1 ox there in a team, and 30 acres of meadow.

BRADELAI [BRADLEY] WAPENTAKE[3]

12. M. In Wivelesbi [Weelsby (Bradley)] Rolf had 4 carucates of land [assessed] to the geld. There is land for 6 teams. Robert, Drew's man, has 2 villeins and 15 sokemen on (*de*) 2 carucates and 5 bovates and the third part of 1 bovate of this land. These men have 2 teams, and 80 acres of meadow. T. R. E. it was worth 6 pounds; now 100 shillings.

SOKE[LAND] OF THIS MANOR

13. S. In Sudcotes [Little Cotes (Bradley)] there are 7 bovates of land [assessed] to the geld. There is land for 14 oxen. 6 sokemen have 1 team there, and 30 acres of meadow.

14.[4] B. In Grimesbi [Grimsby (Bradley)] there is 1 bovate of land [assessed] to the geld. There is land for 2 oxen. It is a berewic [of this manor]. 4 villeins have 1 ox in a team there, and 1 acre of meadow.

15. S. In Leuesbi [Laceby (Bradley)] there is 1 bovate of land [assessed] to the geld. There is land for 2 oxen. It is sokeland [of this manor]. 1 villein has 1 ox in a team there.

16. B. In Itrebi [Itterby (Bradley)] there is 1 bovate of land [assessed] to the geld. There is land for 1½ oxen. 1 villein has 1 ox in a team there.

D. B., f. 360c. *Facsimile, p. la.*

17. M. In Staintone [Stainton le Vale (Walshcroft)] Rolf had 6 bovates of land [assessed] to the geld. There is land for 2 teams and 2 oxen. Geoffrey (*Goisfridus*), Drew's man, has 1 team there [in demesne], and 1 sokeman on (*de*) 1 toft and 7 villeins with 1 team, and the site of a mill, and 45 acres of meadow. T. R. E. it was worth 50 shillings; now 26 shillings.

18. M. In Stimblebi [Thimbleby (Horncastle)] Osmund had 3 carucates and 6 bovates of land [assessed] to the geld. There is land for 5 teams. Geoffrey (*Goisfridus*), Drew's man, has 1 team there [in

---

[1] The land is given under Cotun in *L.S.*, 11/1. The place is now Nun Coton.

[2] This entry is written at the foot of the column, and a sign indicates its proper position in the text.

[3] This title is written in the margin.

[4] In margin against this entry is written 'R*equire* de terra arabili—B. [*rectius* R.] de Mort[emer] et episcopus Baio[censis].

demesne⌋, and 15 sokemen on (*de*) 2 carucates and 6[1] bovates of this land and 4 villeins ploughing with 2 teams and 2 oxen, and 1 mill rendering 9 shillings and 4 pence, and 240 acres of meadow, and 240 acres of underwood. T. R. E. it was worth 4 pounds ; now 3 pounds ; tallage 20 shillings.

19. Two M. In Langetone [Langton by Horncastle (Horncastle)] Archil and Alfric (*Aluric*) had 2 carucates of land ⌊assessed⌋ to the geld. There is land for 3 teams. Geoffrey (*Goisfridus*), Drew's man, has 1 team there ⌊in demesne⌋, and 5 sokemen on (*de*) 2 bovates of this land, and 10 villeins with 1½ teams, and 160 acres of meadow, and 200 acres of wood⌊land⌋ for pannage, and 500[2] acres of underwood. T. R. E. and now worth 40 shillings.

20. Two M. In Ormesbi[3] [North Ormsby (Ludborough)] Ulf and Scemund had 4 carucates and 7 bovates of land ⌊assessed⌋ to the geld. There is land for 8 teams. Geoffrey (*Goisfridus*), Drew's man, has 1 team there ⌊in demesne⌋, and 10 sokemen on (*de*) 2 carucates and 2 bovates of this land, and 1 bordar with 1 team, and 40 acres of meadow, and 10 acres of underwood. T. R. E. it was worth 70 shillings ; now 45 shillings ; tallage 10 shillings.

21. In the same place (*ibidem*) Alwin had 2 bovates of land ⌊assessed⌋ to the geld. There is land for 1 team.

HUNDRED

22. M. In Stroustune [Stroxton (Winnibriggs)] ⌈Earl⌉ Morcar had 2 carucates of land ⌊assessed⌋ to the geld.[4] Guy (*Wizo*), Drew's man, has 2 teams there in demesne, and 4 sokemen and 9 villeins and 1 bordar having 3 teams. There is a church there, and a priest, and 30 acres of meadow. Archbishop Thomas has 15, and Hugh de Grentemaisnel 15. T. R. E. it was worth 6 pounds ; now 100 shillings.

23. B. In Pamtone [Great Ponton (Winnibriggs)] there is a berewic of this manor, 4 carucates of land ⌊assessed⌋ to the geld. There is land for 3 teams. There is 1 bordar there, and 1 mill rendering 6 shillings. There is wood⌊land⌋ of thorns (*silua spineti*) 8 furlongs in length and 1 in breadth.

24. B. In the other Pamtone [Little Ponton (Winnibriggs)] there are 2 carucates of land ⌊assessed⌋ to the geld. There is land for 2 teams. It is a berewic ⌊of this manor⌋. There are 2 bordars there.

HALF HUNDRED

25. M. In Stoches [Stoke Rochford (Winnibriggs)], soke⌊land⌋ of Graham [Grantham (Threo)], Morcar had 1½ carucates of land ⌊assessed⌋ to the geld. There is land for 12 oxen. Colegrim, Drew's man, has half a team there ⌊in demesne⌋, and 3 villeins with 1 team, and 2 mills rendering 10 shillings.

26. M. In Nortstoches [North Stoke (Winnibriggs)] ⌈Earl⌉ Morcar had 10 bovates of land ⌊assessed⌋ to the geld. There is land for 1 team. Colegrim has it of Drew, and the farmers (*censores*) ploughing there render 7 shillings. There are 16 acres of meadow.

---

1 *iii* seems to have been altered to *vi*.

2 There is a space of a quarter of an inch between *quingent'* and *acras*.

3 See 14/64 ; 70/28.

4 A space of one and a half inches is left here for the usual formula about the quantity of land.

HUNDRED

27. M. In Carletune [Carlton le Moorland (Graffoe)] Morcar had 12 carucates of land ⌊assessed⌋ to the geld. There is land for 16 teams. Drew has 2 teams there ⌊in demesne⌋, and 9 sokemen on (*de*) 12 bovates of this land and 9 villeins and 10 bordars with 5 teams. There is a church there, and a priest, and 255 acres of meadow. T. R. E. it was worth 10 pounds ; now 9 pounds.

BELTESLAU [BELTISLOE] WAPENTAKE

D. B., f. 360d. *Facsimile, p. l*b.

HUNDRED

28. M. In Bredestorp [=*probably* Careby *or* Holywell (Beltisloe)] [Earl] Morcar had 7 carucates of land ⌊assessed⌋ to the geld. There is land for 7 teams. It is soke⌊land⌋ belonging to (*in*) Westbitham [Castle Bytham]. The men Ingelran and Ernulf have 1 team there ⌊in demesne⌋, and 6 sokemen and 1 villein and 5 bordars with 2 teams. There is 1 mill there rendering 4 shillings, and 200 acres of underwood. T. R. E. it was worth 3 pounds ; now 40 shillings ; tallage 12 shillings.

29. M. In Westbitham [Castle Bytham (Beltisloe)] Morcar had 9 carucates of land ⌊assessed⌋ to the geld. There is land for as many teams. Drew has 3 teams there ⌊in demesne⌋, and 24 sokemen on (*de*) a moiety of this land and 7 villeins with 8 teams. 7 freemen (*francigene*) have 2 teams there, and 3 iron-worker's shops (*fabricas ferri*) rendering 40 shillings and 8 pence. There is wood⌊land⌋ for pannage throughout the territory 1½ leagues in length and as many in breadth, and 60 acres of meadow. T. R. E. it was worth 19 pounds and 10 shillings ; now 10 pounds.

SOKE⌊LAND⌋ OF THIS MANOR

30. S. In Cudetorp [Counthorpe (Beltisloe)] there are 6 carucates of land ⌊assessed⌋ to the geld. There is land for 6 teams. Walter, Drew's man, has 2 teams there ⌊in demesne⌋, and 12 sokemen and 6 bordars with 3 teams. T. R. E. it was worth 10 pounds ; now 6 pounds. Ulric, his other man, has 5 sokemen there with half a team. T. R. E. it was worth 20 shillings ; now 10 shillings.

HUNDRED

31. M. In Bitham [Little Bytham (Beltisloe)] Edward had 7 carucates of land ⌊assessed⌋ to the geld. There is land for 7 teams. Drew has 2 teams there ⌊in demesne⌋, and 6 sokemen on (*de*) 1 carucate of this land and 18 villeins and 3 bordars with 5 teams, and 1 mill rendering 3 shillings, and an iron-worker's shop (*fabrica ferri*) rendering 40 shillings, and 7 acres of meadow, and 300 acres of wood⌊land⌋ for pannage throughout the territory. T. R. E. and now worth 6 pounds ; tallage 40 shillings.

HUNDRED

32. M. In Witham[1] [Witham on the Hill (Beltisloe)] Wlf had 5 bovates of land ⌊assessed⌋ to the geld. There is land for 5 oxen. Drew has 1 team there ⌊in demesne⌋, and 6 villeins and 2 bordars with 1 team, and 30 acres of meadow, and 40 acres of wood⌊land⌋ for pannage. T. R. E. it was worth 30 shillings ; now 40 shillings. Colegrim holds it. The Abbot of Burg [Peterborough] claims 1 bovate in the soke of Gilbert.

---

[1] See 8/6 ; 24/32 ; 72/6.

HILLE [HILL] WAPENTAKE[1]

33. M. In Hacberdingham [Hagworthingham (Hill)] Adestan had 1 carucate of land [assessed] to the geld. There is land for 14 oxen. Robert, Drew's man, has 1 team there [in demesne], and 8 villeins with 1 team, and 1 mill rendering 18 pence, and 40 acres of meadow. T. R. E. it was worth 50 shillings; now 30 shillings. In this vill Drew has a hall (*aulam*) with sake and soke, and 1 toft.

34. In Haniwic [Anwick (Flaxwell)] he has 5½[2] bovates of land [assessed] to the geld. It is worth 25 shillings.

35. In Rischintone [Ruskington (Flaxwell)] he has 6 bovates of land[3] [assessed] to the geld, and he has 1 team there, and it is worth 20 shillings.

WALECROS [WALSHCROFT] WAPENTAKE

WALESBI [WALESBY] HUNDRED

36. M. In Clachesbi [Claxby by Normanby (Walshcroft)] and Normanebi [Normanby le Wold (Walshcroft)] Ulf had 6 bovates of land [assessed] to the geld. There is land for 12 oxen. Colsuan, Drew's man, has 1 team there [in demesne], and 2 sokemen on (*de*) 1 bovate of this land and 5 villeins and 2 bordars with 1 team, and the fourth part of a mill rendering 8 pence, and 32½ acres of meadow, and 40 acres of underwood. T. R. E. and now worth 30 shillings.

37. In Cuningesbi [Coningsby (Horncastle)] there is 1 bovate of land [assessed] to the geld. It is soke[land] belonging to (*in*) Hacberdingam [Hagworthingham (Hill)]. There are 1 bordar and 1 villein there with 1 ox in a team, and 2 acres of meadow, and 20 acres of underwood.

D. B., f. 361a. *Facsimile, p. lia.*

31. LAND OF WALTER DE AINCURT

HUNDRED

1. M. In Beltone[4] [Belton (Threo)] Tori had 4 carucates of land [assessed] to the geld. There is land for 4 teams. Walter de Aincurt has 2 teams there in demesne, and 8 villeins and 5 bordars with 1 team. There is a church there, and 3 mills rendering 30 shillings, and 60 acres of meadow. T. R. E. it was worth 3 pounds; now 4 pounds; tallage 20 shillings.

HUNDRED

2. M. In Gunfordebi [Great Gonerby (Winnibriggs)] Siward and Elwi had 1½ carucates of land [assessed] to the geld. There is land for 2 teams. Elwi, Walter's man, has 1½ teams there [in demesne], and 6 villeins and 4 bordars with 2 teams, and 2 mills rendering 16 shillings, and 22½ acres of meadow. T. R. E. and now worth 40 shillings.

---

[1] This title is written in the margin.
[2] This land is included in 64/2.
[3] This land is included in 64/1.
[4] See 1/19; 72/59.

3. M. In Summerdebi[1] [Somerby (Threo)] Tori had 2 carucates and 2 bovates of land [assessed] to the geld. There is land for 18 oxen. Raynald, Walter's man, has 2 teams there [in demesne], and 5 villeins with 1½ teams. There is a church there, and a priest with 1 team, and 180 acres of wood[land] throughout the territory. Walter has the defence (*Warram*). T. R. E. it was worth 4 pounds; now 3 pounds; tallage 20 shillings. Tori held this manor T. R. E., and Norman after him in the same time [*i.e.* T. R. E.], but the men of the country and of the wapentake know not on what covenant (*pacto*) he had it, because they have not seen him do any service therefor.

4. S. In Humbi [Great Humby (Threo)] there are 4 carucates of land [assessed] to the geld. There is land for 4 teams and 6 oxen. It is soke[land] belonging to (*in*) Summerdebi [Somerby (Threo)]. There are 15 sokemen and 1 villein and 1 bordar there with 5 teams, and 20 acres of wood[land] for pannage, and 220 acres of underwood.

5. M. In Westorp[2] [Westhorpe (Threo)] Tori had 2 carucates of land [assessed] to the geld. There is land for 2½ teams. Raynald, Walter's man, has 2 teams there [in demesne], and 1 villein and 9 bordars with 1 ox in a team, and 3 mills rendering 40 shillings, and 19 acres of meadow. T. R. E. and now worth 4 pounds.

6. B. In Hogetune [Houghton in Grantham (Winnibriggs)] there is 1 carucate of land [assessed] to the geld. There is land for 1 team. It is a berewic belonging to (*in*) Westorp [Westhorpe]. There is 1 bordar there.

BELTESLAWE [BELTISLOE] WAPENTAKE

7. M. In Sudwelle [*probably* a vill in Swayfield (Beltisloe)] Tori had 2 carucates of land [assessed] to the geld. There is land for 2 teams. Walter has 2 teams there [in demesne], and 7 sokemen and 6 villeins and 1 bordar with 3 teams, and 4 acres of meadow, and 130 acres of wood[land] for pannage throughout the territory. T. R. E. it was worth 40 shillings; now 60 shillings; tallage 10 shillings.

HUNDRED

8. B. In Suamestede [Swinstead (Beltisloe)] there is half a carucate of land [assessed] to the geld. It is a berewic belonging to (*in*) Sudwelle. Odo, Walter's man, has half a team there, and 1 villein, and half an acre of meadow, and 15 acres of underwood. T. R. E. it was worth 10 shillings; now 15 shillings.

HUNDRED

9. Four M. In Bertune [Burton Coggles (Beltisloe)] Archil and Leuric had 3 carucates of land [assessed] to the geld. There is land for 3 teams. Walter has 4 villeins and 3 bordars there with 1 team. Of this land 2 of his men have a moiety, and they have there 2 teams [in demesne], and 6 villeins and 3 bordars with 2 teams, and 31½ acres of meadow, and 323 acres of wood[land] for pannage, and 1 mill rendering 2 shillings. T. R. E. and now worth 60 shillings.

ASWARDETIERNE [ASWARDHURN] WAPENTAKE

10. M. In Goldesbi [Ingoldsby (Aswardhurn)] Siward had 4 bovates and the third part of 1 bovate of land [assessed] to the geld. There is land for 6 oxen. It is waste. T. R. E. [worth] 10 shillings; now 3 shillings. There are 3½ acres of meadow, and 16 acres of underwood there.

---

[1] See 72/55.

[2] See 72/62.

*D. B., f. 361*b. *Facsimile, p. li*b.

HUNDRED

11. M. In Branztune[1] [Branston (Langoe)] Haminc had 12 carucates of land [assessed] to the geld. There is land for 10 teams. Walter has 5 teams there in demesne, and 2 sokemen on (*de*) 2 carucates of this land and 48 villeins and 23 borders with 8 teams. There is a church there, and a priest, and 4 mills rendering (*de*) 27 shillings, and 3 fisheries rendering (*de*) 30 pence, and 60 acres of meadow, and wood[land] for pannage 7½ furlongs in length and 5½ furlongs in breadth. T. R. E. it was worth 20 pounds ; now 26 pounds.

HUNDRED

12. S. In Walecote [Walcot (Langoe)] there are 4 carucates of land [assessed] to the geld. It is soke[land] of this manor. 7 sokemen and 2 bordars have 4 teams there, and 16 acres of meadow.

HUNDRED

13. S. In Timberlunt [Timberland (Langoe)] there are 5 carucates and 6 bovates and the fourth part of 1 bovate of land [assessed] to the geld. There is land for 4 teams. 18 sokemen and 3 bordars have 7½ teams there.

HUNDRED HUNDRED

14. S. In Cherchebi and Scapuic [Kirkby Green and Scopwick (Langoe)] there are 7½ carucates of land [assessed] to the geld. There is land for 6 teams. 14 sokemen and 2 bordars have 5 teams there, and 4 mills rendering (*de*) 21 shillings and 4 pence, and 25 acres of meadow.

15. M. In the same places (*ibidem*) Godric had 10 carucates of land [assessed] to the geld. There is land for 9 teams. Walter has 2 teams there [in demesne], and 32 sokemen on (*de*) 6 carucates and 2 bovates of this land and 7 villeins and 2 bordars with 13 teams. There is a church there, and a priest, and 2 mills rendering 20 shillings, and 26½ acres of meadow. T. R. E. it was worth 70 shillings ; now 4 pounds.

16. M. In Blachene [Blankney (Langoe)], two hundreds, Haminc had 24 carucates of land [assessed] to the geld. There is land for 13 teams. Walter has 3 teams there [in demesne], and 22 sokemen and 10 villeins and 4 bordars with 10 teams. There is a church there, and a priest, and 60 acres of meadow, and underwood 7 furlongs in length and 3 in breadth. T. R. E. it was worth 6 pounds ; now 7 pounds. The tallage belongs to (*in*) Branztune [Branston]. Of this land his knights (*milites*) hold 2 carucates, and they have 1 team there, and 2 bordars ; and it is worth 10 shillings.

HUNDRED

17. Three M. In Haneworde [Potter Hanworth (Langoe)] Aldene and his two brothers had 12 carucates of land [assessed] to the geld. There is land for 6 teams. Walter has 2 teams there in demesne, and 9 sokemen on (*de*) 3 carucates of this land and 22 villeins and 11 bordars having 9½ teams. There is a church there, and a priest, with 1 carucate. Of this land a certain knight (*miles*) of his holds 2 carucates, and has 1 team there [in demesne], and 2 villeins with half a team ; and it is worth 20 shillings. There are 150 acres of meadow there, and 150 acres of wood[land] for pannage. T. R. E. it was worth 3 pounds ; now 4 pounds.

---

[1] See 72/14.

LAGEHOU [LANGOE] WAPENTAKE

18. In Medricesham [Metheringham (Langoe)] there are $8\frac{1}{2}$ carucates of land ⌊assessed⌋ to the geld. There is land for 4 teams and 2 oxen. Wintrehard, Walter's man, has 2 teams there ⌊in demesne⌋, and 10 sokemen and 8 villeins and 16 bordars with 6 teams, and 2 mills rendering 12 shillings, and 150 acres of meadow, and 60 acres of underwood. T. R. E. it was worth 3 pounds; now 4 pounds. It is soke⌊land⌋ belonging to (*in*) Branztone [Branston (Langoe)].

D. B., f. 361c. *Facsimile, p. liia.*

32. NORMAN DE ARCI (*Adreci*)

NORT TREDING [NORTH RIDING]

1. Two M. In Stalinburg [Stallingborough (Yarborough)] Ulf and Ster had $2\frac{1}{2}$ carucates of land ⌊assessed⌋ to the geld. There is land for 4 teams. Norman de Adreci has 2 teams there in demesne, and 1 sokeman and 18 villeins and 1 bordar with 2 teams. There is half a church there, and the site of a mill, and 2 salt-pans rendering 3 shillings, and 400 acres of meadow. T. R. E. it was worth 4 pounds; now 7 pounds; tallage 20 shillings.

2. S. In Brochelesbi[1] [Brocklesby (Yarborough)] there are $1\frac{1}{2}$ bovates of land ⌊assessed⌋ to the geld. There is land for 3 oxen. There are 1 sokeman and 2 villeins and 1 bordar there with 1 team, and 10 acres of meadow.

3. M. In Lobingeham [Lobingham (Yarborough)] Fulcheri had $4\frac{1}{2}$ bovates of land ⌊assessed⌋ to the geld. There is land for 9 oxen. Berewold, Norman's man, has 1 team there ⌊in demesne⌋, and 2 villeins with 3 oxen in a team, and half a mill rendering 4 shillings, and 40 acres of meadow. T. R. E. it was worth 20 shillings; now 30 shillings.

4. M. In Chelebi [Keelby (Yarborough)] Grimchel had 5 bovates and the third part of 1 bovate of land ⌊assessed⌋ to the geld. There is land for $10\frac{1}{2}$ oxen. Geoffrey, Norman's man, has 1 team there ⌊in demesne⌋, and 4 villeins and 2 bordars with 2 oxen in a team. T. R. E. it was worth 40 shillings; now the like amount.

5.[2] S. In Cotes [Great Cotes (Bradley)] there are $4\frac{1}{2}$ bovates of land ⌊assessed⌋ to the geld. There is land for 9 oxen. It is soke⌊land⌋ belonging to (*in*) Chelebi [Keelby]. Richard has 2 villeins and 4 sokemen there with $1\frac{1}{2}$ teams, and 100 acres of meadow.

6. M. In Oresbi [Owersby (Walshcroft)] Ingemund had 2 bovates and the third part of 1 bovate of land ⌊assessed⌋ to the geld. There is land for $4\frac{1}{2}$ oxen. Geoffrey, Norman's man, has half a team there ⌊in demesne⌋, and 1 sokeman and 4 villeins and 2 bordars with 1 team, and 60 acres of meadow. T. R. E. and now worth 20 shillings.

---

[1] See 70/8.

[2] This entry has been inserted at the foot of the next column, and a sign indicates that it should be placed where it is printed in the text.

7. M. In Torgrembi [Thorganby (Walshcroft)] Grinchil had 14 bovates of land ⌊assessed⌋ to the geld. There is land for $3\frac{1}{2}$ teams. Gamelin, Norman's man, has 1 team there ⌊in demesne⌋, and 8 villeins and 2 bordars with 1 team, and $1\frac{1}{2}$ mills rendering 8 shillings, and 13 acres of meadow. T. R. E. and now worth 40 shillings ; tallage 10 shillings.

8. M. In Clachesbi [Claxby by Normanby (Walshcroft)] Chetel had 2 bovates of land and Godwin 1 bovate of land ⌊which are⌋ inland ⌊assessed⌋ to the geld. There is land for 5 oxen. Geoffrey, Norman's man, has half a team there ⌊in demesne⌋, and 2 villeins with 1 ox in a team, and 15 acres of meadow, and 15 acres of underwood. T. R. E. and now ⌊worth⌋ 8 shillings.

9. M. In Crocsbi [Croxby (Walshcroft)] Fulcheri had 3 bovates of land ⌊assessed⌋ to the geld. There is land for 9 oxen. Odo, Norman's man, has half a team there ⌊in demesne⌋, and 3 villeins and 1 bordar with 3 oxen in a team, and 1 acre of meadow. T. R. E. and now ⌊worth⌋ 20 shillings. One bovate belongs to (*est in*) the soke of Berenger de Todeni.

10. B. In Suinhope [Swinhope (Haverstoe)] there is 1 bovate of land ⌊assessed⌋ to the geld. It is inland belonging to (*in*) Crocsbi [Croxby]. There is 1 villein there having 1 ox in a team.

11. M. In Calchewelle [Cawkwell (Gartree)] Chetel had $1\frac{1}{2}$ carucates of land ⌊assessed⌋ to the geld. There is land for 12 oxen. Roger, Norman's man, has 1 team there ⌊in demesne⌋, and 5 villeins and 6 bordars with 1 team. There is a priest there, and a church, and 70 acres of meadow. T. R. E. it was worth 40 shillings ; now 60 shillings.

Sud Treding [South Riding]

12. M. In Bechelinge [Beckering (Wraggoe)] Turolf had 2 bovates of land ⌊assessed⌋ to the geld. There is land for 4 oxen. Herbert, Norman's man, has there 2 oxen in a team ⌊in demesne⌋, and 1 sokeman [on (*de*) 1 toft] having likewise 2 oxen in a team, and 2 acres of meadow. T. R. E. and now ⌊worth⌋ 8 shillings.

West Treding [West Riding]

13. Two M. In Wintrintone [Winterton (Manley)] Fulcheri had 12 bovates of land ⌊assessed⌋ to the geld. There is land for 12 oxen. Norman has 2 teams there ⌊in demesne⌋, and 1 sokeman on (*de*) 2 bovates of this land* and 10 villeins with 1 team. T. R. E. it was worth 4 pounds ; now 3 pounds ; tallage 20 [shillings].

**D. B., f. 361*d. *Facsimile, p. lii*b.

14. S. In Roscebi [Roxby (Manley)] there are 4 bovates of land ⌊assessed⌋ to the geld. There is land for 4 oxen. It is soke⌊land⌋. 1 sokeman has 3 oxen in a team there, and 7 acres of meadow.

15. M. In Walecote [Walcot (Manley)] Fulcheri had 10 bovates of land ⌊assessed⌋ to the geld. There is land for 10 oxen. Robert, Norman's man, has 3 villeins there with 1 team, and 40 acres of meadow, and 10 acres of underwood. T. R. E. it was worth 20 shillings ; now 16 shillings ; tallage 4 shillings.

16. B. In Hedebi [Haythby (Manley)] there are 2 bovates of land ⌊assessed⌋ to the geld. There is land for 2 oxen. It is inland belonging to (*in*) Walecote [Walcot]. There is 1 villein there with 1 ox in a team, and 4 acres of meadow.

17. Four M. In Flichesburg [Flixborough (Manley)] Fulcheri had 11 carucates and 7 bovates of land [assessed] to the geld. There is land for as many teams and oxen. Norman has 4½ teams there in demesne, and 3 sokemen on (*de*) 2 carucates of this land and 29 villeins and 6 bordars with 4½ teams. There are 2 sites of mills there, and 205 acres of meadow, and 120 acres of underwood. T. R. E. and now worth 8 pounds; tallage 40 shillings.

18. B. In Tedulfbi [Thealby (Manley)] there is half a carucate of land [assessed] to the geld. There is land for 4 oxen. It is inland. 3 villeins have there 3 oxen in a team, and 7 acres of meadow.

19. M. In Udetone [Wootton (Yarborough)] Aghete[1] had 6 bovates of land [assessed] to the geld. There is land for 12 oxen. Norman has 1 team there [in demesne], and 2 sokemen and 2 bordars. T. R. E. it was worth 40 shillings; now 20 shillings; tallage 5 shillings.

20. M. In Uluesbi [Ulceby (Yarborough)] Ulchil had 6 bovates of land [assessed] to the geld. There is land for 2 teams and 2 oxen. Norman has, [Odo [holding] of him], 1 team [in demesne], and 4 sokemen on (*de*) 3 bovates of this land, and 2 villeins with half a team, and 9 acres of meadow. T. R. E. and now [worth] 20 shillings; tallage 5 shillings.

21. M. In Cheluingeholm [Killingholme (Yarborough)] Fulcheri had 4 carucates [and 7 bovates] of land [assessed] to the geld. There is land for 10 teams. Norman has 3 teams there [in demesne], and 32 sokemen on (*de*) 3 carucates of this land, and 1 bordar with 4 teams, and 200 acres of meadow. T. R. E. it was worth 5 pounds; now 6 pounds; tallage 40 shillings.

22. S. In Mingeham [Immingham (Yarborough)] there are 5 bovates of land [assessed] to the geld. There is land for 2 teams. It is soke[land]. 3 sokemen have there 3 oxen in a team, and 15 acres of meadow. [It is] soke[land].

23. S. In Haburne [Habrough (Yarborough)] there are 3 bovates and 2 parts of 1 bovate of land [assessed] to the geld. It is soke[land]. There is land for 7 oxen. 1 sokeman has 1 team there.

HUNDRED HUNDRED

24. M. In Cherchebi and Scapuic [Kirkby Green and Scopwick (Langoe)] Gardulf had 6 bovates of land [assessed] to the geld. There is land for half a team. Norman has there 2 oxen in a team [in demesne], and 1 sokeman and 2 bordars having 2 oxen in a team, and 2½ acres of meadow. T. R. E. and now worth 20 shillings.

LANGEHOU [LANGOE] WAPENTAKE

25. S. In Timberlunt [Timberland (Langoe)] there are 2 carucates and 3 bovates and the fifth part of 1 bovate of land [assessed] to the geld. There is land for 12 oxen. 7 sokemen and 2 bordars have 2 teams there. It is soke[land].

LOVEDUN [LOVEDEN] WAPENTAKE

26. M. In Stubetune [Stubton (Loveden)] Tochi had 5½ bovates of land [assessed] to the geld. There is land for 1 team. Now it is waste except 1 bordar and 34 acres of meadow. T. R. E. [worth] 10 shillings; now 5 shillings.

---

[1] The initial letter was first written as *V*; then *A* was inserted inside the upper part of the *V*. *Aghete* is probably the right form.

27. M. In the same place (*ibidem*) Ulchel had 1 carucate of land [assessed] to the geld. There is land for 1 team. Gamelin, Norman's man, has half a team there [in demesne], and 3 bordars, and 5 acres of meadow. T. R. E. and now worth 10 shillings.

GEREBURG [YARBOROUGH] WAPENTAKE

28. M. In Limberge [Little Limber (Yarborough)] Stur had half a carucate of land [assessed] to the geld. There is land for 2 teams. Herbert, Norman's man, has 4 villeins there with half a team. T. R. E. it was worth 20 shillings; now 10 shillings.

*D. B., f. 362*a. *Facsimile, p. liii*a.

29. M. In Scotstorne[1] [Scothern (Lawress)] Godric had 9 bovates of land [assessed] to the geld. There is land for 12 oxen. Norman has 1 team there [in demesne], and 5 villeins and 3 bordars having 6 oxen in a team, and 23 acres of meadow. T. R. E. and now worth 20 shillings; tallage 5 shillings.

30. B. In Cropesbi and Cunesbi [Crosby and North Conesby (Manley)] there are 9½ bovates of land [assessed] to the geld. There is land for as many oxen. It is inland belonging to (*in*) Cunesbi [North Conesby]. 4 villeins have 1 team there.

31. Two M. In Ormesbi [South Ormsby (Hill)] Edric and Gamel had 2½ carucates [of land] [assessed] to the geld. There is land for 3½ teams. Herbert, Norman's man, has 1 team there [in demesne], and 5 sokemen and 3 villeins and 1 bordar with 1 team, and 70 acres of meadow. T. R. E. it was worth 40 shillings; now the like amount.

32. M. In Nochetune [Nocton (Langoe)] Ulf had 23 carucates of land [assessed] to the geld. There is land [*blank*]. Norman has 5 teams there in demesne, and 26 sokemen and 9 villeins and 3 bordars with 9 teams and 2 oxen in a team. There is a church there, and a priest, and 100 less 5 acres of meadow, and 40 acres of underwood. T. R. E. it was worth 6 pounds; now 10 pounds; tallage 40 shillings.

33. M. In the same place (*ibidem*) Osulf had 1 carucate of land [assessed] to the geld. Norman has 1 villein there, and 5 oxen in a team. This is valued (*appreciatur*) in the above-mentioned manor.

34. In Dunestune [Dunston (Langoe)] Ulf had 12 carucates of land [assessed] to the geld. There is land [*blank*]. It is soke[land] belonging to (*in*) Nochetune [Nocton]. Norman found there 3 villeins and 31 sokemen and 13 bordars having 9 teams, and 6 mills[2] rendering 24 shillings, and 12 acres of meadow, and 80 acres of underwood. There is a church there, and a priest.

35. The men of Colebi [Coleby (Boby)] withhold (*retinent*) 6 shillings and 10 pence of the customary render (*consuetudine*).

36. The men of Hermestune [Harmston (Boby)] withhold 8 shillings of the customary render (*consuetudine*).

---

[1] See 71/5. [2] Corrected from *viij teams and ii mills*.

33. LAND OF NORMAN CRASSUS

1. M. In Carletune[1] [Middle Carlton (Lawress)] Agemund had 2 carucates and 2 bovates of land [assessed] to the geld. There is land for 18 oxen. Norman Crassus has 10 sokemen there on (*de*) 12 bovates of this land, and 2 villeins and 3 bordars with 1 team and 2 oxen in a team, and 15 acres of meadow. T. R. E. it was worth 16 shillings ; now 20 shillings ; tallage 40 shillings.

2. M. In Canuic [Canwick (Langoe)] Walrauene had 1 carucate of land [assessed] to the geld. There is land for 6 oxen. Norman has 1 team there [in demesne], and 25 acres of meadow. T. R. E. it was worth 20 shillings ; now the like amount.

*D. B., f. 362*b. *Facsimile, p. liii*b.

34. LAND OF ERNEIS DE BURUN

1. M. In Medeltone [Melton Ross (Yarborough)] Eddeua had 3 carucates of land [assessed] to the geld. There is land for 7 teams. Ernegis de Burun has 5 teams there [in demesne], and 3 sokemen on (*de*) 1 bovate of this land, and 30 villeins and 9 bordars with 4 teams. There is a church there, and a priest, and 78 acres of meadow. T. R. E. it was worth 6 pounds ; now 8 pounds ; tallage 40 shillings.

2. Two M. In Ulvesbi [Ulceby (Yarborough)] Grim and Siward had 4 carucates of land [assessed] to the geld. There is land for 10 teams. Ernegis has 4 teams there [in demesne], and 30 sokemen on (*de*) 1 carucate of this land and 8 villeins and 10 bordars with 9 teams. There is a church there, and a priest, and half a mill rendering 10 shillings, and 500 eels, and 60 acres of meadow. T. R. E. it was worth 5 pounds ; now 8 pounds ; tallage 40 shillings.

3. M. In Messingeham [Messingham (Manley)] Eddiua had 10½ bovates of land [assessed] to the geld. There is land for 12 oxen. Turstin, Ernegis' man, has 1 team there [in demesne], and 8 villeins with 1½ teams, and 1 mill rendering 5 shillings, and 10 acres of meadow. T. R. E. it was worth 60 shillings ; now 20 shillings ; tallage 10 shillings.

4. Three M. In Bernedebi [Barnetby le Wold (Yarborough)] Grim and Ulf and Fin had 7 bovates of land [assessed] to the geld. There is land for 14 oxen. Ulric, Ernegis' man, has 1 team there [in demesne], and 12 sokemen on (*de*) 1 bovate of this land [and 5 tofts] and 5 villeins with 1 team, and half a church. T. R. E. it was worth 20 shillings ; now 16 shillings ; tallage 4 shillings.

---

[1] See 71/3.

5. M. In Torentone and Brune [Thornton Curtis and Burnham (Yarborough)] Grim had 2 bovates of land [assessed] to the geld. There is land for 4 oxen. Ulric, Ernegis' man, has there 3 oxen in a team [in demesne], and 1 sokeman on (*de*) 1 toft and 7 villeins with 3 oxen in a team. T. R. E. it was worth 16 shillings; now 8 shillings; tallage 2 shillings.

6. M. In Golse [Goxhill (Yarborough)] Grim had 10 bovates of land [assessed] to the geld. There is land for 2½ teams. Ulric, Ernegis' man, has half a team there [in demesne], and 25 sokemen and 5 villeins with 2½ teams, and 60 acres of meadow. T. R. E. it was worth 30 shillings; now 40 shillings; tallage 10 shillings.

7. M. In Neteltone [Nettleton (Yarborough)] Gamel had 5 bovates of land [assessed] to the geld. There is land for 15 oxen. There are 3 villeins and 3 bordars there with 2 oxen in a team, and 1 mill rendering 12 pence, and 20 acres of meadow. T. R. E. and now [worth] 20 shillings.

8. M. In Chetelbi [Kettleby (Yarborough)] Eddeua had 3 bovates and the third part of 1 bovate of land [assessed] to the geld. There is land for 1 team. Turstin, Ernegis' man, has there 3 oxen in a team [in demesne], and 1 sokeman on (*de*) 5 acres of this land, and 6 villeins and 1 bordar with 1 team, and 14 acres of meadow, and 3 acres of underwood. T. R. E. it was worth 40 shillings; now 20 shillings.

9. M. In Brochelesbi [Brocklesby (Yarborough)] Eddeua had 3 bovates of land [assessed] to the geld. There is land for 6 oxen. Ranulf, Ernegis' man, has 1 team there [in demesne], and 2 sokemen on (*de*) 1 bovate of this land and 1 villein with 5 oxen in a team, and 80 acres of meadow. T. R. E. and now worth 20 shillings.

10. S. In Haburne and Neuhuse [Habrough and Newsham (Yarborough)] there are 2 bovates of land [assessed] to the geld. There is land for 4 oxen. It is soke[land] of this manor. 2 villeins have there 5 oxen in a team, and 30 acres of meadow.

11. In the same places (*ibidem*) there are 2 bovates of land [assessed] to the geld. There is land for 4 oxen. Ulchil had it. Now it is waste.

12. M. In Waragebi[1] [Wragby (Wraggoe)] [Countess] Gudeta had 6 [and a half] bovates of land [assessed] to the geld. There is land for 12 oxen. Ernegis has 1 team there [in demesne], and 10 villeins with 1½ teams. There is a church there, and a priest, and half a mill rendering 12 pence, and 24 acres of meadow. There is wood[land] for pannage 4 furlongs in length and 4 in breadth. There is underwood 5 furlongs in length and 5 in breadth. T. R. E. it was worth 14 pounds; now 10 pounds; tallage 10 pounds.

D. B., f. 362c. *Facsimile, p. liva.*

SOKE[LAND] OF WARAGEBI [WRAGBY]

13. S. In Hatune [Hatton (Wraggoe)] there are 5 carucates of land [assessed] to the geld. There is land for 8 teams. There are 15 sokemen and 10 bordars there with 4 teams, and 100 acres of meadow, and 230 acres of underwood.

---

[1] See 69/24.

14. S. In Ca[l]decote[1] [Calcote *or* Collow in Legsby (Wraggoe)] there are 1½ carucates of land [assessed] to the geld. There is land for 4 teams. There are 2 sokemen and 4 bordars there having 2 oxen in a team. In demesne Ernegis [has] 1 team, and there are 2 sites of mills, and 8 acres of meadow.

15. S. In Pantone [Panton (Wraggoe)] there are 2 carucates of land [assessed] to the geld. There is land for 3 teams. There are 2 teams there in demesne, and 13 sokemen and 6 bordars with 2 teams. There is a church there, and 40 acres of meadow.

16. S. In Harduic [Hardwick (Wraggoe)] there are 5 bovates and the third part of 1 bovate of land [assessed] to the geld. There is land for 11 oxen. 6 sokemen have 1 team there [in demesne], and 53 acres of meadow.

17. S. In Barcourde [Barkwith (Wraggoe)] there are 2 carucates [and 2 bovates] of land [assessed] to the geld. There is land for 3 teams. 10 sokemen have 1 team there. Ernegis [has] 1 team in demesne, and there is a church, and 33 acres of meadow.

18. S. In Terintone [Torrington (Wraggoe)] there are 2½ carucates and the third part of 1 bovate of land [assessed] to the geld.[2] There is land for 4 teams. Ernegis has 1 team there [in demesne], and there are 12 sokemen who have nothing.

19. S. In Langetone [Langton (Wraggoe)] there are 2 bovates of land [assessed] to the geld. There is land for 4 oxen. 1 villein has there 2 oxen in a team, and 21 acres of underwood.

20. S. In Fulnedebi [Fulnetby (Wraggoe)] there are 3 carucates of land [assessed] to the geld. There is land for 5 teams. 12 sokemen have 3 teams there, and 100 acres of meadow, and 120 acres of underwood.

21. S. In Rande [Rand (Wraggoe)] there are 3 carucates of land [assessed] to the geld. There is land for 5 teams. 8 sokemen and 5 bordars have there 2 teams and 5 oxen in a team, and 40 acres of meadow, and 20 acres of underwood.

22. S. In Grisebi and Burg [Girsby and Burgh on Bain (Wraggoe)] there are 6 bovates of land [assessed] to the geld. There is land for 12 oxen. 3 sokemen have 1½ teams there, and 12 acres of meadow.

23. B. In Chinetorp [Kingthorpe (Wraggoe)] there are 2 bovates and 2 parts of half a bovate of land [assessed] to the geld. There is land for 5 oxen. 1 villein has there 1 ox in a team, and 4 acres of meadow, and 80 acres of wood[land] for pannage throughout the territory.

24. Two M. In Colebi [Coleby (Manley)] Wege and Baret had 2 carucates and 1 bovate of land [assessed] to the geld. There is land for 17 oxen. John, Ernegis' man, has 2 teams there [in demesne], and 1 sokeman on *(de)* 1 toft and 5 villeins and 2 bordars with 2 teams, and 10 acres of meadow. T. R. E. it was worth 40 shillings ; now 50 shillings ; tallage 10 shillings.

BEREWIC

25. B. In Walecote [Walcot on Trent (Manley)] there are 6 bovates[3] of land [assessed] to the geld. There is land for 4 oxen. 1 villein has there 2 oxen in a team, and 24 acres of meadow, and 4 acres of underwood.

---

[1] See 22/37 ; 69/26.

[2] *ad geld'* is duplicated.

[3] See 71/17.

26. B. In Wintritone [Winterton (Manley)] there is 1 bovate of land [assessed] to the geld. There is land for 1 ox. It is waste.

27. M. In Graingeham [Grayingham (Corringham)] Eddeua had 1 carucate of land [assessed] to the geld. There is land for 12 oxen. Ernegis has 2 teams there [in demesne], and 8 villeins and 1 bordar with 1½ teams, and 10 acres of meadow. T. R. E. and now worth 40 shillings.

*D. B., f. 362*d. *Facsimile, p. liv*b.

35. LAND OF RALF PAGENEL

1. M. In Bertone [Broughton (Manley)] Merlosuen had 10 carucates and 6 bovates of land [assessed] to the geld. There is land for 12 teams. Ralf Pagenel has 2 teams there [in demesne], and 29 sokemen on (*de*) 5 carucates and 3 bovates of this land and 34 villeins and 8 bordars with 13 teams. There is a church there, and a priest, and 1 mill rendering 2 shillings, and 240 acres of meadow, and underwood 2 leagues in length and 1 in breadth. T. R. E. it was worth 10 pounds; now 7 pounds; but in the past year it was worth 10 pounds.

2. M. In the same place (*ibidem*) Grinchel had 7 bovates of land [assessed] to the geld. There is land for 1 team. Ralf has 1 team there [in demesne], and 5 farmers (*censarios*) with 1 team, and 10 acres of meadow. T. R. E. it was worth 40 shillings; now [*blank*].

3. M. In Duneham [Dunham (Lawress)] Merlesuen had 2 carucates of land [assessed] to the geld. There is land for 2 teams. A certain knight (*miles*) of Ralf's has half a team there [in demesne], and 4 sokemen on (*de*) 1 carucate of this land and 4 villeins with 1½ teams, and 17 acres of meadow. T. R. E. it was worth 10 shillings; now 16 shillings; tallage 4 shillings.

4. M. In Roxebi [Roxby (Manley)] Merlosuen had 5 carucates and 2 bovates of land [assessed] to the geld. There is land for 6 teams. Ralf has there 2 teams and 2 oxen in a team [in demesne], and 23 sokemen [on (*de*) 21 bovates of this land] and 8 villeins and 4 bordars with 6 teams, and 44 acres of meadow, and 6 acres of underwood. T. R. E. it was worth 6 pounds; now 4 pounds; tallage 20 shillings. Herbert [holds it].

5. B. In Wintritone [Winterton (Manley)] there are 2 bovates of land [assessed] to the geld. There is land for 2 oxen. 2 villeins have there 2 oxen in a team.

6. M. In Rase [West Rasen (Walshcroft)] Merlosuen had 6 carucates and 6 bovates of land [assessed] to the geld. There is land for 9[1] teams. Ralf has 4 teams there in demesne, and 37 sokemen on (*de*) 4 carucates and 7 bovates of this land and 15 villeins with 9 teams, and 1 mill rendering 2 shillings, and 300 acres of meadow. T. R. E. it was worth 16 pounds; now 10 pounds; tallage 6 pounds.

[1] Corrected from *viij*.

7. S. In the other Rase [Middle Rasen (Walshcroft)] there are 14 bovates of land ⌊assessed⌋ to the geld. There is land for 3 teams. It is soke⌊land⌋ of this manor. 16 sokemen have 2½ teams there, and 160 acres of meadow.

8. S. In Wiuilingeham [North Willingham (Walshcroft)] there are 9 bovates of land ⌊assessed⌋ to the geld. There is land for 18 oxen. 19 sokemen have 2 teams there.

9. M. In Tauelesbi [Tealby (Walshcroft)] Merlosuen had 14 bovates of land ⌊assessed⌋ to the geld. There is land for 2½ teams. Ralf has 10 sokemen there on (*de*) 3 bovates, and 10 villeins with 1 team, and 3 mills rendering 12 shillings, and 89 acres of meadow, and 3 sites of mills. T. R. E. it was worth 12 pounds; now 50 shillings; tallage 9 shillings.

10.[1] S. In Osgotesbi [Osgodby (Walshcroft)] there is 1 bovate of land ⌊assessed⌋ to the geld. There is land for 2 oxen. 2 sokemen have half a team there belonging to (*in*) Tauelesbi [Tealby].

11. M. In Witham [Witham on the Hill (Beltisloe)] Merlosuen had 1 carucate of land ⌊assessed⌋ to the geld. There is land for 1 team. Hacun, Ralf's man, has there 2 oxen in a team ⌊in demesne⌋, and 4 villeins and 1 bordar with 1 team, and 10 acres of meadow, and 84 acres of wood⌊land⌋. T. R. E. it was worth 20 shillings; now 10 ⌈shillings⌉ and 8 pence.

12. S. In Suinhamstede [Swinstead (Beltisloe)] Merlosuen had 5 carucates of land ⌊assessed⌋ to the geld. There is land for 5 teams. There was 1 thane (*tainus*) there whom King Edward gave to Merlosuen, as the men of the hundred bear witness. Ralf has 22 sokemen and 4 villeins there with 6 teams, and 18 acres of meadow, and 200 acres of underwood.

13. M. In Bertune[2] [Burton Coggles (Beltisloe)] ⌈Earl⌉ Morcar had 6 bovates of land ⌊assessed⌋ to the geld. There is land for 6 oxen. Oger, Ralf's man, has 1 team there ⌊in demesne⌋, and 5 villeins with half a team, and 12 acres of meadow. There is wood⌊land⌋ 7 furlongs in length and 5½ furlongs in breadth. Besides (*extra*) this there are still 280 acres of wood⌊land⌋ for pannage throughout the territory. T. R. E. it was worth 20 shillings; now 30 shillings.

*D. B., f. 363*a. *Facsimile, p. lv*a.

14. M. In Gerneham [Irnham (Beltisloe)] Merlosuen had 7 carucates of land ⌊assessed⌋ to the geld. There is land for 7 teams. Ralf has 3½ teams there ⌊in demesne⌋, and 7 sokemen on (*de*) 2 carucates of this land and 29 villeins and 9 bordars with 7 teams. There is a church there, and a priest, and 50 acres of meadow. There is wood⌊land⌋ for pannage 1 league in length and 10 furlongs in breadth. Besides (*extra*) this there are still 200 acres of wood⌊land⌋ for pannage throughout the territory. T. R. E. it was worth 12 pounds; now 10 pounds; tallage 40 shillings.

15. M. In Aschebi [Ashby de la Laund (Flaxwell)] Merlosuen had 6 carucates of land ⌊assessed⌋ to the geld. There is land for 6 teams. Ralf has 2 teams there ⌊in demesne⌋, and 17 sokemen and 2 villeins and

[1] This entry has been inserted at the foot of the column, and a sign indicates that it should be placed where it is printed in the text.

[2] See 72/5.

2 bordars with 8 teams, and 50 acres of meadow. T. R. E. it was worth 4 pounds ; now 100 shillings.

16. M. In Scalebi and Stratone [Scawby and Sturton (Manley)] Grinchel had 3 carucates and 2 bovates of land ⌊assessed⌋ to the geld. There is land for 5 teams. Ralf has 2 teams there ⌊in demesne⌋, and 5 sokemen on (*de*) 4 bovates of this land and 7 villeins and 3 bordars with 2 teams. T. R. E. it was worth 60 shillings ; now 40 shillings ; tallage 10 shillings.

17. In Snardesforde [Snarford (Lawress)] there are 3 bovates of land ⌊assessed⌋ to the geld. There is land for 2 oxen. 4 sokemen have half a team there, and 12 acres of meadow. It is soke⌊land⌋ belonging to (*in*) Resne [Rasen].

36. LAND OF RALF DE MORTEMER

1. M. In Grimesbi [and Sualun] [Great Grimsby and Swallow (Bradley)] Eddiue had 2 carucates and 2 bovates of land ⌊assessed⌋ to the geld. There is land for 4½ teams. Richard, Ralf de Mortemer's man, has 2 teams there in demesne, and 7 sokemen on (*de*) 8[1] tofts and 11 villeins and 10 bordars having 1½ teams. There is a church there, and a priest, and 1 mill rendering 4 shillings, and 1 ferry (*passagium*) rendering 5 shillings, and 30 acres of meadow. T. R. E. it was worth 8 pounds ; now 100 shillings.

2. M. In Torentune and Bodebi [and Udetone] [Thornton Curtis and *possibly* Bonby and Wootton (Yarborough)] Eddeua had 10 carucates of land ⌊assessed⌋ to the geld. There is land for 20 teams. Ralf de Mortemer has 3 teams there in demesne, and 58 sokemen on (*de*) 4 carucates of this land and 7 villeins and 7 bordars having 7 teams, and half a mill rendering 3 shillings. T. R. E. it was worth 10 pounds ; now 15 pounds ; tallage 5 pounds. Of this land Odo, Ralf's man, has 2 carucates, and he has 2 teams there ⌊in demesne⌋, and 13 sokemen on (*de*) 1 carucate of this land and 1 villein with 1½ teams ; and it is worth 50 shillings.

3. M. In Bundebi [Bonby (Yarborough)] Copsi had 1 carucate of land ⌊assessed⌋ to the geld. There is land for 2 teams. William, Ralf's man, has 2 teams there ⌊in demesne⌋, and 2 villeins and 1 bordar with 1 ox in a team. T. R. E. and now worth 20 shillings ; tallage 10 shillings.

4. M. In Hermodestone [Harmston (Boby)] Copsi had 3½ carucates of land ⌊assessed to the geld⌋. There is land for as many teams. Ralf has 1 team there in demesne, and 1 sokeman and 4 villeins with 1 team, and 35 acres of meadow. T. R. E. and now worth 40 shillings. Over this land Earl H⌊ugh⌋ has soke as belonging to (*in*) Wadintone[2] [Waddington (Boby)].

5. In Stou [Stow (Well)] Eddiua had 3 mansions with sake and soke. Ralf has them.

---

[1] *vi* is written in the line and *ii* above the line. [2] See 13/34.

*D. B., f. 363*b. *Facsimile, p. lv*b.

37. LAND OF ROBERT DE VECI

1. M. In Helpericham [Helpringham (Aswardhurn)] Eilric had 7 carucates [and 3 bovates] of land ⌊assessed⌋ to the geld. There is land for as many teams and oxen. Robert de Veci has 3 teams there in demesne, and 13 villeins and[1] 9 bordars with 4 teams, and 15 acres of meadow. T. R. E. it was worth 3 pounds ; now 12 pounds.

2. M. In Carltorp[2] [Caythorpe (Loveden)] Eilric had 19 carucates and 2 bovates of land in demesne, and 28 carucates and 6 bovates of land which is soke⌊land⌋ (*de soca*), ⌊assessed⌋ to the geld. There is land for as many teams, that is 48. Hereto belong the three hundreds of Fristun, Normenton, Wilgebi [Frieston in Caythorpe, Normanton, West Willoughby (Loveden)]. Robert de Veci has 3 teams there in demesne, and 113 sokemen with 32 teams, and 50 villeins and 7 bordars with 13 teams. There are 2 churches there, and 2 priests, and half a mill rendering 10 shillings, and 880 acres of meadow. Of the above-said land and soke⌊land⌋ 3 of Robert's men have 12 carucates and 7 bovates, and they have 4½ teams there. One Englishman also has 1 carucate and 5 bovates, and he has 1 team there. T. R. E. it was worth 30 pounds ; now 50 pounds.

Soke⌊land⌋ of this Manor

3. S. In Brandune [Brandon (Loveden)] there are 7 bovates of land ⌊assessed⌋ to the geld. There is land for 11 oxen. 8 sokemen have 2 teams and 2 oxen there.

4. S. In Rosbi [Rauceby (Flaxwell)] there are 3 carucates of land ⌊assessed⌋ to the geld. There is land for 4 teams. 19 sokemen have 3 teams there.

5. B. In Suauitone [Swaton (Aveland)] there is half a carucate of land ⌊assessed⌋ to the geld. There is land for 6 oxen. It is a berewic. 1 villein and 2 bordars have there 3 oxen in a team, and 5 acres of meadow.

6. M. In Steueninge [Stenning in Bicker (Kirton)] Eilric had 6 bovates of land ⌊assessed⌋ to the geld. There is land for 6 oxen. Robert has 1 villein there, and 2 salt-pans rendering (*de*) 2 shillings and 8 pence, and 1 fishery rendering 200 eels, and 18 acres of meadow. T. R. E. and now worth 20 shillings.

Soke⌊land⌋ belonging to (*in*) Catorp [Caythorpe]

7. S. In Hechintune [Heckington (Aswardhurn)] there are 6½ bovates [of land] ⌊assessed⌋ to the geld. There is land for 5½ oxen. 1 villein and 2 bordars have there 6 oxen in a team, and 6 acres of meadow.

---

[1] *and* is repeated in the text.

[2] See 72/36.

D. B., f. 363c. *Facsimile, p. lvia.*

38. LAND OF ROBERT THE STEWARD (*Dispensatoris*)

1. M. In Torintune [Thornton (Horncastle)] Achi had 3 carucates of land ⌊assessed⌋ to the geld. There is land for 6 teams. Robert the Steward has 3 teams in demesne, and 9[1] sokemen on (*de*) 10 bovates of this land and 5 villeins and 5 bordars having 4 teams, and 2 mills rendering 20 shillings, and 80 acres of meadow, and 350 acres of wood⌊land⌋ throughout the territory. T. R. E. it was worth 5 pounds; now 4 pounds; tallage 20 shillings.

2. S. In Rocstune [Roughton (Horncastle)] there are 12 bovates of land ⌊assessed⌋ to the geld. There is land for 12 oxen. It is soke⌊land⌋. 3½ sokemen have 2 teams and 3 oxen ploughing there, and ⌊there are⌋ 15 acres of meadow, and 1 fishery rendering 2 shillings, and 40 acres of wood⌊land⌋ for pannage throughout the territory.

3. M. In Scrivelesbi [Scrivelsby (Horncastle)] Siward had 7 carucates and 5 bovates of land ⌊assessed⌋ to the geld. There is land for 8½ teams. Robert has 6 teams there in demesne, and 30 sokemen on (*de*) 3 carucates of this land and 16 villeins and 11 bordars with 6 teams. There is a church there, and 1 mill rendering 13 shillings and 4 pence, and 200 acres of meadow, and 100 acres of wood⌊land⌋ for pannage throughout the territory. T. R. E. it was worth 12 pounds; now 14 pounds.

4. B. In Cuningesbi [Coningsby (Horncastle)] there are 9 bovates of land ⌊assessed⌋ to the geld. There is land for 9 oxen. It is a berewic. 15 villeins and 3 bordars have 1½ teams there, and ⌊there are⌋ 10 fisheries rendering 8 shillings and 4 pence, and 60 acres of meadow, and 60 acres of wood⌊land⌋ for pannage.

5. B. In Wilgesbi [Wilksby (Horncastle)] there are 1½ carucates [of land] ⌊assessed⌋ to the geld. There is land for 2 teams. It is a berewic. Robert has 1 team there in demesne, and 5 villeins have 2 oxen in a team, and there are 20 acres of meadow, and 40 acres of underwood.

6. S. In Meringhe [Mareham on the Hill (Horncastle)] there is 1 bovate of land ⌊assessed⌋ to the geld. There is land for 2 oxen. It is soke⌊land⌋ belonging to (*in*) Scriwelesbi [Scrivelsby]. [There is] 1 villein there with 1 ox in a team.

7. In Endrebi [Wood Enderby (Horncastle)] Siward had 9 acres of arable land and 8 acres of wood⌊land⌋ with sake and soke. Robert the Steward has it now.

8. M. In Herdertorp [Addlethorpe (Candleshoe)] Wiuelac had 3 carucates of land ⌊assessed⌋ to the geld. There is land for 3 teams. Robert has 3 teams there in demesne, and 32 sokemen on (*de*) a moiety of this land and 12 villeins with 6 teams. There are 2 churches there, and 400 acres of meadow. T. R. E. it was worth 8 pounds; now 10 pounds.

---

[1] Or possibly *x*. The number has seemingly been altered from *ii*.

SOKE⌊LAND⌋ BELONGING TO (*in*) GULDELSMERE [*query* INGOLDMELLS]

9. S. In Partenai and Stepinge [Partney and Great Steeping (Candleshoe)] and Tric [=Skegness (Candleshoe)] and Burg [Burgh in the Marsh (Candleshoe)] there are 2½ carucates of land ⌊assessed⌋ to the geld. There is land for as many teams. 5 sokemen and 2 villeins have half a team there, and ⌊there are⌋ 30 acres of meadow.

10. M. In Butiate [Butyate in Bardney (Wraggoe)] Wiglac had 1 carucate of land ⌊assessed⌋ to the geld. There is land for 12 oxen. Robert has 1 team there ⌊in demesne⌋, and 5 sokemen on (*de*) half a carucate of this land and 10 villeins having 3 teams, and 15 acres of meadow, and 200 acres of wood⌊land⌋ for pannage in the middle (*ex media parte*). T. R. E. it was worth 40 shillings; now 50 shillings.

11. B. In Langetone[1] [Langton by Wragby (Wraggoe)] there are 1½ carucates of land ⌊assessed⌋ to the geld. There is land for 4 teams. Robert has 1 team there ⌊in demesne⌋, and 8 sokemen on (*de*) half a carucate of this land and 4 villeins with 2 teams, and 24 acres of meadow, and 280 acres of wood⌊land⌋ for pannage.

12. M. In Tadewelle[2] [Tathwell (Louthesk)] Siward had 1 carucate of land ⌊assessed⌋ to the geld. There is land for 4 teams. Robert has 1 team there ⌊in demesne⌋, and 8 villeins with 1 team, and 2 mills* rendering 14 shillings, and 100 acres of meadow. T. R. E. and now worth 40 shillings.

**D.B.*, *f. 363*d. *Facsimile*, *p. lvi*b.

[Chetelber[3]]

13. M. In Holtham [Haltham on Bain (Horncastle)] Achi had 2 carucates and 2 bovates of land ⌊assessed⌋ to the geld. There is land for as many teams and oxen. Robert has 1 team there ⌊in demesne⌋, and 3 sokemen on (*de*) half a carucate of this land and 5 villeins with 1 team, and 2 mills rendering 13 shillings and 4 pence, and 24 acres of meadow, and 80 acres of wood⌊land⌋ for pannage. T. R. E. and now worth 30 shillings.

14. M. In Fugelestou[4] [Fulstow (Haverstoe)] Aschil had 14 bovates of land ⌊assessed⌋ to the geld. There is land for 3 teams. Robert has 1 team there ⌊in demesne⌋, and 3 sokemen on (*de*) 9 bovates of this land and 4 villeins and 2 bordars with 1½ teams, and 6 salt-pans rendering 6 shillings. T. R. E. it was worth 100 shillings; now 20 shillings; tallage 10 shillings.

---

[1] See 24/16; 69/23.
[2] See 69/1 and 3.
[3] Written in the bottom margin, probably by way of practice.
[4] See 12/19; 70/22.

39. LAND OF GUY DE REINBUEDCURT

1. M. In Wilgebi [Scot Willoughby (Aveland)] Leuric had 3 carucates and 2 bovates of land ⌊assessed⌋ to the geld. There is land for 4 teams. Guy de Reinbudcurt has 2 teams there in demesne, and 10 sokemen on (*de*) 10 bovates of this land and 3 bordars having 2½ teams. There is a priest there having 37½ acres of land rendering 16 pence in respect of custom. Over a fourth part of the church of the same vill Guy has soke, and ⌊he has⌋ 30 acres of meadow, and 28 acres of underwood. T. R. E. it was worth 7 pounds; now 4 pounds; tallage 20 shillings.

2. S. In Ounesbi [Aunsby (Aswardhurn)] there are 3½ carucates of land ⌊assessed⌋ to the geld. There is land for 7 teams. It is soke[land] of the same manor, and 2 bovates are inland. 25 sokemen have 6½ teams there, and 70 acres of meadow, and 6 acres of underwood.

3. M. In Sidestham[1] [Syston (Threo)] Leuric had 11 carucates and 6 bovates of land ⌊assessed⌋ to the geld. There is land for as many teams and oxen. There is now 1 team there in demesne, and 27 sokemen on (*de*) 8 carucates [and 6 bovates] of this land and 10 villeins with 12 teams. There is a priest there, and a church to which belongs (*iacet*) 1 bovate of land. There are 6[2] mills there rendering (*de*) 50 shillings, and 21 acres of meadow. T. R. E. it was worth 6 pounds; now 4 pounds; tallage 40 shillings.

4. In Beltone [Belton (Threo)] Guy de Ranbudcurt has 10 acres of meadow.

Ingelrann his son holds all these lands of him.

D.B., f. 364a. *Facsimile, p. lviia.*

40. LAND OF RAINER DE BRIMOU

1.[3] Two M. In Limberge[4] [Great Limber (Yarborough)] Jalf and Turuer had 2 carucates of land ⌊assessed⌋ to the geld. There is land for 5 teams. Rayner de Brimou has 1 team there ⌊in demesne⌋, and 2 sokemen on (*de*) 2 tofts and 2 villeins and 11 bordars with half a team. T. R. E. it was worth 4 pounds; now 30 shillings.

2. M. In Ingeham [Ingham (Aslacoe)] Jalf had half a carucate of land. There is land for 6 oxen. Colsuan, Rainer's man, has half a team there ⌊in demesne⌋, and 3 villeins and 2 bordars with 5 oxen in a team, and 8 acres of meadow. T. R. E. and now ⌊worth⌋ 10 shillings.

---

[1] See 72/57.
[2] The number is doubtful: it seems to be a correction of *iiii*.
[3] See 2/25; 70/10.
[4] See 2/24.

3. In Neutone [Newton by Toft (Walshcroft)] there are 3 bovates of land [assessed] to the geld. There is land for 1 team. It is soke[land] of the same manor. 2 sokemen have 3 oxen in a team there, and [there are] 10 acres of meadow.

4. M. In Holtone [Holton le Clay (Bradley)] Jalf had 5 bovates of land and 14 acres of land and 1 virgate [assessed] to the geld. There is land for 10 oxen. Roger, Rayner's man, has 5 oxen there in a team [in demesne], and 4 villeins and 1 bordar having 5 oxen in a team, and 13 acres of meadow. T. R. E. it was worth 30 shillings; now 20 shillings.

5. M. In Staintone [Stainton le Vale (Walshcroft)] Jalf had 6 bovates of land [assessed] to the geld. There is land for 18 oxen. Rayner has half a team there [in demesne], and 4 sokemen on (*de*) 1 bovate of this land and 1 villein and 2 bordars having 5 oxen in a team, and the site of a mill, and 45 acres of meadow. T. R. E. it was worth 60 shillings; now 20 shillings; tallage 5 shillings.

6. M. In Walesbi [Walesby (Walshcroft)] Jalf had 1 carucate of land [assessed] to the geld. There is land for 12 oxen. Baldwin, Rayner's man, has 1 team there [in demesne], and 7 villeins with half a team, and 20 acres of meadow, and 5 acres of underwood. T. R. E. and now worth 30 shillings.

7. M. In Barcuorde [Barkwith (Wraggoe)] Code had 4 bovates of land [assessed] to the geld. There is land for 1 team. Girard, Rayner's man, has 5 oxen there in a team [in demesne], and 1 villein with 1 ox in a team, and 9 acres of meadow. T. R. E. [and now] worth 10 shillings.

8. S. In Ulingeham [South Willingham (Wraggoe)] there are 10 bovates of land [assessed] to the geld. There is land for 2½ teams. It is soke[land] of the same manor. 13 sokemen have 3 teams there, and [there are] 40 acres of meadow.[1]

9. M. In Haintone [Hainton (Wraggoe)] Code had 3½ bovates of land [assessed] to the geld. There is land for 7 oxen. Now Rayner has it, and it is waste. There are 26 acres of meadow there. T. R. E. it was worth 20 shillings; now 30 shillings.

10. M. In Chinetorp [Kingthorpe (Wraggoe)] Jalf had 3 bovates of land [assessed] to the geld. There is land for 6 oxen. Rayner has 1 villein and 1 bordar there with 3 oxen in a team, and 8 acres of meadow, and 100 acres of wood[land] for pannage throughout the territory. T. R. E. and now worth 10 shillings.

11. S. In Strubi [Strubby (Wraggoe)] there are 2 bovates of land [assessed] to the geld. It is soke[land] of this manor. 2 sokemen have 2 oxen in a team there.

12. M. In Sisse [Sixle (Wraggoe)] Jalf had 5 bovates of land [assessed] to the geld. There is land for 1 team. Rayner has 1 team there [in demesne], and 2 sokemen and 1 bordar having 3 oxen in a team, and 80 acres of meadow. T. R. E. and now worth 30 shillings.

13. S. In Houten [Holtham in Legsby (Wraggoe)] there are 2 parts of 1 bovate of land [assessed] to the geld. It is soke[land]. It is waste.

---

[1] See 2/1; 69/29. The letter *K*, probably for *Kalumpnia*, placed in the margin, calls attention to the claim.

14. In Tauelesbi[1] [Tealby (Walshcroft)] Rayner has 1 mill and 4 acres of land, and 1 villein who belongs to (*iacet in*) Sisse [Sixle].

15. M. In Wicham [West Wykeham (Louthesk)] Jalf had 1 carucate of land [assessed] to the geld. There is land for 2 teams. There* Rayner has 10 men who do not plough. T. R. E. it was worth 30 shillings; now 15 shillings.

**D. B., f. 364b. Facsimile, p. lviib.*

16. S. In Ludeforde [Ludford (Wraggoe)] there is 1 bovate of land [assessed] to the geld. There is land for 2 oxen. It is soke[land] belonging to (*in*) Wicham [West Wykeham]. 2 sokemen have half a team there, and 1 acre of meadow.

17. M. In Cadinton[2] [Keddington (Louthesk)] Jalf had 4½ bovates and the fourth part of 1 bovate of land [assessed] to the geld. There is land for 1 team. Baldwin has 1 team there [in demesne], and 7 sokemen on (*de*) 1½ bovates and a fourth part of 1 bovate have 5 oxen in a team, and 1 mill rendering 8 shillings, and 6 acres of meadow. There is a church there, and a priest, with 1 mill rendering 11 shillings. T. R. E. it was worth 20 shillings; now 25 shillings.

18. S. In Cocrinton [Cockerington (Louthesk)] there is half a bovate of land [assessed] to the geld. There is land for 2 oxen. It is soke[land]. 1 man has there 1 ox in a team.

19. S. In Salflatebi [Saltfleetby (Louthesk)] there is half a bovate of land [assessed] to the geld. There is land for half an ox. It is soke[land]. It is waste.

20. M. In Combreuorde [Cumberworth (Calcewath)] Jalf had 6 bovates of land [assessed] to the geld. There is land [*blank*]. Rayner has 1 team there [in demesne], and 9 villeins with 1 team, and 20 acres of meadow. T. R. E. and now worth 50 shillings.

21. B. In Maltetorp [Mablethorpe (Calcewath)] there is half a carucate of land [assessed] to the geld. There is land for 10 oxen. It is a berewic. 5 villeins have 1 team there, and 20 acres of meadow.

22. In Ulesbi[3] [Ulceby (Calcewath)] there are 2 bovates of land [assessed] to the geld. There is land for 1 team. It is soke[land]. It is waste.

23. M. In Cocrinton [Cockerington (Louthesk)] he[4] had 14 bovates of land [assessed] to the geld. There is land for 3½ teams. Rayner has 1 team there [in demesne], and 8 sokemen on (*de*) 1 carucate of land and 2 villeins and 4 bordars with 1 team, and the site of 1 mill, and 60 acres of meadow, and 20 acres of underwood. T. R. E. and now worth 40 shillings; tallage 10 shillings.

24. S. In Summercotes [Somercotes (Louthesk)] there is the third part of 1 carucate [assessed] to the geld. There is land [*blank*]. Three men held this land. Ilbert de Laci has the land of two, [holding] of the bishop of Bayeux (*Baiocensi*). Rayner has the land of the third man, [holding] of the king; and there he has 1 man with 1 ox.

25. S. In Alvingham [Alvingham (Louthesk)] there are 2 bovates and the sixth part of 1 bovate of land [assessed] to the geld. There is land for half a team. There [is] 1 sokeman there, and 7 acres of meadow.

---

[1] See 28/20; 70/18. [2] See 3/27; 69/9. [3] See 69/14.

[4] The name of the pre-Conquest tenant seems to have been missed out.

26. In Widcale[1] [Withcall (Louthesk)] Jalf had 15 bovates [and the third part of 1 bovate] of land [assessed] to the geld. There is land for 3 teams. Rayner has 1 team there [in demesne], and 12 sokemen on (*de*) 13 bovates and the third part of 1 bovate of this land and 2 villeins with 1½ teams, and 1 mill and the third part of 1 mill rendering 4 shillings, and 12 acres of meadow. T. R. E. and now worth 60 shillings. He has the third part of 1 church there, and he claims the other 2 parts by the witness of the wapentake.

41. LAND OF OSBERN DE ARCIS

1. M. In Scallebi and Stratone [Scawby and Sturton (Manley)] [*blank*] [and Grimbold] had 2 carucates and 3 bovates of land [assessed] to the geld. There is land for 4 teams. Alfred, Osbern's man, has 1 team there [in demesne], and 5 sokemen on (*de*) 1 carucate of this land, and 5[2] villeins with 1 team [and 1 ox]. T. R. E. it was worth 30 shillings; now 25[3] shillings; tallage 5 shillings.

2. B. In Reburne [Redbourn (Manley)] there are 2½ bovates [and the fourth part of 1 bovate] of land [assessed] to the geld. There is land for twice as many oxen. It is a berewic belonging to (*in*) Scalebi [Scawby]. [There are] 12 acres of meadow there. It is waste.

D. B., f. 364c. *Facsimile, p. lviiia.*

42. LAND OF OGER THE BRETON (*Britonis*)

1.[4] M. In Brune [Bourne (Aveland)] [Earl] Morcar had 2½ carucates of land [assessed] to the geld. There is land for 2½ teams. Oger [the Breton] has 2 teams there in demesne, and 4 sokemen on (*de*) 4 bovates of this land and 14 villeins and 4 bordars with 5 teams. There is half a church there, and a priest, and 3 mills rendering 30 shillings, and 6 fisheries rendering 2½ thousand eels, and 19 acres of meadow. There is wood[land] for pannage 1 league and 8 furlongs in length and 1 furlong in breadth. T. R. E. it was worth 100 shillings; now 8 pounds; tallage 40 shillings.

2. M. In the same place (*ibidem*) Lewin had 7 bovates of land [assessed] to the geld. There is land for 7 oxen. Oger has 3 sokemen

---

[1] See 69/11.
[2] *v* is a correction superimposed on *ii*, the original number.
[3] *xx* is written in the line, and *v* above the line.
[4] See 72/40.

there on (*de*) 4 bovates of this land and 4 villeins and 2 bordars with 2 teams. There is half a church there, and 6 fisheries rendering 24 pence, and 2 parts of a mill rendering 5 shillings, and 9 acres of meadow. There is wood⌊land⌋ for pannage 1 league and 8 furlongs in length and 4 furlongs in breadth. T. R. E. and now worth 60 shillings; tallage 20 shillings.

3. B. In Dic [Dyke (Aveland)] there is 1 carucate of land ⌊assessed⌋ to the geld. There is land for 1 team. It is a berewic belonging to (*in*) Brune [Bourne]. 2 villeins and 2 bordars have half a team there, and 9 acres of meadow, and 20 acres of wood⌊land⌋ for pannage.

4. S. In Caletorp [Cawthorpe (Aveland)] there are 2½ carucates of land ⌊assessed⌋ to the geld. There is land for as many teams. It is soke⌊land⌋. 10 sokemen have 5 teams there, and 16 acres of meadow, and 24 acres of wood⌊land⌋ for pannage.

5. S. Also in Dic and Caletorp [Dyke and Cawthorpe (Aveland)] there are 1½ carucates of land ⌊assessed to the geld⌋. There is land for 12 oxen. There are 9 sokemen there with 1 team and 2 oxen in a team, and 6 acres of meadow, and 12 acres of wood⌊land⌋ for pannage.

6.[1] S. In the same places (*ibidem*) there are 3½ bovates of land ⌊assessed⌋ to the geld. There is land for as many oxen. It is soke⌊land⌋ belonging to (*in*) Hacunesbi [Haconby].

7. B. In Spanesbi [Spanby (Aveland)] there are 4[2] bovates of land ⌊assessed⌋ to the geld. There is land for 6 oxen. It is a berewic belonging to (*in*) Brune [Bourne]. Oger has 1 team there ⌊in demesne⌋, and 18 acres of meadow. T. R. E. and now worth 10 shillings.

8. In Loctone [Laughton (Aveland)] Oger has 1 carucate of land ⌊assessed⌋ to the geld. Gilbert de Gand has soke over it.

9. Two M. In the same Loctone [Laughton] Toli and Hereward had 4 bovates of land ⌊assessed⌋ to the geld. There is land for half a team. Oger has 2 teams there in demesne, and 4 villeins having half a team, and the fourth part of 2 churches, and 10 acres of meadow, and 6 acres of underwood. T. R. E. and now worth 40 shillings.

10. B. In Aslachebi and Auetorp [Aslakeby and Avethorpe in Aslackby (Aveland)] there are 6 bovates of land ⌊assessed⌋ to the geld. There is land for 1 team. It is a berewic belonging to (*in*) Loctone [Laughton]. 2 villeins have half a team there, and 6 acres of meadow, and 2 acres of underwood.

11.[3] In Ringesdune and Repinghale [Ringstone and Rippingale (Aveland)] Oger has 1 carucate of land ⌊assessed⌋ to the geld. There is land for 1 team.

12. In Ringesdene [Ringstone] there is 1 carucate of land ⌊assessed⌋ to the geld. There is land for 1 team. Oger has it.

13.[4] M. In Repinghale [Rippingale] St. Guthlac had for the sustenance (*uictum*) of the monks 3 carucates of land ⌊assessed⌋ to the geld. There is land for 3 teams. Oger has 2 teams there ⌊in demesne⌋, and 3 sokemen on (*de*) 6 bovates of this land. There are 60 acres of meadow there. T. R. E. it was worth 40 shillings; now 60 shillings.

14.[5] In Haconesbi and Steintone [Haconby and Stenfield (Aveland)] Ulfenisc had 9 bovates of land ⌊assessed⌋ to the geld. There is land for

[1] This entry is *pro tanto* a duplicate of 61/2. See 72/41.
[2] *ii* is written in the line and *ii* above the line.
[3] See 72/46. [4] See 72/48. [5] See 72/44.

as many oxen. It is soke[land] of (*de*) Edeneham [Edenham (Beltisloe)]. Oger has 2 sokemen there on (*de*) 4 bovates of this land and 3 villeins with 1 team, and 12 acres of meadow, and 20 acres of wood[land]. T. R. E. and now worth 20 shillings.

15.[1] In Mortune and Hermodestorp [Morton and Hanthorpe (Aveland)] Ulfenisc had 5 carucates [and half a carucate* and half a bovate] of land [assessed] to the geld. There is land for as many teams. It is soke[land] of (*de*) Edeneham [Edenham (Beltisloe)]. Oger has a moiety of this land, and he has 14 sokemen and 3 bordars there with 6 teams, and 45 acres of meadow, and 40 acres of wood[land] for pannage. It is worth 40 shillings.

**D. B., f. 364*d. *Facsimile, p. lviii*b.

16. M. In the same Mortune [Morton] Quenleue had 2 carucates and half a bovate of land [assessed] to the geld. There is land for as many teams. Oger has 2 teams there [in demesne], and 2 sokemen on (*de*) 2 bovates of this land, and 8 villeins and 4 bordars with 2 teams. There is a church there, and a priest, and 18 acres of meadow, and 16 acres of underwood. T. R. E. it was worth 40 shillings; now 60 shillings.

17.[2] B. In the same Mortun [Morton] there is 1 carucate of land [assessed] to the geld. There is land for 1 team. It is inland belonging to (*in*) Haconesbi [Haconby (Aveland)]. 4 villeins have 1 team there, and 9 acres of meadow, and 16 acres of underwood. T. R. E. and now worth 10 shillings.

18.[2] S. In the same place (*ibidem*) there are 1½ bovates of land [assessed] to the geld. There is land for 2½ oxen. It is soke[land] belonging to (*in*) Haconesbi [Haconby].

19.[3] S. In the same Mortune [Morton] there is half a carucate of land [assessed] to the geld. There is land for 4 oxen. It is soke[land] of (*de*) Corninctone [Quarrington]. There are 4 villeins there with half a team, and 5 acres of meadow, and 8 acres of underwood.

43. [LAND OF] RANNULF DE SANCTO WALARICO

1. M. In Randebi [Ranby (Gartree)] Godric had 13 bovates of land [assessed] to the geld. There is land for 5 teams. Rannulf de Sancto Walarico has 3 teams there in demesne, and 14 sokemen on (*de*) 7 bovates of this land, and 3 villeins and 2 bordars with 2 teams. There is a church there, and a priest, and 1 mill rendering 10 shillings and 8 pence, and 270 acres of meadow. T. R. E. it was worth 40 shillings; now 6 pounds; tallage 40 shillings.

2. B. In Stratone [Great Sturton (Gartree)] there is 1 carucate of land [assessed] to the geld. There is land for 1 team. It is inland of the same manor. There is 1 team there in demesne, and 3 villeins and 3 bordars with 1 ox in a team, and 60 acres of meadow.

---

[1] See 24/77. [2] See 61/3; 72/42. [3] See 72/43.

3. S. In Staintone [Market Stainton (Gartree)] there are 4 carucates of land ⌊assessed⌋ to the geld. There is land for 7 teams. It is soke⌊land⌋ of the same manor. There is 1 team there in demesne, and 16 sokemen and 9 villeins and 3 bordars having 4 teams and 2 oxen in a team, and 2 mills rendering 5 shillings and 8 pence, and 80 acres of meadow.

4. S. In Burgrede [Burreth (Gartree)] there are 3 bovates and the third part of 1 bovate of land ⌊assessed⌋ to the geld. There is land for as many oxen. It is soke⌊land⌋ of the same manor. 3 sokemen and 1 villein have 3 oxen in a team there, and 15 acres of meadow, and 220 acres of wood⌊land⌋ for pannage throughout the terrritory.

5.[1] M. In Refan [Reepham (Lawress)] Godric had half a carucate of land ⌊assessed⌋ to the geld. There is land for 4 oxen. Rannulf has 1 team there ⌊in demesne⌋, and 2 villeins with 2 oxen in a team, and 12 acres of meadow. T. R. E. it was worth 10 shillings ; now 20 shillings.

6. S. In Scotorne [Scothorn (Lawress)] there are 2½ bovates of land ⌊assessed⌋ to the geld. There is land for 4 oxen. It is soke⌊land⌋ of the same manor. There is a church there and a priest having 1 team.

*D. B., f. 365*a. *Facsimile, p. lix*a.

44. LAND OF DURAND MALET

1. M. In Camelingeham [Cammeringham (Aslacoe)] Siward had half a carucate of land ⌊assessed⌋ to the geld. There is land for 6 oxen. And Elnod ⌊had⌋ half a carucate of land ⌊assessed⌋ to the geld. It is soke⌊land⌋ of the same manor. Durand Malet has 1 team there ⌊in demesne⌋, and 8[2] sokemen and 2 villeins having 5 oxen in a team. T. R. E. it was worth 20 shillings ; now 10 shillings ; tallage 3 shillings.

2. M. In Scallebi and Stratone [Scawby and Sturton (Manley)] Edwin had 9 bovates of land ⌊assessed⌋ to the geld. There is land for 2 teams. Alfred, Durand's man, has 1 team there ⌊in demesne⌋, and 3 sokemen and 1 villein and 2 bordars with 1 team. T. R. E. it was worth 15 shillings ; now 20 shillings ; tallage 5 shillings.

Soke⌊land⌋ of the same Manor

3. S. In Wintrintone [Winterton (Manley)] there are 4 bovates of land ⌊assessed⌋ to the geld. There is land for half a team. 1 sokeman has half a team there.

4. M. In Bertone and Mannebi and Castorp [Broughton and Manby and Castlethorpe (Manley)] Edwin had 3 bovates of land ⌊assessed⌋ to the geld. There is land for 1 team. It is waste. There are 10 acres of meadow there, and 10 acres of underwood. T. R. E. it was worth 10 shillings ; now 4 shillings.

5. M. In Neteltone [Nettleton (Yarborough)] Rolf had 14 bovates of land ⌊assessed⌋ to the geld. There is land for 5 teams. 2 of Durand's

[1] See 8/3 ; 71/8.

[2] *iiiii* has been altered into *viii*.

men have 2 teams there [in demesne], and 10 villeins and 5 bordars with 1 team, and 3 mills rendering 5 shillings, and a church, and 60 acres of meadow, and 60 acres of underwood. T. R. E. and now worth 4 pounds.

6. In Toresbi and Aduluesbi [North Thoresby and Autby[1] (Haverstoe)] Durand has 1 salt-pan which belongs to (*iacet in*) Rodowelle [Rothwell (Haverstoe)].

7. M. In Seurebi [Searby (Yarborough)] Rolf had 2½ carucates of land [assessed] to the geld. There is land for 5 teams. Durand has 2 teams there [in demesne], and 15 sokemen on (*de*) 1 carucate of this land and 4 villeins and 2 bordars with 3 teams. There is a church there, and 1 mill rendering 2 shillings, and 80 acres of meadow. T. R. E. it was worth 10 shillings; now 50 shillings; tallage 10 shillings.

8. M. In Cotes[2] [Great Cotes (Bradley)] Rolf had 10½ bovates of land [assessed] to the geld. There is land for 2 teams and 5 oxen. Richard, Durand's man, has 1 team there in demesne, and 10 sokemen on (*de*) 1½ bovates of this land, and 6 villeins with 2 teams. There is a church there, and a priest, and 1 mill rendering 12 shillings, and 500 acres of meadow. T. R. E. and now worth 60 shillings; tallage 20 shillings.

9. M. In Iribi [Irby on Humber (Bradley)] Rolf had 3½ carucates of land [assessed] to the geld. There is land for 7 teams. Durand has 2 teams there [in demesne], and 17 sokemen and 15 villeins with 4 teams. There is a church there, and a priest. T. R. E. it was worth 40 shillings; now 50 shillings; tallage 30 shillings.

10. M. In Lindude [Linwood (Walshcroft)] Rolf had half a carucate of land [assessed] to the geld. There is land for 2 teams. Durand has 1 team there [in demesne], and 7 villeins and 1 bordar with 1½ teams, and the third part of a church, and the third part of a mill rendering 8 pence, and 40 acres of meadow, and 100 acres of underwood. T. R. E. it was worth 30 shillings; now 20 shillings; tallage 5 shillings.

11. M. In Rodowelle [Rothwell (Haverstoe)] Rolf had 13½ bovates and the third part of 1 bovate of land [assessed] to the geld. There is land for twice as many oxen (*dupliciter ad arandum*). Durand has 1 team there [in demesne], and 3 sokemen on (*de*) 2½ bovates of this land and 6 villeins and 1 bordar with 1 team.* There are 18 acres of meadow there. T. R. E. it was worth 40 shillings; now 30 shillings.

**D. B., f. 365*b. *Facsimile, p. lix*b.

12. S. In Cucualt [Cuxwold (Haverstoe)] there are 1 bovate and 3 parts of 1 bovate [assessed] to the geld. There is land for 3½ oxen. It is soke[land] of the same manor. 2 sokemen have half a team there.

13. S. In Caburne [Cabourn (Haverstoe)] there is 1 bovate of land [assessed] to the geld. It is soke[land] of the same manor. It is waste.

14. In Aduluesbi[3] [Autby (Haverstoe)] there is 1 salt-pan. It is that which belongs to (*iacet in*) Rodewelle [Rothwell]. [Durand has it].

---

[1] Cp. 44/14. Though 'Adulvesbi' (cp. 44/14) and 'Aldulvebi' (27/16) must be identified with Autby, an extinct parish and vill, now included in North Thoresby, these names are properly the *D.B.* equivalents of Audleby in the parish of Caistor. It seems probable that the king's clerks confounded the two names

[2] See 27/3; 70/12.

[3] See 44/6.

15. In Clachesbi [Claxby on the Wolds (Walshcroft)] there are 5 bovates of land ⌊assessed⌋ to the geld. There is land for 10 oxen. It is soke⌊land⌋ belonging to (*in*) Wiham [*query* Wykeham Well (Yarborough)].

16. M. In Navenebi [Navenby (Boby)] Rolf had 1 carucate of land ⌊assessed⌋ to the geld. There is land for 10 oxen. Durand has 2 teams there in demesne, and 2 villeins with 2 oxen in a team, and 8 acres of meadow. T. R. E. it was worth 32 shillings; now 50 shillings.

17. B. In Welingoure [Wellingore (Boby)] there are 3 carucates of land ⌊assessed⌋ to the geld. There is land for 3 teams. It is a berewic of this manor. There are 2 sokemen there on (*de*) 1½ bovates of land, and 1 villein, and 11 acres of meadow.

18. S. In Aycle [Eagle (Graffoe)] there are 3 bovates of land ⌊assessed⌋ to the geld. There is land for 2 oxen. 1 sokeman has 2 oxen in a team there, and 4 acres of meadow. It is soke⌊land⌋ belonging to (*in*) Nauenebi [Navenby].

19. In Rasa [Middle Rasen (Walshcroft)] Durand has the third part of half a carucate of land, and he has there 3 villeins with 1 ox in a team.

45. LAND OF MARTIN

1. M. In Glenteurde [Glentworth (Aslacoe)] Gamel had 6 bovates of land ⌊assessed⌋ to the geld. There is land for 10 oxen. Martin has 4 sokemen and 1 villein there with 5 oxen in a team, and 30 acres of meadow. T. R. E. it was worth 8 shillings; now 10 shillings.

2. M. In Helmeswelle [Hemswell (Aslacoe)] Sperri had 10 bovates of land ⌊assessed⌋ to the geld. There is land for 14 oxen. Martin has 1 team there ⌊in demesne⌋, and 1 sokeman on (*de*) 2 bovates of this land and 4 villeins and 4 bordars with 1 team. T. R. E. ⌊it was worth⌋ 40 shillings; now 20 shillings.

3. M. In Hagetorn [Hackthorn (Aslacoe)] Suen had 3 bovates and four parts of 1 bovate of land ⌊assessed⌋ to the geld. There is land for 4 oxen. Martin has 2 villeins there having 3 oxen in a team, and 10 acres of meadow. T. R. E. and now worth 5 shillings.

4. B. In Oustorp[1] [Ewerby Thorpe (Aswardhurn)] Godric had 6 bovates of land ⌊assessed⌋ to the geld. There is land for 5 oxen. It is a berewic belonging to (*in*) Grenebi [Ewerby (Aswardhurn)]. There are 2 villeins there, and 8 acres of meadow, and 1 acre of underwood. T. R. E. it was worth 10 shillings; now 8 shillings.

---

[1] See 72/30.

46. LAND OF WALDIN THE BRETON (*Britonis*)

1.[1] M. In Hazebi [Haceby (Aveland)] Ulviet had 11 bovates of land [assessed] to the geld. There is land for 2 teams. Godwin, Waldin the Breton's man, has there 2 villeins and 2 bordars having 2 oxen in a team, and 8½ acres of meadow, and 17 acres of underwood. T. R. E. it was worth 20 shillings ; now 10 shillings.

2. S. In Orbelinge [Horbling (Aveland)] there are 6 bovates of land [assessed] to the geld. There is land for 6 oxen. It is soke[land] belonging to (*in*) Hazebi [Haceby]. Waldin has 1 bordar there, and[2] 2½ acres of meadow. T. R. E. it was worth 10 shillings ; now 4 shillings. Guy of Craon (*Wido de Credun*) has the soke.

3. M. In Wilgebi [Silk Willoughby (Aswardhurn)] Ulviet had 15 bovates of land [assessed] to the geld. There is land for 3 teams and 6 oxen. Waldin has 2 teams there [in demesne], and 8 villeins with 2 teams, and 56 acres of meadow. T. R. E. it was worth 40 shillings ; now 20 shillings.

4. M. In Stigeswalde [Stixwould (Gartree)] Ulviet had 1 carucate of land [assessed] to the geld.* There is land for 10 oxen. He has 1 team there [in demesne], and 2 fisheries rendering 4 shillings, and 40 acres of meadow, and 80 acres of underwood. T. R. E. and now [worth] 20 shillings.

**D. B., f. 365c.* *Facsimile, p. lxa.*

47. LAND OF WALDIN THE ENGINEER (*Ingeniatoris*)

1. M. In Wilchetone[3] [Willoughton (Aslacoe)] Grimchel had 17½ bovates of land [assessed] to the geld, and Sberne 2 bovates of land [assessed] to the geld. There is land for 3½ teams. Waldin the Engineer has 2 teams there [in demesne], and 17 sokemen on (*de*) 10½ bovates of this land and 7 bordars with 2 teams, and 80 acres of meadow. T. R. E. it was worth 70 shillings ; now 60 shillings ; tallage 20 shillings.

2. M. In Hagetorne [Hackthorn (Aslacoe)] Ernui had 1½ carucates of land [assessed] to the geld. There is land for 2 teams. Waldin has 1 team there [in demesne], and 3 villeins and 7 bordars with 10 oxen in a team, and half a church, and 1 mill rendering 12 pence, and 30 acres of meadow. T. R. E. and now worth 40 shillings.

3. M. In Chilebi [Keelby (Yarborough)] Eiric had 3 bovates and the third part of 1 bovate of land [assessed] to the geld. There is land

[1] See 57/18. [2] The sign for *et* is repeated. [3] See 71/11.

for 6½ oxen. William, Waldin's man, has there 1 ox in a team ⌊in demesne⌋, and 1 sokeman on (*de*) 2 tofts and 2 bordars, and 14 acres of meadow. T. R. E. and now worth 10 shillings.

4. M. In Itrebi [Itterby (Bradley)] Elaf had 2½ bovates of land ⌊assessed⌋ to the geld. There is land for 5 oxen. William, Waldin's man, has 2 oxen there in a team ⌊in demesne⌋, and 14 acres of meadow. T. R. E. it was worth 20 shillings ; now 16 shillings.

5. M. In Torgrebi [Thorganby (Walshcroft)] Ailof had 5 bovates of land ⌊assessed⌋ to the geld. There is land for 10 oxen. William, Waldin's man, has there 1 bordar and 2 sokemen on (*de*) 2 tofts, and four parts of 1 mill rendering 2 shillings, and 9 acres of meadow. T. R. E. it was worth 20 shillings ; now 10 shillings.

6. M. In Ravendale [Ravendale (Haverstoe)] Eilaf had 2 bovates of land ⌊assessed⌋ to the geld. There is land for 4 oxen. William, Waldin's man, has 1 team there ⌊in demesne⌋, and 2 villeins having 2 oxen in a team. T. R. E. it was worth 20 shillings ; now 10 shillings.

7. M. In Belesbi [Beelsby (Haverstoe)] Elaf had 1 carucate of land ⌊assessed⌋ to the geld. There is land for 2 teams. William, Waldin's man, has 1 team there ⌊in demesne⌋, and 8 villeins with 1 team, and half a mill rendering 3 shillings, and 10 acres of meadow. T. R. E. and now worth 40 shillings.

8. In Waragebi [Wragby (Wraggoe)] Godeuert had 5 [and a half] bovates of land ⌊assessed⌋ to the geld. There is land for 2 teams. Waldin has 1 team there ⌊in demesne⌋, and 3 sokemen on (*de*) 2 bovates of this land and 4 villeins and 5 bordars with 1½ teams, and the site of a mill, and 16 acres of meadow, and 240 acres of wood⌊land⌋ for pannage throughout the territory. T. R. E. it was worth 30 shillings ; now 35 shillings ; tallage 5 shillings.

9. S. In Langetone [Langton by Wragby (Wraggoe)] there are 4 bovates of land ⌊assessed⌋ to the geld. There is land for 1 team. It is soke⌊land⌋ belonging to (*in*) Waragebi [Wragby]. 6 sokemen have 1 team there, and 43 acres of underwood.

10. M. In Cheilestorne [Kelstern (Louthesk)] Clac had 2 bovates of land ⌊assessed⌋ to the geld. There is land for 4 oxen. Waldin has there 3 oxen in a team ⌊in demesne⌋, and 8 acres of meadow. T. R. E. it was worth 20 shillings ; now 5 shillings and 8 pence.

*D. B., f. 365*d. *Facsimile, p. lx*b.

48. LAND OF ODO THE ARBLASTER
(*Arbalistarii*)

1. M. In Wilchetone [Willoughton (Aslacoe)] Alestan and Odincar had 3 carucates and 3 bovates of land ⌊assessed⌋ to the geld. There is land for 4½ teams. Odo the Arblaster has 2 teams there in demesne,

and 18 sokemen on (*de*) 13½ bovates of this land and 6 villeins with 2½ teams, and 108 acres of meadow. T. R. E. it was worth 4 pounds; now 3 pounds; tallage 60 shillings.

2.[1] M. In Scallebi [Scawby (Manley)] Sbern and Grimbold had 2 carucates and 3 bovates of land ⌊assessed⌋ to the geld. There is land for 3 teams. Alfred, Odo's man, has 1 team there ⌊in demesne⌋, and 5 sokemen on (*de*) 1 carucate of this land and 4 villeins with 1 team. T. R. E. it was worth 30 shillings; now 25 shillings; tallage 5 shillings.

3. In Reburne [Redbourn (Manley)] there are 2½ bovates of land ⌊assessed⌋ to the geld. It is a berewic belonging to (*in*) Scallebi. It is waste.

4. M. In Suinhope [Swinhope (Haverstoe)] Ainar and his step-mother had 3 carucates and half a bovate and the fourth part (*iiii part'*) of 1 bovate of land ⌊assessed⌋ to the geld. There is land for 6½ teams. Odo has 2 teams there ⌊in demesne⌋, and 10 sokemen on (*de*) 10 tofts and 8 villeins and 2 bordars with 3½ teams, and 12 acres of meadow, and 1 mill rendering 5 shillings. T. R. E. it was worth 3 pounds; now 4 pounds; tallage 20 shillings.

5. M. In Neutone [Newton (Aveland)] Alsi had 7 bovates of land ⌊assessed⌋ to the geld. There is land for 10 oxen. Odo has 1 team there ⌊in demesne⌋, and 1 sokeman on (*de*) 1 bovate of this land and 5 villeins and 4 bordars with 1½ teams. There is a church there, and 12 acres of meadow, and 70 acres of wood⌊land⌋ for pannage throughout the territory. T. R. E. it was worth 4 pounds; now the like amount; tallage 40 shillings.

6. B. In Uuesbi [Ouseby (Aveland)] there are 6 bovates and the third part of 1 bovate of land ⌊assessed⌋ to the geld. There is land for as many oxen. It is a berewic belonging to (*in*) Neutone. William, Odo's man, has 3 bordars there, and half a mill rendering 3 shillings, and 9 acres of meadow.

7. B. In Trichingeham [Threckingham (Aveland)] there are 10 bovates and the third part of 2 bovates of land ⌊assessed⌋ to the geld. There is land for as many oxen. It is a berewic belonging to (*in*) Neutone. Odo has 2 sokemen there on (*de*) 2 bovates of this land and 5 villeins and 1 bordar with 1 team and 2 oxen in a team. There belongs ⌊to him⌋ there the sixth part of 1 church of Saint Peter, and the third part of 1 church of Saint Mary, and the third part of half a carucate which belongs to (*iacet in*) the church of Saint Mary.

8. M. In Hazebi [Haceby (Aveland)] Gunchil had 2 bovates of land ⌊assessed⌋ to the geld. There is land for 2 oxen. Odo has 2 oxen in a team there, and 2 acres of meadow, and 8 acres of underwood. T. R. E. it was worth 10 shillings; now 3 shillings.

9. S. In Torgrebi [Thorganby (Walshcroft)] there are 2 carucates of land ⌊assessed⌋ to the geld. There is land for 4 teams. It is soke⌊land⌋ belonging to (*in*) B[e[2]]lesbi[3] [Bleasby (Wraggoe)]. Herbert, Odo's man, has 12 sokemen there with 2 teams, and 30 acres of meadow, and 1 mill rendering 3 shillings.

---

[1] This entry refers to the same land as 41/1.

[2] Interlined as a correction.

[3] The clerk who compiled the text of nos. 9, 10, and 11 from the original returns from the wapentakes was evidently confused by the similarity of the ancient forms of Bleasby and Beelsby. The fact that Herbert is the sub-tenant in nos. 9 and 11 points to no. 9 as

10. M. In B[i[1]]lesbi[2] [Beelsby (Haverstoe)] Edric had half a carucate of land [assessed] to the geld. There is land for 1 team. Odo has 1 bordar there, and 6 acres of meadow. T. R. E. it was worth 10 shillings; now 2 shillings.

11. M. In Blasebi[2] [Bleasby (Wraggoe)] Alestan had 5 bovates and the third part of 1 bovate of land [assessed] to the geld. There is land for 12 oxen. Herbert, Odo's man, has 1 team there [in demesne], and 1 villein and 3 bordars, and 40 acres of meadow, and 42 acres of underwood. T. R. E. and now worth 20 shillings; tallage 20 shillings.

*D. B., f. 366*a. *Facsimile, p. lxi*a.

12. M. In Suarrebi [Swarby (Aswardhurn)] Godeman had 3½ bovates of land [assessed] to the geld. There is land for 6 oxen. Odo has 2 sokemen there with 10 oxen in teams, and the third part of 1 church, and 20 acres of meadow, and 12 acres of underwood. T. R. E. and now worth 10 shillings.

13. M. In Wilgebi [Silk Willoughby (Aswardhurn)] Ragenald had 2 bovates of land [assessed] to the geld. There is land for 4 oxen. Colegrim, Odo's man, has 1 bordar there, and 1 ox in a team, and 8 acres of meadow. T. R. E. it was worth 10 shillings; now 5 shillings.

14. M. In Turolfbi [Thurlby near Norton Disney (Graffoe)] Botild had 4½ carucates of land [assessed] to the geld. There is land for 3 teams. Odo has 3 sokemen there and 4 villeins and 1 bordar with 2 teams, and 3 acres of meadow. T. R. E. it was worth 20 shillings; now 16 shillings.

15. M. In Aclei [Eagle (Graffoe)] Gonchetel had 7 bovates of land [assessed] to the geld. There is land for 5 oxen. Odo has 2 villeins and 2 bordars there with half a team, and 10 acres of meadow. T. R. E. and now worth 10 shillings.

16.[3] In Duneham [Dunham (Lawress)] Odo the Arblaster has 2 carucates of land [assessed] to the geld. There is land for 2 teams. It is soke[land] belonging to (*in*) Eteleham [Nettleham (Lawress)].

being sokeland of no. 11. We may venture to reconstruct the clerk's experience. Beginning with the return from the wapentake of Walshcroft, he correctly set down *Blesbi* (= Bleasby) in no. 9. Taking the return from the wapentake of Haverstoe, he found *Belesbi* (= Beelsby) which he entered as *Blesbi* (no. 10), probably through confusion with no. 9. Coming to the return from the wapentake of Wraggoe, he found *Blasebi* (= Bleasby) which he entered correctly in no. 11. He then discovered that *Blesbi* in no. 10 referred to Beelsby and, in a clumsy attempt to correct his mistake, inserted *i* after the first letter and, still confusing the places in nos. 9 and 10, made the further mistake of inserting *e* as the second letter of Blesbi in no 9. Comparison with the *Lindsey Survey* proves that no. 10 must not be identified with Bilsby.

[1] Interlined as a correction. [2] See note to no. 9 above. [3] See 1/36.

49. LAND OF WILLIAM BLUND (*Blundi*)

1. M. In Faldingeurde [Faldingworth (Lawress)] Osulf had 2 carucates and 3 bovates of land [assessed] to the geld. There is land for as many teams and oxen. William Blund has 1 team there [in demesne], and 2 sokemen on (*de*) 5 bovates of this land and 6 villeins and 2 bordars having 6 oxen in a team, and 40 acres of meadow, and 12 acres of underwood. T. R. E. it was worth 4 pounds; now 20 shillings; tallage 5 shillings.

2. M. In Crocsbi [Croxby (Walshcroft)] Asford had 1 carucate of land [assessed] to the geld. There is land for 3 teams. William has 1 team there [in demesne], and 1 sokeman on (*de*) 2 bovates of this land and 5 villeins and 1 bordar with 1 team, and 9 acres of meadow. T. R. E. it was worth 60 shillings; now 40 shillings.

3. In Torgrebi [Thorganby (Walshcroft)] William has 1 mill rendering 3 shillings which belongs to Crocsbi, in Turgot's soke.

4. Two M. In Widcale [Withcall (Louthesk)] Godric and Siward had 2 bovates of land [assessed] to the geld. There is land for 6 oxen. William has 1 team there [in demesne], and 3 villeins with 3 oxen in a team, and 8 acres of meadow. T. R. E. and now worth 20 shillings.

5. M. In Catebi [South Cadeby (Louthesk)] Elnod had $2\frac{1}{2}$ bovates of land [assessed] to the geld. There is land for 5 oxen. William has it. T. R. E. it was worth 20 shillings; now 5 shillings.

6.[1] S. In Salflatebi and Schitebroc [Saltfleetby and Skidbrook (Louthesk)] there are 2 bovates of land [assessed] to the geld. There is land for 3 oxen. It is soke[land] belonging to (*in*) Catebi [South Cadeby]. It is waste.

50. LAND OF RESTOLD

1. M. In Glenteurde [Glentworth (Aslacoe)] Sota had 7 bovates of land [assessed] to the geld. There is land for 12 oxen. Restold has half a team there [in demesne], and 4 sokemen on (*de*) 3 bovates of this land and 1 bordar with 1 team, and 25 acres of meadow. T. R. E. it was worth 20 shillings; now 10 shillings.

---

[1] See 27/28 and 29.

*D. B., f. 366*b. *Facsimile, p. lxi*b.

51. LAND OF GODFREY OF CAMBRAI

1.[1] M. In West Depinge [West Deeping (Ness)] Azor had 2½ carucates of land ⌊assessed⌋ to the geld. There is land for as many teams. And Elmer had as much, [2½ carucates], of land ⌊assessed⌋ to the geld. There is land for as many teams. Godfrey of Cambrai has 10 villeins there having 3 teams, and 4 mills rendering 40 shillings, and 100 acres of meadow, and 8 acres of underwood. T. R. E. it was worth 8 pounds; now 6 pounds; tallage 10 shillings.

2. Three M. In Estdepinge [East Deeping (Ness)] Elmer and Erneber and Fredgist had 3 carucates and 6 bovates of land ⌊assessed⌋ to the geld. There is land for as many teams and oxen. Two of Godfrey's men have 2 teams there ⌊in demesne⌋, and 19 villeins and 4[2] bordars having 7 teams, and 93 acres of meadow. T. R. E. and now worth 100 shillings; tallage 35 shillings.

3. In the same place (*ibidem*) Saint Peter of Burg [Peterborough Abbey] had 5 sokemen upon 5 manors of (*de*) 2 carucates and 6 bovates of land ⌊assessed⌋ to the geld. There is land for as many teams and oxen. Two of Godfrey's men have 1½ teams there ⌊in demesne⌋, and 12 villeins with 3½ teams, and 1 fishery rendering 12 pence, and 70 acres of meadow. T. R. E. it was worth 60 shillings; now 50 shillings; tallage 12 shillings.

4. [*f*'[3]] M. In Bercheham [Barholme (Ness)] Aschil had 1 carucate of land ⌊assessed⌋ to the geld. There is land for 1 team. Two of Godfrey's men have half a team there ⌊in demesne⌋, and 5 sokemen on (*de*) the third part of this land, ⌊which is⌋ free soke⌊land⌋ (*frisocam*), having 2 oxen in a team, and 1 acre of meadow. T. R. E. it was worth 20 shillings; now 12 shillings; tallage 12 shillings likewise.

5. S. In Estou [Stowe (Ness)] there are 1½ bovates of land ⌊assessed⌋ to the geld. There is land for as many oxen. Five sokemen have 5 oxen in a team there. It is soke⌊land⌋ belonging to (*in*) Bercheham [Barholme]. It is worth 2 shillings.

6. S. In Griteford [Greatford (Ness)] there are 2 bovates of land ⌊assessed⌋ to the geld. There is land for 2 oxen. Euremar, Godfrey's man, has 3 sokemen there, and 4 oxen in a team, and 4 acres of meadow. Its value [*blank*].

7. M. In Cretun [Creeton (Beltisloe)] Ulf '*cilt*' had 2½ carucates of land ⌊assessed⌋ to the geld. There is land for as many teams. Godfrey has 10 villeins there with 1 team, and 7 acres of meadow, and 100 acres of underwood. T. R. E. it was worth 60 shillings; now 20 shillings.

8. S. In Bintham [Castle Bytham (Beltisloe)] there are 4 bovates of land ⌊assessed⌋ to the geld. There is land for 4 oxen. It is soke⌊land⌋. One villein has 2 oxen in a team there, and 1 acre of meadow.

---

[1] See 51/11.

[2] *ii* is written in the line and *ii* above the line.

[3] This letter in the margin draws attention to the statement that part of the land is *frisoca*.

9. In the wood of Westbitham [Little Bytham (Beltisloe)] Godfrey has 40 acres for 8 pence of warnode.

10. In Tisteltune [Thistleton (Alstoe Wapentake, co. Rutland)] Turuert had 1½ carucates ⌊assessed⌋ to the geld. There is land for 12 oxen. Gleu, Godfrey's man, has 1 sokeman and 3 bordars there with half a team, and 15 acres of wood⌊land⌋, and 40 acres belonging to Drew's warnode (*in warnode Drogonis*). T. R. E. it was worth 20 shillings; now 10 shillings.

11.[1] In Helpericham [Helpringham (Aswardhurn)] Azor[2] had 1 church to which belong (*in qua iacent*) 4 bovates of land and 4 acres of meadow. Godfrey has it, and it belongs to (*iacent in*) Depinge [Deeping⌋.

12. M. In Wiuelesforde [Wilsford (Threo)] Siward had 9 carucates of land ⌊assessed⌋ to the geld. There is land for 12 teams. Of this land Azor his brother had 6 bovates and 1 mill quit from all service except the host (*exercitum*). Godfrey has 3 teams there ⌊in demesne⌋, and 12 sokemen on (*de*) 3 carucates of this land and 6 villeins and 2 bordars having 6 teams. There is a church there to which belong 2 bovates of this land, and 45 acres of meadow, and 20 acres of underwood. T. R. E. and now worth 4 pounds; tallage 20 shillings.

Bishop R⌊emigius⌋ bought this manor of Godfrey for the church of Saint Mary of Lincole [Lincoln].[3]

D. B., f. 366c. *Facsimile, p. lxiia.*

52. LAND OF GUNFRID DE CIOCHES

1.[4] M. In Casuic [Casewick (Ness)] Azor had 10 bovates of land ⌊assessed⌋ to the geld. There is land for 10 oxen. Gunfrid de Cioches has 1 team there ⌊in demesne⌋, and 5 villeins and 5 bordars with 1 team, and half a mill rendering 12 shillings, and 6 acres of meadow. T. R. E. and now ⌊worth⌋ 40 shillings.

2. M. In Pochintone [Pointon (Aveland)] Erneber had 2 bovates of land ⌊assessed⌋ to the geld. There is land for 2 oxen. There is 1 villein there, and 3 acres of meadow, and 40 acres of underwood. T. R. E. it was worth 10 shillings; now 3 shillings.

---

[1] See 51/1.
[2] The clerk first wrote *Ascer*, and then interlined *zor* above the *scer*; but he did not cancel the *scer*.
[3] This sentence is written at the foot of the column, in the bottom margin.
[4] See 24/35; 72/3.

53. LAND OF OSBERN THE PRIEST

1. M. In Faldingurde [Faldingworth (Lawress)] Turuert had 10 bovates of land [assessed] to the geld. There is land for as many oxen. Osbern the priest has 1 team there [in demesne], and 2 sokemen on (*de*) 2 bovates of this land and 2 villeins and 1 bordar, and 12 acres of meadow, and 1 acre of underwood. T. R. E. and now worth 20 shillings.

2. M. In Binnibroc [Binbrook (Walshcroft)] Chetelbar had 9 bovates and 3 parts of 1 bovate of land [assessed] to the geld. There is land [*blank*]. Osbern the priest has 1 team there [in demesne], and 4 sokemen on (*de*) 1 bovate of this land and 13 villeins and 7 bordars with 1½ teams. There is a church there, and 1 mill rendering 5 shillings, and 12 acres of meadow. T. R. E. and now worth 50 shillings.

54. [LAND] OF THE SAME OSBERN AND OF RALPH [THE SEWER]

1.[1] Two M. In Merestune [Marston (Loveden)] Turuert and another Turuert had 6 carucates of land [assessed] to the geld. There is land for 8 teams. Ralph the sewer (*dapifer*) and Osbern the priest have 2½ teams there [in demesne], and 3 sokemen on (*de*) 4½ bovates of this land and 10 villeins and 5 bordars with 2 teams, and 2 mills rendering 22 shillings, and 80 acres of meadow. T. R. E. and now worth 4 pounds.

2. S. In Barchestune [Barkston (Threo)] there is 1 carucate of land [assessed] to the geld. There is land for 1 team. It is soke[land] of this manor. There are 7½ acres of meadow there.

55. LAND OF ANSGOT

1. M. In Buruelle [Burwell (Louthesk)] Godric had 2 carucates of land [assessed] to the geld. There is land for 8 teams. Ansgot has 3 teams there in demesne, and 23 villeins and 6 bordars with 6 teams. There is a church there, and 1 mill rendering 3 shillings, and wood[land] for pannage 1 league in length and 1 in breadth. T. R. E. it was worth 16 pounds; now 15 pounds; tallage 40 shillings.

---

[1] See 72/39.

2. S. In Agetorp [Authorpe (Louthesk)] there are 2 carucates of land [assessed] to the geld. There is land for 3 teams. It is soke[land] of the same manor. There are 4 sokemen and 5 villeins and 1 bordar there with 2 teams, and 8 acres of meadow.

3. M. In Machetone [Muckton (Louthesk)] Turuerd had 12 bovates of land [assessed] to the geld. There is land for 3 teams. Ansgot has 1 team there [in demesne], and 2 sokemen and 5 villeins and 2 bordars with $1\frac{1}{2}$ teams. There is a church there, and 7 acres of meadow. There is underwood 1 league in length and 4 furlongs in breadth. T. R. E. it was worth 30 shillings; now 20 shillings.

4. In Welletone [Welton le Wold (Louthesk)] Ansgot has 1 villein with half a team. There is land there [assessed] to the geld, 2 bovates. There is land for 5 oxen. It is worth 5 shillings.

*D.B., f. 366*d. *Facsimile, p. lxii*b.

56. LAND OF THE COUNTESS JUDITH

1. M. In Widme [North Witham (Beltisloe)] Edward '*cilt*' had 5 carucates of land [assessed] to the geld. There is land for 5 teams. Countess Judith, and Bernard under her, has 2 teams in demesne, and 2 salt-pans rendering 10 shillings,[1] and 41 acres of meadow. T. R. E. it was worth 6 pounds; now 8 pounds; tallage 20 shillings.

2. S. In Tuiuorde [Twyford (Beltisloe)] there are $5\frac{1}{2}$ carucates of land [assessed] to the geld. There is land for 7 teams. It is soke[land]. 8 sokemen and 6 villeins have 4 teams there, and 16 acres of meadow. There is wood[land] for pannage throughout the territory 9 furlongs and 9 perches in length and 6 furlongs in breadth.

3. S. In Suinhamstede [Swinstead (Beltisloe)] there are 2 carucates of land [assessed] to the geld. There is land for 2 teams. It is soke[land]. 8 sokemen have 2 teams there, and 4 acres of meadow, and 100 acres of wood[land] for pannage less 4.

4. In Offintone[2] [Uffington (Ness)] Leuric, abbot of Saint Peter of Burg [Peterborough], had 60 acres of land exempt from geld (*sine geldo*). Countess Judith has this land. On it she has no cattle (*In ea nil pecunie habet*), but tills it as belonging to (*in*) the manor of Belmestorp (*sed colit eam in Belmestorp M.*) [Belmesthorpe (Martinsley Wapentake, co. Rutland)]. It is worth 10 shillings.

5. M. In Hacham [Hougham (Loveden)] Estori had 5 carucates of land [assessed] to the geld. There is land for 3 teams. Bishop Remigius has this manor under (*de*) her, and he has there 9 villeins and 2 bordars, and 1 mill rendering 5 shillings and 4 pence, and the site of 1 mill rendering 13 shillings and 4 pence, and 10 acres of meadow. T. R. E. [it was worth] 20 shillings; now 50 shillings.

---

[1] *x solid'* is seemingly a correction of *ii solid'*.
[2] See 8/33; 72/2.

6. M. In Magna Pantone[1] [Great Ponton (Winnibriggs)] Grimber and Elmer had 8 carucates of land [assessed] to the geld. There is land for 6 teams. Nigel, the countess' man, has 1 team there [in demesne], and 3 villeins and 1 bordar with half a team, and 5 mills rendering 44 shillings. There is underwood 16 furlongs in length and 4 furlongs in breadth, and 3 acres of meadow. T. R. E. it was worth 100 shillings : now the like amount.

7. M. In Parva Pantone [Little Ponton (Winnibriggs)] Turvert had 10 carucates of land [assessed] to the geld. There is land for 10 teams. Nigel has of the countess 1 team there [in demesne], and 8 sokemen on (*de*) 3 carucates of this land and 12 villeins and 3 bordars with 5 teams, and 4 mills rendering (*de*) 63 shillings. There is underwood 6 furlongs in length and 5½ furlongs in breadth. T. R. E. and now worth 6 pounds.

8. M. In Germuntorp [Ganthorpe in Great Ponton and North Stoke (Winnibriggs)] Turuert and Grimbert had 1 carucate and 6 bovates of land [assessed] to the geld. There is land for 2 teams. Nigel has of the countess half a team there [in demesne], and 11 villeins with 1½ teams, and 3 mills rendering (*de*) 25 shillings and 4 pence, and 16 acres of meadow, and 30 acres of underwood. T. R. E. it was worth 50 shillings ; now 40 shillings.

9. M. In Stapleforde [Stapleford (Graffoe)] Morcar had 10 carucates of land [assessed] to the geld. There is land for 5 teams. Osbern has of the countess 2 teams there [in demesne], and 27 sokemen on (*de*) 6 carucates and 6 bovates of this land and 3 villeins and 3 bordars with 7 teams. There is a priest there, and a church, with half a carucate of this land. And there are 5 furlongs of meadow in length and 60 perches in breadth. T. R. E. it was worth 7 pounds ; now 8 pounds ; tallage 40 shillings.

10. S. In Nortune [Norton Disney (Graffoe)] there are 12 carucates of land [assessed] to the geld. There is land for 7 teams. Judith has there 7 sokemen and 11 villeins with 5 teams, and 12 acres of meadow. There is underwood 6 furlongs in length and 1 in breadth.

11. M. In Overtone and Stratone [Market Overton and Stretton (Alstoe Wapentake, co. Rutland)] Earl Waltef had 3½ carucates of land [assessed] to the geld. There is land for 12 teams. Countess Judith has 3 teams there in demesne, and 35 villeins and 8 bordars with 9 teams,* and 40 acres of meadow, and wood[land] for pannage 1 league in length and half [a league] in breadth. T. R. E. it was worth 12[2] pounds ; now 40 pounds.[3]

**D. B., f. 367a.* *Facsimile, p. lxiiia.*

12. M. In Tistertune [Thistleton (Alstoe Wapentake, co. Rutland)] Erich had half a carucate of land [assessed] to the geld. There is land for 1 team. Hugh, the countess' man, has 1 team there [in demesne], and 6 villeins with 1 team. T. R. E. it was worth 20 shillings ; now 40 shillings.[4]

---

[1] See 72/19.
[2] *x* is written in the line and *ii* above the line.
[3] This entry is repeated in the Rutland section of *Domesday Book* (folio 293c), where *berewic* is interlined above *Stratone*, and at the end is added, 'Alured de Lincole calumniatur quartam partem in Stratune,' while the present value is given as 'twenty pounds.' In the Lincolnshire text, the figures of the values seem to have been altered, and the present value might perhaps be read as *xx libras*, as in the Record Commission text of the Rutland section.
[4] This entry is repeated in the Rutland section (folio 293c).

13. M. In Wichingedene [Whissendine (Alstoe Wapentake, co. Rutland)] [Earl] Wallef had 4 carucates of land [assessed] to the geld. There is land for 12 teams. Hugh, the countess' man, has 5 teams there in demesne, and 27 villeins and 7 bordars with 8 teams. There is meadow 10 furlongs in length and 8 furlongs in breadth.[1]

14. M. In Akeley [Eagle (Graffoe)] [Earl] Wallef had 8 carucates of land [assessed] to the geld. There is land for 6 teams. Countess Judith has 2 teams there [in demesne], and 18 villeins and 1 bordar with 4 teams. There is a church there, and a priest, and meadow 15 furlongs in length and 1 in breadth. There is wood[land] 14 furlongs in length and 4 in breadth. T. R. E. it was worth 10 pounds; now 12 pounds.

15. S. and B. In Turulfbi [Thurlby near Norton Disney (Graffoe)] there are 7½ carucates of land [assessed] to the geld. There is land for 3 teams and 6 oxen. It is inland and soke[land] belonging to (*in*) Acley [Eagle]. There are 14 sokemen there with 4 teams.

16. S. In Sunderby [Swinderby (Graffoe)] there are 11 carucates of land [assessed] to the geld. It is soke[land] belonging to (*in*) Acley [Eagle]. There is land for 6 teams. Countess Judith has 49 sokemen there having 13 teams. There is wood[land] for pannage 8 furlongs in length and 5 in breadth, a moiety of it being feeding land (*pascuę*) and the other moiety underwood.

In Rotelande [Rutland]

17. M. In Exentune [Exton (Alstoe Wapentake, co. Rutland)] [Earl] Wallef had 2 carucates of land [assessed] to the geld. There is land for 12 teams. Countess Judith has 3 teams there [in demesne], and 37 villeins with 8 teams, and 2 mills rendering 13 shillings. There is meadow 6 furlongs in length. There is wood[land] for pannage throughout the territory 5 furlongs in length and 5 in breadth. T. R. E. it was worth 8 pounds; now 10 pounds.[2]

Likewise in Rotelande[3] [Rutland]

18. M. In Witewelle [Whitwell (Alstoe Wapentake, co. Rutland)] Besy had 1 carucate of land [assessed] to the geld. There is land for 3 teams. Herbert, the countess' man, has 1 team there [in demesne], and 6 villeins and 4 bordars with 2 teams. There is a church there, and a priest, and 1 mill rendering 12 pence, and 20 acres of meadow. There is wood[land] for pannage 6 furlongs and 6 perches in length and 3 furlongs and 13 perches in breadth. It is worth 40 shillings.[4]

19. M. In Coleby [Coleby (Boby)] Archil had 5 carucates of land [assessed] to the geld. There is land for 5 teams. Countess Judith has 1 team there [in demesne], and 1 sokeman on (*de*) 1 carucate of this land and 6 villeins with 1 team, and 30 acres of meadow. T. R. E. it was worth 60 shillings; now 40 shillings.

---

[1] This entry is repeated in the Rutland section (i, f. 293c), which omits all reference to the meadow, gives the number of pre-Conquest manors as two instead of one, and the number of bordars as six instead of seven. It also gives the name of the countess' tenant as *Hugo de Hotot.*

[2] This entry is repeated in the Rutland section (i, f. 293c).

[3] This title is written in the margin.

[4] This entry is repeated in the Rutland section (i, f. 293c), which adds the value T. R. E., *i.e.* 20 shillings.

20. S. In Wimme [South Witham (Beltisloe)] there are 2 carucates of land ⌊assessed⌋ to the geld. There is land for 2 teams. It is soke⌊land⌋ belonging to (*in*) Ouretone [Market Overton (Alstoe Wapentake, co. Rutland)]. 13 sokemen and 2 villeins [and 1 bordar] have 3 teams there. There is half a church there, and 60 acres of meadow, and 100 acres of wood⌊land⌋.

21. S. In Tisteltone [Thistleton (Alstoe, co. Rutland)] there are 6 bovates of land ⌊assessed⌋ to the geld. There is land for 6 oxen. It is soke⌊land⌋ of the same manor. 2 bordars have 2 oxen in a team there. It is worth 10 shillings. Hugh holds it.

22. B. In Bichere [Bicker (Kirton)] there are 1½ bovates of land ⌊assessed⌋ to the geld. There is land for 2 oxen. It is inland belonging to (*in*) Wime [South Witham]. It is waste except for 1 salt-pan.

23. In Mentinges [Minting (Gartree)] William [the priest] has 2½ bovates and the sixth part of 1 bovate ⌊of land⌋ ⌊assessed⌋ to the geld. There is land for 6 oxen. It is worth 2 shillings.

*D. B., f. 367*b. *Facsimile, p. lxiii*b.

57. LAND OF GUY OF CRAON (*Credon*)

1. M. In Achesbi [Ashby cum Fenby (Haverstoe)] Aslac had 9 bovates of land ⌊assessed⌋ to the geld. There is land for 2½ teams. Alfred, Guy of Craon's man, has 2 teams there ⌊in demesne⌋, and 9 sokemen on (*de*) 3 bovates of this land and 3 villeins with 1 team, and 30 acres of meadow, and 9½ acres of underwood. T. R. E. it was worth 40 shillings ; now 4 pounds ; tallage 40 shillings.

SOKE⌊LAND⌋ OF THIS MANOR

2. S. In Ravenedale [Ravendale (Haverstoe)] there are 10 bovates of land ⌊assessed⌋ to the geld. There is land for 2½ teams. 10 sokemen have 2½ teams there.

3. S. In Brigelai [Brigsley (Haverstoe)] there are 6 bovates of land ⌊assessed⌋ to the geld. There is land for 12 oxen. 8 sokemen and 1 bordar have 1 team there, and 5 acres of meadow.

4. S. In Wade [Waith (Haverstoe)] there are 5½ bovates of land ⌊assessed⌋ to the geld. There is land for as many oxen. 6 sokemen have 1 team there, and 10 acres of meadow.

5. Two M. In Normanebi and Santone [Normanby in Burton on Stather and Santon (Manley)] Sbern and Chetel had 7 bovates of land ⌊assessed⌋ to the geld. There is land for as many oxen. Alfred, Guy's man, has 1½ teams there ⌊in demesne⌋, and 2 villeins and 2 bordars with half a team, and 60 acres of meadow. T. R. E. it was worth 20 shillings ; now 15 shillings ; tallage 5 shillings.

6. M. In Binnibroc and Erforde [Binbrook and Irford (Walshcroft)] Edward had 10 bovates of land ⌊assessed⌋ to the geld. There is land for

3½ teams. Alfred, Guy's man, has 2 teams there ⌊in demesne⌋, and 1 mill rendering 5 shillings, and 12 acres of meadow. T. R. E. and now worth 40 shillings.

7. M. In Lacestone [Laughton (Corringham)] Ulgrim had 2 carucates and 2 bovates of land ⌊assessed⌋ to the geld. There is land for 3 teams. Alfred, Guy's man, has 2 teams there ⌊in demesne⌋, and 9 sokemen on (*de*) 10 bovates of this land and 8 villeins and 4 bordars with 3 teams, and 17 acres of meadow, and 12 acres of underwood. T. R. E. it was worth 60 shillings ; now the like amount ; tallage 40 shillings.

SOKE⌊LAND⌋ OF THIS MANOR

8. S. In Blitone [Blyton (Corringham)] there are 14 bovates of land ⌊assessed⌋ to the geld. There is land for 2 teams.

9. In Scotone [Scotton (Corringham)] Guy has 2 bovates of land.

10. M. In Repinghale [Rippingale (Aveland)] Adestan had 3 carucates of land ⌊assessed⌋ to the geld. There is land for 3 teams. Now Widald, Guy's man, has 1 team there ⌊in demesne⌋, and 10 villeins and 2 bordars with 5 teams, and 60 acres of meadow, and 16 acres of underwood. T. R. E. it was worth 4 pounds ; now 3 pounds.

SOKE⌊LAND⌋ OF THIS MANOR

11. S. In Loctone [Laughton near Folkingham (Aveland)] there are 5 bovates and the third part of 1 bovate of land ⌊assessed⌋ to the geld. There is land for as many oxen. Warner, Guy's man, has 3 bordars there, and 10 acres of underwood. T. R. E. and now worth 10 shillings.

12. M. In Dusebi[1] [Dowsby (Aveland)] Offram had in pledge (*in uadimonio*) 3 carucates of land ⌊assessed⌋ to the geld. There is land for 3 teams. Hernald son of Ansgot redeemed (*disuadiauit*) this land before Guy was seised of Offram's land, and afterwards Guy always had the service. There is 1 team there in demesne, and 3 villeins with 1 team, and 31 acres of meadow. T. R. E. and now worth 30 shillings.

13. M. In Pochintone [Pointon (Aveland)] Adestan had 1 carucate of land ⌊assessed⌋ to the geld. There is land for 1 team. Warner, Guy's man, has 1 team there ⌊in demesne⌋, and 20 acres of underwood. T. R. E. it was worth 20 shillings ; now 30 shillings.

14. M. In Scachertorp [Scottlethorpe (Beltisloe)] Adestan had 1 carucate of land ⌊assessed⌋ to the geld.* There is land for 1 team. Guy until now held it in soke, and now it is deraigned as a chief manor (*est deratiocinatum capitale M.*) to the king's use. There is 1 carucate there in demesne, and 1 villein and 2 bordars having 2 oxen in a team. There is 1 acre of meadow there, and 1 acre of underwood. T. R. E. it was worth 20 shillings ; now 10 shillings.

**D. B., f. 367c.* *Facsimile, p. lxiva.*

15. M. In Osbernedebi[2] [Osbournby (Aveland)] Alfric had 2 carucates of land ⌊assessed⌋ to the geld. There is land for 3 teams. Vitalis, Guy's man, has 1 team there ⌊in demesne⌋, and 1 sokeman on (*de*) 1 carucate of this land and 5 villeins and 3 bordars with 1½ teams, and 24 acres of meadow. T. R. E. it was worth 40 shillings ; now 6 pounds.

---

[1] See 67/23 ; 72/49. [2] See 72/53.

16. S. In Dembelbi [Dembleby (Aveland)] there are 6 bovates of land [assessed] to the geld. There is land for 2 teams. It is soke[land] belonging to (*in*) Osbernedebi [Osbournby]. One sokeman and 2 villeins have 1 team there, and 14 acres of meadow, and 20 acres of underwood.

17. In Wilgebi [Scot Willoughby (Aveland)] Guy has the soke over half a church and over a priest who belongs to Osbernedebi [Osbournby].

18. M. In Hazebi[1] [Haceby (Aveland)] Alfric had 11 bovates of land [assessed] to the geld. There is land for 2 teams. Godwin, Guy's man, has 1 team there [in demesne], and 1 sokeman and 1 villein and 1 bordar having 2 oxen in a team. There is a priest there, and a church, and 8½ acres of meadow, and 18 acres of underwood. T. R. E. it was worth 20 shillings; now 30 shillings. Waldin claims this land of the gift of the king. Guy has soke over 11 bovates of Waldin's land, as the wapentake bears witness.

19. M. In Suavintone [Swaton (Aveland)] Adestan had 1 carucate of land [assessed] to the geld. There is land for 11 oxen. Warner, Guy's man, has 1 team there [in demesne], and 1 villein with 2 oxen in a team, and 8 acres of meadow. T. R. E. it was worth 40 shillings; now 10 shillings.

20. In Horbelinge [Horbling (Aveland)] Guy has soke over 6 bovates of Waldin's land.

21. S. In Haidure [Haydour (Threo)] there are 4 carucates of land [assessed] to the geld. There is land for 5 teams. It is soke[land] belonging to (*in*) Osbernedebi [Osbournby (Aveland)]. 24 sokemen and 3 bordars have 6 teams there, and 80 acres of meadow, and 16 acres of underwood. There is a priest there and a church.

22. M. In Wellebi[2] [Welby (Threo)] Adestan had 4 carucates of land [assessed] to the geld. There is land for 4 teams. Ranulf, Guy's man, has 2 teams there [in demesne], and 5 sokemen on (*de*) 3 carucates and 2 bovates of this land and 3 villeins with 2 teams, and 53[3] acres of meadow, and 80 acres of underwood. T. R. E. it was worth 40 shillings; now 60 shillings.

23. M. In Herigerbi [Harrowby (Threo)] Algar had 1 carucate of land [assessed] to the geld. There is land for 10 oxen. The same Algar [holding] of Guy has 1 carucate there in demesne, and 1 mill rendering (*de*) 4 shillings, and 9 acres of meadow. T. R. E. and now worth 10 shillings.

24. M. In Tudetorp [Towthorpe in Londonthorpe (Threo)] Algar had 2½ carucates of land [assessed] to the geld. There is land for as many teams. Ranulf, Guy's man, has 1 team there in demesne, and 2 sokemen on (*de*) 2 bovates of this land and 5 villeins and 6 bordars with 1 team. There is a priest there, and a church, and 3 mills rendering 40 shillings, and 17 acres of meadow. T. R. E. and now worth 60 shillings.

SOKE[LAND] OF THIS MANOR

25. S. In Beltone[4] [Belton (Threo)] there is half a carucate of land [assessed] to the geld. There is land for 4 oxen. There is 1 sokeman there with half a team, and 9 acres of meadow.

---

[1] See 26/45; 46/1.

[2] See 72/58.

[3] *l* is written in the line and *iii* above the line.

[4] See 72/60; cp. 67/13.

26. S. In Gunfordebi [Gonerby (Winnibriggs)] there are 3 bovates and half a bovate of land [assessed] to the geld. There is land for 3 oxen. 2 sokemen and 1 villein have 1½ teams there, and 7½ acres of meadow, and a mill rendering 5 shillings.

*D. B., f. 367*d. *Facsimile, p. lxiv*b.

27. M. In Wibertone [Wyberton (Kirton)] Adestan had 11 bovates of land [assessed] to the geld. There is land for 14½ oxen. Guy has 2 teams there in demesne, and 10 acres of meadow; and 2 bordars. T. R. E. it was worth 60 shillings ; now 50 shillings.

28. M. In Frantune [Frampton (Kirton)] Adestan had 4 carucates and 2 bovates of land [assessed] to the geld. There is land for 5½ teams. [Guy] has 2 teams there in demesne, and 2 sokemen on (*de*) 4 bovates of this land and 10 villeins and 1 bordar having 2½ teams. There is a church there, and a priest, and 60 acres of meadow. T. R. E. it was worth 70 shillings ; now the like amount ; tallage 10 shillings.

29. M. In Chirchetune [Kirton (Kirton)] Alfric had 14 bovates and 2 parts of 1 bovate of land [assessed] to the geld. There is land for 17 oxen. Guy has 1 team there in demesne, and 2 sokemen on (*de*) 1 bovate of this land having 3 oxen in a team, and 16 acres of meadow. T. R. E. it was worth 20 shillings ; now 30 shillings.

30. M. In Burtun [Burton Pedwardine (Aswardhurn)] Adestan had 10 carucates of land [assessed] to the geld. There is land for 17 teams. Guy has 5 teams there [in demesne], and 30 sokemen and 9 villeins and 12 bordars having 11½ teams. There is a priest there, and a church, and 1 mill rendering 2 shillings, and 120 acres of meadow. T. R. E. it was worth 6 pounds ; now 8 pounds ; tallage 40 shillings.

31. S. In Hechintune [Heckington (Aswardhurn)] there are 4 bovates of land [assessed] to the geld. There is land for 4 oxen. It is soke[land]. There are 2 villeins there and 1 bordar having 3 oxen in a team, and 3 acres of meadow.

32. S. In Aswardebi [Aswarby (Aswardhurn)] there are 4 bovates of land [assessed] to the geld. There is land for 1 team. It is soke[land] belonging to (*in*) Marram [Mareham (Aswardhurn)]. One sokeman and 1 bordar have half a team there, and 20 acres of meadow.

33. M. In Suarrebi [Swarby (Aswardhurn)] Alfric had 2 bovates of land [assessed] to the geld. There is land for 4 oxen. Vitalis, Guy's man, has 1 team there [in demesne], and 16 sokemen and 3 villeins having 2½ carucates, and 80 acres of meadow, and 80 acres of underwood. T. R. E. it was worth 20 shillings ; now the like amount.

SOKE[LAND] OF THIS MANOR

34. S. In Chillebi [Kelby (Aswardhurn)] there is 1 bovate of land [assessed] to the geld. There is land for 2 oxen. There Aschil the priest has under Guy 2 villeins having 3 oxen in a team.

35. B. In Merestune [Marston (Loveden)] there are 6 bovates of land [assessed] to the geld. It is a berewic belonging to (*in*) Hazebi[1] [Haceby (Aveland)]. Osbert has 3 oxen in a team there, and 12 acres of meadow. It is worth 10 shillings.

---

[1] See 57/18.

36. M. In Werangle [Wrangle (Skirbeck)] Adestan had 2 carucates of land [assessed] to the geld. There is land for 1 team. Guy has it, and it is waste on account of the action (*fluxum*) of the sea.

37. M. In Toft [Fishtoft (Skirbeck)] Adestan had 9 carucates of land [assessed] to the geld. There is land for as many teams. Guy has 3 teams there [in demesne], and 1 sokeman and 9 villeins and 1 bordar having 4 teams. There is a church there, and a priest, and 1 mill rendering 10 shillings, and 60 acres of meadow. T. R. E. it was worth 8 pounds; now 10 pounds.

38. M. In Butruic [Butterwick (Skirbeck)] Wlward had 12 carucates of land [assessed] to the geld. There is land for 12 teams. Guy has 2 teams there [in demesne], and 36 sokemen on (*de*) 9 carucates of this land and 6 villeins and 10 bordars having 15 teams. There are 2 churches there, and 2 priests, and 100 acres of meadow. T. R. E. and now worth 10 pounds; tallage 100 shillings.

SOKE[LAND] OF THIS MANOR

39. S. In Fristune [Frieston (Skirbeck)] there are 12 carucates of land [assessed] to the geld. There is land for as many teams. 20 sokemen and 26 villeins and 15 bordars have 15 teams there. Of this soke[land] 2 of Guy's men have 5 carucates and 1 bovate, and they have 2½ teams there [in demesne], and 5 sokemen and 12 villeins having 1½ teams.

40. In Trichingeham [Threckingham (Aveland)] Guy has 2 bovates of Gilbert de Gand's land of which the soke belongs to Folchingham (*de qua est soca in Folchingham*) [Folkingham (Aveland)].

*D. B., f. 368*a. *Facsimile, p. lxv*a.

41. M. In Chisebi [Keisby in Lavington (Beltisloe)] Offram had 2 carucates of land [assessed] to the geld. There is land for 3 teams. Guy has 1 team there [in demesne], and 2 villeins and 4 bordars having 1½ teams, and 24 acres of meadow, and 60 acres of underwood. T. R. E. it was worth 40 shillings; now 30 shillings.

42. B. In Auetorp [Avethorpe (Aveland)] there are 4 bovates of land [assessed] to the geld. There is land for 6 oxen. It is a berewic of the same manor. 2 villeins have 1 team there, and 8 acres of meadow. It is worth 10 shillings.

43. S. In Summerdebi [Somerby (Threo)] Adelid [had] 6 bovates of land [assessed] to the geld. There is land for 6 oxen. This soke[land] was such that it used to render nothing, but used to help in the king's host (*adiuabat in exercitu regis*) on land and at sea. Guy has 5 oxen there in a team, and 5 acres of underwood. T. R. E. and now worth 5 shillings.

44. M. In Bichere[1] [Bicker (Kirton)] Adestan had 10 bovates of land [assessed] to the geld. There is land for as many oxen. Guy has 1 team there [in demesne], and 4 villeins and 4 bordars with half a team, and 1 salt-pan rendering 16 pence, and 20 acres of meadow. T. R. E. and now worth 20 shillings.

45. M. In Sudtorp [Southorpe in Edenham (Beltisloe)] Offram had 2 carucates of land [assessed] to the geld. There is land for 2 teams. Guy has 2 teams there [in demesne], and 10 villeins and 6 bordars with 2

---

[1] See 73/2.

teams, and 1 mill rendering 2 shillings, and 16 acres of meadow, and 200 acres of wood[land] for pannage. T. R. E. it was worth 40 shillings ; now 50 shillings ; tallage 10 shillings.

46. M. In Schillintune [Skillington (Beltisloe)] Colbert had 1 carucate of land [assessed] to the geld. There is land for 12 oxen. Guy has 5 villeins there with 1 team, and 20 acres of meadow, and 20 acres of wood[land] for pannage belonging to Algar's warnode (*in warnode Algari*), and 20 acres of underwood belonging to the warnode of the archbishop (*in warnode archiepiscopi*). T. R. E. and now worth 20 shillings.

47. M. In Chaschingetorp [Casthorpe in Barrowby (Winnibriggs)] Algar had 1 carucate of land [assessed] to the geld. There is land for 10 oxen. The same Algar has it, [holding] of Guy. There is 1 team there [in demesne], and 3 villeins and 2 bordars have 5 oxen in a team, and 8 acres of meadow. T. R. E. it was worth 16 shillings ; now 20 shillings.

48. M. In Hogtone [Houghton in Grantham (Winnibriggs)] Alestan had 3 carucates and 2 bovates [and a half] of land [assessed] to the geld. There is land for as many teams and oxen. Vitalis, Guy's man, has 1 team there [in demesne], and 1 sokeman on (*de*) 1 bovate of this land and 10 villeins and 4 bordars having 2½ teams, and 2 mills rendering 26[1] shillings and 8 pence, and 3 acres of meadow. T. R. E. it was worth 4 pounds ; now 3 pounds.

SOKE[LAND] BELONGING TO (*in*) HOGTONE [HOUGHTON]

49. S. In Tudetorp [Towthorpe in Londonthorpe (Threo)] there are 2 bovates of land [assessed] to the geld. There is land for 2 oxen. There are 3 acres of meadow there.

50. M. In Holobech and Copelade [Holbeach and Whaplode (Elloe)] Alestan had 2 carucates and 2 bovates of land [assessed] to the geld. There is land for 12 oxen.[2] Guy has 1 team there [in demesne], and 4 villeins and 1 bordar with 1 team, and 10 acres of meadow. T. R. E. it was worth 100 shillings ; now 8 pounds.

SOKE[LAND] OF THIS MANOR

51. S. In Stith [*query* Tydd (Elloe)] there are 12 bovates of land [assessed] to the geld. There is land for 1 team. There is 1 sokeman and 1 villein there having 2 oxen in a team.

52. S. In Pincebec [Pinchbeck (Elloe)] there are 2 carucates of land [assessed] to the geld. There is land for 2 teams. Guy has 7 villeins with 1 team there.

53. S. In Westune and Multune [Weston and Moulton (Elloe)] there are 15 bovates of land [assessed] to the geld. There is land for 15 teams. 6 villeins have half a team there.

*D. B., f. 368*b. *Facsimile, p. lxv*b.

54. M. In Spallinge [Spalding (Elloe)] Alestan had 11 bovates of land [assessed] to the geld. There is land [*blank*]. Guy has 1 team there [in demesne], and 5 villeins and 2 bordars with 1 team, and a plot of land with salt-pans (*aream salinarum*) rendering 4 pence. T. R. E. and now worth 40 shillings.

---

[1] *xx* is written in the line and *vi* above the line.

[2] *car'* has been altered into *bou'*, or the reverse. The Record Commission edition has *den*,' which gives no meaning.

55. M. In Bodebi[1] and Summerdebi [Boothby Pagnell and Somerby (Threo)] Alestan had 1 carucate of land [assessed] to the geld. There is land for 1 team. Godwin, Guy's man, has 1 team there [in demesne], and 3 villeins with half a team, and 2 acres of meadow, and 30 acres of pasture, and 80 acres of underwood. To this manor belong 3½ bovates [of land] whereof Siwate has the soke. T. R. E. it was worth 20 shillings ; now the like amount.

56. In Draitone[2] [Drayton (Kirton)] Alestan had half a carucate of land [assessed] to the geld. There is land for 4 oxen. This land was delivered (*liberata*) to Guy for one manor. He has 1 villein and 4 bordars with half a team there, and 2 acres of meadow. T. R. E. it was worth 5 shillings ; now 3 shillings.

57. In Aighelestorp and Bolebi [Elsthorpe and Bulby (Beltisloe)] Offram had 2 bovates of land [assessed] to the geld. Guy has them, and they are vacant (*uacuę*), but none-the-less they are tilled.

58. LAND OF ROBERT MALET

1. M. In Wellebrune [Welbourn (Boby)] Godwin had 12 carucates of land [assessed] to the geld. There is land for 16 teams. Robert Malet has 3 teams there in demesne, and 35 sokemen on (*de*) 7 carucates of this land and 12 villeins and 8 bordars having 12 teams and 2 oxen. There is a priest there, and a church to which belong 5 bovates of land, and 1 mill rendering 2 shillings, and 200 acres of meadow. T. R. E. and now worth 16 pounds ; tallage 40 shillings.

2. M. In Bergebi [Barrowby (Winnibriggs)] Godwin had 8 carucates of land [assessed] to the geld. There is land for 15 teams. Robert has 5 teams there [in demesne], and 2 sokemen on (*de*) 10 bovates of this land and 50 villeins and 2 bordars having 10 teams, and 1 mill rendering 3 shillings. There is a church there, and a priest, and 60 acres of meadow. T. R. E. it was worth 12 pounds ; now 16 pounds.

Soke[land] of this Manor

3. S. In Ingoldesbi[3] [Ingoldsby (Aswardhurn)] there are 6 bovates of land [assessed] to the geld. 4 sokemen have 1 team and 2 oxen there, and 7 acres of meadow, and 52 acres of underwood.

4. S. In Caschingetorp [Casthorpe in Barrowby (Winnibriggs)] there are 6 bovates of land [assessed] to the geld. There is land for 1 team. Ivo holds this soke[land] (*socam*) of Robert, and he has 6 sokemen there with 1 team and 2 oxen, and 2 mills rendering 4 shillings, and 7 acres of meadow.

5. S. In Stanwald [Stainwith in Barrowby (Winnibriggs)] there are 4 carucates of land [assessed] to the geld. There is land for as many teams. 19 sokemen and 2 bordars have 4 teams there, and 1 mill rendering 4 shillings, and 15 acres of meadow.

---

[1] See 24/81. [2] See 73/2. [3] See 24/99 ; 72/35.

6. M. In Sechebroc [Sedgebrook (Winnibriggs)] Godwin had 4 carucates of land [assessed] to the geld. There is land for 9 teams. Robert has 4 teams there [in demesne], and 27 villeins and 5 bordars having 6 teams, and 3 mills rendering 16 shillings, and 60 acres of meadow, and 8 acres of underwood. T. R. E. it was worth 9 pounds ; now 8 pounds ; tallage 40 shillings.

7. S. In Wiuelesforde [Wilsford (Threo)] there are 3 carucates of land [assessed] to the geld. There is land for 4 teams. It is soke[land] of this manor. 9 sokemen and 2 bordars have 3 teams there, and 15 acres of meadow.

8. In Adelinctune [Allington (Winnibriggs)] there are 6 carucates of land [assessed] to the geld. There is land for 5 teams. Godric, [holding] of Robert [Malet], has 2 teams there in demesne, and 11 sokemen and 10 villeins and 3 bordars having 4 teams, and 140 acres of meadow.

D. B., f. 368c. *Facsimile, p. lxvia.*

59. LAND OF ROBERT OF STAFFORD (*Statford*)

1. M. In Dentune [Denton (Winnibriggs)] Uctebrand had 1 carucate and 6 bovates of land [assessed] to the geld. There is land for as many teams and oxen. It is soke[land] belonging to G[r]antham. Robert of Stafford, and Geoffrey [holding] of him, have half a team there [in demesne], and 3 villeins and 2 bordars with 1 team, and 28 acres of meadow. T. R. E. it was worth 40 shillings ; now 20 shillings.

2. M. In Chaschintorp[1] [Casthorpe in Barrowby (Winnibriggs)] Ulfchetel had 6 bovates of land [assessed] to the geld. There is land for 6 oxen. Hugh, Robert's man, has half a team there [in demesne], and 1 villein and 2 bordars with 1 ox in a team, and 7 acres of meadow. T. R. E. it was worth 20 shillings ; now 10 shillings.

3. M. In Buletham [Boultham (Graffoe)] Osmund had 9 bovates of land [assessed] to the geld. There is land for 6 oxen. Now there is 1 villein there with 1 ox, and 8 acres of meadow. T. R. E. it was worth 13 shillings and 4 pence ; now 6 shillings.

4. Two M. In Carlebi [Carlby (Ness)] Dane and Carle had 1 carucate and twice the fourth part of 1 bovate of land [assessed] to the geld. There is land for as many teams and oxen. The land of Carle was free soke[land] (*frigsoca*) under Dane. Geoffrey, Robert's man, has 1 team there [in demesne], and 10 villeins with 2 teams, and 10 acres of meadow, and 40 acres of underwood. T. R. E. it was worth 40 shillings ; now 50 shillings ; tallage 10 shillings.

5. Three M. In Breseburg and Barnetorp [Braceborough and Banthorpe in Braceborough (Ness)] Dane and Carle and Ledflet had 20

[1] See 72/20.

bovates of land ⌊assessed⌋ to the geld. There is land for as many oxen. The land of 2 of these was free soke⌊land⌋ (*frigsoca*) under Dane. Geoffrey, Robert's man, has 1 team there ⌊in demesne⌋, and 4 villeins with half a team, and 2 mills rendering 20 shillings, and the third part of a church, and 7 acres of meadow, and 55 acres of underwood. T. R. E. it was worth 60 shillings ; now 40 shillings.

6. In the same places (*ibidem*) Karle and Dane ⌊had⌋ 4 bovates of land ⌊assessed⌋ to the geld. There is land for 4 oxen. It is soke⌊land⌋ belonging to (*in*) Turgot [the lawman's] manor of Greteford [Greatford (Ness)]. It is waste.

7. M. In Brune [Bourne (Aveland)] Aldene had 6 bovates of land ⌊assessed⌋ to the geld. There is land for 6 oxen. Geoffrey, Robert's man, has half a team there ⌊in demesne⌋, and 3 villeins and 3 bordars with 1 team, and the third part of 1 mill rendering 3 shillings and 4 pence, and 6 fisheries rendering 16 pence, and 7 acres of meadow, and 30 acres of underwood. T. R. E. and now worth 20 shillings.

8. B. In Turoluebi [Thurlby (Ness)] there is half a carucate of land ⌊assessed⌋ to the geld. There is land for 4 oxen. It is a berewic. Two villeins and 2 bordars have half a team there, and 4 acres of meadow, and 30 acres of underwood.

9. Two M. In Cretune [Creeton (Beltisloe)] Fredgist and Brictmar had 12 bovates and 2 parts of 2 bovates of land ⌊assessed⌋ to the geld. There is land for as many oxen. The land of Brictmar ⌊was⌋ free soke⌊land⌋ (*frigsoca*) under Fredgist. Basuin, Robert's man, has half a team there ⌊in demesne⌋, and 5 sokemen and 4 villeins with 1½ teams. T. R. E. it was worth 40 shillings ; now 30 shillings ; tallage 10 shillings.

10. In Bitham [Little Bytham (Beltisloe)] there is half a carucate of land ⌊assessed⌋ to the geld. There is land for 4 oxen. It is soke⌊land⌋ belonging to (*in*) Cretune [Creeton]. It is waste. There is 1 acre of meadow there.

11. M. In Billefelt and Westbi [Bitchfield and Westby (Beltisloe)] Ælmer had 12 bovates of land ⌊assessed⌋ to the geld. There is land for 12 oxen. Basuin, Robert's man, has 2 villeins and 1 bordar there with 6 oxen in a team, and 14 acres of meadow, and 300 acres of wood⌊land⌋ for pannage throughout the territory. T. R. E. it was worth 30 shillings ; now 20 shillings.

12. One M. In Rosbi[1] [Rauceby (Flaxwell)] Ulsi had 3 carucates and half a bovate of land ⌊assessed⌋ to the geld.

Two M. And Osmund [3½ bovates] and Siward [1 carucate] had 11½ bovates of land ⌊assessed⌋ to the geld. There is land for as many teams and oxen. Siward's land ⌊was⌋ free soke⌊land⌋ (*frigsoca*) under Osmund.* Edelo, Robert's man, has 7 sokemen there [on (*de*) 2 carucates and 5 bovates of this land] and 1 villein with 4 teams.

**D. B., f. 368*d. *Facsimile, p. lxvi*b.

13. S. And in the other Roscebi [Rauceby (Flaxwell)] Turuert had 3½ bovates of land ⌊assessed⌋ to the geld. There is land for as many oxen. 6 villeins and 1 farmer (*censarius*) have 2 teams there, and half a church. T. R. E. it was worth 60 shillings ; now 70 shillings.

14. M. In Roscebi [Rauceby (Flaxwell)] Turuert had 9 carucates of

[1] See 72/12.

land [assessed] to the geld. There is land for 9 teams. Brien, Robert's man, has 1½ teams there [in demesne], and 2 villeins and 1 bordar. In the same place (*ibidem*) 5 bovates of land belong to the hall.

15. In the same place (*ibidem*) Osmund had 3 carucates and 1 bovate of land [assessed] to the geld. There is land for as many teams. 3½ bovates used to belong to his hall. The rest was soke[land] of the same manor. Brien, Robert's man, has 20 sokemen and 4 bordars there having 4 teams and 3 oxen in a team. T. R. E. it was worth 40 shillings; now the like amount; tallage 10 shillings.

16. M. In Scredinctun [Scredington (Aswardhurn)] Leuric had 12 carucates of land [assessed] to the geld. There is land for as many oxen. Gulfered, Robert's man, has 1 team there [in demesne], and half a sokeman and 1 villein having 3 oxen in a team, and 3 acres of meadow. T. R. E. it was worth 20 shillings; now 10 shillings.

17. M. In Haconesbi [Haconby (Aveland)] Uluiet had 1 carucate of land [assessed] to the geld. There is land for 1 team. Gulfer, Robert's man, has 1 team there [in demesne], and 5 villeins and 1 bordar with 1 team, and 16 acres of meadow, and 35 acres of underwood.[1] T. R. E. and now worth 30 shillings.

18. M. In Schinende [Skinnand (Boby)] Ulueue had 3 carucates of land [assessed] to the geld. There is land for 3 teams. Colegrim, Robert's man, has 7 villeins there having 4 teams and an ox in a team, and 50 acres of meadow. T. R. E. it was worth 60 shillings; now 20 shillings.

19. M. In Medricesham[2] [Metheringham (Langoe)] Lefsi had 1 carucate of land [assessed] to the geld. There is land for half a team. Ehelo, Robert's man, has 30 acres of meadow there, and 3 acres of underwood. T. R. E. it was worth 16 shillings; now 10 shillings.

20. M. In Wilgebi [Silk Willoughby (Aswardhurn)] Osmund had 6 bovates of land [assessed] to the geld. There is land for 12 oxen. Godwin, Robert's man, has half a team there [in demesne], and 1 sokeman on (*de*) 3 bovates of this land and 1 villein with 5 oxen in a team, and 24 acres of meadow, and 12 acres of underwood. T. R. E. and now worth 10 shillings.

21. S. In Cudetorp [Counthorpe (Beltisloe)] Robert has 2 sokemen on (*de*) 2 acres and 3 perches of land. It is soke[land] belonging to (*in*) Cretone [Creeton (Beltisloe)].

---

[1] The text has *silue prati*, but *prati* is probably a mistake for *minute*, or possibly for *pastilis*.

[2] See 72/16.

60. LAND OF PETER OF VALONGES (*Valongies*)

1. In Burtone [Burton by Lincoln (Lawress)] Godric had 2 carucates of land ⌊assessed⌋ to the geld. There is land for 2 teams. It is soke⌊land⌋ belonging to (*in*) Scantune [Scampton], but nevertheless there was a hall there. Now Peter of Valonges has 1 villein and 4 bordars there with half a team, and 5 acres of meadow. The demesne is tilled and leased (*Dominium colitur et locatur*). T. R. E. it was worth 15 shillings; now 11 shillings.

D.B., f. 369a. *Facsimile, p. lxviia.*

61. LAND OF HEPPO THE ARBLASTER (*Balistarii*)

1. M. In Haconesbi and in Stentuith [Haconby and Stenfield (Aveland)] Leuric had 3 carucates and 2½ bovates of land ⌊assessed⌋ to the geld. There is land for as many teams and oxen. Heppo the Arblaster has 2 teams there ⌊in demesne⌋, and 3 sokemen on (*de*) 12 bovates of this land and 13 villeins and 6 bordars with 6 teams. There is a priest there, and a church, and 1 mill rendering 12 pence, and 40 acres of meadow, and 80 acres of underwood. T. R. E. and now worth 100 shillings; tallage 20 shillings.

2. S. In Dic[1] [Dyke (Aveland)] there are 3 bovates of land ⌊assessed⌋ to the geld. There is land for 3 oxen. It is soke⌊land⌋ of the same manor.

3. S. In Mortune[2] [Morton (Aveland)] there are 9½ bovates of land ⌊assessed⌋ to the geld. There is land for as many oxen. 9 sokemen have 1 team there, and 10 acres of meadow, and 12 acres of underwood.

4. M. In Hermodestorp [Hanthorpe (Aveland)] Turuert had 1 carucate of land ⌊assessed⌋ to the geld. There is land for 1 team. Simund, Heppo's man, has 1 team there ⌊in demesne⌋, and 9 acres of meadow, and 20 acres of underwood. T. R. E. it was worth 20 shillings; now 30 shillings.

5. M. In Suerefelt [Surfleet (Kirton)] Alsi had 4½ carucates of land ⌊assessed⌋ to the geld. There is land for as many teams. Heppo has 1 team there ⌊in demesne⌋, and 11 villeins and 6 bordars with 2½ teams, and 2 salt-pans rendering 12 pence. T. R. E. it was worth 4 pounds; now 66 shillings.[3]

---

[1] See 42/6; 72/41. This entry is duplicated in 42/6.
[2] See 72/42.
[3] The letter *K*, probably for *Kalumpnia*, placed in the margin, calls attention to a claim.

6. **M.** In Cherchebi and Scapeuic [Kirkby Green and Scopwick (Langoe)] Aldene had 5 carucates and 6 bovates of land ⌊assessed⌋ to the geld. There is land for 4 teams. Heppo has 2 teams there ⌊in demesne⌋, and 13 sokemen on (*de*) 4 carucates and 2 bovates of this land and 3 villeins and [7[1]] 2 bordars with 5½ teams, and half a mill rendering 5 shillings, and 20 acres of meadow. T. R. E. it was worth 20 shillings; now 50 shillings; tallage 10 shillings.

7. S. In Timberlunt [Timberland (Langoe)] there are 3 carucates of land ⌊assessed⌋ to the geld. There is land for 2 teams. It is a berewic. Simund, Heppo's man, has half a team there, and 11 sokemen on (*de*) 2 carucates of this land and 1 bordar with 2 teams. T. R. E. it was worth 20 shillings; now 30 shillings.

8. S. In Scapeuic [Scopwick (Langoe)] there are 12 bovates of land ⌊assessed⌋ to the geld. There is land for 12 oxen. One sokeman has 1 team there, and 4 acres of meadow. T. R. E. it was worth 10 shillings; now 6 shillings.

9. M. In Snetrebi [Snitterby (Aslacoe)] Godwin had 10 bovates of land ⌊assessed⌋ to the geld. There is land for 12 oxen. Heppo has 1 team there ⌊in demesne⌋, and 75 acres of meadow. T. R. E. it was worth 20 shillings; now the like amount; tallage 10 shillings.

SOKE⌊LAND⌋

10. S. In Radburne [Redbourn (Manley)] there are 3 bovates of land ⌊assessed⌋ to the geld, and in Staintone [Stainton by Wadingham (Manley)] ⌈and Wadingham⌉ [Wadingham (Manley)] half a bovate of land ⌊assessed⌋ to the geld. There is land for as many oxen. There are 2 villeins there with half a team, and 6 acres of meadow.

62. LAND OF RALPH SON OF HUBERT

1. M. In Gunnebi [Gunby St. Nicholas (Beltisloe)] Godwin had 4 carucates of land ⌊assessed⌋ to the geld. There is land for 4[2] teams. Ralph son of Hubert has 2 teams there ⌊in demesne⌋, and 1 mill rendering 12 pence, and 63 acres of meadow. T. R. E. it was worth 40 shillings; now 70 shillings; tallage 10 shillings.

2. In the same place (*ibidem*) Ulwine had 1 carucate of land ⌊assessed⌋ to the geld. There is land for 1 team. Ansfrid, Ralph's priest, seized (*inuasit*) this land. On it there are 2 villeins, and 10 acres of meadow. A certain William leases (*locat*) it for six shillings. It is soke⌊land⌋ ⌈and a berewic⌉ belonging to (*in*) Wime [Witham (Beltisloe)].

---

[1] *vii* is cancelled by underlining, and *ii* is interlined above it.
[2] *ii* is written in the line and *ii* above the line.

*D. B., f. 369*b. *Facsimile, p. lxvii*b.

63. LAND OF GEOFFREY DE WIRCE

1. M. In Bliburg [Blyborough (Aslacoe)] Leuric ['cilt'] had 2 carucates and 3[1] bovates of land ⌊assessed⌋ to the geld. There is land for 6 teams. Robert, Geoffrey de Wirce's man, has 2 teams there ⌊in demesne⌋, and 13 sokemen on (*de*) 10 bovates of this land and 4 villeins with 2½ teams. There is half a church there, and 1 mill rendering 2 shillings, and 60 acres of meadow. T. R. E. and now worth 40 shillings; tallage 20 shillings.

2. M. In Gainesburg [Gainsborough (Corringham)] Leduin had 8 carucates of land ⌊assessed⌋ to the geld. There is land for 12 teams. Rainald, Geoffrey's man, has 2 teams there ⌊in demesne⌋, and 12 sokemen on (*de*) 4 carucates of this land and 4 villeins with 6 teams, and 40 acres of meadow, and 80 acres of underwood. T. R. E. it was worth 6 pounds; now 3 pounds; tallage 20 shillings.

3. B. In Summerdebi [Somerby (Corringham)] there are 4 bovates of land ⌊assessed⌋ to the geld. It is a berewic. There is land for 4 oxen. There is half a team there in demesne, and 1 villein having 2 oxen in a team, and 10 acres of meadow, and 10 acres of underwood.

4. B. and S. In Ioletorp [Yawthorpe (Corringham)] there is 1 carucate of land ⌊assessed⌋ to the geld. There is land for 1 team. It is inland and soke⌊land⌋. There is 1 team there in demesne, and 6 sokemen have 1 team.

5. M. In Epeurde [Epworth (Axholme)] Leduin had 8 carucates of land ⌊assessed⌋ to the geld. There is land for 12 teams. Geoffrey de Wirce has 2 teams there ⌊in demesne⌋, and 8 sokemen on (*de*) 2 carucates and 5 bovates of this land and 13 villeins and 9 bordars with 6 teams, and 11 fisheries rendering 5 shillings, and 16 acres of meadow. There is wood⌊land⌋ for pannage 1 league in length and 1 in breadth. T. R. E. it was worth 8 pounds; now 5 pounds; tallage 20 shillings.

6. M. In Ostone [Owston (Axholme)] Guede had 4 carucates of land ⌊assessed⌋ to the geld. There is land for 4 teams. Geoffrey has 1 team there ⌊in demesne⌋, and 9 villeins and 6 bordars with 3 teams, and 3 fisheries rendering 3 shillings, and 6 acres of meadow. There is wood⌊land⌋ for pannage 1 league in length and 1 in breadth. T. R. E. it was worth 6 pounds; now 30 shillings; tallage 10 shillings.

7. M. In Acheseia[2] [Haxey (Axholme)] Siward Barn had 3 carucates of land ⌊assessed⌋ to the geld. There is land for 6 teams. Wazelin, Geoffrey's man, has 2½ teams there ⌊in demesne⌋, and 16 villeins and 8 bordars with 3½ teams, and 9 fisheries rendering 7 shillings, and 3 acres of meadow. There is wood⌊land⌋ for pannage throughout the territory 5 furlongs in length and 1 furlong in breadth. T. R. E. and now worth 100 shillings; tallage 20 shillings.

---

[1] *ii* is written in the line and *i* above the line.

[2] See 71/16.

8. Two M. In Lund and the other Lund [Eastlound and Graizelound (Axholme)] Fulcheri and Weghe had 14 bovates of land [assessed] to the geld. There is land for 7 oxen.

9. In the same places (*ibidem*) there are 9 bovates of land [assessed] to the geld. It is soke[land] belonging to (*in*) Epeurde [Epworth (Axholme)].

10. In the same places (*ibidem*) there is 1 bovate of land [assessed] to the geld. It is a berewic belonging to (*in*) Beltone [Belton (Axholme)]. There is land for 5 oxen. There are 4 sokemen and 4 villeins and 2 farmers (*censorii*) there having $3\frac{1}{2}$ teams, and 1 fishery rendering 12 pence. T. R. E. it was worth 20 shillings; now 16 shillings.

11. In Brune and the other Brune [High Burnham and Low Burnham (Axholme)] there are 6 carucates of land [assessed] to the geld. There is land for 6 teams. It is soke[land] belonging to (*in*) Epeurde [Epworth (Axholme)]. 18 sokemen have 7 teams there.

12. Two M. In Beltone[1] [Belton (Axholme)] Ulf and Alnod had 5 carucates of land [assessed] to the geld. There is land for 5 teams. Geoffrey has 1 team there [in demesne], and 17 sokemen and 20 villeins and 6 bordars having 4 teams and 6 oxen, and 11 fisheries rendering 7 shillings. There is wood[land] for pannage throughout the territory 2 leagues in length and 2 in breadth. T. R. E. it was worth 7 pounds; now 4 pounds and 5 shillings and 4 pence; tallage 20 shillings.

13. S. In Beltot [Beltoft (Axholme)] there is 1 carucate of land [assessed] to the geld. There is land for 1 team. 4 sokemen and 16 bordars have 3 teams there. There is wood[land] for pannage throughout the territory 4 furlongs in length and 4 in breadth.

14. S. In Aletorp [Althorpe (Axholme)] there is 1 carucate of land [assessed] to the geld. There is land for 1 team. 6 sokemen have 1 team there.

D. B., f. 369c. *Facsimile, p. lxviiia.*

15. M. In Crule [Crowle (Axholme)] Alwin had 6 carucates less 1 bovate of land [assessed] to the geld. There is land for as many teams; and in the same place (*ibidem*) there is 1 bovate [of land [assessed] to the geld]. It is inland belonging to (*in*) Hubaldestorp [Upperthorpe in Haxey (Axholme)]. Now a certain abbot of Saint German [of Salebi] [Selby abbey] has it, [holding] of Geoffrey. There is 1 team there in demesne, and 15 villeins and 19 bordars have 7 teams, and 31 fisheries rendering 31 shillings, and 30 acres of meadow. There is a church there, and wood[land] for pannage 1 league in length and 1 league in breadth. T. R. E. it was worth 12 pounds; now 8 pounds; tallage 40 shillings.

SOKE[LAND] OF THIS MANOR

16. S. In Amecotes [Amcotts (Axholme)] there are 2[2] carucates of land [assessed] to the geld. There is land for 1 team. 2 sokemen and 6 villeins have 1 team there.

17. B. In the same place (*ibidem*) there are 3 bovates of land [assessed] to the geld. There is land for 3 oxen. It is inland [belonging to (*in*)] Westude [Westwood (Axholme)].

---

[1] See 71/16. [2] *.i. car'* has been altered into *.ii. car'*.

18. S. In the same place (*ibidem*) there are 5[1] bovates of land ⌊assessed⌋ to the geld. There is land for 5 oxen. It is soke⌊land⌋ belonging to (*in*) Gerulftorp [Garthorpe].

19.[2] S. In Gerulftorp [and Ludintone] [Garthorpe and Luddington (Axholme)] there are 4½ carucates of land ⌊assessed⌋ to the geld. There is land for 1½ teams. It is soke⌊land⌋ belonging to (*in*) Crul [Crowle]. Now 12 sokemen have 2 teams there.

20.[3] M. In the same places (*ibidem*) Fulcheri had 1 carucate of land ⌊assessed⌋ to the geld. There is land for half a team; and

21.[4] In the same place (*ibidem*) Ulf had half a carucate of land ⌊assessed⌋ to the geld. It is soke⌊land⌋ belonging to (*in*) Beltone [Belton (Axholme)]. This land is waste; nevertheless it renders 3 shillings. T. R. E. it was worth 10 shillings.

22. S. and B. In Butrewic [Butterwick (Axholme)] there are 3 carucates of land ⌊assessed⌋ to the geld. It is soke⌊land⌋ and inland belonging to (*in*) Ostone [Owston (Axholme)]. There is land for 1 team. One sokeman and 6 villeins have 1 team there, and 1 mill rendering 4 shillings.

23. In Ludintone and Gerulftorp and Maræ and Watretone [Luddington and Garthorpe and the Marshes and Waterton (Axholme)] there are 6 carucates of land ⌊assessed⌋ to the geld. There is land for 2 teams.

24.[2] Of this land 4½ carucates are in the soke of Crul [Crowle (Axholme)]. Now 12 sokemen have 2 teams there.

25.[3] M. There (*ibi*) Fulcheri had 1 carucate of land with a hall. Now it is waste.

26.[4] S. There (*ibi*) Ulfenisc ⌊had⌋ half a carucate, soke⌊land⌋ belonging to (*in*) Beltone [Belton]. Gilbert claims it. Geoffrey has it; and it is waste. T. R. E. it was worth 10 shillings; now 3 shillings.

27. To this island belong marsh lands (*maresc*) 10 leagues in length and 3 in breadth.

[1] The Record Commission edition has *.vi bou'*, but what has been read as *i* seems in fact to be the full stop, in this case smudged, which normally follows a number in the text of *D.B.* If the amount is 5 bovates, the assessment of the hundred to which Amcotts belongs is exactly 12 carucates, and that of the wapentake of the Isle of Axholme 48 carucates. *L.S.* (5/1) and *The Book of Fees* (p. 193) give the same assessment for the Isle. Moreover, the latter document (*ibid.*) puts the assessment of Crowle (*Carul*) at 13¼ carucates, which is the sum of nos. 15-19 above, provided that no. 18 is reckoned as 5 bovates.

[2] Nos. 19 and 24 are duplicate entries.

[3] Nos. 20 and 25 are duplicate entries.

[4] Nos. 21 and 26 are duplicate entries.

*D. B., f. 369*d. *Facsimile, p. lxviii*b.

64. LAND OF GEOFFREY ALSELIN

Laxewelle [Flaxwell] Wapentake

1. M. In Reschintone [Ruskington (Flaxwell)] Tochi had 12 carucates of land ⌊assessed⌋ to the geld. There is land for as many teams. Geoffrey Alselin and Ralph his *nepos* have 2 teams there [in demesne], and 22 sokemen on (*de*) 3 carucates and 2 bovates of this land and 8 villeins and 8 bordars having 8 teams, and 60 acres of meadow, and 240 acres of wood⌊land⌋ for pannage throughout the territory. T. R. E. it was worth 25 pounds; now 50 pounds; tallage 10 pounds. There is a church there, and a priest, and 3 mills rendering 4 pounds and 12 shillings and 8 pence. A certain Drew[1] holds 6 bovates of land in Reschintone, and has 1 team there. It is worth 20 shillings.

2. B. In Amuinc [Anwick (Flaxwell)] there are 6 carucates of land ⌊assessed⌋ to the geld. There is land for as many teams. It is a berewic belonging to (*in*) Reschintone [Ruskington]. Ralph, Geoffrey's *nepos*, has 21 sokemen and 4 villeins there having 7 teams. Drew,[2] his man, holds 5½ bovates of the same land, and has 6 oxen in a team there [in demesne], and 1 villein and 3 bordars with 1 ox. It is worth 25 shillings.

Soke⌊land⌋ of this Manor

3. S. In Derintone [Dorrington (Flaxwell)] there are 12 carucates of land ⌊assessed⌋ to the geld. There is land for 12 teams. Geoffrey has 1 team there in demesne, and 28 sokemen and 8 bordars with 7 teams. One of his men has 9 bovates of land there with 1 team. It is worth 20 shillings. There are 160[3] acres of meadow there, and 50 acres of underwood.

4. S. In Dicbi [Digby (Flaxwell)] there are 12 carucates of land ⌊assessed⌋ to the geld. There is land for as many teams. 35 sokemen have 12 teams there, and 100 acres of meadow, and 10 acres of underwood.

5. S. In Rouestune [Rowston (Flaxwell)] there are 12 carucates of land ⌊assessed⌋ to the geld. There is land for 12 teams. 32 sokemen have 10 teams there. Two knights of Geoffrey's hold 1 carucate of this land, and have there 1½ teams, and 2 bordars, and 150 acres of meadow. It is worth 20 shillings.

6. S. and B. In Branzewelle [Brauncewell (Flaxwell)] there are [soke⌊land⌋] 9 carucates of land and [inland] 2 bovates ⌊assessed⌋ to the geld. There is land for as many teams and oxen. Geoffrey has 1 team there, and 13 sokemen and 3 bordars with 4 teams. Two of his men hold 13 bovates of this land, and have 1 team there, a church, and a priest, and 4½ acres of meadow, and 14 acres of underwood. It is worth 20 shillings.

---

1 See 30/35.
2 See 30/34.
3 *xx* is written in the line and *cxl* above the line.

7. S. In Dunnesbi [Dunsby St. Andrew (Flaxwell)] there are 6 carucates of land [assessed] to the geld. There is land for 6 teams. Geoffrey and his *nepos* have 2 teams there, and 13 sokemen and 1 bordar with 1 team, and 6 acres of meadow.

8. S. In Rosbi [North Rauceby (Flaxwell)] there are 6 carucates and 2½ bovates of land [assessed] to the geld. There is land for as many teams and oxen. There Geoffrey's *nepos* has 25 sokemen and 8 villeins and 5 bordars with 8 teams.

9. S. In the other Rosbi [South Rauceby (Flaxwell)] there is 1 carucate of land [assessed] to the geld. There is land for 12 oxen. There are 7 sokemen there and 2 bordars with 1 team and 3 oxen.

10. B. In Evedune [Evedon (Aswardhurn)] there are 2 carucates of land [assessed] to the geld. There is land for 14 oxen. It is a berewic. Geoffrey and his *nepos* have 1 mill there, and 40 acres of marsh (*maresch*).

SOKE[LAND] OF RESCHINTONE [RUSKINGTON]

11.[1] S. In Rochesham [Roxham (Flaxwell)] there are 3 carucates and 6 bovates of land [assessed] to the geld. There is land for as many teams and oxen.

12.[1] S. In Leuesingham [Leasingham (Flaxwell)] there are 6 carucates of land [assessed] to the geld. There is land for 6 teams. There are 30 acres of meadow there.

13.[1] In Coteland [Coteland in Ruskington, and perhaps in Anwick (Flaxwell)] there are 5 carucates of meadow [assessed] to the geld. There is marsh (*maresc*) 10 furlongs in length and 6 furlongs in breadth.

14.[1] S. In Stobetun [Stubton (Loveden)] there are 5 carucates and 2½ bovates of land [assessed] to the geld. There is land for 7 teams. It is soke[land] belonging to (*in*) Westburg [Westborough (Loveden)]. There are 20 sokemen there and 5 bordars with 7 teams. There is a priest there, and a church, and there are 120 acres of meadow. Of this land 1 knight of his has 6 bovates, and has 1 team there.

15. M. In Westburg [Westborough (Loveden)] Tochi had 12 carucates of land [assessed] to the geld. There is land for 12 teams. Geoffrey Alselin and Ralph his *nepos* have 4 teams there [in demesne], and 5 sokemen on (*de*) 12 bovates of this land and 12 villeins* and 6 bordars with 2 teams. There is a priest there, and a church, and 2 mills rendering 30 shillings, and 200 acres of meadow. Of this land 2 of his men hold 11 bovates, and they have 1 team and 2 oxen there, and 6 bordars with 1 ox. T. R. E. it was worth 15 pounds ; now 25 pounds.

**D. B., f.* 370a. *Facsimile, p. lxix*a.

SOKE[LAND] OF THIS MANOR

16. S. In Dodintone [Dry Doddington (Loveden)] there are 9 carucates and 6 bovates of land [assessed] to the geld. There is land for as many teams and oxen. 5 sokemen and 12 villeins have 7 teams there, and 200 acres of meadow, and 10 acres of underwood.

17. S. In Claipol [Claypole (Loveden)] there are 7 carucates [and 7 bovates] of land [assessed] to the geld. There is land for as many teams and oxen. 34 sokemen and 6 bordars have 8 teams there. There is a

[1] Nos. 11-14 are written at the foot of the preceding column.

church there, and a priest, and 1 mill rendering 10 shillings, and 40 acres of meadow. Of this land Elduin has 2½ carucates of land, and has 1½ teams there. It is worth 40 shillings.

18. M. In Waragebi [Wrawby (Yarborough)] Tochi had 2 carucates and 3 bovates and 5 parts of 1 bovate of land [assessed] to the geld. There is land for 7 teams. Now there are 2 teams there in demesne, and 16 villeins and 15 bordars have 4 teams. There is a church there, and a priest, and 100 acres of meadow, and 100 acres of wood[land] for pannage throughout the territory. T. R. E. it was worth 10 pounds; now 6 pounds; tallage 20 shillings. Ralph holds it of Geoffrey.

19. S. and B. In Eleham [Elsham (Yarborough)] there are 2 carucates and 2 bovates of land [assessed] to the geld; in Chetelbi [Kettleby (Yarborough)] there are 3 bovates and the third part of 1 bovate of land [assessed] to the geld. There is land for 6 teams. It is soke[land] and inland belonging to (*in*) Waragebi [Wrawby]. Now there is 1 team there in demesne, and 11 sokemen and 4 villeins and 8 bordars with 2 teams, and 114 acres of meadow.

65. LAND OF BALDWIN [THE FLEMING]

1.[1] S. In Hadinctune [Haddington (Graffoe)] Ailric had 8½ carucates of land [assessed] to the geld, 7 carucates and 3 bovates [being] soke[land] and 9 bovates inland belonging to (*in*) Dodintune [Doddington Pigot (Graffoe)]. There is land for 4 teams and 2 oxen. Baldwin has 13 sokemen there having 3½ teams. It is worth 20 shillings.

2.[1] S. In Wizebi [Whisby (Graffoe)] there are 6 carucates of land [assessed] to the geld. There is land for 3 teams. It is soke[land] [4 carucates] and inland [2 carucates] of the same manor [Doddington Pigot]. 7 sokemen have 2 teams there, and of meadow 5 furlongs in length and 1 in breadth. It is worth 20 shillings.

3.[1] S. In Hicham [South Hykeham (Graffoe)] there are 4 carucates of land [assessed] to the geld. There is land for 3 teams. It is inland [3 carucates] and soke[land] [1 carucate] of the same manor [Doddington Pigot]. There is 1 team there in demesne, and 2 sokemen and 10 villeins and 2 bordars with 3 teams, and 2 fisheries rendering 3 shillings, and meadow 2 furlongs in length and 2 in breadth, and an equal quantity of underwood. It is worth 40 shillings.

4.[1] B. In Scheldinchope [Skellingthorpe (Graffoe)] there are 12 carucates of land [assessed] to the geld. There is land for 6 teams. 18 villeins and 2 sokemen and 4 bordars have 6 teams there, meadow 1 mile in length and 2½ furlongs in breadth, and an equal quantity of underwood. It is worth 40 shillings.

5.[1] S. and B. In Northhicam [North Hykeham (Graffoe)] there are 8 carucates of land [assessed] to the geld. It is soke[land] [7 carucates] and inland [1 carucate] of the same manor [Doddington Pigot]. 13

[1] See 72/27.

sokemen have 3½ teams there, and 52 acres of meadow. It is worth 20 shillings.

All this land belongs to Dodintune [Doddington Pigot (Graffoe)], to Saint Peter of Westminster's manor.[1] Baldwin holds this of the king, but the abbot claims it to the use of Saint Peter by the testimony of the men of the whole county.

*D. B., f. 370*b. *Facsimile, p. lxix*b.

66. LAND OF WILLIAM TAILGEBOSCH

1. M. In Aschebi [West Ashby (Horncastle)] Turuert had 3 bovates of land ⌊assessed⌋ to the geld. There is land for 5 oxen. William Tailleboscb has there 2 oxen in a team ⌊in demesne⌋, and 40 acres of meadow. T. R. E. it was worth 10 shillings ; now 5 shillings.

2. M. In Alforde [Alford (Calcewath)] Turuerd had 4 bovates of land ⌊assessed⌋ to the geld. There is land for 6 oxen. William has 1 villein there with 2 oxen in a team, and 6 acres of meadow. T. R. E. it was worth 30 shillings ; now 5 shillings.

67. LAND OF COLEGRIM [AND OTHERS]

1. M. In Ieresbi [Ewerby (Aswardhurn)] Colegrim had and has 2 carucates of land ⌊assessed⌋ to the geld. There is land for 14 oxen. Rold, Colegrim's man, has 1 team there ⌊in demesne⌋, and 2 sokemen and 4 villeins with 1 team, and 21 acres of meadow, and 9 acres of underwood. T. R. E. it was worth 20 shillings ; now 40 shillings.

SOKE⌊LAND⌋ OF THIS MANOR

2. S. In Welle [Howell (Aswardhurn)] there are 4 bovates of land ⌊assessed⌋ to the geld. There is land for 4 oxen. There are 4 acres of meadow there.

3. S. In Burg[2] [Burg (Aswardhurn)] there are 6 bovates of land ⌊assessed⌋ to the geld. There is land for 4 oxen. There is a church there.

4. S. In Evedune [Evedon (Aswardhurn)] there are 2 bovates of land ⌊assessed⌋ to the geld. There is land for 2 oxen. There is a church there, and 2 acres of meadow, and 1 acre of underwood, and 5 acres of marsh (*maresc*).

5. M. In Burg[2] [Burg (Aswardhurn)] Archil had 6½ bovates of land ⌊assessed⌋ to the geld. There is land for as many oxen. The same man

[1] See 9/1 ; 72/27.
[2] Probably a depopulated village near Evedon. See 68/26.

has of the king 1 team there [in demesne], and 2 villeins and 5 bordars with 2 oxen, and 1 mill rendering 20 shillings, and 8 acres of meadow, and 3 acres of underwood. T. R. E. it was worth 30 shillings; now 40 shillings.

6. B. In Echintune [Heckington (Aswardhurn)] there are 2½ bovates of meadow belonging to Burg[1] [Burg (Aswardhurn)]. It is inland.

7. M. In Goldesbi [Ingoldsby (Aswardhurn)] Colegrim had 4 bovates and the third part of 1 bovate of land [assessed] to the geld in demesne, and as much land in soke [assessed] to the geld. There is land for 2 teams. Now he himself has 1 team there [in demesne], and 2 sokemen and 6 villeins with 2 teams, and 9 acres of meadow, and 63 acres of wood[land] for pannage throughout the territory, and a church. T. R. E. and now worth 10 shillings.

8. M. In the same place (*ibidem*) Ingulf had 4 bovates of land [assessed] to the geld. There is land for 6 oxen. Now Aschil has it of the king in alms, and he has 2 villeins there with 5 oxen, and 4 acres of meadow, and 16 acres of underwood. T. R. E. and now worth 5 shillings.

9. M. In Brune [Bourne (Aveland)] Uluric had 3 bovates of land [assessed] to the geld. There is land for 3 oxen. Now Suen has it of the king. There are 5 villeins and 1 bordar there with 1 team and 1 ox in a team, and six parts of 1 mill rendering 18 pence, and 3 fisheries rendering 8 pence, and 4½ acres of meadow, and 15 acres of underwood. T. R. E. it was worth 10 shillings; now 16 shillings.

10. M. In Neutone[2] [Newton (Aveland)] Uluric Wild had 3½ bovates of land [assessed] to the geld. There is land for as many oxen. Now Ulviet has it of the king, and [has] half a team there [in demesne], and 3 villeins with half a team, and 6 acres of meadow, and 35 acres of underwood. T. R. E. it was worth 20 shillings; now 25 shillings.

11. B. In Trichingeham [Threckingham (Aveland)] there are 5 bovates and the sixth part of 2 bovates of land [assessed] to the geld. There is land for as many oxen. Now Ulviet has it of the king, and [has] 1 sokeman there on (*de*) 1 bovate and the sixth part of 2 bovates and 3 villeins with half a team, and the twelfth part of 1 church of Saint Peter, and the sixth part of 1 church of Saint Mary and the sixth* part of 4 bovates which belong to (*iacent in*) the church of Saint Mary.

**D. B., f. 370c.* *Facsimile, p. lxxa.*

12. M In Summerdebi [Somerby (Threo)] Ulsi had 6 bovates of land [assessed] to the geld. There is land for 6 oxen. Now Torchil has it of the king, and has there 1 ox in a team [in demesne], and 1 bordar, and 8 acres of underwood. T. R. E. and now [worth] 5 shillings.

13. M. In Beltone[3] [Belton (Threo)] Rold had 2½ carucates of land [assessed] to the geld. There is land for as many teams. Colegrim has 1 team there [in demesne], and 1 sokeman on (*de*) 1 bovate of this land and 7 villeins and 4 bordars with 2 teams, and 2 mills rendering 12 shillings, and 36 acres of meadow, and 16 acres of underwood. T. R. E. it was worth 30 shillings; now the like amount.

---

[1] See note to no. 3 above.
[2] See 3/32; 72/52.
[3] See 57/25; 72/60 and 61.

14. B. In Tuuetorp [Towthorpe in Londonthorpe (Threo)] there are 6 bovates of land [assessed] to the geld. There is land for 6 oxen. It is a berewic belonging to (*in*) Beltone [Belton]. Colegrim has there 1 villein and 1 bordar with half a team, and 5 acres of meadow.

15. B. In Barchestone [Barkston (Threo)] there are 6 bovates of land [assessed] to the geld. There is land for 6 oxen. There is half a team there in demesne, and 2 mills the soke whereof belongs to (*iacet in*) Granham [Grantham (Winnibriggs)].

16. S. In the same place (*in eadem*) there is 1 carucate of land [assessed] to the geld. There is land for 1 team. It is soke[land] of (*de*) Beltone [Belton]. 2 sokemen and 2 villeins have half a team there, and 35 acres of meadow.

17. B. In Lundetorp [Londonthorpe (Threo)] there are 6 bovates of land [assessed] to the geld. There is land for 6 oxen. It is a berewic belonging to (*in*) Beltone [Belton]. Colegrim has 1 villein and 1 bordar there with half a team.

18. S. In Draitone [Drayton (Kirton)] Wider had half a carucate of land [assessed] to the geld. There is land for half a team. It is soke[land] belonging to (*in*) [Count A[lan's] manor] of Draitone [Drayton]. Godric has 3 bordars there, and 2 acres of meadow.

19. In Bichere [Bicker (Kirton)] Wider had 1 carucate of land [assessed] to the geld. There is land for 1 team. Godric has 1 team there in demesne, and 12 villeins. T. R. E. it was worth 20 shillings; now 40 shillings.

20. M. In Hochtune[1] [Houghton in Grantham (Winnibriggs)] Colegrim had 14 bovates of land [assessed] to the geld. There is land for as many oxen. Fredgis, Colegrim's man, has 2 villeins and 3 bordars there with 1 team, and 2 mills rendering 30 shillings, and 3 acres of meadow. T. R. E. and now worth 40 shillings.

21. In the same place (*ibidem*) there are 10 bovates of land [assessed] to the geld. There is land for 10 oxen. Abbot Thorald holds this land of Colegrim, and ploughs it with his own demesne (*dominio*). There are 6 acres of meadow there. It is worth 6 shillings.

22. M. In Ulvesbi [Ouseby in Birthorpe (Aveland)] Uluric had 6 bovates of land [assessed] to the geld. There is land for 6 oxen. Now Suen has it of the king, and has 1 team there [in demesne], and 3 villeins with half a team, and half a mill rendering 3 shillings, and 9 acres of meadow. T. R. E. it was worth 10 shillings.

23. M. In Dusebi[2] [Dowsby (Aveland)] Offram had 3 carucates of land [assessed] to the geld. There is land for 3 teams. Now he himself has 1 team there [in demesne], and 6 villeins with 1 team, and 31 acres of meadow. T. R. E. and now worth 30 shillings.

24. M. In Gunnewordebi [Little Gonerby (Winnibriggs)] Colegrim had 4 bovates of land [assessed] to the geld. There is land for 6 oxen. Now the same man has 1 team there [in demesne], and 2 sokemen and 3 villeins with 6 oxen, and 8 acres of meadow. T. R. E. and now worth 16 shillings.

25. In Suindrebi [Swinderby (Graffoe)] there is 1 carucate of land [assessed] to the geld. There is land for 6 oxen. Colegrim has it with 1

[1] See 8/12.

[2] See 57/12; 72/49.

team there, and ⌊he has⌋ 100 acres of meadow. There is underwood 9 furlongs in length and 3 furlongs in breadth.

26. In Canewic [Canwick (Langoe)] Agemund had 1 carucate of land ⌊assessed⌋ to the geld. There is land for 1 team. There are 2 villeins there with 1 team and 3 bordars, and 55 acres of meadow. T. R. E. and now worth 15 shillings.

27. In the same place (*ibidem*) Quendrud the nun ⌊had⌋ half a carucate of land ⌊assessed⌋ to the geld. There is land for 4 oxen. It is worth 8 shillings.

*D. B., f. 370*d. *Facsimile, p. lxx*b.

68. LAND OF SORTEBRAND AND OTHER THANES

1. M. In Burtone[1] [Burton by Lincoln (Lawress)] Ednod had 3 carucates of land ⌊assessed⌋ to the geld. There is land for 3 teams. Sortebrant has 2 teams there in demesne, and 8 villeins and 3 bordars with 1 team, and 4 farmers (*censores*) rendering 8 shillings. There are 8 acres of meadow there. T. R. E. it was worth 21 shillings; now 40 shillings.

2. M. In Carletune [South Carlton (Lawress)] Gonnewate had 6 carucates of land ⌊assessed⌋ to the geld. There is land for 6 teams. Sortebrant has 6 oxen in a team there, and a certain man of his 1 team, and 8 sokemen and 6 villeins and 4 bordars with 2½ teams, and 30½ acres of meadow, and 100 acres of meadow in Snotingeham [Nottinghamshire]. T. R. E. and now worth 40 shillings; tallage 40 shillings.

3. S. In Nortcarletone [North Carlton (Lawress)] there is 1 carucate of land ⌊assessed⌋ to the geld. There is land for 1 team. 3 sokemen and 3 bordars have 1½ teams there. There is a priest there, and a church, and 22 acres of meadow.

4. M. In Medrichesham [Metheringham (Langoe)] Ragenald had 5½ carucates of land ⌊assessed⌋ to the geld. There is land for 2½ teams. Sortebrand has 1 team there ⌊in demesne⌋, and 2 sokemen and 10 villeins and 4 bordars having 4 teams. There is a church there, and 100 acres of meadow, and 8 acres of underwood. T. R. E. and now worth 40 shillings.

5. M. In Cale [West Keal (Bolingbroke)] Siric had 12 bovates of land ⌊assessed⌋ to the geld. There is land for 14 oxen. Chetelbern has 1 team there ⌊in demesne⌋, and 8 villeins with half a team, and 56 acres of meadow. T. R. E. it was worth 40 shillings; now 50 shillings.

6. B. In Cuningesbi[2] [Coningsby (Horncastle)] there is 1 bovate of land ⌊assessed⌋ to the geld. There is land for 1 ox. It is inland [belonging to (*in*) Cale [West Keal]]. Chetelbern has 1 villein there, and 1 fishery rendering 40 pence, and 20 acres of underwood.

---

[1] See 71/1. [2] See 69/34.

7. In Aschebi [West Ashby (Horncastle)] Chetelber*n* has 1 mill rendering 12 shillings.

8. M. In Calnodesbi [Candlesby (Candleshoe)] Sortebrand had half a carucate of land ⌊assessed⌋ to the geld. There is land for 5 oxen. Chetelbern has half a team there ⌊in demesne⌋. T. R. E. it was worth 20 shillings; now 10 shillings.

9. S. In Breietoft [Braytoft (Candleshoe)] Sortebrand ⌊had⌋ 2 bovates of land ⌊assessed⌋ to the geld. There is land for 2 oxen. 2 villeins have 1 team there, and 60 acres of meadow.

10. B. In Arduluetorp [Addlethorpe (Candleshoe)] there are 2 bovates of land ⌊assessed⌋ to the geld. There is land for 2 oxen. Chetelbern has 4 villeins there who do not plough, and 80 acres of meadow.

11. B. In Frischenei [Friskney (Candleshoe)] Sortebrand ⌊had⌋ 2 bovates of land ⌊assessed⌋ to the geld. There is land for 2 oxen. Chetelbern has 3 villeins there who do not plough, and 4 acres of meadow.

12. S. In Tedlagestorp [Theddlethorpe (Calcewath)] Siric ⌊had⌋ 3 bovates of land ⌊assessed⌋ to the geld. There is land for 3 oxen. Chetelbern has 4 sokemen there having 2 oxen in a team, and 24 acres of meadow.

13. M. In Sudtone [Sutton in the Marsh (Calcewath)] Siric had 5½ bovates of land ⌊assessed⌋ to the geld. There is land for 7 oxen. Chetelbern has 1 team there ⌊in demesne⌋, and 4 sokemen and 6 villeins and 6 bordars with 1 team, and 50 acres of meadow. T. R. E. and now worth 40 shillings.

14. S. In the same place[1] (*ibidem*) Siward ⌊had⌋ 1 bovate of land ⌊assessed⌋ to the geld. There is land for 1½ oxen. It is soke⌊land⌋ belonging to (*in*) Hotoft [Huttoft (Calcewath)]. Chetelbern has 4 sokemen there with half a team, and 4 acres of meadow. It is worth 5 shillings.

15. M. In Grosebi [Grasby (Yarborough)] Chetelbern had half a carucate of land ⌊assessed⌋ to the geld. There is land for 1 team. 4 sokemen and 4 bordars have 1 team there, and 10 acres of meadow. T. R. E. and now worth 20 shillings.

D. B., f. 371a. *Facsimile, p. lxxia.*

16. M. In Cretune [Creeton (Beltisloe)] Leuric had 1 carucate of land ⌊assessed⌋ to the geld. There is land for 1 team. The same man himself has 1 team there ⌊in demesne⌋, and 2 acres of meadow. T. R. E. and now worth 30 shillings.

17. M. In Suinhamstede [Swinstead (Beltisloe)] Ragenald had half a carucate of land ⌊assessed⌋ to the geld. There is land for 4 oxen. The same man himself has 2 villeins there with half a team, and 1½ acres of meadow, and 15 acres of underwood. T. R. E. and now worth 10 shillings.

18. M. In Corby [Corby (Beltisloe)] Bricteua had 1 carucate of land ⌊assessed⌋ to the geld. There is land for 1 team. The same woman herself has 1 team there ⌊in demesne⌋, and 3 bordars, and 1 acre of meadow, and 30 acres of wood⌊land⌋ for pannage. T. R. E. and now worth 20 shillings.

---

[1] See 27/61; 69/17.

19. M. In Westbi [Westby (Beltisloe)] Tochi had 1 carucate of land ⌊assessed⌋ to the geld. There is land for 1 team. Colegrim has 5 oxen in a team there, and 1 villein, and 12 acres of meadow, and 30 acres of underwood. T. R. E. it was worth 20 shillings ; now 10 shillings.

20. M. In Lopintorp [Lobthorpe (Beltisloe)] Algar had 1 carucate of land ⌊assessed⌋ to the geld. There is land for 1 team. He himself has 1 team there ⌊in demesne⌋, and 2 villeins, and 8 acres of meadow, and 20 acres of wood⌊land⌋ for pannage. T. R. E. and now worth 20 shillings.

21.[1] M. In Parva Lavintune [Little Lavington (Beltisloe)] Offram had 2 carucates of land ⌊assessed⌋ to the geld. There is land for 2 teams. He himself pledged (*inuadiauit*) 1 carucate of this land for 9 years for 20 shillings, and there are 14 acres of meadow. T. R. E. ⌊it was worth⌋ 20 shillings ; now 5 shillings.

22. M. In Chisebi [Keisby (Beltisloe)] Offram had 4 bovates of land ⌊assessed⌋ to the geld. There is land for 4 oxen. It is waste, except for 3 villeins with 6 oxen. The men of the hundred say that the soke belongs to (*socam iacere in*) Osgotebi [Osgodby in Lavington]. There are 4 acres of meadow there, and 2 acres of underwood. T. R. E. and now worth 10 shillings.

23. M. In Schillintune [Skillington (Beltisloe)] Carle had 1 carucate of land ⌊assessed⌋ to the geld. There is land for 1 team. The same man has it until now (*adhuc*) in alms, and has 4 villeins there with 1 team, and 20 acres of meadow. T. R. E. and now worth 20 shillings.

24. M. In Colsteuorde [Colsterworth (Beltisloe)] a thane of the queen's had 4 carucates of land ⌊assessed⌋ to the geld. There is land for 4 teams. The same man himself has 3 sokemen and 3 villeins and 7 bordars there with 2 teams, and 2 mills rendering 2 shillings, and 1 acre of meadow, and 80 acres of wood⌊land⌋ for pannage. T. R. E. and now worth 20 shillings.

25. In Widme [South Witham (Beltisloe)] Ernuin [the priest] has of the king in alms 6 bovates of land ⌊assessed⌋ to the geld. There is land for 6 oxen. He has 3 villeins and 2 bordars there with 1½ teams, and 21 acres of meadow, and 1 farmer (*censorium*) with 1 team rendering (*de*) 4 shillings. T. R. E. and now ⌊worth⌋ 10 shillings.

26. M. In Burg [Burg[2] (Aswardhurn)] Archil has 5 bovates of land ⌊assessed⌋ to the geld. There is land for 6 oxen. There are 2 sokemen there with 1 team. T. R. E. and now worth 3 shillings.

WESTRED' [WEST RIDING]

27. M. In Torp and Estorp [Thorpe in the Fallows and Aisthorpe (Lawress)] Suen had 6 bovates of land ⌊assessed⌋ to the geld. There is land for 1 team. Uluuiet has it of the king. One villein and 2 bordars have 1 team there, and 13½ acres of meadow. T. R. E. it was worth 8 shillings ; now 20 shillings.

28. There (*ibi*) Alden the priest, ⌊holding⌋ of the king, has 1 church to which belongs 1 bovate of land. Now it is waste. T. R. E. it was worth 5 shillings and 4 pence.

29. In Chestesbi [Kexby (Well)] Leduin, ⌊holding⌋ of the king, has 6 bovates of land ⌊assessed⌋ to the geld. There is land for 6 oxen. It is waste. There are 32 acres of meadow there, and 6½ acres of underwood.

[1] The whole of this entry is underlined.

[2] See p. 197, n. 2.

30. M. In Ingeham [Ingham (Aslacoe)] Seuen had 2 bovates of land ⌊assessed⌋ to the geld. There is land for 3 oxen. Ernuin ⌊has it, holding⌋ of the king and queen. Now there is 1 sokeman there, and 1 villein having 2 oxen in a team, and 4 acres of meadow. T. R. E. and now worth 10 shillings.

D. B., f. 371b. *Facsimile, p. lxxi*b.

31. M. In Filingeham [Fillingham (Aslacoe)] Godric [the deacon] had 2 bovates of land ⌊assessed⌋ to the geld. There is land for 3 oxen. Ernuin [the priest] held it of the queen. Now it is the king's. Roger of Poitou (*Pict'*) took it without anyone delivering it to him (*accepit eam sine liberatore*). Anschitil ⌊now⌋ holds it. 2 sokemen and 1 bordar have 3 oxen in a team there. T. R. E. and now worth 4 shillings.

32. M. In Cletham [Cleatham (Corringham)] Archil had 6 bovates of land ⌊assessed⌋ to the geld. There is land for 12 oxen. Aldene has 1½ teams there ⌊in demesne⌋, and 3 villeins with 1 team, and 6 acres of meadow. T. R. E. and now worth 20 shillings.

33. M. In Hiboldestou [Hibaldstow (Manley)] Brunier had 2 bovates of land ⌊assessed⌋ to the geld. There is land for 6 oxen. Outi has 1 ox in a team there, and 15 acres of meadow. It is worth 2 shillings.

34. M. In Wadingeham [Wadingham (Manley)] Archil ⌊had⌋ 2 bovates of land ⌊assessed⌋ to the geld. There is land for 2 oxen. Aldene has half a team there, and 2 villeins and 2 bordars with 2 oxen in a team, and 1 mill rendering 2 shillings, and 12 acres of meadow. T. R. E. and now worth 5 shillings and 4 pence.

35. M. In the same place (*ibidem*) Godric [the deacon] had 3 bovates of land ⌊assessed⌋ to the geld. There is land for 3 oxen. Elfain has 3 villeins and 2 bordars there with 1 team, and 14 acres of meadow. T. R. E. it was worth 10 shillings; now 20 shillings.

36. S. In the same place (*ibidem*) Elfain has 2 bovates of land ⌊assessed⌋ to the geld. There is land for 2 oxen. It is soke⌊land⌋ of the same manor. 2 sokemen have half a team there.

37. M. In Iadulftorp [Yaddlethorpe (Manley)] Chetel had 1 carucate of land ⌊assessed⌋ to the geld. There is land for 1 team. It is waste. Waldin had it, but the king gave it back to an Englishman (*reddidit anglico*). There are 16 acres of meadow there, and 13 acres of underwood. T. R. E. ⌊it was worth⌋ 20 shillings.

38. Two M. In Wintrintone [Winterton (Manley)] Grimbol and Fulcheric had 11 bovates of land ⌊assessed⌋ to the geld. There is land for as many oxen. Seuard [the priest] has 1 villein and 1 bordar there having 2 oxen in a team. T. R. E. it was worth 50 shillings; now 15 shillings.

39. M. In Ulvesbi [Ulceby (Yarborough)] Hugh had 4 bovates of land ⌊assessed⌋ to the geld. There is land for 11 oxen. The same man himself has 1 team there ⌊in demesne⌋. T. R. E. and now worth 10 shillings.

40. M. In Golse [Goxhill (Yarborough)] Hugh had 4 bovates of land ⌊assessed⌋ to the geld. There is land for 1 team. The same man has 4 villeins there with 1 team, and 60 acres of meadow. T. R. E. it was worth 20 shillings; now the like amount.

41. M. In Neutone [Newton by Toft (Walshcroft)] Justen had 3 bovates of land [assessed] to the geld. There is land for 1 team. The same man has it, and it is waste. T. R. E. it was worth 5 shillings and 4 pence.

42. M. In Aresbi [Owersby (Walshcroft)] Ernuin [the priest] had half a carucate of land [assessed] to the geld. There is land for 1 team. Siward [the priest] has half a team there [in demesne], and 2 sokemen on (*de*) 2 bovates of this land and 2 villeins with 3 oxen in a team, and 1 mill rendering 3 shillings, and 20 acres of meadow. T. R. E. it was worth 40 shillings; now 10 shillings.

43. M. In Osgotebi [Osgodby (Walshcroft)] Abo had 2½ bovates of land [assessed] to the geld. There is land for 5 oxen. It is waste. Seward has it. There are 6 acres of meadow there. T. R. E. [it was worth] 10 shillings; now 3 shillings.

44. M. In Cucualt [Cuxwold (Haverstoe)] Stanchil had 6 bovates of land [assessed] to the geld. There is land for 10 oxen. Seward has 3[1] sokemen and 2 bordars there with 6 oxen in a team. T. R. E. it was worth 20 shillings; now 5 shillings.

45. M. In Belesbi [Beelsby (Haverstoe)] Agemund had 4 bovates of land [assessed] to the geld. There is land for 1 team. Godric his son has there 2 oxen in a team, and 6 acres of meadow. T. R. E. [it was worth] and now worth 5 shillings.

46. M. In Osgotebi [Osgodby (Walshcroft)] Summerlede [had] 1 bovate of land [assessed] to the geld. There is land for 2 oxen. Siward [the priest] has 1 villein and 1 bordar there with 1 ox. T. R. E. it was worth 5 shillings; now 2 shillings.

D. B., f. 371c. *Facsimile, p. lxxii*a.

47. M. In Risun [Riseholme (Lawress)] Agemund [the priest] [had] half a carucate of land [assessed] to the geld. [There is land for 4 oxen]. The same man himself has 1 team there [in demesne]. This belongs to the church of Saint Michael. T. R. E. it was worth 10 shillings; now 20 shillings.

48. M. In Neteltone [Nettleton (Yarborough)] Leueua [had] 5 bovates of land [assessed] to the geld. There is land for 2 teams. She herself has half a team there [in demesne], and 2 villeins and 1 bordar and 1 sokeman with half a team, and 1 mill rendering 12 pence, and 20 acres of meadow. T. R. E. it was worth 20 shillings; now 5 shillings.

D. B., f. 372a-d. *Facsimile, pp. lxxiv, lxxv [blank].*

D. B., ff. 373a-374 *[relates to Yorkshire].*

D. B., f. 374c-d *[blank].*

---

[1] The first *i* of *iii* has been altered from the sign for *et*.

[DISPUTES]

D. B., f. 375a. *Facsimile, p. lxxva.*

[69]. CLAMORES QUE SUNT IN SVDTREDING LINCOLIE ET CONCORDIA EORUM PER HOMINES QUI IURAUERUNT.

1. In Tadeuuelle hundred clamant homines episcopi Baiocensis .i. carucatam terre super Robertum dispensatorem . et homines de Wapentac dicunt quod ipse episcopus iure debet habere.

2. In eodem hundred clamant homines eiusdem episcopi super Hugonem comitem iii. bouatas terrę . et Wapentac dicit quod ipse episcopus debet habere.

3. In eodem hundred . molendinum quod fuit Agemund . et post eum habuerunt Lanbertus et Gozelinus filius eius . dicit Wapentac quod Robertus dispensator debet habere cum terra sua.

4. In Lvde hundred clamat episcopus Lincolie .i. molendinum super Alanum comitem . et Wapentac testatur eiusdem episcopi esse debere.

5. Terras[1] illas quas habuerunt Alsi et Olgrim in Lindesi[1] . posuerunt ęcclesię sancte Marię Lincolię . et in misericordia Wluui episcopi . et ideo clamat eas . R. episcopus . quia habuerunt pro ipsis terris octies .xx. libras . T. R. E.

6. In Bvruelle hundred clamant ministri regis [super Hugonem comitem] in Hecham et Welle terras .ii.orum fratrum Godric et Edric . et homines de Wapentac deratiocinauerunt eas ad opus regis.

7. In Carleton hundred . clamat Willelmus Perci dimidiam carucatam terrę super Colsuan . et Wapentac testificatur eidem Willelmo.

8. In Summercotes hundred clamat Aluredus de Lincole dimidiam carucatam terrę super regem in Gereburg . set Treding dicit quod non habet ibi nisi .ix. acras et dimidiam . et unam toft . unde iacet soca in Gedtune manerio regis.

9. In eodem hundred clamat Siuuard Buss .i. molindinum super Aluredum . et homines de Treding [dicunt] quod Aluredus habet medietatem in Cadint' . R. de Brimou . et aliam medietatem habet episcopus Dunelmensis socam in Cadintone.

10. In Schitebroc hundred clamat Aluredus .iii. bouatas terrę in Stiueton . super Ilbertum . dicunt homines de Treding quod ipse Aluredus debet habere.

---

[1] There are spaces left here on account of a defect in the vellum.

D.B., f. 375a. *Facsimile, p. lxxva.*

[69]. DISPUTES WHICH THERE ARE IN THE SOUTH RIDING OF LINCOLN, AND THEIR SETTLEMENT BY THE JURORS.

[WAPENTAKE OF LOUTHESK]

1. In Tathwell hundred the Bishop of Bayeux' men claim 1 carucate of land against Robert the Steward; and the men of the Wapentake say that the said bishop ought by right to have it. [See 38/12].

2. In the same hundred the same bishop's men claim 3 bovates of land against Earl Hugh; and the Wapentake says that the said bishop ought to have them. [See 13/28].

3. In the same hundred the Wapentake says that Robert the Steward ought to have with his land the mill which was Agemund's, and after Agemund, Lambert and Gocelin his son had it. [See 38/12].

4. In Louth hundred the Bishop of Lincoln claims 1 mill against Count Alan; and the Wapentake bears witness that it ought to be the same bishop's.

5. Those lands which Alsi and Olgrim had in Lindsey they placed in the church of Saint Mary of Lincoln, and at the discretion of Bishop Wulfwig; and therefore Bishop Remigius claims them because they [Alsi and Olgrim] had 8 score pounds for these lands T. R. E.

6. In Burwell hundred the king's officers claim [against Earl Hugh] in Haugham [see 13/44] and Maidenwell [see 13/33] the lands of the two brothers Godric and Edric; and the men of the Wapentake have deraigned them to the king's use.

7. In Little Carlton hundred William Perci claims half a carucate of land against Colsuan; and the Wapentake bears witness in favour of the said William. [See 22/29].

8. In Somercotes hundred Alfred of Lincoln claims half a carucate of land against the king in Yarborough; but the Riding says that he [Alfred] has nothing there except 9½ acres and 1 toft whereof the soke belongs to the king's manor of Gayton le Wold. [See 1/87].

9. In the same hundred Siward Buss claims 1 mill against Alfred; and the men of the Riding say that Alfred has a moiety belonging to (*in*) Rayner de Brimou's [manor of] Keddington, and that the Bishop of Durham has the other moiety whereof the soke belongs to Keddington. [See 3/27; 40/17].

10. In Skidbrooke hundred Alfred claims 3 bovates of land in Stewton against Ilbert. The men of the Riding say that the said Alfred ought to have it [See 4/73; 27/26].

11. In Widcale hundred clamat Rayner totum monasterium . et homines de Treding [dicunt] quod antecessoris sui fuit . et tercia pars [de] soca . et Ilbertus de Laci .ii. partes soce super ecclesiam . et terram quę illuc iacet. Require [*in margin*].

12. In Svabi hundred clamat Robertus Dispensator super Hugonem comitem in Clactorp .i. carucatam terre . homines de Treding dicunt quod soca iacet in Grethàm . et fuit Witlac . et ipse terram exiuit . et foris fecit . et dicunt quod Robertus dispensator nil ibi habet.

13. In Richesbi hundred clamat Losuardus super Gislebertum de Gand in Welle .i. carucatam terre . Homines de Treding dicunt quod T. R. E. habuit Turolf cum saca et soca . et post habuit Tonna . et ista terra fuit deliberata episcopo Odoni per cartam . set non uiderunt inde breuem regis . et ipse habebat ea die qua fuit captus . et postea fuit dissaisitus.

14. In eodem hundred clamat Rayner de Brimou super Hugonem comitem in Vlesbi .ii. bouatas terrę . et homines de Treding dicunt [quod] non debet habere nisi socam in Combreuorde . et comes terram.

15. In Tedlagestorp hundred clamat episcopus Dunelmensis super Hugonem comitem in Maltorp .ii. bouatas . Homines de Treding dicunt quod non habet nisi .i. bouatam que fuit Bertor . et soca . est . H. comitis in Gretham . *et ibidem Willelmus Blundus .iii. bouatas quę fuerunt Summerdi et Godrici et Siuuardi . et soca . est in Gretham . testimonio totius Treding.

**D.B., f. 375*b. *Facsimile, p. lxxv*b.

16. In Hotot hundred . clamat Aluredus .ii. bouatas terrę . et dicunt homines de Treding quod unam debet habet[1] habere cum saca et soca . et alia similiter eius est . set socam habet . H. comes in Gretham.

17. In eodem hundred socam unius bouate quam clamat Aluredus super Ketelber in Sutune . dicit Treding quod isdem Aluredus debet habere.

18. In Mundbi hundred clamat . A. comes super Gislebertum de Gant .ii. bouatas terrę . set Treding dicit quod antecessor . G. habuit inde sacam et socam . T. R. E. et ipsius debet . esse.

19. In Wilgebi hundred clamat episcopus Dunelmensis super . G. de Gand terram Alnot presbiteri . et dicunt homines de Treding quod nunquam uiderunt antecessorem episcopi fuisse saisitum neque per breuem neque per legatum . et testantur ad opus Gisleberti.

20. In eodem hundred testantur homines de Tredinc quod Ketelber debet habere .xx. acras siluę in Humbi . et Iuo [Taillebo] socam.

---

[1] *habet* is inserted in error.

11. In Withcall hundred Rayner claims the whole of the church; and the men of the Riding [say] that it was his predecessor's, as was a third part of the soke; and that Ilbert de Laci has two parts of the soke over the church, and the land which belongs thereto. Inquire [*in margin*]. [See 4/72; 40/26].

[WAPENTAKE OF CALCEWATH]

12. In Swaby hundred Robert the Steward claims against Earl Hugh 1 carucate of land in Claythorpe. The men of the Riding say that the soke belongs to Greetham, and was Witlac's, and that Witlac himself departed from the land, and made forfeiture; and they say that Robert the Steward has nothing there. [See 13/3].

13. In Rigsby hundred Losuard claims 1 carucate of land in Well against Gilbert de Gand. The men of the Riding say that T. R. E. Turolf had it with sake and soke; and afterwards Tonna had it; and this land was delivered to Bishop Odo by charter; but they have not seen the king's writ therefor; and he [Odo] had it on the day on which he was taken; and he was afterwards disseised. [See 4/62; 24/68].

14. In the same hundred Rayner de Brimou [claims] 2 bovates of land in Ulceby by Spilsby against Earl Hugh; and the men of the Riding say that he ought to have nothing except the soke, which belongs to Comberworth, and the earl the land. [See 40/22].

15. In Theddlethorpe hundred the Bishop of Durham claims 2 bovates against Earl Hugh in Mablethorpe. The men of the Riding say that he has only 1 bovate which was Bertor's, and that the soke belongs to Earl Hugh in Greetham.* And in the same place [*sc.* Mablethorpe] William Blund has 3 bovates which were Summerd's and Godric's and Siward's; and the soke belongs to Greetham by the testimony of the whole Riding. [See 13/7].

**D. B., f.* 375b. *Facsimile, p. lxxv*b.

16. In Huttoft hundred Alfred claims 2 bovates of land. And the men of the Riding say that he ought to have one with sake and soke; and the other is his in like wise, but Earl Hugh has the soke in Greetham. [See 27/60].

17. In the same hundred the Riding says that Alfred ought to have the soke of 1 bovate which he claims against Ketelber in Sutton in the Marsh. [See 27/61; 68/14].

18. In Mumby hundred Count Alan claims 2 bovates of land against Gilbert de Gant; but the Riding says that Gilbert's predecessor had the sake and soke thereof T. R. E., and that it ought to be his. [See 12/93; 24/55].

19. In Willoughby in the Marsh hundred the Bishop of Durham claims the land of Alnot the priest against Gilbert de Gand; and the men of the Riding say that they never saw the bishop's predecessor seised of it, either by writ or by deputy; and they testify in Gilbert's favour. [See 24/54].

20. In the same hundred the men of the Riding testify that Ketelber ought to have 20 acres of wood in Hamby, and Ivo [Taillebois] the soke. [See 14/85, 100].

21. De calumnia inter episcopum Dunelmensem et Eudonem filium Spireuuic . portauerunt testimonium homines de Hornecastre wapentac annuente toto Treding . quod .iii. fratres Herold et Godeuert et Aluric diuiserunt dominicam terram patris sui ęqualiter et pariliter . et solummodo Herold et Godeuert diuiserunt socam patris sui sine tercio fratre . et equaliter et pariliter tenuerunt eam . T. R. E.

22. De soca .vi. bouatarum unde . est calumnia inter episcopum et Eudonem in Langetone et in Torp' : dicunt homines de Waragehou Wapentac quod predicti duo fratres equaliter et pariliter habuerunt socam . T. R. E. sed eo anno quo isdem rex mortuus est filii Godeuert habebant socam totam . sed nesciunt qua ratione eam habebant . utrum ui . uel dono patrui sui.

23. De calumnia quam Robertus dispensator . facit super Gislebertum de Gant de silua quę . est in Langetone . dicit Waragehou Wapentac quod Tonna habebat T. R. E. cum saca et soca in Badeburg . et ideo iure habet .G. de Gand . annuente toto Treding.

24. De silua minuta quam clamat Robertus dispensator super regem in Gaintone . et super Ernegis de Burun in Waragebi . nihil ibi habet testimonio Wapentac . Sed super .xii. acras comitis . Hugonis . et super viii. acras episcopi Baiocensis . habet socam per testimonium hominum Wapentac et Treding.

25. Clamorem quem faciebat Rayner de Brimou super Aluredum de Lincolia de soca .iii. bouatarum et dimidie . nil ibi debet habere ut testantur homines de Wapentac et Treding . sed Rogerus Pictauensis debet habere in domo Clac antecessoris sui in Haintone.

26. De calumnia quam facit Ernegis de Burun super Willelmum de Perci*. in Lagesbi . [de soca .iiii. bouatarum .] dicit Wapentac quod isdem Ernegis debet eam iure habere.

*D. B., f. 375c. *Facsimile, p. lxxvia.*

27. De calumnia quam archiepiscopus Thomas faciebat . hoc est quod debebat habere socam super terram Siuuard antecessoris Iuonis Tallebosc . dicit Wapentac et Treding quod Siuuard tam bene tenuit terram suam cum saca et soca . sicut tenuit Goduinus antecessor archiepiscopi . et ideo non recte clamat.

28. Archiepiscopus Thomas debet habere socam super terram Aschil quam habet episcopus Baiocensis in Vlingeham . quia sicut testatur totus Comitatus . antecessor archiepiscopi habuit sacam et socam super eandem terram . et homines episcopi iniuste auferunt eidem archiepiscopo eandem socam.

[WAPENTAKE OF HORNCASTLE]

21. Touching the dispute between the Bishop of Durham and Eudo son of Spirewic, the men of the Wapentake of Hornecastle bore witness, with the assent of the whole Riding, that the three brothers Herold and Godevert and Alfric divided their father's demesne land equally and share and share alike; and that Herold and Godevert only, without the third brother, divided their father's soke, and that they held the soke T. R. E. equally and share and share alike.

[WAPENTAKE OF WRAGGOE]

22. Touching the soke of 6 bovates, whereof there is a dispute between the bishop and Eudo in Langton by Wragby and [*query* Low] Langton, the men of the Wapentake of Wraggoe say that the aforesaid two brothers had the soke T. R. E. equally and share and share alike; but in the year in which the same king died, the sons of Godevert had the whole soke, but they know not on what ground they had it, whether by force or by their uncle ⌊Harold's⌋ gift. [See 3/10].

23. Touching the claim which Robert the Steward makes against Gilbert de Gant touching the wood which is in Langton by Wragby, the Wapentake of Wraggoe, with the assent of the whole Riding, says that Tonna used to have it T. R. E. with sake and soke in Baumber; and therefore that G. de Gand has it by right. [See 24/16; 38/11].

24. Touching the underwood which Robert the Steward claims against the king in Hainton, and against Ernegis de Burun in Wragby, Robert has nothing there according to the testimony of the wapentake; but, by the testimony of the men of the Wapentake and Riding, he has the soke over 12 acres of Earl Hugh's and over 8 acres of the Bishop of Bayeux'. [See 34/12].

25. Rayner de Brimou ought to have nothing in respect of the claim which he made against Alfred of Lincoln touching the soke of 3½ bovates, as the men of the Wapentake and Riding testify; but Roger of Poitou ought to have it as belonging to the house of his predecessor Clac in Hainton. [See 16/14].

26. Touching the claim which Ernegis de Burun makes against William de Perci* in Legsby [concerning the soke of 4 bovates], the Wapentake says that the said Ernegis ought by right to have it. [See 22/37; 34/14].

**D. B., f. 375c.* *Facsimile, p. lxxvia.*

27. Touching the claim which Archbishop Thomas made, that is, that he ought to have the soke over the land of Siward, the predecessor of Ivo Tallebosc, the Wapentake says, and the Riding too, that Siward held his land with sake and soke as well as Godwin, the archbishop's predecessor ⌊held his⌋, and therefore the archbishop does not claim it rightly. [See 2/16; 14/58].

28. Archbishop Thomas ought to have the soke over Aschil's land which the Bishop of Bayeux has in South Willingham, because, as the whole County testifies, the archbishop's predecessor had sake and soke over the same land, and the bishop's men unjustly withdrew the same soke from the same archbishop. [See 2/1; 4/53].

29. T. R. E. fuit saisitus Almær antecessor archiepiscopi Thomę de soca .x. bouatarum in Vlingeham. Hec terra fuit Code. et modo est Rayner de Brimou. et pro .iii. libris fuit inuadiata. T. R. E. et modo affirmant homines de Treding. quod archiepiscopus iure debet habere hanc socam. quousque ei reddantur .iii. libre.

30. Gislebertus de Gand et Norman de Areci calumniantur super. W. de Perci socam .xii. bouatarum in Steinfelde quę pertinet ad Berlinge. et fuit Tonne. Sed Wapentac et Comitatus dicit quod Gislebertus debet habere non Normannus. Willelmus uero de Perci tenet eam dono regis. sicut tenuit Robertus filius Stigandi.

31. Eandem rationem testantur de soca .vii. bouatarum in Apelei. quia iacet in Berlinga. et Tonna tenuit eam. T. R. E.

32. In eadem Apelei calumniatur episcopus Dunelmensis socam .ii. bouatarum super W. de Perci. et Wapentac dicit quod antecessor eiusdem episcopi habuit. et ipse debet habere in Bolintone.

33. Wapentac de Hornecastre dicit quod iniuste facit calumniam Robertus dispensator super Gislebertum de Gand. de dimidia carucata terrę in Badeburg. et de alia dimidia carucata in Ellingetone. T. R. E. habuit Tonna ipsam terram.

34. Robertus Dispensator debet habere socam super piscariam et super toftam quam tenet Ketelbern in Cuningesbi. quia Achi antecessor Roberti. habuit eam T. R. E.

35. Calnodeshou Wapentac dicit quod Iuo Tallebosc debet habere in Aschebi quod clamat super. H. comitem hoc. est .i. molindinum et .i. bouatam terrę. Sed soca pertinet ad Gretham.

36. De .ii. carucatis terrę quas calumniatur Robertus dispensator super. G. de Gant in Screnbi per Wiglac antecessorem suum ⁝ dicit Wapentac non eum habuisse nisi .i. carucatam. et soca de ipsa erat in Bardenai. Wiglac autem forisfecit eam terram contra dominum suum. G. et ideo Robertus nil habet ibi testimonio Treding.

37. In eadem Screnbi clamat Chetelber .i. carucatam [super. G. de Gand.] per Godricum. sed dicunt quod non habuit nisi dimidiam carucatam. et soca eius erat in Bardenai. et Chetelber iniuste clamat ut dicit Wapentac. quia antecessor eius eam forisfecit.

38. Testificantur homines de Calnodeshou Wapentac consen*tiente toto Treding ⁝ quod Siuuate et Alnod et Fenchel et Aschil equaliter et pariliter diuiserunt inter se terram patris sui. T. R. E. et ita tenuerunt ut si opus fuit expeditione regis et Siuuate potuit ire. alii fratres iuuerunt

29. T. R. E. Almær, Archbishop Thomas' predecessor, was seised of the soke of 10 bovates in South Willingham. This land was Code's, and now it is Rayner de Brimou's; and it was given in pledge for 3 pounds T. R. E.; and now the men of the Riding assert that the archbishop ought by right to have this soke until the 3 pounds are rendered to him. [See 2/1; 40/8].

30. Gilbert de Gand and Norman de Areci claim against William de Perci the soke of 12 bovates in Stainfield which belongs to Barlings, and was Tonna's; but the Wapentake says, and also the County, that Gilbert ought to have it, not Norman. William de Perci however holds it by the king's gift, as Robert son of Stigand held it. [See 22/16].

31. They put forward the same argument touching the soke of 7 bovates in Apley, because it belongs to Barlings, and Tonna held it T. R. E. [See 22/19].

32. In the same Apley the Bishop of Durham claims the soke of 2 bovates against William de Perci; and the Wapentake says that the said bishop's predecessor had it, and he himself ought to have it as belonging to Bullington. [See 22/20].

[WAPENTAKE OF HORNCASTLE]

33. The Wapentake of Hornecastle says that Robert the Steward makes an unjust claim against Gilbert de Gand touching half a carucate of land in Baumber [see 24/20] and touching another half carucate in Edlington [see 24/22]. Tonna had this land T. R. E. [see 24/20].

34. Robert the Steward ought to have the soke over a fishery and over a toft which Ketelbern holds in Coningsby, because Achi, Robert's predecessor, had it T. R. E. [See 38/4; 68/6].

[WAPENTAKE OF CANDLESHOE]

35. The Wapentake of Candleshoe says that Ivo Tallebosc ought to have in Ashby by Partney what he claims against Earl Hugh, that is, 1 mill and 1 bovate of land; but the soke belongs to Greetham. [See 13/6].

36. Touching 2 carucates of land which Robert the Steward claims against Gilbert de Gant in Scremby through Wiglac his predecessor, the Wapentake says that Wiglac had only 1 carucate, and the soke of that belonged to Bardney; but Wiglac forfeited that land to Gilbert his lord, and therefore, by the testimony of the Riding, Robert has nothing there. [See 24/47].

37. In the same Scremby Chetelber claims 1 carucate through Godric [against Gilbert de Gand]; but they say that Godric had only half a carucate, and its soke belonged to Bardney; and Chetelber claims unjustly, as the Wapentake says, because his predecessor forfeited it. [See 24/47].

[WAPENTAKES OF CANDLESHOE AND BOLINGBROKE]

38. The men of the Wapentake of Candleshoe, with the consent* of the whole Riding, testify that T. R. E. Siwate and Alnod and Fenchel and Aschil divided their father's land amongst them equally and share and share alike, and held it in such wise that if there were a call to the king's army, and Siwate could go, the other brothers assisted him. After Siwate,

eum . Post istum ! iuit alter . et Siuuate cum reliquis iuuit eum . et sic de omnibus . Siuuate tamen fuit homo regis . Hoc idem testificantur de Bolimbroc cum supradictis . annuente [sud] Treding.

**D. B., f. 375*d. *Facsimile, p. lxxvi*b.

39. In Salfluet et in Mare et in Suine . est nouum theloneum assuefactum . et accepit illud Ansgerus de Schitebroc . et Rainaldus et Hunfridus et Goisfridus et hoc dicit Ludes Wapentac et totum Sudtreding quod hoc theloneum non fuit . T. R. E. Godricus dedit theloneum .i. denarii testimonio Vlchil de Estrebi qui uidit . et hoc testatur Archil de Widerne quod ipse uidit Ansgerum recipere theloneum de nauibus de Hasting' .xxiiij.

40. In Salfluet accipit Hugo seruiens consuetudines nauium quę ibi ueniunt gratis et ingratis . que non fuerunt ibi . T. R. E. et hoc inceperunt nouiter . et hoc dicunt homines de Treding . quod uiderunt inde clamorem fieri.

[70]. CLAMORES IN NORTREDING

1. In Bertune et in Ferebi accipiunt homines Gisleberti de Gand theloneum aliud quam acceperunt . T. R. E. de pane . piscibus . coriis . et aliis rebus plurimis . unde nunquam datum fuit.

2. In Castre faciunt similiter homines regis.

3. In Limberge clamat Iuo Tallebosc super regem .vi. bouatas terre . dicunt homines Comitatus quod ipse debet habere terram . et rex socam.

4. Pro xxx. acris prati quas Aluredus clamat in Vluesbi . debet habere in eadem uilla unam culturam terrę.

5. Testatur Gereberg Wapentac . quod Morcar dedit Hugoni cum saca et soca .iiii. bouatas terre in Golsa . quas clamat Drogo de Beurere . De ipsa terra clamat Aluredus .i. bouatam . Dicit Wapentac quod Hugonis . est terra . et Aluredi est soca.

6. Wapentac testatur quod ęcclesiam [de Castre] dedit rex W. sancte Marię Lincolię in elemosinam . ad quam ęcclesiam pertinent .ii. bouate terre in dominio . et ii. uillani . et i. molindinum . et in Hunidune soca .i. carucate.

7. Gozelinus clamat .iii. bouatas terre in Seurebi . super .A. comitem . Dicit Comitatus quod Gozelinus habere debet non Alanus.

a second went, and Siwate with the rest assisted him; and thus with respect to them all. Siwate however was the king's man. [The men] of Bolingbroke bear witness to the same with the aforesaid [men of] Candleshoe, the South Riding assenting.

**D. B., f. 375*d. *Facsimile, p. lxxvi*b.

[WAPENTAKE OF LOUTHESK]

39. In Saltfleet Haven and in Mare and in Swine[1] a new toll has been established, and Ansger of Skidbrook has taken it, and Raynald and Humphrey and Geoffrey also; and the Wapentake of Louthesk says, and the whole South Riding also, that this toll did not exist T. R. E. Godric gave a toll of 1 penny, according to the testimony of Ulchil of Asterby who saw it. Archil of Withern testifies that he saw Ansger receive the toll in respect of 24 ships from Hastings.

40. In Saltfleet Hugh the serjeant takes the customs of ships which come there, whether it is admitted or not, which custom did not exist there T. R. E.; and these men began this as a new practice. And the men of the Riding say that they saw the claim made therefor.

[70]. DISPUTES IN THE NORTH RIDING

[WAPENTAKE OF YARBOROUGH]

1. In Barton on Humber and South Ferriby Gilbert de Gand's men take another toll than they took T. R. E. in respect of bread, fish, hides, and very many other things, for which nothing was ever given T. R. E. [See 24/13, 14].

2. In Caistor the king's men do in like manner. [See 1/65].

3. In Limber Ivo Tallebosc claims 6 bovates of land against the king. The men of the County say that he ought to have the land, and the king the soke. [See 1/67; 14/31].

4. Instead of 30 acres of meadow which Alfred claims in Ulceby near Brigg, he ought to have 1 shot of land in the same vill.

5. The Wapentake of Yarborough bears witness that in Goxhill [Earl] Morcar gave Hugh 4 bovates of land with sake and soke, which Drew de Beurere claims. Alfred claims 1 bovate of this land. The Wapentake says that the land is Hugh's, and the soke is Alfred's. [See 27/1; 30/2].

6. The Wapentake bears witness that King William gave the church [of Caistor] to Saint Mary of Lincoln in alms; to which church belong 2 bovates of land in demesne, and 2 villeins, and 1 mill, and in Hundon the soke of one carucate. [See 1/65].

7. Gocelin claims 3 bovates of land in Searby against Count Alan. The County says that Gocelin ought to have it, not Alan. [See 12/10].

[1] For these places, see Index.

8. Hugo . filius . Baldri clamat dimidiam bouatam terre in Brochelesbi . Dicunt homines de Treding quod eius esse debet terra . et Normanni soca . per suos antecessores.

9. In Stalinburg .ii. maneria [Elaf .] dicit Wapentac quod Raynerus diaconus [ea] tenebat . ea die qua exiuit de hac patria .

10. Raynerus de Brimou debet habere socam in Limberge de dimidia bouata terre quam habet archiepiscopus Thomas in Stalingeburg.

11. De uno manerio [Elaf] quod modo habet Thomas archiepiscopus in Chelebi . erat saisitus Raynerus diaconus ipsa die qua de hac terra exiuit.

12. In Cotes debet Aluredus habere terram de .ii. bouatis . et Durandus Malet socam . cum .iii. uillanis qui pertinent ad eam.

13. De .i. carucata terrę in Sualun . fuit Raynerus [diaconus] saisitus quando exiit* de hac terra . Similiter de terra Æiric erat saisitus . [isdem Raynerus diaconus .] quę . est in Grimesbi hundred . modo habet episcopus Baiocensis.

**D. B., f. 376a.* *Facsimile, p. lxxviia.*

14. Homines Radulfi de Mortemer et homines Losoardi . accipiunt nouum theloneum in Grimesbi . quod non fuit T. R. E. sed Losoardus negat suos homines fecisse per eum.

15. Episcopus Baiocensis et episcopus Lincoliensis debent habere socam super ii. bouatas terrę et dimidiam . quę iacet in ęcclesia de Wingeham.

16. In Oresbi hundred . habet episcopus Baiocensis socam super dimidiam carucatam terrę quę fuit Ernuini presbiteri . et modo est Siuuardi presbiteri.

17. In Osgotebi debet habere Gozelinus filius Lanberti . socam super dimidiam bouatam terrę. Require [*in margin*].

18. In Tauelesbi hundred . habuit Raynerus [diaconus] terram Eiric cum omnibus ibidem pertinentibus . Gozelinus eam tenet . et Raynerus calumniatur . Treding testatur quod antecessor comitis Alani habuit socam . sed nesciunt qualem.

19. In Clachesbi debet habere Gozelinus filius Lanberti .i. molindinum . quod Goisfridus homo Iuonis Taillebosc inuasit super eum.

20. In Crosbi debet habere Willelmus Blundus unum hortum . in terra Iuonis Tallebosc . sed impeditur propter molendinum quod non fuit ibi . T. R. E.

21. In Fugelestou debet episcopus Dunelmensis habere .xl. acras terrę [prati[1]] . et iiii. toftas . et comes Alanus inde socam . sicut dicit Wapentac.

---

[1] *prati* is probably meant to be a correction of *terrę*.

8. Hugh son of Baldric claims half a bovate of land in Brocklesby. The men of the Riding say that the land ought to be his, and the soke Norman's, through their predecessors. [See 32/2].

9. In Stallingborough touching [Elaf's] 2 manors, the Wapentake says that Rayner the deacon held them on the day on which he departed from this country. [See 2/6].

10. Rayner de Brimou ought to have as belonging to Limber the soke of half a bovate of land which Archbishop Thomas has in Stallingborough. [See 2/25; 40/1].

11. Touching 1 manor of [Elaf's], which Archbishop Thomas [of York] now has in Keelby, Rayner the deacon was seised of it on the same day on which he departed out of this land. [See 2/8].

[WAPENTAKE OF BRADLEY]

12. In Great Cotes Alfred ought to have the land of 2 bovates, and Durand Malet the soke, with 3 villeins who belong to it. [See 27/3; 44/8].

13.* Rayner [the deacon] was seised of 1 carucate of land in Swallow when he departed* from this land. [See 2/10]. Likewise [the same Rayner the deacon] was seised of Eiric's land which is in Grimsby hundred. Now the Bishop of Bayeux has it. [See 4/70, 71].

**D. B., f. 376*a. *Facsimile, p. lxxvii*a.

14. Ralph de Mortemer's men and Losoard's men take a new toll in Grimsby, which did not exist T. R. E.; but Losoard denies that his men took it on his account. [See 36/1].

[WAPENTAKE OF WALSHCROFT]

15. The Bishop of Bayeux and the Bishop of Lincoln ought to have the soke over $2\frac{1}{2}$ bovates of land which belongs to the church of Winghale.

16. In Owersby hundred the Bishop of Bayeux has the soke over half a carucate of land which was Ernuin the priest's, and now is Siward the priest's. [See 4/74].

17. In Osgodby Gocelin son of Lanbert ought to have the soke over half a bovate of land. Inquire [*in margin*]. [See 28/24].

18. In Tealby hundred Rayner [the deacon] used to have Eiric's land with all that belongs to it there. Gocelin holds it, and Rayner claims it. The Riding bears witness that Count Alan's predecessor had the soke, but they know not of what sort. [See 28/20; 40/14].

19. In Claxby by Normanby Gocelin son of Lanbert ought to have 1 mill upon which Geoffrey, Ivo Taillebosc's man, entered in despite of him. [See 14/11; 28/23].

20. In Croxby William Blund ought to have 1 garden in Ivo Tallebosc's land; but he is obstructed on account of a mill which was not there T. R. E. [See 14/15].

[WAPENTAKE OF HAVERSTOE]

21. In Fulstow the Bishop of Durham ought to have 40 acres of [meadow[1]] and 4 tofts, and Count Alan the soke thereof, as the Wapentake says. [See 3/6].

22. In eadem uilla in terra Roberti dispensatoris iudicant habere socam Alanum comitem super unam carucatam terrę . et ibi debet habere Drogo .i. salinam quam clamat . et inde Alanus comes socam.

23. De terra Fulcheri in Cucualt fuit saisitus Raynerus diaconus quando exiuit de hac terra . Modo tenet eam Thomas archiepiscopus . Raynerus de Brimou calumniatur.

24. In eadem Cucualt in terra Hugonis filii Baldrici . debet habere Willelmus de Perci .ii. bouatas terrę quas clamat . Wapentac testificatur ei.

25. Dicit Wapentac quod Comes Alanus debet habere socam super aulam Grimchel . cuius terram habet episcopus Dunelmensis in Neutone.

26. Terram Ingemund et fratrum eius non liberauit Colsuan Alano comiti . sed isdem Ingemund subiugauit eam ipsi comiti . propter aliam terram quam tenebat de eo.

27. Nortreding et omnis Comitatus testatur . quod terra Vlf de Ormesbi idest .iiii. carucate terrę et dimidia fuit uenundata in Sancta Maria de Stou T. R. E. et in illa iacuit ipsą die quá isdem rex fuit mortuus . et Re . episcopus postea inde fuit saisitus.

28. In Schemin[1] in terra Iuonis Tallebosc clamat Drogo .iii. man*suras* . quas debet habere testimonio Wapentac . cum saca et soca.

29. In Fodrebi terra Berenger de Todeni debet habere episcopus Dunelmensis .v. bouatas terrę . et Berenger socam inde.

30. Testatur Wapentac et totus Comitatus . quod episcopus Dunelmensis debet habere terram .iii. fratrum cum saca et soca . et Eudo . filius . Spireuuic terram quarti fratris . similiter cum saca et soca . Nomina eorum Siuuate [filius Goduin] . Ælnod Fenchel et Aschil.

22. In the same vill they adjudge that Count Alan has the soke over 1 carucate of land in Robert the Steward's land; and Drew ought to have there 1 salt-pan which he claims, and Count Alan the soke thereof. [See 12/19; 38/14].

23. Rayner the deacon was seised of Fulcheris land in Cuxwold when he departed from this land. Now Archbishop Thomas holds it, Rayner de Brimou claims it. [See 2/9].

24. In the same Cuxwold William de Perci ought to have 2 bovates of land which he claims in the land of Hugh son of Baldric. The Wapentake bears witness in his favour. [See 22/9; 25/10].

25. The Wapentake says that Count Alan ought to have soke over the hall of Grimchel, whose land the Bishop of Durham has in Newton le Wold. [See 3/7; 12/30].

26. Colsuan did not deliver the land of Ingemund and his brothers to Count Alan, but the said Ingemund placed it under the said Count because of other land which he was holding of him. [See 12/31].

[WAPENTAKE OF LUDBOROUGH]

27. The North Riding, and the whole County, bears witness that the land of Ulf of North Ormsby, that is 4½ carucates of land was sold to Saint Mary of Stow T. R. E., and it belonged thereto on the day on which the same king died; and afterwards Bishop Remigius was seised thereof. [See 7/25].

28. In Ivo Tallebosc's land in North Ormsby[1] Drew claims 3 messuages which, by the testimony of the Wapentake, he ought to have with sake and soke.

29. In Fotherby, the land of Berenger de Todeni, the Bishop of Durham ought to have 5 bovates of land, and Berenger the soke thereof. [See 3/20; 18/9].

[WAPENTAKES OF BOLINGBROKE AND CANDLESHOE]

30. The Wapentake, and the whole County, bears witness that the Bishop of Durham ought to have the land of 3 brothers with sake and soke, and Eudo son of Spirewic the land of the fourth brother with sake and soke likewise. Their names are Siwate [son of Godwin], Ælnod, Fenchel, and Aschil. [See 3/21-25, 43-46; 69/38].

---

[1] The three messuages seem to be in North Ormsby (see 14/64; 30/20), and the copyist appears to have taken the name of Scemund (see 30/20), one of the pre-Conquest tenants, as the name of the vill; unless we may hazard the conjecture that some words have been omitted, and amend the text as follows: 'In eadem uilla per Schemin in terra,' etc.

D. B., f. 376b. *Facsimile, p. lxxvii*b.

[71]. CLAMORES IN WESTREDING

1. Lagvlris Wapentac testatur . quod Elnod habuit socam et sacam super terram suam .iii. carucatas in Burton . Modo habet Sortebrant post eum.

2. Abbas de Burg clamat .iiii. bouatas terrę in Risun terra Colsuani . et Wapentac testatur quod T. R. E. iacuerunt in ęcclesia Omnium Sanctorum in Lincolia.

3. Terram quam Gozelinus . filius . Lanberti clamat in Carletone super Normannum Crassum ⁝ inuadiauerunt[1] .iii. burgenses Lincolię . Gudret et Leuuinus et Siuuinus . de Agemund T. R. E.

4. In Scantone Normannus Crassus supermisit .iii. libras et unam markam auri . et hoc uadiauit Iuoni uicecomiti.

5. In Scotstorne hundred . T. R. E. habebat Godric antecessor Normanni .iiii. bouatas terre et dimidiam ut Wapentac testatur.

6. Unam carucatam terrę in eodem hundred clamat Gislebertus de Gand super abbatem de Burg . Wapentac uero testatur quod ipsam terram cum soca sua habebat Sanctus Petrus . die qua . R. E. fuit uiuus et mortuus.

7. In Netelham hundred clamat Remigius episcopus .ii. bouatas terre . et Wapentac testatur quod ipse debet habere.

8. Quartam partem siluę quam calumniantur Rannulfus et Colsuan in Refam . dicit Wapentac quod Sanctus Petrus de Burg debet habere.

9. Wapentac testatur quod Vlchil et Asfort et Restef et Vlmer habuerunt sacam et socam super terras suas . et super homines suos in Stratone hundred . et super forisfacturam de Wapentac habet Sancta Maria ii. partes soce . et comes terciam . Nunc Rex . Similiter de heriete . Et si terram suam forisfecissent ⁝ Sancta Maria ii. partes habuisset . et comes terciam.

10. Scira testatur quod terra Gonneuuate .i. manerium . i. carucate in dominio . fuit forisfacta .ii. partes Sancte Marie . et tercia pars ad opus comitis . Similiter de omni soca quę pertinet ab[2] Bortona . [uel Brogtone .] Similiter et de terra Stangrim .xviii. bouatis terrę . De omnibus tainis qui terram habent in Welle wapentac . habet Sancta Maria .ii. partes de forisfactura et comes terciam . Similiter de heriet .

---

[1] This is a highly unusual use of *inuadio*, but no other construction seems possible.
[2] *Rectius* ad.

*D. B., f. 376*b. *Facsimile, p. lxxvii*b.

[71]. DISPUTES IN THE WEST RIDING

[WAPENTAKE OF LAWRESS]

1. The Wapentake of Lawress bears witness that Elnod had soke and sake over his land, 3 carucates in Burton by Lincoln. Sortebrant now has it after him. [See 68/1].

2. The Abbot of Peterborough claims 4 bovates of land in Riseholme, [namely] Colsuan's land; and the Wapentake bears witness that T. R. E. they belonged to the church of All Saints in Lincoln. [See 8/13; 26/2].

3. Three burgesses of Lincoln, Gudret, Lewin, and Siwin, T. R. E., held in pledge from Agemund the land in Middle Carlton which Gocelin son of Lanbert claims against Norman Crassus. [See 33/1].

4. In Scampton Norman Crassus added 3 pounds and 1 mark of gold, and he pledged all this to Ivo the sheriff.

5. In Scothorne hundred Godric, Norman's predecessor, used to have 4½ bovates of land T. R. E., as the Wapentake bears witness. [See 26/5; 32/29].

6. In the same hundred Gilbert de Gand claims 1 carucate of land against the Abbot of Peterborough. The Wapentake however bears witness that Saint Peter had this land with its soke on the day on which King Edward was alive and dead. [See 8/2].

7. In Nettleham hundred Bishop Remigius claims 2 bovates of land, and the Wapentake bears witness that he ought to have them.

8. The Wapentake says that Saint Peter of Peterborough ought to have the fourth part of a wood in Reepham which Ranulf and Colsuan claim. [See 8/3; 43/5].

[WAPENTAKE OF WELL]

9. The Wapentake bears witness that Ulchil and Asfort and Restef and Ulmer had sake and soke over their lands and over their men in Sturton by Stow hundred. And touching forfeiture in the wapentake, Saint Mary [of Stow] has two parts of the soke, and the earl the third part. Now the king has the third part. Likewise with respect to heriot. And if men forfeited their land, Saint Mary used to have two parts, and the earl the third part. [See 4/3].

10. The Shire bears witness that Gonnewate's land, 1 manor, having 1 carucate in demesne, was forfeited, two parts to Saint Mary of Stow, and the third part to the earl's use. Likewise with respect to all the soke which belongs to Gate Burton [or Broughton]. Likewise also with respect to Stangrim's land, 18 bovates of land. With respect to all the thanes who have land in Well wapentake, Saint Mary has two parts of their forfeiture, and the earl the third part. Likewise with respect to heriot. Likewise if

Similiter si terram suam forisfecissent ! ii. partes in Sancta Maria . et tercia pars in manu comitis . Nunc habet rex . In hac consuetudine non est Gislebertus de Gant . nec Robertus de Todeni . neque Radulfus de Mortemer . per antecessores suos.

11. T. R. E. habuit Grinchel super terram suam sacam et socam . sed anno quo mortuus . est isdem rex fuit ipse forisfactus . et dedit illam Merlosuen uicecomiti pro reatu regis . et de illo fecit hęredem.

12. In Ounebi de terra Agemund habet Gozelinus .ix. bouatas . et Iuo .i. bouatam . Remigius episcopus de his debet habere socam.

D. B., f. 376c. *Facsimile, p. lxxviiia.*

13. In Torp . hundred . T. R. E. habuit Siuuardus [Rufus] .i. carucatam terre . cum saca et soca . et modo tenebat Radulfus de Neuilla de abbate Turoldo . sed non habuit inde liberatorem . Nunc est deratiocinata ad opus regis.

14. In eodem hundred in Lactone uilla . clamat Wido de Credun socam super terram Suen . per antecessorem suum Wilgrim . et Wapentac testatur quia ipse Wilgrim habuit sacam et socam super eundem Suen . T. R. E.

15. Scira testatur quod Aschil habebat ea die qua rex . E. fuit uiuus et mortuus et post . hęc tria maneria . Scotune . Scotre . et Ragenaltorp . in propria libertate . de rege Edwardo . Similiter habebat Muscham in Snotinghamscire . et unum manerium Malmetune tenebat de fratre suo Brand [m*odo*] in presto.

16. Westreding testatur . quod calumnię quę sunt in Epeurde Wapentac recte factę sunt.

(a) Normannus Crassus clamat .vii. bouatas terrę super Goisfridum de Wirce . in Acheseia.

(b) Gislebertus [de Gand] clamat super ipsum Goisfridum .iiii. carucatas terre et vi. bouatas . Hec est terra Vlfenisc in Beltone.

(c) Henricus de Ferrariis clamat super ipsum Goisfridum .iii. bouatas terre . Hec est terra Siuuardbar in Amecotes.

(d) Item Gislebertus de Gand clamat dimidiam carucatam de soca in Beltone . super eundem Goisfridum . quę fuit Vlfenisc.

17. Testatur Wapentac quod in Wintringeham hundred debet

men have forfeited their land, two parts belong to Saint Mary, and the third part is in the earl's hand. Now the king has the third part. Neither Gilbert de Gant nor Robert de Todeni nor Ralf de Mortemer, through their predecessors, are subject to this custom. [See 12/1].

[WAPENTAKE OF ASLACOE]

11. Grinchel had sake and soke over his own land[1] T. R. E., but in the year in which the same king died, he made forfeiture, and he gave it to Merlosuen the sheriff for his offence against the king, and made him his heir. [See 47/1].

12. In Owmby by Normanby Gocelin has Agemund's land, 9 bovates, and Ivo has 1 bovate. Bishop Remigius ought to have the soke of these. [See 7/6; 14/20; 28/4].

*D. B., f. 376*c. *Facsimile, p. lxxviii*a.

[WAPENTAKE OF CORRINGHAM]

13. In Northorpe hundred Siward [Rufus] had 1 carucate of land with sake and soke T. R. E.; and Ralf de Nevill lately held it of Abbot Thorald; but he had not livery thereof. Now it is deraigned to the king's use. [See 8/16].

14. In the same hundred in the vill of Laughton near Gainsborough Guy of Craon, through his predecessor Wilgrim, claims soke over Suen's land; and the Wapentake bears witness that T. R. E. the said Wilgrim had sake and soke over the same Suen. [See 16/28].

[WAPENTAKES OF CORRINGHAM AND MANLEY]

15. The Shire bears witness that, on the day on which King Edward was alive and dead and afterwards, Aschil had these 3 manors, Scotton, Scotter, and Raventhorpe, at his own disposal of King Edward. In like manner he had Muskham in Nottinghamshire. And he held 1 manor, Manton, of his brother Brand by way of lease [only]. [See 8/15, 17, 23].

[WAPENTAKE OF AXHOLME].

16. The West Riding bears witness that the claims which are put forward in Epworth Wapentake[2] are rightly made:

(a) Norman Crassus claims 7 bovates of land against Geoffrey de Wirce in Haxey. [See 63/7].

(b) Gilbert [de Gand] claims 4 carucates and 6 bovates of land against the said Geoffrey. This is Ulf Fenisc's land in Belton in Axholme. [See 63/12].

(c) Henry de Ferrars claims 3 bovates of land against the said Geoffrey. This is Siward Bar's land in Amcotts. [See 63/16].

(d) Also Gilbert de Gand claims against the said Geoffrey half a carucate of soke[land] in Belton in Axholme, which was Ulf Fenisc's. [See 63/21, 26].

[WAPENTAKE OF MANLEY]

17. The Wapentake bears witness that in Wintringham hundred

[1] The land was in Willoughton (see 47/1).

[2] The usual name of the wapentake is *Axholme*.

habere Erneis de Burun terram Wege . idest .vi. bouatas terre et i. toft . in soca Gisleberti de Gand . et aliam toftam cum saca et soca.

18. In Tedulbi hundred clamat Radulfus Pagenel .i. toftam . Wapentac dicit quod ipse debet habere eam . et rex socam in Chirchetone.

19. Super Drogonem clamat Norman de Adreci .iii. bouatas terrę . in Normanebi . Dicit Wapentac quia ipsius debet . esse . terra . et Drogonis soca.

*D. B., f. 376*d. *Facsimile, p. lxxviii*b.

[72]. CLAMORES IN CHETSTEVEN

1. Nesse Wapentac et totum Treding testificauerunt terram Vluiet et Vlflet matris eius non fuisse Erneberne sororii sui . nec eum habuisse nisi in custodia . donec Vluiet terram posset tenere . Idest in Offinton .vii. carucate . In Talintune vi. carucate et dimidia . In Casuic .vi. bouate . In Estdeping iiii. bouate [dimidia carucata].

2. Sexaginta acras terrę quas Iudita comitissa habet et colit cum carucis de Belmestorp . dicit Wapentac quod Sanctus Petrus de Burg habuit . T. R. E. De his . lx acris terre et de .xlviii. acris prati ⁝ iacet warnode in Offintone Aluredi de Lincolia . sed ui est retenta.

3. Dimidiam carucatam terrę Azor in Bercham ⁝ dicit Wapentac debere . esse Gunfridi de Ciochis.

4. Terram Asford in Bercham hundred . dicit Wapentac non habuisse Herewardum die qua aufugiit.

5. Sex bouatas terrę de terra Morcar in Bertone hundred . Radulfus Pagenel habet . sed Merlesuen non habuit T. R. E.

6. Unam bouatam terre clamat abbas de Burg super Drogonem in Witham hundred . dicit Wapentac quod Sancti Petri debet . esse terra . et soca . Gisleberti de Gand in Edeham.

7. In Bintham hundred debet Ratbodus habere .i. carucatam terrę quam clamat . sed soca . est Sancti Petri de Burg.

8. Warnode .iiii. denariorum de .lx. acris siluę quę iacet ad Schillintone . dicunt pertinere in Bitham.

9. In Gerneham dicunt Gerneber habuisse .xiii. acras siluę . et xxv. acras terrę arabilis . et pertinere ad Aslachebi quam habet Robertus de Todeni.

Erneis de Burun ought to have Wege's land, that is 6 bovates of land and 1 toft in the soke of Gilbert de Gand, and another toft with sake and soke. [See 24/12 ; 34/25].

18. In Thealby hundred Ralf Pagenel claims 1 toft. The Wapentake says that he ought to have it, and the king the soke thereof as belonging to Kirton in Lindsey. [See 1/64].

19. Norman de Adreci claims 3 bovates of land in Normanby in Burton on Stather against Drew. The Wapentake says that the land ought to belong to him, and the soke to Drew. [See 30/3].

*D. B., f. 376*d. *Facsimile, p. lxxviii*b.

[72]. DISPUTES IN KESTEVEN

[WAPENTAKE OF NESS]

1. The Wapentake of Ness and the whole Riding have borne witness that the land of Ulviet and his mother Ulflet did not belong to Erneberne his sister's son, and that Erneberne only had it in wardship until Ulviet could hold land ; that is, in Uffington 7 carucates [see 27/34], in Tallington $6\frac{1}{2}$ carucates [see 27/38], in Casewick 6 bovates [see 27/37], and in East Deeping 4 bovates, [half a carucate] [see 27/39].

2. The Wapentake says that T. R. E. Peterborough Abbey had 60 acres of land which Countess Judith has and tills with the teams of Belmesthorpe [Witchley Wapentake, co. Rutland]. The warnode of these 60 acres of land and of 48 acres of meadow belongs to Alfred of Lincoln in Uffington, but it is forcibly withheld. [See 8/33 ; 27/34 ; 56/4].

3. The Wapentake says that Azor's half carucate of land in Barholm ought to belong to Gunfrid de Ciochis. [See 24/35 : 52/1].

4. The Wapentake says that Hereward had not Asford's land in Barholm hundred on the day on which he fled. [See 8/35].

[WAPENTAKE OF BELTISLOE]

5. Ralf Pagenel has 6 bovates of land of Morcar's land in Burton Coggles hundred ; but Merlesuen did not have it T. R. E. [See 35/13].

6. The Abbot of Peterborough claims 1 bovate of land against Drew in Witham on the Hill hundred. The Wapentake says that the land ought to belong to Peterborough Abbey, and the soke to Gilbert de Gand in Edenham. [See 8/6 ; 24/32 ; 30/32].

7. In Bytham hundred Ratbod ought to have 1 carucate of land which he claims ; but the soke belongs to Peterborough Abbey. [See 8/7].

8. They say that the warnode of 4 pence from 60 acres of wood[land], which lies at Skillington, belongs to Bytham. [See 2/37].

9. They say that Gerneber had 13 acres of wood[land] and 25 acres of arable land in Irnham ; and that it belongs to Aslackby, which Robert de Todeni has. [See 18/19].

10. Archiepiscopus Ældredus adquisiuit Lauintone et Schillintone cum berewic Harduic . de Vlf Tope sune . per pecuniam suam quam ei dedit uidente Wapentac . et postea uiderunt sigillum regis per quod resaisitus est de ipsis terris . quia Hilboldus eum dissaisierat de eis.

11. Wapentac dicit Aschil fuisse tainum regis . nec habuisse unquam sub Merlesuen terram suam.

12. Sex bouatas [socam] de terra Archil in Rosbi hundred tenuit Robertus de Stadforde iniuste sicut dicit Wapentac.

13. Calumniam . Re. episcopi quam facit de soca Archil [in Rosbi hundred .] dicunt iniustam esse . quia ipse de terra [eiusdem] Archil non habuit nisi .x. bouatas de dominico in escangio . et tota alia terra liberata . est Dunelmensi episcopo.

14. Nouem bouatas terrę quas clamat Walterus de Aincurt . dicit Wapentac esse socam in Branztun terram Elsi diaconi . quam Walterus modo habet . et ideo iuste calumniatur.

15. Homines de Nauenebi detinent per uim .xvi. solidos de consuetudinibus pascuarum quę sunt in Scapeuuic et Cherchebi . et non dederunt eos in die regis Eduuardi.

16. Robertus de Stadford clamat terram Outi hominis archiepiscopi Thomę debere . iacere in socam Lepsi antecessoris sui . sed Wapentac dicit quod nunquam uiderunt Outi dare socam Lepsi.

17. De clamore Hugonis comitis dicunt quod Houden habebat terram T. R. E. et soca iacebat in Haneuuorde.

D. B., *f.* 377a. *Facsimile*, *p. lxxix*a.

18. In Canuic clamat Sortebrand .cxl acras . Wapentac fert ei testimonium . quia pater suus Vlf dedit pro hac terra unam markam auri in uadimonium.

19. In Pamptune . tenet Iudita comitissa .ii. maneria quę fuerunt Ælmeri et fratrum eius . Robertus de Todeni calumniatur . et Wapentac portat ei testimonium quod deliberata sunt ei in escangio pro Merestune.

20. In Chaschingetorp clamat Robertus de Todeny .ii. bouatas et ii. toftas super Robertum Malet . et Wapentac dicit debere iacere in Vlestanestorp . In eadem uilla dicunt de uno horto quod iacere debeat in Chaschingetorp Roberti de Stadford.

21. Dicunt Norman[us] Mereuuine sune habuisse .vii. hortos in Grantham . de quibus pertinet soca ibidem . sed ipsi horti pertinent ad Gouerdebi [*sic*] . Similiter dicunt de .ii. bouatis terrę quę pertinent ad Gouerdebi [*sic*] et soca iacet in Grantham.

10. Archbishop Ældred acquired Lavington [see 2/42] and Skillington with the berewic of Hardwick [co. Rutland] from Ulf Tope's 'sune' by his own money, which he gave him in the sight of the Wapentake; and afterwards they saw the king's seal by which the archbishop was re-seised of those lands, because Hilbold had disseised him of them. [See 2/37, 38].

[? WAPENTAKE OF FLAXWELL]

11. The Wapentake says that Aschil was the king's thane, and that he never had his land under Merlesuen.

[WAPENTAKE OF FLAXWELL]

12. Robert of Stafford unjustly held 6 bovates, [which were sokeland], of Archil's land in Rauceby hundred, as the Wapentake says. [See 59/12].

13. They say that the claim which Bishop Remigius makes with respect to Archil's soke in [Rauceby hundred] is unjust, because he had only 10 bovates of the demesne of [the same] Archil's land in exchange, and all the rest of the land was delivered to the Bishop of Durham.

[WAPENTAKE OF LANGOE]

14. The Wapentake says that 9 bovates of land which Walter de Aincurt claims, the land of Elsi the deacon which Walter now has, are soke[land] belonging to Branston; and therefore he claims justly. [See 31/11].

15. The men of Navenby forcibly withhold 16 shillings of customary dues of the feedings which are in Scopwick and Kirkby Green; and they did not give them in King Edward's day.

16. Robert of Stafford claims that the land of Outi, Archbishop Thomas's man, ought to lie in the soke of his predecessor Lepsi; but the Wapentake says that they never saw Outi give soke to Lepsi.

17. Touching Earl Hugh's claim, they say that Houden used to have the land T. R. E., and the soke used to lie in Potterhanworth..

D. B., f. 377a. *Facsimile, p. lxxixa.*

18. In Canwick Sortebrand claims 140 acres. The Wapentake bears witness in his favour because his father Ulf gave 1 mark of gold, receiving this land as pledge. [See 6/1].

[WAPENTAKE OF WINNIBRIGGS]

19. In Great and Little Ponton Countess Judith holds 2 manors which were Ælmer and his brothers'. Robert de Todeni claims them; and the Wapentake bears witness in his favour that they were delivered to him in exchange for Marston. [See 56/6, 7].

20. In Casthorpe [see 58/4] Robert de Todeny claims 2 bovates and 2 tofts against Robert Malet; and the Wapentake says that they ought to lie in Woolsthorpe. Touching 1 garden in the same vill, they say that it ought to lie in Robert of Stafford's [manor of] Casthorpe. [See 59/2].

21. They say that Norman Merewin's 'sune' had 7 gardens in Grantham of which the soke belongs to the same place, but the gardens themselves belong to Gonerby. They say the same with respect to 2 bovates of land which pertain to Gonerby, and the soke lies in Grantham.

22. Ivo Taillebosc calumniatur super Robertum de Todeni .ii. carucatas terre .xxx. acras minus in Stanuualt . unde ipse dat geldum . De hoc dicunt rectum . esse . ut ipsi eant super ipsam terram . et partiantur eam recte sicut dant geldum.

23. In Stoche dimidio hundred clamat Robertus de Stadford terram Carle .iii. carucatas terre . Dicit Wapentac quod hec terra fuit Radulfi Stalre . et [predictus] Robertus nil habet ibi.

24. Dicunt pertinere ad ęcclesiam de Grantham decimas et ęcclesiasticas consuetudines de Winebruge Wapentac et de Treos Wapentac . de omnibus socis et inlandis quas rex habet ibi.

25. Osbernus legatus regis clamat .i. carucatam terre in Turoluebi . quam testimonio Wapentac debet habere . et socam in Achelei reddere manerio Judite comitisse.

26. Super Osbernum de Arcis clamat Drogo de Beurere . [socam] .x. bouatas terrę in Turoluesbi . sed dicit Wapentac quia clamat iniuste.

27. De calumnia quam facit abbas Westmonasterii super Balduinum de terra et soca Ælric Meriete sune . dicunt se audisse quod isdem Ælric dedit eam Sancto Petro . sed nesciunt utrum totam aut dimidiam . Dicunt autem quod in Hadinctune sunt viii. carucate [terre] et dimidia soca et inland in Dodintune . et in Hicham .iiii. carucate terrę [socam[1]] in Dodinctone . et in Schellingop .xii. carucate socam[1] in Dodint' . et in Wizebi .vi. carucate terrę inland et soca in Dodinctone . Totum hoc clamat abbas de Westmonasterii . quia capitale manerium datum est Sancto Petro . Omnis comitatus fert Sancto Petro testimonium.

28. Dicit Wapentac habuisse Cofsi .x. bouatas terrę . et i. ecclesiam in soca de Torp. Require [*in margin*].

29. Manerium .iiii. carucatarum terrę in Northicam . dicit Wapentac habuisse Siuuardum . non Vlf patrem Sortebrand . et ideo clamor eius non . est rectus.

30. Sex bouatas . terre in Oustorp . que fuerunt Godric et modo est[2] Martini ! dicunt esse . debere inland in Grenesbi.

31. Terram .vi. bouatarum clamat Radulfus Pagenel in Hechintune super Colsuen que fuit Ælger [diaconi] . dicit Wapentac quia[3] Merlesuen* eam non habuit . antecessor Radulfi.

**D. B., f.* 377b. *Facsimile, p. lxxix*b.

32. In Corninctun clamat Waldinus Brito super abbatem de Ramesy xiiii. bouatas terrę . sed dicit Wapentac quia non recte clamat.

---

[1] *Rectius* soca.

[2] *Rectius* sunt.

[3] In 72/31, 32, 34, 35, 38, 41, 44, 49, 51, 53, 56, and 62, *quia* is used as the equivalent of *quod.*

22. Ivo Taillebosc claims 2 carucates of land less 30 acres in Stenwith against Robert de Todeni for which he [Ivo] gives the geld. Touching this, they say that it is right that they themselves should go upon that land and divide it rightly as Ivo and Robert pay the geld.

23. In Stoke Rochford half hundred Robert of Stafford claims Carle's land, 3 carucates of land. The Wapentake says that this land was Ralf the Staller's, and [the aforesaid] Robert has nothing there. [See 12/91].

24. They say that the tithes and ecclesiastical customs of Winnibriggs Wapentake and Threo Wapentake, in respect of all the sokes and inlands which the king has there, belong to the church of Grantham.

[WAPENTAKE OF GRAFFOE]

25. Osbern, the king's messenger, claims 1 carucate of land in Thurlby which, by the witness of the Wapentake, he ought to have, and for which he ought to render soke in Eagle, Countess Judith's manor. [See 56/15].

26. Drew de Beurere claims 10 bovates of land, [soke[land]], in Thurlby against Osbern de Arcis; but the Wapentake says that he claims unjustly.

27. Touching the claim which the Abbot of Westminster makes against Baldwin with respect to the land and soke of Ælric Meriete's 'sune,' they say that they heard that the same Ælric gave it to Saint Peter, but they know not whether he gave the whole or the half. They say, however, that in Haddington there are 8 carucates and a half [of land], which are soke[land] and inland belonging to Doddington Pigot; and in Hykeham 4 carucates of land, which are [soke[land]] belonging to Doddington Pigot; and in Skellingthorpe 12 carucates, which are soke[land] belonging to Doddington Pigot; and in Whisby 6 carucates of land, which are inland and soke[land] belonging to Doddington Pigot. The abbot of Westminster claims the whole of this because the chief manor was given to Saint Peter. All the County bears witness in Saint Peter's favour. [See 9/1; 65/1–5].

28. The Wapentake says that Cofsi had 10 bovates of land and 1 church in the soke of Thorpe on the Hill. Enquire [*in margin*]. [See 9/2].

29. The Wapentake says that Siward, not Ulf, Sortebrand's father, had a manor of 4 carucates of land in North Hykeham; and therefore his [Sortebrand's] claim is wrong. [See 12/92].

[WAPENTAKE OF ASWARDHURN]

30. They say that 6 bovates of land in Ewerby Thorpe which were Godric's, and now are Martin's, ought to be inland belonging to Ewerby. [See 45/4].

31. Ralf Pagenel claims against Colsuen in Heckington 6 bovates, the land which was Ælger [the deacon's]. The Wapentake says that Merlesuen,* Ralf's predecessor, did not have it. [See 26/27].

**D.B.*, *f.* 377b. *Facsimile*, *p. lxxix*b.

32. In Quarrington Waldin the Breton claims 14 bovates of land against the abbot of Ramsey; but the Wapentake says that he claims unjustly. [See 10/1].

33. In eadem Corninctu[n]e clamat . Re. episcopus se inuadiasse terram Archel . sed ipse hoc negat . et de rege tenet.

34. Colsuan calumniatur .ii. bouatas terrȩ et i. hortum super regem in Cherchebi . de terra Morcari [comitis] que tenuit Torchil . dicit Wapentac quia et soca fuit comitis Morcari et neque iacet hec terra in aliud manerium.

35. In Ingoldesbi clamat Robertus Malet socam super .iiii. bouatas terre quas habet Gislebertus de Gant . Dicit Wapentac quia ipse Robertus debet habere per Azor antecessorem suum.

36. In Catorp hundred . clamat Gislebertus de Gand super Robertum de Ueci pratum quod fuit Eilric antecessoris sui . sed Wapentac dicit quod isdem Ælric totum pratum habuit . nec antecessor Gisleberti inde aliquid habuit . nisi per locationem mercedis.

37. Testatur Wapentac quod decima et alie consuetudines de Carletune iacent in ȩcclesia eiusdem uillȩ.

38. In Beninctun clamat Alanus comes .x. bouatas terre . sed Wapentac dicit quia pertinent ad Carletun manerium Willelmi de Warenna . et [comes] Heroldus antecessor eius habuit ita.

39. Episcopus Dunelmensis clamat .ii. bouatas terrȩ in Merestune de terra Turuert . et de hoc dicunt quod Normannus pro ipsa terra dedit ipsi Turuerd .iii. markas auri . T. R. E. et post mortem eiusdem regis . iiii^{tam}. marcham dedit.

40. Homines de Auelunt Wapentac testificantur quod Brune manerium fuit Morcari [comitis] T. R. E. Modo Ogerus habet de rege . Drogo calumniatur sed iniuste.

41. Tres bouate et dimidia quas habet Ogerus in Dic . dicit Wapentac quia iacent in Hacunesbi et sunt per rectum Hepponis balistarii.

42. Unam carucatam terre in Mortune [inland] . et i. bouatam et dimidiam in Hermodestorp [soca] . dicunt pertinere ad Haconebi . et ibi fuisse . T. R. E. et has habuit Leuric.

43. In eadem Mortune dicunt habere debere Sanctum Benedictum de Ramesy di[midiam] carucatam terrȩ cum saca et soca . Hanc Ogerus tenet iniuste.

44. In Haconesbi dicunt quod Ogerus tenet iniuste .ix^{uem} bouatas terrȩ . quia Gislebertus de Gant debet habere per Vlf fen*isc* antecessorem suum . qui eas habuit . T. R. E.

45. Terram Aldene in Dunesbi quam tenet Re. episcopus et abbas de Burg calumniatur . dicit Wapentac non fuisse Sancti Petri . T. R. E.

46. In Repinghale tenet Ogerus .i. carucatam terre . quam Wapentac dicit fuisse antecessoris Roberti de Todeni.

33. In the same Quarrington Bishop Remigius claims that he received Archel's land in pledge; but Archel himself denies this; and holds of the king. [See 7/48].

34. Colsuan claims against the king in Kirkby by Laythorpe 2 bovates of land and 1 garden of [Earl] Morcar's land, which Torchil held. The Wapentake says that both the soke was Earl Morcar's, and this land did not lie in another manor. [See 1/1].

[WAPENTAKE OF LOVEDEN]

35. In Ingoldsby Robert Malet claims the soke over 4 bovates of land which Gilbert de Gant has. The Wapentake says that the said Robert ought to have it through Azor his predecessor. [See 24/99; 58/3].

36. In Caythorpe hundred Gilbert de Gand claims against Robert de Veci the meadow which was Eilric's, his [Robert's] predecessor; but the Wapentake says that the same Æilric had the whole meadow, and Gilbert's predecessor had nothing therein except by a lease at rent. [See 37/2].

37. The Wapentake bears witness that the tithe and other customary dues of Carlton Scroop lie in the church of the same vill. [See 15/1].

38. In Long Bennington Count Alan claims 10 bovates of land; but the Wapentake says that they belong to Carlton Scroop, William of Warenne's manor, and that [Earl] Harold, his predecessor, had them in this way. [See 12/49; 15/2].

39. The Bishop of Durham claims 2 bovates of land of Turuert's land in Marston; and touching this they say that T. R. E. Norman gave the said Turuerd 3 marks of gold for the said land; and, after the same king's death, he gave him a fourth mark. [See 54/1].

[WAPENTAKE OF AVELAND]

40. The men of Aveland Wapentake bear witness that T. R. E. the manor of Bourne was [Earl] Morcar's. Now Oger has it of the king. Drew claims it, but unjustly. [See 42/1].

41. The Wapentake says that 3 bovates and a half which Oger has in Dyke [lie] in Hacconby, and are rightly Heppo the Arblaster's. [See 42/6; 61/2].

42. They say that 1 carucate of land in Morton [which is inland], and $1\frac{1}{2}$ bovates in Hanthorpe [which are soke[land]], belong to Hacconby, and belonged to that place T. R. E.; and that Leuric had them. [See 42/17, 18; 61/3].

43. They say that in the same Morton Saint Benedict of Ramsey ought to have half a carucate of land with sake and soke. Oger holds it unjustly. [See 42/19].

44. They say that Oger holds 9 bovates of land in Haconby unjustly because Gilbert de Gant ought to have them through Ulf Fenisc, his predecessor, who had them T. R. E. [See 42/14].

45. The Wapentake says that Aldene's land in Dunsby, which Bishop Remigius holds, and the Abbot of Peterborough claims, did not belong to Saint Peter T. R. E. [See 7/30, 33].

46. In Rippingale Oger holds 1 carucate of land, and the Wapentake says that it belonged to Robert de Todeni's predecessor. [See 42/11].

47. Terram Offra*n* in Cherchebi . dicunt non fuisse in soca Erneberni.

48. Terram Sancti Guthlaci quam tenet Ogerus in Repinghale . dicunt fuisse dominicam firmam monachorum . et Vlchel abbatem commendasse eam ad firmam Hereuuardo . sicut inter eos conueniret uno quoque anno* . sed abbas resaisiuit eam antequam Hereuuardus de patria fugeret . eo quod conuentionem non tenuisset.

**D. B., f.* 377c. *Facsimile, p. lxxx*a.

49. Socam .iii. carucatarum terrę in Dusebi quam Offra*n* in uadimonio habuit et post deuadiata fuit . dicunt quia iacere debet in Repingale manerio Sancti Guthlaci . et ita dicunt fuisse . T. R. E. et postea usque Wido de Credon eam saisiuit.

50. Clamores quos Drogo de Beurere facit super terras Morcari . dimittunt in iudicio regis.

51. Dicunt quod Robertus de Stadford iniuste clamat terram Carle in Billingeburg . quia isdem Carle tenuit de Radulfo stalre.

52. Terram Wluric Wilde in Walecote hundred dicunt debere . esse mediam episcopi Dunelmensis . et dimidiam Vluiet cuiusdam hominis . qui habet per elemosinam regis.

53. Radulfus Pagenel clamat socam[1] et socam super terram Aluric quam habet Wido de Credun in Osbernebi . dicit Wapentac quia isdem Radulfus debet habere de hac terra unum equum in expeditione quando uadit.

54. In Picheuorde sunt .ii. carucate terrę . quę fuerunt Outi et modo sunt Colsuen . Hę non sunt in numero alicuius hundret . neque habent pares in Lincole scire.

55. De terra Thori in Summerdebi quam habet Walterus de Aincurt . dicunt quod T. R. E. uiderunt habere eundem Thori . sed ipso [anno] quo isdem rex mortuus . est inuadiauit eam Normannus . homines de Wapentac nesciunt quo pacto quia nullum seruitium inde uiderunt eum facere.

56. Dicunt quia decima et alię ęcclesię consuetudines de terra Thori in Ropeslai hundred . pertinent ad ęcclesiam Sancti Petri.

57. Walterus de Aincurt clamat seruitium hominum Widonis de Re*n*budcurt in manerio Sidestan . sed non habet rectum clamorem.

58. In Wellebi hundred clamat Drogo .iiii. carucatas terre super Widonem de Credun . sed Wapentac portat Widoni testimonium quod iure eius sunt.

59. Dicunt quod Walterus de Aincurt non debet habere dimidiam carucatam terre quam clamat super regem in Beltone . sed rex.

60. In eadem Beltone debet habere Colegrim .i. bouatam terre de terra Algar quam habet Wido de Credon . sed soca pertinet ad Widonem in Todetorp.

---

[1] *Rectius* sacam.

47. They say that Offra*n*'s land in Kirkby Underwood was not in Ernebern's soke. [See 27/55].

48. They say that Saint Guthlac's land, which Oger holds in Rippingale, was the monks' demesne farm, and that Abbot Ulchel let it to Hereward at rent, as might be agreed between them each year* ; but the abbot took possession of it again before Hereward fled the country, because he had not kept the agreement. [See 42/13].

**D. B., f.* 377c. *Facsimile, p. lxxx*a.

49. They say that the soke of 3 carucates of land in Dowsby, which Offra*n* had in pledge, and which was afterwards redeemed, ought to lie in Rippingale, Saint Guthlac's manor, and they say that it was thus T. R. E., and afterwards until Guy of Craon seised it. [See 57/12 ; 67/23].

50. The claims which Drew de Beurere makes upon Morcar's lands they remit to the king's decision.

51. They say that Robert of Stafford claims Carle's land in Billingborough unjustly, because the same Carle held it of Ralf the Staller. [See 12/55].

52. Touching Wluric Wilde's land in Walcot hundred, they say that a moiety ought to belong to the Bishop of Durham, and a moiety to a man named Uluiet who has it by the king's alms. [See 3/32 ; 67/10].

53. Ralf Pagenel claims sake[1] and soke over Alfric's land which Guy of Craon has in Osbournby. The Wapentake says that the same Ralf ought to have 1 horse from this land when he goes to war. [See 57/15].

54. In Pickworth there are 2 carucates of land which were Outi's, and are now Colsuen's. These are not reckoned in the tale of any hundred, nor have they their like in Lincolnshire. [See 26/53].

[WAPENTAKE OF THREO]

55. Touching Thori's land in Somerby by Grantham, which Walter de Aincurt has, they say that T. R. E. they saw that the same Thori had it ; but in the very [year] in which the same king died, Norman took it in pledge. The men of the Wapentake know not on what condition, for they did not see him do any service for it. [See 31/3].

56. They say that the tithe and other customary dues of the church in respect of Thori's land in Ropsley hundred belong to the church of Saint Peter. [See 18/24].

57. Walter de Aincurt claims the service of Guy de Re*n*budcurt's men as belonging to the manor of Syston ; but he has no just claim. [See 39/3].

58. In Welby hundred Drew claims 4 carucates of land against Guy of Craon ; but the Wapentake bears witness in Guy's favour that they rightly are his. [See 57/22].

59. They say that Walter de Aincurt ought not to have the half carucate of land which he claims against the king in Belton, but that the king ought to have it. [See 1/15 ; 31/1].

60. In the same Belton Colegrim ought to have 1 bovate of land of Algar's land which Guy of Craon has ; but the soke belongs to Guy in Towthorpe. [See 57/24, 25 ; 67/13].

61. Dicunt quod T. R. E. detinuit Leuric cilt Warnode de .x. acris prati . in eadem Beltone . De his .x. acris clamat Colegrim socam.

62. Totas ęcclesię consuetudines et decimam de Westorp . dicunt quia[1] pertin' ad ęcclesiam de Grantham . sicut clamat Osmundus episcopus.

63. In Hundinton hundred clamat Gislebertus socam de .ii. carucatis terre et dimidia per Vlf antecessorem suum . sed Wapentac dicit quod Iuo debet habere socam sicut habuit Azor antecessor suus . de Vlf.

64. Duos molindinos qui sunt in Barcheston clamat Robertus de Stadford . et Colsuin similiter clamat . Wapentac dicit quia iacent in Mereston . et soca eorum in Grandham.

D. B., f. 377d. *Facsimile, p. lxxx*b.

[73]. [CLAMORES IN HOILAND]

1. In Draitone hundred habet Alanus . comes .i. carucatam terre de Sancto Benedicto de Ramesy . Re . episcopus clamat . et Wapentac portat ei testimonium quod Wluui antecessor suus eam tenuit de Sancto Benedicto . T. R. E.

2. Wido de Credone tenet in Draitone .iiii. bouatas terrę . et in Bichere hundred .x. bouatas . de terra Adestan Godramesune . Has calumniatur comes Alanus . et Algęr homo eius dedit uadimonium baronibus regis . ad confirmandum per iudicium aut per bellum . quod ipse Adestan de his xiiii. bouatis saisitus [non] fuit . T. R. E. E contra homo Widonis Alestan de Frantone dedit suum uadimonium ad conuincendum quod inde saisitus erat cum saca et soca . et Wido inde fuit saisitus ex tempore Radulfi Stalre usque nunc . et modo tenet.

3. Homines de Hoiland testantur quod Aldene antecessor Remigii episcopi habuit [quiete] in Steueninge .iii. carucatas terrę . quas modo habet Alanus comes . et iniuste . quia episcopus inde saisitus . fuit.

4. Vnam carucatam terrę in Quedhaueringe clamat Aluredus de Lincolia super Alanum comitem . Homines de Hoilant concordant eidem Alueredo . quia et antecessoris sui fuit . et ipse saisitus inde fuit tempore Radulfi comitis.

5. Guerd homo Alani comitis dedit [uadimonium] ad affirmandum quod antecessor Alani comitis habuit .vi. bouatas terrę cum saca et soca in Gosebertcherche . et ideo Wido de Credun non recte eas clamat.

6. Soca monasterii Ketel de Sudtone . iacet in Tid manerio regis . Testantur homines de Hoiland.

7. Sex carucatas terrę quas clamant ministri regis in Holobec . iacuerunt in Gadenai . manerio regis . Nunc habet regis dono comes Alanus pro uno manerio.

---

[1] *quia* seems to be superfluous.

61. They say that T. R. E. Leuric '*cilt*' withheld the warnode of 10 acres of meadow in the same Belton. Colegrim claims the soke of these 10 acres. [See 67/13].

62. They say that all the ecclesiastical dues and tithe of Westhorpe belong to the church of Grantham, as Bishop Osmund claims. [See 31/5].

63. In Honington hundred Gilbert claims the soke of 2½ carucates of land through Ulf his predecessor; but the Wapentake says that Ivo ought to have the soke as Azor his predecessor had it of Ulf. [See 14/88; 24/84].

64. Robert of Stafford claims 2 mills which are in Barkston, and Colsuin makes a like claim. The Wapentake says that they lie in Marston, and their soke in Grantham.

*D. B., f. 377*d. *Facsimile, p. lxxx*b.

[73]. [DISPUTES IN HOLLAND]

[WAPENTAKE OF KIRTON]

1. In Drayton hundred Count Alan has 1 carucate of land of Saint Benedict of Ramsey. Bishop Remigius claims it; and the Wapentake bears witness in his favour that Wlfwig his predecessor held it of Saint Benedict T. R. E. [See 12/59].

2. Guy of Craon holds 4 bovates of land in Drayton and 10 bovates in Bicker hundred of the land of Adestan Godramesune. Count Alan claims these; and Alger his man has given to the king's barons a pledge to prove by ordeal or by battle that the same Adestan was [not] seised of these 14 bovates T. R. E. On the other hand, Alestan of Frampton, Guy's man, has given his pledge to prove that he was seised thereof with sake and soke, and Guy was seised thereof from the time of Ralf the Staller until now, and holds it at the present time. [See 57/44, 56].

3. The men of Holland bear witness that Aldene, the predecessor of Bishop Remigius, had 3 carucates of land [quietly] in Stenning, which Count Alan has now, and unjustly, because the bishop was seised thereof. [See 12/89].

4. Alfred of Lincoln claims 1 carucate of land in Quadring against Count Alan. The men of Holland agree with the said Alfred, both because it was his predecessor's and also he himself was seised thereof in the time of Earl Ralph. [See 12/90].

5. Guerd, Count Alan's man, has given [a pledge] to maintain that Count Alan's predecessor had 6 bovates of land with sake and soke in Gosberton, and therefore Guy of Craon does not claim them justly. [See 12/76].

6. The men of Holland bear witness that the soke of Ketel's church of Long Sutton lies in the king's manor of Tydd Saint Mary. [See 1/28].

7. Six carucates of land which the king's officers claim in Holbeach lay in the king's manor of Gedney. Count Alan has them now for one manor by the king's gift. [See 12/83].

[The Lindsey Survey]

Folio 1.

In the West Riding (West Triding)

1. In MANELI [MANLEY] WAPENTAKE

THERE ARE RECKONED TO BE . . . . . .[1] HUNDREDS AND A HALF.

1. Earl Richard has 34 carucates and 2 bovates and half a bovate in Halton [West Halton] and the soke.[2]

2. Walter de Gant in Wintringham [Winteringham] 11 carucates, which Robert Marmion holds; and in Risebi [Risby] 2 carucates and 2 bovates; and in Santuna [Santon] 1 bovate, which Walter de Sancto Paulo holds.

3. Roger Marmion in Wintringeham [Winteringham] 1 carucate.

4. Ralph Painel in Bertuna [Broughton] 11 carucates and 5 bovates; and in Cheistorp [Castlethorpe] 3 bovates; and Rochesbi [Roxby] 5 carucates; and in Scallebi [Scawby] 3 carucates and 6 bovates and a half; and in Wintringt' [Winterton] 3 bovates.

5. Ranulf Mischin [5[3]] carucates; and in Redburna [Redbourne] 1 carucate and a half; and in Hibaldestoua [Hibaldstow] 1 carucate; and in Rainelestorp [Raventhorpe] half a carucate; and Saier has 3 bovates of his fee.

6. The Abbot of Peterborough (*Burc*) in Alchebarua [Alkborough] 1 carucate; and in Walecota [Walcot] 6 carucates and 6 bovates; and in Massingeham [Messingham] 4 carucates and 6 bovates and a half; and in Holm [Holme] 3 carucates; and in Ragheniltorp [Raventhorpe] 1 carucate [and] 1 bovate; and in Malmetuna [Manton] 2 carucates; and in Hibaldestoua [Hibaldstow] 1 carucate and 2 bovates; and in Risabi [Risby] 3 bovates; and in Nordmanab[i] [Normanby in Burtôn on Stather] . . . . .[4]; and in Aschebi [Ashby in Bottesford] 3 bovates and a half which . . . . .[1] H . . . . .[1] holds.

Folio 2.

7. Geoffrey son of Payne between Massingham and Walecota and Risabi [Messingham and Walcot and Risby] 5 [carucates and] . . .[5] bovates.

8. Saint Mary of Lincoln 1 carucate and 2 bovates.[6]

---

[1] The surface of the parchment has perished.

[2] *et scocha* has been added by a fifteenth century hand.

[3] The figure is illegible. It corresponds to Ivo Taillebois' 5 carucates in Alkborough in 1086 (*D.B.*, 14/28).

[4] The assessment is illegible; but cp. *Book of Fees*, p. 191.

[5] The figure is illegible.

[6] The land was in Redbourne.

9. Stephen de Albamara in Tedolfbi [Thealby] 1 carucate; and in Normanebi [Normanby in Burton on Stather] 9 carucates.

10. The Bishop of Durham in Steintuna [Stainton by Wadingham] 3 bovates.

11. The Bishop of Lincoln in Massingham [Messingham] 1 carucate and 7 bovates.

12. Robert de Haia in Scallebi [Scawby] 1 carucate.

13. The King in Aplebi [Appleby] 9 carucates and 2 bovates; and in Santuna [Santon] 1 carucate; and of this 2 carucates and 6 bovates are in the demesne of Helle. In Witena [Whitton] 12 carucates, [⌊which⌋ Robert de Fereris ⌊holds[1]⌋].

14. Norman de Areceio in Ualecot' [Walcot] 1 carucate and 2 bovates; and in Flichesburc and Cunigesbi [Flixborough and North Conesby] 12 carucates; and in Wintringtuna [Winterton] 2 [carucates]; and in Cuningesbi and C[r]oc[hes]b[i][2] [? North Conesby and Croxby] 1 carucate and 1 bovate and half a bovate; and in Rochesbi [Roxby] 4 bovates; and in the hundred of Tedolfbi [Thealby] 4 bovates; and in Risabi [Risby] 1 bovate; and in Walecota [Walcot] 1 bovate in litigation, [⌊which⌋ Bernard son of Adam ⌊holds⌋].

15. Alfred of Laughton (*Lachtuna*) in Hibaldastowa [Hibaldstow] 2 bovates.

16. The Abbot of York (*de Eboraco*) in Edoluestorp [Yaddlethorpe] 1 carucate; and in Wintringtuna [Winterton] 1 carucate and 3 bovates.

17. Gilbert son of Gocelin in Botlesforda and Asebi [Bottesford and Ashby in Bottesford] 1 carucate and 4 bovates; and in Scallbi [Scawby] 2 carucates and [3] bovates; and in Wadingham [Wadingham] 5 bovates; and in Redburna [Redbourne] 7 carucates. Total—11 carucates and 3 bovates.

18. William de Arcis in Scallabi [Scawby] 2 carucates and 1 bovate; and in Redburna [Redbourne] 3 bovates; and in Hibaldestowa[4] and Gameltorp [Hibaldstow and Gainsthorpe] 2[5]

Folio 3.

19. William Mischin in Scallabi [Scawby] 1 carucate, which Alfred of Laughton (*Lactuna*) holds; and in Cheistorp [Castlethorpe] 3 bovates.

20. Count Stephen of Mortain (*Moreton*) in Wadingham [Wadingham] 1 carucate and 3 bovates, which Roger de Montebegon holds.

21. Hugh de Vallo in Steintuna [Stainton by Wadingham] 6 bovates and half a bovate.

22. Helpo the Arblaster (*balistarius*) in Redburna [Redbourne] 3 bovates; and in Steintuna [Stainton by Wadingham] half a bovate.

23. Alan of Craon (*Credon*) in Santuna [Santon] 7 bovates, which Alfred of Laughton (*Lactuna*) holds.

---

[1] The interlineation was probably made *temp.* Henry II.
[2] The name is partly illegible, and the missing letters have been supplied conjecturally.
[3] The number of bovates has been omitted. It should probably be 2.
[4] Corrected from *Habaldestowa.*
[5] The word *bouatas* seems to have been omitted.

2. IN ASLOCAHOU [ASLACOE] WAPENTAKE

THERE ARE RECKONED TO BE 7 HUNDREDS AND A HALF.

1. Ralf Paganel in Glenteworda [Glentworth] 5 bovates.

2. Ranulf Meschin in Nordmanabi [Normanby by Spital] 5 carucates; and in Glentheim [Glentham] 3 carucates [⌊which⌋ Reinfrei holds[1]]; and in Ounebi [Owmby by Spital] 5 bovates [⌊which⌋ Gilbert de Calz ⌊holds[1]⌋]; and in Bliburc [Blyborough] 4 bovates and half a bovate.

3. Gilbert de Calz and[2] in Wadingeheim[3] [Wadingham] 4 bovates [⌊which⌋ Gilbert himself ⌊holds⌋].

4. Stephen de Albamara in Helmeswella [Hemswell] 1 carucate and 2 bovates. And in Glenteworda [Glentworth] 1 carucate and 3 bovates; and in Hacatorn [Hackthorn] 6 bovates and half a bovate, which Anscetil de Scuris holds.

5. Bishop Ranulf [of Durham] in Bliburc [Blyborough] 7 bovates.

6. Robert bishop of Lincoln in Nordtuna [Bishop Norton] 6 carucates; and in Glemtheim and Casnabi [Glentham and Caenby] 7 carucates and 6 bovates; and of these Martel de Taneio holds 2 carucates and 4 bovates. And in Ounabi [Owmby by Spital] 3 carucates and 1 bovate; and in Ingheham [Ingham]* 6 bovates [⌊which⌋ Simon ⌊holds[4]⌋]; and in Cotes [Cotes by Stow] 4 bovates [⌊which⌋ Simon ⌊holds[4]⌋].

**Folio 4.*

7. Nigel de Albeneio in Bliburc [Blyborough] 2 carucates and 4 bovates and the fourth part of 1 bovate.

8. William son of Rastold[5] ⌊holds⌋ of the king 1 carucate and 1 bovate.

9. Gilbert son of Gocelin in Bliburc [Blyborough] 7 bovates; and in Harpeswella [Harpswell] 2 carucates and 4 bovates; and in Glenteworda [Glentworth] 5 bovates; and in Ingeham [Ingham] 1 carucate and 4 bovates; and in Cotis [Cotes by Stow] 5 bovates; and in Hachetorna [Hackthorn] 4 carucates and 1 bovate; and in Ounebi [Owmby by Spital] 1 carucate and 5 bovates,[6] which Robert de Haia holds. Total—10 carucates and 2 bovates.

10. William Meschin in Camringham [Cammeringham] 1 carucate,[6] which Robert de Haia holds of him.

11. Robert de Haia ✠ in Cotis [Cotes by Stow]; and in Camringham [Cammeringham] 4 carucates; and in Spridlinctuna [Spridlington] 2 carucates and 2 bovates; and in Figlingaham [Fillingham] 6 carucates and 6 bovates; and in Ingheham [Ingham] 6 bovates; and in the same vill 4 bovates[7] of (*de*) Ralph de Crioil; and in Hacatorna [Hackthorn] 3

[1] The interlineation was probably made *temp.* Henry II.
[2] *and* seems to be superfluous.
[3] Though Wadingham is in the wapentake of Manley, the tenement is entered here on account, as it seems, of Gilbert's holding in Owmby in the preceding entry.
[4] The interlineation seems to be contemporary with the text.
[5] *Rastaldi* has been corrected into *Rastoldi.*
[6] The 1 carucate and 5 bovates in Owmby and the 1 carucate in Cammeringham in entries 9 and 10 are duplicated in no. 11 below.
[7] These 4 bovates are duplicated in no. 22 below.

bovates; and in Ounabia [Owmby by Spital] 1 carucate and 5 bovates; and in Haneworda [Cold Hanworth] 4 bovates.

[✠ Be it remembered that there are in the vill of Cotis [Cotes by Stow] 53 bovates of land, to wit, of the fee of Kyma 15 bovates; also of the fee of the Bishop of Lincoln 15 bovates; also of the fee of Orreby 15 bovates; also of the fee of Saint Katherine 4 bovates; also of the fee of Cameryngham 4 bovates].[1]

12. Simon son of William in Hachethorna [Hackthorn] 1 carucate and 4 bovates.

13. Hugh de Laval in Cotis [Cotes by Stow] 4 bovates and a half; and in Hacatorna [Hackthorn] 6 bovates and a half; and in Frisabi [East and West Firsby] 3 carucates and 4 bovates and a half and the fifth part of 1 bovate; and in Ounebi [Owmby by Spital] 2 bovates and half a bovate; and in Saxsebi [Saxby near Market Rasen] half a bovate; and in Nordmanabi [Normanby by Spital] 1 carucate, which Payne holds, and Geoffrey his brother; and in Ingheham [Ingham] 1 carucate.

14. Anfrid de Canceio in Wilgatuna [Willoughton] 3 carucates and 5 bovates and half a bovate, which William de Bussa holds.

15. The Abbot of Saint Nicholas [of Angers] 2 carucates and 2 bovates and a half.

16. The Archbishop of York in Harpeswella [Harpswell] 5 bovates and a half; and in Hachetorna [Hackthorn] 1 carucate and 4 bovates,* which Gregory holds. In the same vill 1 carucate and 7 bovates and a half, which Hugh holds.

*Folio 5.

17. Hugh son of Eudo in Saxsabi [Saxby near Market Rasen] 2 carucates and 5 bovates.

18. Count Stephen of Brittany in Spritlingtuna [Spridlington] 2 carucates and 3 bovates and the third part of 1 bovate; and in Halmeswella [Hemswell] 4 bovates.

19. Manaset Arsic in Ounabi [Owmby by Spital] 2 bovates; and in Glentheim [Glentham] 10 bovates; and in Gleintaworda [Glentworth] 7 bovates, and Walter son of William holds [them].

20. Helpo the Arblaster (*Balistarius*) in Snitrebi [Snitterby] 10 bovates; and in Figlingheim [Fillingham] 2 bovates and a half and the fourth part (*ferding*) of 1 bovate.

21. The Count of Mortain (*Moreton*) in Figlingheim [Fillingham] 2 carucates and 3 bovates and the fifth part of 1 bovate, which Rannulf Bilion holds. And in Ingheham [Ingham] 6 bovates; and in Haneworda [Cold Hanworth] 2 bovates, which Renald Purcell holds, and Godfrey.

22. Ralph de Criol in Ingeham [Ingham] 4 bovates.

3. In LAGOLFRIS [LAWRESS] WAPENTAKE

THERE ARE RECKONED TO BE 12 HUNDREDS.

1. The canons of Saint Mary [of Lincoln] have in Wellatuna and in Risu*n* and in Wllingheim [Welton by Lincoln and Riseholme and Cherry

[1] These 5 lines are interlined above entry no. 11 in a fifteenth century hand.

Willingham] 14 carucates and 2 bovates; [and of these the church [holds] 4 bovates, and Robert de Haia 2 bovates[1]].

2. The Bishop of Lincoln in Netelham [Nettleham] 12 carucates; and in Dunham [Dunham] 5 carucates and 3 bovates; and in Carletuna [North and South Carlton] 7 carucates; and in Scotstorna [Scothorn] 2 bovates, [[which] Gilbert Nevill (*de nova villa*) [holds][1]]; and in Refham [Reepham] 4 bovates, which Gilbert Nevill (*de Noua uilla*) holds.

3. Alan de Perceio in Saxlabi [Saxilby] 2 carucates and 1 bovate and the third part of 1 bovate.

4. Robert de Haia in Scotstorna [Scothorn] 5 carucates; and in Faldinguorda [Faldingworth] 2 carucates and 4 bovates; and in Risu*n* [Riseholme] 3 carucates; and in Refham [Reepham] 6 bovates; and in Barlinga [Barlings] 2 carucates and 5 bovates; and in Torp [Thorpe in the Fallows] 1 carucate; and in Englabi [Ingleby] 2 carucates and 5 bovates and* the third part of 1 bovate; and in Frisatorp [Friesthorpe] 7 bovates, [which] William son of Anschetil holds; and in Brotolbi [Brattleby] 2 carucates and 2 bovates.

**Folio 6.*

5. William Meschin in Faldinguorda [Faldingworth] 2 carucates and 4 bovates, which Ralph Malet holds.

6. Saint Mary [of Lincoln] in Frisætorp [Friesthorpe] 2 carucates and 1 bovate, which Nigel held.

7. William Turniant in Faldinguorda [Faldingworth] 1 carucate.

8. Robert de Insula in Esatorp [Buslingthorpe] 2 carucates, which Buselin holds; and in Carletuna [North Carlton] 6 carucates, which Alan de Twit holds; and in Burtuna [Burton by Lincoln] 1 carucate, which Richard de Munte Pinchun holds.

9. Alfreit de Canceio in Duneham [Dunham] 2 carucates and 5 bovates, which Ralf the canon, brother of Osbert the sheriff holds.

10. Ranulf bishop of Durham in Snarteforde [Snarford] 3 carucates, which Goslin the Sewer (*dapifer*) holds.

11. Hugh de Vallo in Duneham [Dunham] 2 carucates, and in Scotstorne [Scothorn] 7 bovates.

12. Ralf Paganel in Duneham [Dunham] 2 carucates, which Goslin the sewer (*dapifer*) holds.

13. Norman de Araceio in Holm [Sudbrooke Holme] 1 carucate and 1 bovate.

14. The Abbot of Peterborough (*Burc*) in Scotstorne [Scothorn] and Sutbroc [Sudbrooke] 4 carucates and 4 bovates; and in Fischertune [Fiskerton] 3 carucates; and in Refham [Reepham] 4 carucates and 6 bovates.

15. Roger Marmion in Wllingeheim [Cherry Willingham] 1 carucate and 6 bovates.

16. Wigot of Lincoln (*Lincolię*) in Broxholm [Broxholme] 4 carucates; and in Englebi [Ingleby] 3 carucates and 5 bovates and the third part of 1 bovate.

[1] The interlineation seems to be contemporary with the text.

17. Manasiet Arsic in Saxlebi[1] [Saxilby] 1 carucate and 4 bovates, which Turstin de Renni holds.

18. Robert the king's son in Esttorp [Aisthorpe] 6 bovates, which Hundefot Robert holds of William Turniant.

19. Walter de Ganto in Burtuna [Burton by Lincoln] 5 carucates; and in Scantuna [Scampton] 6 carucates; and in Turuluestorp[2] [Thorpe in the Fallows] 2 carucates and 7 bovates;* and in Astorp [Aisthorpe] 3 carucates and 2 bovates, which Walter son of Ragemer holds; and in Netelham [Nettleham] 2 bovates, which Robert de Haia holds; and in B[ar[3]]linga [Barlings] 3 bovates, which Robert de Haia holds; and in Risu*n* [Riseholme] 2 carucates, [[which] Robert holds[4]]; and in Brotulebi [Brattleby] 1 carucate and 6 bovates, [which Robert de Haia holds[4]]; and in Carletune [Middle Carlton] 6 bovates, which Fulk Albus holds.

**Folio 7.*

20. William de Rollos in Burtuna [Burton by Lincoln] 3 carucates, which Sortebrand son of Ulf holds.

21. Hugh de Luvetot in Gretwella[5] [Greetwell] 3 carucates.

22. Roger de Ganto 4 carucates, which Fulk Albus holds and Roger Macherel.

23. Roger de Valoniis 2 carucates, which Hårcher holds in Burtuna[6] [Burton by Lincoln].

4. IN CORINGEHAM [CORRINGHAM] WAPENTAKE

THERE ARE RECKONED TO BE 5 HUNDREDS.

1. Nigel de Albaneio has in Gleinesburc [Gainsborough] 8 carucates; and in Ioltorp [Yawthorpe] 1 carucate; and in Sum*er*debi [Somerby in Corringham] 4 bovates.

2. Count Stephen of Brittany in Le and Sum*er*debi and Iopheim [Lea and Somerby and Heapham] 5 carucates, which Geoffrey (*Gosfr'*) son of Treatune holds.

3. Robert de Insula in Coringheham [Corringham] 2 carucates, which Richard de Monte Pinchun (*dem'. pinc'.*) holds.

4. The Bishop of Lincoln in Greingheham [Greyingham] 1 carucate, which Richard son of Malg*er* holds.

5. Ranulf bishop of Durham in Cletham [Cleatham] 6 bovates.

6. Hugh de Vallo in Torp [Northorpe] 6 bovates; and in Cletham [Cleatham] 6 bovates.

7. Alan of Craon (*de Credun*) in Blituna [Blyton] 1 carucate and 6 bovates; and in Lactuna [Laughton] 3 carucates and 2 bovates; and in Scottuna [Scotton] 4 bovates.

---

1 *Saxlabi* has been corrected into *Saxlebi*.
2 Corrected from *Tutuluestorp*.
3 Illegible.
4 The interlineation seems to be comtemporary with the text.
5 Corrected from *Grewella*.
6 *in Burtunia* seems to have been added *temp*. Henry II.

Folio 8.

8. The Count of Mortain (*Moreton*) in Lactuna [Laughton] 2 carucates and 6 bovates; and in Torp [Southorpe and Northorpe] and in Tuneic and Tunstal [Thonock and Dunstall] 6 carucates; and in Scottuna [Scotton] 4 bovates; and in Iolthorp [Yawthorpe] 4 bovates; and in Blituna [Blyton] 2 bovates; all of which Roger de Mont*e* holds.

9. The Abbot of Peterborough (*Burc*) in Scottune [Scotton] 6 carucates: and in Scotra [Scotter] 8 carucates; and in Saltorp [Scotterthorpe] 3 carucates; and in Ioltorp [Yawthorpe] 4 bovates, [⌊which⌋ Herbert ⌊holds⌋[1]]; and in Torp [*probably* Northorpe] 1 carucate, [⌊which⌋ R. Nevill (*de Villa*) ⌊holds⌋[1]]; and in Cletham [Cleatham] 1 carucate ⌊which⌋ Herbert ⌊holds⌋.

10. Ralf Mischin in Dunestal [Dunstall] 2 carucates; and in Scottuna [Scotton] 2 carucates, ⌊which⌋ Guy de U*er*mis ⌊holds⌋.

11. Geoffrey son of Payne (*Pagani*) in Greingheham [Grayingham] 1 carucate.

5. In HAXEHOLM [AXHOLME WAPENTAKE]

THERE ARE RECKONED TO BE 4 HUNDREDS, ⌊AND⌋ IN EACH ⌊HUNDRED⌋ 12 CARUCATES OF LAND. AND NIGEL DE ALBENEIO HOLDS THEM IN DEMESNE.

6. In WELLE [WELL] WAPENTAKE

THERE ARE RECKONED TO BE 7 HUNDREDS, ⌊AND⌋ IN EACH ⌊HUNDRED⌋ 12 CARUCATES OF LAND.

1. Robert bishop of Lincoln has in the hundred of Neotuna [Newton on Trent] 12 carucates; and in the hundred of Stowa and Brantuna [Stow and Brampton] 10 carucates; and in Normannæbi and Chezbi [Normanby by Stow and Kexby] 8 carucates and 4 bovates; and in the hundred of Uppetune [Upton] 8 carucates and 5 bovates; and in Martuna [Marton] 4 carucates; and in Fentuna [Fenton] 2 carucates which geld at Sturton by Stow (*astrettuna*). And Hugh the canon 6 bovates. And of the king's barons the bishop holds in Stowa [Stow] 1 carucate of Gilbert son of Gocelin; and in Wiflingeheim [Willingham by Stow] 3 bovates of the Bretons (*des Britinis*); and in Uiflingeheim [Willingham by Stow], the same vill, 2 bovates of Hugh de Valo; and of Walter de Ganto 2 bovates in demesne.

Folio 9.

2. Hugh de Vallo in Strettuna [Sturton by Stow] 8 carucates; and in Uiflingheheim and Stowa [Willingham by Stow and Stow] 3 carucates and 4 bovates, which Hamelin and Robert de Haia hold, but Hugh de Luvetot holds 2 bovates thereof.

3. Gilbert son of Gocelin in Uiflingheheim [Willingham by Stow] 6 carucates.

4. Robert de Haia in Chet[l[1]]esbi [Kexby] 3 carucates.

---

[1] The interlineation seems to be contemporary with the text.

5. Robert de Insula in Branzbi [Bransby] 2 carucates, ⌊which⌋ Richard de Monte Pinceoni (*dem' pinceoni*) holds.

6. Count Stephen of Brittany in Burtuna [Burton by Lincoln] 4 carucates and the third part of 1 bovate; and in Martuna [Marton] 6 bovates, which Hacon son of Eluric holds; and in Uptuna [Upton] 1 carucate and 6 bovates and 2 parts of 1 bovate; and in Wiflingham and Stowa [Willingham by Stow and Stow] 3 carucates and 4 bovates, which Hugh's wife holds.

7. The Count of Mortain (*Moreton*) in Uptuna [Upton] 1 carucate and 5 bovates, which Payne de Vilers holds.

8. Odo Sancte Crucis 8 carucates between the increment and the team-lands of arable (*inter crementum et carucat' terre*).[1]

9. Stephen of Brittany 5 carucates and 2 bovates between the increment and the team-lands of arable (*inter incrementum et terram*).[1]

10. Columban 3 carucates and 4 bovates between the increment and the team-lands of arable (*inter inplement' et terram*).[1]

11. Rayner de Euermou 6 carucates.

In the North Riding (Nortriding)

7. In Walescroft [Walshcroft] Wapentake

THERE ARE RECKONED TO BE 8 HUNDREDS, AND IN EACH ⌊HUNDRED⌋ 12 CARUCATES.

1. Stephen earl of Albemarle (*Albamara*) in Torgrimebi [Thorganby] 1 carucate and 7 bovates; and in Steintuna [Stainton le Vale] 6 bovates, [which Herbert of Saint Quintin holds[2]]; and in Clachesbi [Claxby by Normanby] 6 bovates.

2. The Bishop of Lincoln in Torgrimbi [Thorganby] 5 bovates, [⌊which⌋ Gerard de Belesbi ⌊holds⌋[2]]; and in Ouresbi [Owersby] 2 carucates; and in Chimerebi [Kingerby] 2 carucates; and in Clachesbi [Claxby by Normanby] 1 bovate.

3. Norman de Areceio in Torgrimbi [Thorganby] 1 carucate and 6 bovates; and in Crochesbi [Croxby] 3 bovates; and in Ouresbi [Owersby] 2½ bovates* and the fourth part (*ferding*); and in Nordmanabi [Normanby le Wold] 2 bovates; and in Clachesbi [Claxby by Normanby] 1 bovate.

*Folio 10.

4. Ranulf Meschin in Torgrimbi [Thorganby] 6 bovates; and in Crochesbi [Croxby] 5 bovates; and in Wiflingham [North Willingham] 2 bovates; and in Houtuna [Holton le Moor] 1 carucate; and in Nordmanabi and Clachesbi [Normanby le Wold and Claxby by Normanby] 3 carucates; and in Ouresbi [Owersby] 1 carucate; and in Toresweia [Thoresway] 2 bovates; and in Nordmanabi [Normanby le Wold] 3 bovates, which Alan holds.

[1] The *carucat' terra*, *terra*, probably means the established team-lands of arable land; and the *crementum*, *incrementum*, *inplementum*, the land brought into cultivation of recent date.

[2] The interlineation seems to be contemporary with the text.

5. Robert de Insula in Torgrimbi [Thorganby] 1 carucate; and in Crochesbi [Croxby] 1 carucate; and in Binnabroc [Binbrook] 5 carucates and 7 bovates; and in Iraforda [Irford] 3 carucates and 5 bovates and half a bovate.

6. And William Turniant 1 carucate in Binnabroc [Binbrook].

7. William Meschin in Crochesbi [Croxby] 1 carucate, which William *nepos* of Osbert the sheriff holds; and in Media Rasa [Middle Rasen] 3 bovates, which Ralf Malet holds; and in Lindwda [Linwood] 4 bovates; and in Nordmanabi [Normanby le Wold] 5 bovates; and in Media Rasa [Middle Rasen] 1 bovate and the third part of one bovate, which Walter Malet holds.

8. Alan of Craon (*Credun*) 1 carucate and half a bovate[1]; and ⌊in⌋ Ireforde [Irford] 2 bovates, which Alfred of Laughton (*Lactuna*) holds.

9. The Abbot of York in Osoluabi [Usselby] 4 bovates; and in Osgotabi [Osgodby] 4 bovates.

10. William Torniant in Newetuna [Newton by Toft] 3 bovates.

11. Ralf de Criol in Steint' [Stainton le Vale] 5½ bovates; and in Wiflingham [North Willingham] 1 bovate; and in Ottebi [Otby] 1 carucate; and in Newetuna [Newton by Toft] 3 bovates, which Robert de Haia holds.

12. Alan de Perci in Steintuna [Stainton le Vale] 4½ bovates; and in Wiflingham [North Willingham] 2½ bovates; and in Ouresbi [Owersby] 6 bovates and half a bovate and the third part of 1 bovate; and in Torntuna [Thornton le Moor] 1 carucate and 4 bovates.

13. Ralf Painell in Teflesbi [Tealby] 1 carucate and 6 bovates; and in Wiflingham [North Willingham] 1 carucate; and in Rasa [West Rasen] 7 carucates and 2 bovates and 2 parts of 1 bovate; and in the other Rasa [Middle Rasen] 1 carucate and 6 bovates; and in Osgotebi [Osgodby] 1 bovate; and in Osoluebi [Usselby] half a bovate beyond the beck (*ultra bec*).

14. And Gilbert son of Gocelin in Teflesbi [Tealby] 1 carucate; ⌈and in Wiflingeham [North Willingham] 1 carucate[2]⌉ and 4½ bovates; and in Nordmanabi [Normanby le Wold] 1 carucate and 1 bovate; and in* Blesebi [Bleasby] 3 carucates[3]; and in Osgotebi [Osgodby] 1 bovate; and in Media Rasa [Middle Rasen] 3 bovates, which Robert de Haia holds.

**Folio 11.*

15. The Count of Mortain (*Moretonia*) in Teflesbi [Tealby] 1 carucate and 4 bovates, and in Cheleseia and Torntuna [Kelsey and Thornton le Moor] 4 carucates and 4 bovates, and in Houtuna [Holton le Moor] 1 carucate, and in Walesbi [Walesby] 2 carucates, and in Parua Rasa [Market Rasen] 1 carucate and 1 bovate, and Roger de Montebegun holds them all; and in Osgotabi [Osgodby] 3 bovates; and in Sixla[4] [Sixle] 2 carucates and 3 bovates; and in Ouresbi [Owersby] 1 carucate and 4 bovates, which the monks of Wighala [Winghale] hold.

---

[1] The land was in Binbrook.
[2] The interlineation was probably made *temp.* Henry II.
[3] Bleasby is in the wapentake of Wraggoe. The 3 carucates should probably be 2 carucates. The entry is duplicated in 16/11.
[4] Sixle is in the wapentake of Wraggoe.

16. Alan of Lincoln [his daughter Margaret married Ralf Bayous from whom [descend] Hugh, William, and Alan[1]] in Lindwda [Linwood] 1 carucate and 4 bovates; and in Toreweia [Thoresway], [in demesne[2]], 5 carucates and 6 bovates; and in Parua Rasa [Market Rasen], [demesne[2]], 4½ bovates and the third part of 1 bovate; and in Media Rasa [Middle Rasen], [demesne[2]], 2½ bovates and the third part of 1 bovate.

17. The Count of Mellent in Steintuna [Stainton le Vale] 1 carucate.

18. Count Odo in Newetuna [Newton by Toft] 1 carucate and 3 bovates; and in Osgotabi [Osgodby] 5 bovates; and in Risabi [Risby in Walesby] 1 carucate.

19. The Count of Brittany in Teflesbi [Tealby] 4 bovates.

20. Manaset Arsic in Toft [Toft by Newton] 1 carucate and 6 bovates and the third part of 1 bovate, and in Ouresbi [Owersby] 2 carucates and 6 bovates, and Walter son of William holds them all; and in Media Rasa [Middle Rasen] 2 carucates and 2 bovates, which Gilbert Nevill (*de Nova Villa*) holds.

21. Anfrid de Canceio in Walesbi [Walesby] 2 carucates.

22. Hugh de Laval in Newetuna [Newton by Toft] 6 bovates, which Richard son of Losward holds.

[8]. In HAWARDESHOU [HAVERSTOE] WAPENTAKE

THERE ARE RECKONED TO BE 7 HUNDREDS AND HALF A HUNDRED, AND IN EACH [HUNDRED] 12 CARUCATES OF LAND.

1. The Count of Brittany in Waltham 6 carucates; and in Bernetebi [Barnoldby le Beck] 6 carucates; and in Belesbi [Beelsby] 4 carucates and 4 bovates; and in Hadecliva [Hatcliffe] 4 carucates; and in Gunresbi [Gunnerby in Hatcliffe] 2 carucates; and in Ravendala [East and West Ravendale] 3 carucates; and in Brigesla [Brigsley] 1 carucate and 4 bovates; and in Aschebi [Ashby by Fenby] 6 bovates; and in Wada [Waith] 1 carucate and 3 bovates; and in Aluoldebi [Autby] 1 carucate and 1 bovate; and in* Fembi [Fenby] 3 carucates; and in Besabi [Beesby] 3 carucates; and in Catebi [North Cadeby] 3 carucates [[which] Walter [holds][2]]; and in Hawardabi [Hawerby] 2 carucates and 2 bovates; and in Newetuna [Newton le Wold] 3 carucates and 4 bovates; and in Greinesbi [Grainsby] 3 carucates [[which] Wim*und* [holds][2]]; and in Newetuna [Newton le Wold] 2 bovates—3 hundreds and 6 carucates and 2 bovates[3] in the count's demesne (*dominio*). And in Suinahopa [Swinhope] 2 carucates and 2½ bovates [[which] Anfrid [holds][2]].[4]

**Folio 12.*

2. Picot de Laceles in Fuglestowa [Fulstow] 2 carucates and 2 bovates.

---

[1] This note was probably made by a fifteenth century hand.

[2] The interlineation seems to be contemporary with the text.

[3] This is the sum of the preceding items, excluding North Cadeby and Grainsby, which were not held in demesne.

[4] The 2 carucates and 2½ bovates are duplicated in no. 12 below.

3. Walbert 4 bovates[1] [[which] Bishop Ranulf [holds][2]]; and in Newetuna and in Aluoldabi [Newton le Wold and Autby] 1 bovate,[1] which Roger de Laci holds.

4. Earl Richard in Fuglestoua [Fulstow] 6 bovates.

5. Ranulf Mischin in Caburna [Cabourne] 4 carucates and 3 bovates, which Hugh holds.

6. William Mischin in Rodewella [Rothwell] 1 carucate and 7 bovates; and in Caburna [Cabourne] 1 bovate; and in Cucuwalt [Cuxwold] 2 bovates and the third part of 1 bovate.

7. Ralf Paganel 2 bovates, which Gocelin holds in Rodwella[3] [Rothwell].

8. Alan de Perci in Caburna [Cabourne] 1 carucate; and in Cucuw[a]ld [Cuxwold] 2 bovates, which Robert de Araceia holds.

9. Alan of Lincoln in Rodewella and Caburna [Rothwell and Cabourne] 5 carucates and 1 bovate.

10. The Archbishop of York in Cucuwald [Cuxwold] 1 carucate, [[which] Alan de Muntcell [holds][2]].

11. The Bishop of Lincoln in Belesbi [Beelsby] 1 carucate; and in Ravendala [Ravendale] 2 bovates.

12. Anfrid de Canci in Suinopa[4] [Swinhope] 2 carucates and 4½ bovates, [which he holds] of the king; and in the same vill 2 carucates and 2½ bovates,[5] [which he holds] of the Count of Brittany.

Folio 13.

13. Alan of Craon (*Credon*) in Ravendala [Ravendale] 1 carucate and 2 bovates, and in Aschebi [Ashby by Fenby] 1 carucate and 1 bovate, and in Brighesla [Brigsley] and in Wada [Waith] 5½ bovates, and Walter son of Alfred holds all these.

14. Hugh de Laval in Ravendala [Ravendale] 1 carucate and 2 bovates; and in Ascbi [Ashby by Fenby] 1 carucate and 1 bovate; and in Brighela [Brigsley] 6 bovates; and in Uada [Waith] 5½ bovates; and in Toresbi [North Thoresby] 4 carucates and 3 bovates.

15. William son of Hacon in Cucualt [Cuxwold] 7½ bovates, [[which he holds] of the king[2]], of Ranulf Mischin, and of Alan de Perci, and the Count of Mortain (*Moreton*).

16. Manasiet Arsic in Rodewella and in Nordcotis [Rothwell and North Cotes] 3 bovates, which Gilbert Nevill (*de Nova Villa*) holds, and Richard son of Roolf.

17. Roger Marmion in Fuglestoua [Fulstow] 1 carucate and 6 bovates, which Pigot holds, [and Jordan the canon holds 1 bovate of these[6]].

---

1 These 4 bovates and 1 bovate are included in Bishop Ranulf's 2 carucates and 7 bovates in no. 18 below.

2 The interlineation was probably made *temp.* Henry II.

3 *In Rodwella* seems to be an addition: perhaps contemporary.

4 Corrected from *Suineopa*.

5 Duplicated in no. 1 above.

6 The interlineation may possibly relate to no. 16. It seems to be contemporary with the text.

18. Ranulf bishop of Durham 2 carucates and 7 bovates, which Pinceon the sewer (*dapifer*) holds of him.

19. Carbonell 4 bovates in Belesbi [Beelsby].

[9]. In BREDELAI [BRADLEY] WAPENTAKE

THERE ARE RECKONED TO BE 3½ HUNDREDS AND 3 BOVATES, AND IN EACH [HUNDRED] 12 CARUCATES OF LAND.

1. Hamon the sewer (*dapifer*) has 14 carucates and 4 bovates. [In Leyseby [Laceby] and the soke[1]].

2. Stephen of Albemarle (*Albaemara*) 5 carucates and 3 bovates, [to wit[2]], in Uiflesbi [Weelsby] 4 carucates; and in Sut Cotun [Little Cotes] 7½ bovates; and in Bredelai [Bradley] half a bovate; and in Grimesbi [Great Grimsby] 2 [bovates[2]]; and in Hol [Hole] 1 bovate.

3. Ranulf Mischin in Tatenai and Humberstein and Tirnesco and Uada [Tetney and Humberstone and Thrunscoe and Waith] 15 carucates and 3 bovates, [to wit[2]], in Humberstein 12 carucates in demesne, and in Tirnesco 1 carucate, and in Wada 1 carucate, and in Alsebi [Aylesby] 3 bovates. That is 12 carucates are* in demesne. And Heinfred [holds] in Irebi[3] [Irby on Humber] 1 carucate.

**Folio 14.*

4. Hugh de Vallo in Cle and Tirnesco [Clee and Thrunscoe] 1 carucate and 4 bovates, which William son of Hacon holds.

5. The King in Grimesbi [Great Grimsby] and in Sualwa [Swallow] 2 carucates and 5 bovates. [It is reckoned in the 14 carucates and 4 bovates of Hamon the sewer (*dapiferi*) above[4]].

6. Earl Richard in Irebi [Irby on Humber] 1 carucate and 4 bovates, which William the Constable holds.

7. The Count of Brittany in Alesbi [Aylesby] 2 carucates and 4 bovates; and in Sualwa [Swallow] 1 carucate and 6 bovates.

8. Norman de Araceio in Cotun [Great Cotes] 4 bovates.

9. The Archbishop of York in Heghelinga and Cle [Healing and Clee] 5 bovates [[of which] Ralf holds 4[5]]; and in Sualwa [Swallow] 6 bovates, which Richard de Verli holds.

10. Manasiet Arsic in Heghelinga and Cle [Healing and Clee] 1 carucate and 4½ bovates, which Gilbert Nevill (*de Nova Villa*) holds and Osbert holds of them.

11. Alan Perci the fourth part of 1 bovate.

12. Robert bishop of Lincoln in Hol [Hole] 2 bovates.

13. William Mischin in Cotis and Irebi [Great Cotes and Irby on Humber] 4 carucates and 7 bovates—in [I]rebi 4 bovates and in Cotis 1 carucate and 3 bovates.

---

1 An addition: probably made *temp.* Henry II.

2 The interlineation was probably made *temp.* Henry II.

3 Two letters have been erased before this name. Perhaps the scribe began to write *Itrebi*.

4 A note *temp.* Henry III.

5 The interlineation seems to be contemporary with the text.

14. Ralf de Criol in Houtuna [Holton le Clay] 7 bovates.

15. Geoffrey (*Goisfridus*) son of Payne in Sualwa [Swallow] 1 carucate and 2 bovates, which Wimund holds.

16. Alan of Lincoln in Heghelinga and in Sualwa [Healing and Swallow] 3 carucates and [1 bovate[1]] 2 parts of 1 bovate.

17. Bishop Ranulf [of Durham] in Alesbi [Aylesby] 6 bovates.

Folio 15.

[10]. In LUDEBURC [LUDBOROUGH] WAPENTAKE

THERE ARE RECKONED TO BE 3 HUNDREDS, AND IN EACH [HUNDRED] 12 CARUCATES OF LAND.

1. Robert de Insula in Ludeburc [Ludborough] 8 carucates; and in Fotrebi [Fotherby] 4 carucates and 4 bovates, which Walter holds.

2. Robert bishop of Lincoln in Wihum [Wyham] 2 carucates; and in Ormesbi [North Ormsby] 2 carucates and 2 bovates.

3. Stephen of Albemarle (*Albamara*) in Ormesbi [North Ormsby] 4 carucates and 4 bovates.

4. Ranulf Mischin in Ormesbi [North Ormsby] 2 carucates and 2 bovates; and in Parva Grimesbia [Little Grimsby] 1 carucate and 3 bovates; and in Wihum [Wyham] 2 carucates.

5. Ranulf bishop of Durham in Fotrebi [Fotherby] 7 bovates.

6. The monks in Coevham [Covenham] 3 carucates; and in Ludena[2] [Ludney] 1 carucate.

7. Alan de Perci in Caletorp [Cawthorpe in Covenham] 1 carucate; and in Grimesbi [Little Grimsby] 1 carucate and 4 bovates; and in Fotrebi [Fotherby] 4 bovates; and in Coveham [Covenham] 2 carucates.

[11]. In IERBURC [YARBOROUGH] WAPENTAKE

THERE ARE RECKONED TO BE 14 HUNDREDS, [AND] IN EACH [HUNDRED] 12 CARUCATES OF LAND.

1. Stephen of Albemarle (*Albemara*) 25 carucates and 5 bovates[3]—In Barwa [Barrow] 11 carucates; and in Torentuna [Thornton Curtis] 8 carucates; and in Cotun [Nun Coton] 1 carucate; and in Chiluingheholm [Killingholme] 1 carucate; and in Linberga [Limber] 1 carucate; and in Golsa [Goxhill] 2 carucates and 4 bovates; and in Chirnigtuna [Kirmington] 6 bovates; and in Chetlebi [Kettleby] 3 bovates and the third part of 1 bovate.

2. Ranulf Mischin [earl of Lincoln[4]] in Haltun [East Halton] 3 carucates and 4 bovates; and in Lopingheham [Lobingham] 6 bovates; and in Parva Linberga [Little Limber] 1 carucate; and in Chelebi

[1] A contemporary interlineation.
[2] Ludney is in the wapentake of Louthesk. This 1 carucate is duplicated in 18/5 below.
[3] A third of a bovate has been omitted in this total.
[4] The interlineation was probably made in the fifteenth century.

[Keelby] 2 bovates; and in Haburc [Habrough] 3 bovates; and in Broclesbi [Brocklesby] 3 bovates; and in Chelebi [Keelby] 2 bovates, [[which] Gilbert de Chaz [holds][1]]; and in Haburc [Habrough] 3 bovates; and in Neosum [Newsham] 5 bovates; and in Brochesbi [Brocklesby] 3 bovates.

Folio 16.

3. Ralf de Criol in Magna Linberga [Great Limber] 2 carucates.

4. Walter de Ganto in Bartuna [Barton on Humber] and Ferebi [South Ferriby] and the dependencies (*pendiciis*) 17 carucates; and in Horchestou [Horkstow] 4 carucates, which Alan de Perci holds.

5. Geoffrey (*Gosfridus*) Murdac in Torp and Bechebi [Kettleby Thorpe and Bigby] 1 carucate and 6 bovates.

6. Alan de Perci in Horchestou [Horkstow] 4 carucates; and in Immingeham and Torentuna [Immingham and Thornton Curtis] 5 carucates; and in Sumerdebi [Somerby by Bigby] 2 carucates and 4 bovates; and in Ounebi [Owmby by Searby] 2 carucates and 3 bovates; and in Haburc [Habrough] 1 carucate; and in Wituna [Wootton] 1½ bovates; and in Brunum [Burnham] 4 bovates; and in Seurebi [Searby] the fourth part of 1 bovate; and in Cadenai [Cadney] the fourth part of 1 bovate; and in Grossebi [Grasby] the fourth part of 1 bovate.

7. Robert de Chalz and Geoffrey (*Gosfridus*) Halselin in Wragebi [Wragby] 4 carucates and 5 bovates and the third part of 1 bovate.

8. Norman de Araceio in Stalinburc [Stallingborough] 2 carucates and 2 bovates; and in Immigheham [Immingham] 4 bovates; and in Lopingheham [Lobingham] 4 bovates; and in Chiluingheholm [Killingholme] 4 carucates and 3 bovates; and in Wttuna [Wootton] 6½ bovates; and in Ulesbi [Ulceby] 6 bovates; and in Parva Linberga [Little Limber] 4 bovates; and in Broclesbi [Brocklesby] 2 bovates; and in Chelebi [Keelby] 5 bovates and the third part of 1 bovate; and in Haburc [Habrough] 4 bovates.

9. Robert bishop of Lincoln in Golsa and Wttuna [Goxhill and Wootton] 3 carucates; and in Elesham [Elsham] 2 carucates and 2 bovates; and in Wlfriohebi[2] [Worlaby near Brigg] 1½ carucates; and in Bechebi [Bigby] 1 carucate, [[which] Gilbert Nevill (*de Nova Villa*) holds[1]]; and in Chelebi [Keelby] 5 bovates, [[which] the same Gilbert [holds][1]]; and in Ulesbi [Ulceby] 4 bovates, [[which] the same Gilbert [holds][1]]; and in Stalinburc [Stallingborough] 2 bovates, which Gilbert holds.

10. Robert [de Humet], the bishop's nephew (*nepos*), in Linberga [Great Limber] 3 carucates; and in Bondebi [Bonby] 7 carucates; and in Stalinburc [Stallingborough] 1 carucate.

11. Hugh de Vallo in Helesham [Elsham] 1 carucate, which Richard son of Osbert the sheriff holds.

12. The Count of Brittany in Cadenai [Cadney] 1 carucate and 4 bovates; and in Nordchelesia [North Kelsey] 1 carucate; and in Cherlingtuna [Kirmington] 4 bovates; and in Seurebi [Searby] 3 bovates; and in Chiluingheholm [Killingholme] 2 carucates and 2 bovates.

---

[1] A contemporary interlineation.

[2] Probably a clerical error for *Wlfrichebi*. *Cp.* no. 13 below.

13. The Count of Mellent 3 carucates and 4 bovates in Crosthestuna and Cherligtuna and Wlfrechebi [Croxton and Kirmington and Worlaby near Brigg].

14. Count Odo, [of the fee of the Earl of Albemarle (*Albemerle*), pertaining to Burtiwich'[1]] in Aldolbi [Audleby] 1 carucate and 2 bovates; and in Grossebi [Grasby] 2 carucates.

Folio 17.

15. Geoffrey (*Gosfridus*) son of Payne in Golsa [Goxhill] 1 carucate and 2 bovates; and in Meltuna [Melton Ross] 3 carucates; and in Chelebi [Keelby] 3 bovates and the third part of 1 bovate; and in Uttuna [Wootton] 7 bovates; and in Brunum [Burnham] 2 bovates; and in Haburc [Habrough] 2 bovates; and in Broclosbi [Brocklesby] 3 bovates; and in Ribi [Riby] 1 carucate and 4 bovates; and in Ulesbi [Ulceby] 4 carucates and 3 bovates; and in Ribi [Riby] $4\frac{1}{2}$ carucates,[2] [which are held] of Earl Richard.

16. Robert de Haia in Ulesbi [Ulceby] 4 bovates; and Robert Greslet 5[3] bovates in Neteltuna [Nettleton], [which are held] of the king.

17. Earl Richard, [[which the] Constabulary of Chester [holds][4]], in Bernetebi [Barnetby le Wold] 6 carucates; and in Wlfrichesbi [Worlaby] 2 carucates; and in Bechebi [Bigby] 1 carucate and 1 bovate; and in Sumerdebi [Somerby near Brigg] 4 bovates; and in Bertuna [Barton on Humber] 2 bovates; and in Haburc [Habrough] $1\frac{1}{2}$ bovates; and in Ribi [Riby] $4\frac{1}{2}$ carucates,[2] which Geoffrey (*Gosfridus*) son of Payne holds; and in Chiluingheholm [Killingholme] 3[5] carucates and 4 bovates, which Reinar de Sali held.

18. Ralf Mortimer (*de mortuo mari*) 2 carucates in Wittuna [Wootton].

19. Ranulf bishop of Durham in Broclosbi [Brocklesby] 1 carucate.[6]

20. Manasiet Arsic [of the honour of Dover[4]] in Chellebi [Keelby] $4\frac{1}{2}$ bovates; and in Stalinburc [Stallingborough] 4 bovates; and in Neteltuna [Nettleton] 1 carucate and 2 bovates, which Gilbert Nevill (*de Nouauilla*) holds and Richard son of Mobs.

21. The Archbishop in Stalinburc [Stallingborough] 6 bovates; and in Chelebi [Keelby] $4\frac{1}{2}$ bovates.

22. The Count of Mortain (*Moreton*) in Neteltuna [Nettleton] 5 bovates, and in Elesham [Elsham] 1 carucate and 2 bovates, and in Clifsebi [Clixby] 4 bovates, and in Husum [Howsham] 4 bovates; and all these Roger de Monbegon holds; and in Crochestuna [Croxton] 6 bovates, which Hugh of Croxton (*Crochestuna*) holds.

23. William de Vesci (*Veceio*) in Bondebi [Bonby] 4 bovates.

24. William Mischin in Neteltuna [Nettleton] 5 bovates; and in Uicheim [Wykeham in Nettleton] 1 carucate and 2 bovates; and in Huneduna [Hundon] 1 carucate; and in Safrebi [Searby] 2 carucates and 3 bovates.

---

[1] A fifteenth century interlineation.
[2] These $4\frac{1}{2}$ carucates are duplicated in nos. 15 and 17.
[3] The figure has been corrected from query *b*[*ouatas*] by a contemporary hand.
[4] The interlineation was probably made in the fifteenth century.
[5] *4* has been altered into *3*.
[6] This entry seems to be a contemporary interpolation.

25. Gilbert Ticio 2 carucates and 6 bovates in Ferebi [South Ferriby] and half a bovate, and Nigel de Albaneio holds [them].

26. Alan of Lincoln in Golsa [Goxhill] 1 carucate and 2 bovates; and in Barua [Barrow on Humber] 1 carucate; and in Neosum [Newsham] 5 bovates; and in Broclesbi [Brocklesby] 1 bovate; and in Haburc [Habrough] 2 bovates.

27. Richard of Lincoln, son of Osbert the sheriff, in Elesham [Elsham] 3 bovates.

28. William Torniant in Neteltuna [Nettleton] 5 bovates; and in Grossebi [Grasby] 3 bovates.

Folio 18.

[12]. IN BOLINBROC [BOLINGBROKE] WAPENTAKE

THERE ARE RECKONED TO BE 8 HUNDREDS.

1. Ranulf Mischin [Earl of Lincoln[1]] has 79 carucates of land and 6 bovates.

2. Bishop Ranulf [of Durham] 5 carucates and 2 bovates.

3. Robert the canon of Greinvilla 3 carucates.

4. Walter de Ganto 3 carucates, which Wigot holds.

5. Hugh son of Eudo 3 carucates between Endrebi [Mavis Enderby] and Cal' [West Keal] and Oustcal'[2] [East Keal].

6. Ketelbern 1 carucate and 7 bovates in Cal' [East and West Keal].

7. The Count of Brittany in Torp [Thorpe St. Peter] 3 bovates, which Eudo of Mumby (*Monbi*) holds.

[13]. IN CHEIRETRE [GARTREE] WAPENTAKE

THERE ARE RECKONED TO BE 6 HUNDREDS.

1. Ranulf Mischin has 47 carucates and 3 bovates.

2. Ralf Tasson 6 carucates.

3. Earl Richard 2 carucates, which Richard of Hemingby (*Heninghebi*) holds.

4. Robert de Haia 1 carucate, which Ernis holds; and in Mintingis [Minting] 5 bovates, which Terricus held.

5. Ralf Paganel in Strettuna and Randebi and Steintuna [Great Sturton and Ranby and Market Stainton] 5 carucates and 2 parts of 1 bovate.

6. Robert bishop of Lincoln in Randebi and Steintuna [Ranby and Market Stainton] 6 carucates.

7. Norman de Araceio in Calchewella [Cawkwell] 1 carucate and 4 bovates.

---

[1] A fifteenth century interlineation.
[2] Corrected from *Oustcal'*.

8. Alan of Lincoln 6 bovates, ⌊which⌋ Gilbert son of G[ocelin] and Gerard ⌊hold⌋, in Sticheswald [Stixwould].

9. Hugh son of Eudo 5 bovates in Strettuna [Great Sturton].

Folio 19.

In Suttriding (South Riding)

[14]. In CALNODESHOU [CANDLESHOE] WAPENTAKE

THERE ARE RECKONED TO BE 10 HUNDREDS.

1. Gilbert son of Gocelin 2 carucates in Welletuna [Welton le Marsh], which Richard of Lincoln holds; and in Freschena [Friskney] 4 bovates.

2. Hugh de Vallo 4 carucates and 6 bovates[1]; and 2 bovates, ⌊held⌋ of the Archbishop [of York] as of his manor of Rigesbi [Rigsby] (*de archiepiscopo de Rigesbi*).[2]

3. The Count of Brittany 3 carucates in Burc [Burgh le Marsh].

4. Hugh son of Pinceon 4 bovates[3] in Freschena [Friskney].

5. Roger de Ganto in Croft [Croft] 2 carucates and 4 bovates.[4]

6. Walter de Ganto 48 carucates, ⌈and 4 bovates and they are in Welletuna [Welton le Marsh], and Hugh Pilat holds them[5]⌉; and of all these Wigat holds 4 bovates; and of these Roger de Ganto holds 6 carucates and 4 bovates, and Hugh son of Eudo 1 carucate.

7. Earl Richard in Sutrebi [Sutterby] 2 carucates and 4 bovates; and in Brincla[6] 2 carucates; and in Calesbi[6] 2 carucates and 4 bovates; and in Freschena and Weinflet [Friskney and Wainfleet] 8 carucates and 6 bovates; ⌈and in Dalbi and Forthintuna [Dalby and Fordington] 11 carucates; and in Aschebi [Ashby by Partney] 5 carucates; and in Breitoft and Irebi [Braytoft and Irby in the Marsh] 11 carucates[7]⌉; Total—3 hundreds and 6 carucates and 6 bovates.

8. Ketelbern 1 carucate.

9. Ranulf bishop of Durham 4 carucates and 3 bovates, and Pinceon holds them.

10. Hugh son of Randulf 7 carucates and 2½ bovates.

11. Robert de Haia 4 bovates, which Terricus held.

12. Hugh son of Eudo 4 carucates and 5 bovates, and 1 carucate[8] of the fee (*fedio*) of Walter de Ganto which Hervey (*Hurueius*) holds.

13. Ranulf Mischin in Waletuna [Welton le Marsh] 2 carucates.

---

[1] In Ingoldmells.
[2] These 2 bovates were in Addlethorpe, and were sokeland of the manor of Rigsby.
[3] This is included in the Bishop of Durham's 4 carucates and 3 bovates in no. 9 below.
[4] This is included in Roger's 6 carucates and 4 bovates in no. 6 below.
[5] A contemporary interlineation.
[6] *Brincla* seems to be a mistake for *Dexthorpe*, and *Calesbi* for *Ulceby by Alford.*
[7] The interlineation was probably made *temp.* Henry II.
[8] This is included in Walter's land in no. 6 above.

Folio 20.

[15]. In CALSWAT [CALCEWATH] WAPENTAKE

THERE ARE RECKONED TO BE 10 HUNDREDS, ⌊AND⌋ IN EACH ⌊HUNDRED⌋ 12 CARUCATES OF LAND.

1. Earl Richard in the hundred of Suabi [Swaby] 12 carucates; and in the hundred of Lecheburna [Legbourne] 10 carucates; and in Tedolftorp [Theddlethorpe] 10 carucates and 6 bovates; and in the hundred of Hotoft [Huttoft] 8 carucates; and in the hundred of Calesbi [Calceby] 6 carucates; and in the hundred of Widerna and of Stein [Withern and Stain] 1 carucate and 4 bovates; and in Drebi[1] 4 bovates; Total—4 hundreds and 10 carucates[2].

2. Walter de Ganto 18 carucates and 4 bovates, and of these the sons of Ragemer hold 14 carucates.

3. Alan of Craon (*de Credon*) 10 carucates.

4. The Count of Mortain (*Moreton*) 2 carucates.

5. The Archbishop of York in Rigesbi [Rigsby] 3 carucates and 6 bovates.

6. The Count of Brittany in Rigesbi [Rigsby] 2 carucates and 2 bovates, which Richard son of Losward holds; and in Mumbi [Mumby] and its dependencies (*pendiciis*) 9 carucates, which Eudo holds.

7. Ketelbern of Keal (*Cal'*) 2 carucates and 4 bovates in Suttuna and Marchebi and Dedloncstorp [Sutton in the Marsh and Markby and Theddlethorpe]; and in Hotoft [Huttoft] 4 bovates.

8. Manasiet Arsic 3 carucates, which Wimund of Aby (*Abi*) holds.

9. Ranulf Mischin in Humbi [Hamby] 2 carucates, which Walter son of Roger holds.

10. Bishop Ranulf 1 carucate and 4 bovates in Burnetorp [Bonthorpe], which William son of Anschetil held; and in Ulesbi [Ulceby by Alford] 2 bovates, which Pinceon ⌊holds⌋.

11. Hugh son of Eudo in Aghetorp [Authorpe in Mumby] 6 bovates.

12. Gilbert son of Gocelin in Marchebi [Markby] 4 bovates; and in Maltebi [Maltby le Marsh] 4 bovates, ⌊which⌋ Walter son of Rag*emer* holds.

Folio 21.

13. Randulf de Criol in Maltorp and Cumberworda and Suttuna and Ulsebi [Mablethorpe and Cumberworth and Sutton in the Marsh and Ulceby by Alford] 1 carucate and 6½ bovates.

14. Robert de Brus in Alworda [Alford] 4 bovates.

15. Alan of Lincoln in Hotoft [Huttoft] 5 bovates, ⌊which⌋ Ansch*etil* holds.

16. Hugh son of Randulf 1 carucate and 2 bovates.

17. Richard of Lincoln, son of Osbert the sheriff, 2 bovates, which Ralf of Calceby (*Chalchesbi*) holds.

---

[1] *Rectius* Aby.

[2] The total exceeds the sum of the details by 9 carucates and 2 bovates.

[16]. In WRAGHEHOU [WRAGGOE] WAPENTAKE

THERE ARE RECKONED TO BE 9 HUNDREDS, ⌊AND⌋ IN EACH ⌊HUNDRED⌋ 12 CARUCATES OF LAND.

[*Sic* est in alio rot*u*lo cu*m*puta hu*n*dr' et o*m*nes . . . .[1]]

1. Earl Richard in Steintuna iusta Langwat [Stainton by Langworth] [and Reresby [Reasby] 5 carucates which the sons ⌊hold⌋ as below[2]] [3[3]] carucates, which the sons of Rocelin hold; and in Neobole [Newball] 2 carucates and 2 bovates, which Hugh holds; and in Bolingintuna [Bullington] 6 bovates, which Robert son of Humfrey held; and in Langhetuna [Langton by Wragby] 3 bovates, which Simon holds.

2. Bishop Ranulf [of Durham] in Bulingtuna [Bullington] 1 carucate, which William son of Ansch*etil* held; and in Biscopetorp [Biscathorpe] 3 carucates and 2 bovates [in Langetuna [Langton by Wragby][3]], which Pinceon holds; in Chesfremu*nd*[4] [Kirmond le Mire] 3 carucates; and in Ludesfort [Ludford] 5 carucates and 1 bovate; and in Apeleia [Apley] 2 carucates [emina[5]]; and in Steinfelda [Stainfield] 3 carucates [ei tuna[5]].

3. Alan de Perci in Ludeforda [Ludford] and its dependencies (*pendiciis*) 13 carucates and 1 bovate; and in Uichenbi [Wickenby] 3 carucates, which Richard holds; and in Westletebi [Westlaby] 1 carucate and 1 bovate; and in Becheringa [Beckering] 1½ bovates; and in Snelleslund [Snelland] [2 bovates[3]]; and Reresbi[6] [Reasby] [2 bovates[3]] of land; and in Oteun [Holtham in Legsby] 1 carucate and 2 bovates.

4. The Archbishop of York in Benigworda [Benniworth] 2 carucates and 4 bovates, which Richard of Lincoln holds; and in Pantuna and Barcworda [Panton and Barkwith] 2 carucates and 6 bovates, which Gilbert Ticio held; and in Lissigtuna [Lissington] and its dependencies 7 carucates, which Herbert son of Albri holds; and in Wllingheham [South Willingham] 2 carucates and 1½ bovates, which Richard de Verli holds; and in Grisebi and Burc [Girsby and Burgh on Bain] 2 carucates and 2 bovates, which Richard de Verli holds; and in Heintuna [Hainton] 1 carucate and 4 bovates, which the same Richard de Verli holds; and in Barcworda [Barkwith] 6 bovates, which the same Richard de Verli holds.

Folio 22.

5. The Count of Mortain (*Moreton*) in Heintuna [Hainton] 3 carucates, which Albert holds.

6. Geoffrey (*Gosfridus*) son of Payne in Wragebi [Wragby] 6 [carucates[7]]; and in Fulnetebi and Randa [Fulnetby and Rand] 6 carucates;

---

[1] Interlineated by a fifteenth century hand above the first line of the entry. The reading is doubtful. The words may be a continuation of the interlineation printed in the second line of entry no. 1.

[2] A fifteenth century interlineation.

[3] A contemporary interlineation.

[4] Kirmond, Ludford, Apley, and Stainfield were part of Alan de Perci's fee (no. 3 below), and are wrongly placed here. The four items are an analysis of the 13 carucates and 1 bovate in no. 3.

[5] These interlineations are probably contemporary with the text. Whether or no they represent the names of sub-tenants cannot be determined.

[6] The name is written on an erasure, and another erasure follows it.

[7] *carucatas* is a contemporary correction from *bovatas*; but nevertheless perhaps *bovatas* should be read. Cp. *D.B.*, 34/12.

and in Hattuna [Hatton] 5 carucates; and in Langhetuna [Langton by Wragby] 1 bovate; and in Pantuna [Panton] 2 carucates; and in Barcworda [Barkwith] 2 carucates and 2 bovates; and in Becheringa [Beckering] 4 bovates; and in Houtuna [Holton] 1 carucate; and in Chinetorp [Kingthorpe] 2 bovates; and in Burc [Burgh on Bain] 6 bovates; and in Tirigtuna [Torrington] 7 bovates, which Richard of Lincoln holds; and in Herduic [Hardwick in Panton] 5½ bovates; and in the other Tirigtuna [Torrington] 2 carucates and 2 bovates.

7. Walter de Ganto in Bardanai [Bardney] 2 carucates; and in Suderei [Southrey] 2 bovates; and in Osgotebi [Osgodby in Bardney] 2 carucates.

8. Robert Greslet 1 carucate and 4½ bovates in Caldecota [Calcote *alias* Collow in Legsby], [which are held] of the king.

9. Roger Marmion between Leghetuna [Langton by Wragby], [1 carucate and 4 bovates[1]], and Buteita and Ansgotebi [Butyate in Bardney and Osgodby in Bardney] 2 bovates.

10. Ranulf Mischin in Beniguorda [Benniworth] 3 carucates and 4 bovates; and in Strutebi [Strubby in Langton by Wragby] 2 bovates; and in Buligtuna [Bullington] 5 bovates; and in Chintorp [Kingthorpe] the third part of 1 carucate of land; and in Ludeford [Ludford] 4½ bovates, which the monks of Spalding (*Spaldingis*) hold; and in Westletebi [Westlaby] 6 bovates.

11. Gilbert son of Gocelin in Houtuna [Holton by Beckering] 1 carucate; and in Becheringa [Beckering] half a bovate; and in Snelleslund [Snelland] 1 carucate; and in Reresbi [Reasby], [1 carucate[1]], and Sunetorp [Swinthorpe] 2 carucates; and in Blesebi [Bleasby] 2 carucates.[2]

12. Norman de Araceio in Becheringa [Beckering] 2 bovates.

13. Robert bishop of Lincoln in Uichinghebi [Wickenby] 1 carucate; and in Snelleslund [Snelland] 2 bovates; and in Reresbi [Reasby] 1 bovate; and in Sunetorp [Swinthorpe] 1 carucate; and in Langhetuna and Wraghebi [Langton by Wragby and Wragby] 1 carucate and 2 bovates, which Simon [of Kyme] son of William holds.

14. Ralf Paganel between Heintuna and Barcworda and Strubi and Suderebi [Hainton and Barkwith and Strubby in Langton by Wragby and Southrey] 2 carucates and 5 bovates.

15. Manasiet Arsic in Wllingeheim [South Willingham] 6 bovates and half a bovate, which Walter son of Walter holds and Willlam son of Hacon.

Folio 23.

16. Ralf de Criol in Wllingheheim [South Willingham] 1 carucate; and in Strubi[3] [Strubby in Langton by Wragby] 2 bovates; and in Chintorp [Kingthorpe] the third part of 1 carucate of land and the fourth part of 1 bovate; and in Barcworda and Heintuna [Barkwith and Hainton] 1 carucate; and in Ludeford [Ludford] half a bovate; and 5 bovates in Sixla [Sixle].

---

1 A contemporary interlineation.
2 These 2 carucates are duplicated in 7/14.
3 Corrected from *Sutrebi* probably *temp.* Henry II.

17. Alfræit de Canci in Blesebi [Bleasby] 5 bovates and the third part of 1 bovate, which Wilgrip holds; but these belong to the geld of the North Riding (*ille iacent ad geldum de Nortridingio*).

18. The King in Sotebi [Sotby] 4 carucates.

19. Alan of Lincoln in Tiringtuna [Torrington] 2 carucates and 4 bovates, which Gocelin holds.

20. Saint Mary [of Lincoln] in Suderei [Southrey] 2 bovates.

21. Ansgot of Burwell (*Burewella*) in Ludeford [Ludford] 3 bovates, which his wife holds.

22. Hugh son of Eudo in Langhetuna [Langton by Wragby] 2 bovates, [which] Robert de Haia holds.

23. Hugh de Vallo 1 carucate in Sixla [Sixle].

[17]. In HILLA [HILL] WAPENTAKE

THERE ARE RECKONED TO BE 6 HUNDREDS, [AND] IN EACH [HUNDRED] 12 CARUCATES OF LAND.

1. Earl Richard in the hundred of Langhetuna [Langton by Partney] 12 carucates; and in the hundred of Hamringheheim [Hameringham] 11 carucates and 4 bovates; and in Hagwordingheheim [Hagworthingham] 3 carucates; and in Salmonebi [Salmonby] 1 carucate; and in Brinche [Brinkhill] 2 carucates; and in Ormeresbi [South Ormsby] 3 carucates; and in Chetlesbi [Ketsby] 3 carucates and 4 bovates; and in Ualmeresgara [Walmsgate] 1 carucate; and in Tedforda [Tetford] 6 bovates; and in Fuledebi [Fulletby] 2 carucates; and in Oxecum [Oxcombe] 1 carucate and 6 bovates; and of these Wigot holds 10 bovates in Wincebi [Winceby]. Total—3 hundreds and 5 carucates and 4 bovates.

Folio 24.

2. The Archbishop of York in Tedforda and Ormesbi [Tetford and South Ormsby] 3 carucates and 7 bovates; and in Wlfrichesbi [Worlaby by Louth] 2 carucates and 2 bovates, which the Archdeacon [of York] holds.

3. Norman de Araceio in Ormesbi [South Ormsby] 3 carucates and 7 bovates.

4. The Count of Brittany in Agwordingheheim [Hagworthingham] 4 bovates, which Wigot holds.

5. Bishop Ranulf [of Durham] in Fuletebi and Oxcum [Fulletby and Oxcombe] 4 carucates and 6 bovates, which Pinceon holds.

6. Ansgot of Burwell (*Borewella*) in Walmeresgara [Walmsgate] 2 carucates.

7. Walter de Ganto in Wincebi [Winceby] 1 carucate and 2 bovates, which Wigot holds; and in Hagwordingheheim [Hagworthingham] 4 bovates.

8 Alan de Perci in Wlfrichebi [Worlaby by Louth] 6 bovates.

9. Gilbert son of Gocelin in Ascbi [Ashby Puerorum] 1 carucate and 1 bovate and Sumerdebi [Somersby] 2 carucates and in Tedforda [Tetford]

15 bovates and in Hamrigheheim [Hameringham] 4 bovates and in Endrebi [Bag Enderby] 6 bovates.

10. Stephen de Albemara in Hagwordingheheim [Hagworthingham] 1 carucate ; and in Ascbi [Ashby Puerorum] 4 carucates ; and in Endrebi [Bag Enderby] 4 bovates.

[18]. In LUDESC [LOUTHESK] WAPENTAKE

THERE ARE RECKONED TO BE 10 HUNDREDS, ⌊AND⌋ IN EACH ⌊HUNDRED⌋ 12 CARUCATES.

1. The Count of Brittany in Gertuna [Gayton le Wold] 3 carucates; and in Welletune [Welton le Wold] 4 carucates; and in Mannebi [Manby] 3 carucates; and in Grimolbi [Grimoldby] 3 carucates and 1 bovate; and in Salfletebi [Saltfleetby] 3 carucates; and in Schitebroc [Skidbrook] 3 carucates; and in Sumercotis [Somercotes] 3 carucates; and in* Ghermudtorp [Grainthorpe] 2 carucates; and in Ierburc [Yarburgh] 2 carucates and 5 bovates and the third part of 1 bovate; and in Alvingheheim [Alvingham] 1 carucate and 2 bovates and the third part of 1 bovate; and in Welletune [Welton le Wold] 1 carucate, which Alan son of Landri held.

**Folio 25.*

2. Earl Richard in Tadewella [Tathwell] and the soke 20 carucates and $5\frac{1}{2}$ bovates, and of these Wigot holds 10 bovates in Maltebi [Maltby in Raithby], and Ingelram 5 bovates in Tadewella and Haligtune [Tathwell and Hallington].

3. Ansgot of Burwell (*Borewella*) [in Burewella [Burwell][1]] 2 carucates; and in Haghetorp [Authorpe] 2 carucates; and in Munchetune [Muckton] 1 carucate and 4 bovates; and in Carletune [Castle Carlton and Great Carlton] 4 carucates; and in Wicheim [West Wykeham] [⌊in right of his⌋ wife[2]] 1 carucate[3]; and in Welletuna [Welton le Wold] 4 bovates; and in Sumercotis [Somercotes] 1 bovate.

4. Alan de Perci in Ristuna and Carletuna [Reston and Little Carlton] 2 carucates and 4 bovates, which Richard of Lincoln holds; and in Helchingtuna [Elkington] 8 carucates; and in Ludena [Ludney] 4 bovates.

5. And the monks of Couenam [Covenham] in Ludena [Ludney] 1 carucate.[4]

6. Bishop Ranulf [of Durham] in Cledi*n*gtuna and Cheilestorp [Keddington and Calcethorpe] 2 carucates; and in Welletuna [Welton le Wold] 2 bovates; and in Scitebroc [Skidbrook] 2 bovates; and in Salfletebi [Saltfleetby] 2 bovates; and in Coringtuna [Cockerington] half a bovate.

7. Alan of Lincoln in Catebi [South Cadeby] 1 carucate, [demesne[2]]; and in Wicheim [East Wykeham] $5\frac{1}{2}$ bovates; and in Chelestuna [Kelstern]

---

[1] The interlineation was probably made *temp.* Henry II.
[2] A contemporary interlineation.
[3] This carucate is duplicated in no. 13 below.
[4] See 10/6, note.

2 carucates and 6½ bovates, [demesne[1]]; and in Stiuetuna [Stewton] 2 carucates, [demesne[1]]; and in Cocrigtuna [Cockerington] 4 bovates, [demesne[1]]; and in Grimolbi [Grimoldby] 7 bovates, ⌊which⌋ Ansch*etil* Healing (*Egheling*[2]) ⌊holds⌋.

8. Geoffrey (*Gosfridus*) son of Payne in Grimchiltorp and Cateby [Grimblethorpe and South Cadeby] 1 carucate and 4 bovates, [which Ralf Malet holds[1]]; and in Welletuna [Welton le Wold] 6 bovates.

9. William Mischin in Uitcala [Withcall] 2 bovates, [which William son of Albreda holds[1]]; and in Salfletebi and Scitebroc [Saltfleetby and Skidbrook] 2 bovates, [which the same William holds[1]]; and in Catebi [South Cadeby] 1½ bovates, [⌊which⌋ Ralf Malet holds[1]].

10. Ranulf Mischin in Helchingtuna [Elkington] 4 carucates, and Walter de Beningheborda holds 3 carucates ⌊thereof⌋, and Alan Olliet 1 carucate.

11. The Bishop of Lincoln in Luda [Louth] 12 carucates; and in Parua Wicheheim [East Wykeham] 2 bovates; and the same holds of Earl Richard 4 bovates.

12. Hugh de Vallo in Uitcala [Withcall] 3 carucates and 7½ bovates; and in Cocringtuna [Cockerington] 3 carucates and 2 parts of 1 bovate; and in* Alvingheheim [Alvingham] 3 bovates and half a bovate; and in Sumercotis [Somercotes] 1½ bovates; and in Salfletebi [Saltfleetby] 3 bovates. **Folio 26.*

13. Ralf de Criol in Alvingheheim [Alvingham] 2½ bovates; and in Cocringtuna [Cockerington] 1 carucate and 6 bovates; and in Sumercota [Somercotes] 1 bovate; and in Salfledebi [Saltfleetby] 1⅓ bovates; and in Chedingtuna [Keddington] 4 bovates; and in Wicheheim [West Wykeham] 1 carucate[3]; and in Uitcala [Withcall] 1 carucate and 7 bovates and the third part of 1 bovate.

14. Roger Marmion in Tadewella [Tathwell] 1 carucate, which Thorald de Bolebec holds.

15. Robert de Haia in Carletuna and Sumercotis [Great Carlton and Somercotes] 6 bovates, ⌊which⌋ Ansgot [of Burwell] holds.

16. Ralf Paganel in Sumercotis [Somercotes] 2½ bovates; and in Welletuna [Welton le Wold] 4 bovates, ⌊the subject⌋ of litigation; and in Sumercotis [Somercotes] 2 parts of 1 bovate; and in Scitebroc [Skidbrook] half a bovate, ⌊the subject⌋ of litigation.

[19]. IN HORNECASTRA [HORNCASTLE] WAPENTAKE

THERE ARE RECKONED TO BE 6 HUNDREDS AND 6 CARUCATES, ⌊AND⌋ IN EACH ⌊HUNDRED⌋ 12 CARUCATES.

1. Earl Richard in Scriflebi and Conighesbi [Scrivelsby and Coningsby] 5 bovates.

---

[1] A contemporary interlineation.

[2] What seems to be the letter *i* is written above the last letter of this name. Anschetil's holding was in Brackenborough (*Book of Fees*, 1081; cp. *Lincs. Notes & Queries*, viii, 85). Perhaps we should read "in Grimolbi [*query*] bovates; and in Brackenborough 7 bovates, which Anchetil of Healing holds."

[3] See no. 3 above, note 3.

2. Roger Marmion between Scriflebi and Torentuna and Ructuna and Dalbi and Wilghebi and Coningesbi and Holteim [Scrivelsby and Thornton by Horncastle and Roughton and Dalderby and Wilksby and Coningsby and Haltham on Bain] 17 carucates and 2 bovates. The same Roger holds 9 carucates and 6 bovates thereof [in demesne[1]], and Uluiet holds 3 carucates and 4 bovates thereof, and Thorald and Alsie 2 carucates.

3. The Bishop of Durham between Chirchebi and Torp and Martuna and Wispigtuna [Kirkby on Bain and Tattershall Thorpe and Martin by Horncastle and Wispington] 9 carucates and 6 bovates.

4. Walter de Ganto between Baburc [Baumber], and Hedlingtuna [Edlington], and Ascbi [West Ashby] 1½ carucates, and Timlebi [Thimbleby], 24 carucates.[2]

Folio 27.

5. Ranulf Mischin 1 carucate and 4 bovates, which Ralf of Stixwould (*Stichesweld*) holds in Edlingtuna [Edlington].

6. Robert de Brus 4 bovates in Aschebi [West Ashby].

7. Stephen of Albemarle (*Albamara*) between Timlebi and Langhetuna and Coninghesbi [Thimbleby and Langton by Horncastle and Coningsby] 5 carucates and 6 bovates, and 2 bovates which William de Alost holds thereof; and Osbert of Hagworthingham (*Hawordinghcham*) holds 2 bovates in Coninghesbi [Coningsby].

8. Alan of Lincoln between Langhetuna and Timlebi and Bochelanda [Langton by Horncastle and Thimbleby and Buckland] 2 carucates, [which] Alan's kinsman (*cognatus*), Alan, holds.

9. Ralf Paganel in Chirchebi [Kirkby on Bain] 1 carucate and 2 bovates, which Alba[3] holds.

10. Hugh son of Eudo between Tatesala and Tumbi and Martuna and Strettuna and Wispingtuna and Wadigworda [Tattershall and Tumby and Martin by Horncastle and Sturton and Wispington and Waddingworth] 15 carucates and 4 bovates.

---

[1] A contemporary interpolation.
[2] The 24 carucates include the 1½ carucates in West Ashby.
[3] The last two letters have been altered and must be treated as uncertain.

INDEX OF PERSONS AND PLACES

INDISPENSABLE DIRECTIONS

The roman numerals refer to the pages of the Introduction and Appendixes.

The text of *Domesday Book* is indexed according to the chapters into which it is divided, and the entries which have been numbered in this edition; except that the page is sometimes specified in place of the chapter: thus 4/3 refers to the last entry on page 37; and p. 3/8 signifies the last entry on page 3.

The text of the *Lindsey Survey* is similarly indexed according to the chapters and entries, the references being distinguished from those to *Domesday Book* by the letter *L*: thus L 1/23; 2/11 mean the last entries on pages 238 and 239 respectively.

FURTHER DIRECTIONS

The King, and the barons who held direct of him, in 1086, are distinguished by **heavier type.**

The King, and the barons who held direct of him, in 1115–18, are marked by SMALL CAPITALS.

An asterisk (*) distinguishes pre-Conquest tenants and their contemporaries.

A dagger (†) marks pre-Conquest tenants who still held land in 1086.

A double dagger (‡) marks the names of persons whose date is later than the *Lindsey Survey* (1115–1118).

Where a person is indexed under his surname, a reference is given from the christian name to the surname, or *vice versa*, unless the date is later than the thirteenth century.

In such a form as 'Aschil son of Toke,' the reference is generally given under 'Aschil,' with a cross-reference from 'Toke'; but occasionally *vice versa*. *Son* is represented by *s.*

References to the current forms of place-names have been supplied from the more important of their medieval variants.

The name of the wapentake, enclosed in round brackets, has been added to the Lincolnshire and Rutland place-names; and, in the case of Lincolnshire, the county has been omitted.

In early records, there is often confusion between personal names beginning with the respective stems *Æthel* and *Ælf*. The stem *Æthel*, under Norman influence, often appears as *Ail* or *Eil*, and is frequently reduced further to *Al* or *El*. In names beginning with *Ælf*, the *f* usually disappears when the second element of the name begins with a consonant. *Ælfnoth*, for example, will probably appear as *Alnoth*, *Alnod*, or *Elnod*. When this change has happened, there is nothing to shew whether the name originally began with *Ælf* or with *Æthel*. In this Index, therefore, all the forms between which there may be confusion have been brought together for convenience of reference.

Index of Counties and Countries

LINCOLNSHIRE—*continued*

MIDDLESEX

NORFOLK

Index of Subjects

For references to persons and places, see the Index of Persons and Places.